Anthropology
in Theological Perspective

Anthropology
in Theological Perspective

Wolfhart Pannenberg

Translated by
Matthew J. O'Connell

The Westminster Press
Philadelphia

Book design by Gene Harris

First edition

Published by The Westminster Press®
Philadelphia, Pennsylvania

PRINTED IN THE UNITED STATES OF AMERICA

9 8 7 6 5 4 3 2 1

Library of Congress Cataloging in Publication Data

Pannenberg, Wolfhart, 1928–
  Anthropology in theological perspective.

  Translation of· Anthropologie in theologischer
Perspektive.
  Includes bibliographies and indexes.
  1. Man (Christian theology) 2. Man.
I. Title.
BT701.2.P33713 1985   233   84-22048
ISBN 0-664-21399-5

Contents

Abbreviations

ANET	*Ancient Near Eastern Texts,* ed. J. B. Pritchard (3d ed.; Princeton, 1969)
CR	Corpus Reformatorum
DS	H. Denzinger, ed., *Enchiridion symbolorum,* 32d ed. by A. Schönmetzer (Freiburg, 1963)
HWP	J. Ritter, ed., *Historisches Wörterbuch der Philosophie*
HZ	*Historische Zeitschrift*
KuD	*Kerygma und Dogma*
NZST	*Neue Zeitschrift für systematische Theologie*
PG	Patrologia Graeca
PhB	Philosophische Bücherei
PhilJb	*Philosophisches Jahrbuch*
PL	Patrologia Latina
rde	Rowohlts deutsche Enzyklopädie
RGG	*Die Religion in Geschichte und Gegenwart,* 3d ed.
TDNT	*Theological Dictionary of the New Testament*
TLZ	*Theologische Literaturzeitung*
TRE	*Theologische Realenzyklopädie*
WA	Weimarer Ausgabe (standard edition of Luther's works)
ZEE	*Zeitschrift für evangelische Ethik*
ZST	*Zeitschrift für systematische Theologie*

Introduction:
Theology and Anthropology

The understanding of the human being has increasingly played a foundational role in the history of modern theology.

In Protestant theology this development can be traced through various stages, from the early bias toward a "praxis" springing from the human need of redemption, through Deism and the moral rationalism of the later Enlightenment, into the classical period of German evangelical theology that began with Schleiermacher's redefinition of religion. The line continued through revivalist theology and its successors into liberal theology and the debates occasioned by dialectical theology in our own century. In the recently concluded phase of this long history, the debates culminated in the victory of an existentialist interpretation of the Christian message as a result of Rudolf Bultmann's opposition to Karl Barth.

After the holding action of the neo-Scholastic revival, Catholic theology has finally run the same course. The theology of Karl Rahner may serve as an example.

This concentration on anthropology in dealing with the problems of fundamental theology reflects the modern development of the philosophical idea of God. Insofar as modern philosophy did not turn in the direction of atheism or persist in keeping an agnostic distance, it showed increasing determination in conceiving God as a presupposition of human subjectivity and to that extent it thought of him in terms of humanity and no longer of the world. Not the natural world as such but human experience of the world and of the individual's existence in it repeatedly supplied the point of departure for discussing the reality of God. Human beings seemed able to understand themselves in relation to the world only if they presupposed God as the common author of both themselves and the world.

This frame of mind can be seen as early as the fifteenth century in Nicholas of Cusa. In the history of modern thought the same outlook was adopted, with varying emphases, by Descartes, Leibniz, Kant, Fichte, Schelling, and Hegel.[1] The same pattern is observable throughout the

[1] W. Schulz has described and summarized this process in his lectures "Der Gott der neuzeitlichen Metaphysik" (1957). On the anthropological concentration that has taken

entire modern history of philosophical theology. Thinkers no longer took the cosmos as their starting point in order to demonstrate in a quasi-experimental way that God is the first cause of the natural order. Instead, they argued from the existence and experience of human beings in order to show that God is inevitably presupposed in every act of human existence.

In patristic and medieval philosophy and theology this approach had provided only a secondary line of argument. It did not have to bear the whole burden of proof for the idea of God. Thinkers in that age had also found it possible to argue directly from the order of being. Modern thought, however, had to renounce the claim that there is a physical necessity of accepting the existence of God as first cause of the natural process. The reason was that once the principle of inertia was introduced or, at the latest, once the mechanistic theory of the origin of the planets was accepted, modern physics seemed no longer to need "the God hypothesis."

The concentration on understanding of the human in modern fundamental theology thus reflected both the general intellectual outlook of the modern age and the development of this outlook as it found its characteristic expression in the course of modern philosophy. The development of modern philosophy was itself one of the stimuli for the growing anthropocentrism of modern theology. The philosophical concentration on the human person as subject of all experience and of philosophical reflection itself could not but have an impact on theology. By comparison, the theological physics of the seventeenth and eighteenth centuries, which looked to the teleology of the cosmos for evidence of a wise Architect of the World, represented a byway that was gradually abandoned.

The growing anthropocentrism that has marked the development of Christian theology has not, however, been due solely to the influence of philosophy. It has also had another and genuinely theological cause: the fact that Christian theology is a response to the human question of salvation. The foundation for a theological concentration on the human person was already laid in the early Christian faith in the incarnation of God.

In the Augustinian tradition, which set its mark on Western theology, the focus was on the problem of individual salvation. The penitential piety of the Middle Ages only strengthened this emphasis, which reached its most intense form in the Lutheran Reformation and was continued in Pietism. In this thinking, the theme of sin and grace was narrowly con-

---

place in philosophical theology in the course of this process, see my essay "Anthropology and the Question of God," in my *The Idea of God and Human Freedom,* trans. R. A. Wilson (Philadelphia, 1973), 80–99.

ceived as *the* vital religious question for the individual person. By comparison, God's rule over the world in creation and in his future eschatological kingdom became secondary. This tendency found its purest expression in the Lutheran tradition. In the Calvinist tradition, on the other hand, the social context of human life and a corresponding conception of God's reign continued to exercise a greater influence.

While, then, the individualistic approach to the religious question of salvation represented only one line of development among others in Protestantism, it was nonetheless especially characteristic of the development as a whole. The correspondingly narrow anthropocentric focusing of theology found its classical expression in the revivalist theology of conscience. By contrast, Schleiermacher's theology of conscience once again linked the individual with the religious community. Yet this theology was not spared in the indictment subsequently leveled at the entire nineteenth-century theological development, namely, that it had succumbed to an anthropological egoism in the matter of salvation and thus to religious individualism. This accusation was set forth at the beginning of the twentieth century in Erich Schaeder's *Theozentrische Theologie* (vol. I, 1909). Hegel's similar criticism of the revivalist theology of his day had not exerted any notable long-term influence on theology. Schaeder's theocentrist emphasis, on the other hand, was continued in early dialectical theology; as a result, it left an ineradicable impress on the theological consciousness of our century.

The anthropological concentration in the history of modern theology is therefore not traceable solely to philosophical influences; it has also, and indeed principally, been stimulated by properly theological motifs, although it is only in the recent period that these have exerted their full influence. This makes it clear that this development in theology can be understood only as an expression of the overall intellectual situation in the modern era. The same conclusion follows from the fact that the anthropological concentration in theology has been strongly influenced by the social history of the modern period.

I am referring here to the privatization or at least segmentation of religion in modern society. After the religious wars of the sixteenth and seventeenth centuries the Christian confessions to a greater or lesser extent lost their position as state religions. The state became religiously neutral, and the choice of a religious confession became the private concern of the individual or of free associations of individuals. Even where the privatization of the religious confessions was not carried out as radically as it was in, for example, the United States, states did sooner or later accept the principle of religious neutrality. In these cases too, the result was a segmentation of the religious thematic, a restriction of religion to the private sphere and to the institutions dealing with this, while the political and economic order of society was relieved of any connection with religious views.

This tendency is observable throughout the modern period despite divergences peculiar to some countries. It is also independent of the question whether the life of society as a whole can thus be indifferent to the religious thematic or whether on the contrary the process is accompanied by an element of self-deception. The trend to the segmentation and privatization of religion is one of the dominant currents in modern history.

The privatization of religion also explains why pietism has acquired such an important place in the modern history of religious devotion. For the pietistic devotion of the heart took possession precisely of the sphere of private interiority which the modern state still allowed religion to occupy. Pietism turned the problem created by the privatization of religion into a virtue by making of human interiority a preserve, so to speak, for the themes of the religious life. Of course, pietistic devotion could hold its own in the religious debates of the modern age only if it could successfully show the *universal human validity* of religious interiority.[2]

It managed to do this initially in the theological moralism of the Enlightenment, especially in the form of the theology of conscience. This last, instead of reducing religion to morality, derived theological profit from the moralistic justification of religion which Rousseau and, following him, Kant had provided. But the independence of religion as based on private devotion achieved its classical expression only in Schleiermacher, beginning with his *Addresses on Religion* (1799).

Here Schleiermacher showed the universal human validity of religion by claiming for it "a special province in the soul" which is not reducible to morality or metaphysics and in which nonetheless the unity of the individual has its basis. As seen from the standpoint of a sociology of knowledge, religion, which had been reduced to the private sphere, was here asserting itself by claiming a universal human validity precisely for this private sphere. The question of the universally human had, after all, become what Christian revelation had been for the Middle Ages: the basis on which the legitimacy of all opposing views was decided.

---

[2]With reference to J. S. Semler's distinction between public religion and private religion, T. Rendtorff has justly observed, in his *Church and Theology: The Systematic Function of the Church Concept in Modern Theology,* trans. R. H. Fuller (Philadelphia, 1971), 35ff., that the relation between private and public has been reversed in comparison with the earlier development: The official confessional churches, which at that time still enjoyed great public authority, were demoted to the rank of private institutions, while the private religious consciousness became the general form of theological perception and in the modern age is universally acknowledged as valid. This point has recently been emphasized by F. Wagner, who refers to T. Luckmann, *Das Problem der Religion in der modernen Gesellschaft* (1963), 59 and 63.

This explains how anthropology, or in any case the discussion of anthropological themes, became so fundamentally important to the public life of the modern age. For, just as the Christian religion had been the basis for the spiritual unity of society in the days before the internal division of Christianity and the horrors of the confessional wars, so from the seventeenth century on, a shared conception of the human person, human values, and human rights became the basis for social coexistence.

It is understandable that not only Christians but also modern atheists who deny any and all religious faith should seek an anthropological basis for the universal validity of their claims. This was the path taken by Ludwig Feuerbach and the Marxists, as well as by Nietzsche, Freud, and the followers of both. If it can be shown that religion is simply a product of the human imagination and an expression of a human self-alienation, the roots of which are analyzed in a critical approach to religion, then religious faith and especially Christianity with its tradition and message will lose any claim to universal credibility in the life of the modern age. The Christian faith must then accept being lumped together with any and every form of superstition.

Without a sound claim to universal validity Christians cannot maintain a conviction of the truth of their faith and message. For a "truth" that would be simply my truth and would not at least claim to be universal and valid for every human being could not remain true even for me. This consideration explains why Christians cannot but try to defend the claim of their faith to be true. It also explains why in the modern age they must conduct this defense on the terrain of the interpretation of human existence and in a debate over whether religion is an indispensable component of humanness or, on the contrary, contributes to alienate human beings from themselves.[3]

For these reasons, Christian theology in the modern age must provide itself with a foundation in general anthropological studies. We are not dealing here with a position that one may or may not decide to accept. Individuals are not free to choose the problematic situation in which they prefer to play a part and make a contribution, whatever form this may take. Given the state of the discussion as it has developed in modern times, the general principle just enunciated holds true even for Christian theology today.

In this situation there is admittedly the danger of an anthropological bracketing of theology. Schaeder and especially Karl Barth saw the danger and saw it correctly. It is the danger that human beings doing theology

[3]For a more detailed discussion, see my essay "Speaking of God in the Face of Atheist Criticism," in my *The Idea of God and Human Freedom*, 99–116. See also P. Berger, *A Rumor of Angels: Modern Society and the Rediscovery of the Supernatural* (Garden City, N.Y., 1969).

may be concerned only with themselves instead of with God and thus let the true subject matter of theology go by the board. Nonetheless, if theologians are not to succumb to self-deception regarding their proper activity, they must begin their reflection with a recognition of the fundamental importance of anthropology for all modern thought and for any present-day claim of universal validity for religious statements. Otherwise they will, even if unintentionally, play into the hands of their atheistic critics, who reduce religion and theology to anthropology, that is, to human assumptions and illusions. By narrowly focusing on the question of human salvation (especially under the influence of pietism), theologians have undoubtedly forgotten in great measure that the Godness of God, and not human religious experience, must have first place in theology. This is true at least for any theology that is mindful of the First Commandment and takes as its norm the message of Jesus: "Seek first the kingdom of God."

Theologians will be able to defend the truth precisely of their talk about God only if they first respond to the atheistic critique of religion on the terrain of anthropology. Otherwise all their assertions, however impressive, about the primacy of the Godness of God will remain purely subjective assurances without any serious claim to universal validity.

Such has been the sad fate of dialectical theology and in particular the theology of Barth. It disdained to take a position on the terrain of anthropology and argue there that the religious thematic is unavoidable. As a result, it was defenseless against the suspicion that its faith was something arbitrarily legislated by human beings. As a result, its very *rejection* of anthropology was a form of *dependence* on anthropological suppositions. That is, when Barth, instead of justifying his position, simply decided to begin with God himself, he unwittingly adopted the most extreme form of theological subjectivism. Nothing could show more clearly how indispensable a rational justification of theology is and in particular, given the modern situation, an anthropological justification of the mode of theological argumentation. Only on this basis is it possible to show that the theological assertion of God's sovereignty is more than an arbitrary assumption of the part of a pious heart or even a theologian.

The considerations thus far offered show that in the modern age anthropology has become not only in fact but also with objective necessity the terrain on which theologians must base their claim of universal validity for what they say.

But what is the nature of this terrain? Are we dealing with a kind of neutral foundation, or rather one that already predetermines—and predetermines prejudicially—the special character and stability of the theological structure to be erected on it? The latter is precisely what Barth suspected. The results reached by philosopher O. Marquard in studying the history of the concept "anthropology" point in the same direction,[4] even though Marquard's interest in the question was the opposite of Barth's.

According to Marquard, the term "anthropology" first entered into common use in the sixteenth century as the name for a subordinate discipline within metaphysical psychology. This metaphysical psychology for its part took for its object not only the human person but God and the angels as well, and even the souls of animals. Then "anthropology" came to refer specifically to human psychology. This made it possible for the doctrine on the nature of the human being *(doctrina humanae naturae)* to be removed from its earlier metaphysical setting and made independent. And in fact (according to Marquard) under the title "anthropology" the philosophy of the schools did cut itself free from the metaphysical tradition with its theological ties and ask itself the question: "How is the human being to be defined, if not (any longer) by metaphysics and not (yet) by the mathematico-experimental sciences?" (363). The French and English moralists, he says, laid the groundwork for a metaphysically neutral and uninhibitedly secular conception of the human being. The latter was no longer defined in primarily theological or metaphysical terms but was viewed empirically as part of the natural world and in a context provided by the resuscitated Stoic philosophy of late antiquity.[5]

The "new anthropology" became the basis for the secular culture that arose after the end of the confessional wars of the sixteenth and seventeenth centuries. This culture developed in detachment from the Christian churches that were still battling each other. Marquard's description of the development is accurate insofar as the very concept of anthropology represented an answer to the question of the human being that was independent of Christian dogma and any metaphysics determined by that dogma. In opposition to Marquard, however, I must stress the point that the development was not automatically accompanied by any opposition to Christian-

---

[4]O. Marquard, "Zur Geschichte des philosophischen Begriffs 'Anthropologie' seit dem Ende des 18. Jahrhunderts," in *Collegium Philosophicum* (1965), 209–39; idem, "Anthropologie," *HWP* 1 (1971), 362–74. The page reference that follows in the text is to the latter article.

[5]W. Dilthey emphasized this point in his landmark study (1891), "Auffassung und Analyse des Menschen im 15. und 16. Jahrhundert" (*Gesammelte Schriften* II, 1–89), and especially in the essay (1904) "Über die Funktion der Anthropologie in der Kultur des 16. und 17. Jahrhunderts" (ibid., 416–92, esp. 442ff.). According to Dilthey, the discovery of the soul's interiority and its development in medieval mysticism (420f.) were connected with "the doctrines of the Stoa regarding a teleological coherence of nature, self-preservation, the dispositions of our being in which nature is at work teleologically, the human fall into the turbulence of the emotions and into a resultant enslavement by these, and finally liberation through the knowledge of 'vital values'" (450). Dilthey says that this new vision of humanity then became the "basis for the works that a natural system of law, state, and religion undertook to set in place and make effective in practice" (ibid.).

ity. In fact, motifs derived from the Christian faith played a part, implicitly and explicitly, in the new anthropology. This will subsequently be shown in detail.

It is correct, nonetheless, to say that the new anthropology with its empirical orientation did detach itself from confessional dogmas and from traditional Aristotelian metaphysics. As anthropology became thus detached and independent, the constitutive importance of the religious dimension of humanness receded more and more into the background as time went on, if indeed it was recognized at all. Modern anthropology reflects this independence of modern men and women from the confessionally divergent doctrinal systems of Christian theology and thus from any explicit religious thematic.

From this it is clear how ambivalent a procedure it would in fact be to try to base a Christian dogmatics on conceptions of the human person that arose in the course of a turning away from Christian dogma. As Barth correctly observed in his critique of the anthropocentrism of nineteenth-century theology, the theologians of that time showed an excessive naïveté and lack of discrimination when they adopted philosophical positions that were in turn based on a detachment of the human being from theology and its subject matter. This is true, for example, of Kant's moral philosophy, but it is true as well of his doctrine that timeless structures within the rational subject are the basis of all experience.[6]

A disregard of the theological question concerning the human person is, then, implicitly, even if more or less unreflectively, at work in most contributions to modern anthropology. But let us not be tempted to conclude rashly that theologians should not involve themselves at all in that kind of anthropology but should instead go unperturbed about what they like to call their own proper business. It is indeed true that despite all the differences in its various disciplines and in the individual contributions made to it, modern anthropology has been historically characterized by a certain tendency and will not allow theologians to claim it as a neutral basis for theological reflections making use of its results. But the only conclusion theologians should draw from this situation is that they may not undiscriminatingly accept the data provided by a nontheological anthropology and make these the basis for their own work, but rather must appropriate them in a critical way.

This kind of critical appropriation is necessary in dealing with a nontheological anthropology because, for the reasons already given, the relations between anthropological findings and the subject matter of theology

---

[6]F. Delekat has shown this in detail in his *Immanuel Kant. Historisch-kritische Interpretation der Hauptschriften* (1963). See my review, "Theologische Motive im Denken Immanuel Kants," *TLZ* 89 (1964), 897–906.

have in large measure been lost from sight. Theologians, moreover, must expect that a critical appropriation of these findings for theological use is also possible, if the God of the Bible is indeed the creator of all reality. It is not possible, on the other hand, to decree a priori that the expectation will actually be fulfilled. This must wait upon the anthropological phenomenon itself, but the question is both meaningful and necessary even if it should turn out that no simple and definitive answer is possible. In fact, the lack of a definitive answer is really to be antecedently expected, given the special character of the idea of God in its relation to the still incomplete totality of the world and our experience of it, a totality that transcends every finite experiential standpoint we can adopt.

A critical appropriation of nontheological anthropological research by theologians is not to be confused with the theological search for a "point of contact" in the self-understanding of the human person, as called for since the end of the twenties by Emil Brunner[7] and in a limited way by Rudolf Bultmann as well,[8] in opposition to Barth. The idea of a point of contact presupposes, especially for Brunner, that the subject matter of theology is fixed in itself but must still be somehow brought home to human beings. In the light of this conception a concern for missionary effectiveness requires that theology establish contact with the situation of the human beings to whom the proclamation is directed, just as God himself has done in his revelation.

When "contact" is conceived in this fashion the nontheological anthropology being used is not critically transformed and in this way appropriated by the theologian. It stands over against theology as something different from the latter, and theology, which in turn stands over against the anthropology as something different from it, is supposed to establish contact with this very different thing. The demand that anthropology be critically appropriated means something quite different. The aim is to lay theological claim to the human phenomena described in the anthropological disciplines. To this end, the secular description is accepted as simply

---

[7]E. Brunner, *Natur und Gnade* (1934; 1935[2]).

[8]R. Bultmann, "Points of Contact and Conflict", in *Essays Philosophical and Theological*, trans. J. C. G. Greig (New York, 1955), 133–50. For Bultmann, unlike Brunner, the subject matter of theology can only be elaborated *existentially* in the form of anthropology. Since Bultmann sees the point of contact as resolving the opposition of revelation to the human being as sinner, he adopted a position midway between Barth and Brunner in this question. But because he understood revelation to be unqualifiedly a judgment on and negation of the human, he did not achieve a critical appropriation of an anthropology based on existential philosophy, though he regarded this anthropology as normative, but accepted as valid the pretheological interpretation of the person already given in Heidegger's analysis of Dasein and this without any critical discussion of the individual claims made in that analysis. He simply offered a *global* negative evaluation of it as a description of the sinner's understanding of Dasein and used it in this form as a negative foil for theology.

a provisional version of the objective reality, a version that needs to be expanded and deepened by showing that the anthropological datum itself contains a further and theologically revelant dimension.

The assumption that such aspects can be shown to exist in the facts studied by the other disciplines is the general hypothesis that determines the procedure followed in my own study; the hypothesis must, of course, prove its validity in the discussion of the particular themes discussed. These aspects have not already been developed in the nontheological disciplines making up anthropology or are mentioned only peripherally and usually not made central. This situation is to be explained by the motives that have directed the development of modern anthropology in its various disciplines. These disciplines have developed in separation from the dogmatics of the contending confessions and from any theologically influenced metaphysics. Their aim, moreover, has been to place even the peripheral statements they do make about human religious behavior on a new and empirical foundation, in the establishment of which the religious themes of human existence seemingly play no part as yet.

What is the relation between this task of appropriating nontheological anthropological research and theory and the traditional dogmatic anthropology that was developed in the framework of the theological doctrine of creation and took the form of a doctrine regarding the original state and the fall of Adam?

Dogmatic anthropology has had two central themes: the image of God in human beings, and human sin. Also discussed have been the relation of soul and body, as well as a series of other questions for the most part connected with the soul-body question, but these have not been the specifically dogmatic themes in the theological doctrine of the human person. The two main anthropological themes of theology—the image of God and sin—will also prove to be central in the attempted theological interpretation of the implications of nontheological anthropological study.

We must be careful, however, not to think of these two themes as having no validity outside the framework of the old doctrine of the original state and the fall, a doctrine reflecting a now outdated worldview. If we avoid this prejudice, we will see that the doctrines of the image of God and sin thematize the two basic aspects found in the most varied connections between anthropological phenomena and the reality of God. To speak of the image of God in human beings is to speak of their closeness to the divine reality, a closeness that also determines their position in the world of nature. To speak of sin, on the other hand, is to speak of the factual separation from God of human beings whose true destiny nonetheless is union with God; sin is therefore to be thematized as a contradiction of human beings with themselves, an interior conflict in the human person.

The opposition between closeness to God and distance from God leaves its impress on the whole of religious life. It finds expression in the fundamental polarity of holy and unholy, clean and unclean, as well as in the opposition between holy and profane. The concepts of image of God and sin describe the anthropological manifestation of this basic opposition that marks all of religious life. At the same time, however, they give the basic opposition a specific nuance that is characteristic of the Judeo-Christian tradition.

In reminding the reader that an opposition and tension far more universal in application manifests itself here in a particular setting, I am for the moment simply making one point: that we ought not to be surprised if an investigation of the religious and therefore theologically relevant implications of anthropological data leads us to the concepts of image of God and sin. But there is a further possibility which we may not exclude in advance: that the specifically Christian stress, as conveyed in these two concepts, on the opposition and tension between closeness to God and distance from God may shed a special light on the empirically derived anthropological phenomena. As we shall see, even historically the two concepts pointed the way to the discovery of these phenomena.

Nonetheless it is not my intention here to offer a *dogmatic* anthropology. Traditional dogmatic anthropology presupposes the existence of God when it speaks of the image of God in human beings. Furthermore, it develops this concept on the basis not of anthropological findings but of what the Bible says. Since it supposes the reality of God as it sets about speaking of human beings, it surrenders the possibility of joining in the discussion at the level of anthropological findings, for at this level a divine reality can be introduced, if at all, only as a problematic point of reference for human behavior, not as the object of apodictic dogmatic assertion. In addition, an anthropology that would suppose the reality of God could not help to ground theology as a whole, since the theme of theology is precisely the reality of God.

In contrast to traditional dogmatic anthropology, the studies undertaken here may be summarily described as a *fundamental-theological* anthropology. This anthropology does not argue from dogmatic data and presuppositions. Rather, it turns its attention directly to the phenomena of human existence as investigated in human biology, psychology, cultural anthropology, or sociology and examines the findings of these disciplines with an eye to implications that may be relevant to religion and theology.

What method is best suited to such studies as these? Can one of the disciplines dealing with the human person claim a primacy in the sense that it provides a groundwork to which the contributions of all the other disciplines must then be related? Does any single discipline thematize the reality of the human in a way at once comprehensive and diversified, so that the contributions of the other disciplines can find a place in the framework it supplies?

Human biology certainly cannot suitably play such a role. The question it asks about the human being is undoubtedly fundamental, but it is not comprehensive in a rounded way. Biology studies human beings only as a species and must prescind from individual features. Even the social relations of the human entity enter, if at all, only in a very general way into the perspective adopted in human biology. Sociology, for its part, devotes its attention especially to these relations, but it too prescinds from the individual and therefore from the concrete form which human reality takes. Something similar must be said of psychology.

The closest approach to concrete human reality is to be found in historical science, since this deals with the concrete lives of individuals and the way in which they interact in the process that is their history. Yet even the reconstructions produced by historical science must prescind from many details that belong to the concrete reality of the events being investigated. Even a biography, which represents the closest approach of history to the individual life, must focus on the events and occurrences regarded as important in the life that is being presented.

In history too, therefore, abstraction still plays a fundamental part. This does not alter the fact that historical science approaches more closely to the concrete reality of human life than does any other of the anthropological disciplines. In comparison with history, these other disciplines thematize only partial aspects of the human reality: biology, the special character of human beings as compared to the animals; sociology, the basic forms of social relations among human beings; psychology, the general structures of human behavior.

On the other hand, historical science presupposes in principle all these partial aspects when it undertakes to describe human existence in its individual concrete forms. Consequently, history cannot be the basis for the other anthropological disciplines; rather, it absorbs them all into itself as partial aspects. The history of humankind thus comes at the end of anthropological reflection, precisely because it alone thematizes the concrete reality of the human being. Knowledge must always begin with the universal and abstract and only at the end reach the concrete as the object to which all the previous, abstract approaches were ultimately directed.

From this point of view, the fundamental anthropological discipline is the one that deals with humans beings at the highest level of generality and thus first delimits the concept of human being. even if at the cost of remaining very abstract. That discipline is human biology. My investigation will therefore begin with what biological research tells us about the special character of human beings as opposed to the animals most closely related to them and to the animal world generally. Since such a definition of the human being looks less to the doctrine of evolution than to behavioral research, we find ourselves in very close proximity to psychology. Psychology in turn proves to have close ties with the anthropological perspectives of sociology, while conversely sociology presupposes biological anthropology and psychology.

These studies will lead finally to human history as the history of human existence itself. In the process it will become clear that the question of the anthropological significance of history is linked with the central anthropological problem in pedagogy: How to form human beings.[9]

[9]I presented the substance of these methodological considerations in 1962 in the concluding chapter of my book *What Is Man? Contemporary Anthropology in Theological Perspective,* trans. D. A. Priebe (Philadelphia, 1970). But at that time I did not so consistently correlate the findings of the discipline of anthropology from the standpoint of the question of the *concept* of the human being.

Part One
THE PERSON IN NATURE

1

The Uniqueness
of Humanity

Modern anthropology no longer follows Christian tradition in defining the uniqueness of humanity explicitly in terms of God; rather, it defines this uniqueness through reflection on the place of humanity in nature and specifically through a comparison of human existence with that of the higher animals. To some extent this represents a revival of the ancient and in particular the Stoic approach which understood humanity in the framework of the cosmic order as a microcosm that reflects the macrocosm of the physical universe. Democritus was the first to describe the human being as "a world in miniature," a microcosm (Diels, Frag. 34). A human being is an image of the macrocosm by virtue of containing all the strata of reality (body, soul, and spirit).

An integration of humanity into nature along these lines still played an important part in the anthropology of the Renaissance, and echoes of it could still be heard at the beginning of the modern age. Here, nonetheless, as was true of the Christian tradition, the question of the special place of humanity in nature had become independent of the idea of the human being as microcosm. The question of humanity's special place in nature still dominates modern anthropology even when human beings are understood in terms of their relation to the animals; for in the study of this relationship the aim is precisely to determine what is distinctively human. In asserting this special place, the Christian and metaphysical tradition had appealed to the concept of an immortal spiritual soul with which only human beings are endowed. This individual, immortal soul was conceived, not as simply a participation in a world soul that permeates the cosmos, but, in biblical and Christian terms, as a supraterrestrial distinguishing mark and dignity that elevates humanity above the entire cosmos and sets it at God's side over against the cosmos.

In the course of the nineteenth century the interpretation of humanity's special place as owing to a soul that is united to an animal body became increasingly dubious. An attempt was made—here again in continuity with earlier insights—to overcome the body-soul dualism and to understand human uniqueness in terms of corporeality. A foundation was thus laid for

a comparison between animal and human. We know the animals, however, only from outside, via their bodily form and bodily behavior. The
decision to adopt the same approach to human uniqueness represents the
decisive turn in the direction of present-day anthropology, for, like Darwin in his theory of the origin of the species, the method of contemporary
anthropology postulates a continuity between human and animal and then
endeavors to determine the special place of humanity within this continuity, instead of allowing the uniqueness to depend on the introduction of
an alien principle into the world of nature.

This approach had its predecessors in the eighteenth and nineteenth
centuries. Among the philosophers who adopted it, J. G. Herder and
Friedrich Nietzsche deserve special mention. But the decisive breakthrough came when psychologists no longer sought access to the psyche
through introspection but through observation of *external behavior*. This
trend started at the beginning of the present century in American behaviorism, on the one hand, and, on the other, in the biological (animal-psycho-
logical) investigation of behavior that became the starting point
of German "philosophical anthropology." Max Scheler is regarded as
the originator of this discipline, which was developed by Helmuth
Plessner along with Scheler himself and, later on, especially by Arnold
Gehlen.

I. The Behaviorist Approach and Its Critics

After preliminary work by William McDougall (1912), behaviorism
was launched in 1913 by John B. Watson, whose aim was to renew
psychology on the basis of the natural sciences.[1]

> Watson, a student of animal behavior, wished to pursue the study of psychology
> with the objective methods proper to the natural sciences. In his view, this
> meant the limitation of psychological investigation to an analysis of behavior in
> terms of stimulus and response and the variations in these. The object of
> psychological research was no longer to be the life of the psyche or the data of
> consciousness but the adaptation of the organism.[2]

In 1953 the American behaviorist B. F. Skinner wrote an essay, "Behaviorism at Fifty," in which he looked back to the beginnings of the new

[1]J. B. Watson, *Behaviorism* (New York, 1930; Norton Library, 1970); see especially ch.
2, "How to Study Human Behavior," which dates from 1913. See also his article "Behaviorismus," *HWP* 1 (1971), 817f.

[2]Thus F. Graumann in his Introduction to the German translation of J. B. Watson,
Behaviorismus (1968).

psychology inaugurated by Watson.[3] According to Skinner, the point of departure for this psychology was Darwin's theory of evolution. In substantiation of that theory it had to be shown that humanity is not fundamentally different from the lower animals and that on the contrary all human characteristics are simply variants of animal forms of life and modes of behavior. Even intelligence is not something completely new in human beings, but is found in rudimentary form in our closest relatives in the animal world, as can be seen from the occasionally discerning behavior of animals. But if it is possible to conclude from the behavior of animals that they possess intellectual powers, why should not the same procedure be applied to human beings and the same methodology thus be used in studying both human and animal behavior? Watson wrote in 1913: "Everyone admits that the behavior of animals can be studied without any appeal to a consciousness. . . . What I am proposing here is that the behavior of man and animal alike must be placed on the same level."[4] Watson believed it possible to abandon the concept of consciousness in the psychological sense; this renunciation would, he thought, "do away with the separation between psychology and the other sciences." In his description of behavior as an adaptation to environmental conditions Watson made use of the correlation of stimulus and response, especially as discovered by the Russian scientist I. P. Pavlov in his famous experiments with dogs and formulated in his theory of "the conditioned reflex." Watson hoped to explain the whole range of human behavior in a similar way, especially with the aid of the assumption that behavioral habits arise from this kind of reflex.

It is now clear that behaviorism was a primarily negative response to the modern question of humanity's special place in nature inasmuch as it sought to avoid and replace the concept of consciousness. As a result, the very limitations of behaviorism became, conversely, arguments for the special place of humanity in nature. Today, however, the concern to maintain this special place can no longer be defended with the arguments used in the old metaphysics of the soul, but, like behaviorism itself, must appeal to the bodily conditions and peculiar characteristics of human behavior. Here we see the abiding significance of behaviorism: its attempt to reduce human activity to observable behavior that is stimulated from without has dictated the terrain and mode of argumentation for all efforts to deal with humanity, even if these efforts have a different orientation from that of behaviorism. For if human behavior could be satisfactorily

[3]B. F. Skinner, "Behaviorism at Fifty," in T. W. Wann, ed., *Behaviorism and Phenomenology: Contrasting Bases for Modern Psychology* (Chicago, 1964), 79ff., esp. 80f.

[4]Watson, *Behaviorism.* [I have not been able to find these sentences in the English original and have translated them from the German version, 27f.—Tr.]

and fully explained by a behaviorist analysis, all other assumptions regarding human uniqueness would be rendered superfluous.

As early as 1935, F. J. J. Buytendijk and Helmuth Plessner criticized the application of Pavlov's conditioned reflex as a principle for explaining all behavior without exception.[5] Following the American psychologist Edward C. Tolman, Buytendijk raised the objection against behaviorism that the stimulus-response scheme does not display an unambiguous causal relationship, since the same constellations of stimuli can elicit a variety of movements in response, while, conversely, different constellations of stimuli can elicit the same response. In his later studies of human behavior and activity Buytendijk wrote that a concrete activity such as running or jumping does not come into existence as a chain of reflexes but is to be understood as an integrated feat that is "determined by the state or condition being sought as a goal."[6] Because of this objective orientation to a goal, which Tolman had demonstrated in detail, even the behavior of animals is never a causal sequence in the sense of a chain of reflexes, but is "always a conducting-*oneself.*"[7] This finding is of wide-ranging significance, for it means that even simple animal movements such as running, grasping, and jumping cannot be described in purely external terms as a sequence of changes of state caused by stimuli but only as the activity of a "subject": animal behavior is always a conducting-*oneself.*

G. H. Mead, the founder of social psychology, developed the same point of view, although with a somewhat different emphasis.[8] Externally observable behavior, said Mead in opposition to Watson, is simply the expression of something internal, namely, a subjective act. Mead made the point that in the special case of human behavior the subjective acts that are at the basis of this behavior make themselves known especially through the connection between human behavior and speech.[9] Charles W. Morris in his neobehaviorism attempted to meet this difficulty by describing the connections between speech and behavior with the aid of concepts based on externally stimulatable behavior and without appealing, as Mead did,

[5]"Die physiologische Erklärung des Verhaltens. Eine Kritik an der Theorie Pawlows," *Acta Biotheor.* (Leiden), Series A 1 (1935), 151–72.

[6]F. J. J. Buytendijk, *Allgemeine Theorie der menschlichen Haltung und Bewegung* (1948; German tr., 1956), 12. M. Merleau-Ponty had undertaken (1942) a similar critique of the reduction of behavior to a stimulus-reflex mechanism in his *The Structure of Behavior,* trans. A. L. Fisher (Boston, 1963). In a manner similar to Buytendijk's later arguments, Merleau-Ponty's introduction of the concepts of gestalt (33ff.) and structure (145ff.) showed the irreducibility of the whole to a mere sum of its parts (e.g., 69), without thereby succumbing to the kind of mystification found in vitalism (cf. 151, etc.).

[7]Buytendijk, 14.

[8]G. H. Mead, *Mind, Self and Society* (Chicago, 1934), 2ff.

[9]Ibid., 6.

to an acting subject.[10] In response, Jürgen Habermas raised the same objection that Buytendijk had raised in a more generalized form: it is impossible in principle to assert that the stimulus-response link is an unambiguous one, that is, that a specific response is always given to a specific stimulus. Habermas emphasized the *uncertainty* of the stimulus-response connection, especially in human behavior as mediated through speech: "Identical stimuli can elicit divergent responses when diversely interpreted by the one responding."[11] The response to a stimulus is univocally determined only (if at all) by constant factors at work in the subjective attitude. This consideration leads away from an extremely empiricist toward an aprioristic interpretation of behavior that makes the peculiar features of a response to stimuli depend on the individuality of the living entity in question, that is, on its innate behavioral schemata which prior to any experience determine its responses to possible stimuli and thus its behavior as well.

II. Is the Structure of Behavior Peculiar to the Species?

Whereas American behaviorism stands in the tradition of British empiricist philosophy and its tendency to reduce all knowledge to sense perceptions and sense observations, a decisive part of the behavioral study done by German-speaking scientists has been influenced by the philosophy of Kant and its thesis that all experience depends on the experience of the pregiven forms by which our spirit apprehends. When Konrad Lorenz, the leading contemporary German student of behavior, wrote a summary (Königsberg, 1942) of his conception of behavioral research he entitled it "The Innate Forms of Possible Experience."[12] In this essay Lorenz expressly adopts Kant's view, but at the same time he both modifies and generalizes the latter's transcendental approach. According to Lorenz, Kant had "discovered both that our forms of intuition and categories are independent of any prior experience and that we are in a position to 'read as experiences' only what can be written on the keyboard of the categories and forms of intuition" (237). But, he says, Kant did not see that these forms of intuition and categories depend on the peculiar character of our bodily organs. Moreover, since the latter are the product of the evolution of life, it seems probable that the experience of all living things is in like manner preformed by the form of their organs. The transcendental philosophy of Kant is here transferred to the empiricobio-

---

[10]C. W. Morris, *Signs, Language and Behavior* (New York, 1955).
[11]J. Habermas, *Zur Logik der Sozialwissenschaften* (1967), 107.
[12]*Zeitschrift für Tierpsychologie* 5 (1943), 235–409.

logical order: every animal has its *innate behavioral pattern* (241).

In adopting these theses, Lorenz contradicts behaviorism, but not to the extent that he must completely reject behaviorist analyses. Rather, the acceptance of innate behavioral patterns serves merely to supplement the behaviorist presentation of behavior as fitting the stimulus-response schema.

> Whenever a living being, without prior experience, seemingly "understands" a situation and responds to it in a meaningful way, this response is dependent only on very specific stimuli that operate like a key. . . . To such obviously mechanistic and physiological correlations with specific stimuli situations, such innate "predispositions" to react with regularity to certain key stimuli, we may give the name *innate schemata* (240).

These innate schemata "at one and the same time *characterize* and *simplify*" situations of vital importance to the organism. The acceptance of innate schemata serves here to solve the problem that behaviorism had been unable to solve: the ability of the same stimulus to elicit divergent responses. According to Lorenz, the response depends not only on the stimulus but also on the behavioral schema of the particular organism. It is this behavioral schema that unequivocally determines the stimuli to which an animal will respond under a given set of conditions and what its specific reactions will be.

A similar acceptance, inspired by transcendental philosophy, of a priori behavioral schemata is found in a modified form in Lorenz' disciple, I. Eibl-Eibesfeldt.[13] An analogous perspective characterizes Jean Piaget's studies for a genetic theory of knowledge that is based especially on research into the psychology of children.[14] The generative grammar of Noam Chomsky[15] and certain trends in structuralism show a concurrence with these views inasmuch as they accept the idea that human behavior is determined by peculiarly human structures which precede all experience and are therefore to be regarded as a priori or transcendental.[16] Here too is to be located the doctrine of Habermas and K. O. Apel on interests as governing knowledge.[17] The multiplicity of these important concepts which differ among themselves yet are in agreement on this fundamental

[13]Compare I. Eibl-Eibesfeldt's essay on "Stammesgeschichtliche Anpassungen im Verhalten des Menschen," in *Biologische Anthropologie* II (1972) (series Neue Anthropologie 1, ed. H. G. Gadamer and P. Vogler).

[14]See the comprehensive presentation by H. G. Furth, *Piaget and Knowledge: Theoretical Foundations* (Englewood Cliffs, N.J., 1969).

[15]N. Chomsky, *Language and Mind* (New York, 1968; enlarged ed., 1972).

[16]C. Lévi-Strauss, *Structural Anthropology.* trans. C. Jacobson and B. G. Schoepf (New York, 1963).

[17]J. Habermas, *Knowledge and Human Interests.* trans. J. J. Shapiro (Boston, 1971); K. O. Apel, *Transformation der Philosophie* II (1973), 155ff.

point of view shows how broad is the spectrum of contemporary efforts to interpret human behavior in transcendental terms as directed by a priori behavioral schemata that precede any and all experience. Despite their diversity, all these approaches have in common an inflection of Kant's transcendental-philosophical statement of the problem, comparable to that seen in Konrad Lorenz' biological study of behavior. The question of the structures that determine behavior is broadened so as to move beyond the Kantian problematic of subjectivity as the ground of all experience and thus become a radical acceptance of empirical theory formation, so that the Kantian opposition between the empirical and the transcendental is now abandoned.

Biologist Jacob von Uexküll had developed views materially similar to those of Lorenz.[18] According to Von Uexküll, every animal experiences its surroundings in a specific way, that is, with its attention focused on the presence of features that are positively or negatively important for its own survival and the life of the species. In the case of the lower animals, these features comprise a very small part of the multiplicity that is to be found in the actual surroundings. A tick, for example, experiences its surroundings in an extremely simple form. With the aid of its skin's sensitivity to light it finds its way to a tree branch. Its sense of smell and temperature tell it when a warm-blooded animal is under the branch. At this signal the tick drops onto the animal in order to suck its blood. These features, then, form the "feature world" or "environment" of the tick. Thus the concept of environment *(Umwelt)* does not refer in Von Uexküll and subsequent writers to the actual "surroundings" *(Umgebung),* with all the multiformity we know them to have, in which the animal in question lives. Rather, the environment of an animal is the subjective perspective, the subjective sector of the world, that is defined by the set of features to which the animal reacts according to its species, that is, according to the innate behavioral schema of that species.

According to Von Uexküll, human beings, like the animals, are limited in their behavior to an environment and therefore to a sector out of the total reality of the world, a sector that is determined by the vital interests of the species and corresponds to an innate behavioral schema. In his book *Streifzüge durch die Umwelten von Menschen und Tieren* (Expeditions through the environments of man and the animals; 1958), Von Uexküll speaks of environments proper to specific occupations. Now, the forest is certainly a different place for the hunter than it is for the woodcutter or the Sunday excursionist. There is, however, no question here of a limited perspective that is innate and peculiar to a species, but rather an effect of culture, that is, of occupational specialization. This shows that the concept of environ-

[18]J. von Uexküll, *Umwelt und Innenwelt der Tiere* (1921).

ment in the special sense it has in behavioral research can be applied only metaphorically to humankind.

The concept of environment cannot be transferred without further ado from animal to human behavior. If there are innate behavioral schemata in the human being, then they exist only in a singularly rudimentary and attenuated form. They influence the free play of human behavior in only a small degree. Konrad Lorenz, who observed a similar reduction of instinctual mechanisms in domesticated animals as a consequence of their domestication, sought to interpret the analogous situation in human behavior as the result of a "self-domestication." But the objection was raised to this interpretation that "the plasticity of the instinctual life and its readiness to deteriorate are obviously primary and not secondary in the case of man."[19] As evidence for this claim, Gehlen pointed to the fact that cannibalism is documented among early hominids, whereas among animals restraints proper to the species keep them from eating other members of the species. It is clear that even in the early phases of human evolution, the behavior of the human being was characterized by the "*natural* instability" of the human being's instinctual life (59) and that this gives the human being a special place in the animal world. To describe this special place Gehlen and others before him have used the concept of "openness to the world," in distinction from the dependence of the animals on their environment. The concept of "openness to the world" is central to what is known as "philosophical anthropology," a phrase that is understood in this context not simply in a broad sense that includes all philosophical efforts to define the nature of the human being but in a narrow sense as the name of a particular philosophical trend of our century in which the focus of attention has been the philosophical interpretation of empirical anthropological research.

III. Philosophical Anthropology

The concept of philosophical anthropology in the narrow sense of the phrase describes the type of anthropological reflection that originated in Max Scheler's groundbreaking book *Die Stellung des Menschen im Kosmos* (1928).[20] Independently of Scheler, Helmuth Plessner developed a similar conception.[21] The positions taken by Scheler were then further developed by Arnold Gehlen in particular.[22] Some biologists too have associated themselves with this philosophical anthropology, especially the

[19]A. Gehlen, *Anthropologische Forschung* (rde 138, 1961), 59.

[20]ET: *Man's Place in Nature*, trans. H. Meyerhoff (Boston, 1961). The quotations from Scheler farther on in the text are from the ET.

[21]H. Plessner, *Die Stufen des Organischen und der Mensch* (1928; 1965²).

[22]A. Gehlen, *Der Mensch* (1950).

zoologist Adolf Portmann[23] and the Dutch behavioral scientist F. J. J. Buytendijk.[24]

Philosophical anthropology shares with behaviorism and German behavioral research the principle that human beings must be interpreted in terms of their corporeality and in particular of their bodily and therefore observable behavior. It also agrees with German behavioral research and the social psychology of G. H. Mead (in contrast to classical behaviorism) that even the behavior of animals and certainly that of human beings must be understood as a conducting-*oneself,* that is, as the expression of a subjective center. On the other hand, philosophical anthropology differs from behaviorism and from the science of behavior as represented by Jacob von Uexküll and Konrad Lorenz, inasmuch as it recognizes humanity's special place in the domain of animal life. In Scheler and Gehlen this place is described by the concept of "openness to the world." Plessner, for his part, prefers the expression "exocentricity"; he intends to express the same content, however, and the new term points only to a critical limitation of that content and represents an effort to define it more precisely.

Scheler's anthropological thought was strongly influenced by Henri Bergson and especially by his *Matière et mémoire* (1896; ET: *Matter and Memory,* 1911). As a vitalist philosopher, Bergson had devoted special attention to the intimate connection of body and spirit. Scheler developed the same line of thought by linking the phenomenology of Edmund Husserl with the behavioral research of Von Uexküll. In so doing, he still took as a starting point the principle that human beings as persons are spiritual beings whose spirituality cannot be derived from the biological factors that condition their being. But at the same time Scheler looked for a bodily correlate of this human spirituality, that is, for a datum in which the special character of humankind finds a corporeal expression. Scheler found it in human openness to the world. In this phrase he was describing the fact that "the spiritual being is . . . no longer subject to its drives and its environment" but is "free from the environment" (37). Human beings are no longer limited by a set of drives and instincts to a determinate feature world so that their senses would perceive only those features of the environment which are important for their own life and that of the species, while all the other qualities of the objective world would be already filtered out. Human perception does not function primarily as releaser of reactions that are pre-imprinted in an innate behavioral schema. What is characteristic of

[23]A. Portmann, *Zoologie und das neue Bild des Menschen* (rde 20, 1956). Originally published as *Biologische Fragmente zu einer Lehre vom Menschen* (1944).

[24]F. J. J. Buytendijk, *Mensch und Tier. Ein Beitrag zur vergleichenden Psychologie* (rde 74, 1958).

human beings is, rather, that they can dwell on the contents of intuitions and ideas *as such,* in their "objective nature" (37) and not simply insofar as they are the objects of instincts. Human instinctual impulses can therefore be inhibited by the person, and this "voluntary inhibition" (39) points, according to Scheler, to the person or spirit as its origin; that is, it points to an origin which, according to Scheler, "transcends what we call 'life' in the most general sense" (36). This voluntary inhibition of instincts—which at every point is presupposed in all freedom from inhibition and indeed makes the latter possible to begin with—points precisely, according to Scheler, to that "which gives man his unique characteristics," that is, to a "principle opposed to life as such, even to life in man" (36). This is the spirit, and the appearance of the spirit in humanity cannot, in Scheler's view, be accounted for by the natural evolution of life but must be attributed, "if reducible to anything, . . . to the ultimate Ground of Being of which 'life' is a particular manifestation" (36). The center from which human beings are in a position to oppose their own life and drives and thus objectify themselves "can only be located in the highest Ground of Being itself" (47).

When Scheler asserts that humanity's special place in nature is due to its openness to the world, he understands this openness as requiring for its intelligibility the presence of spirit as a principle that is opposed to life and intervenes from outside as it were in the process of evolution, so that it can be traced directly to God.[25] Scheler found the idea of God an indispensable one if he was to answer the question of the origin of spirit and thus the question of humanity's special place. The situation changed in subsequent work in "philosophical anthropology."

Helmuth Plessner, in his *Die Stufen des Organischen und der Mensch,* which likewise appeared in 1928, was showing himself much more reserved than Scheler. It has justly been said "that Plessner supplies conceptual help at a point at which Max Scheler's discourse turns particularly metaphysi-

[25]In the dualism of spirit and life, K. Lenk sees the early Scheler's theistic metaphysics of the person continuing to influence his later work in anthropology; cf. K. Lenk, *Von der Ohnmacht des Geistes. Kritische Darstellung der Spätphilosophie Schelers* (1959). The increasing emphasis on the dynamism of the vital drives, against which the life-transcending spirit is "helpless" (ibid., 6), has been connected by F. Hammer, *Theonome Anthropologie? Max Schelers Menschenbild und seine Grenzen* (The Hague, 1972), with Scheler's express appeal to Freud's doctrine of the instincts (137). Compare Scheler's *Man's Place in Nature,* 57, 59f. W. Schulz, in his comprehensive presentation of "philosophical anthropology," *Philosophie in der veränderten Welt* (1972), 419–67, gives the reasons why Scheler retained the traditional view: the inevitability of the question of meaning and the capacity for repressing instinct (431). The judgment that this second function in particular contradicts Scheler's thesis of the "helplessness of the spirit" would be valid only if Scheler had denied all motivational power to the spirit.

cal."[26] Instead of using the concept of spirit, Plessner speaks of humanity's *exocentric position.* The meaning is that whereas the higher animals, unlike the plants, have the center of their vital manifestations in themselves (a center that became more clearly defined as such as the course of evolution brought the progressive development of a central nervous system), human beings are at the same time exocentric as well. They have their center not only within themselves but at the same time outside themselves. In this somewhat obscure description Plessner is pointing to the ability of human beings to adopt an attitude toward themselves, a capacity for self-reflection, which at the same time is the basis for the human ability to stand back from things and treat them as objects, *as* things. The relation of priority between human objectivity, unencumbered by instinctual drives, toward the world of things, on the one hand, and human self-objectification, on the other, is the converse in Plessner of what it is in Scheler. Plessner sees the capacity for self-reflection (exocentricity) as the original condition from which the capacity for objective, dispassionate dealing with environing reality is derived. On the other hand, Scheler's concept of spirit is by no means completely absent from Plessner's thought. In the final analysis, exocentricity is simply another name for self-consciousness and therefore for spirit. Plessner, however, is not thereby introducing a separate and independent principle opposed to all life, as Scheler does in his concept of spirit, in keeping with the entire tradition from which he takes the concept. In Plessner, exocentricity is, rather, a structural modification of life itself at the stage of development that life has reached in humanity. Plessner does not make clear, however, what the "outside" is in which human beings properly have their exocentric center, especially since they obviously have the most highly developed central nervous system of all. The relationship and interconnection of centrality and exocentricity remain singularly vague. It is not surprising, then, that Plessner's replacement of the idea of openness to the world with the idea of exocentricity has found little favor. On this point, Arnold Gehlen in particular has followed Scheler's terminology and not Plessner's.

Gehlen too intends first of all to avoid "the theme of 'spirit,' which calls for the adoption of a metaphysical position," by "bracketing" it.[27] At the same time, however, he also intends to face the question of humanity's special place in nature, but without using the concept of spirit in his answer. He avoids "either assuming that human beings are distinct only in degree from the animals or defining them by 'spirit' alone . . . in the

[26]D. Claessens, *Instinkt. Psyche. Geltung. Bestimmungsfaktoren menschlichen Verhaltens. Eine soziologische Anthropologie* (Cologne, 1968), 23.
[27]Gehlen, *Der Mensch.* 11. The page references that follow in the text are to this book.

sense of an essential attribute that is opposed to nature" (29). But when
Gehlen insists, against Scheler, that the difference between human beings
and the beasts cannot be located solely in the spirit and that on the contrary
the difference is "just as evident in the physical forms of movement" (24),
the supposed disagreement with Scheler probably rests on a misunderstanding. According to Scheler, spirit not only manifests itself in human
consciousness but also finds expression first of all in human bodily behavior. Consequently Gehlen is proceeding fully in accord with Scheler's
intentions when he endeavors to discover humanity's special place by the
peculiar characteristics of human bodily behavior. Otherwise he could not
have accepted Scheler's concept of openness to the world and made it the
central concept in his own thinking. Gehlen found a way of doing this,
however, which rendered superfluous a recourse to Scheler's concept of
spirit.

In order to achieve this goal, Gehlen needed, above all, to find another
explanation for the singular "inhibition" of human impulses and instincts,
which Scheler accounted for by introducing the spirit. But does this inhibition really need to be explained by assuming some force that does the
inhibiting? Gehlen found a way out of the difficulty by explaining the
inhibition as a central structural feature of the human form of life, a feature
that is connected with a good many other peculiarities of human organization and behavior. We are no longer dealing, then, with a special effect
produced by some force, but rather with the specific structure of the
human mode of existence itself.

Gehlen broadens Scheler's idea of an inhibition of instinct in human
beings into the thesis that the human species as a whole shows the characteristics of "an inhibition of evolution" (109). This is Gehlen's well-
known thesis of the human beings as "deficient beings." The idea was
suggested to him by the work of Amsterdam anatomist Ludwig Bolk, who
had described the primitive state of human organs (108) as "fetal states
or conditions that have become permanent" (109). Gehlen sees this state
of affairs as the expression of "an inhibition of evolution" that is characteristic of the human species. Gehlen subsequently appealed as well to the
demonstration by Basel zoologist Adolf Portmann[28] that in comparison
with the other higher mammals human beings are born a year too soon
and in a still unfinished state. As one who is "physiologically premature,"
a human being is already exposed in the final stage of development as an
embryo to the influences of a social environment. From the latter the
human being receives decisive impressions during the "extrauterine
springtime." In Gehlen's mind, these results of Portmann's research fitted

---

[28]Portmann, *Biologische Fragmente zu einer Lehre vom Menschen* (1944), 46ff.

in with the information received from Bolk regarding the primitive state of human organs. Now he had the explanation of why human beings are born prematurely as "deficient beings" and, if not supported by the world of social culture, are exposed without protection to the multiplicity of impressions that pour in upon them ("an inundation of stimuli"). In this way, and without having recourse to the spirit, Gehlen deduces the basic human situation that Scheler had described as the inhibition of vital impulses by the spirit. Instead of the term "inhibition," which suggests the question of an inhibiting force, Gehlen prefers the neutral term "hiatus." He speaks of a hiatus, a gap, between perceptions and impulses. What this means becomes clear from a comparison with the dependence of animals on their environment, for in animals perceptions serve to release innate behavioral mechanisms, the instincts. In this process the sense organs serve as filters which by their nature allow only those impressions to pass through to the animal which are important, positively or negatively, for its life. The life of perception and instinct thus forms a closed functional circle in the behavior of animals.[29]

It is precisely here that the situation is different in human beings. Our instincts are for the most part deficient in development and at the same time blended with one another; for both reasons they operate in an uncertain way as compared with those of our animal relatives. Our perceptions do not release precise instinctual reactions. For this very reason our perceptions can develop a life of their own and turn to things without being limited by instinctual interests that guide our behavior. As a result, the "inundation" of stimuli and perceptions that do not have a direct instinctual importance is intensified. Such is the "hiatus" between stimulus and reaction which Gehlen observes and which is analogous to Scheler's "inhibition" of animal instincts in human beings. Gehlen need no longer trace this hiatus back to an inhibiting cause, namely, Scheler's spirit, because he understands it in purely biological terms as a result of the human bodily constitution, the primitive condition of human helplessness as "a deficient being."

Gehlen therefore sees it as humanity's basic task to compensate for the deficiencies of the species. In Gehlen's view, it is language and culture, above all, that make this compensation possible. They are the result of human action. Now at last we have come to the key concept in Gehlen's anthropology: in his view, the human being is the "acting being." Through action and specifically through the development of language, culture, and technical skills human beings convert the disadvantages of their initial biological condition into advantages. Through their action

[29]On this, see V. von Weizsäcker, *Der Gestaltkreis* (Leipzig, 1943).

they ease the burden of the complex multiplicity of stimuli that pour in on them by creating in language a symbolic universe that enables them to render manageable the profusion of impressions. In Gehlen's view, language is the fundamental instance of human creative cultural activity. The concept of action includes, for Gehlen, all cognitive processes and cultural achievements. Action has replaced Scheler's spirit. This means that for Gehlen human beings are beings who create themselves by gaining control of their world. While for Scheler human beings as spirits owe their existence to "the highest Ground of Being," for Gehlen they are self-creative in the strict sense of the term, and religion and God can become thematic only as human creations, as by-products of the human conquest of the world. Corresponding to this contrast between creation and self-creation there is also a reversal of the relation of priority which led Scheler from spirit to the inhibition of animal instincts. For Gehlen, the direction is from the hiatus between perception and impulse, via the actions of human beings themselves to spirit and the formation of a cultural world, the contents of which are the foremost help human beings have in directing their impulses.[30]

Gehlen's conception of humanity has often been criticized, but it has nonetheless established itself as the classical form of modern philosophical anthropology. Criticism has been directed first of all at Gehlen's concept of human beings as deficient beings. Thus Portmann, implicitly dissociating himself from Gehlen's view, has pointed out that "the relative weakness in the organization of the instincts" in human beings is accompanied by "an immense increase in the mass of the cerebral cortex and its synapses." Nor should the slow pace of human development be seen only as something negative; rather, it is correlative with the peculiar psychic nature of human beings as beings with a social culture.[31] Portmann has once again been able to use the concept of spirit as a way of describing this human peculiarity. Buytendijk too continues to interpret the human being as "incarnated spirit."[32]

Criticism has been directed not only at Gehlen's one-sidedly negative interpretation of the initial human biological condition but also at the concept of openness to the world, which he shares not only with Scheler but also with Portmann, Buytendijk, and others. Thus Plessner, in his

[30]The understanding of the human person as the being who acts is explicable in the light of Gehlen's idealistic beginnings in his *Theorie der Willensfreiheit* (1933). For a transposition of this idea into a "biological metaphysics," see Schulz (n. 25, above), 442ff.

[31]Portmann, *Zoologie und das neue Bild des Menschen.* 62f. and 92f. See also idem, "Der Mensch—ein Mängelwesen?" in his *Entlässt die Natur den Menschen? Gesammelte Aufsätze zur Biologie und Anthropologie* (Munich, 1970), 200–209.

[32]Buytendijk, *Mensch und Tier.* 45.

Introduction (written in 1961) to the Propyläen history of the world, says of human beings:

> An unlimited openness to the world cannot be ascribed to human beings. Such an openness would be possible only for a subject which, like the angels of medieval theology, would be incorporeal or possess a spiritualized body; in this case, "world" would be the embodiment of the truly divine in its revealedness. As a matter of fact, however, our world is given to us only in phenomena in which reality manifests itself in a fragmentary manner through the medium of our modes of perception and courses of action.[33]

The assumption of an unqualified openness of human beings to the world fails to take into account the "indirect and fragmentary character of our relation to the world," a character made clear to us in the process of knowledge with its detours and uncertainties.

Plessner's thesis that our openness to reality is a halting openness because of the limited and partial ways in which we grasp the real (ways resulting from our corporeality and from the perspectival nature of our experience) is confirmed by the present state of behavioral research as summarized by I. Eibl-Eibesfeldt in his contribution to the series Neue Anthropologie.[34] According to contemporary research, and contrary to the thesis of an unlimited human openness to the world, human beings do in fact have innate behavioral dispositions, as can be seen especially in the behavior of infants, whose weeping, smiling, clutching, sucking, and babbling are based on innate behavioral schemata. Then, too, the universal occurrence in all cultures of certain modes of behavior, such as the so-called eye contact, can be traced back to similar behavioral schemata proper to the species. But Eibl-Eibesfeldt also confirms the thesis that "human beings can impose a new cultural form on almost everything" (48) and can even "suppress such basic instinctual movements as those of sex and hunger." Therefore Eibl-Eibesfeldt is able to accept Gehlen's statement that human beings are by nature cultural beings (54). The presence of innate behavioral dispositions does not mean, therefore, that these surround human behavior with insurmountable barriers and thus determine it. These dispositions set no definitive limits on "freedom" and on the human capacity in principle to alter and transcend the antecedent conditions of the human situation. Innate behavioral dispositions, rather, designate, as it were, the place that is the abiding point of departure for the human adventure of self-transcendence and historicity. It is an open question how successful human beings are in imposing a new form on

[33]H. Plessner, *Conditio Humana* (1964), 47.

[34]*Biologische Anthropologie* II, 3–59, esp. 11ff., 19ff. The page references that follow in the text are to this book.

these initial conditions proper to the species, not only by individual efforts but also and especially by dint of cultural tradition. Human "openness to the world" thus loses the character of a given state which it has in many remarks of Scheler and even of Gehlen; instead, it is seen as describing a direction in the process of human "self-realization," a process through which alone a human being takes form as a self and which therefore may not, with Gehlen, be one-sidedly reduced to human action.[35] The special place of humanity in the animal world is not achieved abruptly, as though by a single bound, but is, rather, the result of a history in the course of which alone human beings attain to selfhood and their specific nature. At this point we are close to a view of things developed by Herder.

[35]On this point, see B. Liebrucks' discussion of Gehlen's theory of action in *Sprache und Bewusstsein* I (1964).

2

Openness to the World
and Image of God

I. Herder as the Point of Departure
for Modern Philosophical Anthropology

Arnold Gehlen has called attention to the fact that Herder, in his prize essay, *Abhandlung über den Ursprung der Sprache* (1772), sketched the main outlines of the view of humanity that Gehlen himself has developed in his work. Thus Herder notes: "It seems assured that man is by far inferior to the animals in the intensity and reliability of his instincts and indeed that he does not have at all what in many animal species we regard as innate artifactive skills and drives."[1] The life of animals is confined to an ever narrowing "sphere," the more specialized its sense organs become. According to Gehlen, this observation shows that Herder had seen the dependence of the animals on their environment. Of human beings, on the other hand, Herder says that the "distinctive trait of the human species" is "gaps and wants." In comparison with the animals, the newborn human infant is "the most orphaned child of nature. Naked and bare, weak and in need, shy and unarmed" (89; Herder, 108, 107). Such observations remind us of Portmann's description of the "extrauterine springtime" of a human infant.[2] No wonder, then, that Gehlen can sum up by saying, "Philosophical anthropology has not advanced at all beyond Herder, and his is, in outline, the conception I shall be developing with the tools of modern science." And he adds, "And in fact philosophical

[1] Cited in A. Gehlen, *Der Mensch* (1950), 88. German text of Herder in *Joh. Gottf. Herders Sprachphilosophie. Ausgewählte Schriften,* ed. E. Heintel (1960), 15ff. The English translation is from J. G. Herder, *Essay on the Origin of Language,* in J. J. Rousseau and J. G. Herder, *On the Origin of Language,* trans. J. H. Moran and A. Gode (New York, 1967), 103. The page references that follow in this paragraph in the text are to Gehlen's book and, where indicated, to the ET of Herder.

[2] References to Herder are provided by S. H. Sunnus in his dissertation, *Die Wurzeln des modernen Menschenbildes bei J. G. Herder* (Nürnberg, 1971). Herder was already emphasizing the point that the human body and soul are not divided from each other by "iron bars" and that the person is to be understood as a unified being.

anthropology need not advance further, since its present position is the true one" (90).

But Herder's assessment of the phenomena he observes is notably different from Gehlen's. The difference was quickly noted. Herder does not proceed as one-sidedly as Gehlen does in taking as the starting point of his interpretation the "wants" that typify the human life form as compared with that of the animals. Herder regards these "wants" as simply the necessary counterpart of the highly developed human brain, or reason. The lack of keenness of our senses is counterbalanced by the advantage of being able to use them in a free manner. Herder too, seemingly like Gehlen, can say, "We are not yet men, but are daily *becoming* so."[3] He is here close to the Enlightenment idea of human self-perfectibility, an idea to be found not only in Rousseau but also in Leibniz and his school.[4] In fact, this view of a human self-improvement had already been contrasted with the behavior of animals, especially in Hermann Samuel Reimarus' *Allgemeine Betrachtungen über die Triebe der Tiere* (1760), in which the author anticipates many of Herder's observations.[5] Yet Herder's version of the idea of human self-improvement is not identical with Gehlen's one-sided recourse to action as the source of human self-realization. Like Gehlen, Herder can indeed write of the human being that nature "drives him out, to construct his own nest."[6] But according to Herder, human beings never owe their development first and foremost to their own action. Herder presupposes reason and freedom as germ or source and disposition for the process of human self-improvement, whereas Gehlen has reason and freedom making their appearance as a product of human activity, for otherwise the concept of action could not replace Scheler's concept of spirit. If in understanding the process of human self-improvement we were to join Herder in presupposing reason and freedom as at least a disposition, then it would not be possible to reject so absolutely the need felt by Scheler of tracing this novelty in the evolution of life back to an origin located beyond the whole development of life up to this point, to an origin which therefore, according to Scheler, can be sought and found only in the highest Ground of all things.

[3]J. G. Herder, *Outlines of a Philosophy of the History of Man,* trans. T. Churchill (London, 1800; New York, 1966), 229.

[4]Sunnus, 82 and 28ff.

[5]G. Buck, in his essay "Selbsterhaltung und Historizität," in R. Koselleck and W. D. Stempel, eds., *Geschichte—Ereignis und Erzählung,* in Poetik und Hermeneutik 5 (Munich, 1973), 29–94, esp. 32, refers to these dependences and especially to the judgment of Herder's contemporaries (e.g., J. N. Tetens) who denied the originality of his theses. On this point, see also Sunnus, 15ff.

[6]Herder, *Outlines* VIII, 4, 3 (210).

Herder's ideas on this point are closer to Scheler's than to Gehlen's. In Herder's view, the animal instincts are replaced by a divinely supplied direction for human life. God did not abandon human beings, whose instinctual life had retrogressed, to an absence of all direction from which they must now rescue themselves with no support from outside; rather, according to Herder, God put in the human heart a direction to be followed in the course of self-improvement, and this direction takes the form of God's image in human beings, as understood by Herder:

> No, benevolent God, thou didst not leave thy creature to murderous chance. To the brute thou gavest instinct; and on the mind of man thou didst impress thy image, religion and humanity: the outline of the statue lies there, deep in the block; but it cannot hew out, it cannot fashion itself. Tradition and learning, reason and experience, must do this; and thou hast supplied sufficient means.[7]

It will be worth our while to break down this very substantial formulation into its elements:

1. As instinct guides the behavior of the animals, so the image of God guides human beings: instinct and image of God alike have as their function to give a direction to the life of the creature, instead of leaving it a prey to the "murderous chance" of random impressions.

2. The image of God, which is impressed "on the mind" of human beings, functions as a teleological concept and standard for their behavior. It can exercise this function because the image of God represents the goal of human existence as such, in keeping with Herder's conviction that "we are not yet men, but are daily *becoming* so."[8] Thus the image of God and the selfness or humanness of human beings belong together: "religion and humanity" are intimately connected for Herder.

3. What human beings possess initially is only "the disposition to reason, humanity, and religion,"[9] the outline of the statue. How, then, are they to become the fully formed statue and realize their humanity? Herder does not answer this question by appealing to the idea of action; in fact, he says explicitly that human beings are *unable* to "hew out" or "fashion" themselves. Herder's answer to the question of how they are to reach the self that is their goal is to be found rather in the line of the great Enlightenment idea of the education of the human race. It is the "specific character" of the human race "that born almost without instinct, we are formed to manhood only by the practice of a whole life, and both the perfectibility and corruptibility of our species depend on it." What is involved here is

---

[7]Ibid., IX, 5 (256). According to Sunnus, it was in the *Outlines* that Herder first introduced the idea of the image of God (Sunnus, 40).

[8]Ibid., IX, 1, 2 (229).

[9]Ibid., IX, 5 (151).

"an education .   of the human species; since every one becomes a man only by means of education, and the whole species lives solely in this chain of individuals."[10]

4. In this process whereby the human species is educated, three factors play a part.

a. "Tradition and learning": these terms sum up the influence we experience others as exercising on us, for "no one of us became man of himself: the whole structure of his humanity is connected by a spiritual birth, education, with his parents, teachers, friends; with all the circumstances of his life, and consequently with his countrymen and their forefathers; and lastly with the whole chain of the human race."[11]

b. In addition, "reason and experience" play a part. These are the "organic powers"[12] in human beings themselves that contribute to their education, for they are not just passively exposed to external influences but are stimulated by these to a process of self-formation. To that extent the formation of the human being "is left to himself and his fellows."[13] Thus human beings play a part in the process; it does not take place without their cooperation. These first two factors are brought into unity by divine providence.

c. Divine providence: it is faith in the rule of providence that justifies for Herder the idea of an education of the human race toward a goal set before it. Herder considers that "God's purpose with regard to the human species on earth remains evident even in the most perplexing parts of its history."[14] The purpose perdures in the "divine character of its [each of God's works] destination."[15] Learning and tradition, on the one hand, and reason and experience, on the other, contribute to the achievement of this destiny only because in the collaboration of these factors divine providence is also at work and, through the mediation of other human beings, forming individuals for the goal to which they are destined, educating them, that is, to be the images of God.

Only in the context of faith in providence does Herder's conception of the image of God in human beings become fully intelligible. On the one hand, this image is the human goal and destination, although in its definitive form, "a form truly that of the godlike man,"[16] it will be reached only in another existence. On the other hand, the image of God is already present in outline form and thereby gives human life a direction, just as

[10]Ibid., IX, 1 (226).
[11]Ibid., 227.
[12]Ibid.
[13]Ibid., 229.
[14]Ibid.
[15]Ibid.
[16]Ibid., V, 5 (125).

the instinctual apparatus gives an animal's life its direction. But the connection between this present anticipation and the future fulfillment of human destiny has its basis in the plan of divine providence, which coordinates the influences coming from other human beings with the impulses of the person's own reason and experience and thereby turns these into means contributing to a single result, the formation of human beings.

II. Herder's Relation to the Traditional Conception of the Image of God in Humanity

Before discussing the current relevance of Herder's linking of instinctual reduction and image of God, I must consider how this view is related to the traditional theology of the image of God in human beings. It is in fact his characteristic departure from this tradition that makes fully clear the function which the idea of God's image has for Herder in understanding the original human situation as already described by other writers before him. And only when this function of the idea in Herder has been understood will it be possible to consider his potential significance in contemporary anthropological discussion.

It is clear at first glance that Herder does not speak of an original state of human perfection. In this he departs from traditional Christian dogmatics. According to the teaching of the theologians on the creation, original state, and fall of humanity, human beings had originally been created in the perfect image of God but had then lost this original perfection through the fall. According to a more precisely dogmatic definition, this original perfection consisted in an original justice, an actual communion with God (*iustitia originalis*). But the relation between this justice and the image of God had been defined in divergent ways in the dogmatic tradition and has today once again become a subject of confessional differences. Latin Scholasticism distinguished between original justice, that is, the actual union of the first human being with God, and the image of God. In the original human state, to the *imago Dei* as the distinctive *condition* of human nature there was added original justice, that is, actual union with God, as the grace proper to the original state. In the view of the medieval Scholastics, this additional grace of original justice was lost through original sin, whereas the image, being a property of human nature as such, continued to exist. The image belongs to humanity as such, and human beings did not cease to be human even as a result of the fall.

The distinction made here between the destination to God as a condition and distinctive trait of human nature and an actual communion with God goes back to Irenaeus of Lyons toward the end of the second century. As Irenaeus read the words of the Old Testament story of creation in Gen. 1:26 he saw a distinction being made between the image of God and the likeness of God. The text tells us that God said, "Let us make man in our image, after our likeness." Even today it is not exegetically clear whether the Hebrew terms used here, *ṣelem* and *dᵉmūt*, are intended to call attention to different aspects or whether they are simply two synonyms for the same idea.[17] If there is a difference in accent and if the use of two terms is not simply a way of being emphatic,[18] then "likeness" *(dᵉmūt)* would signify, rather, a limitation on the human role as God's representative to the rest of creation as expressed in the concept of image. Irenaeus, however, interprets *dᵉmūt* as an enhancement of the concept of image, since he translates the two words with the Platonic terms *eikōn* and *homoiōsis*. Accordingly, the *eikōn* is the image or copy, but as such it is distinct from the exemplar and falls short of it. *Homoiōsis*, on the other hand, describes an *actual* communion with the exemplar.[19] According to Plato, the greatest possible assimilation to God *(homoiōsis Theō kata to dynaton)* is the life's task and longing of human beings, and the subject matter of ethics.[20] In this Platonic perspective it is but a step to ascribe the image of God, in the sense of a copy of the divine, to human nature and to connect this image with the rational nature that sets human beings apart from the brute animals, while identifying the *homoiōsis* with justice or the moral perfection for which they are to strive. But since in the Christian vision of things human beings are justified only by grace, Christian theology conceived the *homoiōsis* as a gift of grace that was given to the first human being, was lost through sin, and has been restored by Christ in the justification of the sinner. Medieval Latin Scholasticism was thus continuing Irenaeus' exegesis of Genesis in its distinction and correlation of *imago* and *similitudo*.[21]

The Reformation view of the image of God in humanity departs from this hitherto prevailing interpretation. It regards the image of God not as

[17]See H. W. Wolff, *Anthropology of the Old Testament,* trans. M. Kohl (Philadelphia, 1974), 159–61.

[18]According to G. von Rad, *Genesis, A Commentary,* trans. J. H. Marks (Philadelphia, 1972²), by the addition of the idea of likeness the basic word "image" is "more closely explained and made precise . . . with the simple meaning that this image is to correspond to the original image, that is, to resemble it" (58). According to W. H. Schmidt, *Die Schöpfungsgeschichte der Priesterschrift* (Neukirchen, 1964), 133f., there is no difference of content between the two words; on the concept of image, see ibid., 136ff.

[19]Irenaeus, *Adv. haer.* IV, 38, 12, and esp. V, 6, 1. On this second passage, see W. D. Hauschild, *Gottes Geist und der Mensch. Studien zur frühchristlichen Anthropologie* (Munich, 1972), 208f. On the preparation in Tatian for the idea of a formation of the human being by the Spirit of God (but without as yet any distinction between "image" and "likeness"), see ibid., 199f.

[20]Plato, *Republic* 613a4ff.; *Theaetetus* 176a5.

[21]Thus, for example, the distinction is taken over by Thomas Aquinas, *Summa theologiae* I, q. 93, a. 9, in the form it has in John Damascene. On the Scholastic teaching, see also B. Cairns, *The Image of God in Man* (Louvain, 1953), and A. Burghart, *Gottes Ebenbild und Gleichnis* (Freiburg, 1962).

the foundation of a distinct, actual communion with God, namely, the divinely given justice of the first human being *(iustitia originalis)*, but as identical with this actual relation to God.[22] Consequently, the fall was regarded as bringing the loss not only of the *similitudo* but of the *imago* itself. The difference between the Reformed and the medieval Catholic views in the question of whether human nature itself was corrupted by the fall is therefore to be explained by different views on the relation between *iustitia originalis* and *imago Dei*. The latter difference also explains the dispute in our own century between Karl Barth and Emil Brunner on the question of whether the image of God was completely lost in the fall or whether (as Brunner claimed) a "remnant" was left which consists in human rationality and the capacity for being addressed by God, for in these Brunner sees summed up the distinctive formal human characteristic that perdures even after the fall, although affected by some degree of material corruption.[23] In the theological discussion of that period this disputed question was directly connected with another: whether there is "a point of contact" for revelation.

According to Brunner, a point of contact does exist and consists precisely in that formal "remnant" of the image of God; it consists, that is, in the fact that despite sin human beings remain human, so that God's revelatory action in its turning to them can establish contact with the original destination of their being and remind them of this. This would be impossible if sinners were wholly immersed in hostility to God. Barth, for his part, could not allow that any anthropological conditions which would be distinct from and prior to God's gracious action could be under-

[22]M. Luther, WA 42:46: "The likeness and image of God consists in the true and perfect knowledge of God, supreme delight in God, eternal life, eternal righteousness, eternal freedom from care." Melanchthon, *Apol.* II, 18ff. In the Formula of Concord the original justice, that is, the actual relation to God, is identified with the image of God; see *The Book of Concord,* trans. and ed. T. G. Tappert (Philadelphia, 1959), 510. Analogous statements of Calvin are collected in W. Niesel, *The Theology of Calvin,* trans. H. Knight (London and Philadelphia, 1956), 67ff.

[23]See Luther's statements in R. Niebuhr, *The Nature and Destiny of Man* I (New York, 1941), 160f. The idea of remnants of the *imago* in the sinner is clearer in the writings of Calvin; see J. Verburg, *Adam. Een onderzoek naar de betekenis van de figur van een eerste mens in het christelijk geloof* (Wageningen, 1973), 96f. Inasmuch as the image of God was recognized as being specific to human beings and constitutive of their humanity, its complete loss could not be too readily asserted. Attention to the presence of this realization in early Lutheran dogmatics led P. Althaus to revise his concept of the image of God and to understand it as the human destiny rather than the original human state: *Die christliche Wahrheit* (1947; Gütersloh, 1952³), 338ff., esp. 342. The question of the remnants of the created image of God in humanity had given rise to theological disagreement once again, this time between Barth and Brunner: E. Brunner, *Natur und Gnade* (1934; 1935²), 10ff.; K. Barth, *Nein! Antwort an E. Brunner* (1934), esp. 16f., 24ff.; E. Brunner, *Man in Revolt* (1937), trans. O. Wyon (New York, 1939), 172ff.

stood as a point of contact which the divine action must respect. God's action is not dependent on anything outside himself; such a dependence would be an infringement on his sovereignty. Even Barth of course had taught that God was faithful to his own intention as originally connected with the creation of humanity. But he was unwilling to think of the divine action as dependent on circumstances that are previously regarded in themselves and thus rendered independent in relation to that action. In the background of this dispute is thus the question whether a theologically neutral description of human reality can be accepted as objectively valid by Christian thought or whether, on the contrary, the actual relation to the divine reality must be judged to be constitutive for the special character of human beings and for their fulfillment.

The medieval Catholic and the Reformed conceptions of the image of God differ, therefore, in that for the Reformers the image of God consists in the *actual relation* to God, while for medieval Latin Scholasticism it is, rather, a presupposition for this actual relation to God and is a formal structural property of human nature, somewhat as the "remnant of the image" is for Brunner. The two confessional interpretations of the image of God are, however, in agreement that this likeness to God was present at the beginning of human history, namely, in the perfection of the original state of the first human being before the fall. Herder's idea of an image of God in human beings that "becomes" or develops is thus clearly different from what is maintained in the two confessional doctrinal traditions. Herder departs from them because he does not share the teaching on the original state that is common to them and is so difficult to reconcile with a modern evolutionary view of the human species and its appearance in the history of life.

But the idea of an "evolving image of God," which in many respects anticipates the evolutionary perspective of modern biology, was not first conceived by Herder. Marsilio Ficino, founder of Florentine Platonism, in his book *De religione Christiana* (1476) explained the incarnation as the fulfillment of the human religious destiny.[24] In Ficino's disciple Pico della Mirandola the dynamism of this process of the fulfillment of human destiny, a process culminating in the incarnation, is even more strongly associated with the voluntaristic emphasis found in Renaissance humanism. Pico spoke indeed of a destruction of God's image in humans through the fall and of its restoration by Christ. He continued, therefore, to maintain the doctrine of the original state, but the dynamism inherent in his conception of humanity reaches its goal, nonetheless, only in Christ; only in

---

[24]C. E. Trinkaus, *In Our Image and Likeness: Humanity and Divinity in Italian Humanist Thought* II (London, 1970), 734ff., esp. 740.

Christ does the creation of humanity reach its completion.[25] It is characteristic of this view of the creation of humanity that Pico no longer distinguishes between *imago* and *similitudo* but uses the two words as synonyms. Also connected with this is the voluntaristic emphasis proper to his view: the dynamic process of assimilation to God, of becoming like God *(similitudo),* which is the ethical content of a human life properly lived, becomes in Pico the theme of the humanization of the human being, which finds its perfect form only in the ethical life-style of Jesus Christ.

In the same way the Reformers too identified *imago* and *similitudo.* In Melanchthon, however, this point is discussed only in the context of the original state and of the creation and fall of the first human being. The broader conception of a hominization or creation of the human being that is completed only in Christ is not to be found in Melanchthon, although it is found in Calvin and, earlier, in Luther.[26] This dynamic concept provides a point of contact for the modern idea of a process of hominization, in the sense of a self-perfecting, that extends to the entire race, although this idea has not always been linked to the concept of the image of God. In the eighteenth century the idea of a process of human improvement was taken over by Leibniz in the form of the concept of perfectibility, in the sense of a capacity for a moral self-improvement that is the ethical task of a properly human way of life, and was connected with a moral interpretation of the kingdom of God as the goal of moral action.[27] In this

[25]Ibid., II, 505ff., 516ff. Also important is Pico's idea that human dignity, which is based on the image of God in humanity and achieves its fullest form in the incarnation, elevates the human person even above the angels (512). On the eschatological orientation of the idea, see also II, 517, on Pico's *Heptaplus* (1488–89), IV, 6–7.

[26]J. Calvin, *Inst. rel. christ.* (1559), I, 15, 4 (CR 30:138f.). Further references in T. F. Torrance, *Calvin's Doctrine of Man* (Grand Rapids, 1967[2]), and W. Krusche, *Das Wirken des Heiligen Geistes nach Calvin* (Berlin, 1957), 281. For Luther, cf. the statements in his disputation *De homine* (1556) on the eschatological destiny of the human person (WA 39/1, 175ff.); on this point, see W. Joest, *Ontologie der Person bei Luther* (1967), 348ff., 192f. Nevertheless the historico-salvational and eschatological approach of the Reformers to the image of God remained linked to Augustinian views on the perfection of the original state and its restoration in Christ; see A. Peters, *Der Mensch* (1979), 194f.; also 47f., 82f.

[27]Leibniz, in his *Principles of Nature and Grace* (1714), in *Philosophical Papers and Letters,* ed. and trans. L. E. Loemker (2 vols.; Chicago, 1956), II, 1033–43, wrote that all things receive their limited perfection (no. 9: "some perfection") from God as the supremely perfect being, and that the perfection of God elicits within each thing the highest measure of perfection it can attain (no. 12; cf. no. 10). It is not surprising, therefore, that the human soul, which, being the image of God, imitates him in its activity (no. 14), finds its happiness in a perpetual progress "to new pleasures and new perfections" (no. 18). Leibniz had given a very carefully nuanced version of this relationship in his *Discourse on Metaphysics* (1685) (in *Philosophical Papers and Letters* I, 464–506). There it is said that through their activity things immediately pass to a higher degree of perfection (no. 15; see *Monadology,* no. 49; *Theodicy,* nos. 32, 66, 386); spirits, however, are the substances capable of perfection in the

thesis of the harmony between nature and grace the objective fact of the
perfecting of humanity becomes the human moral task of self-improvement. In the eighteenth century even Rousseau, despite his pessimism
about culture, was unwilling to deny the human capacity for this task,[28]
and it was precisely against this background that the question of human
perfectibility became the object of widespread discussion.

Herder, however, looked with increasing skepticism on the idea of a
human moral perfectibility through "self-enhancement."[29] During the
period when he was writing his *Outlines* he realized indeed that "both the
perfectibility and corruptibility of our species" have their basis in the
flexibility or plasticity of the human being, who is "born almost without
instinct."[30] But according to Herder, who differs in this from Rousseau,
the positive surmounting of this ambivalence is not simply a matter of
moral action. Herder disputes the idea that "the mere actuation of a
capacity is able to change something merely possible into something
real."[31] Here Herder is objecting to the whole idea of a self-improvement
to be accomplished by human beings themselves, the idea of a "self-
perfecting" in this sense. The human lack of instinct does not mean for
Herder, as it does for Kant, that the individual should "bring everything

---

highest degree (no. 36: "the most perfectible of substances"). Now since in spiritual beings
or persons happiness corresponds to what perfection is for mere things (no. 36: "since
happiness is to persons what perfection is to things"), God's primary intention "in the moral
world, or the city of God," is the happiness of persons (no. 36), and it was in this sense that
Christ revealed to us the kingdom of God "or that perfect republic of spirits which deserves
the title of the city of God" (no. 37). The interpretation of the city of God as the moral world
is also found elsewhere in Leibniz (*Monadology,* nos. 85ff.). Hobbes had prepared the way
for the moral interpretation of the kingdom of God with his distinction between a natural
kingdom of God based on the dictates of reason and a supernatural or prophetical kingdom
of God (*De Cive* XV, 4f.). Spinoza, however, had disputed the distinction on the grounds
that the content of the reign of God—whether this was made known naturally or supernaturally—can in any case consist only in justice and love (*Theologico-Political Treatise,* ch. 19);
Spinoza thereby reduced the supernatural reign of God to the natural reign. The same fusion
resulted from Leibniz' theory of harmonization: "Nature leads to grace, and grace perfects
nature by using it" (*Principles of Nature and Grace,* no. 15).

[28]Rousseau, *Diskurs über den Ursprung der Ungleichheit unter den Menschen* (1755), French
text with German tr. by K. Weigand (Hamburg, 1955), 107ff.

[29]On this concept, see Buck (n. 5, above), 37f.

[30]Herder, *Outlines* 226. Analogous statements of Rousseau in Buck, 31, n. 17. On this
point Herder did not need instruction from Schlözer, who called attention to it in a response
(1785) to a review of his universal history (Buck, 31).

[31]Herder, *Werke* (ed. Suphan), V, 33, cited in Buck, 32; but the latter unjustly parallels
this argument with Reimarus' observation that the capacity for perfectibility is simply a
potentia remota and not an "active, efficacious power of the soul." Herder was not concerned
with whether human beings needed such an active power in order to improve, but *whether
they could achieve this improvement at all by themselves.*

forth out of his own resources";[32] it means, rather, that human beings depend on external forces for their formation, whether on impressions received and experiences that stimulate their reason or on the influence of other human beings, and especially on their bringing them "tradition and learning." But that such influences from outside should activate an innate destination to humanness and not, rather, allow this to atrophy seemed to Herder something ensured only by faith in the operation of a divine providence that brings the manifold factors involved in such influences into harmony with the interior human disposition. It may even be that Herder's recourse in the *Outlines* to the idea of the image of God in the human being is motivated by the indispensable role of divine providence in the formation of human beings. The image of God idea here gives expression to the fact that human beings are by their natural disposition interiorly ordered to such an operation of providence.

Herder's recourse to the idea of the divine image seems thus to be an expression of his opposition to the idea of a human self-fulfillment through active self-enhancement. In order to realize their human destiny, their humanity, human beings remain dependent on the most varied influences from outside and on the harmonious contribution of these to the advancement of their humanity. Their disposition to be like God is therefore fulfilled only by God himself, through the operation of his providence. This is an important development of the humanistic idea of an evolving image of God in humanity. On the one hand, Herder "secularized" the idea by linking it with the human relation to the world and with the shape taken by human destiny as realized in this manner. In this way he set aside the restriction of the problems of human life to a moral task. But in so doing he was not content to reduce the supernatural elevation of human nature by grace to the natural strivings of nature, as the Enlightenment thinkers before him had been. Rather, he succeeded in removing the restrictions imposed by a purely moral description of the thematic of human life. Precisely in this way he was able to express in a new manner the dependence of human beings on God's gracious action. For, according to Herder, in the process of fulfilling their destiny, human beings remain dependent on the action of divine providence. Therefore, in Herder's view, the special nature and destiny of human beings continue to be linked to the religious content of their life. The concept of the image of God is here not replaceable by anything else, contrary to the Promethean emphasis in the Enlightenment idea of a human self-realization and self-fulfillment. Yet Herder need not for that reason neglect the active participation

---

[32] I. Kant, *Idea for a Universal History from a Cosmopolitan Point of View*, trans. L. W. Beck, in I. Kant, *On History*, ed. L. W. Beck (Indianapolis, 1963), 14.

of human beings in the process of their own formation; rather, this participation remains an essential factor in the complex of causes through which
divine providence works.

Herder's ideas thus have surprising relevance to the contemporary
discussion of theological anthropology. Once the saga character of the
Yahwist story of the creation and fall of Adam had been discovered (a
discovery due in part to Herder), nineteenth-century Evangelical theology no longer regarded the image of God as a *perfection of the original state*
that was lost by the fall, but regarded it rather as the *destiny* that human
beings have still to attain. Kant had said of the human person: "When it
is said, Man is created good, this can mean nothing more than: He is
created *for good* and the original *predisposition* in man is good."[33] H. Ph.
K. Henke had made the point with terse brevity: A human being is not
born like God but becomes like him *(Homo similis Deo haud nascitur, sed
fit)*.[34] In this context K. G. Bretschneider was already introducing the
concept of human "destiny,"[35] and it was to prevail, although Schleiermacher, for example, did not yet use it. Thus I. A. Dorner wrote that the
human being "is destined to a communion of life with God or to religion.
The likeness of God is thereby realized in the personal creature, so that
the latter becomes an *image of God.* This image is to be thought of partly
as an original gift, partly as a destiny." But the dispositions for this image

---

[33]I. Kant, *Religion Within the Limits of Reason Alone,* trans. T. M. Greene and H. H. Hudson
(Chicago, 1934), 40.

[34]H. Ph. K. Henke, *Lineamenta institutionum fidei christianae historico-criticarum* (1793;
1795[2]), 86.

[35]K. G. Bretschneider, *Handbuch der Dogmatik der evangelisch-lutherischen Kirche* (1814;
1829[3]), I, 756f. "The end for which God created human beings tells us what their *destiny*
is. As in the case of every being, this is determined by the God-given powers and dispositions
and is achieved through the full development of these. . . . And the destiny of human beings
is to form themselves to knowledge and love of the true, the good, and the beautiful and
to make of this knowledge the unalterable rule of their entire activity." For the concept of
human "destiny" Bretschneider appeals to J. J. Spalding, *Bestimmung des Menschen* (1748).
There we are told that in the presence of the immensity of nature and the still greater
immensity of the divinity the human individual says: "To such sublimity I am destined, and
I am determined to seek to approach it ever more nearly" (ed. H. Stephan [Diessen, 1908],
25). In an appendix to the 3d ed. of 1789, Spalding added that this conception of the human
person did not in any way make the Christian religion superfluous: "The higher the concept
and the more lively the impression human beings have of their great destiny and of virtue,
law, and eternal order, the more affecting and valuable will they find the divine instructions
to be which afford them so much help to this goal" (ibid., 34). But neither in Spalding nor
in J. G. Fichte's *Bestimmung des Menschen* (1800), to which Bretschneider likewise refers
(ibid., n. 517), is any connection made between the concept of human "destiny" and the
dogmatic concept of the image of God in human beings. On the concept of human destiny
and its prehistory in antiquity, see also the article on this term by C. Grave in *HWP* 1 (1971),
856–59.

"are not yet the true image of God, but only a potentiality for it. The higher meaning of the word 'image' points to the future."[36]

In opposition to this dissolution of the doctrine of the original state into a doctrine of human destiny, a destiny for which the person is interiorly disposed, the dialectical theology of the present century harked back to the Reformation thesis of a loss of the image of God through sin; thereby it also renewed the doctrine of the original state as having preceded the loss. In 1937, Emil Brunner objected that Schleiermacher "actually gives up the fundamental Christian view of the origin of man, and substitutes for it an idealistic, evolutionary theory with a strongly naturalistic bent; for the idea of the origin in Creation he substitutes that of a goal of evolution of a universal spiritual process."[37] Brunner was using "origin" (or "origin in Creation") in terminological contrast to "empirical beginning."[38] For Brunner regarded the picture of a historical initial state in which humanity lived in paradisal perfection and communion with God as "absolutely destroyed." To be distinguished from that state is a human "origin" in the divine creative will, and this origin is a necessary presupposition for an understanding of the present human state: "Even as a sinner man can only be understood in the light of the original Image of God, namely, as one who is living in opposition to it."[39] Only thus is it possible to understand human reality as "*a life in conflict* between his origin and the contradiction."[40]

The destiny of human beings is here thought of as one that is presently lost to them and therefore, once again, as a kind of original state, even if in the sense not of an initial historical state but rather of a suprahistorical and to some extent mythical point of departure which is presupposed,

[36]I. A. Dorner, *System der christlichen Glaubenslehre* I (1879–80; 1886²), 515 (sec. 41). Dorner goes on to say that human destiny is to be distinguished as "the *idea* of likeness to God" from its realization (517). In the tradition of speculative theology Hegel, in his *Vorlesgungen über die Philosophie der Religion* (ed. G. Lasson; vol. IV [PhB 63], 130f.), had used the idea of human destiny in this sense (but see ibid., 99, where, using a different set of concepts, he speaks of "two destinies"). A. E. Biedermann, *Christliche Dogmatik* (1869; 1885²), says pithily: "The element of the divine destination of human beings to spirit becomes in the teaching of the church a real and perfect original state" (sec. 665).

[37]Brunner, *Man in Revolt*, 87. Schleiermacher, in *The Christian Faith*, § 60, to which Brunner refers, speaks of a "predisposition to God-consciousness" that is given to human beings. This predisposition includes "the consciousness of the faculty of attaining, by means of the human organism, to those states of self-consciousness in which the God-consciousness can realize itself" (Schleiermacher, *The Christian Faith*, ed. H. R. Mackintosh and J. S. Stewart [Edinburgh, 1928; Philadelphia, 1976]).

[38]Brunner, 89.

[39]Ibid., 85 and 105.

[40]Ibid., 83. This sentence of Brunner provides the key for understanding the title *Man in Revolt*.

simply as a lost origin, in their present existence. As R. Prenter showed,[41] this conception of Brunner goes back to Søren Kierkegaard, who in his book *The Concept of Dread* (1844) attempted to give a new form to the doctrine of the original state. He agreed with Schleiermacher in rejecting the view that the biblical primeval history is to be taken as an account of the historical beginnings of the human race; according to Kierkegaard, such an interpretation is simply "fantastic."[42] Nonetheless he wanted to "adhere" to the figure of Adam and not "leave him in the lurch," because "Adam is the first man; he is at once himself and the race," just as man as individual "is at once himself and the race."[43] Regarded as a "state," this fact is the perfection of the human being; however, it is also a contradiction and, as such, "the expression for a task."[44] In his *The Sickness Unto Death* (1849), Kierkegaard then went on to show that this task cannot be accomplished and leads to despair. As a result, the conflict between human beings as individuals and their consciousness of themselves as one with the species takes the form of a consciousness of lost identity.

Is it possible in the light of these considerations to construct a viable defense of the dogmatic teaching on the original state of Adam, this being understood no longer as a historical beginning but rather as the divine "origin" of the human race? Is it possible on such a basis to make a meaningful claim that human beings have "lost" an original perfection?[45] Helmut Thielicke has spoken rather guardedly of a "loss of a positive relation to God": not a loss of the image of God as such (the image being understood as the divine destiny given to human beings) but rather a passage to "a negative mode of the divine likeness." But A. Nordlander has not been able to discover in this view a convincing answer to the basic problem of the doctrine of the original state. According to Nordlander, the removal of the "fall" from the dimension of the historical beginnings of the human race "into a suprahistorical, supratemporal and supraempirical dimension, a metaphysical dimension called 'origin,' " does indeed render the dogmatic doctrine of the original state immune to direct criti-

---

[41]R. Prenter, *Creation and Redemption*, trans. T. I. Jensen (Philadelphia, 1967), 257–58. Prenter himself accepts this interpretation. R. Niebuhr had followed the same view in its essentials in his *The Nature and Destiny of Man* I (n. 23, above), 267ff., 269ff. But for him the concept of the image of God was secondary to that of original justice.

[42]S. Kierkegaard, *The Concept of Dread*, trans. W. Lowrie (Princeton, 1957²), 23; see the remark on Schleiermacher, 18.

[43]Ibid., 26–27.

[44]Ibid., 26.

[45]Thus Brunner, *Man in Revolt*, 135ff., 170. See also his *The Christian Doctrine of Creation and Redemption: Dogmatics II*, trans. O. Wyon (Philadelphia, 1952), 48ff., 73–74. It is doubtless not only the Reformed teaching on the loss of the *imago Dei* (in the strict sense) that Brunner was maintaining; the traditional church doctrine of the "fall" of Adam implies the loss of a previous perfection.

cism from the theory of evolution maintained by the natural sciences. But "we may ask whether it is any less disputable than the view that the original state and the fall are to be seen as historical events . . . or any less speculative than the idea of a preexistent fall."[46]

As a matter of fact, it seems possible to retain the idea of an original state of union with God that was lost by sin only if that state may also be claimed to have been the initial state of humankind at the beginning of human history. Talk of a loss presupposes a state prior to the loss, and then the question cannot be avoided of whether or not such a state ever existed. A refusal to allow this question, even though one continues to talk of a loss through sin of an original human state of union with God, can only be regarded as a trick to gain immunity, an effort to use obfuscation as a way of avoiding the logical implications of one's claims and their weaknesses. There can be no loss of something that never existed. As a historical claim about the beginnings of human history, the idea that there was an original union of humankind with God which was lost through a fall into sin is incompatible with our currently available scientific knowledge about the historical beginnings of the race. This being the case, we should renounce artificial attempts to rescue traditional theological formulas; one such attempt is the idea of an origin that is supposedly nonhistorical. The point of departure for a return to the idea of an original state on the part of Kierkegaard and those who appeal to him is the experience of humanness as entailing an obligation. In the language of Kierkegaard: The individual is humanity as such, the species, and at the same time the individual is not the species, and this conflict is "the expression for a task" at which human beings have always failed. But, for this very reason, union with the species is not a state that at one time actually existed in perfection but now exists no longer. Rather, the species itself is still in becoming through the course of human history, and to this extent it is a "task" for the individual.

The idea that the fulfillment of the human in the unity of individual and species was once a reality in primordial time is an idea that originates in mythical thinking, which looks to a primordial past as the time when all currently valid orders and relations were established.[47] This orientation of mythical thinking to a primordial time also finds expression in the Yahwist's story of the original paradisal state of the first human being,

[46]A. Nordlander, *Die Gottesebenbildlichkeit des Menschen in der Theologie Helmut Thielickes* (Uppsala, 1973), 174. In H. Thielicke "the original good creation is somehow present as a future reality" (173). See Thielicke, *Theologische Ethik* I (1951), 261–88; esp. 281f., as well as 823ff. (The ET is an abridgment: *Theological Ethics* I, ed. and trans. W. H. Lazareth [Philadelphia, 1966].)

[47]See my essay *Christentum und Mythos* (Gütersloh, 1972); now in my *Grundfragen systematischer Theologie* II (1981), 13–65.

although in this story there is the question not of a myth connected with a cult but of a saga developed with the aid of novelistic traits. But this kind of orientation to a primordial time is contradicted even within the process of biblical tradition itself by the increasing importance assigned to history and therefore to the future as the horizon for the fulfillment of humankind. Within this horizon of thought, which Christianity has communicated to the human race as a whole, the essence of the human being is seen as a *destiny* that will be achieved only in the future. This destiny finds expression for the individual in the experience of an obligation to live as a human being. The connected experience of actual failure, to the point even of the infidelity of human beings to their human destiny, does not mean that this destiny had been fulfilled at one time and that this fulfillment now lies behind us in an irretrievable past. That kind of notion is in keeping with mythical thinking and not with the historical experience that human beings have of themselves and their world.

The experience of actual nonidentity, of failure, and of infidelity to one's human destiny does, however, have another and in fact very radical consequence: it removes any credibility from a faith in human self-fulfillment by human powers alone. Human beings who are not identical with themselves cannot generate their own identity; the attempt to achieve self-realization on the basis of nonidentity can only produce new forms of the loss of self, as Kierkegaard has impressively shown in his *The Sickness Unto Death*. The goal for which human beings are destined is one they cannot reach by themselves. If they are to reach it, they must be raised above themselves, lifted above what they already are. But they must also be *participants* in this process, and this in interaction with their world and their fellow human beings, who, like them, are on the way to their own human destiny. And the harmonious working of all these factors is guaranteed solely by the fact that in all of them God himself, the origin and goal of our destiny to communion with him, is influencing us. This was Herder's conception, and it has not been outdated by the criticism leveled by the theology of our century against the idealistic thesis of human self-fulfillment (or what was regarded as such).

Herder was also, of course, a child of his time to the extent that he regarded evil in human beings as a disfiguration but not as a destructive contradiction of their very humanness itself; as a result, he underestimated the threat that evil represents for humankind. This has justifiably been urged as a criticism of Herder.[48] But, contrary to what Brunner thought, the criticism does not touch the interpretation of the image of God as a human destiny that is to be realized only in the future. Brunner's view would be correct only if Herder and his successors understood this destiny

---

[48]Sunnus (n. 2, above), 142.

as to be realized solely by human beings themselves through their own activity. But, as we saw, precisely on this point Herder opposed the ideas of his age on human perfectibility, as defended by Kant for example. Even Schleiermacher and the nineteenth-century theologians who interpreted the image of God in terms of human destiny thought of human beings as dependent on God for the fulfillment of this destiny. These nineteenth-century theologians also realized that sin contradicts this human destiny. It is not sensible to try to establish oppositions in principle on this point.

The decisive question is, rather, whether the image of God is to be regarded as having been realized in the beginning and then lost through sin. In their answer to this question the majority of twentieth-century theologians have not followed Brunner. Thus Paul Althaus held to the conception of the image of God as the destiny of human beings and judged that this "essential destination of human beings to God, a destination that is theirs by their creation," is "neither lost nor able to be lost."[49] In like manner, Thielicke writes that "there can *not* in fact be any such loss [of the image thus defined]."[50] W. Trillhaas also denies a loss of the image of God and speaks instead of its restoration by Christ.[51] Not least, Barth himself places the image of God under the heading of the human "determination as the covenant-partner of God" and likewise denies its loss through the fall; the image is not to be thought of as a human possession that could be lost. "And on the other hand, the divine intention at the creation of man, and the consequent promise and pledge given with it, cannot be lost or subjected to partial or complete destruction."[52]

Of course, while Barth accepts the interpretation of the image of God as promise and as human destination in God's intention, he also objects to all views that link this image with any quality and endowment of human beings themselves.[53] At this point there is a material difference from Herder's view. Herder had been at great pains to show that a disposition for the likeness to God exists in factors in the initial human natural state, and not to let the image be thought of as existing only in a realm beyond natural human existence, even though at the same time Herder emphasized the dependence of this disposition and destiny and its fulfillment on

[49]Althaus (n. 23, above), 343. Despite this judgment, Althaus speaks of the destination as an "original state of our existence" from which "we fall through sin at every moment" (ibid.).

[50]Thielicke, *Theological Ethics* I, 167. On the other hand, as I mentioned earlier, Thielicke does claim a "loss of a positive relation to God" (ibid.), because he refuses to surrender the conceptual scheme of original state and fall.

[51]W. Trillhaas, *Dogmatik* (1962), 214f.; see the criticism on 210.

[52]Karl Barth, *Church Dogmatics* III/1, trans. J. W. Edward, O. Bussey, and H. Knight (1958), 200; see III/2 trans. H. Knight et al. (1960), 323, and the title of sec. 45 (203).

[53]Ibid., III/1, 192f.

God. Since human beings themselves are involved in the question of their human destination, it is not possible that this destination, though grounded in the divine creative intention, should remain purely external to them; rather, their being must be understood as constituted by the divine creative intention. Otherwise the intention would remain ineffectual and would therefore not be understood as a true intention of God in his creative activity. Even Barth did not remain as closed to this objective logic in giving his positive explanation of his view of the image of God in the human being as we might expect from the limits he established in his polemic against modern theological anthropology. Nevertheless in Barth's theology the externality of God's creative intention in relation to "the phenomenon of the human" prevents the divine creative intention from showing itself, to the same extent as in Herder, as determining the entire range of natural human dispositions and existential conditions and thus as an *effective* creative action.

III. The Significance of Herder's Thought
for Contemporary Philosophical Anthropology

In Herder's fully developed anthropology the idea of the image of God has for its function to describe the unfinished humanity of human beings in such a way as simultaneously to counter the difficulty that the fulfillment of human destiny cannot be thought of as the accomplishment of the very ones in whose lives that destiny is to become a reality. If they were able to accomplish this destiny, they would have to be already what they have still to become. On the other hand, the future of their destination to humanness is also to be thought of as already playing a constitutive role in establishing their characteristic natural being; only under this condition can that future be understood as the fulfillment of the human destiny as such. Both of these conditions are fulfilled in the idea of the image of God, because it makes it possible to think of the goal of essential human realization as at the same time constitutive of the initial human state.

In view of the unfinished state not simply of one capacity or another but of human nature itself in its initial form, Helmuth Plessner's criticism of the concept of human openness to the world brings him close to the ideas of Herder in the context of the modern discussion of philosophical anthropology. Plessner pointed out that human beings are not unrestrictedly open to the reality of things outside them. A capacity and readiness for objectivity are indeed present in principle, but are in practice always limited. In any event, human beings are in a position to recognize, always in specific ways and even if to a limited degree, the partisan character of their perspectives and thus to move beyond these, to expand and, at least partially, to break through the boundaries set by their own interests. This is why it is also possible for them to impose new cultural forms on innate behavioral dispositions, along the lines indicated by I. Eibl-Eibesfeldt. For this same reason, finally, it is not possible to set firm limits to further advances in this kind of change and imposition of new forms.

This human self-transcendence presupposes a reduction in instinct, the primitive condition of the human organs, an unfinished state at birth, and a lengthy period of maturation. But the space for free movement that is thus created provides only the occasion for what Konrad Lorenz calls "fulguration," the "flashing out" of the specifically human. The question of how the passage to this fulguration is to be effected is highlighted by Plessner's emphasis on the limitations of human openness to the world. The passage cannot appropriately be described as accomplished by human activity, since the concept of a *human* activity presupposes the identity of human beings as its subject. Those who act already exercise some control over the circumstances and factors of their activity. Therefore the process whereby they originally become themselves cannot be conceived as action. For the same reason, action as such cannot be that which is specifically human. We will have to come back to this question in another context. But what name are we to give to the specifically human, to that which forms the positive content of that space for free movement which is conditioned by the reduction of instinct and the unfinished state of human organization? Shall we join Scheler (and Portmann) and call it "spirit"? At least at the present stage of our reflections this would be to decide too much in advance, and to do so without having surveyed the difficulties we would be letting ourselves in for. The concept of spirit is a muddied one today and burdened with a limitless multiplicity of associations that would have to be critically examined before a judgment could be made on the usefulness of the concept.

Let us therefore set the concept of spirit aside for the time being and limit ourselves to the peculiarity of human behavior which Scheler sought to explain by introducing the concept of spirit: Human beings are natively always already present to *what is other than themselves.* That is what Scheler means when he speaks of the capacity of the spirit for objectivity, a capacity actuated by the "objective nature" of the object. But when I say that the structure of this objectivity can be described as the presence of human beings to what is other than themselves, this is not yet precise enough, since it is true even of the animals and in fact of all living things, that they live "ecstatically," that is, by entering into their environing reality. In fact, animals are even more keenly susceptible than humans are to impressions from their environment, because they live wholly in the present moment, ignorant of both future and past.[54] Human beings, on the other hand, have past and future, because unlike the animals, including even the chimpanzees, they are able "to loosen the bonds imposed by the situation and to distance themselves from it."[55] Yet precisely for this reason they also have the ability to be present in a new way to what is other than themselves, that is, in such a manner that they are not absorbed into that other through being wholly at the mercy of the content of their perceptions.

Human beings are present to what is other *as* other. When they attend to an object, they are conscious of its differentness, its otherness. And in one and the same act I grasp the otherness of the object not only in its difference from me but also in its distinction from other objects; thus the object is grasped in its own special determination.[56] This in turn does not exclude reflection from attending specifically to the otherness of the object of perception as distinct from other such objects or as distinct from me, the perceiving subject. This is, at another level, one more example of attention to an objective content on the basis of its distinctness as such an object. Since the distinguishing of an objective content is a condition for attention to it, for this very reason such attention can be based on a conscious, even if temporary, turning away from all other objects. This means that the absorption of pure objectivity, the surrender to a thing, becomes possible only as a result of knowledge of the otherness of the thing.

The capacity of human beings for objectivity, for dwelling on the other as other, contains an element of self-transcendence, an element of disregard for their own impulses, and this element is specifically distinct from the ecstatic dynamism common to all living things. This element of self-transcendence is not yet achieved in the life of the higher animals, at least not as a way of life, even if there is a hint of it in the play of young animals. Even in humans this self-transcendence attains to its evolved form only in the course of the individual's development, and we may assume that in the development of the species too this human self-transcendence has not at all times been exercised with the same clear consciousness. It is the consciousness of it—not so much an abstract, theoretical consciousness as a

---

[54]D. Katz, *Animals and Men: Studies in Comparative Psychology,* trans. A. I. Taylor and H. S. Jackson (New York, 1937), F. J. J. Buytendijk, *Mensch und Tier. Ein Beitrag zur vergleichenden Psychologie* (1958), also notes that "an animal has no memories and no notions of the future" (50). This is not inconsistent with the fact that many animals recognize objects and persons encountered previously, and may even spontaneously seek them out. This phenomenon does not yet mean that such objects or persons are known by the animal in question as familiar from a past situation, so that the past situation would be distinguished from the present in the consciousness of the animal.

[55]Buytendijk, 49.

[56]On this point, see M. Merleau-Ponty, *Phenomenology of Perception,* trans. C. Smith (New York, 1962), Part 2, ch. 4, and, earlier, 3f., where the relatedness of each distinct perceptual content (e.g., a point) to a background is emphasized.

consciousness accompanying concrete life—that brings this self-transcendence to its full form, inasmuch as it is now linked to an act of distinguishing. Consciousness is therefore an essential factor in the exercise of human self-transcendence, and even if such consciousness is not always and everywhere fully developed, it can be awakened in every human being. At the same time, however, cultural improvement does not necessarily signify a progress in the clarity of self-transcendence at the level of concrete life. The reason for this will become clearer later on.

The concept of human self-transcendence—like the concept of openness to the world which is to a great extent its equivalent—summarizes a broad consensus among contemporary anthropologists in their effort to define the special character of the human. At the same time, however, opinions vary when it comes to the question of the internal constitution of the peculiarly human form of life, and my reflections will presuppose a certain position adopted in this debate. Explicit clarification is necessary here. The clarification will start most appropriately with the different emphases within the one phenomenon in the presentations of Plessner and Scheler regarding the relation between perception of the object and the distancing of the perceivers from themselves.

Scheler stresses the fact that the various elements making up behavior that is open to the world form "an inseparable structural unity."[57] Nonetheless, for Scheler, the fundamental datum in the analysis of the phenomenon is undoubtedly the objectivity of human perception. Self-consciousness—and the consciousness of God as well—is implicit in this datum. But even though the objectivity of perception is of basic importance for the course of the phenomenological analysis,[58] in the essential structure of the human form of life exocentricity is nonetheless the most generalized and to that extent fundamental characteristic of the properly human.[59] There is a dislocation, however, when, as with Plessner, the element of exocentricity is explained as the peculiarity of the human mode of existence, that is, of the human being as subject. For then the central place in the structural organization of the human life form is assigned in advance to the concept of subject (something Scheler avoided doing), and as a result the special character of human perception can by comparison be given only subordinate importance. In fact, Plessner effects the transition from the centralism of animal life to the exocentricity of human life by raising the question of the conditions required if "a living thing is to

[57]Scheler, *Man's Place in Nature* (Boston, 1961), 90; cf. earlier, 40.

[58]See Scheler's three-stage schema, ibid., 38. Only at the third stage, in the "third reflex" movement (90), does the simultaneity of the exocentric consciousness of the world, self-consciousness, and consciousness of God come into the picture.

[59]Scheler too says (ibid., 90) that at the stage of the "third reflex" the central core of the person has become (!) "anchored in something beyond this world."

be given its center [outside itself]" and he finds that for "the givenness of a subject to itself" the basic condition is that it "is able to distance itself from itself."[60] But in thus starting with the subject Plessner is unable to explain its exocentricity.[61] Scheler, on the other hand, by focusing his

[60]H. Plessner, *Die Stufen des Organischen und der Mensch* (1928; 1965[2]), 289ff.

[61]Plessner himself sees the difficulty that the claim of a simultaneous "centrality" and "exocentricity" suggests a "multiplication of the core of the subject," but he thinks he can avoid this absurd consequence by showing that the subject is not a "fixed reality which is completely given" but is, rather, "linked to a completion or establishment" and may be defined as "that through which mediation takes place" (ibid., 298f.). But how this "that through which" is to be conceived as a subject of action remains obscure. In order to manifest itself as a subject of action, the subject must already have passed through the process whereby it is constituted a subject.

The leading role of the concept of subject and the reminiscences of idealism that are connected with it have led W. Schulz (*Philosophie in der veränderten Welt* (1972), 435ff.) to criticize the "ambiguity" of Plessner's argument. According to Schulz, Plessner's claim to be proceeding in a purely descriptive way as a biologist cannot without further ado be combined with the analytical concept used in an idealistic philosophy of subjectivity, namely, "the human being as exocentric neither by nature nor antecedently to any mediation" (436; see 438).

But in connection with his rejection of Scheler's dualism and with the fact of Gehlen's turn away from philosophy to empirical research, Schulz broadens this criticism into a claim that philosophical anthropology has given way to empirical research in the one case and to the practice of introspection in the other (457ff.). He says that philosophical anthropology represents only "a transitional intermediate stage" between the dualistic picture of the human being in the metaphysical tradition and the research carried on in the specialized sciences (462). In Scheler, and in Plessner and Gehlen as well, the description required for a comparison of human beings with animals on the basis of external observation is not carried through: "If human beings are initially asserted to be beings that are self-relating and that independently build their world for themselves, this is not a statement that can be understood as strictly empirical, since a relation of the self to the self is not a verifiable fact. All three thinkers thus move out of the realm of biological research. Their guiding intention is to show the *differentness* of human beings, and the means by which this is to be proved are ultimately derived not from biology but from the philosophical tradition" (458).

This criticism is most readily applicable to Scheler's concept of spirit. It is not valid, however, for Plessner and Gehlen and certainly not for the procedure followed in philosophical anthropology as a whole. The thesis of the differentness of human beings is not introduced as a postulate but emerges in the context of the question regarding the specific character of the human form of life as compared with other forms of life. The empirical character of the investigation into the specificity of a phenomenon may not be rejected out of hand. For, despite the difficulties in which Plessner entangles himself by adopting the concept of subject, it must be noted that while the concept is idealistic in origin, he uses it as a tool of empirical description. I do not understand why the assumption of a relation of the self to the self must be excluded in principle as a means of explaining the peculiarities of a being's bodily behavior when these peculiarities cannot be rendered intelligible except by assumptions of this kind. What Plessner and other thinkers in the field of anthropology are doing is to argue from externally observable human behavior to the conditions that make such behavior possible. This approach cannot be considered outmoded simply as a result of criticism leveled at the concepts used by one author or another. Its rejection can in fact only

analysis on the objectivity of human perception necessarily starts from the exocentricity of human life, so that he need not let himself be led astray by the aporias in the concept of subject (which can be thought of as simultaneously in itself and outside itself).

Admittedly, Scheler's presentation of this objectivity is encumbered by the obscurities in the concept of spirit, which, on the one hand, in a manner reminiscent of Aristotle, supposedly intervenes from without in the life process of the human organism, while, on the other, spirit as person must be the center from which the acts of this living entity flow. Nonetheless Scheler's point of departure, as is clear from its development in Gehlen, has the advantage of greater accessibility, because the weaknesses in his own interpretation of the phenomenon of the unique objectivity of human perception could stimulate other interpretations of the same situation. This advantage remains despite the problems raised even by Gehlen's conception. For even Gehlen's interpretation of "openness to the world" as the point of departure for appropriation of the world through human action remains entangled in the thematic of the subject, and this in a manner notably similar to Plessner's. According to both, the subject supposedly comes into being only in the process of its behavior, but at the same time the subject must be thought of as the source of this behavior and therefore would have to exist fully at the beginning of the process. At least, however, Gehlen, like Herder and later Scheler, has taken the openness of the human relation to the world as the point of departure for his description, and this provides the opportunity to keep this approach from getting entangled in the problems connected with the subject and to develop it in a description of the process that has the human subject for its result. In adopting this approach, I am following, via Scheler and Gehlen, the way pointed out by Herder.

Herder's theme was human becoming, in the process of which subjectivity comes into existence, so that the result of the process cannot be understood as a product of the subject. He took as the key concept for describing such a process the idea of the human destination to likeness to God. Herder interpreted the initial human biological situation as a disposition for this destination and in this way he linked the two. But if we

---

lead back into the dualism of positivistic research into details, on the one hand, and "introspection" (even if for practical ends), on the other. The advance of philosophical anthropology beyond the narrow limits of the philosophy of consciousness on the one hand and the positivism of the behaviorists on the other consists precisely in its insistence on the indispensable intellectual penetration of empirical data. No one can seriously seek to avoid this task, nor, on the other hand, can it be left solely to the empirical researcher, because when this second course is adopted, the result is that undiscussed and inadequately differentiated philosophical presuppositions all too easily take control, as happened both in behaviorism and in German behavioral research.

examine the matter more closely, we find that the idea of the image of God in Herder is not mediated through a description of the initial human biological situation, but, like the idea of providence, is introduced into the anthropological data from outside. On this point Herder's line of thought can no longer satisfy present-day requirements for rendering plausible the introduction of theological concepts into the description of empirical anthropological matters. If there is to be any justification for Herder's procedure, it must be shown that the religious and theological concepts are not extrinsic to the phenomena but correspond to a dimension exhibited by the latter.

In this area both Scheler and Plessner have argued with greater rigor than Herder did. Both were of the opinion that the essential structure of the human form of life implies the religious thematic. Thus according to Scheler intercourse with divine reality "belongs to the *essence* of man just as much as self-consciousness and consciousness of the world." Religion is not a secondary addition to behavior that is open to the world, but *"at the very moment"* when this behavior came into being "man was also driven to anchor his own central being in something beyond this world."[62] But Scheler did not regard it as necessary to develop in a detailed argument this claim of simultaneity and essential correlation. If he had not followed the supposedly shorter road of the concept of spirit and its transcendent origin, he could have taken as his starting point the openness to the world or objectivity of the human perception of objects. In any case, it is advisable to join Plessner in taking the concept of exocentricity as a way of describing behavior that is open to the world[63] and not to introduce it only for justifying a turning to a divine reality which is "something beyond the world." For only in this way does the connection of the two phenomena or, rather, of the two sides of one and the same phenomenon emerge into full clarity.

By this orientation to an object, by this presence to the other as other, human beings prove themselves to be exocentric in Plessner's sense of the term. But the dwelling of perceptive intuition in its object is only one of the ways in which human beings exist outside themselves and thus exocentrically. It is, however, the fundamental form, and the other forms of exocentric behavior may be understood as developments of it. To begin with, the grasping of an object *as* other means that human beings are present to the objects of their world. At the same time, however, because

---

[62]Scheler, *Man's Place in Nature*, 89f. (italics added). See also Scheler, *On the Eternal in Man*, trans. B. Noble (New York, 1960), 250ff. Plessner, on the other hand, does not regard exocentricity as directly religious; rather, the religious thematic emerges from the exocentric manner of life because of the experience that this brings of the contingency of all things and of one's own existence.

[63]I bracket here, however, the problem of the subject in Plessner.

they are aware of the otherness of the object, they can also distance themselves from every object and turn their attention to other objects which are defined as "other" in relation to the first.[64] For in the consciousness of the otherness of the object, that other which stands over against the first object and is distinct from it is always implicitly present, even if only in a vague and undefined way. This structure of behavior which allows human beings to direct themselves to the object *as* other also makes it possible for them to distance themselves from it in favor of still another. To this extent Plessner's short formulation of the human situation is to be accepted: "Being positioned exocentrically, human beings stand where they stand and at the same time do not stand where they stand."[65]

The act of distancing, which has its basis in the free selectivity of attention and is not reducible, for example, to new impressions that immediately make their presence felt, is in turn mediated through the knowledge, implicitly given with the perception of an object, of other objects from which the intuited object is by its nature distinct. This object is distinct not only from other objects but also from the perceiver. Consequently, attention can turn not only to other objects but back to the perceiver. The fact that such self-consciousness is conditioned by the perception of the perceiver's own body[66] and by the social environment[67] may be left aside here. I shall concern myself in this context only with the fact that perception itself provides the platform for a return from experience of the object to the self or ego. There is here a transcending of the whole sphere of objective perception, but one that nonetheless is based on the perception of the object *as* other and in which the existence of the perceiver is initially grasped as one object among others. If I am to be able to grasp the

[64]At the same time, the free "selectivity" of attention (see A. Treismann, "Selective Attention in Man," *British Medical Bulletin* 20 [1964], 12–16) has the same basis as the objectivity of perception, namely, the relative freedom from the pressure of instinct; see U. Neisser, *Cognitive Psychology* (Englewood Cliffs, N.J., 1967), 87ff., 94ff., and P. Bakan, ed., *Attention: An Enduring Problem in Psychology* (Princeton, 1966).

[65]Plessner, 342. The implicit accompanying presence of phenomena that are not the focus of attention has been brought out by Merleau-Ponty in his *Phenomenology of Perception* (n. 56, above), 26ff. See also Neisser, *Cognitive Psychology*, 86–104, on the relation of "focal attention" to the "preattentive" processes.

[66]The reintroduction of the concept of the absolute subject in the idea of a situatedness of the ego that has its basis in corporeality and provides the standpoint for a limited finite perspective in experience of the world characterizes the position of Merleau-Ponty in his *Phenomenology of Perception*. The role played by knowledge of one's own body in the development of self-consciousness had, strangely enough, not yet become a problem for Merleau-Ponty. This may be connected with the fact that he thought of the relation to one's own body as being simply "pre-objective" and habitual in a primordial way, so that body was not grasped as an object (compare Part 3, ch. 1, with Part 1, ch. 4). On this subject, see below, pp. 293f.

[67]See below, chapter 3.

individual object *as* this individual object and thus as other in relation both to other objects and to myself, I must have reached beyond the individual object and acquired a perspective in which it can be viewed together with others and which by its very generality is of a higher order than the individual object and embraces this simultaneously with others.[68]

This step into the universal is, of course, placed initially at the service of the perception of the individual thing. It need not yet take the distinct form of knowledge of species and genera. Such knowledge is reached only when reflective attention turns thematically to the universal which is given simultaneously with perception of the object, just as such attention can turn to other objects and back to the perceiver, guided by the implications of the primary data of perception. But for this very reason that the step into universality is as yet unaccompanied by a distinct consciousness of genera and species, the step also has no limitations put upon it. The exocentric structure of human living has therefore an openness that is not restricted to the things of the world. The openness of the step which first makes possible the very perception of an object reaches beyond the totality of all given and possible objects of perception, that is, beyond the world. Only in reflection, of course, do we become conscious of this, in the same reflection in which the formation of definite specific and generic concepts takes place and the transcendence marking the initial step loses its indeterminate character. Only at this level too do we reach beyond species and genera and form the idea of the totality of the world and of a divine reality that is the ground of the world. But this level of reflection

[68]In his *Phenomenology of Perception,* Merleau-Ponty speaks of a "field" that is constitutive for the individual sensation at any given moment (e.g., the field of vision, 5). Correspondingly, through the body and its situatedness the world is manifested as an indefinite, openended unity which is the horizon for all perceptions. The fact that the individual perception is conditioned by the world as a horizon corresponds, at the level of conceptual reflection, to the priority of the universal over the particular, even where the universal forms only the implicit horizon within which the particular is grasped. For this reason, Aristotle not only regarded the knowledge of first principles as the logical presupposition of knowledge of particular things (*Analytica Posteriora* 100b8ff.) but doubtless also regarded a knowledge— even if only provisional and diffuse—of the universal and the whole as the epistemological starting point for the knowledge of particulars (*Physica* 184a21). In any event, medieval Aristotelianism systematized Aristotle's ideas along these lines. Thomas Aquinas therefore distinguished a diffuse knowledge of the universal, which precedes knowledge of the particular, from a precise knowledge of the universal, which emerges only through abstraction from the particular (*Summa theologiae* I, q. 85, a. 3). Modern transcendental Thomism speaks of a "stepping out" *(excessus)* or a "preapprehension" of being in general as a condition for the knowledge of an individual object; see K. Rahner, *Spirit in the World.* trans. W. V. Dych (New York, 1967), 142ff., 183ff., and see earlier, 60f., 120ff. But the connection with the use of the idea of *excessus* in Thomas Aquinas (*Summa theologiae* I, q. 84, a. 7 ad 3) seems a very loose one (142).

is not something supplementary. It is the very field of attention, a field in which attention is at home as it turns in this or that direction.

It was this transcending of every particular object—a transcending that is already a condition for the perception of the individual object in its determinacy (and thus in its otherness and distinctness)—that I had in mind when I wrote in 1962 that the so-called openness of the human being to the world signifies ultimately an openness to what is beyond the world, so that the real meaning of this openness to the world might be better described as an openness to God which alone makes possible a gaze embracing the world as a whole. Is this step justified? Are not human beings related, in their open-ended transcendence of themselves and all the objects of their experience, only to a very broad horizon containing all of these? Is it not always a leap from there to an intuition of divine reality? The answer: Even when they move beyond all experience or idea of perceptible objects they continue to be exocentric, related to something other than themselves, but now to an Other beyond all the objects of their world, an Other that at the same time embraces this entire world and thus ensures the possible unification of the life of human beings in the world, despite the multiplicity and heterogeneity of the world's actions on them. A mere very general horizon containing all objects would have no inherent existence. In fact, when human beings reach out to a very general horizon embracing all the individual objects of actual or possible perception, they are relating themselves exocentrically to a *reality* prior to them; in this reaching out they are therefore implicitly affirming at the same time the divine reality, even though they have not yet grasped this thematically as such, much less in this or that particular form.

For Plessner too the question of God arises in view of the experience that I have already transcended every finite content in the very act of grasping it. This experience need not mean that I abandon the finite objects; rather, I can become conscious that these objects do not have their root in themselves. Thus the experience of transcending all finite contents leads "to the consciousness of the unqualified contingency of existence and thus to the idea of a ground of the world . . . or to God."[69] According to Plessner, however, even in the idea of God the exocentricity of human beings does not automatically come to rest; for they can distance themselves even from this idea and turn away from every concept of God. I must agree with this argument, but with the restriction that Plessner neglects to keep separate two distinct situations under this heading. On the one hand, when discussing the exocentric behavior of human beings, we are dealing with a real relation to the unconditioned or the infinite.

[69]Plessner, *Die Stufen des Organischen und der Mensch.* 341.

This relation is implicit in the awareness of the contingency, conditioned-ness, and transcendibility of all finite contents. The experience of the finite as such already implies—to use the language of Hegel—the transcending of it and, ultimately, the elevation of consciousness to the idea of the infinite. But on the other hand, every intellectual determination of this infinite by means of such concepts as ground of the world, absolute, or God is in fact itself finite and therefore able to be transcended and ne-gated, just as other finite ideas are. This means that the relation of human exocentric existence to the infinite or unconditioned is always given only through the mediation of a finite content. But it may be said conversely that every human relation to finite objects implies a relation to the infinite and therefore has in the final analysis a religious foundation and that from the transcending of all finite realities it always returns to the reality given in each instance.

It is not difficult to see the connection between these considerations and Herder's idea. For if according to Plessner the human exocentric structure presupposes, in one manner or another, "an extreme of power and gran-deur" which alone can form the "counterweight" to the "openness" of the exocentric mode of life and provide the "appropriate support" for it,[70] it is also true that this infinite is always given only in the context of the moment's experience of finite reality, whether it is given merely implicitly or in explicit religious thematization but then always in relation to contents derived from finite experience. The way of human beings to the (divine) reality in which they can ultimately ground their exocentric existence and thereby attain to their own identity is thus always mediated through the experience of the external world. This is especially true of the relationship with the other human beings, that is, with beings whose lives are character-ized by the same question and experience. But having said this, we are back in principle with Herder's conception according to which human beings need to be *educated* to be themselves—educated to reason, human-ity, and religion—and that such education comes to them through their experience of their world but especially through dealings with other human beings, because the theme of those other lives is or has already been the same as that of their own. Human beings do not realize them-selves in a Promethean manner through self-enhancement by their own power. They must continue to depend on achieving their destiny, which directs them beyond the world of finite things, by dealing with the things of their world which, as a world inhabited by society, is mediated to them through the social relations in which they live. The considerable contribu-tion of society to the process of the individual's self-becoming will have to be evaluated in detail.

[70]H. Plessner, *Conditio Humana* (1964), 67.

In the process, then, of their education to be themselves human beings are dependent on natural and social conditions, although they can also affect these in their turn. Certainly their own action also contributes in a positive or negative way to the process of their education. This has to be admitted in view of the fact that it is a world and an environment which have been changed by their action that now, in their altered form, in turn act upon the agents themselves. But in the history of the education of human beings their own action remains only one factor among others, and its contribution to the process is more indirect than direct. They cannot be totally the object of their own action if for no other reason than that they are always the agents as well. Therefore even when human beings direct their action to themselves, the influence of this action on their process of self-education is of a more indirect kind: what emerges is only partially under our control.

As we have seen, the principle that in a specific way human beings exist exocentrically or *extra se* ("outside themselves") is not true only of the religious side of their practical life. It may be, however, that the point was first discovered in connection with this dimension, when Luther described the existence of believers by saying that they exist in faith *extra se in Christo* ("outside themselves in Christ").[71] This is precisely a description of the essential structure of faith as trust; for whenever we trust, we "abandon ourselves" and build on the person or thing in which we trust. Through our trust we make our existence dependent on that to which we abandon ourselves.[72] Luther must have regarded this *extra se* of faith as something paradoxical, since Aristotelian psychology knew nothing of such a structure of human life. Its wider significance has been brought to light only by contemporary philosophical anthropology, although the latter for its part has not been aware of the analogy between its concept of human exocentricity and Luther's description of faith.

The "being present to the other" which characterizes the objectivity of our dealing with things has the same structure as the *extra nos* of faith. It is true in both cases that human beings not only relate themselves to something outside themselves but find themselves "translated" into what is other than themselves or, rather, are present to the other from the

---

[71]On this point, see Joest (n. 26, above), 273–74.

[72]On this, see my *What Is Man? Contemporary Anthropology in Theological Perspective,* trans. D. A. Priebe (Philadelphia, 1970), 28ff. This fact is not taken into account in N. Luhmann's study, *Vertrauen, ein Mechanismus der Reduktion sozialer Komplexität* (1968), although Luhmann recognizes that trust first becomes necessary because of the limits set on the instrumental control of events (13, 87ff.). His description of social relations based on trust and of their fundamental importance for the social system presupposes the concept of the self and of self-presentation (59ff.), so that the question of the meaning of trust for very constitution of the self remains unsettled.

beginning and are therefore able to find themselves only in the light of the other. The experience of the object is admittedly only a first aspect of the human existential structure, for the reason that when the object is grasped as *this* object, it has already been transcended, since only within a limitless horizon of meaning is it possible to grasp the determinate character of an individual object. When human beings direct their attention to a particular object, they are in that very act reaching out beyond all that is finite; for only in the context of the whole can we determine the meaning of the individual thing. But when we become aware of the fact that in every turning to an individual, determinate object we have reached beyond all that is determinate and therefore all that is limited and finite, we are in the presence of the religious thematic and therefore of the question about the *basic trust* that supports our life. That which can become the explicit object of religious consciousness is implicitly present in every turning to a particular object of our experience.

Human openness to the world, the capacity for objectivity in relation to the objects of our world, thus has an implicitly religious dimension of depth. This is true even of those who take an irreligious view of themselves in their explicit consciousness, for then they understand themselves by opposition to the express thematization of certain implications of their own life. The broad significance of this situation for human behavior will be the object of the next chapter. But first I must point out the connection between the deeper religious meaning of so-called openness to the world and the question of existence as a self.

Speaking very generally, experience of the world is the way by which human beings reach experience of themselves. The objectivity that characterizes their relation to the world is correlative to the indeterminate character of their spontaneous impulses: they must direct their impulses with the aid of the experience of objective reality. As I shall show later in more precise detail, this always happens in the context of a social world. And because their impulses are not directed along hard-and-fast lines by inherited behavioral dispositions and because the roles assigned them in the life of society do not all have the same indisputable validity, they become a question to themselves. They seek the answer to this question of themselves from the objects and relationships of their world; that is, they seek to orient themselves through information regarding their world. In the process they are led beyond all particular finite objects and relationships. If and when they become conscious of this, they experience that the question of their own destiny—the question of themselves—*and* the question of the ground beyond the world that sustains it and their life are one and the same question. The question of human beings about themselves and the question of the divine reality belong together. Herder saw this inner connection between *humanity and religion* more clearly than was often the case later on. The fundamental importance of this connection for the idea of the image of God occupied us earlier. This idea says in any case that only in relation to God can human beings become fully themselves.

All that I have been saying does not amount to a kind of anthropological proof of God's existence. The fact that the question of God belongs to the humanity of human beings does not yet signify that a God exists and what kind of God he is. It is only insofar as it is a problem that the question of God cannot be separated from the humanity of human beings. In this sense human beings are in fact, as Cicero said, religious by nature. The unavoidableness of the God question as a problem means nonetheless that we are not dealing with a theme from which human beings can quite well distance themselves and which they may pass over without having to pay for this distancing with a loss of openness to their own reality. For in one way or another, as long as human beings live, they live on the basis of a fundamental trust which sustains their life—whether it is God or an idol in which they put their trust (to use the language of Luther's explanation of the First Commandment). The progress of their life will either demonstrate the carrying capacity of their trust or show that they have built on sand.

The connection between the question of human beings about themselves and the question of God appears with special clarity in the question of the ultimate human destiny. Under one aspect this theme is articulated in the idea of the image of God. From another point of view—namely, in the context of the knowledge that human beings have about their own end—it finds expression in hope that reaches beyond death. This hope has taken many forms: faith in reincarnation, the immortality of the soul, the resurrection of the dead. But in all these forms it gives expression to the fact that the question of God goes together with the question of human beings about themselves. If that is the case, then we must face the possibility that the human destination to communion with God is superior to and outlasts human transiency and death.

Hegel justly remarked that the idea of God and some form of faith in immortality are two sides of one and the same thing. This is why the religious thematic in human life has been connected since early times with burial rites and belief in the continued existence of the dead. Even the initial results, often regarded as sensational, of modern research on death[73] offer confirmation on this point: when the dying have the feeling of casting loose from the body, a feeling of lightness and of entering into a realm of light, we must see in this first of all—and prior to any further inferences that may be drawn—an expression of that consciousness, which

[73]E. Kübler-Ross, *Was können wir noch tun?* (1975²); J. Chr. Hampe, *Sterben ist doch ganz anders. Erfahrungen mit dem eigenen Tod* (1975²).

is already constitutive of the living person even if it is frequently camouflaged, of belonging to a sphere of divine reality that transcends this transient life. Reports of such experiences speak, to be sure, of a second phase, a phase of experience of judgment, in which their whole life, from end to beginning, passes before the inner gaze of the dying, who stand now in the light of that divine reality. Such an experience of judgment amid consciousness of the person's unsuitability in relation to the divine reality is the unavoidable reverse side of the consciousness that the person's life belongs to a divine reality that transcends this life. To have a share in eternity entails experiencing one's own life with its inner contradictions and its opposition to the divine eternity.[74]

Thus the idea of a divine reality that transcends everything finite is part of the religious thematic of human life, as is the idea of some kind of immortal destiny for one's own being, beyond transiency and death. Even in the theological tradition the human destination to immortality, unlike the image of God with which it is nonetheless materially closely connected, has been understood as future and not yet realized in a complete initial state.[75]

IV. Relation to the World as Expression of the Image of God

In the previous sections of this chapter I have used the expression "image of God" in the general sense of a human destination to communion with God. This usage corresponds to the interpretation given of the concept in Christian theology since the second century, and certainly the idea of closeness to God is also contained in the statement in the biblical story of creation on which the theological concept is based. However, nothing has been said here as yet of the specific interpretation given of the biblical statement by the Priestly account of creation in Gen. 1:26f.

The exegetes of the early church and the Middle Ages looked for the content of the image of God in a kinship of the human soul with God, while the Reformers found it rather in the union of the human will with God's will which the first human being had by reason of original justice. But the dominant exegetical tradition at the present time began with the

---

[74]See my *What Is Man?* 54ff.

[75]Irenaeus, *Adv. haer.* IV, 38, 2f. Human beings could not have complete likeness to God at the outset but only reach it through a process of assimilation to him; only in this way could they obtain "eternal permanence" (38, 3). Irenaeus could also state in this context that only in the course of the process could human beings become "the image and likeness of God" (ibid.; see V, 16, 1), while in another passage he says that human beings originally possessed the image of God but not the likeness, which is communicated by the Spirit (V, 6, 1). For the background in Tatian and for Irenaeus' recasting of Tatian's thought, see Hauschild (n. 19, above), 198f., 212f.

observation of the Socinians that in the biblical story of creation the human likeness to God and the human destination to be ruler of the earth are closely connected. In fact, the identification of the image of God with the role of master has not prevailed.[76] Nonetheless present-day exegetes do regard the authority and commission to rule as an immediate consequence of the biblical statement about humanity as made in the image of God.[77] The real content of the notion probably has to do with the likeness of human beings in their bodily form to God, an idea that is rendered intelligible only if we assume "that in the broader background of this Priestly statement about God's image in man is the notion of Yahweh's human form." The Priestly text shows less interest, however, in the question "of the nature of God's image than of its purpose."[78] The objective connection that exists between the image of God and the human function as ruler of creation, which is grounded in the image, becomes clear when we realize that in the ancient Near East the idea of likeness to God and that of divine sonship were the special privilege of the king and the mark of his position; only in the Old Testament were they extended to humankind generally.[79] For in the ancient Near East the king was regarded as the earthly representative of God and of the divine rule over the world. By making the statement about the image of God in the human being the Priestly document is thus assigning the human being as such the role of king in the context of creation.

On the other hand, this same background enables us to understand the New Testament when it sees the human destination to be the image of God as brought to focus in the person of Jesus Christ.[80] For in the Messiahship of Jesus and in his divine Sonship the influence is still felt of those ancient sources of the idea of the divine image that are closely bound up

[76]In twentieth-century theology it is represented by Thielicke, *Theologische Ethik* I, 268, n. 781 (ET: *Theological Ethics* I, 157), who agrees that the biblical text offers no basis for a distinction between the image of God as such and the function the image bestows.

[77]Thus von Rad (n. 18, above), 57. O. H. Steck, *Der Schöpfungsbericht der Priesterschrift* (1975), 155, makes a distinction between the function of ruling, which follows from the likeness to God, and the capacity for this task, which is bestowed by the added blessing. On Barth's interpretation of the image of God as connected with the sexual differentiation of human existence into male and female, which is mentioned (Gen. 1:27) in the context of the image and likeness, see the critical response of W. H. Schmidt (n. 18, above), 146, n. 4.

[78]Von Rad, 57.

[79]W. H. Schmidt, 136ff., has shown this in detail. "What is elsewhere said only of the king is here transferred to all human beings" (139).

[80]2 Cor. 4:4 (see 3:18; Rom. 8:29); Col. 1:15; etc. On this point, see O. Cullmann, *The Christology of the New Testament,* trans. S. C. Guthrie and C. A. M. Hall (rev. ed.; Philadelphia, 1963), 166ff., who also discusses Phil. 2:5–11 in this same context; and J. Jervell, *Imago Dei. Gen 1, 26f. im Spätjudentum, in der Gnosis und in den paulinischen Briefen* (Göttingen, 1960), 256ff., who emphasizes the links with Hellenistico-Judaic wisdom.

with the religious basis of kingship. Of course, when the royal rule of Christ is understood as the rule of the love of God that is revealed in the crucified Jesus, the customary notions of sovereignty among human beings are turned upside down: "Whoever would be great among you must be your servant, and whoever would be first among you must be slave of all" (Mark 10:43f.).

Is the connection between the image of God and the call to rule the world as God's representative an objective connection that can be recognized in the phenomenon called "openness to the world"? If Herder's linking of the theologoumenon about God's image with the anthropological data which thinkers today like to sum up in the concept of openness to the world is objectively justified, then we should expect that the biblical linking of the image of God and human rule over the earth would also have something to do with openness to the world—unless, of course, we were to assume that the Priestly document and the tradition of ideas behind it brought together ideas that had no objective connection, or that at least the Priestly document's extension of the image of God found in the king to humankind as such is inappropriate in the light of the anthropological data.

It seems now that in fact there is a connection between the relation of human beings to God and their increasing mastery of the natural conditions of their existence. Only because in their exocentric self-transcendence they reach beyond the immediately given to the broadest possible horizon of meaning that embraces all finite things—only because of this is it possible for them to grasp an individual object in its determinateness that distinguishes it from other objects. Later on we will have to reflect more carefully on the fact that we are dealing here with the action of reason which conceives the individual in the light of the universal as it stands out in its particularity against the background of the universal. This process of defining the individuality of things[81] has become the basis for all human mastery of nature. Precisely because human beings reach beyond the given, and therefore ultimately because human exocentricity is characterized by an impulse, inconceivable except in religious terms, to the unconditioned do they have the ability to rule over the objects of their natural world.

This linkage of religious thematic and human rule over nature is comprehensible only in a religion that sharply contrasts the divine reality with the reality of the world and does not confuse God with the forces of nature and that in addition locates human beings on the side of God and thus sets

---

[81]Exegetes have rightly pointed out that God's invitation to Adam to name the animals in the older or Yahwist account of creation is analogous to the commission to rule the earth in the Priestly account of creation.

them too over against the world.[82] It is likely that in the religious veneration of the forces of nature human beings were implicitly concerned to make themselves masters of nature. But this element in the human destiny could become an explicit theme only in a religion that draws a line of division between the divine reality and the forces of nature, as was the case in the religion of Israel.

Recently the accusation has been leveled against the Jewish-Christian tradition that with its idea of humanity being destined to rule over the earth it has promoted a destructive development that has led finally to our present-day problems of human threats to the environment. Thus the reckless technological exploitation of the environment by the West has been traced back by Lynn T. White, an American historian writing in 1970, to the disastrous influence exercised by the Jewish-Christian linking of human destiny to the image of God with the commission to exercise mastery over nature.[83] This same traditiohistorical connection had earlier been displayed as positive in its significance, and it used to play an important role in the apologetic argument in defense of the Christian faith against the suspicion that it was hostile or at least alien to the spirit of modern science and technology.[84]

Today, however, the theologians are suddenly seeing the dubious aspects of the biblical provenance of the modern technological world situation and are admitting a share of the responsibility for the present-day reckless quest of mastery over nature. Thus one of the leading American theologians, John B. Cobb, demands that Christians accept more responsibility for the preservation even of nonhuman nature and especially of nonhuman life.[85] To this end, Cobb appeals to the fact that in the story of creation in Genesis it is creation *in its entirety* and not just humanity that

[82]It is a merit of F. Gogarten in his later work to have repeatedly called attention to this point; see, e.g., *Despair and Hope for Our Time,* trans. T. Wieser (Boston, 1970), 13ff. C. F. von Weizsäcker, in *Die Tragweite der Wissenschaft* (1964), has provided extensive confirmation of this thesis of Gogarten by his investigation of the historical roots of modern conceptualization in the natural sciences (esp. 196f.). See also G. Altner, *Schöpfung am Abgrund* (1974), 72ff.

[83]Lynn T. White, "The Historical Roots of Our Ecological Crisis," in *The Environmental Handbook* (New York, 1970). In Germany this view has been accepted especially by C. Amery in his book *Das Ende der Vorsehung. Die gnadenlosen Folgen des Christentums* (1972).

[84]F. Gogarten, *Der Mensch zwischen Gott und Welt* (1952), 149ff., 325, 338ff.

[85]J. B. Cobb, *Is It Too Late? A Theology of Ecology* (Beverly Hills, Calif., 1972). The remarks that follow in the text refer especially to the chapter entitled "A New Christianity" (48ff.) and in particular to what the author says on 50 and 55f. In a Preface to the German edition of the book, K. Scholder voices a criticism that is directed especially against Cobb's hoped-for "reintegration of human beings into the natural process" and "decreased emphasis on Christology" and that calls instead for a "radicalization of the *dominium terrae* ["mastery of the earth"]" (12f.). But G. Altner (n. 82, above), 18f., rightly objects that our biblical commission to master the earth is precisely not an unlimited one.

is called very good, and from this standpoint he criticizes the humanistic absolutization of the human individual to the disregard of the rest of nature. A new Christianity must "substitute a vision of a healthy biotic pyramid with man as its apex for the absoluteness of man."

Although this notion is perhaps not adequately secured against the dangers of a resacralization of nature, it is nonetheless closer to the biblical faith in creation and to the true meaning of the divine commission given humanity to be master than is the reckless exploitation of nonhuman nature by arbitrary human choice. The mastery of nature to which human beings are called according to the account of creation in the Priestly document must be exercised in awareness of the creator's own dominion over his creation. This means that human beings have not been given carte blanche for the selfish pillage and exploitation of nonhuman nature. Rather, their rule over creation as the creator's representative must take God's creative will as its norm.[86]

Only beginning in the eighteenth century did the commission given to human beings to represent God in their dominion over nature turn into a claim that they have unlimited power to dispose of nature. This happened, in other words, at the very time when modern humanity in its self-understanding was cutting its ties with the creator God of the Bible. It is therefore incorrect to charge Western Christianity as a whole with this distortion of the biblical commission of domination, this failure to recognize the role of human beings as fiduciaries. It was in fact only the emancipation of modern humanity from biblical revelation that turned the biblical commission of domination into a subjugation of nature to human beings on their own authority and for their own arbitrary use.[87]

Friedrich Gogarten has aptly described the basic structure of this development as a turn from "independence [of the human person] as the son," via a desacralized and to this extent secular world, to secularism.[88] In

[86]Thus Altner, 58ff., 81f.

[87]When Cobb makes the combination of Christian individualism and the commission to be master of nature responsible for these consequences (n. 85, above, 32), he allows himself to be overly impressed by Lynn T. White's flawed arguments. I cannot agree with him in his criticism of the absolute value set on the individual in the Christian tradition. The supreme value set on the human individual is in fact connected with the image of God in human beings (see Gen. 9:6). This same value plays a central role in the preaching of Jesus, as the parables of the lost sheep, the lost coin, and the prodigal son show in an especially impressive way (Luke 15). This high esteem for the individual finds expression not least in the Jewish and Christian hope of resurrection, insofar as this includes the hope that those individuals who had been united with God in earlier generations will also participate in the fulfillment of human history in the kingdom of God. This high value placed on the individual human life does not necessarily lead, as Cobb seems to think, to contempt for nonhuman nature.

[88]Gogarten, *Despair and Hope for Our Time,* 142ff.

working out his explanation, Gogarten did not indeed have the ecological crisis in mind. But this crisis provides the most striking illustration and justification of his distinction between secularization and secularism. The "independence as the son" implies the respect of a fiduciary for the creator's own dominion over his creation as well as the exercise of a rule that affirms and protects nature. The expression "independence as the son" is also a reminder that the meaning of the commission of dominion that is given to human beings in the account of creation in Genesis finds its full realization only in the Sonship of Jesus, that is, in the way in which Jesus as Son of the Father perceived his relation to the world and in which this relation is continued in the Lordship of the risen Christ. Jesus Christ, the Son of God, thus became the prototypical fulfillment of the image of God; all other human beings are to bear his image, the image of the second Adam (1 Cor. 15:49). This holds true also of their relation to the world. Human beings are to rule over the world in a spirit of responsibility to the Father. It is impossible to argue to a right of limitless exploitation of nature for whatever ends human beings may arbitrarily choose. The usurpation of such a power of disposition is based, rather, on the assertion of human beings that they themselves are the ultimate goal of their own actions. The modern principle of human autonomy guarantees nature far less protection against its limitless exploitation by human beings than does Christian anthropology. This is especially the case when the idea of autonomy is connected not with a concept of reason to which the individual is subordinate, but with the modern understanding of individual freedom as an unlimited power of self-disposition which is subject to factual limitations only by the demands of life together in society. The human claim, derivable from such an understanding of human autonomy, to an unrestricted control of nature has, in fact, been unsettled by the ecological crisis. This does not mean, however, that humanity can or should renounce any and all rule over nature, for only through a responsible exercise of dominion can the ecological crisis be overcome.

3

Centrality and Sin

I. Brokenness and Distortion of Human Identity

The ambiguity of human dominion over nature brings us back to a more general ambiguity in human behavior. Dominion can be accepted as a duty and exercised by incorporating a particular sphere of responsibility into the individual's own existential goal, that is, by expanding self-interest to include this sphere of responsibility. But dominion may also mean the unscrupulous exploitation and oppression of what is ruled to the advantage of the private self-interest of the ruler. The difference between these two forms of dominion consists in this, that in the case of dominion as oppression the will of the ruler is opposed to the integrity, inherent character, and inherent rights of the sphere that is ruled, while in the case of dominion accepted as a duty, the will of the ruler extends beyond any special interests to assume into pursuit of the goal a prudent care for the objective requirements of this new sphere of responsibility.

The more inclusive root of this ambiguity in human behavior is made evident in the basic structure of the human form of life as described by Helmuth Plessner. Other analyses found in contemporary anthropology, even those of Arnold Gehlen and Adolf Portmann, take hardly any account of this ambiguity and brokenness of human behavior. It is perhaps the most important merit of Plessner's description of the human form of life that it provides a way of interpreting the ambiguity of human behavior, namely, in the light of the tension between centrality and exocentricity in the human being. Plessner himself has not fully developed the potentialities of his anthropological approach in this direction, because he has not thought out in a fully radical way the implications of the tension between centralized position—subjection to the here and now—and exocentricity in human beings. The peculiar brokenness of the human relation to the world, which the later Plessner has rightly emphasized against the claim of a limitless human openness to the world,[1] was,

[1]H. Plessner, *Conditio Humana* (1964), 47.

of course, seen even in his groundbreaking early work and explained by the structure of the human form of life. At that time Plessner had realized that the structure of exocentricity is accompanied by a break in the relation of human beings to themselves and he understood the danger that this break represents for human identity. But he had not grasped the full extent to which this break represents an interior human conflict, and the reason for this failure is probably the fact that the break seemed to him to exist primarily in the relation of human beings to their bodies.

The thinking of Max Scheler had been moving in this direction; he in turn was following a path broken by Friedrich Nietzsche and L. Klages in the "philosophy of life" *(Lebensphilosophie)*. In Scheler's perspective the human person is characterized by the opposition between spirit and vital impulses. The inadequacy of this description is due to the fact that it takes insufficient account of the form this human brokenness takes in human self-consciousness. In our consciousness of ourselves we are aware not only of identity but also of nonidentity with ourselves, in the form of a tension between the ego and the self. One possible way in which this opposition may manifest itself is, to be sure, the opposition between spirit and vital impulses as understood by Scheler. But this opposition can appear in two different basic forms: I can experience myself as spirit in opposition to my natural instincts, but conversely I can experience myself as a subject of needs that are denied their satisfaction by the strict demands of a superego. The dialectic of this opposition that we experience in ourselves arises precisely from the fact that the ego may take the side of the vital instincts against the demands of the spirit or, conversely, the side of spirit against instinct. This means that the tension manifested here must have a deeper basis even than the opposition between spirit and instincts. The reduction of the tension to this last-named opposition signifies a reification of the human problem of identity, thus concealing the true nature of the problem. Perhaps this is due to the fact that in Scheler the human person is always identified in too self-evident a way as a spiritual being, so much does he emphasize the opposition between this latter aspect and the vital instincts; in fact, it is perhaps for this very reason that this opposition has the special intensity it does in Scheler.

Unlike Scheler, Plessner makes self-consciousness an explicit theme in his description of the basic structure of the human. He regards the process of reflection that takes the form of self-consciousness as the place where animal centrality and exocentricity are brought into unity.[2] But Plessner considers it even more basic that self-consciousness as manifestation of exocentricity is the place where human beings are separated from them-

[2]H. Plessner, *Die Stufen des Organischen und der Mensch* (1928; 1965²), 290.

selves,[3] and at bottom this in turn means the place where they are separated from their own bodies. Self-consciousness is the basis of the knowledge that human beings have of themselves as soul set over against body. According to Plessner, this twofold aspect of the life of human beings represents "a real break in their nature,"[4] one that is continued in the duality of soul and individual personal experience: "The real interior world is the quarrel with the self, from which there is no escape and for which there is no compensation."[5] In his brilliant phenomenological study of laughing and crying Plessner has described these admittedly specifically human phenomena as forms of expression of that "break"[6] that comes with human exocentricity and thus with human self-consciousness and makes it possible for human beings to be inferior to the animals in control of their own bodies. Here again, what we are dealing with primarily is the "break" between the exocentric ego and the body which persons know themselves to be and from which at the same time they know themselves to be separated.[7] According to Plessner, laughing and crying are ways of escape in situations in which the control of the body by reason and language breaks down in the person's own self-consciousness: then the person "falls" into laughter or "lets himself go" into crying. "And in the loss of control over himself and his body, he reveals himself at the same time as a more than bodily being who lives in a state of tension with regard to his bodily existence yet is wholly and completely bound to it."[8]

Enlightening though Plessner's analyses of laughing and crying are in many respects, his interpretation of the brokenness of the human form of life in terms of the relation of human beings to their bodies seems one-sided. Human exocentricity as manifested in self-consciousness is not co-extensive with the fact that the ego knows itself as different from its body. It can also know itself to be nonetheless identical with its body, yet separated from it by the demands of the social superego. Such variability in the identification of the ego, with the resultant diverse determinations of the contents in relation to which the ego lives in the "break," although all of them belong to the ego in one way or another, suggests that the brokenness in human life is to be conceived in terms of a tension within the ego itself, in its structure of centrality and exocentricity, rather than

[3]Unlike all the animals or at least all the higher animals, human beings are not the center of their own life, but they "know this center, experience it, and therefore [!] transcend it" (ibid., 291).

[4]Ibid., 292.

[5]Ibid., 299; see 296.

[6]H. Plessner, *Laughing and Crying: A Study of the Limits of Human Behavior,* trans. J. S. Churchill and M. Grene (Evanston, Ill., 1970), 32.

[7]Ibid.

[8]Ibid., 31.

in terms of a specific content such as the difference from its own body. This viewpoint may even be applied to the study of the phenomena of laughing and crying. Even if we accept Plessner's basic idea that in both cases we are dealing with expressions of a breakdown in the identity of individuals and, at the same time, of escapes that make it possible for them (by reason of their exocentricity, through a distancing from themselves) to rescue themselves from this breakdown, nonetheless it need not be the control over the body that breaks down. Rather, the autonomy given to the body in the collapse into laughter or tears may be the result of extremely varied identity crises of other kinds in which the issue is not primarily the relation to one's own body. Only as a result of these other identity crises would control of the body then be lost.

In his development of the theses of "philosophical anthropology" into an anthropological basis for morality, Dieter Wyss diverges from Plessner and describes the split in consciousness, which develops in reflection on the self as a result of openness to the world, as the locus of the experience of a "primary alienation of human beings from themselves."[9] According to Wyss, it is not the difference from one's own body but the alienation of the products of one's own activity that first comes to the fore in self-consciousness. Just as human beings experience the things of their environing world as other than themselves, so the products of their own activity present themselves to them as other and alien. According to Wyss, herein is to be found "the decisive reason for the alienation of human beings from themselves" or their "estrangement from themselves in their action" (60). They experience this estrangement in reflection, and at the same time the estrangement in activity is, according to Wyss, "one of the essential motives for the rise of reflection itself" (ibid.). The estrangement manifests itself in, for example, the experience of "being disunited from the self" that may be observed even in newborn infants, but also in the experience of hearing one's own voice. Reflection therefore involves "not only the experience of a break between agent and activity but also the shattering and calling in question of a unity (identity) previously given, which, however, was not yet aware of itself as a unity" (61). Among the "primary brokennesses" that result from this basic situation of human activity Wyss lists—along with the oppositions between will and reflection and between will and the experience of impulse—the "disinhibiting" of the human "life of impulse and instinct" (135), with the results flowing from this: the destructive tendency of the "incorporative" impulses ("sadistic" inclination to aggression), the self-tormenting ("masochistic") inclination of the "discorporative" impulses (turning of aggression inward),

[9]D. Wyss, *Strukturen der Moral. Untersuchungen zur Anthropologie und Genealogie moralischer Verhaltensweisen* (1968), 60. The page references that follow in the text are to this book.

and in general the "explosive-ecstatic" basic tendency of the impulses to excess and irrationality, and, finally, the interchange of instinct and goal of instinct, a phenomenon that in Wyss's thinking is probably likewise to be understood as a consequence of the growing independence of the instincts from the goals of the instincts.

But can these "brokennesses of human nature" (134) be really derived from the experience of one's own activity as analogous to objectivity in perception, that is, from "estrangement in one's action"? After all, human beings can also know themselves to be one with themselves in their activity. This is shown by one of the examples that Wyss himself uses: the hearing of one's own voice, which is so important for the little child who is learning to speak (61). A child that babbles aloud is expressing its satisfaction at hearing the sounds produced by its own voice. Therefore the alienation of products that is connected with human behavior cannot by itself make intelligible the brokennesses that emerge in human experience of the self. As a matter of fact, Wyss sees himself obliged to broaden his original range of data: "The split in human existence shows itself in the discrepancy between the striving after the 'perdurance of pleasure' and the simultaneous canceling of this striving by the action itself" (82). It is no longer simply the "ego's objectification in action of its experience of impulse," as we read in the immediately preceding sentence, but rather the tension between this peculiarity of human activity, which comes with openness to the world, and the striving of the ego for pleasure that is now made responsible for the "primary brokenness of human beings as compared with the existence of the animals." Only in this perspective do the forms of this brokenness which I mentioned above (and which Wyss explains subsequently, 135) become intelligible: the tensions between will and reflection and between will and experience of impulse, as well as the "disinhibiting" of the human "life of impulse and instinct" along with the results of this. These phenomena yield their meaning not in the light of the structure of human action as such nor in the light of our knowledge of this structure through reflection on ourselves, but only in the light of the opposition between the striving for pleasure and the objectivity of the human relation to the world, insofar as this objectivity characterizes not only the perception of external objects but also the perception of the results of our own behavior.

This opposition may now be described as a conflict between basic factors in the structure of human existence, as an expression of a tension between the centralized organization of human beings and their exocentricity. The intensity of the tension does not emerge when exocentricity is grounded, as it is in Plessner, solely in the fact of self-consciousness. The fact of self-consciousness yields only a difference between the self-knowing ego and its own body, and this difference is immediately canceled by the consciousness of identity as well. The fact that in self-consciousness human beings experience an opposition of the ego to itself is not yet made intelligible. Light is shed on this phenomenon only by the fact that exocentricity by its nature means a being present to the other; it is then from the vantage point of the other that the ego approaches its own body and, in its body, the embodiment of its impulses and its striving for pleasure.

In its exocentric self-transcendence the ego is originally present to what is other than its body, but it is in knowing the otherness of the other, which is identical with its body, as distinct from all else, that it knows itself to be distinct from itself. Being present to the other *as* other opens up the dimension of self-consciousness with its distinction from self and unity with self; this dimension remains nonetheless full of contradiction because the ego makes its appearance on both sides of the distinction, being both different from and identical with its body, while in this contradiction which the ego is, its unity too remains an open question.

This exocentric self-transcendence, this being present to what is other than the self (i.e., originally what is other than the body) constitutes the ego or person. At the same time, however, the ego, in its identity with "itself," also places itself over against the other. This is the root of the break in the ego, the root of its conflict with its own exocentric destiny. Initially, of course, there is question only of a tension. Even the act by which the ego sets itself against the other is made possible by the exocentric constitution of the ego, and the act can therefore remain integrated into the process of exocentric experience as one phase of that process. As a matter of fact, however, the ego's setting of itself against the other—and therefore also against its own exocentricity—becomes the organizing principle of the unity of the individual's experience. The ego continues to be constituted as exocentric, but its presence to the other now becomes a means for it to assert itself in its difference from the other. Presence to the other becomes a means by which the ego can dominate the other and assert itself by way of this domination.

Even this domination is still ambivalent. It can be at the service of the exocentric destination of the ego. Only when the setting of the ego against the other becomes total and *everything* else must be made a means to the self-assertion of the ego, only then does the break of the ego from itself and its still constitutive exocentricity become acute. It is only the locking up of the ego in its opposition to everything else that fixes it in a contradiction of its exocentric destination. When the ego becomes certain that it is itself the truth of the contents of its consciousness and that therefore "it is all reality," when it becomes certain that it possesses within itself the truth of all reality, and when it endeavors to implement this arrogant claim in its relation to the world, then the ego distorts its own makeup, inasmuch as it subordinates its consciousness of objects, that presence to the other by which it is natively constituted, to itself as distinct from everything else, instead of finding its unity in the exercise of its exocentric destiny and allowing its particularity to be canceled out and rediscovered at a higher level in the process. To be sure, the attempt of self-consciousness to implement its arrogant claim in its relation to the world has in fact the ironic consequence that the ego wears itself out in the effort to integrate its world and thus becomes something different, contrary to the intention behind its self-assertion; this happens no matter how doggedly the ego holds to this intention.

Kant gave the name "radical evil" to the distortion in the constitution of the ego which I have just sketched. On the other hand, Kant has in mind only the distorted behavior of the ego in its moral experience, not in its whole relation to the world.[10] Therefore his description extends only to a distortion in the hierarchy of the mainsprings of human action, not a distortion in the underlying structure of the ego itself, although he does conclude from the distortion of action to a "perversity of the heart."

Yet despite these limitations in the Kantian description, the phenomenon of "radical evil" which he describes is indeed one way in which the exocentric destination of human beings is distorted by their own ego, despite the fact that the latter owes its very constitution to the exocentricity which marks its way of life. For, despite the limits set by Kant's formalism and in general by his abstract handling of morality, his concept of the moral law must, by reason of its universality, be judged to be an expression —though an imperfect one—of the human exocentric destination in the medium of its totalizing thematization. Therefore the subordination of respect for the law to the "natural" inclinations (in the sense of Kant's concept of "radical evil") is in fact one form taken by the distortion of the relation between centrality and exocentricity in the self-assertion of the ego. The only question is whether in his description, limited as it is to a transcendental-philosophical moral doctrine, Kant really grasped the radicalness of evil and its root in human life. If he had clearly grasped in its comprehensive significance for all aspects of human life the contradiction present in the self-realization of the ego, his theoretical philosophy with its doctrine of transcendental subjectivity would probably have been supplemented by further distinctions apt to anticipate the later criticism leveled at it by Hegel.

The explanation of the moral perversity of the ego in the light of a general distortion of its relation to the world is present in Augustine's classical development of the Christian teaching on sin. To this my study must now turn.

---

[10]I. Kant, *Religion Within the Limits of Reason Alone*, trans. T. M. Greene and H. H. Hudson (Chicago, 1934), 15, 27ff.

II. Egoism and the Failure of Selfhood

In classical Christian theology the distortion of the human relationship to the world took the form of covetousness or concupiscence *(cupiditas* or *concupiscentia)*. According to the apostle Paul, it is against this that the commandments of the divine law are directed, for he sums up all the prohibitions in a single prohibition: "You shall not covet" (Rom. 7:7). But is covetousness or concupiscence itself the sin forbidden by the law? To the early Christian writers the evil desire that always reaches out beyond what falls to one's lot at any given moment was in fact a consequence of sin, that is, of Adam's disobedience of God's command.[11] At times, Augustine too described concupiscence as a punishment and therefore a consequence of sin: human beings who turn away from God are abandoned to their own desires. At other times, however, he could describe concupiscence itself as sin and the cause of further sins.[12]

This fact has given rise to divergent and contradictory interpretations of Augustine. Latin Scholasticism distinguished between sin and concupiscence, regarding the latter as simply the material element in sin *(materiale peccati);* the Reformers and the Jansenists, on the contrary, identified concupiscence and sin. Each interpretation is one-sided and fails to do justice to the complex thought of Augustine. Even the superficially accurate observation that "the Augustinian concept of concupiscence is inconsistent"[13] is unsatisfactory, because it fails to analyze the reason for Augustine's different uses (of which he himself was evidently aware) of the concept. The reason is to be found, I believe, in Augustine's psychological analysis of concupiscence. For his analysis of the concupiscence that Paul considers to be the very essence of all that is forbidden by the divine law shows it to be both sin and a consequence of sin.

Concupiscence *(cupiditas)* is itself a sin insofar as it represents a perverse form of love or volition.[14] This "perverse will" *(perversa voluntas)*[15] dis-

---

[11]See J. Gross, *Entstehungsgeschichte des Erbsündendogmas. von der Bibel bis Augustinus* (Geschichte des Erbsündendogmas I; 1960), esp. 111 (Methodius of Olympus), 133 (Athanasius), 142 (Basil).

[12]Ibid., 325ff. Especially informative here are some statements in the writings of the later Augustine against Julian of Eclanum: *C. Julianum* V, 3, 8, and *Opus imperf.* I, 47 (in Gross, 320).

[13]Ibid., 328.

[14]Augustine, *Enarr. in Ps.* 9, 15: "The soul's 'foot' is rightly understood to be its affection. When this is depraved it is called cupidity *(cupiditas)* or lust *(libido);* when it is virtuous it is called love *(dilectio)* or charity *(caritas)*." In the *Confessions.* Augustine had written: "From the perverse will came lust" *(Conf.* VIII, 5, 10). In the *De div. quaest. 83* (396) we read: "That [love] is base with which the soul pursues what is less than itself; it is more correctly called cupidity *(cupiditas)* which is the root of all evils" (q. 35, 1; PL 40:23f.). See also *De lib. arb.*

torts the order of the universe by turning to inferior goods and for their sake abandoning better and higher goods—namely, God, his truth and his law. That is how Augustine described the sinful will even in his early writings.[16] In the *City of God* he still describes the evil will by saying that it desires lower things in a depraved and disordered way.[17] Contrary to the order of nature, it turns away from the higher and to the inferior.[18] The perversion in this act consists psychologically in a reversal of means and end *(uti* and *frui),* for whereas we ought to use transitory things as means of attaining to the enjoyment of the imperishable goal, the sinner inverts the relation by using God as a means to secure enjoyment of money.[19]

Concupiscence is thus identical with the perverse will and therefore sinful. On the other hand, the fact that the perversity is defined by an inversion of the end-means relation shows that something else lurks at the heart of the corrupt turning to transitory things. That is, the reversal of end and means is inspired by a high-handed attitude to the natural order, and this high-handedness in turn points to an excessive esteem of self or, in Augustine's vocabulary, to pride or egoism *(amor sui).* The arrogant claim an ungrounded superiority that they do not possess; they are excessively pleased with themselves as they make themselves the origin of things instead of attaching themselves to the real origin of all things.[20]

I, 3, 8 (PL 32:1225): "For it is clear that it is naught but lust *(libido)* that reigns in every kind of evildoing." The terms *cupiditas* and *libido* are here used as synonyms and in a very comprehensive sense; see also Gross, 324.

[15]Augustine, *De civ. Dei* XIV, 7, 2.

[16]Augustine, *Conf.* II, 5, 10: "Sin is committed because due to an unrestrained attraction to these lowest of goods better and supreme goods are abandoned: you, Lord our God, and your truth and your law." See *De lib. arb.* II, 19, 50–53.

[17]Augustine, *De civ. Dei* XII, 6.

[18]Ibid., XII, 8: "Where there is a defection the evil is not in the object but in the manner of acting, for there is no such thing as an evil nature; rather the action is disordered because contrary to the natural order the will separates itself from the supreme being and turns to what is lesser in its being."

[19]Ibid., XI, 25: "Nor am I unaware that 'fruit' belongs properly to those who enjoy, and 'use' to those who use. The difference seems to be that we are said to enjoy a thing that gives delight by itself without reference to anything else, while we are said to use something that is desired for the sake of something else. Temporal things are therefore to be used rather than enjoyed, in order that we may deserve to enjoy eternal blessings—unlike the wicked who want to enjoy money and use God, for they do not use their money for the sake of God but instead honor God for the sake of money."

[20]Ibid., XIV, 13, 1: "What is it that gives rise to an evil will except pride? For pride is the beginning of all sin *(Sirach* 10:15). And what is pride but the desire for an illusory greatness? It is a perverse form of greatness to abandon the source to which the soul should cling, in order to become as it were one's own source. This is what happens when one takes excessive satisfaction in oneself." For the equation of *superbia* and *amor sui,* see *Serm.* 96,

This attitude lies behind the distorted desire for transitory things, since the latter are no longer desired as means of serving God but are desired instead as means of obtaining the enjoyment of the one desiring them. Therefore egoism or pride *(superbia)* is at the very heart of all perverse desire.[21] When the ego which is proud in the sense described wills itself to be the center and ultimate end, it usurps the place in the order of the universe that belongs solely to God, its creator and supreme good. Therefore egoistic pride *(superbia)* is implicitly hostile to God, and by its inner logic leads the sinner ultimately into open hostility to God.[22]

In view of what Augustine says about the relation between egoism and concupiscence, it is easy to see how the latter could itself be called sin or, on the contrary, be called a consequence of sin (in the strict sense of the term). To the extent that egoism is implicit in concupiscence and that the assertion of the ego as ultimate end is implicit in perverse desire, such concupiscence can well be called sin, because this egoism is (even if only implicitly) hostile to God. On the other hand, the element in concupiscence that makes it sinful can also be the object of explicit attention in the form of *superbia* and to that extent be distinguished from the concupiscence that uses all things for the ego's self-centered purposes. Augustine has not stated these relations of implication and explication with complete clarity, but there is in fact no material contradiction in what he says, provided we attend to the material consistency of seemingly contradictory statements.

It is not only in the interpretation of Augustine that the reciprocal implication of perverse desire and egoism has been the object of misunderstandings. The discussion of the nature of sin in the history of modern theology has likewise not shown the same clarity of thought that we find in Augustine. Thus rationalism and idealism tended to reduce evil to sensuality, which human beings must control and transcend with the help of their spiritual powers. But even a theologian such as Richard Rothe took as his starting point the differing relations of human beings to "their material nature," on the one hand, and to their (spiritual) individuality, on the other; he then distinguished between sensuous and egoistic sin and

---

2; for the thesis that *superbia* is the root of sin, see also the discussion of the fall of the wicked angels in *De Genesi ad litt.* XI, 15(19).

[21]Augustine, *De Trin.* XII, 9, 14. See Cicero, *De fin.* III, 5: "It would be impossible for them to desire anything unless they had an awareness of themselves and therefore loved themselves and what is theirs."

[22]Thus the opposition of two loves, two orientations of the will, is the basis of the opposition between the city of God and the city of Satan: "And so two loves built two cities: self-love unto contempt for God built the earthly city, and love of God unto contempt for self built the heavenly city" (*De civ. Dei* XIV, 28); see *De Genesi ad litt.* XI, 20, 20.

reduced all sin to the former,[23] giving as his reason that "in the individual human being there is a natural predisposition to selfishness." According to Rothe, this natural selfishness exists antecedently to the spirit's moral self-determination which he, like the idealists, expects will rise above such natural limitations.

Julius Müller, on the other hand, was a good Augustinian to the extent that he understood selfishness or egoism to be a corruption of the human spirit and insisted that sin has its basis in this selfishness.[24] Moreover, he rejected Rothe's position that the selfishness of human beings is to be explained by their sensuous nature,[25] and claimed instead that it represents a distortion of human self-consciousness which is founded upon the consciousness of God. For it is in God that "human self-consciousness has the source of its nature and existence," and we are conscious of God "in an utterly primordial and unmediated way."[26] In this way Müller safeguarded the responsibility of human beings as the cause of sin,[27] since, given these presuppositions, the origin of sin becomes completely unintelligible. On the other hand, by following this line of thought, Müller failed to recognize the sensuous mediation of self-consciousness and the way the latter is interwoven with the experience of objects (something Augustine saw much more clearly). As a result, he not only rendered impossible any empirical description of and judgment upon the subject of his theological anthropology but also renounced any guiding principle with the help of which he could make the possibility of sinful behavior empirically intelligible.[28] It is precisely in this area that the teaching of Augustine was so persuasive.

At least in its essentials, the Augustinian analysis of the distortion in the structure of human behavior still retains its power to illuminate. But in order to grasp and acknowledge this, we must disregard the tendency toward hostility to the body and to sex that marks Augustine's thought and distorts what he has to say about concupiscence. In this respect, Augustine was influenced by an ascetical mentality that was widely prevalent in late

[23]R. Rothe, *Theologische Ethik* III (1870²), 2ff.; citation from 7.

[24]J. Müller, *Die christliche Lehre von der Sünde* I (1839; 1849³), 177ff.

[25]Ibid., 199.

[26]Ibid., 103f.

[27]Ibid., 266ff.

[28]I. A. Dorner emphasized this point in his critique of Müller's position; see Dorner's *System der christlichen Glaubenslehre* II/1 (Berlin, 1886²), sec. 77, 3, p. 88. But his own concept of sin as "distorted love of creatures," which includes both corrupt forms of devotion and corrupt self-assertiveness (ibid., no. 4, pp. 90f.), does not replace the one-sidedness he criticizes with any concrete principle of sin that is comparable to the Augustinian *superbia*. The reason for this lack is that the relations of implication and explication between *amor sui* and *concupiscentia* as a pair of concepts never become thematic.

antiquity and found far coarser expression in other Christian writers. The intellectual structure of his description of sin as pride and concupiscence is in its broad outline independent of the fact that he liked to use sexual lust as the model of concupiscence. Despite this preference, he could protest that Julian, one of his adversaries, was wrongly attributing to him a concept of concupiscence that restricted it to the area of sex.[29] In addition, Augustine acknowledged a "praiseworthy concupiscence" *(concupiscentia laudabilis)*, a phrase suggested to him by biblical expressions found, for example, in Ps. 118[119]:20, 40, or Gal. 5:17.[30] In such contexts the formal structure of the concept of concupiscence emerges with special clarity, since the difference between good and evil desire depends on the end to which the desire is ultimately ordered, in accordance with the scriptural statement: "The desire *(concupiscentia)* of wisdom leads therefore to an everlasting kingdom" (Wisd. of Sol. 6:21). Desire as such is not evil; a desire is sinful only when it is the expression of a pride that subverts the order of nature.

The Augustinian presentation of human sinfulness as a corruption of desire has two important advantages that still make it superior to other forms of the Christian doctrine of sin. The first advantage is the empirical orientation of Augustine's psychological description. The other advantage also depends on this psychological approach and has to do with the relevance of sin to the relation of human beings to themselves.

Let me consider first the way in which the description of sin focuses on empirical psychological data. There is no doubt, of course, that in Augustine's view the essence of sin consists in its opposition to God. Nonetheless the human behavior whose catastrophic significance emerges fully only when its radical meaning as hostility to God is recognized is first of all an empirical datum and only as such is it something that cannot be evaded. One cannot dismiss the empirical proof of the connection between pride and concupiscence by saying that one does not believe it. The reality of this type of behavior is an object not of faith but of psychological description and observation. Even the theological interpretation of it as a turning from God to the point of hostility to God derives its persuasiveness from the fact that it can be shown to be necessarily implied by the empirical data, even though the radical perversity represented by such behavior will be grasped only in the light of biblical revelation.

Karl Barth saw fit to renounce any such connection between Christian statements about human sinfulness and empirical data which no human

---

[29]References in Gross (n. 11, above), 324. But Gross also emphasizes Augustine's inclination to use sexuality to illustrate concupiscence (ibid. and 335ff.).

[30]Augustine, *Enarr. in Ps.* 118, 8, 3; see *De spir. et litt.* 4, 6.

observer can deny. "Only when we know Jesus Christ do we really know that man is the man of sin, and what sin is, and what it means for man."[31] But in this approach the Christian assertion of human sinfulness depends for its validity on the decision of faith; it seems to be simply the shadow that faith in reconciliation in Christ casts on the judgment that human beings pass on themselves. This means that those who refuse to believe in Christ can no longer be expected to have any realization of the broken-ness that characterizes the human mode of existence. Are those who refuse to believe in Christ also spared the confrontation with the distortion of their human destiny as seen in the structure of their own behavior? May we even say that in their case there need not be any such distortion and that they can reject Christian statements of faith to that effect as based on an objectively groundless, subjective "decision" to see things in this way? Why, they might even appeal to what Christian theology itself has to say about the subject! But what, then, is to be thought of a message proclaim-ing reconciliation and deliverance from an evil whose oppressive power and catastrophic consequences are not undeniable facts but must instead be believed so that we can then let ourselves be rescued from them? Must not the response to such a message be that other chains weigh more heavily upon us and that deliverance from them seems a more pressing need?

There is certainly an element of truth in Barth's view. Only in the light of a knowledge of God is it possible to see that the perversity of the behavior that Christian tradition calls sin is due to the fact that this behav-ior represents a turning from *God* and that a fully clear knowledge on this subject can come only from God's self-revelation, since a knowledge of God based on anything but an initiative of God himself would cancel out the very concept of God. To that extent, M. Kähler, to whom Barth appeals in this context, was right when he said that "only the revelation of salvation can fully illumine the state of estrangement." But, unlike Barth, Kähler limited himself to speaking of the "confused self-under-standing human beings have when left to their own resources";[32] he did not regard as irrelevant any and every consideration of the experience that human beings have of their brokenness (a brokenness which he diagnosed solely in terms of "immorality").

In addition to the point made by Kähler, there is a further reason that makes it difficult for the Christian doctrine of sin to appeal directly to the experience that human beings have of themselves. It is that if human corruption is really as radical as the Christian doctrine of sin says it is, it

---

[31]Barth, *Church Dogmatics* IV/1, trans. G. W. Bromiley (1956), 389.

[32]M. Kähler, *Die Wissenschaft der christlichen Lehre vom dem evangelischen Grundartikel aus* (1883; 1893[2]), 270.

must inevitably prevent human beings from gaining insight into their own condition. This is why Luther could write in the Smalkaldic Articles (1537) that original sin is "so deep a corruption of nature that reason cannot understand it. It must be believed because of the revelation in the Scriptures."[33] This statement is very close in its formulation to the thesis I am criticizing here, namely, that human sinfulness is known only through faith. Luther did not mean, of course, that those who refuse to believe can also avoid the burden of their sinfulness. In Luther's mind such a possibility was excluded by his unshakable conviction regarding the universal efficacy of the divine law, which in his view was identical with natural law and therefore extended to all human beings. It is an aspect of their perverse condition that human beings shut their eyes to their own wretchedness and delude themselves regarding their state. But this is not to say that the reality of their own lives cannot be called upon to give witness against them. Luther's statements on sin in the Smalkaldic Articles leave this side of the subject untouched and must therefore be regarded as one-sided, though not as incorrect. The relative superiority of Augustine's teaching on sin becomes clear from the fact that it allows us to do justice to both aspects, that is, both the empirical manifestation of sin and its radical character, the full discovery of which is made possible only by the light of grace.

It is an easy step from the statement that sin can only be an object of faith to the further statement that sin consists first and foremost in a turning away from God and that therefore unbelief is the root of sin. This view is also found in Luther. It follows, *first,* from the position that all sin can be traced back to the "disobedience" of the first human being, who thereby lost the "original" union with God for both himself and the rest of the human race. I shall return later to this notion of a fall. The priority given to unbelief in defining the concept of sin follows, *secondly,* from the fact that the expressions of sin are listed in the order of the Ten Commandments and in a negative correspondence to these. As a result, the violation of the First Commandment by "unbelief, false belief, idolatry," as well as by a lack of fear of God, comes at the beginning.[34]

A different presentation of sin results, however, when we take as our point of departure the present human condition, as Augustine does in many passages. Then it is concupiscence or the inversion of the end-means structure in the human relation to the world that is in the foreground; moreover, at the center of this inversion is evidently *superbia,* the baseless

[33]*The Book of Concord.* trans. and ed. T. G. Tappert (Philadelphia, 1959), 302.
[34]Ibid. In the definition of original sin in the Augsburg Confession (1530), Art. 2, the lack of fear of God and of trust in God again comes first in the Latin text and is followed by concupiscence, whereas in the German text the order is reversed (ibid., 20).

high-handedness and egocentricity of human beings, which in turn implies a turning away from God. Once again, this approach to sin is to be preferred, because it is closer to the real experience of human life. The distortion in human behavior does not begin with a conscious turning from God; rather, the estrangement from God takes place in an obscure manner and is for long periods more or less unnoticed, being simply implicit in the distortion of our relation to the world and to ourselves. Augustine's teaching on sin, despite all its weak points, does greater justice to this state of affairs than do most later treatments of the doctrine.

The psychological obviousness of Augustine's description of sin as a distortion in the relation of human beings to the world and to themselves depends indeed, in his presentation of it, on contextual presuppositions which have lost their validity in the modern development of the anthropological problematic. Among these presuppositions is the thesis of a hierarchical order embracing the entire universe, an order in which everything comes forth from God and strives to return to him. As a result of this order, there is a distinction between higher and lower goods, and it is in the inversion of this relationship that the distortion produced by concupiscence consists, while concupiscence itself can only spring from the high-handedness of desire in its dealings with the natural order established by the creator. But the modern era has made the knowledge of nature independent of the idea of God and in so doing has deprived this conception of a universal natural order of its claim to validity as a fundamental philosophical principle. Reflection on a divine origin of nature, if entertained at all, is regarded as secondary to the knowledge of nature provided by the natural sciences. This state of affairs is connected with the fact that the modern knowledge of nature no longer provides us with objectives for our action in dealing with nature, but on the contrary makes natural processes available for purposes that are practically arbitrary or in any case justifiable on grounds unconnected with nature.

For the modern mind the question of God has as its philosophical context the question of the constitution of human subjectivity, and only when the question of the relation of this subjectivity to nature is raised can there also be a reflection on the scientific knowledge of nature that would connect nature with God as with its source. This means that the assertion of a distortion in human behavior can no longer find contextual support in the idea of a divinely established order of nature and of a hierarchy of goals for action that is based on such an order. Even if one were to try to justify such a conception in the framework of the modern state of the discussion, one would have to trace it back to human subjectivity in its relation to the world. It is therefore typical that Kant should see human perversity taking the form no longer, as in Augustine, of a distortion of the order of the cosmos, but of a distortion rather of the internal order of human nature itself, as the divinely commanded subordination of the sensuous striving for happiness to the moral law is replaced by a merely conditional acceptance of morality insofar as it is compatible with the natural striving for happiness.[35]

Even the thesis of a distortion in the human relation to the world, as this emerged in the previous section from the discussion of the brokenness of human life that Plessner has noted, has to do with a distortion taking place within human subjectivity when exocentricity is made to serve self-centeredness whereas the ego should be living in accordance with its exocentric destiny. In distinction from the Kantian doctrine of radical evil, the distortion here affects not only the moral consciousness and moral action but the whole of the human relation to the world. Yet even here we have what is present in prototypical form in Kant: a conflict of human beings with themselves and their own destiny. Whether this conflict signifies a distortion of the order of the universe as well must remain a distinct question. But the establishment of the anthropological findings does not depend on this further question. Here we can see how far removed we are from the state of the question in terms of which Augustine developed his argument. Given the profoundly different situation, it is astounding that modern descriptions of the psychological structure of the distortion in human behavior should be in fundamental accord with Augustine's description of it. In all the descriptions, human perversity is seen as consisting in the priority given to human egocentricity over a destination that transcends self-centered human existence, whether this destination is to live according to moral reason or whether it is the formal destination of exocentricity, the integral contents of which include the religious thematic.

As compared with the Augustinian thematic, the modern approach to the problem represents a shift to a concentration on the relation of human beings to themselves. But here again it was Augustine's psychological description of the human situation and of human behavior that paved the way. For Augustine, sin is not only a transgression of a divine commandment; inasmuch as it is a distortion of the natural order of creation it is also, as it had been for Paul, a failure of human beings in relation to themselves. Paul derived this notion from the very content of the divine

[35]Analogously, sin according to Schleiermacher consists in a reversal of the relation between immediate self-consciousness (consciousness of God) and the consciousness of objects: *The Christian Faith*, ed. H. R. Mackintosh and J. S. Stewart (Edinburgh, 1928; Philadelphia, 1976), § 66; see § 11, 2. According to Hegel, it consists in a reversal of the relation between finiteness and infinity as elements in self-consciousness (*Vorlesungen über die Philosophie der Religion*, ed. G. Lasson, III, 102ff.). Even in Julius Müller, who follows Augustine in defining sin as egoism, this last is itself defined as an interior contradiction of the immediate human knowledge of God.

commandments, since these are given so that human beings may have life (Rom. 7:10). According to Augustine, when human beings distort the natural order of creation through their volitional action they reject their own happiness, since they can obtain this only from God, who is their supreme good as he is the supreme good of all created being.[36] Therefore "it is their own works that bring harm" to the wicked.[37] Through sin the human soul is "locked out of itself and driven into exteriority."[38] For this reason, concupiscence is not only sin but at the same time a punishment for sin.

Despite these insights, Augustine defined the *essence* of sin not as a failure in relation to the self but as a distortion of the order of the universe. The interior failure he saw as a consequence of this distortion, a punishment for sin. Only when the idea that human beings are integral parts of a universe hierarchically ordered to God had lost its power and when modern interpretations of the human person as a self-conscious being had made their appearance could the opposition of human beings to themselves become the central theme in the anthropologically structured concept of sin.

This point of view received its most penetrating development from Søren Kierkegaard in his analysis of dread and despair. Kierkegaard distinguished dread from fear, because dread has no definite external object. In dread the concern of human beings is with themselves,[39] and specifi-

[36]For Augustine's teaching on the supreme good as the background of his moral theology and therefore of his teaching on sin as well, see J. Mausbach, *Die Ethik des hl. Augustinus* I (Freiburg, 1909), 51ff.

[37]Augustine, *Conf.* II, 6, 13; see *De civ. Dei* XIV, 4, and Mausbach, I, 119ff.

[38]Augustine, *Serm.* 142, 3.

[39]S. Kierkegaard, *The Concept of Dread,* trans. W. Lowrie (Princeton, 1957²), 39; see also 86 and 88. According to Freud too, anxiety [as the phenomenon that Kierkegaard calls "dread" is known in Freud and in post-Freudian literature.—Tr.] serves the ego as "a signal to give a warning of dangers threatening its integrity" (*An Outline of Psychoanalysis,* trans. J. Strachey [New York, 1949], 111). But Freud does not always explicitly maintain this relation of anxiety to the ego. Thus he speaks of an anxiety about losing a parent's love (112). Kierkegaard's terminology with its distinction between dread (= anxiety) and fear is more precise, even though dread and fear are actually separable only in borderline cases. An object that rouses fear always stirs, in one manner or another, the primordial existential human dread regarding the self; this does not, however, invalidate the conceptual distinction between them (contrary to R. Denker, *Angst und Aggression* [Stuttgart, 1974], 28). Moreover, while there may be no fear without an accompanying dread, dread without an object to awaken fear does occur. One may be unable to say why one experiences dread, but one may experience it nonetheless. This is enough to justify a conceptual distinction between fear and dread. Also and not least, the distinction makes it possible to render a better account of the primordial role of dread in relation to the (not yet definitively realized) self than is possible if the analysis is limited to a consideration of objects that threaten danger. In the emptiness of dread that cannot say why it is afraid, the threat to human existence and the knowledge of this threat emerge in their pure form as the object of the human care *(Sorge)* for the self.

cally with their own unity. Kierkegaard describes this human unity first of all, in the traditional language of a trichotomist anthropology, as a "synthesis" of soul and body that is effected by the spirit.[40] As a synthesis of soul and body, human beings are spirit. On the other hand, only by making this synthesis a reality can they attain to self-realization, and this exercise of freedom brings dread in its train. "Thus dread is the dizziness of freedom which occurs when the spirit would posit the synthesis, and freedom then gazes down into its own possibility, grasping at finiteness to sustain itself. In this dizziness freedom succumbs."[41] This grasping at their own finiteness entails for human beings the loss of the infinity for which they are destined. The loss takes place because the spirit seeks to accomplish by its own resources the synthesis between its finite body and the soul that clings to the infinite, but is able to accomplish it only on the basis of its own finiteness.

Kierkegaard expressed these thoughts even more clearly five years later in his book *The Sickness Unto Death* (1848). Here again the human being is described as a synthesis, but now as a "synthesis of the infinite and the finite."[42] Kierkegaard here has in mind the same phenomenon that is today described as human self-transcendence or finds expression in such terms as "openness to the world" or "exocentricity." Human beings are finite beings, but at the same time they reach beyond their finiteness to the infinite, which for Kierkegaard is also the eternal. This reaching out would not be possible if human beings were simply finite, nor would it be possible if in their finiteness they stood in a purely factual relation to the infinite. They must, rather, be conceived as a relation between these two concepts, and, further, as a relation of such a kind that it can itself become thematic for them. A relation, however, is a third entity in relation to the two extremes that it links.

With this insight Kierkegaard advances beyond *The Concept of Dread* in which the spirit still supervenes upon soul and body as the third element that is their synthesis but also must make the synthesis a reality. In that earlier book the synthesis of time and eternity seemed to Kierkegaard to

[40]Ibid. See 76, where the synthesis of the temporal and the eternal in the human being is compared to the synthesis of soul and body.

[41]Ibid., 55. See 81–82. The succumbing of the individual can be described (65–66) as a consequence of the *weakness* caused by dread (see also and esp. 55, and a diary entry for December 1840 in *Søren Kierkegaard's Journals and Papers*, ed. and trans. H. V. Hong and E. H. Hong [Bloomington, Ind., 1967], I, no. 94, p. 39). This probably explains the connection Kierkegaard saw between dread and sensuousness as well as his interpretation of the role of the female sex in the biblical story of the fall. On Kierkegaard's interpretation of sensuousness, see J. Holl, *Kierkegaards Konzeption des Selbst* (1972), 122ff.

[42]S. Kierkegaard, *The Sickness Unto Death*, trans. W. Lowrie (Princeton, 1941), 17. Kierkegaard here identifies this synthesis with the synthesis "of the temporal and the eternal," which had already been mentioned in *The Concept of Dread*.

lack such a third element. But in *The Sickness Unto Death* he says of the synthesis of the infinite and the finite, which is equivalent to the synthesis of the temporal and the eternal, that in it the relation between them is itself the third element, and this not simply as a negative unit whereby the two related entities are distinguished from each other but as a positive unit that is related to the relation between the two opposed members. This notion yields Kierkegaard's well-known definition of the self: "The self is a relation which relates itself to its own self." The "spirit" is now conceived as being this self (and therefore is no longer conceived primarily in terms of the soul-body relation): "Spirit is the self."[43]

This means that "spirit" is also understood to be self-consciousness; for the relation of the self to itself as a synthesis of the finite and the infinite occurs in the form of self-consciousness.[44] On the other hand, the concept of self-consciousness is now related in turn to that of the relation between the finite and the infinite, and this determination of the content of the relation of the self to itself provides the springboard for raising seemingly insoluble difficulties. Thus human beings are constituted as a relation to the infinite, not by themselves but by something else, and they are related to this something else, namely, to "that power which constituted the whole relation" and which originally Kierkegaard explicitly identified as the power of God.[45] But when human beings relate themselves to themselves in their self-consciousness, they are at the same time *constituting* themselves. For self-consciousness is also freedom, and the synthesis of the finite and the infinite in the self therefore becomes for the self the "task . . . to become itself, a task which can be performed only by means of a relationship to God."[46] But since human beings are to effect by means of

[43]Ibid. E. Hirsch, in his German translation of Kierkegaard's works, Abteilung 24 (Düsseldorf, 1954), observes that in his preliminary sketches Kierkegaard treated the two relationships of soul-body and temporal-eternal as parallel. J. Holl, in his presentation of "Kierkegaard's Conception of the Self" (n. 41, above), unfortunately pays no attention to the development in Kierkegaard's understanding of the synthesis that is the human being, namely, the shift in emphasis from the soul-body relation to the temporal-eternal relation. Kierkegaard's varying identifications of the elements in the synthesis are too hastily placed on one and the same formal level and systematized into an undifferentiated view (119ff.). H. Fischer, on the other hand, in his dissertation, *Subjektivität und Sünde. Kierkegaards Begriff der Sünde mit ständiger Rücksicht auf Schleiermachers Lehre von der Sünde, Itzehoe (Die Spur)* (1963), 101, emphasizes the advance in Kierkegaard's thinking as seen in the "broadened formulation" of the anthropological synthesis and in the introduction of the concept of the self.

[44]Ibid., 43.

[45]Ibid., 18. See also Hirsch's n. 4, p. 67. The words about the "dependence" of the self on the other by which it is constituted are reminiscent, and probably not by chance, of the theory of consciousness of God that Schleiermacher develops in his *The Christian Faith*.

[46]Ibid., 44. Hirsch (p. 171, n. 4) points out the parallel with Fichte's *Bestimmung des Menschen* (1800).

their freedom that which does not have its ground in themselves, namely, their self, it is an easy step to the distortion which Kierkegaard describes as a despairing will to be the self, that is, an attempt to ground the self in the self instead of in God. The attempt brings despair, because precisely by making it, human beings fall short of their true selfhood. "That self which he despairingly wills to be is a self which he is not . . . ; what he really wills is to tear his self away from the Power which constituted it."[47] This means that in order not to despair, human beings "must annihilate the possibility every instant" of succumbing to this distortion. This annihilation is ensured when "the self is grounded transparently in the Power which posited it."[48] But is such a grounding a real possibility for human beings, inasmuch as God "lets this [relationship] go as it were out of His hand, that is, in the fact that the relation relates itself to itself"?[49]

For dogmatic reasons Kierkegaard wanted to maintain that human freedom could in fact overcome the temptation to despair, since he thought that human responsibility and even despair itself presupposed a perfect original state or origin of human beings.[50] Yet it is not easy to coordinate this dogmatic concern with his own analysis, for how are human beings to use their freedom to effect the synthesis of the finite and the infinite, when the synthesis has its ground not in themselves but in the infinite and eternal? The synthesis can in fact be effected only in the form of faith, as Kierkegaard explains farther on in the book.[51] But faith is not a possibility available to human freedom on its own terms; it is always a possibility made available to freedom by God alone. How, then, is it possible for human beings to avoid freedom when left to their own resources?

Kierkegaard's *The Sickness Unto Death* is related to the theme of self-consciousness and self-preservation which has been so intensively discussed in recent years. According to Dieter Henrich, this theme provides

[47]Ibid., 29. This presupposes the fundamental form of despair: "in despair to will to be rid of oneself" (ibid.), i.e., of the self that one actually is.

[48]Ibid., 21 and 19.

[49]Ibid., 22. The relation to oneself is identical with freedom (ibid., 43).

[50]See below, n. 66. H. Fischer, in his *Subjektivität und Sünde,* 115ff., see 103, rightly emphasizes the point that in Kierkegaard (unlike Schleiermacher) sin is always actual sin. For this reason, Kierkegaard, like Augustine before him, had to presuppose a state of innocence prior to sin. There could not be, therefore, as Fischer believes, "a complete agreement with Schleiermacher's criticism of the *status integritatis* and of the doctrine of the fall" (86). Though Kierkegaard criticized the "fantastically" mythological character of the church's teaching and gave an existential interpretation of the fall as a depiction of the history of *every* human being, he did not thereby destroy the character of the primordial history as primordial, since in the first human being the history of the race was lived for the first time and therefore in a paradigmatic manner.

[51]Kierkegaard, *The Sickness Unto Death,* 132: "Faith is: that the self in being itself and in willing to be itself is grounded transparently in God." See the comparable formulation on p. 18.

16000

the "basic structure of modern philosophy."[52] In Henrich's view, the
theme of self-preservation (which can be traced back to Stoicism), as
contrasted with the idea of a purely passive dependence on the conserving
action of God,[53] should not be regarded as deriving "from the consciousness, on the part of a self-grounding subject, of a power usurped from the
concept of God."[54] "For that which would preserve itself must recognize
that it does not at every moment have its ground in itself and that it
certainly does not have its ground solely in itself."[55] The task of self-
preservation, which presupposes a measure of familiarity with the self
(self-consciousness), arises "insofar as the existence *(Dasein)* of human
beings depends on their own activity, which may be neglected or mis-
guided."[56] The thesis of the self-grounding of subjectivity thus loses its
role as descriptive of the typical outlook of the modern age and is reduced
to being one possible, but extreme, articulation of the fundamental theme
of the modern age, alongside other forms that this theme takes.

The modern experience that human beings are to depend only on
themselves, and this even in relation to that "which grounds" their selfhood "yet is not at their disposition,"[57] provides the platform on which
Kierkegaard's argument is developed. But in this question of the self
human beings are not concerned solely with self-preservation (this presupposes the existence of the self and is concerned only with its continued
existence), but with the very constitution of this self. In some sense or
other those beings already "are" which nonetheless regard their selfhood
as still problematic because it is a "synthesis" still to be achieved by
themselves and *as* themselves. The result of this situation is the almost

[52]See Henrich's essay "Die Grundstruktur der modernen Philosophie," in H. Ebeling,
ed., *Subjektivität und Selbsterhaltung. Beiträge zur Diagnose der Moderne* (Frankfurt, 1976),
97–121.

[53]H. Blumenberg develops this contrast in his essay "Selbsterhaltung und Beharrung"
(originally 1970; repr. in Ebeling, 144–207), esp. 156 and 185ff. Blumenberg is here
continuing the argument of his book *Die Legitimität der Neuzeit* (1966), which presents the
modern age as originating in an act of human self-assertion against the "absolutism" of the
God of the late Middle Ages. For a criticism of this construct, see my review, which is
reprinted in my *The Idea of God and Human Freedom*, trans. R. A. Wilson (Philadelphia, 1973),
144–77.

[54]D. Henrich, "Über Selbstbewusstsein und Selbsterhaltung," in Ebeling, 128. See, in the
essay cited in n. 52, above, the criticism of Heidegger's interpretation of modern consciousness as "a conviction of the limitless power of subjectivity" (109ff.).

[55]Ibid., 111; see 112f. Henrich thus broadens the thesis of his study *Fichtes ursprüngliche
Einsicht* (1967) according to which self-consciousness cannot be grounded in an act of
self-positing by the ego by way of the task of self-preservation which results from this state
of affairs, given the presupposition of a relation to the self, which at the same time registers
it.

[56]Ibid., 133.

[57]Ibid., 115.

unavoidable illusion that the synthesis which is the self must be the act of an already existing subject and a creation of its freedom.

Kierkegaard's own utterances not infrequently suggest such a misunderstanding, as when he speaks of the synthesis of the self as a "task" to be "performed"[58] or when he describes sin as an activity of freedom (even if an activity which is the "succumbing" of freedom).[59] Yet closer examination reveals that it is not freedom itself but only its possibility that precedes the event in which freedom is at the same time lost.[60] Even when the "condition" which is not at the disposal of human beings—namely, that they have a glimpse of their eternal destiny—is given to them or restored to the sinner,[61] the "decision" of which Kierkegaard so often speaks is not to be understood in the traditional sense as a manifestation of a faculty or power which by its nature is indifferent in regard to the various possibilities set before it and therefore itself tips the scales in choosing among them. For "the possibility of freedom does not consist in being able to choose the good or the evil"; it is therefore not an act of *liberum arbitrium* ("free will").[62] Freedom is, rather, identical with the spirit, with the eternity that is present in the "instant."[63] Prior to the reality of the instant, freedom is present only as a possibility, and it is from this possibility of freedom that dread springs.

In his statements about selfhood and freedom Kierkegaard came very close to dissolving the transcendental concept of the subject that was developed in idealistic philosophy. For if the subject is in a state of becoming with regard to its selfhood and therefore its freedom, it cannot already be a condition and prior ground of all experience. But Kierkegaard did not travel this path to its end; instead, he stopped short at his well-known paradoxical utterances about subjectivity being, on the one hand, untruth and, on the other, the very essence of truth for human beings. As a result, he laid his thinking open to an interpretation that has the person positing itself in the very act of choice,[64] an interpretation that seemingly finds ready confirmation in the concept of "Stages on Life's Road." But as understood by Kierkegaard, the movement by which subjectivity posits

[58]Kierkegaard, *The Sickness Unto Death*, 44.

[59]Kierkegaard, *The Concept of Dread*, 55. Further references are in n. 41, above.

[60]Ibid., 40, 52f. Therefore freedom is "given prior to self-realization but takes the form of a becoming between possibility and reality" (Holl [n. 41, above], 127; see 129f. and 181ff.).

[61]S. Kierkegaard, *Philosophical Fragments or Fragments of a Philosophy*, trans. D. F. Swenson (2d ed.; Princeton, 1962), 17–19.

[62]Kierkegaard, *The Concept of Dread*, 44, 45. Yet he can say in his diaries that in sin there is, in addition to finitude, "an element of freedom" (*Søren Kierkegaard's Journals and Papers* [n. 41, above], vol. IV, no. 4004, p. 106).

[63]See Holl, 135f., on Hirsch, Abteilung 11, pp. 90ff. *(The Concept of Dread).*

[64]See, e.g., J. Anz, *Kierkegaard und der deutsche Idealismus* (1956), 35ff., 71f.

itself in this way is simply the existential form that despair takes.

When Vigilius Haufniensis criticized the concept of freedom as *liberum arbitrium* in *The Concept of Dread,* his primary concern was merely to substitute the concept of dread for the role played by a freedom of indifference that is an "intermediate state" between innocence and guilt. Kierkegaard's intention in so doing was to defend the concept of original sin and the biblical story of the original state and the fall against the kind of criticism voiced by Schleiermacher. Schleiermacher had raised the objection against the biblical story of the fall that it is impossible to explain the sin of Adam and Eve "apart from an already existent sinfulness."[65] For if Eve listened to the whisperings of the serpent and if Adam ate the apple offered to him, there must have already been an "inclination toward sin." The hypothesis of a *liberum arbitrium* that is responsible for the origin of sin is useless here, since this hypothetical freedom of indifference is an abstraction based on the concrete human situation, and what the latter displays is not an indifference but an inclination to sin.

Kierkegaard thought he could counter this kind of criticism by showing that a "transition" from innocence to guilt is in fact conceivable and that it is possible to save the biblical story, not indeed as referring to a historical beginning which preceded the entire subsequent history of the human race but as referring to a history of humanity which is repeated in each human life.[66] Kierkegaard thought he could show that dread is the psychological "intermediate determination" between innocence and guilt because in dread there occurs that "dizziness of freedom" in which human beings fall back into their false subjectivity.[67] But does not dread for the self, that feeling of dizziness when freedom is left to its own resources, presuppose sin, which consists in human beings making themselves the center and standard of their own lives?[68]

[65]Schleiermacher, *The Christian Faith,* § 72, 2 (p. 65). On this, see Kierkegaard, *The Concept of Dread,* 39f.

[66]See Kierkegaard's criticism in *The Concept of Dread,* 23f., of the extrinsicism of the relation between the first human being and the human race as seen in the dogmatic teaching on the original state. According to this teaching, the human race had a "fantastic beginning" because Adam "was kept fantastically outside" of the race. For the interpretation, see n. 50, above.

[67]Kierkegaard, *The Concept of Dread,* 54–55. See n. 41, above.

[68]Kierkegaard himself calls dread "the most egoistic thing" (*The Concept of Dread,* 55), but does not see in this the essence of sin, because he relates the concept of egoism to the concept of the self in which there is a "positing [of] the general as the particular" (70). Therefore he considers the definition of sin as egoism (a definition that goes back to Augustine) to be useless (ibid.), because all that is being said in it is that sin has to do with the individual. Above all, this definition does not explain sin, "since on the contrary it is truth that by sin and in sin selfishness comes into being" (71). When the sin of Adam is said to be caused by egoism or selfishness, "the intervening state," namely, dread, "has been leapt over" (71). As a matter of fact, when egoism or selfishness is not understood simply as "selfness" but

Dread or anxiety gives expression to an understanding of existence *(Dasein)* which has for its central theme the care *(Sorge)* of human beings with regard to themselves. Thus Martin Heidegger in his *Being and Time* (1927) takes the phenomenon of anxiety as a paradigm for the basic structure of human existence in the world, a structure determined by care with regard to the self.[69] But care with regard to the self can be a basic structure of life only if the ego wills itself as the quintessence of its existence, that is, if self-love *(amor sui)* is the focus of human existence. Insofar as care for ourselves, in the sense of Heidegger's attentive caution, dominates us, our lives are no longer characterized by a trust that becomes the basis for behavior but by a striving for security. When our lives are completely dominated by such a striving for security and for control of the conditions of our existence, then they are ruled by *amor sui,* by sin.

It is true, of course, that a striving for self-preservation is to be regarded as a direct result of the self-consciousness of a finite being, because its knowledge of itself includes a knowledge of its own finiteness and the precariousness of its existence.[70] Such a striving for self-preservation is fully compatible with trust in the source that is constitutive of one's existence and selfhood while at the same time it transcends these. To that extent the saying of Jesus about worries (Matt. 6:25ff.) by no means applies to all human life-preserving activity. Only when self-preservation

---

as a distortion of selfness, it is already sin and therefore does not explain the origin of sin. But neither does the concept of dread provide such an explanation, since, according to Kierkegaard, dread is "the most egoistic thing." To that extent, Kierkegaard mistakenly regards the concept of dread as superior to that of concupiscence by reason of "the ambiguity in which the individual becomes both guilty and innocent" (65).

[69]M. Heidegger, *Being and Time,* trans. J. Macquarrie and E. Robinson (New York, 1962), 226ff., 235ff.

[70]With Henrich, "Die Grundstruktur der modernen Philosophie," in Ebeling (n. 52, above), 97ff., esp. 111ff., I assume that self-preservation (as distinct from simple persistence in a state) presupposes self-consciousness or at least a "primordial awareness of oneself" (112). In his Postscript on "Self-Consciousness and Self-Preservation," Ebeling himself emphasizes the difference between self-preservation based on self-consciousness and an intransitive "maintenance" as understood in the laws of conservation in modern physics (130ff.). Ebeling's critical observation that the priority given by Henrich to self-consciousness over self-preservation is plausible only "in the perspective of an idealistic theory of subjectivity" (32), to which Ebeling himself wishes to oppose a "materialistic" theory of subjectivity, seems to overlook the fact that self-preservation as distinct from mere persistence presupposes a difference between preserver and preserved, without, however, destroying the unity of the two. When in the history of modern philosophy, beginning with Spinoza, a perseverance in existence is already understood as a *conservatio sui,* or self-preservation (on this, see Blumenberg, "Selbsterhaltung und Beharrung" in the Ebeling volume, 144ff., esp. 185ff.), then indeed there is probably an "idealistic" projection of a situation found only in the case of self-conscious subjectivity into the whole of nature. The fact that the impulse to such a view came from the Stoic philosophy of nature (through its doctrine of the *oikeiōsis* or at-homeness of things with themselves) can only confirm this judgment.

is no longer based on trust but proceeds from anxiety and worry does it become an expression of the distortion of human behavior that results when love for one's own ego, a love that cares for nothing but the self, takes possession of the center of existence. This distortion in the structure of human behavior finds expression in anxiety, if indeed Heidegger was right in claiming that in anxiety the basic structure of human existence manifests itself in the form of care. His analysis thus provides confirmation that anxiety or dread is to be understood as already an expression of sin,[71] and cannot be, as Kierkegaard would have it, an "intermediate determination" in the transition from an original innocence to sin.

III. Human Nature, Sin, and Freedom

Kierkegaard's analysis of sin as dread or anxiety, along with his analysis of despair, has classical value for Christian anthropology only as a description of sin's effects in self-consciousness and not as a psychology of the origin of sin. When it is taken as such an explanation of the origin of sin, as it is in Paul Tillich,[72] Kierkegaard's interpretation of anxiety is linked to an essentialist conception of human reality that has the human essence preceding human existence. The passage from essence to existence is then seen as the step from creatureliness as willed by God to sin. In the process, something that is more appropriately viewed as a human characteristic manifesting itself in religious and ethical experience is projected back to the beginning of human life and presented as an originally given state.

In his philosophy of the will Paul Ricoeur has developed a similar conception in the form of a philosophical anthropology. Rejecting other trends that look for the origin of evil and wickedness in human finitude and its tension with the infinite, Ricoeur looks for this origin in the passage from the structure of human finitude to actual living via decisions of the will. The structure of human finitude includes the possibility of falling but not fallenness or a fall as an event.[73] Because of its irrational character this

---

[71]See also R. Bultmann, *Theology of the New Testament,* trans. K. Grobel (2 vols.; New York, 1953, 1955), I, 243–44 on fear *(phobos)* in Paul, and 241–42 on care *(merimnān).*

[72]P. Tillich, *Systematic Theology* II (Chicago, 1957), 33ff. See his *The Courage to Be* (New Haven, 1952), 32–63. On this subject, see H. Elsässer, *Paul Tillichs Lehre vom Menschen als Gespräch mit der Tiefenpsychologie* (dissertation; Marburg, 1973), 38ff., 56ff., and esp. 116ff.

[73]P. Ricoeur, *Fallible Man,* trans. C. Kelbley (Chicago, 1965), 201ff.; see 216ff. and the criticism of Kant's concept of radical evil, 115ff., 154f. See also Ricoeur's essay on the concept of original sin in his *The Conflict of Interpretations: Essays in Hermeneutics,* ed. D. Ihde (Evanston, Ill., 1974), 269–86. According to Ricoeur, the symbol of the fall is irreplaceable because it makes it possible to combine the voluntary character of evil with its "quasi-nature," which consists in the fact that evil is already there before we produce it. In the teaching of the church the failure to attend to the symbolic character of the biblical story of the fall has led to "a monstrous combination of a juridical concept of imputation in order

event and human fallenness cannot, according to Ricoeur, be described in conceptual language but only in the symbolic language of mythical images. How this is to be done is explained in detail in the second volume of his work on the will, *The Symbolism of Evil.*

But the thesis that evil is inaccessible to conceptual description seems to be conditioned by the fact that Ricoeur takes as his starting point a phenomenological description of the "pure" essential structure of the will. If one proceeds in this manner, then the transition to reality can be made only by a leap; and if this leap is assigned not to the viewer but to the human will itself, then it is understandable that it can only take the form of an irrational decision. But the essential structure of the will, which Ricoeur takes as the starting point of his work, is derived, as Ricoeur himself emphasizes, by a process of abstraction, and as an abstraction it enjoys no priority over concrete reality. It does not make sense, therefore, to ask about a *real passage* from the abstract essential structure of the human will to its concrete reality, as though such a passage were a real step and specific event in human reality. Rather, the distortion that always codetermines human behavior is to be regarded as itself a structural element of the human form of life and its behavior, which is marked by a tension between the centralist organization which human beings share with all animal life and especially with its more highly organized forms, and the exocentric character which is peculiar to human beings.[74]

If the peculiarity of human beings among the higher animals is correctly captured in the concept of exocentricity or is correctly described as an objectivity that is open to the world and helps human beings achieve distance from themselves and therefore self-consciousness or reflection on themselves, then such a description calls for a clarification of human identity in terms of the twofold reference of human self-consciousness that corresponds to the tension between centrality and exocentricity. What is being answered here is the question of how human beings, who are

---

for evil to be voluntary, and a biological concept of inheritance in order for it to be involuntary, acquired, contracted" (286).

[74]Ricoeur describes the human situation as fundamentally characterized by the disproportion in the life of a being that is finite and yet is at the same time infinite by reason of its destiny (*Fallible Man*, xx, 4ff., 192). But for Ricoeur this "non-coincidence of man with himself" (4) is not yet evil but initially only human fallibility, although he admits that this fallibility comes to light only through the fault that has already occurred. He goes so far as to describe as possible "only in an imaginary mode" the idea of a "primordial structure" that in fact precedes any fault and that while marked by fallibility is still innocent (220–21). But does this not mean that the failure to achieve one's destiny is inherently connected with the factual natural conditions of human existence? What, then, can it still mean to say that evil originates in an act of human freedom (xxv), if not that by confessing their sins and doing penance, human beings *subsequently* take responsibility for the facticity of their existence (see Ricoeur, xxvff.)?

unified living entities, exist in view of, on the one hand, their centralized organization, which they share with the higher animals, and, on the other, their exocentricity. The question of human unity carries over into self-consciousness, and it makes itself felt at every point in the form of anxiety about the self and of care with regard to its self-affirmation. Self-consciousness thus manifests a dominance of the centrality aspect of human organization, which reaches its highest point in the central ego, over the exocentricity element in the definition of the human. The central ego turns exocentricity, or the capacity for objectivity that is open to the world, into a means in the service of its own ends.

The distortion of the relation between the central ego and the exocentric aspect means a failure of human beings in relation to themselves, since in their striving to win themselves they neglect their exocentric side. The self-positing of the ego finds expression primarily in the effort to gain control somehow of everything, including, above all, the conditions of its own existence. Over against this effort to gain control stands the necessity of trusting, of mooring oneself to a reality outside oneself.[75] To be sure, this opposition too is marked by the ambiguity that is connected with human exocentricity and permeates all the phenomena of human behavior. For the decision to put one's trust in this or that can itself become a means in the service of a basic outlook that seeks control of life. In other words, even trust can become distorted, just as conversely the exercise of control over the things of the world can be inspired by a basic attitude of pure trust in the power that sustains life and guarantees its fulfillment, and thus can be an exercise of that rule over creation in which the image of God consists.

Despite this ambiguity which attaches in principle to all human behavior, it must be said that in their pregiven existential structure all human beings are determined by the centrality of their ego. They individually experience themselves as the center of their world. Thus they experience space as in front and in back, right and left, with their vantage point at any given moment functioning as the center to which all is related. They experience time as past and future that are divided by the point which is their present, and are thus relative to them. And we experience everything else as being, like time and space, relative to our ego as to the center of our world. It is clear, then, what deep roots egocentricity has in our natural organization and in our sensible perception.[76] It is not at all the case that

<hr/>

[75]This thesis is set forth in greater detail in my *What Is Man? Contemporary Anthropology in Theological Perspective,* trans. D. A. Priebe (Philadelphia, 1970), 28ff.

[76]Ricoeur describes the perspectivity at work in the actions of human life (including self-love) as an expression of human finitude which must be distinguished from actual fault (*Fallible Man,* 28ff., 72ff.). This position would be justified if the ego were constantly mindful of the limitations of its perspective at any given moment and thus, by the very fact of

egocentricity first makes its appearance in the area of moral behavior; rather, it already determines the whole way in which we experience the world. If this relatedness of everything to the ego is, in the form of *amor sui,* the essential element in sin or the failure of human beings in regard to themselves, then sin is not simply or first of all something moral but is closely connected with the *natural conditions* of our existence.

At this point three questions arise:

1. If *sin* is anchored in the natural conditions of human existence, then is not human nature as such already "sinful"? But how is it possible to speak here of "sin," since sin consists in the perversity of the will?

2. If human beings share their centralized organization with the higher animals, why is it only in relation to human beings that we speak of sin in the context of this existential structure? Why do we not speak of sin in the case of the animals as well?

3. If sin is linked to the natural foundations of our existence, what responsibility do we human beings have for our sinful behavior?

1. If the Augustinian analysis of sin as unrestrained egoism *(amor sui)* and concupiscence is correct, then human life in its natural origins is already characterized by the structure of this sinfulness. The earliest form of the ego, that is, the narcissistic pleasure ego as understood by Freud, corresponds to the *homo incurvatus in se* ("the human person bent back upon itself") and the *amor sui* of the theological tradition, a love which, according to that tradition, initially makes its appearance in human sin only implicitly, being concealed in concupiscence. But even if human beings are in this sense sinners *by nature,* this does not mean that their nature as human beings is sinful.

In this seemingly paradoxical statement the word "nature" has two different senses. In the first half it means the *natural conditions* of our existence; in other words, those limitations which human beings transcend in virtue of their exocentricity as they transform the natural conditions of their lives by dint of the behavior that creates culture. In the second half of the statement, on the other hand, the word "nature" means the essence, the essential nature of the human being as the kind of exocentric being just described. The theological tradition has repeatedly insisted that

---

admitting these limits, were at the same time to transcend them. Ricoeur has indeed convincingly shown that in the transcendental synthesis of object-perception the ego does at the same time transcend the limits of its perspectives in that it is "set among the things of the world" (46). "Perspective and transgression" are in fact "the two poles of a single function of openness" (62). But in its anticipation of things (41) as well as in its reaching out to happiness (98ff.) the finite ego is constantly taking as definitive reality what is in fact only a finite perspective, and this self-enclosed perspective, which is not aware of its own finitude, is an expression no longer simply of human finiteness but of human fault.

human *nature,* in this second sense of the word "nature," is not sinful as such.[77] As a matter of fact, "according to their nature," that is, in respect of their destination to humanity, human beings are exocentric beings who by creating cultures are to impose a new form, both within themselves and outside themselves, on the pregiven conditions of their existence and thus transcend these under the guidance of experiences of meaning that are, in the final analysis, religious. It is precisely the natural conditions of their existence, and therefore that which they are by nature, that human beings must overcome and cancel out if they are to live their lives in a way befitting their "nature" as human beings.

The essential nature is seen here not as something that is always and everywhere already realized, but rather as something that is to characterize all the manifestations of human life insofar as human beings are to be human and live in keeping with their destination as human. The essential concept of the human person is an "ought" concept, not, however, one that is applied extrinsically to the actual living of human life but one that is operative in the exocentric structure of this life. Ought and is are not to be opposed here, for the actual knowledge (of whatever kind) of an ought is characteristic precisely of the specifically human form of existence with its incompleteness. Human beings are given their "what they are," but only in the form of a task still to be completed. From this point of view the general conviction is correct that sin is located in the will. The conviction is valid despite the fact that sin has its roots in the natural conditions of human existence, because the destination to humanity directs human beings to transcend these conditions. In our wills, on the other hand, there is brought to pass that which we affirm as an element of our lives, even though we are not already directly that which we affirm. The will is thus that wherein here and now we correspond or do not correspond to our destiny.[78]

The traditional theological doctrine on sin was unable to grasp in their unity both the voluntary character of sin and its rootedness in the natural conditions of human existence. Since the will transcends the natural conditions of our existence, any assertion that sin is rooted in nature seemed to contradict its connection with the will. But when human beings do not accept the self-transcendence which their destiny requires of them, or accept it only in the form of its distortion, they are perpetuating their initial existential state in relation to their destiny as human beings. Now, this is hardly the object of an express act of the will, but it does qualify

[77]The Formula of Concord (1580), Art. 1, is typical in its rejection of the view of M. Flaccius that after Adam's fall sin became the very nature *(ipsissima natura)* of the human being; see *The Book of Concord.* 468; also 512, 515, 520.

[78]See Ricoeur's remarks (*Fallible Man.* 52ff.) on the contrast between the infinitude of the will and the finitude of the understanding in Descartes's fourth *Meditation.*

the character and result of those acts of the will in which human beings do not act according to their destiny. Thus the perpetuation of natural centrality is accomplished in the will itself and does not befall it as a fate that is alien to it.

2. The higher animals, and not human beings alone, are directed from a center. Why, then, is the egocentricity of human beings regarded as sin but not the analogous forms of centrally guided behavior that are found in animals? The answer is closely connected with the special character of human beings in the world of the higher animals. Only human beings, it seems, know themselves to be selves; only they know that they are given to themselves as both gift and task. Only beings for whom their own identity, their own selfhood, is the theme of their behavior can also fail themselves. Only because the destination of human beings is exocentric and finds fulfillment solely in the radical exocentricity proper to them as religious beings can the egocentricity that is analogous in them to animal centrality turn into a failure of their existence, their destination as human beings.

It is to be noted that even the centrality proper to human living bears the stamp of the specifically human life form. For this reason, egocentricity as the human form of behavior is only analogous to the centralized organization found in other forms of animal life. The structure of the ego is determined by exocentricity, insofar as human beings can be present to themselves only by being present to what is other than themselves. But to the extent that even when present to others the ego is, in the final analysis, present only to itself and not truly present to others, it shuts itself up in a quasi-animal centrality. Also relevant is the fact that it seemingly becomes wholly merged in the other precisely because its attention is not on the other as other but only to itself in the other. For this reason, the ego that is shut up in itself is wholly at the mercy of the otherness of the other, whether this is the effect of alcohol or the grind of professional life or the emptiness of distractions. Animal centrality, which lacks self-consciousness, is spared subjection to this kind of dialectic. The animal lives in its environment without any interior break. Despite its centralized organization, or rather in virtue of it, it is open to its environment. It is self-consciousness that makes possible an ambiguous presence to the other and therefore also a closing off of the self to the otherness of the other in consequence of the self-constituting of the ego. For when human beings experience self-consciousness as immediate identity with themselves and therefore as constitutive of the self, they close themselves against the divine power that establishes their existence and, in consequence, against the otherness of others within the world.

3. The sin of human beings is imputed to them as guilt. When the law of God reveals the estrangement of human beings from God, that is, their

sin, it reveals at the same time their guilt (Rom. 3:19f.). Sin is not a fate that comes upon human beings as an alien power against which they are helpless. The concept of sin is inseparable from the ideas of responsibility and guilt. It is this fact which gives rise to the most serious objection against linking the idea of sin to the natural conditions of human existence. It would seem that individual human beings cannot be held responsible for the conditions in which they begin to live their lives, since these conditions are not the result of their choice and decision. Thus individuals cannot be held responsible for the egoism of their narcissistic beginnings, as though they could have avoided such egocentricity before any beginning.

True enough, if we had to accept this concept of responsibility, the concept of sin could not without contradiction be applied to the natural conditions in which human life begins. That for which I am not responsible cannot be imputed to me either as sin or as guilt. The linking of the concept of sin with the natural conditions of human life would seem, then, to be a contradiction, since the concept of sin becomes meaningless when the concept of responsibility cannot be applied.

This view is essentially dependent on the underlying concept of responsibility. For if I am responsible only for what my free choice has preferred when the opposite was just as possible, then nothing can be sinful that is part of the natural conditions in which I find myself from the outset. Ever since the time of the antignostic fathers the concept of responsibility has been linked to the concept of freedom of choice, this last being understood as a decision-making power that stands apart from the alternatives between which a choice must be made. Thus Clement of Alexandria wrote: "There would be neither praise nor blame, neither rewards nor punishments, if the soul were not capable of striving for or rejecting something and if the actions of the wicked were involuntary."[79] The reduction of sin to human freedom of choice made it possible to overcome the metaphysical dualism of the gnostics, because it permitted the fact of evil in the world to be reconciled with the goodness of the creator and of his work as it originally came from his hand.[80]

But was this really the only possible solution of the problem? In any case, the early Christian theologians evidently did not give adequate thought to the price being paid for this solution. The price takes the form of the aporias in the idea of a human freedom of choice that stands beyond the alternatives of evil *and* good. For how can human beings thus fashioned be themselves originally good, and how can they be independent

[79]Clement of Alexandria, *Stromata* I, 83, 5; see IV, 153, 2; as well as Origen, *De princ.* I, 3, and, even earlier, Justin, *Apol.* 43, 4f.

[80]Origen, *De princ.* I, 8, 2 (ed. Koetscher, 98, 8ff.).

in relation to the good and at the same time masters of themselves through their decisions? As we saw, any explanation of Adam's sin presupposes sinfulness, while the assertion that a will thought of as neutral toward God has the capacity to choose the good offends against the Christian idea of grace.

As a matter of fact, even in the Scriptures the responsibility of human beings for their sins is not based on such a freedom of indifference. "Freedom" in the New Testament is not thought of as something that human beings have from the beginning and "by their nature" but as an effect of the redemptive presence of Christ and his Spirit (John 8:36; 2 Cor. 3:17).[81] In the history of modern theology Julius Müller was one man who realized this, even though his book on the concept of sin is completely traditional in seeing freedom of choice as the origin of sin.[82] Freedom in the biblical sense of the term is identical with the true nature of the human being; it describes, as Müller recognized, "the highest possible selfhood."[83] But Müller believed that in addition to this "real" concept of freedom he must also hold fast to the "formal" concept of freedom, according to which freedom is "conceived as a power, belonging to the original nature of human beings, whereby they are able to *choose between good and evil.*" Admittedly, this concept of freedom, unlike the other, cannot be substantiated from sacred Scripture; it is, however, implicitly contained in what Scripture says. For the gospel "appeals at every point to the human consciousness of guilt . . . and rightly leaves it to the further development of Christian thought to bring to light *the necessary presupposition for the consciousness of guilt.*"[84]

The key question, however, is precisely this: Is this "formal" freedom a necessary presupposition for responsibility, imputation, and the consciousness of guilt? The question cannot be answered by referring, for

[81]On the Pauline concept of freedom, see F. Mussner, *Theologie der Freiheit nach Paulus* (Freiburg, 1976), as well as R. Schnackenburg, "Befreiung nach Paulus im heutigen Fragehorizont," in L. Scheffczyk, ed., *Erlösung und Emanzipation* (Freiburg, 1973), 51–68. For the understanding of freedom in the New Testament as a whole, see K. Niederwimmer, *Der Begriff der Freiheit im Neuen Testament* (Berlin, 1966). For a systematic interpretation of these data, see P. C. Hodgson, *New Birth of Freedom: A Theology of Bondage and Liberation* (Philadelphia, 1976), 101ff., 216ff., 253ff.

[82]Müller (n. 24, above), II, 12.

[83]Ibid., 28.

[84]Ibid., 17f. On the relation between the two concepts of freedom, see 66: "Human beings must start with formal freedom in order to attain to real freedom; the passage from the one to the other requires a gradual development." Müller also rejects the idea of an unlimited freedom of indifference (12), but it is not clear how his notion of *formal* freedom can do without such indifference. This freedom can be thought of as limited only by the concrete situations of life in which it is actually used, unless the whole hypothesis of indifference is to become untenable.

example, to the fact that human beings choose when they exercise their wills. Willing and the choosing of what is willed are one and the same thing. It is not, however, the fact of choice that is disputed, but the interpretation of the fact. What I mean is that choosing does not require the will to stand apart from the alternatives between which it chooses, certainly not in the sense of being indifferent to them. What finds expression in the act of choice is, rather, the native and, for human behavior, constitutive phenomenon of a transcendence of the given, in the sense of a capacity for *distancing* oneself from impressions and conceptions, turning to others, and thus moving beyond the immediately given. It is not inconsistent with this basic phenomenon that human beings should always have as their starting point an initial natural situation, that is, the natural conditions of their existence, which in the process of self-transcendence they likewise transcend inasmuch as they come back to them and alter them in the light of their experience of the world. One may of course give the name of "formal freedom" to this kind of self-transcendence. However, now that the element of indifference to the alternatives presented for choice has been eliminated, this self-transcendence, or formal freedom, no longer explains responsibility. The latter requires a different and more profoundly based explanation.

The hypothesis of a freedom of indifference that stands apart from the alternatives presented for choice could be regarded as explaining human responsibility to the extent that it was regarded as the ultimate *cause* of the tilt to one or another of the alternatives. If this explanation of responsibility is presupposed, then human beings cannot be responsible for the natural conditions of their existence which precede any and all choices. But is responsibility in fact based on being the author or originator of something? When we say that someone "accepts" or "shirks" responsibility,[85] we are speaking of actions that cannot be translated into judgments regarding causality. Those who are the authors of actions may well refuse responsibility for them and may be relieved of responsibility by showing the motives that led to the actions; the closely woven net of motives can always be used to show why the actions had to occur as they did. This does

[85]Thus K. E. Logstrup in his article "Verantwortlichkeit," *RGG*[3] VI (1962), 1254f. It is here that the so-called "responsibility independently of any fault" has its context. R. D. Pfahl's study of this subject, *Haftung ohne Verschulden als sittliche Pflicht* (Düsseldorf, 1974), unfortunately does not go into the connected problem of the concept of responsibility. Ricoeur, on the other hand, states that the consciousness of responsibility "does not proceed from a consciousness of being the *author of.* . . . Man had the consciousness of responsibility before having had the consciousness of being cause, agent, author. It is his situation in relation to interdictions that first makes him responsible" (*The Symbolism of Evil*, trans. E. Buchanan [New York, 1967], 102). See also and especially P. Fauconnet, *La responsabilité. Étude de sociologie* (Paris, 1920), 247–81 and 392f.

not mean, however, that the result might not and should not have been different. The only point I am making here is that the question of causality can be raised just as well in order to remove responsibility as in order to demonstrate it. This shows that the real basis for human responsibility is not to be sought in this direction.

Only in connection with an entirely different point of view can authorship become significant for the imputation of an action. The viewpoint to which I refer is the *identity* of the agent. It is this which gives rise to the demand that agents acknowledge their actions as their own and thus *accept* responsibility for them. This is a demand which does not impose itself on agents from outside; it is one under which their lives are always lived at every point, insofar as all human beings claim an identity and cannot wholly deny their identity with their own body and its behavior. As human beings they stand therefore under the moral demand that they acknowledge their behavior as their own.

Responsibility does not first come into play where a fault has been committed; rather, the converse is true, that it is possible to speak of a fault only where responsibility is accepted or can be demanded but the action in the individual case is not in harmony with the requirement contained in such responsibility. Responsibility and the demand or expectation of responsibility have their basis in legal or moral imperatives that prescribe what the character of my action *ought* to be. But these imperatives are binding only if they are accepted by agents as conditions for their own identity. The injunctions in question may be connected with a person's identity as a member of a particular group or society. They may be consequences entailed by a conviction or faith that is regarded as constitutive of the person's identity, so that the person's behavior ought to be in tune with them. Both viewpoints usually come into operation where agents acknowledge imperatives as binding on them.

The fact that the binding force of imperatives depends on their relevance to the identity of the agents involved points in turn to something further, namely, that the experience of responsibility has to do with the relation of human beings to themselves. This relation is a relation to a selfhood that is not yet completely possessed, for otherwise consciousness of it could not express itself in the form of an ought. It is a selfhood in which human beings come to know their proper destiny, which is a destiny that is to be attained through their own behavior. To that extent an original indebtedness of existence finds expression in the experience of being responsible. This is how Martin Heidegger describes the phenomenon[86]: Human beings owe it to themselves—that is, to the true self of their as yet unrealized destiny—to correspond to this destiny of theirs and so

[86]Heidegger (n. 69, above), 329ff.

to themselves. To that extent all responsibility is responsibility to the self.[87] A responsibility that was not a responsibility to the self could have only a heteronomic basis; it could be based only on a norm that is forced upon human beings and has no relation to their selfhood. And in fact agents can feel responsible in relation to a truly heteronomic norm only as long as they (mistakenly) regard this norm as a condition for their true selfhood. It must not be said, therefore, that human responsibility to God is opposed to responsibility to the self.[88] Responsibility to God can be meaningfully asserted only as a particular form of responsibility to the self, on the ground that the true selfhood, the destiny, of human beings is grounded in God and can be achieved only by his power.

These considerations make clear the connection between responsibility and freedom. It is not, however, a so-called "formal" freedom that proves to be fundamental for the experience of responsibility but rather a freedom that is essential and has a determinate content—in other words, the presence of the being, destiny, and selfhood of the human being. The study of this substantial freedom has rightly been made central even in philosophical reflection on the nature of freedom.[89] "Formal" freedom becomes something concrete in one fashion or another only as the result of a given understanding of "real" or essential freedom. Therefore Müller's assertion that we must begin with formal freedom in order to reach real freedom needs to be turned around, for it is according to a given understanding of real freedom that the "formal" capacity for transcending the immediate data of a real-life situation will be evaluated. This is the profound truth contained in Kant's statement, "You can because you ought," for when the categorical imperative gives expression to the identity of human beings in relation to their behavior, it at the same time supplies a motive for meeting its demands in action. Whether this motive is adequate in every case to secure a corresponding behavior is an entirely different matter. As everyone knows, Kant's own answer to this question was a no. Nonetheless, when consciousness of the moral law can be understood not as a set of demands from outside but as the call of the person's own selfhood, it adds a new motive for action to the other motives inspiring human behavior.

[87]W. Weischedel, *Das Wesen der Verantwortung. Ein Versuch* (1933).

[88]While Weischedel objects to Kierkegaard's reduction of the positing of the subject to God as the positer (65 and 81) and thus presents responsibility to self and responsibility to God as alternatives, M. Henschel in his debate with Weischedel rightly does not get himself involved in such alternatives, despite the suggestion in his title, "Verantwortung oder Autonomie des Menschen?" *KuD* 8 (1962), 46–55, esp. 49ff. Henschel says with Kierkegaard that responsibility to self points "in the final analysis beyond itself to a power that established the basic ego" (54).

[89]See "Freiheit," *HWP* 2 (1972), 1064–98.

It may be doubted, however, whether Kant's categorical imperative with its formal universality is able to effect the kind of constitution of the individual self from which the motivation for free action will spring. The fact that the call of the self is heard in conscience, summoning persons to accept responsibility for their own behavior and their world and enabling them to transcend the factual state of their own existence together with all the aspirations linked to it—this fact is independent of the specifically Kantian theses on the foundations of ethics. In any case, the reality that grounds selfhood also makes itself known in the summons of selfhood. J. Splett offers a theological interpretation of these facts. He describes human beings as "free beings" who "nonetheless do not begin solely with themselves but are awakened to themselves by a creative summons."[90] In one way or another, freedom is to be understood as self-determination in the sense that individuals allow their actions to be determined by the call of their selfhood. In this connection Splett emphasizes the point that this is also the original meaning of freedom as self-constitution. Thus the definition *Liber enim est qui sui causa est* in Thomas Aquinas is a Latin version of the Aristotelian statement, *Anthrōpos eleutheros ho heautou heneka ōn,* or "They are free who exist for their own sakes." Thus self-causality was originally understood as final causality, and the goal that determines freedom is one's own self.[91] There is question not of positing the acting ego by effective causality but of the effect of the human destination on the life situation of any given moment.

Neither, therefore, is freedom to be understood as an indifference that is neutral in the face of possible objects of choice and that nonetheless (or even precisely because of this neutrality) is able repeatedly to undertake new sequences of effects. Even in Catholic theology this kind of freedom of indifference is being rejected today in the light of the connection between freedom and selfhood.[92] Freedom has to do with personal existence as a single whole which manifests itself in individual actions and decisions, with the result that human beings claim their present life situation as their own in the light of their human destiny. Therefore in keeping with their consciousness of their own destination they know themselves to be responsible for their own condition and activity and for turning the natural and social givens of their own life situation into a fulfillment of their destiny. Since, moreover, the destiny of individuals as human beings

[90]J. Splett, *Konturen der Freiheit. Zum christlichen Sprechen vom Mensch* (Frankfurt, 1974), 44; see 28ff., 73f.

[91]Ibid., 70, n. 3, with references to Aristotle, *Meta.* 982b25f., and Aquinas, *In I. Meta.*, lect. 3, no. 58, and *Summa contra gentes* III, 112, and often. Splett points out, however, that Aquinas himself sometimes uses the formula *causa sui* without reference to its final meaning.

[92]For example, K. Rahner, *Foundations of Christian Faith,* trans. W. V. Dych (New York, 1978), 38, 94.

links them with others in the common life of a community, these individuals accept responsibility not only for their separate actions and destinies but also for spheres of responsibility that extend beyond these to embrace the life situations and behaviors of other human beings.

The call of freedom is always to a harmonization of one's behavior with one's own destiny. This call is therefore the basis of a freedom to do good, not of a freedom to choose between good and its opposite. It can happen, of course, that what is chosen is not the good but the bad or evil. Evil is preferred, being chosen with the idea that it is good (*sub ratione boni*— insofar as it is good), that is, that it is good for the one choosing it. The belief may be objectively erroneous. The mistake may even be a culpable mistake when gauged by the standard of the true human destiny of the persons who in this way fail themselves. But it is not culpable, because, despite a full awareness of what is good, the opposite is supposedly chosen. The claim that choice takes such a form as this is a construct that is alien to reality.

Moreover, just as there is no freedom *against* the good, so there is no freedom *against* God as the ground of the person's own future selfhood and therefore as the very embodiment of all that is good.[93] Human beings can indeed close themselves against God as they can against the good, but this closure does not take the form of a direct confrontation. Rather, when God is rejected, he is rejected because of the view that the idea of God is merely a human construct. When, on the other hand, God is believed to be real and yet his will and commandment are scorned, this is due to doubt about whether this or that is in fact God's will ("Can God really have said . . . ?"). But it may subsequently become clear to such agents that their action was in fact directed against God. Then they cannot excuse themselves on the grounds of ignorance; rather, they must subsequently become aware that they have sinned against God and are responsible for this sin.

Responsibility does not depend, then, on a choice having been made between good and evil as clear alternatives, and this by a will that could

---

[93]Rahner, 98, takes a different view. He recognizes, of course, that freedom always "takes place as mediated by the concrete world which encounters us," but he adopts the position that in every such act there is present "an *unthematic 'yes' or 'no'* " to God, so that freedom "is also and in truth . . . a freedom which decides about God and with respect to God himself." But is this decision, unthematically co-elicited in the confrontation with the concrete world which encounters us, to be thought of as a decision against its object? If so, is not the distinction between conscious thematization and its unthematic implications once again blurred, inasmuch as the latter present themselves in the same form as the former? The distinction between the thematic and unthematic aspects of human living permits the latter to be thematized only at a second stage, in an act of subsequent reflection. It is consistent with this that human beings become aware only at a later stage of the opposition to God implied in their lusts.

just as well have chosen either good or evil. As I said above, such an interpretation is an artificial construct. It confuses the relation of the chooser to good and evil with the relation of the chooser to the concrete objects of choice. Human beings do confront these concrete objects in order to choose among them. But the criterion for the choice is whatever these individuals regard as good. Therefore the idea of a choice *against* the good or *against* God is a contradiction in terms. To outside observers the behavior of such individuals may suggest that they are choosing between what is good for them and in itself and other possibilities and that in the process they forgo the good. Observers can look at the situation in this way because they can judge what has in fact been chosen to be bad or evil. But the persons making the choice cannot but regard the object chosen as a good; otherwise they would not have chosen it.

It is possible, however, that the persons choosing are mistaken about what is good for them. Then they choose, though unwittingly, what is in fact evil. Interpreters have judged this Socratic explanation of moral evil to be intellectualist and then have frequently rejected it as superficial. But the deception with regard to the good need not be understood in a superficially intellectualist way. It can even be the result of compulsion, a consequence of conditioning or even of an instinctual orientation that exists prior to any conditioning and no longer allows the individual to admit good to be good and evil to be evil. Where a behavioral disposition of this compulsive type exists, such as is to be seen in all addictions, the power to choose is often or even in most cases not subjectively affected. That is, choice turns constantly to that which the addiction calls for, because it seems good to the one choosing.

The capacity for self-transcendence is of course diminished in fact, but it is not damaged from the formal standpoint, for if those addicted were to realize, and then could hold on to the realization, that alcohol (for example) is bad for them, they might derive from this insight the strength to overcome the addiction. In fact, however, while in sober moments they may realize what is happening, they are unable to hold on to the insight, and in the moment of temptation the object of their addiction once again seems attractive and "good." When Paul writes that human beings agree in their minds with the law of God but experience in their members another law which contradicts the first (Rom. 7:22f.), we should not take him to mean that human beings *always and everywhere* agree with the law of God at the level of rational understanding, while at the same time their actions are in opposition to that law. In that case, there would be a completely split personality, and this is certainly not usually the case in human behavior. It is, rather, the case that in a moment of sober reflection we (perhaps) agree with the law of God but are inclined either to regard his directives as not applying to our situation or even to doubt that such

laws can have God's authority behind them ("Can God really have said
. . . ?"), once the content of his demands is in opposition to a fixed
behavioral orientation based on instinct.

Only the power of the lie that says that good is evil and evil good and
deceptively offers us life as the reward for sin[94] (when in fact the outcome
of sin is death)—only this deceitful character of sin enables us to understand how, even though the power to choose remains intact from the
formal standpoint, human beings can nonetheless choose what is objectively evil, and choose it not through negligence but by compulsion.[95]
This is the bondage of the will. It does not mean that human beings are
not (or are no longer) capable of choosing and hence of deciding between
alternative possibilities. The bondage of the will consists in that human
beings regard as good what is objectively bad for them and therefore
choose it.[96] This situation makes it clear that—unless there is question in
a particular case of a simple error—human beings are the kind of beings
who can find pleasure in what is objectively evil (not only in itself but even
for them themselves). The observation that such is the case need not stir
others to moral outrage. Such a reaction has its place, of course, especially
when the structures of social life are being endangered. But those who
realize that a failure to achieve the good is always a failure of the self as
well will feel sadness more than anything else. In addition, there is little
they can do to bring about a change. Good advice is of little avail in such
cases, since deception with regard to the good is not simply an intellectual

---

[94]G. Bornkamm, *Das Ende des Gesetzes. Paulusstudien* (1952), 56f. (on Rom. 7:11), in
agreement with Bultmann, *Theology of the New Testament* I, 147f. It is in connection with the
law that Paul speaks of the deceitful nature of sin. The promise of life which accompanies
the law becomes an "occasion" for sin to misuse the law in the service of its own lusts. But
this need not mean, as Bornkamm believes, that "only with the help of the divine commandment" is sin able to mislead the sinner with false promises of life.

[95]A variant of this self-deception that is inseparable from sin is what Niebuhr has described
as the element of dishonesty in the self-glorification of the sinner. See his *The Nature and
Destiny of Man* I (New York, 1941), 203ff.: "Since his determinate existence does not
deserve the devotion lavished upon it, it is obviously necessary to practice some deception
in order to justify such excessive devotion." When explaining the priority of self-deception
over deception of others, Niebuhr adds this interesting observation: "The fact that this
necessity exists is an important indication of the vestige of truth which abides with the self
in all its confusion and which it must placate before it can act" (203; see 206).

[96]This point is not sufficiently clear in Ricoeur's "recapitulation" of the symbolism of evil
(defilement, sin, guilt) in the concept of the servile will (*The Symbolism of Evil*, 151ff. He is
content to speak of a "contamination" of the will by evil, which, moreover, human beings
regard as external to themselves (155). This externality of evil is important for the moments
when human beings identify themselves with the good, which is likewise something objective in their eyes. The difficulty is that the identification is not a stable one. Only this fact
renders intelligible what Ricoeur leaves much too vague by using the image of contagion
or contamination. Above all, this image surrenders too much to the thesis of the externality
of evil; it suggests that apart from this contamination human beings are in themselves healthy.

matter. The bondage of the will calls, therefore, for a liberation and, in the radical case, for a redemption that will establish the will's identity anew.

IV. The Universality of Sin:
The First Sin,
Original (Inherited) Sin, Death

The will's bondage, which leaves intact the power to choose, that is, the formal act of self-transcendence, but reduces its range, points to a motivational structure that precedes and underlies individual decisions and actions, as being the source of human failure in regard to the self. It is to this structure that Christian theology has given the name "original sin."[97] The enslavement of the will in this case is due to an addiction that is not merely partial but is connected with the egoism of human beings, inasmuch as the ego experiences itself as the center of its world and wills itself to be this center, even though it must then come into inevitable conflict with other such self-appointed centers and, above all, with the one real center of all reality. The Augsburg Confession (1530), following Augustine,[98] therefore describes concupiscence in its second article as the "positive" essence of sin, which is the counterpart of the lack of fear of God and trust in God and which marks human beings in their conception and birth.

Roman Catholic teaching has shown reserve with regard to this formula to the extent that it refuses to regard as sin in the proper sense the concupiscence that continues to exist even in the baptized. But the confessional difference here has to do more with the relation between baptism and sin[99] than with the professed belief that a sinfulness, known as original sin, attaches to every human being from birth.[100] Human beings do not first become sinners through their own actions and by imitating the bad

---

[97][The English term "original sin" is used both for the "first sin" (German: *Ursünde;* Latin: *peccatum originale originans*) and for "inherited sin" *(Erbsünde; peccatum originale originatum)*. The context will make clear which of the two is meant.—Tr.]

[98]See J. Gross, *Geschichte des Erbsündendogmas* I (1960), 322ff., 327ff.

[99]Thus P. Schoonenberg, "Der Mensch der Sünde," in J. Feiner and M. Lohrer, eds., *Mysterium Salutis* II (1967), 915 and 920ff. on the fifth canon of the Council of Trent on original sin (DS 1515): "The holy Council, however, professes and thinks that concupiscence or the inclination to sin remains in the baptised. . . . Of this concupiscence which the apostle occasionally calls 'sin' the holy Council declares: The Catholic Church has never understood that it is called sin because it would be sin in the true and proper sense in those who have been reborn, but because it comes from sin and inclines to sin" (trans. in J. Neuner and J. Dupuis, eds., *The Christian Faith in the Documents of the Catholic Church* [Staten Island, N.Y., 1982], no. 512, p. 139). On this subject, see below, n. 168.

[100]DS 1513.

example of others; they are already sinners before any action of theirs.

This, then, is the first and fundamental element in the concept of original sin as opposed to actual sin (sin of act). With it a second is closely connected: the radicalness of sin. Sin is located at a deeper level than the individual act, deeper than any transgression. In this insight the Jewish tradition gave expression to that spirit of repentance which according to Paul Ricoeur is the lasting legacy of the prophets: "The Jew repents not only for his actions, but for the root of his actions."[101] The idea of original sin as a sinfulness that affects the whole of human existence from birth may be taken as an extreme expression of that Jewish spirit of repentance. At the same time, of course, the idea of original sin breaks through the boundaries of the Jewish religion as a religion of law, since the unconditionality of original sin leaves no room for a human righteousness, unless human beings are first redeemed from their sin.

Ricoeur considers the discovery of the communal dimension of sin to be linked to the insight into its radicalness and to the confession of the wickedness of the heart. But the dismay of an entire people at the actions done in its midst probably had its roots originally rather in a not yet fully individualistic understanding of sin as a defilement; it is an understanding to which the prophets appeal. Once again there does not seem to be any direct line from the idea of a communal domination by sin to the Pauline thesis of sin's universality. Even though the Baptist's preaching of repentance and the outlook of other sects of the day that separated themselves from the multitude of the lost may have been more or less close to such a view, yet in the mainstream of Jewish piety the way of conversion to fidelity to the law was open to every individual. This way becomes closed only when, as in Paul, the law itself becomes suspect as an instrument of sin. It is only faith in redemption and a concern for the universality of redemption that make possible the idea that God has consigned all to disobedience in order that he may have mercy on all (Rom. 11:32; see 3:23f.).

The universality of sin, which is the third and decisive element in the concept of original sin, is a presupposition for the universality of the redemption wrought by Jesus Christ. It is in this light that we can comprehend the new importance that the biblical story of Adam's sin and, therefore, the figure of Adam as such had for Paul. The importance he assigned to Adam was new even by comparison with Philo, because in Paul the heavenly man of Gen. 1:26 is no longer linked to creation in a contrast with the earthly man of the second creation story but reveals himself only in the resurrection of Jesus as *eschatos Adam* ("the last Adam"). In Paul,

---

[101]Ricoeur, *The Symbolism of Evil.* 240–41.

Adam becomes the author and representative of sin as affecting all human beings.

In the Old Testament, on the other hand, Adam was "not an important figure,"[102] at least as author of sin. The myth of the crime and downfall of the Primal Man, which is in the background of the poem in Ezek. 28:11ff. and may also be behind the Yahwist story of paradise,[103] has been completely historicized by Ezekiel, who refers it to the king of Tyre. "Man" without qualification (Adam) is not even mentioned, and the crime leads only to the downfall of the criminal himself. Adam's fall is not mentioned again until The Wisdom of Solomon, and there it is said that Wisdom rescued Adam from his fall (Wisd. of Sol. 10:1). Death is said to have been the result of his fault, but nothing is said about the power of sin itself (2:24).

Jesus the son of Sirach likewise knows that death is the destiny imposed by the first sin, but he ascribes the sin to Eve alone and says nothing of Adam (Sir. 25:24). In addition to the mention of death, this verse speaks of the spread of sin as the disastrous effect of that first transgression. The fact that "sin [or: sins] had its beginning" in a woman is emphasized here as one piece of evidence for the rhetorical commonplace, or topos, of female wickedness, but even here there is no idea of the whole race being subject to inevitable sin. In the apocalyptic story of the life of Adam and Eve (ch. 44), on the other hand, the author laments not only the calamities but also the "transgressions and sins" that Eve has brought upon the entire race. We might seem to be coming close here to what Paul says, but in fact the purpose of the story is to tell of the *repentance* of Adam and Eve, which God finally accepted. Similarly in 2 Esdras we read, on the one hand, that Adam's fall affected not only himself but also his descendants (7:48 [118]) and, on the other hand, that each individual can win the victory over sin (7:57 [127ff.]). Paul, on the contrary, sees sin coming from Adam on all his descendants in such a way that no repentance can break its power and human beings can be delivered only from without, through the redemptive work of Christ.

Even in Paul himself sin does not yet appear as a fated universal legacy that proliferates generation after generation like a congenital disease. He does indeed use the figure of Adam in showing the *universality* of sin and even traces this universality back to him (Rom. 5:12), but a simple reference to Adam did not yet suffice Paul as a basis for this thesis. This is quite

---

[102]Ibid., 237.

[103]On Ezek. 28:11ff., see W. Zimmerli, *Ezekiel II*, trans. J. D. Martin (Philadelphia, 1983), II, 812–95, esp. 889ff. On the importance of the myth of the Primal Man for the Yahwist story of paradise, see O. H. Steck, *Die Paradieserzählung* (Neukirchen, 1970), 43ff.

understandable in the light of the way in which the story of paradise is presented in the Jewish tradition. A simple reminder of the story could not therefore be an argument for the universality of sin. It is probably for this reason that when introducing Adam, Paul also immediately mentions death which "spread to all men" as a result of Adam's sin. This was an idea familiar to the Jewish tradition[104] and one that went back to the story of paradise itself (Gen. 3:22).[105] Paul then turns the universal occurrence of death into an argument for an equally universal spread of sin, since sin is the cause of death: Death has spread to all because all have sinned (Rom. 5:12).[106] But nothing is said here, any more than it is in the Jewish documents, of an inheritance of sin; individuals sin on their own account and suffer death in consequence.[107] The universality of death does show, however, the actually universal spread of sin, in keeping with the relation of the race as a whole to Adam.

Adam is seen here as the prototype of all human beings, as their embodiment, as the Human Being pure and simple. In every individual, Adam's journey from sin to death is repeated as in a copy. In like manner the Greek fathers understood "the sin of Adam to be an act of the whole race," but they did not link to this notion the idea of an inheritance of sin.[108] A similar meaning might have been extracted from the Latin translation of Rom. 5:12, according to which all human beings sinned in Adam *(in quo omnes peccaverunt).* But once Augustine had turned from a doctrine of the inheritance of evil (the transmission of death to Adam's descendants) to a doctrine of the inheritance of sin,[109] he interpreted this statement as referring to a transmission of Adam's sin, through concupiscence, to all his descendants.

What role did this interpretation of the connection between Adam's sin

---

[104]Further references are in R. Bultmann, "Zaō," *TDNT* 2:856, n. 191.

[105]Steck insists that while "the story of paradise nowhere supposes that humanity was originally meant to be immortal" (81), yet the connection, introduced by the Yahwist, between the expulsion from paradise and the tree of life is to be understood as God's definitive decree of human mortality in consequence of sin (64ff.). Not until the book of Wisdom is it said that God created the human race for incorruption (Wisd. of Sol. 2:23).

[106]See Rom. 6:23 and 7:9f. But the direction of the argument is the converse in Rom. 5:12ff.: "Paul concludes from the fact of death in the period between Adam and Moses to the fact of sin in that same period" (Bornkamm [n. 94, above], 84).

[107]W. G. Kümmel, *The Theology of the New Testament,* trans. J. E. Steely (Nashville, 1973), 179, rightly emphasizes this point.

[108]Gross (n. 98, above), 92f.

[109]Ibid., 269ff. On Augustine's exegesis of Rom. 5:12ff., see ibid., 304ff. It is interesting that Julian, Augustine's adversary at that time, proposed the interpretation of Rom. 5:12ff. that is recognized today as the correct one (ibid., 305). Subsequently, the councils of Carthage in 418 (DS 223), Orange in 529 (DS 372), and Trent in 1546 (DS 1512) also appealed to Rom. 5:12.

and the sins of his descendants play in the thinking of Augustine? No substantiating reference back to Adam would have been needed in order to explain the universality of sin; Augustine had already explained this universality by his analysis of the concupiscential structure of human behavior together with the universality of inevitable death as the consequence of sin.[110] The thesis of the universality and radicalness of sin would not have required for its proof the acceptance of a *transmission* of the *individual* sin of the first parents of the human race. However, the recourse to Adam did have another function which must have seemed an important one to Augustine in view of the emphasis he puts on the rootedness of individual sins in the concupiscential structure of human behavior. I mean that the participation of Adam's descendants in him and his sin seemed to offer an appropriate way of answering the question of the responsibility of human beings for their sins.

If sin is connected with the naturally transmitted concupiscential structure of behavior, so that human beings are sinners from their birth and before any individual actions of theirs, then they can hardly be responsible for their sinful actions with the kind of responsibility that is *based on the principle of causality.* For there is no way of explaining how those who are born into a life context already marked by concupiscence and who share from birth this concupiscential behavioral structure could avoid sin. How can I be held responsible if my activity has a characteristic that I have no way of keeping it from having?

Augustine answers this question by referring to Adam. Unlike the later members of the race, Adam, the first human being, could have avoided sin in virtue of the state of original perfection in which he was created.[111] The reference to Adam thus grounds the responsibility that all later individuals have for their sin despite its radicalness that precedes all individual actions. In Adam "all sinned at that time when they were all still that one man in virtue of the power in his nature by which he could beget them."[112] This argument of Augustine can be regarded as plausible to the extent that Adam is regarded not as the historical ancestor of the race but as a mythical prototype and embodiment of the entire race. When he is taken as a mythical prototype, his history manifests what is repeated in the history of each individual human being. On the other hand, as a mythical

---

[110]Augustine, *De civ. Dei* XIII, 15.

[111]Augustine, *De nuptiis et concupiscentia* II, 26, 43: "Marriage is not the cause of the sin that is contracted by birth and expiated in rebirth [i.e., baptism]; rather the voluntary sin of the first and originating human being is the cause of this sin." When Julian asked how infants shared in sin, Augustine answered by referring to Rom. 5:12: "in Adam, in whom all sinned."

[112]Augustine, *De pecc. mer. et rem.* III, 7, 14 (PL 44:194).

prototype Adam has no authentic individuality such as is required if there is to be talk of responsibility for sin in the sense of a responsibility based on the principle of causality.

For his purpose, therefore, Augustine needed an Adam who was also historically the first human being. Consequently he had to give the mythical participation expressed in "in whom" *(in quo)* a naturalistic interpretation and make it refer to the preexistent presence of Adam's descendants in the loins of their ancestor. The combination of mythical participation with descent from a single historical ancestor seems to render plausible the responsibility of the descendants for their sin. But the elements combined are much too heterogeneous; and in the measure that they drifted apart and the mythical component lost ground to the relation of descent, new problems arose which more than a millennium later finally led to the disintegration of the doctrine of original sin. For if Adam is understood as the historical ancestor, his situation necessarily ceases to be a paradigm for the human situation as such, since prior to the fall he was in a situation that differed in principle from that of all his descendants, whose history has been decided in advance by his, and this in a negative way. How, then, can the individual fault of Adam be imputed to his descendants, that is, as their own guilt and not as a purely inherited guilt in the sense of a joint liability for the consequences of another's action? It is impossible for me to be held jointly responsible, as though I were a joint cause, for an act that another did many generations ago and in a situation radically different from mine.

In summary, the Augustinian doctrine of original sin is unable to accomplish the purpose for which it was elaborated. It cannot prove the responsibility of individuals for their sinfulness even though the latter already has roots in the natural conditions of human existence prior to any action of their own. Nor is this defect remedied in the Scholastic and early Protestant theory of imputation, according to which the sin of Adam is ascribed to his descendants.[113] There is no answer to the objection that Pelagius raised long ago in his commentary on the Letter to the Romans: How can God, who forgives the sins committed by individuals themselves, impute to them the sins of another?[114] The theory of imputation presupposes that Adam's sin is not extrinsic to his descendants but is instead their own. At this point the Augustinian idea of a physical transmission of sin had already

[113]A good presentation and defense of this teaching in its early Lutheran form is given by G. Thomasius, *Christi Person und Werk. Darstellung der evangelisch-lutherischen Dogmatik vom Mittelpunkt der Christologie aus* (1886³), 221ff. But for the reasons given in the text here, Thomasius' arguments do not prevail against the penetrating criticism of Müller (n. 24, above), II, 417–94, esp. 447ff.

[114]Pelagius on Rom. 5:15 according to R. Seeberg, *Lehrbuch der Dogmengeschichte* II (1923³), 491. See also the remark of Müller, II, 449.

broken down, and the imputation theory represents no advance at all. Nor does the combination of the two theories in early Lutheran dogmatics break out of the impasse, since the theories have the common defect of being unable to explain the co-responsibility of Adam's descendants for the sin of their ancestor. For this reason, the criticism voiced against the traditional doctrine of original sin since the time of the Arminians has been generally accepted in the modern age.[115] This is not to say that the object which the doctrine of original sin was intended to explain, namely, the radicalness and universality of sin, must be abandoned. It does, however, need to be explained in new ways.

The path generally taken in modern Protestant theology has been to provide a substitute for the doctrine of original sin; the characteristic idea adopted has been that of a "kingdom" of sin or evil. The concept of a "kingdom of evil" occurs in Kant's philosophy of religion,[116] where it functions as the counterpart of the kingdom of God, the latter being understood as "an ethical commonwealth under divine moral legislation."[117] In Kant the idea of a "kingdom" of evil replaces the doctrine of original sin insofar as the latter has the function of describing the unity and agreement among human beings in their distortion of the proper order among motivations (therefore in radical evil). In this context Kant has no need of disputing the biblical teaching on the descent of all human beings from Adam. Instead, he says that "all men, descended (in natural wise) from Adam, became subject" to this kingdom of evil, "and this, too, with their own consent, since the false show of this world's goods lured their gaze away from the abyss of destruction for which they were reserved."[118] Precisely because of this human community in evil the good principle can win out only by forming an ethical community, since among human beings each is interiorly dependent on the others and since they "mutually corrupt each other's predispositions and make one another evil."[119]

To an astonishing degree these thoughts of Kant have a parallel in Schleiermacher's ideas of a "corporate life" of sin and a corresponding

[115] Among the Arminians, S. Curcelläus in particular rejected the imputation whereby Adam's sin becomes a burden on his descendants, as well as the transmission of his corruption; see his *Institutio religionis christianae* (1675). On this, see O. Ritschl, *Dogmengeschichte des Protestantismus* III (Göttingen, 1926), 363, who also recalls Zwingli's earlier criticism of the idea of a transmission of sin. The critical attitudes of Enlightenment theologians in the question of the imputation of Adam's sin are collected in Ch. K. R. Olearius, *Die Umbildung der altprotestantischen Urstandslehre durch die Aufklärungstheologie* (theological dissertation; Bochum, 1968), 120ff.

[116] Kant, *Religion Within the Limits of Reason Alone* (n. 10, above), 74.

[117] Ibid., 92; see 113.

[118] Ibid., 74.

[119] Ibid., 85.

"new corporate life" of grace. Since Schleiermacher did not explain universal sinfulness by an original fall into sin,[120] he considered it to be "an arrestment of the determinative power of the spirit due to the independence of the sensuous functions" (§ 66, 2) that is part of the initial natural stages of human development (§ 67) but is at the same time a "derangement of our nature" (§ 68) in relation to our spiritual destiny. The development of the disposition to sin by the individual's own activity is thus conditioned, "with respect to each later generation," by "the action of the one before it" (§ 69, 3). As a result, sinfulness is "something genuinely common to all," being "in each the work of all, and in all the work of each" (§ 71, 2). Individuals are therefore caught in "the corporate life of sin"; only through participation in a "new divinely effected corporate life" can they be freed from this entanglement (§ 87). The establishment of such a new corporate life requires, however, a historical beginning, which Schleiermacher, unlike Kant, regards as possible only through the work of a real historical redeemer (§ 88; see § 93). This redeemer cannot have developed out of a corporate life marked by sinfulness (§ 93, 3); on the other hand, he must be the "ideal" for all members of a new corporate life. It is in the consciousness of the reality of this new corporate life that Christ is "taken as Redeemer" (§ 91, 1).

The parallel between Schleiermacher and Kant consists in the fact that the universal original sin which the two men claim to see in both society and individuals is not explained by a relation of natural descent but by the reciprocal involvement of individuals and generations in ongoing human society. It was as a prolongation of this thinking that Albrecht Ritschl developed his doctrine of the "kingdom of sin," which was now expressly described as "a substitute for the hypothesis of original sin."[121] Augustine had made "the human collectivity as a natural species . . . the subject of sin" (318). But against such a view stands the fact that only through its actions does the will acquire its peculiar nature, on which, in turn, "any and every kind of responsibility for evil" depends (319). On the other side, Pelagius saw "sin taking form solely in the will of the individual" (318). The idea of a "kingdom of evil" resolves this dilemma, for it takes the human collectivity, not as a natural species but "as the sum total of all individuals," to be the subject of sin, "inasmuch as the egoistic actions of each individual, whereby each is part of an immense web of reciprocity with all other individuals, is directed in one degree or another to the

---

[120]Schleiermacher, *The Christian Faith* (n. 35, above), § 72. The references that follow in the text are to the sections and subsections of this book.

[121]A. Ritschl, *Die christliche Lehre von der Rechtfertigung und Versöhnung* III (1874; 1888³), 317ff.; citation here from 326. Schleiermacher, to whom Ritschl attributes the "idea of a corporate sin," is reproached for his attempt "to locate this under the traditional rubric of original sin, to which it bears very little resemblance" (321).

opposite of the good, and leads to individuals being bound together in corporate evil" (317f.). According to Ritschl, this conception "does justice to everything . . . that the concept of original sin rightly intended to explain" (326), although unlike the latter this new approach necessarily takes the sins of individuals as its point of departure and presupposes the concept of individual sin (310).

Ritschl's theory of the "kingdom of sin" exercised a lasting influence. Even when it was not accepted as a substitute for the doctrine of original sin, it was recognized as being a necessary complement to it with reference to the social context in which individuals live their lives.[122] According to the Second Vatican Council, similar views had emerged even in Catholic theology, though there does not seem to have been an awareness of the points of contact with Ritschl.

P. Schoonenberg in particular has described original sin as the "being-situated" of human beings in their social context. "The fact of being situated by original sin precedes the personal choice of those who carry original sin within them, and belongs essentially to the interpersonal realm, since it results from personal decisions (taken by others)." From this vantage point, Schoonenberg, like Ritschl, can "circumscribe original sin in relation both to the realm of the purely natural and the not yet moral and to that of personal decision." At the same time, however, he insists that being-situated is to be regarded not as something extrinsic to individuals but as an intrinsic determination of their existence.[123] In like manner, Karl Rahner interprets "original sin" as "the universality and the ineradicable nature of the co-determination of the situation of freedom by guilt in the single history of the human race." He too insists that "freedom inevitably appropriates the material in which it actualizes itself as an intrinsic and constitutive element which is originally co-determined by freedom itself, and incorporates it into the finality of the existence which possesses itself in its freedom."[124]

Against such modern interpretations of the dogma of original sin the same objections must be raised that were raised against Ritschl. Paul

---

[122]Thus, for example, P. Althaus, *Die christliche Wahrheit* (1952³), 371ff. Brunner, too, considers the idea to be a "valuable" one, even though Ritschl's substitution of it for the doctrine of original sin represents "a form of Pelagianism, intensified by social psychology" (*Man in Revolt*, 125; see his *The Christian Doctrine of Creation and Redemption: Dogmatics II*, 117). Oddly enough, Barth says nothing at all about Ritschl when presenting the doctrine of sin in his *Church Dogmatics*. In 1912, H. Stephan could sum up the initial extensive influence of Ritschl's views by saying they had become "a common property in dogmatics" at that time; *Lehrbuch der evangelischen Dogmatik*, by F. A. B. Nitzsch, 3d ed. rev. by H. Stephan (Tübingen, 1912), 334.

[123]Schoonenberg (n. 99, above), 931, 928, and 924. See also his *Theologie der Sünde* (Einsiedeln, 1966).

[124]Rahner (n. 92, above), 110 and 107.

Althaus has justifiably singled out as the "basic defect" of Ritschl's view the fact that "it takes as its starting point sins rather than sin, actions rather than the being of the person." The whole point of original sin is that "we become subject to the power of evil in the heart not simply as a result of the laws governing the ongoing historical influence of evil, for example, enticement, tradition, environment, and the atmosphere in which we grow up; we are subject to it 'before' any of those things enter the picture, and 'by nature,' that is, simply by our humanity, no matter at what point in human history we are located." Precisely at this level, antecedently to any and all actions of any individual, there is a corporate will, a "unity of the human race in its willing," that precedes the reciprocal historical relationships of individuals.[125] The same point is being made in the Augustinian formula taken over by the Council of Trent, namely, that Adam's sin was transmitted "by propagation, not by imitation" *(propagatione, non imitatione).* [126] Augustinian ideas about the transmission of sin need not be regarded here as essential to the dogma itself. The important thing is that a sinful perversity is part of individuals from birth and therefore common to all human beings as "children of Adam." This is the radicalness of sin that precedes any attitude adopted by the person.

Schoonenberg is able to point out, of course, that the interpersonal being-situated precedes the adoption of any attitude by the individual, but to the extent that this is the case, the being-situated can no longer be regarded as an *intrinsic* determination of individual existence in respect of its decision about itself. Individuals can very well distinguish and distance themselves from the social context into which they grow as being a world that is alien to them and that estranges them from their real selves; they can do this even though it does not remove them from that world. Only if sinfulness in the sense of a distortion of the subjectivity that underlies all action is linked from the outset to the ego in its becoming will there be no longer any right to such a distancing. If this distortion must be regarded as "a natural biological datum," it is also a datum essential to the concept of original sin.

The "moral and religious nature" of original sin must not be presented in such a way as to exclude any connection with that kind of "natural biological datum."[127] Schoonenberg's remark that there is "no basis in Scripture for a biological or natural interpretation of original sin" is to the point only with reference to the specifically Augustinian view linking the transmission of original sin with sexual desire. In addition, of course, the

---

[125] Althaus (n. 122, above), 372 and 373.
[126] DS 1513; see Augustine, *De pecc. mer. et rem.* (412), I, 9, 10 (PL 44:114); also I, 9, 12.
[127] Thus Schoonenberg, 931; Rahner, 110f., could be misunderstood as maintaining this.

biblical writers lacked our present-day understanding of biological life. But do not Paul's statements about the connection between sin and death contain in their own manner a "natural" aspect, since it is not possible to exclude so-called natural death as not being cointended in these statements?[128] Then too, Paul's words, echoing Gen. 2:7, about Adam as earthly and from the earth (1 Cor. 15:44ff.) may also imply a "natural" understanding of sin.[129] Finally, such an understanding may without difficulty be cointended in the Pauline view of the relation of sin to the "flesh" and its desires.[130] A dualism between an ethical and religious sphere, on the one hand, and a "natural and biological sphere," on the other, cannot appeal to Pauline thinking; it likewise finds little support elsewhere in the New Testament writings.

Those modern theologians who regard the traditional theology of original sin as untenable for the reasons given but who nonetheless maintain that all human beings are sinners from birth and not simply in consequence of their entanglement in a corrupt social context have often attempted to solve the problem of human responsibility for this state of affairs with the hypothesis of a suprahistorical, mythical fall into sin. In its existentialist form this hypothesis is the one most frequently accepted in contemporary Evangelical theology.[131]

This view originated with Julius Müller.[132] He started with a dilemma: on the one hand, "a sinfulness innate in all human beings" actually exists in the form of egoism; on the other hand, personal guilt can be asserted only when individuals "are the authors of their sin by their personal decisions." Müller thought it possible to reconcile personal guilt and innate sinfulness only by presupposing a guilty decision made prior to birth. In this way he arrived at the "concept of a sinfulness that has its basis *beyond our individual existence in time*"; he found support here in Kant's interpretation of the fall as an *"intelligible act"* that "precedes all experience."[133]

---

[128]On this question, see Schoonenberg's cautious remarks, 935, where he refers to L. Boros and K. Rahner (on the theme of "sin and death," see also my Excursus at the end of this section). On the possibility of a distinction in Paul between "death as the natural end of physical life" and a death through judgment, Bultmann (*Theology of the New Testament* [n. 71, above], I, 251) observes laconically in connection with Rom. 5:12 that "Paul makes no such distinction."

[129]Bultmann, *Theology of the New Testament*. I, 251.

[130]Ibid., 239ff., esp. 241f.

[131]On what follows, see H. Fischer, *Grundlagenprobleme der Lehre von Urstand und Fall. Ein Beitrag zur Methodenfrage der Theologie* (dissertation; Marburg, 1959), 9ff.

[132]Müller (n. 24, above), II, 495ff.

[133]Kant, *Religion Within the Limits of Reason Alone.* 34, n*; see Müller, II, 97f., 100ff. (with a positive appraisal of the Platonic and Origenist doctrine of the fall of souls, 101f.), 103ff.

But if the act in question is to be taken as an act that really precedes our temporal life—and that is how Müller takes it—Richard Rothe's objection becomes unavoidable: "A contradictory requirement is being imposed on us when we are asked to think of a created and therefore *finite* being as having an *extratemporal* kind of existence and positing a *timeless* act of self-determination, simply because *temporality* is an *essential* element in *all* that is finite."[134] Such a hypothesis is in fact a contradictory one, since an action *preceding* the historical existence of a creature can be thought of only as temporal in relation to what follows it as well as in relation to what precedes it.

On the other hand, a further objection against Müller is less to the point, namely, that "his intellectual approach is too individualistic" and that "consideration of the race as a whole" is completely lacking.[135] The fact is, rather, that Müller wanted to connect the guilt of the individual and the universality of sin with the aid of Kant's description of the propensity to evil as "woven into human nature" but at the same time "brought by man upon himself."[136] Kierkegaard indeed gave a simpler and clearer formulation of this situation in his *The Concept of Dread,* in the thesis that every human being—and therefore Adam too—"is at once himself and the whole race, in such wise that the whole race has part in the individual, and the individual has part in the whole race."[137] Here the fall which precedes the existence of the individual is connected with the priority of the human race over the individual, while at the same time the humanity that thus precedes the existence of individuals is not alien to them since it is, rather, "itself and the whole race." Therefore not only do all other individuals share in the fall of Adam (in keeping with the traditional idea that all were in Adam); it is also the case that the fall is repeated anew in every individual life, in the passage from dread to the act of freedom in which individuals choose and posit themselves—and at the same moment lose themselves.

And yet, attractive and illuminating though this idea seems to be at first sight, closer examination makes it doubtful whether it comes down to the idea that every human being is born a sinner. For the anxiety that would make it possible to identify the two is not yet sin according to Kierke-

[134]Rothe, *Theologische Ethik.* III, 53 (§ 480).

[135]Thus Fischer, 10, probably in agreement with K. Heim and P. Althaus (*Die christliche Wahrheit.* 385f.).

[136]Müller, II, 497; see Kant, 25 and 24. Müller develops the connection into his hypothesis of a threefold original state of humanity (II, 528), in which the intimate connection between the individual and universal aspects of human existence corresponds to the hypothesis of a nontemporal original sinfulness of the human race (531).

[137]Kierkegaard, *The Concept of Dread.* 26.

gaard.[138] His argument shows, rather, that individuals *repeat* by their own actions what is characteristic of the entire race and was already to be found in its first ancestor. This means, on the one hand, that the sinful acts of individuals, and not an innate sinfulness, are the foundation of their sin and, on the other, that in their acts individuals are not free to be righteous before God but can only illustrate anew the inevitable truth: that clinging to finiteness brings in its train the distortion of selfhood. The decision of which Kierkegaard is speaking is not at all the origin of sin in the sense of a *posse non peccare* ("to be able not to sin") such as Müller requires. As a result, Kierkegaard's thesis, which was meant to resolve the dilemma of original sin and responsibility, is caught between the alternatives of innate sinfulness and the reduction of all sin to the actions of individuals. If, as was maintained in the interpretation given earlier (pp. 96ff.), sin is to be understood as constitutive of dread itself, then what Kierkegaard is describing is at every point the effect of an already existing sinfulness, and sin has only apparently been traced back to an original act of freedom.

In twentieth-century Evangelical theology the idea of a suprahistorical fall into sin has found wide acceptance, whether in dependence on Müller's interpretation of Kant's derivation of radical evil from an intelligible act prior to all experience or in the line of Kierkegaard's idea of a presence of the entire human race in the individual's action. K. Heim [139] and Paul Althaus[140] carried Müller's thesis farther by accentuating more strongly the role of humanity in original sin. In Althaus, this was accompanied by an increasing reaction against the "speculative" acceptance of "another world" behind history. "We know of the sin of humanity only in history, and we invent no other world behind it." In his "interpretation of the existential character of sin" Althaus nonetheless considered the idea of an original state, known through our consciousness of sin to be a lost state, as "indispensable," since it alone prevents sin from being taken as part of creation instead of as due to human culpability. But this original state does not take the form of something prior to time or history. Every human being sins in "contemporaneity" with the entire race as an expression of a corporate "primordial decision."[141] As Althaus develops his idea, it can be said, objectively speaking, that he inflects the starting point derived from Müller in the direction of Kierkegaard.

[138]See above, pp. 101f.

[139]K. Heim, *Leitfaden der Dogmatik,* Part 2 (1921), 45ff.

[140]P. Althaus, *Religiöser Sozialismus* (1921), 69; idem, *Die letzten Dinge* (1922), 82f.; idem, "Zur Lehre von der Sünde," ZST (1923), 314ff.

[141]See Althaus, *Die christliche Wahrheit,* 386, 382 (see 383f.), and 385. "The first human beings, we today, and the last human beings live in their sin as *one* human being, a single will before God" (385). For a critique, see Fischer's remarks, 37f.

There has been a similar development in the writings of Barth. In the second edition of his *The Epistle to the Romans* he spoke of the historical reality of sin as the expression of a nonhistorical "fall" from union with God.[142] But in his *Church Dogmatics* this distinction disappears in the idea of an "evil life" *(Lebenstat)* of the individual who as this individual at the same time sums up humanity and repeats the history of Adam.[143] There is no previous time "in which man is not a transgressor and therefore guiltless before God,"[144] although insofar as this evil life is a violation of the original destiny of the human being as a creature, it is at the same time the individual's "fall." The difficulty with these statements of Barth is that the ideas of a "fall" and a "transgression" presuppose some prior moment; otherwise the transgression would not really be understood as a human "act." The element of truth in Barth's statements becomes accessible, therefore, only through an interpretation that strips them of their contradictions.

The same is true of the other forms that the existentialist interpretation of the "fall" takes in contemporary theology. Among the many examples of it[145] I shall here mention only Emil Brunner's version. Brunner too initially adopted the ideas of Müller,[146] but he moved away from them in 1937 on the grounds that Müller's doctrine of "a sinfulness which lies beyond our individual and temporal existence" represents "a metaphysical and speculative transgression of the boundary which is set for our knowledge, even our knowledge in faith" and "leads onto paths trodden by the speculations of Origen."[147] Even in 1927 Brunner had thought of sin as "a determination of the whole" of the human being in the unity of its individual acts and the person, but also of the individual and the race, so that "the individual as an individual is always at the same time the

---

[142]K. Barth, *The Epistle to the Romans,* trans. E. C. Hoskyns (London, 1933), 168: Concrete sin is "the ever-widening appearance and expression and *abounding* (v. 20) of this Original Guilt. It points to the Fall which lies behind time."

[143]Barth, *Church Dogmatics* IV/1, 556 (rejection of the concept of original sin, 557) and 509–10.

[144]Ibid., IV/1, 495; see III/1, 307f. Materially speaking, Barth's intention here is comparable to Althaus' in his rejection of a temporal and historical interpretation of the "original state," although in Barth the rejection takes the form of a denial of the original state as a "state" of humanity as such.

[145]See also Niebuhr, *The Nature and Destiny of Man* I, 269, 277ff., and R. Prenter, *Creation and Redemption,* trans. T. I. Jensen (Philadelphia, 1967), 253ff.

[146]E. Brunner, *Die Mystik und das Wort* (1924). Critical response in W. Künneth, *Die Lehre von der Sünde* (1927), 82ff.

[147]Brunner, *Man in Revolt,* 142, n. 3. In his *The Christian Doctrine of Creation and Redemption: Dogmatics II,* 117, Brunner seems to put Müller and approaches taking him as their point of departure into the category of gnostic and dualistic conceptions of original sin.

representative of the species."[148] This is a curtailed version of Kierkegaard, inasmuch as Brunner, like Barth later on with his similar concept
of sin as an "evil life" *(Lebenstat),* reduces everything to human decision,
while ignoring the dread which precedes decision in Kierkegaard. As a
result, Brunner, again like Barth later on, fails to explain how the whole
of life can be thought of as an "act" *(Tat)* (and therefore possibly also as
guilt) and how the elements of the individual and the universally human
therein are related to the fact that guilt attaches to the individuality of the
agent and the agent's action.

Brunner too interprets the "total act" of human life as a "fall," inasmuch as in his view sin presupposes "a God-given being" which is "prior
to our empirical sinful existence" but which "we know only in connexion
with its contrast with sin."[149] This priority of an original state, which
the concept of sin supposedly requires and in opposition to which we now
live, makes it appear that Brunner is always speaking of a temporal
priority, although he expressly denies this.[150] It seems clear, then, that if
one wishes to join Müller in retaining the concept of a fall while not
making the fall a historical event at the beginning of time, it is not
so easy to avoid Müller's "speculations" and the problems they entail.
But Müller's argument has at least the advantage of logical clarity and
stringency.

As time went on, Brunner was increasingly concerned—this is especially true in his *Dogmatics*— to see sin as sin before God and therefore
in relation to the human destiny that has been revealed in Christ. As a
result, he developed a new interpretation of the universality of sin in the
light of the human solidarity that has been established through the revelation given in Christ. Just as "it is only through the Christian revelation that
. . . the individual can be perceived, in the full sense, as an individual
person," so in the same light "before God we men are all one in Christ,"
and it is this unity of our destiny as revealed in Christ that explains the
unity and solidarity of all human beings in Adam. "The knowledge of
Christ creates unity both in the past and in the future. Looking back, in
Christ, we see ourselves as a closely-knit sinful body of mankind which is
under sentence of death; when we look forward in Christ, we see our-

---

[148]E. Brunner, *The Mediator,* trans. O. Wyon (Philadelphia, 1947), 174. See also *Man in
Revolt,* 145–53 ("Original Sin and Sins of Act," esp. 149), as well as the citation from
Kierkegaard on 140 with the interpretation of it under the title "Solidarity in Sin." See also
The Christian Doctrine of Creation and Redemption, 107f. and 113ff.

[149]Brunner, *Man in Revolt,* 104 and 111; see 129ff. Barth differs from Brunner only in
that he will not allow this presupposition to be a being or state of humanity. Since, however,
Brunner likewise denies a *temporal* priority (104), the two men are really in basic agreement.

[150]See also the critique of Fischer, 27f.

selves as a redeemed humanity, which shares in the life of Christ."[151]

The "retrospective unity" of human beings from the standpoint of Jesus Christ [152] can perhaps throw light on the paradoxes that are linked to the concept of the first sin in modern theology. A first justification of this viewpoint is that it fits in with the Pauline interest in the figure of Adam, since this interest is due to the universality of the redemption accomplished by Jesus Christ. But the knowledge of Christ does not simply "create"— to use Brunner's term— its negative counterpart in the universal domination of sin that is summed up in the sin of Adam, the Human Being as such. It is, rather, the case that the universality of redemption *presupposes* the universality of sin. The universal rule of sin must therefore be explained as such; it cannot simply be postulated to support the universalist claim expressed in the Christian message of redemption. On the contrary, this latter claim must be verified anthropologically. That is precisely what Paul did when he took the universality of inevitable death as proof of the universality of human sinning and when he assigned to the law the function of revealing, through its "You shall not covet," the universal character of sin as seen in unrestricted concupiscence. It is precisely by way of the anthropological proof of the universality of sin that the universal relevance of redemption through Christ becomes convincing. Conversely, however, it is also true that only in the light of the concern for a universal redemption have the signs of the universality of sin manifested their comprehensive and radical character. The doctrine of the universality of sin was not taught until the advent of Christianity.

The fact that the universality of sin becomes known in the light of Christian revelation and as a *presupposition* of this revelation justifies us in looking for the root of human sin in the universal natural conditions of human existence, namely, in the immoderation of concupiscence or, to use Paul's word, the "flesh," in which in turn the ultimate root of egoism is hidden. It was in this way that Augustine showed the universal sinfulness that makes its appearance in all human beings; the demonstration is independent of his hypothesis regarding the transmission of the sinfulness. Once modern criticism had demolished the hypothesis of an inheritance of sin with its source in Adam, Schleiermacher returned to the Augustinian proof, inasmuch as he described sinfulness as emerging, together with the initial natural conditions of all human life, in "the independent activity of the flesh,"[153] and Richard Rothe followed him in this approach.

---

[151]Brunner, *The Christian Doctrine of Creation and Redemption,* 96 and 99. Similar idea three years later in Barth, *Church Dogmatics* IV/1, 570ff. and esp. 572: "It is in relation to the last Adam that the first Adam, the unknown of the Genesis story, has for Paul existence and consistence."

[152]Brunner, *The Christian Doctrine of Creation and Redemption,* 98.

[153]Schleiermacher, *The Christian Faith* (n. 35, above), § 67, 2.

Müller too acknowledged that this hypothesis yielded a solidarity of all individuals in sin, in the sense that each of them "would likewise have committed the sin" that one of them committed in the beginning.[154] Only the question of the guilt of the individual for this primordial sinfulness becomes difficult to answer, at least as long as the concept of guilt is restricted to the effects of the free voluntary activity of the individual.

As a matter of fact, Schleiermacher too distinguished between universal sinfulness (or the first sin) and personal guilt,[155] and in this he was followed by Rothe and O. Pfleiderer, as well as by J. Kaftan and other theologians of the Ritschl school.[156] Kaftan, who went into this distinction in an especially thorough way, based it on the Pauline statement that where there is no law, sin is not accounted sin (Rom. 5:13; see 7:7). "For sin is all human willing and acting that is in opposition to the divine will. It is sin even when it is not known, willed and done as sin." But there is personal guilt only when there is an awareness of the divine law and a determination to transgress it.[157] Müller, on the other hand, saw sin as directly connected with the doing of what is sinful,[158] and this position is admittedly a plausible one when all sin is regarded as the consequence of responsible decisions of the human will. For Thomasius too, guilt "is correlative with sin and inseparably tied to it."[159] The same view is to be found in the twentieth century in Brunner and Barth but also in Althaus.[160] These theologians see the sense of the radicalness and totality of sin as being undermined when the concept of sin is separated from the concept of guilt.

Even advocates of a sharper distinction between sin and guilt have unreservedly conceded that in an ultimate perspective "all sin is in fact to be understood as guilt."[161] It is admittedly not fully clear how such a position is compatible with a distinction in principle between the two

[154]Müller (n. 24, above), II, 464 on § 76, 6 of Schleiermacher's *The Christian Faith* (with formulations taken word for word from this source).

[155]Schleiermacher, § 71, 1, as compared with § 72, 5 and 6.

[156]Rothe (n. 134, above), 58ff., esp. 60f.; see 55f., but also 33. O. Pfleiderer, *Grundriss der christlichen Glaubens- und Sittenlehre* (1898⁶), 125. J. Kaftan, *Dogmatik* (1897; 1901³), 322f., 329ff. (§ 35); see 320f. (§ 34). On Kirn, Häring, Reischle, and other points of view, see Nitzsch-Stephan, *Lehrbuch der evangelischen Dogmatik* (1912³), 328f., and 327ff. generally. See also Niebuhr, *The Nature and Destiny of Man* I, 219ff.

[157]Kaftan, 322; see 325f. and 330.

[158]Müller, I, 280ff. and 269f., where stress is also laid on the fact that sin refers to the act, whereas the resultant guilt is attributed to the person. The supposition for Müller is that all sin, even the sin innate in every human being, is based on an intelligible act.

[159]Thomasius (n. 113, above), 195; see 226f.

[160]Brunner, *The Christian Doctrine of Creation and Redemption*, 106. Same idea earlier in *The Mediator*, 147–48, as well as in Barth, *Church Dogmatics* IV/1, 484f., but also in Althaus, *Die christliche Wahrheit*, 357f.

[161]Kaftan, 323; see 334f. Schleiermacher, *The Christian Faith*, § 71, 2.

concepts. But there seems to be a material convergence here with the thesis of Brunner and Barth according to which it is in looking back from the Christian revelation and its universality that we substantiate the universality of sin.

We may, to begin with, agree with this thesis to the extent that in Paul the *knowledge* of the universality of sin is arrived at in this way, although, on the other hand, he treats the universal spread of the corruption of sin as a *presupposition* for the dependence of all human beings on the redemption wrought in Jesus Christ. Now the concept of guilt also has to do with the knowledge of sin as sin. The law brings knowledge of sin because it reveals the opposition of concupiscence to the will of God and thus to the destiny of human beings. Initially this opposition is present only implicitly, not explicitly, in concupiscence. Only through the law do human beings become conscious of it. Yet it is not even through the law but only through the cross of Christ—the cross of the One whom God raised up, thus putting the stamp of approval on his mission—that this opposition is revealed in its full depth and universality. That this opposition, as well as the opposition to the demand of the law on the part of one who is aware of the demand, should have the character of guilt is something that becomes intelligible only in view of the fact that what is at issue in Jesus Christ as the "new man" is the real destiny of human beings and therefore the identity of the individual as a human being.

This is also the basis for the law's claim on human beings and for the expectation, based on this claim, that they will take upon themselves the responsibility not only for their actions but also for their omissions and consequently for the entire state in which they find themselves, insofar as they are not in accord with the demands of the law (understood as the expression of true human destiny).[162] However, only a concept of responsibility that is not one-sidedly linked with the concept of action but also extends to omissions and therefore to the person's own state can do justice to this approach. Only a concept of guilt that, insofar as it involves the "acceptance" of responsibility by individuals for their own lives, is based on a consciousness of the demands connected with their destiny can be true to the perspective, justified by Christian revelation, that is operative in the Pauline thesis of the universality of sin. Only in the light of the revelation of the "new man" in Jesus Christ as being the fulfillment of the specifically human destiny is it possible to know "retrospectively" the universality of the sin seen in the figure of Adam as representative of all

---

[162]Kaftan, 34f., aptly describes the way in which the consciousness of guilt "gradually" spreads from the misuse of freedom in particular actions "to embrace the entire life of the sinner," but he does not bring out the concept of responsibility herein implied.

human beings.[163] Only then is it possible or acceptable to judge that individuals share the guilt for their state. Only in this perspective—and therefore as confessional statements—are the formulas of dialectical theology about sin as "the total act of the human person"[164] justified. The Scholastic concept of the essence of sin as being a "lack of the righteousness that should be there" *(carentia iustitiae debitae)* is likewise to be understood in the perspective of the human destiny that has its ground in God and has been revealed in Christ. Thus while sin has an empirically verifiable universality and must be asserted as a universal presupposition for the Christian message of redemption, it also has a more hidden side. The opposition of sin to God, which is revealed first in the light of the law and then radically by the cross of Christ, is concealed in the immoderation of concupiscence; even the egoism which in its ultimate logic implies hatred of God is initially only implicit in concupiscence. Only in this obscure form is sin universal by empirical standards.

The universality of sin is discovered as such in the light of the revelation of human destiny by the law and by the crucified and risen Christ. The material situation thus brought to light can also, however, be shown to be universal at the empirical level, even if not under the name of sin. One pointer in this direction is the universal rule of death, while the content of this universal sin is to be seen in the universality of concupiscence as a characteristic of human behavior. Therefore the thesis of the radicalness and universality of sin, which is fundamental to the Christian dogma of original sin, does not need the supplementary hypothesis of "monogenism," that is, the descent of all human beings from a single first human pair who are also the authors of sin in the human race.[165]

Earlier in this book (pp. 57ff.), I described the traditional dogmatic teaching on the original state of Adam as the result of considering the human destiny to have been fulfilled in a mythical original situation. Moreover, the traditional teaching on the original state is not consistent

[163]Therefore Schleiermacher could say that original sinfulness can rightly be linked to guilt only "if the individual is the representative of the whole race" and if the guilt therefore attaches to "the totality of the whole race" (*The Christian Faith*, § 71, 2). The Council of Trent also teaches the element of guilt in original sin (DS 1513).

[164]Thus Brunner, *The Christian Doctrine of Creation and Redemption*, 93 and 110.

[165]As late as 1950 the encyclical *Humani generis* insisted on the necessity of this hypothesis in Catholic theology (DS 2897). But as a result, on the one hand, of the increasing acceptance of the theory of evolution as taught in the natural sciences and, on the other, of a critical historical understanding of Genesis 3 and Romans 5, doubts have arisen even in Catholic dogmatics as to whether this hypothesis is defensible. See the remarks of J. Feiner, "Man's Origin and Contemporary Anthropology," in J. Feiner et al., eds., *Theology Today*, vol. I: *Renewal in Dogma*, trans. P. White and R. H. Kelly (Milwaukee, 1965), 27–65, as well as the same writer's essay in *Mysterium Salutis* II (n. 99, above), 562–81, esp. 546ff., and Schoonenberg, ibid., 925f.

with the biblical story of paradise in key respects, for the story is interested in "explaining not the origin of universal *sinfulness* but the origin of the universal rule of *evil.*"[166] On the one hand, the universality of sin is empirically verifiable in concupiscence and its implications,[167] as Augustine realized, following Paul. On the other hand, it is recognized as guilt before God in the light of the human destiny revealed in Jesus Christ. The figure of Adam is simply a symbolic expression of this guilt. A historical descent of the human race from Adam as its historical ancestor (along the lines of monogenism) yields place here to the viewpoint of the unity of human destiny that is revealed in Jesus Christ and is reflected in the Adam of the Genesis saga only as in its antitype.[168]

Excursus: Sin and Death

According to Paul, the decisive proof of the universal spread of sin is the fact of death and its dominion over all life (Rom. 5:12). Paul adopted the outlook of Old Testament thought, according to which death is the natural consequence of sin. In Rom. 6:23 he calls it the "wages" which sin pays out to human beings because they have been in its service. It is quite evident that the connection Paul asserts here between sin and death causes difficulties for contemporary theologians. Is death, then, not a natural phenomenon? Everything that lives must die. Whereas until recently it was assumed that the living cell is not necessarily disposed to grow old and die, recent research makes the contrary plausible, even for these most primitive beginnings of life. As a matter of fact, at least pluricellular living things are doomed to die, even without any influence in this direction being exerted on them from outside. Is it possible that this state of affairs has anything to do with human sin? Death seems to accompany the *finitude* of life, and finitude cannot as such be called *sin.*

Contemporary theologians have thought that they must look to distinc-

---

[166]Thus Müller, II, 482. On this point, see also the still valid remarks in L. Köhler, *Old Testament Theology,* trans. A. S. Todd (Philadelphia, 1957), 175ff., esp. 175: "No question is posed or answered in the passage concerning the origin of sin or guilt."

[167]K. Rahner, "The Theological Concept of Concupiscentia," in his *Theological Investigations* I, trans. C. Ernst (Baltimore, 1961), 347–82.

[168]This approach also makes possible a new answer to the question of the significance of baptism in relation to original sin, a question on which there is disagreement among the confessions. The Reformers insisted that the concupiscence which remains in the baptized is truly sin, while the Council of Trent (DS 1515) asserted that baptism removes all that is sin in the proper sense of the term *(Tolli totum, quod veram et propriam peccati rationem habet).* We ought to allow the teaching of Augustine and the Reformers that concupiscence in itself is in fact sin. This does not prevent our acknowledging that through baptism this phenomenon is inserted into the new vital context of the human destiny revealed in Christ and is thereby also really changed.

tions for help in this area. They distinguish between a "natural" death that has nothing to do with sin and a death that results from a curse or judgment and represents a special intensification of natural death; only where the second kind of death is present does the first lead to separation from God.[169] Karl Rahner has developed this view in an especially profound way (1958). Following Heidegger, Rahner is of the opinion that because life comes to an end in death, it attains to its fulfillment through death. The only question, then, is whether in death there is an opening to God as there was in the death of Jesus, or whether on the contrary there is a closing of the self to God, so that the death is under the sign of sin. Rahner's view presupposes an idea taken from Heidegger, that human life attains to its fulfillment in death. But this presupposition seems dubious: death does not bring life to its fulfillment but terminates it and prevents its fulfillment.[170] This is why in the eyes of Christian faith the resurrection we hope for means a victory over death, which Paul calls the "last enemy" (1 Cor. 15:26), and not simply a revelation of what is already the real meaning of death itself.[171]

If death does not bring life to its fulfillment but terminates it, there is little reason to doubt the hostility to life that is the predominant characteristic of death in the Bible. As a result, especially in some of the psalms, the realm of death is described as the realm of separation from God, who is, for Israelite faith, the source of life: "Is thy steadfast love declared in the grave, or thy faithfulness in Abaddon?" (Ps. 88:11). The separation from God that is caused by the power of death does not mean that Yahweh's own power does not reach into the kingdom of the dead or that even there anyone can hide from him (Ps. 139:8; etc.). Nor does the fact

[169]On what follows, see my essay "Tod und Auferstehung in der Sicht christlicher Dogmatik" (1974), now reprinted in my *Grundfragen systematischer Theologie* II (1980), 146–59, esp. 151ff. The hypothesis of a "natural" death as distinct from a "death through judgment," with the Pauline statements on the connection between sin and death being then taken as referring only to the latter, is accepted especially by the following writers: Althaus, *Die letzten Dinge*, 87f.; idem, "Tod," *RGG*³ VI (1962), 918; Barth, *Church Dogmatics* III/2, trans. H. Knight et al. (1960), 587ff., esp. 629ff.; Tillich, *Systematic Theology* II 66ff.; K. Rahner, *On the Theology of Death*, trans. C. H. Henkey (Quaestiones Disputatae 2; New York, 1961), 43ff.; L. Boros, *The Mystery of Death*, trans. G. Bainbridge (New York, 1965); G. Schunack, *Das hermeneutische Problem des Todes im Horizont von Röm. 5 untersucht* (1967); E. Jüngel, *Death: The Riddle and the Mystery*, trans. I. and U. Nicol (Philadelphia, 1974).

[170]For detailed discussion, see my remarks in *Basic Questions in Theology*, trans. G. H. Kehm (2 vols.; Philadelphia, 1970, 1971), vol. I, and in my *Grundfragen systematischer Theologie* II, 146–59, esp. 151ff.

[171]Thus Rahner, with a noteworthy resemblance to Bultmann's proposition that the message of the resurrection of Jesus is a way of expressing the significance of the cross: Rahner, "Dogmatic Questions on Easter," in his *Theological Investigations* IV, trans. K. Smyth (Baltimore, 1966), 121ff.; Bultmann, "New Testament and Mythology," in K. Bartsch, ed., *Kerygma and Myth: A Theological Debate*, rev. trans. R. H. Fuller (New York, 1961), 38ff.

that in death human beings no longer have any relation to God[172] mean that conversely Yahweh's relation to his creatures must likewise come to an end in death.

The logic of the biblical view of death is based on the idea that life is due to the action of the divine spirit.[173] If life comes from God, then death, which is separation from life, is also, in the proper sense, a radical separation from God. According to H. W. Wolff, in the Old Testament the passage from life to death occurs "at the precise moment when the praise of God falls silent" (111). As a result, even uncleanness and illness separate human beings from life and hand them over to death. But, given this logic, sin in particular must have death for its natural consequence, inasmuch as the opposition to God contained in sin reaches its logical term in a complete separation from God that is sealed by death. Paul's thinking follows this same logic when he writes in Rom. 5:12 that like Adam all human beings have sinned and therefore die and when in Rom. 6:23 he calls death "the wages" which sin pays its servants.

Is it possible to maintain this conception of life and death even in the framework of contemporary views of life and especially of the human form of life? Only if it is, will it be possible to derive from the biblical characterization of death as the consequence of sin a meaning that can impose itself on our present-day understanding of life. We must not underestimate the difficulties to be faced in an elucidation of this question. The difficulties arise chiefly from the fact that biologists understand life to be a function of the living cell, whereas a religiously shaped understanding of life, such as finds expression in the biblical writings, believes the life of every living thing to depend on the operation of a transcendent and divine life-giving power. For the biblical writings, this power is the divine spirit or breath. The modern understanding of life as found in biology no longer assumes that life comes from God; therefore it is no longer obvious that separation from God has death as its natural consequence.

But is it at all possible to compare such different conceptions of life and death? In another context I have drawn upon Pierre Teilhard de Chardin and Paul Tillich in an effort to relate the biblical understanding of spirit

---

[172]See H. W. Wolff, *Anthropology of the Old Testament.* trans. M. Kohl (Philadelphia, 1974), 107ff. According to Wolff, the power of God even over death was the starting point in the Old Testament for belief in the conquest of death. On the other hand, Wolff restricts the negative judgment on death to *premature* death; he claims that this negative judgment does not apply to death in old age when human beings "die satisfied with life" (115). But the question must be asked whether remarks about the death of the patriarchs after a full life do not reflect the outlook of an earlier period according to which individuals were still closely linked to the clan as far as the meaning of their lives was concerned, and lived on in the clan.

[173]On this, see my *Grundfragen systematischer Theologie* II, 149ff.

and life to the understanding of life that has been shaped by modern scientific biology.[174] I shall not repeat or develop here the relationships that I sketched in that essay, since I must limit myself in this excursus to the subject of human death as the end of human life. For this purpose it will be enough to call attention to Tillich's important observations on the subject. It is true, of course, that Tillich acknowledged his acceptance of the doctrine of death as natural and could therefore insist that "sin is the sting of death, not its physical cause."[175] At the same time, however, he developed a set of concepts that connect sin and death much more closely than might have been expected in view of the statement just cited, and that enable us to relate biblical statements on the subject to the modern understanding of life and death.

According to Tillich, sin leads to the "self-destruction" of human beings (II, 58ff.). How are we to understand this statement? Sin consists in the individual's "estrangement from God in the center of his being" (48). In sin, therefore, "man is outside the divine center to which his own center essentially belongs." This is so because the sinner has become "the center of himself and of his world" (49). This is the *hubris* that makes human beings want to be like God (50). *Hubris* corresponds to the Augustinian concept of *amor sui. Hubris,* in which human beings *separate themselves* from God and make themselves the center of their world, has for its result that they are in contradiction to themselves, since their own center belongs *essentially* to the divine center (49). Thus the attempt of human beings to ground their self-centered existence in themselves by making themselves the center of their own world leads to the very opposite of the result intended, namely, to the loss of themselves and the failure of self-integration (61f.). Tillich has given a more detailed description of this process in the third volume of his *Systematic Theology* (1963) in connection with his treatment of life and its ambiguities. Whereas in the second volume he had used psychopathological phenomena to illustrate the disintegration of the self that results from estrangement (II, 61–62), he now describes all sickness as a disintegration of the organism's centeredness; this takes place as the specialized processes in the organism become independent (III, 34ff.), as can be seen especially in infections and cancers.

Tillich's interpretation of sickness as a dissolution of the self-integration that is constantly renewed moment by moment in a healthy life is confirmed by views that have emerged especially in psychosomatic medicine. Thus, according to V. von Weizsäcker, the "essence" of illness is

---

[174]See the essay "The Spirit of Life," in my *Faith and Reality,* trans. J. Maxwell (Philadelphia, 1977), 20–39.

[175]Tillich, *Systematic Theology* II, 67–68. The page references that follow in the text are to this book.

generally to be seen "in a kind of estrangement from oneself." "The common factor in all illnesses is therefore to be found in a departure from the right order of life."[176] The agreement with Tillich's viewpoint is not only noteworthy; it also substantiates the impression that Tillich's thought on this subject can explain more than Tillich himself thought it could. By its inner logic his thought clearly leads to the conclusion that physical death, which is the final outcome of the dissolution of the organism, is a consequence of sin and not simply that sin is the sting of death.[177]

Tillich simply suggests a connection between sin and death via the collapse of the self-integration proper to human life. The idea would have to be studied in detail and tested against empirical data of the most varied kinds, especially with a view to a phenomenology of the different kinds of sickness and death. The viewpoint of self-integration and its dissolution fits into the argument of the present book inasmuch as the image of God, conceived as the destiny of human beings, is to be understood as providing direction for the process of self-integration in the living of human life, while sin, being the failure to achieve this destiny, destroys human identity. The way in which the relation between sin and the destiny given by the image of God influences the process of identity formation will be studied further in the course of this book.

V. Sin and Wickedness

In the German title of one of his most successful books, Konrad Lorenz describes aggression as "evil, so called" (*Das sogenannte Böse*, 1963). The title intimates two things. First, it suggests that aggression is identical with what is generally regarded as evil. At the same time, however, it says that this judgment needs to be revised; aggression is not evil in an unqualified sense, but only evil "so called." The purpose of the book is to show that

[176]V. von Weizsäcker, *Der kranke Mensch. Eine Einführung in die medizinische Anthropologie* (1951), 330 and 368; see also 283 on the "nomotropy" of the organism.

[177]Tillich's observations on sin, sickness, and death suffer from a lack of terminological clarity, especially in his use of the concept of centeredness. On the one hand, human beings are said to be by nature (in their "essential" being) *fully centered* beings (II, 49, 62, etc.); on the other, it is said that only through sin does the individual become "the center of himself and of his world" (49). The context shows that Tillich's idea of the natural centeredness of human life might be more appropriately expressed in the concept of exocentricity or self-transcendence. Thus Tillich writes that the center of the human being belongs essentially to the divine center (II, 49) and that the human being has no environment but transcends every given environment in the direction of the world (62). Tillich's point is evidently that only from the divine center beyond themselves can human beings obtain the full self-integration of their lives. It is precisely this human destiny which is frustrated by the attempt to make the self the center of its world, because such an attempt leads to the disintegration of human life to the point where it is dissolved in death.

aggression with its instinctual roots originally had the preservation of the species for its purpose and was limited in its manifestations. According to Lorenz, aggression "is an instinct like any other and in natural conditions it helps just as much as any other to ensure the survival of the individual and the species." It is only the removal of aggression from the natural conditions for the life of the species that has let loose its "injurious effects" in human beings.[178]

Fundamental to Lorenz' interpretation of aggression is the hypothesis that it is an independent primitive instinct. This hypothesis, which is also accepted by many others,[179] is derived by Lorenz and other contemporary writers from Freud's theory of the death instinct, to which Lorenz expressly appeals for confirmation.[180] It was also Freud who identified aggression and evil. The human propensity to aggression caused Freud to judge "an untenable illusion" the supposition that human beings are by nature "wholly good."[181] This judgment was also the basis for Freud's critical attitude toward communism, since, according to the latter, it was only the "institution of private property" that corrupted human nature. According to Freud, the defect is much more deeply rooted in human nature. At the same time, however, human beings tend, according to Freud, to suppress from consciousness the ugly side of human nature that is manifested in aggression. This tendency provided Freud with an expla-

---

[178]K. Lorenz, *On Aggression,* trans. M. K. Wilson (New York, 1963), X and 56. Lorenz considers the functions of intraspecific aggression against fellow members of the species—functions originally aimed at the survival of the species—to be, first, the preservation of a balanced distribution of the species, as individuals dispute the boundaries of their territory, which is the primal form of property (30ff.); second, the function of effecting a selection through the struggle for a sexual partner (39ff.); and, third, the protection of the offspring (43), which increases the chances for survival of the posterity of the most powerful members of the species. All these functions are closely connected with the social hierarchy. Lorenz considers the dysfunctional development of the aggressive instinct in human beings to be the consequence of what he claims is a "self-domestication" of the human being. As a result of the formation of vast social systems which the individual's mind cannot comprehend and which demand peace on the part of the individual, the aggressive instinct has partly or even entirely lost its functions and therefore finds an outlet in harmful ways (236ff.). In addition, a highly developed weapons technology has led to the loss of the inhibiting mechanisms that in other circumstances would prevent aggressivity from gaining the upper hand.

[179]In addition to the Freudian school (e.g., A. Mitscherlich), mention should be made here of A. Gehlen, who in 1969 (*Moral und Hypermoral,* 42f.) limited his thesis on human openness to the world by acknowledging innate predispositions such as aggressiveness; but, unlike Lorenz, Gehlen does not see the destructive effects of these predispositions as resulting from a human "self-domestication." I. Eibl-Eibesfeldt, *Love and Hate: The Natural History of Behavior Patterns,* trans. G. Strachan (New York, 1974), has likewise modified the view of Lorenz, his teacher, by taking friendship and love of neighbor to be a principle originally opposed to aggressivity and having for its purpose to alleviate its effects.

[180]Lorenz, X.

[181]S. Freud, *Civilization and Its Discontents,* trans. J. Strachey (New York, 1961), 60.

nation not least of the rejection he encountered in his hypothesis of a death instinct of which aggression is "the derivative and main representative": "For 'little children do not like it' when there is talk of the inborn human inclination to 'badness,' to aggressiveness and destructiveness and so to cruelty as well."[182]

The closeness of Freud to the Christian doctrine of sin, a point emphasized by Tillich,[183] is made quite clear in the sentence just quoted. The same can be said of Freud's presentation of the opposition between the aggressive inclination to harm one's fellows and the commandment of love; in Freud's presentation, this opposition defines the evil aspect of aggression, which "forces civilization into such a high expenditure [of energy]." For "in consequence of this primary mutual hostility of human beings, civilized society is perpetually threatened with disintegration." And according to Freud, "the fateful question for the human species" is whether human beings will succeed "in mastering the disturbance of their communal life by the human instinct of aggression and self-destructiveness." Freud hoped they would with the help of "eternal eros."[184]

Freud was not the first to describe wickedness as an inclination to harm others. Schopenhauer had said of wickedness that, unlike simple egoism, it "seeks, quite disinterestedly, the hurt and suffering of others, without any advantage to itself."[185] On the other hand, tradition regards a pure destructiveness, a completely disinterested wickedness, to be humanly impossible. That is how Kant looked at the matter, and as a result he passed on the view that has been dominant in Christian tradition. Such extreme wickedness was conceived as being realized only in the idea of Satan. Yet even in this instance the destructiveness was regarded not as original but as derivative. This is probably connected with the fact that Christian theology did not conceive Satan as being a primordial power opposed to God's love, as part of a metaphysical dualism, but understood him rather as a fallen creature of God. According to Augustine, the root of Satan's wickedness was his inability to make himself God. The boundless self-love that put itself in place of God led, according to Augustine, to a hatred not only of God but of all that God had created. Destructive-

---

[182]Ibid., 68 and 67. Since 1915, Freud had assumed the existence of a death instinct that opposes the life instinct (see "Thoughts for the Times on War and Death," in his *Collected Papers* IV, trans. J. Riviere [New York, 1959], 288–317). H. Nolte, "Über Aggression," in Lepenies and H. Nolte, eds., *Kritik der Anthropologie* (1971), 103ff., esp. 105, calls attention to the temporal context in which Freud adopted this idea.

[183]Tillich, *Systematic Theology* II, 53.

[184]Freud (n. 181, above), 59 and 92.

[185]A. Schopenhauer, *The World as Will and Idea*, Book 4, 61, trans. R. B. Haldane and J. Kemp (3 vols.; London, 1883), I, 429.

ness was a consequence and manifestation, not the origin, of Satan's wickedness.

Much less, then, can there be any question, from the standpoint of Christian teaching, of a native human disposition to pure destructiveness.[186] Just as the sin even of Satan was only indirectly against God and led to hatred of God only as a consequence of unbridled egoism, so too the indirectness characteristic of human sin points to another break. As sensuous beings, humans are primarily turned toward the objects of their world. Their sin therefore primarily takes the form of greed for the possession and enjoyment of things that appear desirable to them. Only implicitly is an unlimited self-love operative as the ultimate impulse behind human concupiscence.

Human beings can, of course, burst out into blind destructiveness directed against everything that is detrimental to their self-love. But according to the Christian understanding of it, such destructive wickedness does not spring from a primordial instinct either in the case of human beings or in the case of any other creature. The Christian belief in creation rejects this kind of mythologizing exaggeration of evil in human beings into something primordially opposed to the divine goodness. Evil in human beings comes from their created nature, but it comes because they fail to achieve their destiny to be the images of God. Only in a broad sense of the term is this human weakness that manifests itself as sinfulness to be itself described as "evil"; it is evil only in view of its extreme consequences as seen in hatred of God and one's fellow human beings. This means, admittedly, that sin is evil even in its root, which is usually hidden from human beings themselves; and this fact is explicitly acknowledged in the confession of sins. But this wickedness does not always come to the surface in its manifestations, that is, in the behavior of human beings toward their fellows. If we limit the concept of evil, in the sense of moral evil, to the intention of harming others, then sin itself is not yet to be understood as (intentional) evil but rather as the root and origin of evil. Sin is then evil in its root, but it is not to be equated with moral evil. Only in the retrospective confession of their guilt do sinners recognize that sin's spearhead, which is hidden from them, is aimed from the outset at God: "Against thee, thee only, have I sinned" (Ps. 51:4).

How does sin as egoism and concupiscence turn into destructive wickedness? In describing the connection, Augustine made use of the very

---

[186]There is therefore no justification for reckoning the Christian "legend" of an "innate sinfulness" or original sin among the hypotheses of a native human instinct of aggressivity and savagery, as M. F. A. Montagu does in his essay "The New Litany of 'Innate Depravity,' or Original Sin Revisited," in idem, ed., *Man and Aggression* (New York, 1968), esp. 16.

ancient idea of envy, which goes back to Plato. Because of the pride that separated him from God, the angel Lucifer was seized by envy, and as a result enjoyed having others subject to his tyrannical arrogance instead of making himself subject to God. Because of envy, he could not bear having human beings remain innocent; therefore he led them astray.[187] Augustine's doctrine of sin may thus be adduced as evidence for Helmut Schoeck's thesis that envy is the "basic phenomenon" behind such forms of behavior as "aggression, hostility, conflict, frustration," and so on.[188]

But Augustine went back beyond envy itself and showed that it in turn originated in egoism and, more specifically, in frustrated egoism. At the same time, however, Augustine took a limited and one-sided view of the connection between egoism and aggression. The one-sidedness is due precisely to taking the concept of envy as the motive for aggression. For, on the one hand, the psychological link between egoism and the envy motive seems possible but not compelling. On the other, the envy motive does not explain the entire range of aggressive behavior. In particular, it does not take into account the aggression that is turned inward against the subject itself. In fact, the envy motive even blocks our vision of this inner-directed aggression, since one can envy only other people.

Augustine did indeed emphasize the helplessness of the envy born of Satan's egoism, insofar as this envy was directed against God, since God's enemies are incapable of harming him; their rebellion harms no one but themselves.[189] But this very thought, which is offered as an example of the seemingly paradoxical working of divine providence, shows how far Augustine was from the idea that the pride of sinners might lead even to the *intention* of harming themselves. Here we see once again that Augustine had not yet fully thought out the consequences of sin for the relation of human beings to themselves. As I pointed out earlier (p. 93), only in the modern age has sin been described in a consistent way as a distortion of human subjectivity. This development attained a previously unreached high point in Kierkegaard's analyses of dread and despair; it is here that the Christian concept of sin crosses paths with the development of modern research into aggression.

[187]Augustine, *De civ. Dei.* XIV, 11, 2: "But when the proud *and therefore envious* angel, whose pride turned him away from God and to himself, preferred, in a kind of tyrannical and scornful contempt, to have subjects rather than to be himself a subject, he fell from the spiritual paradise. . . . With criminal treacherousness he then sought to insinuate himself into the senses of the first man, whom he envied for standing when he himself had fallen. . . . He addressed the woman. . . ." On the destructive intention of Lucifer's behavior, see XI, 13, where the seduction of human beings is described as murder (i.e., of the soul).

[188]H. Schoeck, *Envy: A Theory of Social Behavior,* trans. M. Glenny and B. Ross (New York, 1970), 8; see 87ff., 116ff.

[189]Augustine, *De civ. Dei* XII, 3.

Since 1939, theories of aggression as a drive or instinct have been opposed by the frustration theory, which does not regard aggressive behavior as an expression of an independent instinct of aggression but connects it rather with the ego instincts.[190] Alfred Adler had pointed in this direction as early as 1908 with his essay "The Aggression Instinct in Life and in Neuroses," since he explained the instinct of aggression as an impulse that is in charge of all the particular instincts and "ensures the dynamism that carries behavior through to success."[191] But this reduction of aggression to the instinct of self-preservation and self-expansion (which is reminiscent, and probably not by chance, of Nietzsche's basic concept, the will to power[192]) cannot explain the peculiar ambivalence of aggressivity, which can be turned not only against others but also inward against the subject itself. Freud's hypothesis of a death instinct did account for this ambivalence. But when frustration is adopted as the basic standpoint, the ambivalence can also be understood in the light of the instinct of self-expansion. Aggressivity is no longer regarded here simply as an expression of a vital dynamism. "In the perspective of the instinct of self-expansion" aggressivity "reacts in a destructive way only in situations in which the acceptance of claims meets with resistance."[193]

The reduction of aggression to the instinct of self-preservation and self-expansion has frequently been accompanied by a tendency to excuse aggressive behavior and regard it as innocuous. The more one is inclined to grant individuals the right to an unlimited development of their natural tendencies, the more one will find aggressive behavior to be understandable and even justified, since it is simply an expression of the reaction against a restriction and impairment of this natural striving for self-assertion and self-expansion. The questionable aspect of such views emerges with special clarity in their application to penal law and the infliction of punishment, but also to the task of education, when the plea is made for a wide acceptance and even encouragement of aggressive behavior by children as a means of strengthening their egos. It is true that the still weak ego which is now being formed needs strengthening and encouragement, but the assumption that the toleration and even encouragement of aggressive behavior should be part of the process is a questionable one.

It has turned out that a permissive type of education is particularly conducive to the further development of aggressive behavior. This must seem paradoxical to those who regard aggressivity (or at least its destruc-

---

[190]J. Dollard, R. S. Sears et al., *Frustration and Aggression* (New Haven, 1939).

[191]Nolte (n. 182, above), 118.

[192]In Nietzsche, as opposed to later simplistic popularizations of his thought, the concept of the will to power contains a phase of self-conquest and therefore self-transcendence and does not mean simply self-assertion.

[193]Nolte, 115.

tive expression) as simply the result of frustration. Given such a presupposition, the avoidance of any constraints on the striving for self-assertion should in fact lead to the disappearance of destructive aggressivity. But the psychology of learning has shown that, contrary to the frustration theory, destructively oriented aggressivity does not spring solely from frustration. Wherever aggressive behavior is tolerated or even rewarded, it spurs imitation. This insight from the psychology of learning explains the failure of permissive education as far as the avoidance of destructive aggressivity is concerned; at the same time it tells us that other factors besides the frustration of the ego instincts must be at work in destructive aggressivity. On the other hand, it has been shown that the suppression of aggressivity by means of social sanctions need not lead to a "damming up of aggressivity" which must then be violently released in one manner or another. It is, rather, the case that pedagogical and social sanctions can help the individual to achieve self-development through self-conquest. In this process the individual evidently needs the support that the community gives or should give.

This last consideration brings us back to the question of the anthropological foundations of the frustration hypothesis. According to H. Nolte, the promotion of the capacity for aggression "assists the successful development of self-preservation and self-realization as accomplishments connected with individuation." On the other hand, "when there is external resistance" these same energies are "given a destructive direction in accordance with innate patterns of reaction that have a physiological basis"; "in the last resort" they will be turned "back upon the person."[194]

The development of the ego seems to be conceived, in this view, as a development, with as little interruption as possible, of initially given dispositions. Freud's theory of ego formation, on the other hand, emphasized the necessity of a failure of the initial narcissistic self-centeredness with its "wishes for omnipotence." In the process of ego development the initial ego which is the object of wishes must be overcome so that the real ego may be formed. In this view, allowance is made for the need of self-conquest in the process of self-becoming. The frustration hypothesis, on the other hand, with its call for the unhampered development of all original dispositions readily ignores the question of whether many of our innate dispositions ought perhaps not to be developed at all. The hypothesis seems so convinced of the goodness of human nature in its original state that any opposition from society is viewed as an infringement upon the integrity of the individual's development. This psychology is naïve in regard to the fallibility and actual brokenness of the human striving for

---

[194]Ibid., 131.

self-realization. Primary responsibility for defective development is assigned to external opposition that constricts self-development rather than
to a tendency within the ego itself that causes an unsuccessful self-development. No heed is paid to the ambiguity of the striving for self-development, which may mean either self-conquest or a mere persistence of the
ego in the securing of the acceptance of its claims.

Such objections do not, of course, justify us in rejecting without qualification the interpretation of aggressive behavior as being linked to frustra-
tions of the ego instincts. An interpretation of aggression that drew solely
upon the psychology of learning would be even more superficial than the
frustration theory in accounting for the anthropological roots of aggressive behavior, and a return to the instinct theory of aggression would
sacrifice the most important advance made in the frustration theory,
namely, the linking of the analysis of aggression with the problems of ego
development. The criticism I have been offering should lead not to an
abandonment of the frustration hypothesis but to an expansion and
nuanced deepening of it, and this specifically in regard to its foundations
in ego psychology.

In particular, the introduction of the phenomenon of anxiety into the
psychological discussion of aggression leads in that direction. In this context, attention must of course be paid not only to the anxiety that is a result
of aggression[195] but also and above all to the universally present existential anxiety that precedes any actual aggression and takes the form of a
vague realization of the vulnerability of one's own existence and of the
threats to it. In fact, it is only thus that the anxiety aroused by experiences
of frustration becomes understandable, since such experiences are cal-
culated to intensify the primordial existential anxiety. This may lead to
aggressive behavior, but it may just as well make the person choose flight
and depression.[196] Yet even aggressive behavior that is not the result of
frustration can always be explained as having a connection with anxiety.
Thus anxiety about one's ability to achieve recognition by the group may
be an essential factor in the imitation of examples of aggressivity, while
at the same time the overreactions of anxiety in the form of violations of

---

[195]Thus R. Denker (n. 39, above), 89; see 37. Denker's restrictive use of the concept of
anxiety or dread seems to be connected with his neglect of Kierkegaard's distinction between
an unfocused general dread and a fear related to a concrete object (28). Denker's argument
that fear is inseparable from anxiety is correct. The object that threatens danger always
focuses the primordial existential anxiety in one way or another. But this does not disprove
the point that anxiety, on the other hand, always precedes such a relation to a particular
object. For there is a such a thing as anxiety that is unaccompanied by any fear of a
threatening object, whereas fear is always accompanied by anxiety.

[196]Denker has shown this, 30ff.

taboos in defense of group solidarity can lead to ostentatious self-display.[197] Anxiety may be taken as a universal condition for aggressive behavior, even though the passage from anxiety to aggression depends on other conditions as well.

The introduction of anxiety into the description of the motives for aggressive behavior can also contribute to a nuanced understanding of the anthropological bases of the frustration hypothesis. In anxiety the ego experiences itself as involved not only in the process of developing innate dispositions but also in the process of becoming an ego; this second process is concerned with selfhood as such, and for the sake of the attainment of this selfhood it can demand a self-conquest and sublimation of the ego. On the other hand, however, as a result of anxiety the ego may be thrown back upon itself in such a way that—to use Kierkegaard's language—it clings to its own finiteness and thereby loses itself. This clinging and loss may find expression both in aggression and in depression. In both cases, there is a failure of self-conquest and therefore of access to the formation and preservation of an independent real ego.

While anxiety is the basic form in which sin manifests itself in human self-consciousness, both (destructive) aggression and flight depression are also to be seen as expressions of human sinfulness. Human decisions regarding action are preconditioned by these dispositions or sentiments. Must not this realization itself have a depressing effect in view of the universal presence of anxiety in all the activities of human life? This brings us to the question of whether the Christian doctrine of sin is not itself an expression of aggression in the form of aggression against the self.

It can hardly be denied that features of aggression against the self have played a part in the history of Christian teaching on sin. This is especially true of the stigma put on sexuality in the Augustinian doctrine of the transmission of sin. Only when the motivational level of aggression against the self is removed (by removing the supplementary hypothesis regarding the transmission of sin from the description of the essence or disorder of sin) does the traditional doctrine of sin, which was so profoundly influenced by Augustine, reveal that deepest level which is to be regarded as the root of aggression: I mean the anxiety experienced by the self-centered ego. Admittedly, in the teaching on original sin this sinfulness that structures human behavior has frequently not been carefully distinguished from views on the more limited problem of the transmission of sin. As a result, it is understandable that the whole complex of ideas on

---

[197]Denker's thesis (57f.) that anxiety can be at the bottom even in the cases, described in the psychology of learning, of direct imitation of aggressive behavior without any intervening frustration, presupposes that the process of identity formation is permeated by anxiety in the sense of the universal human anxiety about the individual's capacity for existence.

sin and guilt could be interpreted as an expression of aggression against the self.

That is precisely the interpretation we find in Nietzsche's criticism of the Christian doctrine of sin. Of course, his criticism embraces substantially more than this point. In his view, bad conscience is "the serious illness that man was bound to contract under the stress of the most fundamental change he ever experienced—that change which occurred when he found himself finally enclosed within the walls of society and of peace." In what does the illness consist, according to Nietzsche? "All instincts that do not discharge themselves outwardly *turn inward*. . . . Hostility, cruelty, joy in persecuting, in attacking, in change, in destruction—all of this turned against the possessors of such instincts: *that* is the origin of the 'bad conscience.' "[198] Decades later, Alfred Adler and Sigmund Freud gave an analogous explanation of the genesis of conscience from aggression against the self.

In his *On the Genealogy of Morals* (1887), Nietzsche likewise anticipated the derivation of the idea of God from *"fear* of the ancestor and his power" and from "the consciousness of indebtedness to him,"[199] a thesis put forth by Freud twenty-five years later in his *Totem and Taboo* (1912). And just as, on the one hand, Nietzsche saw belief in God as originating in the aggression against the self that is manifested in the feeling of guilt, so, on the other hand, he assumed that, conversely, belief in God intensifies the feeling of guilt. "The advent of the Christian God, as the maximum god attained thus far, was therefore accompanied by the maximum feeling of guilty indebtedness on earth."[200] For Nietzsche, then, not only the phenomenon of the judging conscience and the idea of guilt incurred in relation to God but, in close connection with these two, even the idea of God itself, culminating in the Christian belief in God, was to be explained as a product of aggression that had turned inward. This is why he could think of atheism as promising liberation from the burden of guilt feelings.

Nietzsche's "hypothesis" that "bad conscience," the idea of God, and the idea of "indebtedness to God" all originate in an "illness" in the original "animal soul" of human beings does, of course, have one presupposition. It is that the original animal situation in which human history had its start was a state of health and integrity. Here, to our surprise, we find

---

[198]F. Nietzsche, *On the Genealogy of Morals,* Essay II, no. 16, trans. W. Kaufmann (New York, 1967), 84–85. Oddly enough, L. Kofler, *Aggression und Gewissen* (Munich, 1973), opposes conscience as "regulative of relations between individuals" (57; see 66) to the propensity to aggression, but says nothing about Nietzsche's (and Freud's) derivation of ("bad") conscience itself from aggression that has turned inward.

[199]Nietzsche, II, 19 (Kaufmann, 89).

[200]Ibid., II, 20 (Kaufmann, 90).

remnants in Nietzsche of a theological doctrine of the original state, although in a secularized form. But it is neither empirically demonstrable nor probable that human history began with a state of health and psychic identity on the part of human beings. Once this presupposition is eliminated, then "bad conscience" continues indeed to point to a nonidentity of human beings, but this nonidentity is no longer to be interpreted as a loss of an original identity.

On the contrary, the consciousness of nonidentity is more readily to be understood as pointing to the knowledge of a human identity not yet attained. "Bad conscience" then becomes the reverse side of the fact that from early in their history human beings have projected images of themselves that reach boldly beyond their de facto present condition. And the history of religious experience of the divine power is then to be understood as the history of experiences whereby human beings are encouraged to strive for this kind of self-transcendence and as the history of a journey to freedom rather than, as in Nietzsche, the history of an illness and a loss of a supposed original harmony of human beings with themselves. The consciousness of guilt then gives expression to the fact that human beings are not identical with the idea of their destiny, and the concept of sin describes this condition in the form of anthropological reflection. The consciousness of this nonidentity is then seen not as the product of aggression against the self but as the realistic reverse side of the consciousness of their destiny which human beings acquire in the act of religious self-transcendence. Consequently, the experience of religious liberation and the elevation of human beings above what they already are to a higher view of their existence are necessarily accompanied by a consciousness of the distance still natively separating them from this divine destiny. At the same time, their consciousness that this destiny is really theirs justifies their acceptance of responsibility for the fact that their existence and behavior are still far removed from this goal; it justifies, in other words, a consciousness of obligation with reference to what ought to be.

If we understand the doctrine of sin as functioning in the context of a still unfinished process which has human identity as its goal, we will not misinterpret this doctrine as a product of aggression turned inward. The consciousness of the failure of the self—that is, of sin—is a necessary phase in the process whereby human beings are liberated to become themselves. This consciousness breaks the spell exercised by the distorted view that personal identity is unattainable; at the same time, it lends human beings the strength to accept their own reality with the consciousness that they are responsible for themselves, and to do so in an act of repentance which makes it possible for them to identify themselves with that in them which they must judge to be incompatible with their selfhood. The consciousness of guilt and failure is indeed easily linked to elements of aggression against the self, so that it becomes distorted. It is only a step from realization of one's nonidentity to hatred of oneself.

Too little heed has been paid to these connections in the traditional Augustinian teaching on sin. Otherwise Augustine himself would surely have been more on guard against the influence of motives for self-aggression in his own teaching on sin. It is a fact, of course, that he explicitly rejected as sinful the extreme form of self-aggression, which is suicide. But the reasons he gives—that suicide is a form of murder; that (as in the case of Judas) suicide expresses a despair of divine mercy; and that the suicide allows himself no chance to repent[201]—do not connect suicide with the psychological analysis of sin as egoism and concupiscence. And yet the connection between pride and aggression against the self is an obvious one. The proud cannot easily tolerate the awareness of their own nonidentity and existential failure. The inclination of the proud to identify their own existence with the perfect attainment of their destiny and to ignore the difference made by their own imperfection facilitates the passage from consciousness of nonidentity to self-hatred. This shows that aggression against the self is just as much an expression of sin as is aggression against others. The point of departure in both cases is the consciousness of being God's equal; the proud take pleasure in pluming themselves on this, and they take offense at any infringement upon it.

It is important for us to become more clearly aware of the ambivalence in the consciousness of sin and in the doctrine of sin even in the history of Christianity; it is important especially for the preacher and the pastor. Even the consciousness that human beings have of their own nonidentity can become an expression and instrument of distortion and self-failure, and Christian preaching on sin, as well as the Christian doctrine of sin, can unwittingly help in this process or even become an exercise ground for aggressive feelings. Preaching and teaching on sin are protected against that kind of perversion only if they limit themselves strictly to fulfilling their function in the formation of human identity, where they serve as factors in the process of human liberation.

[201]Augustine, *De civ. Dei* I, 17.

Part Two
THE HUMAN PERSON AS A SOCIAL BEING

4

Subjectivity and Society

I. Self-Consciousness and Sociality

The question of self-consciousness arose in the previous chapter. Self-consciousness appeared there, however, not in the perspective of identity —that is, as the place where ego and self are identified—but in the perspective of the nonidentity that marks the relation of human beings to themselves. The discussion of this point ranged from Helmuth Plessner's observations regarding a brokenness—which reveals itself in self-consciousness as such—in the relation of human beings to their own corporeality, all the way to the Christian teaching on sin, according to which in an offense against God there is always the question as well of the relation that human beings have to themselves and of a failure of the self. In those reflections self-consciousness was not yet thematized as such; rather, it appeared simply as evidence of brokenness, as the place where human nonidentity comes into view. As soon as self-consciousness becomes directly thematic, the aspect of identity that it contains becomes unavoidable. In fact, the very knowledge of nonidentity, insofar as it is a nonidentity with the person's "own" being, is always accompanied by a knowledge of identity, even if this is known as also distorted by nonidentity.

It may be, however, that nonidentity is the primary way in which self-consciousness manifests itself as it develops. If so, then to take the aspect of nonidentity as the starting point for reflection is to align such reflection with the genesis of self-consciousness, and this both in the individual and in the history of culture.[1] In the next chapter I shall explain in detail how nonidentity is indeed the starting point in the genesis of individual self-consciousness. That the same is true in the history of culture is suggested by a point whose significance for the history of the concept of self-consciousness, at least in our cultural tradition, is far too little appreciated, namely, that the fact of self-consciousness first emerges into

[1]This point has just been made on pp. 151ff. in connection with Nietzsche and Freud.

awareness, or at least is first articulated in speech, in the *synoida emautō* ("I am conscious to myself").[2] This is the experience that not only in someone else but in my very self I have a confidant of my thoughts and actions. Moreover, this experience is, not indeed exclusively but certainly preeminently, one of being criticized or even accused.[3]

In the method followed in the present book, reflection on this state of affairs has taken a more abstract form. The analysis of the basic form of human behavior as a being "present to the other *as* other" led us back to the otherness, therein revealed, of the behaving entity itself, which knows that it is *not* the other. That this consciousness itself is socially mediated is shown by the fact that the *synoida emautō* originates in the knowledge that others have of me in my social context. When the matter under discussion is the genesis of self-consciousness, the *being-present* to things should not be viewed in isolation but must be taken with its social reference. This insight finds expression in Hegel's *Phenomenology of Spirit,* since the development of self-consciousness that begins with the struggle for recognition between master and slave must be understood as a description of its concrete development, while the previous general characterization of this stage in the experience of consciousness is simply an abstract advance summary of the history of its formation.

In modern psychology, the significance of the social environment for the genesis of self-consciousness has been increasingly recognized ever since William James proposed his concept of the social self.[4] This has been due, on the one hand, to the influence of the ego psychology of Freud and his school[5] and, on the other, to the added influence of the social psychol-

---

[2]See O. Seel, "Zur Vorgeschichte des Gewissensbegriffes im altgriechischen Denken," in *Festschrift für F. Dornseiff* (1953), 291–319. The Stoic enlargement of *syneidēsis* into the *hēgemonikon* ("ruling principle") of the soul already gives expression to an age-old theory of self-consciousness.

[3]Thus H. Reiner in *HWP* 3 (1974), 576, especially on the first appearance of the substantive, *syneidēsis,* in Democritus (Frag. B 297), while Chr. Maurer in *TDNT* 8: 898, emphasizes the possibility of a morally neutral use of the term. But in the tragedians and Socrates (as Maurer himself shows), the negative, moral emphasis is already to the fore (895ff.). This is quite understandable in view of the witness function of this tribunal, though the same function also permits a morally neutral meaning for the word. In any case, there is the question here of an authority "within" me, although there is as yet no reflection on its identity with "myself."

[4]W. James, *The Principles of Psychology* (1890; repr. in 2 vols., New York, 1950), I, 293ff. These considerations acquire their specific meaning in the framework of James's conception of human self-becoming as taking place in a passage from "nature" to "society"; the idea of society eliminates the idealist concept of the objective self. See E. Herms, *Radical Empiricism. Studien zur Psychologie, Metaphysik und Religionstheorie William James'* (Gütersloh, 1977), 26ff., 35f.

[5]On this, see for the time being D. Wyss's survey, *Die tiefenpsychologischen Schulen von den Anfängen bis zur Gegenwart* (1961). In 1956, H. Hartmann, who played a leading part in the

ogy of G. H. Mead, who further developed James's concept of the social self.[6] This social reference underlies the experience of nonidentity as well as the process of individual identity formation in which that experience is transcended. But the social reference could not explain the genesis of self-consciousness were it not that a being "present to the other *as* other" were presupposed as a universal basic structure of human behavior. This basic form of human behavior implies the distinction of this (material or personal) other not only from still other objects but also from my "self." In a further step, the question then arises of the relation between my being present to the other and my being in myself. The concrete explicitation of these relations that are implicit in the structure of human behavior takes place, of course, in the context of social life.

In the transition to the theme of the individual's self-consciousness in its social context, behavioral research and its methodology are not simply abandoned and replaced by a psychology of consciousness or even a psychology that penetrates behind consciousness or a social psychology. Behavioral research deals with behaving—that is, "self"-comporting—individuals and therefore with "subjects" in their entirety. At the level of the human mode of life this subjectivity shows itself in the tension between centrality and exocentricity, which is the structural condition for the appearance of self-consciousness. To that extent the appearance of self-consciousness corresponds fully to the peculiarities that characterize the bodily behavior of the living human being. At this point, then, the approach taken in behavioral research leads without any break into the thematization of self-consciousness.

In fact, behavioral research even provides the reason for taking this step. For at the level of human behavior the subjective unity of the "self"-comporting living entity is not simply given in advance but is, rather, acquired only in the very process of human behavior itself. This process is one of identity formation, the result of which at any given moment is the form taken by self-consciousness at that moment. Unless behavioral research assessed the function of self-consciousness for the human form of life, it could not fulfill its task of describing the externally observable behavior of human beings as a self-comporting. For the special contribution of self-consciousness to human behavior in its entirety is to be seen in the fact that in it the otherwise unfulfilled task of unifying centrality and exocentricity and thus at the same time achieving selfhood becomes thematic for human beings themselves and takes shape as an act of their

development of psychoanalysis into ego psychology, described "The Development of the Ego Concept in Freud's Work." This paper is now available in a collection of Hartmann's essays, *Essays on Ego Psychology: Selected Problems in Psychoanalytic Theory* (New York, 1964), 268–96.

[6]G. H. Mead, *Mind, Self and Society,* ed. C. W. Morris (Chicago, 1934), esp. 135–226.

freedom. It is true that the tension between centralized organization and exocentric destiny is initially and recurrently resolved in a one-sided way to the advantage of centrality and therefore in a form biased in favor of the ego, so that the tension constantly rises anew and the theme of human identity makes its presence known primarily in the form of care and anxiety. Nonetheless human self-consciousness remains the place where the struggle for identity must be carried on. We will have to inquire into the role played in this process by the social context in which individuals live their lives. Is the social world perhaps the place where their exocentric destiny is achieved and therefore also the place where their identity as subjects and persons is established?

In the considerations offered in the first part of this book I prescinded from the fact that the existence of human individuals is determined by social relations. My subject there was the peculiarity of the human form of life as compared with that of the animals closely related to humanity. For this reason, even though concrete, socially differentiated behavior also provides material for that kind of investigation, I had to proceed as though the human as such finds expression in every individual no matter whom and therefore in every individual taken in isolation. This methodological abstraction was required in order to work out the main structural features of the human form of existence with its centrality and exocentricity. These features must now be incorporated into an understanding of the social context of human behavior. To this end the methodological abstraction just mentioned will be set aside.

The social relations of individuals can be thematized even at the level of biological theory, to the extent that biology deals not only with morphology but also with the theory of evolution. Behavioral research and genetics play a mediating role here. As a matter of fact, the behavior of the individual always has social referents, even though the attention of the student may be focused on the peculiarities of the individual's behavior. To the extent that genetic research presupposes sexual differentiation, it too implies social relations between individuals, although it need not pay any special attention to these.

This is the reason why, not long ago, a "new synthesis" called sociobiology could combine the seemingly widely divergent approaches of behavioral research and genetics in the form of an expanded theory of evolution.[7] The behavior of individuals, which cannot in every case be explained from the standpoint of the struggle for individual survival, is here traced back to an interest in the diffusion of the individual's genes, even if through the medium of other individuals. E. O. Wilson and other sociobiologists find in this the key to an understanding of "altruistic"

[7] E. O. Wilson, *Sociobiology: The New Synthesis* (Cambridge, Mass., 1975).

behavior even in human beings, and they think that in this way they can reduce human ethics, along with the bases of cultural formation, to biology.[8]

The cultural anthropologists objected strongly to this view of things.[9] In this approach, they claimed, individual behavior is interpreted on the model of a capitalistic maximization of profit, the capital in this case being the genes; the propagation of the genes becomes the dominant consideration, and the individual is subordinated to this. In addition to such ideologically inspired criticism, there is, above all, the convincing argument that the various kinship systems and familial communities, to which the loyalty of individuals is primarily given at the human level, are already products of human cultural activity and in many cases do not fit in with the biological criterion of the maximal propagation of genes.[10]

This fact is enough to invalidate a reduction of cultural systems of human behavior to the explanatory principles of sociobiology. This means that a new type of approach is needed in dealing with the transition from prehuman evolution to human history with its phenomenon of culture. "Culture is biology plus the symbolic faculty."[11] We must come back to this point later on. For the moment, it follows that the investigation of human social relations must operate at a new level of categories, distinct from those of general zoology, inasmuch as ever since the rise of human culture out of the spirit of religion human social relations have always been carried on in the framework of cultural systems and the changes these undergo. Only a biological theory of evolution that accepted the perspective of the activity of the divine spirit in all living things could trace the evolution of life on into human cultural history without being compelled to pass to a new methodological level at the threshold where humanity as such begins its development.

None of this is to deny that even a study that is biological in a restrictive sense can reach the conclusion that human beings are not simply individuals with social relations in the same sense as the other animals but are social beings in a sense specific to them. This point of view is implicit in Arnold Gehlen's statement that human beings are by nature cultural beings.[12] His point is that human beings are oriented and disposed to culture just as other animals are to an environment peculiar to their species. Moreover, he means from the outset that human beings are disposed to *create* culture and that culture therefore originates in the peculiar character of human

---

[8]Ibid., 562ff.; see 551ff.

[9]M. Sahlins, *The Use and Abuse of Biology: An Anthropological Critique of Sociobiology* (Ann Arbor, 1976).

[10]Ibid., 17–67.

[11]Ibid., 65.

[12]A. Gehlen, *Der Mensch* (1950), 86; see earlier, 39f.

beings as beings who act. For the moment, however, there is the question simply of an orientation to social relations which are always institutionalized in the form of a cultural world. The question of the constitution of the social world as a cultural world may provisionally be left open.

Adolf Portmann has shown himself reserved on this last point, but he has laid all the greater emphasis on the importance of social relations for the development of the human individual. The fact, mentioned in chapter 1, that the human being, unlike the other animals, is "physiologically premature" at birth shows, according to Portmann, "to what extent" the specifically human "qualities of behavior, speech and mode of action," which develop in the first year of life, "are from the outset phenomena that have a social imprint, and how from the very beginning they are influenced in their formation by the fact of social contact."[13] The incomplete state of human beings as "physiologically" premature beings is connected in particular with the fact that unlike all the other higher mammals the human child at birth reminds us of those birds which are "insessorial" and need a somewhat lengthy rearing before they are "fledged," that is, before they have fully developed the modes of behavior peculiar to their species. Similarly, "a series of ontogenetic idiosyncrasies" of human beings "can be properly understood only in the context of the way in which they are formed to social behavior."[14]

In contrast to a naturalistic reduction of human social behavior in terms of a maximal propagation of genes, the specifically human orientation to a social world points to what is qualitatively new in the human process of culture formation, a process that is able to integrate the biological conditioning factors in an entirely new and different way. On the other hand, the specifically social orientation of the human individual also motivates a skepticism with regard to theses that would have human beings be at the same time the creators of their cultural world. The concept of action always presupposes a subject already completely formed. But human individuals in the incomplete state proper to the newborn are not able to be acting subjects; they acquire this ability only through the process of ego development and self-becoming. This point has been emphasized in connection with Herder's idea of a developing image of God (see above, p. 60.).

In this second part of my study, therefore, I must describe in greater detail the process of the development of the ego or subjectivity as this takes place in the field of social relations. In so doing, I shall not only go farther into the question of individual identity but also provide the starting point for the presentation, in the third part of the book, of the social world

[13]A. Portmann, *Zoologie und das neue Bild des Menschen* (rde 20, 1956), 76.
[14]Ibid., 109.

as the basis of individual identity. Clarity on the structural foundations and theologically relevant implications of cultural anthropology cannot be achieved unless the question of the identity of individuals is first cleared up in at least a provisional way. This involves the problem of the relation between the establishment of individual identity and the establishment of the cultural world. The conclusion that this relation is like that between chicken and egg is indeed correct, but it also remains vague and superficial and is likely to conceal the religious implications both of individual identity formation and of the cultural world in which human life is lived. It seems obvious to cultural anthropologists that in the final analysis human beings have created the system that makes up their cultural world, but social psychologists also regard as evident the thesis that the identity of individuals is the product of their social and cultural environments. As a result, each of these disciplines saddles the other with responsibility for answering the basic anthropological question.

Any clarification of this complicated state of affairs must start with a sociopsychological investigation of individual identity formation. For, while this formation presupposes the existence of a cultural world, this presupposition itself can be left provisionally vague in general social psychology, without the specific thematic of this discipline becoming blurred on that account. The theory of culture, on the other hand, cannot attain to clarity on its own object without a precise description of how individual identity is established.

Just as, therefore, at this point in my discussion of anthropology an attempt to explain the presupposition for the description of human behavior, namely, the concept of the human subject and its identity, obliges me to rescind the provisional abstraction from the social dimension of human life, so in the third part of the book the restriction of attention to individual behavior with its abstraction from the cultural system as such will have to be set aside in the course of a further thematization of the foundations of individual identity. Conversely, the preceding reflection on the biological uniqueness of human behavior will prove fruitful for the discussion of the sociopsychological problems of identity. The result will also be the subsequent justification of the procedure followed here of defining the special place of human beings in the animal world, first while bracketing the social dimension of human life and then with this bracketing removed. In an analogous manner, the discussion of the themes of individual identity will prove fruitful for a more exact grasp of the concept of culture. Finally, a similar problematic will make its appearance once more in the transition to the concrete historicity of human life. It is a fact, of course, that sociologists frequently take the historicity of human life into account, somewhat as biologists may introduce into their reflections as biologists the social relations attaching to the behavior not only of individuals but of whole populations. But the history of humanity with its nonrecurring course is not reducible to the universal structures of social relations and to a sociological study of the modifications of these structures.

It is now clear that as I carry my presentation farther I will not simply be leaving behind the material elaborated in the first part but will be going into it more deeply. I shall be continuing to deal with the tension between centrality and exocentricity in human behavior, a tension wherein still another tension has revealed itself: the tension between the destiny of human beings to be images of God and the egocentricity that marks the living of their empirical lives. This latter tension will make its appearance in the process of *identity formation* as a tension in the relation between ego and self and as a source of disturbance in the realm of moods and affects; finally, it will form the field of reference for interpreting the *problems of alienation.* Only in the third part will the social world be discussed in its own right. Then, too, *language* and *reason* as the factors that give life to the supraindividual structures of meaning that are proper to the cultural world will be discussed for the first time, even though, of course, it is impossible, apart from language and reason, to conceive either the social nature of human beings and the stages of human identity formation or the special place of human beings in the world of nature.

As part of the further discussion and exploration of what was said in chapter 3 about the tension between exocentricity and self-centeredness in human behavior I turn in the present chapter to the determination of the ego itself by the community or, as the case may be, by the persons who serve as points of reference for individuals in their development. The I, or ego, does not simply stand as an independent entity over against the Thou or against the broader social context of its life, a context that for individuals is represented by the persons in proximate relation to them. Rather, the ego proves to be dependent on its social context for the determination of its identity. Therefore the question raised at the beginning of this section must be faced: Is human exocentricity perhaps to be defined as sociality? Do human beings perhaps live outside themselves, *extra se,* to the extent that they live by participating in the enveloping context of their social and cultural world with its traditions?

The question is not meant to imply, however, that individuals might disappear completely into the function they exercise in the life of a society whose collective understanding of reality would allow individual lives no independent and inviolable worth. The determination of the relation between individual and society, which is presupposed by the question of the individual's identity, is the result of a specific historicocultural development that has produced a consciousness of the special dignity of the individual within the social world and makes this dignity a criterion for judging the order of society.

The question of individual identity can nonetheless claim to be a universally valid one, even though in modern Western society, as in hardly any other culture, this identity has become so much of an open question, even for individuals themselves. In other cultures this question seems to be concealed from individuals to a far greater extent by the answers given in their cultural traditions, which assign individuals their place in the life of society. But the possibility of such an interpretation of the data in other and especially in archaic cultures justifies the assertion that the theme of individual identity may claim universal anthropological validity even though it is not expressly posed in all cultures. There is need, nonetheless, of a preliminary understanding of the historicocultural process whereby the relation of individual to society became explicitly thematized; only then, in section III, will I be in a position to discuss how the individual emerges from the relation to the other, the I from the relation to the Thou.

II. The Independence of the Individual in Society

1. The Way to the Independence of the Individual

In archaic societies "the relation of individual and society was not thematized as such, nor therefore did it become a problem."[15] To the peoples of the archaic world, society seemed to be "part of a cosmic order," in relation to which individuals enjoyed no independence. Rather, they "lived 'unreflectingly' in society" (169) and, more specifically, in a wide-branched kinship system within which the place of the individual and the rights and duties associated with this place were exactly determined. In the early high cultures, however, with their greater spatial extension, their advanced division of labor, and their much more prominent polarization in the hierarchy of power, the integration of the individual into the "cosmic order" to which the society belonged had already become thematic. But we must surely agree with Thomas Luckmann's opinion that even here there was not as yet "a general crisis in the relation of the individual to society" (171).

Luckmann believes that no such crisis arose before the beginning of the modern age in the West. Here for the first time, in his opinion, there was a break in the relation of the individual to society as a result of the "value neutrality" of modern social structures; this neutrality reflects the fact that " 'private' interpretations of reality are chosen with an abitrariness only inadequately captured in the idea of cultural pluralism" (174).

---

[15]T. Luckmann, "Zwänge und Freiheiten im Wandel der Gesellschaftsstruktur," in *Sozial-anthropologie.* Neue Anthropologie 3 (1972), 168–98 at 168. The page references that follow in the text are to this essay.

Luckmann rightly sees this as "something fundamentally new" by comparison with not only primitive societies but also the early high cultures. But in his argument he makes somewhat too long a jump from the high cultures of the fourth to the first millenniums before Christ to the modern age in the West. In fact, long before the modern age, back in the first millennium before Christ individuals and the problems affecting their lives achieved autonomy over against society in China and India and in the Mediterranean world—Greece and Israel—as well.

The temporal proximity to one another of these various breakthroughs to an individualization of human self-understanding so impressed Alfred Weber and Karl Jaspers that they spoke in this context of a "synchronistic world-age" and of a "pivotal age" of world history.[16] In Israel the development in this area came during the exile, and its result was the demand that God's justice manifest itself in the lifetime of each individual (and not only in succeeding generations) in the form of a correspondence between action and consequence.[17] No longer henceforth must children and grandchildren atone for the sins of their parents. No longer must it be said, "The fathers have eaten sour grapes, and the children's teeth are set on edge" (Jer. 31:29; Ezek. 18:2). The prophet Ezekiel proclaimed a new order of divine justice (in this he went beyond even Jeremiah, who had promised this reform of justice for the future time of salvation): henceforth individuals would die for their own sins. "The righteousness of the righteous shall be upon himself, and the wickedness of the wicked shall be upon himself" (Ezek. 18:20).

This was the point of departure for the hope of resurrection in postexilic Judaism. The fact, so shocking to the devout, that the righteous suffered while the wicked prospered showed that in fact action and consequence often do not correspond during the earthly life of the individual. There must therefore be a balancing of accounts in the other world if God's justice is not to be violated. The expectation of the resurrection of the dead that developed in postexilic Judaism was the most pointed expression of the idea that the meaning of life and the justice of God must be fulfilled in the life of the individual human being. It is not only as members of their clan or people that individuals participate in the meaning of reality; this meaning must be fulfilled in their individual lives as well.

This notion went considerably beyond the Greek belief in the immortality of the soul that arose at about the same time. Plato and probably his

---

[16]A. Weber, *Kulturgeschichte als Kultursoziologie* (1935; 1950²), 24; K. Jaspers, *The Origin and Goal of History,* trans. M. Bullock (New Haven, 1963), 1–21.

[17]On what follows, see the reflections in my *Die Bestimmung des Menschen. Menschsein, Erwählung und Geschichte* (1978), 8ff.

Orphic sources as well did not think of the soul in individual terms in the sense of a unique and unrepeatable human life on its journey from birth to death. Rather, the soul goes through a series of reincarnations, and the Platonic doctrine of immortality is closely connected with this conception. Orphism and, later on, the mystery cults of late antiquity doubtless did give expression to a certain autonomization of the individual in relation to the life of the community; and with respect to the individual's moral obligation to society, this process may even have gone farther there than it did in Judaism. Greek thought nonetheless did not have as profound a grasp as Jewish belief did of individuality in its bodily concreteness, nor did it affirm it as strongly.

Christianity then went a step even beyond Jewish hope, since, according to the preaching of Jesus, God seeks out each individual lost soul with infinite love and since individuals in their decision of faith decide the eternal meaning of their lives without regard to their membership in a people. Hegel and more recently Adolf von Harnack were right therefore in considering the assertion of the infinite value of the individual to be a central idea in Christianity.[18] The full development of this idea came, of course, only at the Reformation which made individuals in their faith consciousness independent even of the church and its tradition.

It is incorrect therefore to say that individuals achieved autonomy only with the coming of modern secularized society, as Luckmann seems to do in his somewhat brief presentation of the subject. Specifically modern, on the other hand, is the "value neutrality" of the shared public areas of life in society, especially the law, the state, and the economy; this is something that stands out when we compare modern society with the ancient cultures or even with the premodern history of Christianity. In this context the independence which the "institutional spheres"—political power, family, law, economy, and religion—have in relation to one another and which heightens the chances that individuals have of freely deciding how to shape their own lives is to be understood as a *consequence* of this value neutrality which marks the general foundations of social life.[19] At its source, however, stands the disengagement (for which the way was paved in the seventeenth century) of the state and its laws and thus of the economy as well from its former ties with religion.

[18]A. von Harnack, *What Is Christianity?* trans. T. B. Saunders (rev. ed., New York, 1901), 63ff.

[19]Differing from the view presented here, N. Luhmann, *Die Funktion der Religion* (1977), 228, 232ff., explains the differentiation of the subsystems of society and their resultant "secularization" as the effect of tendencies toward differentiation that are structurally inherent in the development of society. See my review in *Evangelische Kommentare* 11 (1978), 99ff., esp. 103.

The initial phases of this process of secularization should not be taken either as the expression of a revolt against Christianity[20] or as a direct consequence of the Reformation principles of freedom of conscience and the separation of the spiritual from the secular.[21] The call for freedom of conscience and Luther's doctrine of the two realms did not in the beginning cause any change in the conviction that the unity of the social order depended on unity in religion and therefore demanded a single profession of religious faith. Then, when the demand for a single profession of religious faith was abandoned (not voluntarily and lightheartedly but under the pressure of the failure of other solutions to confessional conflicts), there was the question not of an emancipation from Christianity as such but rather of a bracketing of the intra-Christian confessional disputes that for more than a century had been forcing the European states into hopeless political and military conflicts. The questions of faith on which there was disagreement must no longer henceforth be allowed to harm social peace and the common life of society. Individuals were therefore left free to choose their own religious confession; this happened first in Holland and later (with limitations) in England as well.

Given the general persuasion that religion was of fundamental importance for the unity of the social system, such a step would not have been possible without some legitimation that had a basis in religious tradition itself. Such a legitimation came from linking the Reformation idea of the freedom of the Christian with the right of resistance and with the idea of freedom that was found in the natural law tradition, this last being understood as an expression of the creaturely destination of all human beings to the freedom made accessible through Christ.[22] Thinkers were here

[20]Thus H. Blumenberg, *Die Legitimität der Neuzeit* (1966); see my review-essay, "Christianity as the Legitimacy of the Modern Age" (1968), reprinted in my *The Idea of God and Human Freedom*, trans. R. A. Wilson (Philadelphia, 1973), 178–91.

[21]The first of these approaches is taken in the idealist philosophy of history and especially by Hegel; the second by F. Gogarten, *Despair and Hope for Our Time*, trans. T. Wieser (Boston, 1970).

[22]The importance of the right of resistance for the beginnings of constitutional democracy in the Netherlands (the Intentie of William of Orange, 1572; the Dutch Declaration of Independence, 1581; the Deductie van Vrancken, 1587) has recently been brought out by W. Fikentscher, *Methoden des Rechts in vergleichender Darstellung* IV (1977), 501–67. See also the same author's incisive summary in his lecture, *Der Gegensatz von Grundwerten und "täglichen Dingen" bei der Entstehung der modernen Demokratie* (Schriftenreihe des niedersächsischen Landtags 5; Hannover, 1978). His presentation is based especially on R. H. Murray, *The Political Consequences of the Reformation* (London, 1926). See also A. Kaufmann and L. E. Backmann, eds., *Widerstandsrecht* (Darmstadt, 1972), as well as the further literature listed in Fikentscher's book, 500f., n. 24. Calvin already derives the right of resistance from the priority of the divine law over human law and the action of superiors (thus E. Wolf in Kaufmann and Backmann, 152ff.).

moving beyond the "relative" natural law of the Christian Middle Ages, which was related to fallen humankind, to the "absolute" natural law of the original state and of Stoic philosophy, although with corrections that had to do chiefly with the inclusion of property among the freedoms of the original state.[23]

As a result of being linked to the right of resistance, under the influence of the idea of the universal freedom of the Christian, the principles of natural law were transformed into "constitutional rights" of the individual, rights guaranteed against the power of the state and even against the will of the majority. But once the Christian background of these constitutional rights of the individual against the state had dimmed in John Locke, constitutional or human rights came to be regarded as an expression of the precivic freedom of the isolated individual who was not yet subject to any kind of obligation to the community; this view had made its appearance in Thomas Hobbes.

The secularization of human rights thus produced that "spirit of modern natural law" which is "no longer in the older tradition of political thought with its ethical obligations," but instead thinks unilaterally "in terms of the individual" and, in fact, of an individual who is conceived as "presocietal" and endowed with "natural rights," an individual who is completely free of any duties and obligations and confronts the state as one who makes claims upon it.[24] In the Christian understanding of freedom the basic rights of individuals in the face of state and society were always connected with their obligations to the neighbor. The abstract individualism of modern natural law seems to have sprung from the secularization of the Christian idea of human rights; in the political reality and theory of the bourgeois-liberal age the new outlook led to an antagonism between individual and society.

---

[23]This question played an important part in the discussion of the "Consensus of the People" that was presented to the military council of Cromwell's army in 1547, as J. Bohatec showed in his study "Die Vorgeschichte der Menschen- und Bürgerrechte in der englischen Publizistik der ersten Hälfte des 17. Jahrhunderts" (1956), now in R. Schnur, ed., *Zur Geschichte der Erklärung der Menschenrechte* (Darmstadt, 1964), 267–331, esp. 292ff. In 1690, John Locke, without further ado, listed the control of property among the freedoms guaranteed by nature; see his *Two Treatises of Civil Government*. ed. W. S. Carpenter (London, 1924), II, 4ff., pp. 118ff. For Locke's teaching on property, see W. Euchner, *Naturrecht und Politik bei John Locke* (1969), 81ff.

[24]This is how H. Maier, *Die Grundrechte des Menschen im modernen Staat* (Osnabrück, 1973), 23, describes the "spirit of modern natural law." Even allowing for the fact that he did not know of Fikentscher's researches into the Dutch origins of constitutional democracy, and though he justifiably criticizes G. Jellinek's theses regarding a religious origin of the American Bill of Rights, Maier nonetheless underestimates the importance of Christianity for the rise of modern constitutional democracy (see 18ff.).

2. The Antagonism Between Individual and Society

Once natural law is interpreted in an individualistic manner, the social and political organization of human life in common ceases to be something self-evident. It is no longer simply a reflection of a cosmic order, and it becomes necessary to ask on what grounds and for what purpose individuals had to pass from a state of nature to a corporate life. To this question an answer was supplied by the theories of the *social contract*. These originated a good deal earlier than the appearance of the individualistic interpretation of natural law,[25] but from the seventeenth century on the idea of the social contract acquired a new function: "to establish social relations for the first time between individual human beings."[26]

The result was that the idea of the social contract became fundamental for the political theory of the modern age. It provided a means of passing from the natural law conception of an original "state of nature" in which there was universal freedom and equality, to the present reality which is one of social inequality and dependence. The idea thus fulfilled a function similar to that of the doctrine of the fall in Christian natural law, since in the latter the fall marked the dividing line between the absolute natural law of the original state and the relative natural law of fallen humanity.[27] When examined more closely, however, the doctrine of the social contract proves, rather, to be continuing the theological interpretation of the rise of civic authority as a *remedium peccati* ("remedy for sin"), and it has the function of marking the dividing line between natural state and present social reality only because no one talks anymore of the fall. But for the same reason, the origin of political authority is seen no longer as a simple consequence of the action of other human beings, but as the object of an action marked by unlimited free self-disposal.

This view of the matter emerges with particular clarity in Hobbes, to whom, according to Jürgen Habermas, we owe the "foundation of social philosophy as science."[28] Hobbes uses the idea of a social contract in

[25]G. W. Gough, *The Social Contract: A Critical Study of Its Development* (Oxford, 1957), finds the rudiments of the individualistic contract theory as early as the beginning of the sixteenth century in the Italian writer, Marius Salamenius (47f.).

[26]W. Euchner, "Gesellschaftsvertrag, Herrschaftsvertrag," *HWP* 3 (1974), 476–80 at 478.

[27]For this distinction, see E. Troeltsch, *The Social Teaching of the Christian Churches.* trans. O. Wyon (London, 1931; 2 vols. repr., Harper Torchbooks, 1960), I, 158ff., 197 (n. 76), and see II, 673ff. with 936, n. 416, on the preference given to absolute over relative natural law in the "Neo-Calvinism" of seventeenth-century England.

[28]J. Habermas, "The Classical Doctrine of Politics in Relation to Social Philosophy," in his *Theory and Practice.* trans. J. Viertel (Boston, 1973), 62.

connection with his conception of a naturalistic grounding of social philosophy, after the model of mechanics. To this end, he starts with individuals as the basic components, as he tells us in the Preface (1647) of his *De Cive* (1642), which was published during his exile in Paris. The interaction of these components makes clear why a state became necessary. Hobbes describes the natural state of human common life before the formation of society as a *bellum omnium contra omnes* ("a war of all men against all men").[29] All seek their own advantage at the cost of everyone else, and in so doing they use others as means. Their attitude includes a readiness to harm their fellow human beings: *Voluntas laedendi omnibus quidem inest in statu naturae* ("All men in the state of nature have a desire and will to hurt").[30]

Hobbes's anthropological point of departure is therefore, in theological terms, the nature of fallen humanity. However, he avoids the theological concept of the fall and, in the Preface to *De Cive,* emphasizes the connection between the conduct described as characteristic of the original state and our animal nature. He will not allow this nature to be designated as already evil, because the distinction between good and evil in behavior between human beings presupposes the existence of human laws, which did not yet exist in the state of nature.[31] Nonetheless Hobbes's views are strikingly similar to the theological vision of fallen humanity, and Hobbes himself recognized this.[32]

In the situation just described, human beings were moved by reason, which has its eye on self-preservation,[33] to submit themselves by contract to laws that would bind all. Precisely because in the state of nature every human being had to fear being killed by others, all decided on a social contract, that is, a surrender by all of unlimited freedom. All surrendered this freedom to a ruler, in order that he might secure the prosperity and

---

[29]T. Hobbes, *De Cive* I, 12; tr. by Hobbes himself in T. Hobbes, *Man and Citizen.* ed. B. Gert (New York, 1972), 118. See also *Leviathan* (1651), I, 13 and 14. The individualistic character of Hobbes's anthropology is also emphasized by W. Förster, *Thomas Hobbes und der Puritanismus. Grundlagen und Grundfragen seiner Staatslehre* (1969), 137f.

[30]Hobbes, *De Cive* I, 4 (p. 114).

[31]Ibid., note on I, 10 (2d ed., 1647).

[32]Ibid., Preface of 1647.

[33]Reason usually appears in Hobbes as an agency that is free of the biases of the passions (Förster, 139f.; see 146ff., etc.). There is a contradiction on this point between Hobbes's anthropology and that of Christian theology, which Hobbes nonetheless acknowledges as having paved the way for the early Enlightenment. On the other hand, Hobbes makes the instinct of self-preservation the normative principle of his anthropology, thus displacing the doctrine, which is fundamental for Scholastic natural law, of a human orientation to the divine *lex aeterna;* this point is emphasized by Euchner (n. 23, above), 17ff., who is following L. Straus, *Natural Right and History* (Chicago, 1953).

freedom of every individual in the highest degree compatible with the prosperity and freedom of all the other citizens. Thus Hobbes derived "from the causality of human instinctive nature the norms of an order, whose function is precisely to compel the renunciation of primary satisfaction of those instincts."[34]

There is visible in Hobbes a peculiar ambivalence in the theory of the social contract when it comes to the relation between individual and society. Hobbes starts indeed with a state of nature that is conceived in an individualistic way, but he ends with the assertion of an unlimited sovereignty for the ruler to whom the citizens have irrevocably surrendered their right to dispose freely of themselves and, consequently, to follow their own judgment.[35] Yet many interpreters, Habermas among them, are able to see in Hobbes not only the advocate of absolute monarchy but also the originator of liberalism, that is, of the basic liberal idea that the selfish interests of individuals will, under the guidance of reason, ultimately work together for the common peace and prosperity. The only consequence of Hobbes's anthropological pessimism is that this goal is not to be reached except by way of a surrender on the part of all individuals of their freedom to dispose of themselves, whereas later liberalism, from Locke on, had a more optimistic vision of the human and assumed a less halting kind of harmonization among properly understood individual self-interests for the common good.[36]

Locke's theory of the social contract differs from Hobbes's in that, according to Locke, the individuals entering into this contract do not sacrifice their *freedom* in order to obtain *security;* on the contrary, the social contract serves to preserve freedom itself. Locke's explicit argument is concentrated, however, on the preservation and undisturbed enjoyment of *property.* Human beings enter into a social order "for the securing and

[34]Habermas, 66.

[35]Hobbes, *De Cive* VI, 12ff.; XII, 1ff. Hobbes acknowledges no limit on the supreme power except that it is impossible for individuals to neglect their own preservation (II, 18). See the discussion in Förster, 150ff., of the right to resist. Moreover, the idea that the sovereign determines what is right and wrong has for a consequence (or a presupposition) that Hobbes must reject any independence of religion from the power of the state (*Leviathan* II, 29; *De Cive* XII, 5; Förster, 142ff.). But this is inconsistent with his negative answer to the question of whether we must obey the state when it orders us to offend God (*De Cive* XV, 18; see XVIII, 1). It is evident here that, given the existence of the Christian religion, even Hobbes was unable to hold consistently to a complete surrender of individual freedom in favor of the state.

[36]With truly classical clarity and balance, R. Niebuhr has given expression to the theological criticism of this thesis, in his *The Children of Light and the Children of Darkness* (New York, 1944), esp. 42ff.: "The Individual and the Community."

regulating of property."[37] In the state of nature they were indeed unrestricted masters of their own persons and property, but the use of these was extremely uncertain and continually exposed to attacks by others (ch. 9, n. 123). Therefore they entered into a social union and, to the extent necessary (!), renounced the exercise of their original unhampered freedom (ch. 8, n. 99; 9, n. 129). Because individuals in entering into this association consented to the limitation of their original unhampered freedom (ch. 9, nn. 129 and 131), Locke is not able immediately to use the idea of freedom as the motivation for the association, but he manages to do so indirectly by way of property. His concept of property is, however, a very broad one. Property includes not only material goods but also the life and freedoms of the individual (ch. 9, n. 123). It may be said, then, that property as understood by Locke is a concretization of freedom and that individuals therefore accept the limitation on their power of self-disposal in the interests of their freedom, "with an intention in every one the better to preserve himself, his liberty and property" (ch. 9, n. 131).

In another passage Locke expressly says that in its true meaning law is "not so much the limitation as the direction of a free and intelligent agent to his proper interest, and prescribes no farther than is for the general good of those under that law" (ch. 6, n. 57); "the end of the law is not to abolish or restrain, but to preserve and enlarge freedom" (ibid.).[38] Because freedom is not really surrendered in the societal association but only accepts an order for its exercise, it can continue to serve as a criterion and a right reserved against the power of the state and can be made to prevail: "The power of the society . . . can never be supposed to extend farther than the common good, but is obliged to secure every one's property" (ch. 9, n. 131). Unlike Hobbes, Locke therefore elaborates precautionary measures for the control and limitation of the exercise of political power, especially by calling for a division of powers and the subjection of the executive office to general laws.

In Locke's liberal theory of the state, the abstract individualism that forms the basis of the idea of the social contract is fully apparent. But for that very reason, individuals, still viewed just as abstractly, are regarded as equal and are made subject to the general rules of a reason that is the same for all and to a majority principle that is purely quantitative. Locke sees and discusses the obvious objection that in historical reality human

[37]J. Locke, *Second Treatise of Government* (1690), ch. 8, n. 120. The references that follow in the text are to this work. In connection with Locke's theory of property, Euchner, 80ff., refers to the theory of the value of work that Locke took over from Shaftesbury, but he does not go further into the singular extension of the concept of property in Locke and its connection with the idea of freedom.

[38]On Locke's concept of freedom, see Euchner, 112ff.

beings always live and grow up within authority systems, at least that of the family (ch. 8, nn. 113ff.). He thinks he can meet this objection with a distinction: the natural subjection into which all human beings are born must be distinguished from a voluntary subjection binding them to rulers and their successors.[39] But do not natural community ties, as well as momentous encounters among human beings, have power to impose duties on the individual? Is it right to limit the scope of ethical obligation to contractual relations? From this point of view, Reinhold Niebuhr was doubtless correct in his sharp judgment of the social contract theory: it "completely obscures the primordial character of the human community."[40]

No one emphasized more than Jean Jacques Rousseau the constitutive importance of the community for individuals themselves within the framework of the social contract theory. In his *Contrat social* (1762) the idea of the social contract was transformed so as to serve the contrary of its original individualistic intention. According to Rousseau, the single comprehensive clause to which the social contract may be reduced signifies "the total alienation of each associate . . . to the whole community" (I, 6).[41] Moreover, since individuals here, differently from in Locke, hold back no rights against the state, each person is, according to Rousseau, dependent on all the others. For the social contract "tacitly" includes the undertaking that "whoever refuses to obey the general will shall be compelled to do so by the whole body" (I, 7; p. 18).

Rousseau is closer here to Hobbes than to Locke,[42] although with the important difference that in the social contract human beings do not surrender their freedom (I, 4). They only exchange their unhampered natural freedom for civic or moral freedom. Of the latter it can be said that "obedience to a law which we prescribe to ourselves is freedom" (I,

---

[39]See Locke, ch. 8, n. 114: "It is plain mankind never owned nor considered any such natural subjection they were born in, to one or to the other, that tied them, without their own consents, to a subjection to them and their heirs." History, he says, is full of examples of human beings removing themselves from obedience to the jurisdiction under which they were born and founding new societies elsewhere (n. 115). See also ch. 2, n. 15.

[40]Niebuhr (n. 36, above), 53.

[41]J. J. Rousseau, *The Social Contract and Discourses,* trans. G. D. H. Cole (New York, 1950), 14. The references that follow in the text (with page references) are to this work.

[42]This proximity finds expression in the fact that the idea of the general will comes from Hobbes (see *De Cive* V, 6ff.). I. Fetscher, *Rousseaus politische Philosophie* (1960), 112, rightly emphasizes the difference between the two thinkers: in Hobbes the general will is only a "juridical fiction," whereas in Rousseau it is understood as an anthropological reality. This difference is connected with Hobbes's individualism, from which Rousseau departs, as will be shown in the text. Regardless of this difference, the absorption of the individual into society can be even more radical in Rousseau than in Hobbes, because in the former it is based not only on a contractual right but on the moral origin of individual freedom as well.

8; p. 19). Therefore it can also be said that the action by which society as a whole forces the individual to obey the general will "means nothing less than that he will be forced to be free" (I, 7; p. 18). Locke had touched only in passing on the connection between law and freedom; Rousseau develops this into the idea that individual freedom itself is established or reestablished by society. It is in this sense that he speaks of a "change" that takes place in human beings in the passage to a social condition. The change consists in the birth in them of the moral sense which "they had formerly lacked" (I, 8; p. 18). In view of this moral reconstitution of the individual as citizen (see II, 7), Rousseau can, with Hobbes, assert the absorption of the natural individual into the general will and yet at the same time hold freedom to be inalienable.

In thus basing moral freedom on the law that expresses the general will, Rousseau anticipated and gave stimulus to the ethics of Kant and German idealism. But the absorption of the individual into the *volonté générale* ("general will") was also the point of departure for the totalitarian twist to the democratic idea, a twist that under the aegis of Rousseau emerged for the first time in the French Revolution.[43] Kant, on the contrary, with his distinction between morality and external legality avoided the attraction of totalitarianism and continued to regard the individual as the authority through whose mediation alone the moral law can be operative in historical and political reality. The effects of this approach are to be seen even in Hegel's philosophy of right.[44] Ludwig Feuerbach's return to natural philosophy would soon, of course, interpret Hegel's Universal in a one-sided way as signifying the suppression of the individual,[45] and Feuerbach's own dismissal of individual immortality led finally to the Marxist theory of society. This theory has its anthropological foundations in an "anthropology of the species"[46] and looks back beyond Feuerbach's naturalism to the thought of Rousseau. As a result, Rousseau's idea that individuals are so dependent on society that they retain no freedom *against* it is represented nowadays chiefly by Marxism.

The Polish Marxist philosopher Adam Schaff, in his study of the place of the individual in Marxist anthropology, comes to the conclusion that in the Marxist perspective the human individual, "far from being 'autonomous' in relation to society, . . . is, on the contrary, its product, dependent

[43]See H. Arendt, *On Revolution* (New York, 1963), 73ff.

[44]This is rightly emphasized by J. Ritter, "Moralität und Sittlichkeit. Zu Hegels Auseinandersetzung mit der kantischen Ethik" (1966), reprinted in Ritter's collected essays, *Metaphysik und Politik. Studien zu Aristoteles und Hegel* (1969), 281–309.

[45]P. Cornehl, *Die Zukunft der Versöhnung. Eschatologie und Emanzipation in der Aufklärung bei Hegel und in der Hegelschen Schule* (1971), 221ff., esp. 233.

[46]On this, see A. Wildermuth, *Marx und die Verwirklichung der Philosophie* I (The Hague, 1970), 244–448, esp. 364ff.

on it."[47] The individual is regarded as a "function" of social relations (68), and Schaff explicitly calls attention to the opposition between this conception and "Christian personalism" (69). Within the framework thus established, Schaff nonetheless energetically defends the individual's freedom of choice (152f.) and reacts in particular to any restrictions on intellectual freedom for political reasons (154ff.).

Yet one must ask whether the thesis of the complete dependence of individuals on society does not imply as well their unconditional subjection to those institutions which claim to represent society as a whole to the individual. Schaff believes that the alternative, an antagonism between society and individual, "can only arise when society and individual have become alienated from each other, when the interests of the individual differ from those of society" (165). In connection with a citation from Marx's essay on the Jewish question,[48] Schaff writes: "It is enough to transform social relations, to overcome the dramatic cleavage of the individual into *bourgeois* and *citoyen,* to bring about an identification of private with public interest—and the dilemma loses all meaning" (165). Yes, that is all that is needed—but the condition is not easily fulfilled as long as the interests of society must be imposed by some individuals upon the rest. And it is difficult to see how this situation can change. Every mere transfer of power changes only the agents who are to identify their actions with the overall interests of society against the divergent judgment of others. Kant rightly observes that each individual "will always abuse his freedom if he has none above him to exercise force in accord with the laws."[49] It is in this same context that Kant wrote the famous words: "From such crooked wood as man is made of, nothing perfectly straight can be built."

Kant's reservations, directed at an early stage against Rousseau's theory of the state, are all the more noteworthy since, unlike Rousseau,[50] Kant assumed an original inclination to gregariousness. "Man has an inclination to *associate with others,* because in society he feels himself to be more than man, i.e., as more than the developed form of his natural capacities."[51] According to Rousseau, the behavior of primitive human beings springs

[47]A. Schaff, *Marxism and the Human Individual,* trans. O. Wojtasiewicz (New York, 1970), 143. The page references that follow in the text are to this book.

[48]K. Marx, *On the Jewish Question.*

[49]I. Kant, *Idea for a Universal History from a Cosmopolitan Point of View,* trans. L. W. Beck, in I. Kant, *On History,* ed. L. W. Beck (Indianapolis, 1963), Thesis 6, p. 17.

[50]It is clear from the Appendix on the social condition that accompanies Rousseau's *Discourse on the Origin of Inequality* (1755), 273ff. (in Cole's translation, n. 41, above), as well as from the conclusion of the debate with Locke in the early part of the *Discourse,* that Rousseau did not accept an original inclination to social life in primitive human beings, such as was asserted by Grotius and afterward by the English moral philosophers, especially Shaftesbury.

[51]Kant, *Idea,* Thesis 4, p. 15.

from *amour de soi* ("self-love"), which is directed to self-preservation and is not to be identified with selfishness in the strict sense or *amour propre* ("pride").[52] It was association with others, which began with the introduction of property,[53] that, in Rousseau's view, caused natural self-love to degenerate into selfishness. Association with others here takes over the function that was exercised, in Rousseau's theological predecessors, by the doctrine of the fall.[54]

But the formation of a moral sense, which counteracts that development, is not, in Rousseau's mind, simply the development of a natural disposition. It is true that the original self-love includes an *amour de l'ordre* ("a love of order") that would later (in society) develop into conscience.[55] But the transition from the one to the other takes the form of a leap; if people "are not willing to introduce religion as the support of morality and to let God's will intervene in a direct way in order to unify human society," then, since the crowd will always evade the moral prescriptions of religion, there is at least need of something analogous to God's will, namely, the general will, that will play a role comparable to that of the "voice of heaven" in calling human beings into association with one another.[56]

Kant avoids these difficulties because, like the English moral philosophers, he assumes that human beings have an original inclination to associate with their fellows—although this is accompanied by an inclination to isolation that corresponds to Rousseau's *amour propre* and persists alongside the inclination to social life. In regard to the relation between these two inclinations, Kant speaks of an "antagonism" that is based in human nature itself. According to Kant, the antagonism has this positive role to play: that (very much in the line of Rousseau's thinking) the asocial inclination to isolation fosters the development of talents and culture, and thus "the beginnings . . . for a way of thought which can in time convert the coarse, natural disposition for moral discrimination into definite practical principles, and thereby change a society of men driven together by their natural feelings into a moral whole."[57] The dualism of Rousseau,

[52]Rousseau, *Discourse,* Part I. Fetscher (n. 42, above), 50ff., has shown the connection of this distinction with Malebranche and Vauvenargues.

[53]Rousseau, *Discourse,* Part II.

[54]Fetscher, 56f.

[55]Appendix to the *Discourse.* See note 18 of the editor, K. Wiegand, of the German version of the *Discourse,* in *J. J. Rousseaus Schriften zur Kulturkritik* (PhB 243; 1971²), and Fetscher, 70ff.

[56]Appendix and *Discourse,* Part I; see also Fetscher, 72 and 113. It is in connection with such statements as these that the fundamental systematic importance of the chapter on "Civil Religion" in the *Social Contract* (Book IV, ch. 8) needs to be evaluated.

[57]Kant, *Idea,* Thesis 4, p. 14. This antagonism is empirically observable, but it is obviously related to the opposition between sensuous propensity and morality, insofar as practical

who could not conceive of a transition to society and morality without the mediation of a divine intervention, is replaced in Kant by a monistic teleological conception which starts with the assumption that "all natural capacities of a creature" are destined "to evolve completely to their natural end," and leads up to the demand that "man should, by himself, produce everything that goes beyond the mechanical ordering of his natural existence."[58] Kant thus makes the antagonism part of the very concept of the human subject as such. The antagonism takes the form here of a tension, unresolved in Kant, between the universality of the transcendental subject and the particularity of the existing ego.[59]

In keeping with this view, the universal moral "destiny" of human beings in the historicosocial world makes its appearance as an abstract ought which confronts them. Rousseau, on the other hand, had thematized the becoming of subjectivity itself, that is, of its moral freedom, as taking place in the transition from primitive condition to society,[60] somewhat as Herder did later on in his idea of a developing image of God in humanity. The abiding contribution of Rousseau to the theme of human self-becoming consists in the demonstration of its—negative and positive—connection with the formation of society. Rousseau did, of course, connect the law of God so closely with the general will of society[61] that no room was left for an independence of the individual from society, while Kantian apriorism, on the other hand, was able to preserve this independence of morality, but only at the cost of removing the transcendental subject from

---

reason, being universal, must have the human community as its goal. Thus Kant's teaching, in his philosophy of religion, on radical evil and its tension with the "legal claim on human beings of the good principle" is to be compared with the antagonism that stands at the beginning of his sketch of the philosophy of history. His teaching on a universal church as an ethical commonwealth of God can therefore be read as a counterproposal to Rousseau's *Social Contract.* See especially Kant's remark in his *Religion Within the Limits of Reason Alone* that "the concept of an ethical commonwealth is extended ideally to the whole of mankind and thereby distinguishes itself from the concept of a political commonwealth" (88). In the background here is Kant's restriction of the purpose of the state to the safeguarding of justice. On this conception, which goes back to Thomasius, as opposed to that of M. Mendelssohn, which is based on Chr. Wolff, see A. Altmann, *Prinzipien politischer Theorie bei Mendelssohn und Kant* (Trierer Universitätsreden 9; Trier, 1981), 22ff.

58Kant, *Idea,* Theses 1 and 3, pp. 12–13.

59This tension has been set forth by H. Jahnson, *Kants Lehre von der Subjektivität. Eine systematische Analyse des Verhältnisses transzendentaler und empirischer Subjektivität in seiner theoretischen Philosophie* (1969), 182ff.

60Rousseau's picture of the human being "is dualistic—like that of Christianity. But in him the dualism is not complete from the outset but develops" (Fetscher, 86).

61See Fetscher, 113ff. Typical here is Rousseau's agreement with Hobbes's elimination of the Christian distinction between church and state, as well as his inability to understand the political relevance of the distinction, which he misinterprets as implying an abstract atemporality and otherworldliness (*Social Contract* IV, 8).

empirical reality and thus from the very reality of the subject. Kant's philosophy was unable to avoid the questions here raised for critical reflection, because the unity of the subject and the question of its constitution remained open in this philosophy. As this theme was developed, Hegel's *Phenomenology of Spirit* finally returned to the viewpoint of the becoming of subjectivity in the passage through the process of the formation of society. Here both the connection between religion and society and the difference between them are seen in a more nuanced way than in Rousseau, and yet this unity-in-difference did not take systematic shape in Hegel's philosophy of right but in the final analysis was dissolved in the concept of the ethical state along the lines of Rousseau.

The dialogical personalism of the twentieth century brought a new approach to this theme, but the significance of this approach can be appreciated fully only in the framework of the sociohistorical and sociophilosophical developments discussed in this section. The antagonism between society and individual is here reconciled through the investigation of the personal relations in which the ego, or I, participates and through which it is in fact constituted. The abstract private mode which frequently characterizes the style of discussion in dialogical personalism makes it difficult to grasp this relevance of its theses to the philosophy of society. At the same time, however, it is precisely these relations which guarantee the abiding interest of such discussions, as does their connection with the philosophy of subjectivity of German idealism, a connection that emerged in the application of this philosophical tradition as dialogical personalism sought to give a new answer to the question of the constitution of the ego.

III. The Constitution of the Ego by Its Relation to the Thou

Since the end of the nineteenth century there has been a growing desire to avoid taking as the starting point of thought either the isolated subject or an abstract, supraindividual subject which exists only in the form of individual subjects but which is asserted to be the basis of all experience. The anthropological perspective of European liberalism, which was still operative in Kant and after him in the methodology of the transcendental philosophy of consciousness, was felt to be too narrow. The way was prepared for this shift not only in the philosophy of the species as developed by Feuerbach and especially Karl Marx but even earlier in Hegel's doctrine of the objective spirit and Schleiermacher's teaching on the constitutive significance of sociality for the development of individuality, and later on by the philosophy of life and the youth movement. The breakthrough, however, came only in the present century.

What is especially significant in all of this is that quite varied approaches to the subject were all in agreement on one point: the age of individualism is over. There is still disagreement, however, about what is to take its place. Is there no alternative to abstract individualism except to give society priority over the individual after the manner of Rousseau or Marxism or nationalist ideas of one kind or another? Misgivings about such solutions are not caused solely by the fact that in these models the personal dignity of the individual can no longer be asserted as a critical principle for judging social institutions. In addition, the model in which society is made superior to the individual is threatened by an internal contradiction, inasmuch as even here social institutions must be represented by individuals. The programmatic setting of society over the individual therefore easily becomes an ideological camouflage for the domination of those individuals who claim to be acting in the name of society and who allow no individual freedom to be invoked against them but, on the contrary, treat all opposition as a crime against society.

The priority of society over individual in this unmediated form does not lead to an understanding of the constitution of individuality nor, therefore, to an appreciation of the rights proper to the individual. When Rousseau identified the general will with the freedom of the individual, he was not speaking of the individual's freedom *as an individual* but of the individual's freedom as a rational being, and therefore of a general freedom. The idea of the individual, including the idea of moral individuality, cannot be attained along these lines. Neither Hegel nor Marx advanced appreciably beyond Rousseau in this matter. The assurance that the moral state or the classless society is the embodiment of human freedom and therefore of the freedom of the individual does not answer the question of what is the basis for freedom in its individual form, even against state and society.

It is possible to gain an understanding of the social constitution of individuals as such only if we do not relate them immediately to society as a whole as it encounters them in its institutions and their interrelationships, but rather relate them initially to *another individual,* the Thou or person(s) to whom they are related in the orbit of their personal lives. Then it becomes clear that individuals do not exist simply by themselves but are always constituted by their relation to the other, the Thou. This is the basic idea of "dialogical personalism," which Ferdinand Ebner and Franz Rosenzweig, working along different lines, founded after World War I and which Martin Buber made familiar to a wide circle of readers.[62]

Ebner and Buber, in particular, distinguish between the I-Thou rela-

---

[62]F. Rosenzweig's *Stern der Erlösung* and F. Ebner's *Das Wort und die geistigen Realitäten* appeared in 1922, and M. Buber's *Ich und Du* two years later. B. Casper, *Das dialogische Denken* (1967), presents the development and interrelationships of these three types of dialogical personalism as formulated in these three books. Also to be mentioned in this context is the personalism of Gabriel Marcel from a later time.

tion, in which the I as such is first constituted by the call and claim of the Thou, and the I-It relation, in which the human being as subject disposes of objects. The assertion of the I-Thou relation against a philosophical perspective that restricts itself to the I-It relation is linked to a penetrating criticism of idealistic transcendental philosophy, since to the extent that this philosophy has the world of objects being constituted by the subject and to the extent that its thinking moves solely within this framework, the thinkers of transcendental idealism, from Kant to Neo-Kantianism and on to the phenomenology of Edmund Husserl, remain entangled in the I-It relation. They pass over not only the reality of the Thou but also, and by that very fact, the entire dimension in which the I itself is founded.

In 1965 the problems of dialogical personalism were given a penetrating analysis by M. Theunissen, who focused his attention especially on Buber's conception of it.[63] Theunissen emphasized the immediacy that marks Buber's contrast between the I-Thou and the I-It relations. The result is that Buber, like Ebner before him, once past the concept of "encounter" and the way in which the I is affected by the Thou that encounters it, is able to give only a *purely negative* description of the I-Thou relation, that is, by defining it against the I-It relation. But for this very reason, even in his rejection of transcendental philosophy Buber remains a prisoner of it and is unable to develop an alternative, independent philosophical approach. His insistence on the immediacy of the encounter with the Thou leaves the entire mediation of this encounter to be described in terms of the I-It relation; his statements about the encounter with the Thou itself remain on the same level. Consequently, even the increasing emphasis in Buber's later writings on language as the medium of encounter is of no help, since all the contents expressed in language belong to the I-It relation, with the result that the claim of the Thou is experienced only in a negative way and in fact, as Buber expressly says, is experienced in its purest form in silence.[64]

---

[63]M. Theunissen, *Der Andere. Studien zur Sozialontologie der Gegenwart* (1965).

[64]Thus Theunissen, 287, on M. Buber, *Das dialogische Prinzip* (1973³), 42. J. Bloch, *Die Aporie des Du. Probleme der Dialogik Martin Bubers* (1977), responds to Theunissen with the objection that Buber expressly denies silence to be the ultimate recourse (25, n. 40). Buber, he says, is interested rather in the way the human being is "addressed" by the "mystery" that is mediated through "the world as sacramental" (48) inasmuch as the world in its totality is "more than world" and precisely herein has its reality as world (68). Yet though Bloch is able to bring out in an impressive way the "pansacramentality" of the world as Buber sees it, even he must admit that according to Buber the "address" by the mystery cannot be "reproduced in words" (29f.) and takes place "apart from any communicated or communicable content" (26, n. 40). But, then, how can the "substance" of the linguistic event be stated as a linguistic substance, as Bloch claims (25, n. 40)? Even Bloch's interpretation is unable to rescue Buber from Theunissen's critique of his constant dependence on a language that operates at the level of the I-It relation. Casper, 344 and 359, agrees with Theunissen.

This criticism of Buber affects Ebner as well, but not Rosenzweig. The reason is that Rosenzweig does not oppose the idea of encounter to the I-It relation directly but rather through reflection on the temporal nature of language—or, more exactly, of speech—as contrasted with the atemporality of Western thinking about objects.[65] In the temporality of dialogue the eschaton of the world is anticipated at every moment,[66] and yet is also opened to the future of the "kingdom." With this explanation of the reality of the world in the light of language understood as speech and "dialogue," Rosenzweig looks far beyond Ebner's and Buber's narrowly circumscribed realm of personalism, although he too believes that he can in an all too facile and summary way get behind thinking that is oriented to the object and its "nature," with the help of the general consideration that such thinking is due to a refusal to face up to death.[67] The fact that he himself also argues on the basis of this kind of thinking and its intersubjective character and indeed can argue only on this basis is something that he accepts too readily, as he does the resultant necessity of proving each step in his thinking in a debate with tradition and with the degree of reflection already attained in the tradition. The end result is that in Rosenzweig too "dialogue" becomes all too much a magical key. To this extent there is a bridge leading from Rosenzweig to Buber. Nonetheless his thinking on language with its thematization of time opens a way out of these limitations to a new and deeper view of reality; it is a view, however, that still awaits its conceptual development.

Unfortunately theology, and in particular Evangelical theology, in the first half of the twentieth century has been more responsive to stimuli from Ebner and Buber than from Rosenzweig. The opposition established between the I-Thou relation and the theories of the philosophical tradition regarding objective reality seemed to provide theologians with an opportunity to liberate the relation of human beings to God from the critical

---

[65]For Rosenzweig's theology of language, see *The Star of Redemption.* trans. W. W. Hallo (New York, 1970, 1971), 124ff., 150ff., and the excellent presentation in Casper, 120ff. and 151f. In an essay, "Franz Rosenzweigs Kritik an Bubers *Ich und Du*," *PhilJb* 86/2 (1979), 225ff., Casper shows that, contrary to Buber, Rosenzweig expressly insists on talking of God in the third person.

[66]Rosenzweig, 205ff.

[67]This is the thought with which *The Star of Redemption* begins; on it see Casper, 91ff. If we reflect on the importance that the conscious acceptance of death has in Hegel's dialectic of negativity, this diagnosis, though impressively stated, seems all too unnuanced, and we may ask how Rosenzweig, a specialist in Hegel, could fail to realize this. In any case, the result is that his criticism of objective thinking and especially of the form given to it in speculative idealism becomes questionable. A further result is that Rosenzweig's own ideas for a more penetrating interpretation must first be related in a more nuanced way to traditional philosophy.

demands and questions of modern philosophy up to that point, while at the same time enabling them to relate it to modern philosophy, so that theological thinking, as thinking that has a personal character, might even feel itself to be intellectually superior to the philosophical tradition.

In the process the theologians have not gone along with Buber's tendency to look for the reality of God in the mystery that is "between" the I and the Thou, a mystery in which both the I and the human Thou are involved.[68] Instead, Friedrich Gogarten and Emil Brunner, following in the steps of Ebner,[69] understood the human I as constituted by the Thou, with the divine Thou ultimately standing behind the human Thou. This position could be interpreted either as grounding an unconditional claim of the human Thou on the I[70] or as a relativization of the human Thou.[71] In either case the concept of the word of God as a challenge, by the divine Thou, which is not at the individual's beck and call, could be connected with this position. To this, Theunissen has legitimately objected that in this conception of the constitution of the I by the Thou the Thou itself is thought of simply as *another I* along the lines of the traditional philosophy of the subject and that therefore the Thou does not take us out of this realm of the subject.[72] In this respect, the theology of Gogarten and of Brunner as well falls short of Buber, who, as is now clear, had a deeper reason for describing the mystery *between* the I and the Thou as the origin that constitutes *both* of them and grounds the special nature of the I-Thou relation.[73]

[68]Thus Theunissen, 278ff., who is followed by Casper, 299f. See also Casper's essay on Rosenzweig's critique of Buber (n. 65, above), 226. Bloch, however, suggests that the Between is not simply given in advance to the I and the Thou, but "is realized by both" (231, n. 53), whereas Theunissen at this point brings in a Christian concept of grace (293ff.). There remains, according to Theunissen, only a questioning that is directed to the divine mystery. Buber himself, moreover, speaks of humans being "addressed" by the mystery, which thereby "becomes their own" (see Bloch, 28f.), although the restlessness that finds expression in questioning is not thereby removed. Bloch's criticism of Theunissen's presentation is, therefore, unconvincing.

[69]On Ebner, see Casper, 235ff., 245f., and, for a critique, 259ff.

[70]Thus F. Gogarten, *Politische Ethik* (1932).

[71]Thus E. Brunner, *Truth as Encounter* (rev. and much enlarged ed. of *The Divine-Human Encounter*), trans. O. Wyon (Philadelphia, 1964).

[72]Theunissen, 361ff. (specifically on Gogarten).

[73]Barth is the Evangelical theologian closest in his thinking to Buber, at least in his *Church Dogmatics* (III/2). Barth does not interpret the human I as constituted by the Thou, but makes the combination of I and Thou in its totality point to God, that is, to the Trinitarian coexistence of Father and Son. But in Barth the interhuman I-Thou relation is simply *repeated*. Barth himself, of course, presents the intradivine relation as the prototype of the human and, as far as the provenance of the dialogical understanding of the person in the history of ideas is concerned, he may well be correct. But in any case, whichever of these two analogous

It is clear, then, that neither the dialogical philosophy of Buber nor its theological variants in Brunner and Gogarten succeeded in getting beyond the idea of the self-positing ego. Buber did not succeed, because he was able to describe the special character of the I-Thou relation in only a *negative* way and therefore did not move on to a positive alternative. Personalist theology, on the other hand, simply inverted the I-Thou relation and treated the Thou, and especially the divine Thou, as the real, sovereign I. The idealist philosophy of the autonomous subject was simply transposed into a thinking centered on a heteronomous subject.

Dialogical personalism thus proves to be rather a pointer in a direction that calls for further investigation than an alternative that intellectually transcends the philosophy of the isolated ego. Its merit is to have shown the dependence of the ego, previously regarded as a sovereign subject, on the encounter with a Thou. In practice, dialogical personalism has shown at the same time the dependence of the individual on society, which meets it in the form of a human Thou. But it has rarely thematized this link in an explicit way and instead has often restricted itself to the private realm. In this way it could become an ideology that justifies a withdrawal from the modern technicized world which is controlled by the I-It relation and from the anonymity of social mechanisms. On the other hand, when the connection between the relation to the Thou and the relation of the individual to society became thematic, as in Gogarten's book on political ethics (1932), the "bondage" of the individual to the Thou was transferred immediately to the relation to the state, insofar as the latter represented all others in their claims on the ego.

The limitation shared by both variants of personalism is their insistence on the immediacy of the claim of the Thou and their exclusion of the shared objective world from any mediation in the encounter with the Thou. The objective world is excluded because it is considered to belong to the I-It relation. But this opposition between the relation of the I to the Thou and the relation of the It to its world of objects must be avoided if the introduction of the Thou is to lead to an enlargement of the traditional philosophy of the subject and its understanding of the ego.

G. H. Mead, the American philosopher and social psychologist, advanced farther in this direction than did dialogical personalism. He does not posit any opposition between the ego's relation to the Thou and its relation to objects. On the contrary, it was precisely in the social relation

---

relations is given priority, the relation of Father and Son in the Trinity is not, any more than the human I-Thou relation, to be explained in terms of the "between them," whether this "between" be the unity of the divine being or the Spirit who unites Father and Son. At the decisive point, then, Barth too stops short of Buber's position.

to the other that Mead looked for the key to an understanding both of the relation of human beings to their world and of its genesis.

IV. G. H. Mead's Theory of the Self[74]

George Herbert Mead taught philosophy and, in particular, social psychology at the University of Chicago from 1894 until his death in 1931. Only after his death, however, was his principal work, *Mind, Self and Society,* edited and published by Charles W. Morris. The heart of the book is his theory of the self, which is portrayed as conditioned by the process of socialization: "The self . . . is essentially a social structure, and it arises in social experience."[75]

This proposition presupposes a distinction between ego and self, which Mead took over from William James. James's psychology distinguishes between the spontaneous ego, or "I," and the ego that is given to itself as an object in reflection on itself; the second ego is the "me," or self. James had also stressed the social conditioning of the self which I know myself to be in my self-consciousness.[76] The novelty and special character of Mead's theory does not consist, then, in the distinction between self and ego or in the idea of the self as socially conditioned. Mead's real contribution to the subject is to be found in his effort to explain the state of affairs that James had described. He was concerned to explain in general the objectification of the self that is to be seen in the fact of self-consciousness: "How can an individual get outside himself (experientially) in such a way as to become an object to himself?" (138).

The object of this question is nothing less than the *genesis* of the human form of life which we have already seen, with Plessner, to be characterized by *exocentricity.* In contrast to the philosophical idealists, Mead does not take the fact of self-reflection and self-consciousness as a primordial datum of human subjectivity but, rather, attempts to understand it as the result of a becoming. And his answer is that self-reflection is a product of social intercourse with other individuals: "The individual experiences himself as such, not directly, but only indirectly, from the particular standpoints of other individual members of the same social group, or from the generalized standpoint of the social group as a whole to which he belongs" (138).

How is it possible for individuals to view and understand themselves

---

[74]On what follows, see K. Raiser, *Identität und Sozialität. George Herbert Meads Theorie der Interaktion und ihrer Bedeutung für die theologische Anthropologie* (1971). Mead's theory of the self is central in G. Winter, *Elements for a Social Ethic* (New York, 1966).

[75]G. H. Mead, *Mind, Self and Society* (n. 6, above), 140. The page references in the paragraphs that follow are to this book.

[76]Raiser, 97.

from the standpoint of others? Such a procedure evidently requires that individuals be in a position to put themselves in the place of others. But how is this possible? Mead finds that the first presupposition for doing so—and therefore the foundation of the phenomenon of self-conscious-ness—is the human ability to understand the gestures or movements of others. This kind of understanding is found in the beasts, as when the leader of a herd lifts its head to smell the air and in this way signals some danger to the herd. The gesture can indicate that the leader will in a moment turn and flee; to this extent, the gesture has meaning: "If that gesture does so indicate to another organism the subsequent (or resultant) behavior of the given organism, then it has meaning" (76).

The leader does not, however, itself grasp the meaning its gesture has for the herd. It is not aware of its own gesture. The simultaneous percep-tion both of its own gestures and of the reaction of the other organism is required if a living being is itself to perceive the significance of its own gestures for the other and thus be able to put itself in the situation of the other. This presupposition—that the living being perceives its own ges-tures—is verified in a particular class of manifestations, namely, vocal utterances which the being that makes likewise hears. At the same time, this being experiences the reactions of others and experiences them *as* reactions to its own vocal utterance.[77] Consequently, human beings, for whom vocal utterances are the most important vehicles of social communi-cation, can hear their own utterances and put themselves in the place of others and understand their reactions.[78] "We are, especially through the

[77]The result, for Mead, is a "significant symbol" (46). At this point Mead makes a questionable transition: the connection between the vocal utterance and the reaction of the other is mediated, according to his description, by the fact that the vocal utterance supposedly evokes in the being who makes it the *same* reaction as in the other. A vocal gesture is "one of those social stimuli which affects the form that makes it in the same fashion that it affects the form when made by another" (62; see 69f.). This similarity functions subsequently as the basis for the possibility of understanding the other's reaction (68f.). But the linking of the individual's own vocal gestures with the reaction of the other could take place in experience even independently of the similarity of reactions, in those cases in which the other always reacts in the same way to a particular vocal utterance; for example, the mother always comforts the screaming child. The connection between vocal gestures and the reaction of the other that thus occurs regularly in experience could in turn be the basis for our connect-ing with our gestures the expectation of a particular behavior by the other.

[78]This presupposes, however, that there is a fixed reciprocal relation between *particular* vocal utterances and particular reactions. But the establishment of such a relation would require the evaluation of a great deal of experience and, in addition, the possibility of choosing among various associations of expectations with a specific vocal utterance. It is understandable, therefore, that Mead should have sought a simpler solution by adopting the viewpoint of the similarity of reaction in myself and in the other to my vocal utterance. Later in this book (p. 407), I shall explain that the structure of meaning of a shared environment that is disclosed through language is presupposed in the act of putting myself in the place

use of the vocal gestures, continually arousing in ourselves those responses which we call out in other persons, so that we are taking the attitudes of the other person into our own conduct" (69). This is true even when a particular vocal utterance can elicit a whole range of responses from the other.

The possibility of self-reflection in human beings is based, therefore, on the fact that they perceive their own vocal utterances and experience the reaction of others to these *as* a reaction to the sound they have produced. They thereby put themselves in the situation and role of the other and are able to see themselves from the vantage point of the other and thus from a distance, as it were. All this does not, of course, explain the origin of human exocentricity as such, nor does it mean a derivation of the human exocentric structure from prehuman forms of behavior. On the contrary, the very fact of being able to attend, unburdened by instinct, to the connection between one's own sounds and the determinate reactions of others presupposes exocentricity.

Mead's reasoning does, however, describe the genesis of self-reflection, in which the relation of individuals to themselves that is implied in the exocentric form of life becomes thematic. In a manner similar to that which we saw earlier in speaking of Scheler, self-reflection is derived from a *being present to the other,* but this other is now not simply the being of things but specifically another human being. As a matter of fact, however, a surrender to the object in the form of a curiosity that is unburdened by instinct is not enough to explain the genesis of self-reflection, although it is the presupposition for the passage to self-reflection. If self-reflection is actually to develop, there is need of a motivation as well, and this arises out of the social context. The fact that the first and foremost of the objects that human beings turn to and observe is another human being and that in doing so they are able to put themselves in the place of the other and understand actual and possible reactions to themselves—*this* is the basis for the passage to self-consciousness and to the inspection of one's own being from outside, from the standpoint of another.

It follows from this theory of the genesis of self-consciousness that the human being as self-conscious ego is not grounded in itself and independently of others. Rather, self-consciousness and the self-conscious ego are constituted through relation to the other. This is not to say that the ego is a creation of the Thou; the point is, rather, that individuals comprehend themselves by putting themselves in the place of others over against themselves.

The self of which we are conscious in self-consciousness depends there-

---

of another. See also the critical reflections of J. Habermas, *Theorie des kommunikativen Handelns* II (1981), 23ff.

fore on the image others have of us. But if so, how can our self be a unity for us? Must we not receive different images of our self from the various others with whom we deal at any given moment? According to Mead, this is in fact the case. Nonetheless we are also unified in our own minds because we experience ourselves not only as seen by individual others but also as members of the social *group* to which we belong. Mead calls this new perspective that of the "generalized other."[79] My self thus acquires continuity and identity, insofar as I see it from the standpoint of the "generalized other," the social group, or, ultimately and in the most generalized form possible, from the standpoint of the human race.

The self that we grasp ourselves as being in self-reflection is thus a social reality. It is "established through the internalization of the social act."[80] This holds both for the "real, true" self—that is, the normative or ideal self which expresses what the group or humanity expects of us—and for the actual self which expresses the way in which our actual behavior is seen by the group or humanity.

According to Mead, there exists not only a self but an I, and in his view the I is not constituted by the social process. Nor is it ever a direct object of my experience (178), but is the spontaneous source of my behavior, including my self-reflection.[81] In particular, we become conscious of our I as that power in us which reacts to social reality and therefore to our self as well: "The 'I' reacts to the self which arises through the taking of the attitudes of others" (174). "It is the answer which the individual makes to the attitude which others take toward him" (177). The self as mirror of society's assessment does not therefore constitute by itself the whole of the individual personality. In addition, there is the reaction of the I, which modifies the social assessment. Only the two together make up the individual personality. "Taken together they constitute a personality as it appears in social experience" (178).[82]

But how do I know that "I" am identical with "me," that is, with my socially constituted self as this appears to me in self-reflection? For the answer, Mead appeals to the power of memory: "It is in memory that the 'I' is constantly present in experience, . . . so that the 'I' in memory is there

---

[79]"The organized community or social group which gives to the individual his unity may be called 'the generalized other.' " More details in Raiser, 124ff. Habermas, 73f., points out that Mead did not supply the needed account of the foundations of group identity. For this, Habermas turns to the explanation given of these questions by E. Durkheim, who found the identity of society to be originally articulated in the religious consciousness. On this, see below, chapter 8, n. 231.

[80]Raiser, 131.

[81]On this, see Raiser, 128f.

[82]In this passage Mead uses "self" not (as elsewhere) for the object of self-reflection (the "me" as distinct from the "I") but for the unity of both (178).

as the spokesman of the self of the second, or minute or day ago."[83] But the structural possibility of a unity of ego and self through memory does not emerge very clearly in Mead. His concept of the ego is marked by shifting functions: subject of self-reflection and action, "spokesman" for the past "self," power of reaction to the self (me) as a social product. "The unclear status of the 'I' in Mead has elicited a good deal of critical comment."[84] But then the self too is seen now as object of self-reflection and thus as sum total of the assessments of my individuality by others, now as the unity of the object of self-reflection (the "me") with the ego that does the reflecting.

The main difficulty in understanding the unity of the ego (the I) and the self (me) is that the ego is supposedly not mediated through social relations, whereas the self in the narrow sense of the word (the object of self-reflection) is the summary of the picture others have of me, a picture that is composed and organized by the reflecting ego and therefore also *mediated* through the attitude that the ego takes in response. The self, which is supposed to be the expression of how others see me, is therefore constituted by the ego, which for its part is not a power that depends on the social process for its constitution. Yet at the same time it is the ego that puts itself in the place of others and from their perspective looks upon itself as a *self*. In other words, it is the ego that is present outside of itself to the other. Moreover, only through the *mediation* of the socially constituted self-consciousness is the ego accessible to the person's own experience, namely, in memory and as "spokesman" (174) of the self of earlier moments. All of this amounts to saying that, contrary to Mead's claim, not only the self but also the ego is always mediated to itself through social relations. In particular, the unity of the ego and the self cannot be understood unless the ego too is conceived as the product of a developmental process that is conditioned by social relations.

As we shall see, the way to such an understanding was prepared by Freudian psychoanalysis and traveled by the American Neo-Freudians, Erik H. Erikson in particular, who combined the teaching of Freud with suggestions from Mead.[85] The abiding merit of Mead is that he went beyond the broad personalist thesis that the ego is constituted by its

---

[83]Mead, 174. The thesis that the identity of the person depends on memory goes back to Locke (*Essay Concerning Human Understanding* II, 27, 11). It has recently been advocated by B. Russell and A. J. Ayer. For criticism, see S. Shoemaker, *Self-Knowledge and Self-Identity* (Ithaca, N.Y., 1963), 123ff., esp. 130, 151ff.

[84]Raiser, 170.

[85]Especially important for the treatment of this problem is E. H. Erikson, *Identity and the Life Cycle: Selected Papers* (New York, 1959). The discussion will show, however, that because of inadequate reflection on the relation between ego and self, even Erikson fails to make his genetic theory of ego identity bear fruit in an understanding of the ego.

relation to the Thou and undertook a concrete and nuanced description of this dependence. But in the end only a self that is detached from the ego proved to embody the dependence of individual self-consciousness on the processes of social life. In the final reckoning, then, Mead too failed to do justice to the thesis—admittedly too inclusive in its terms—of dialogical personalism that the ego as such is constituted by the relation to the Thou.

Precisely because of its ambiguities and problems Mead's description is the indicated starting point for any nuanced discussion and development of the claim that is programmatic for personalism: that the ego is constituted through its relation to the Thou. Any attempt to solve this problem must do justice to the phenomena which Mead described, but also eliminate the ambiguities in his terminology. The two most important problems that Mead's description left unresolved are, first, the social conditioning even of the ego and, second, the question (which cannot be raised until that first problem is solved) of the unity of ego and self. But the discussion of the social conditioning of the ego requires that a new level of reflection be found, lest this social conditioning prove to be once again, as in Mead, *something extrinsic* and therefore having no connection with the center from which the individual's action proceeds. Psychoanalysis, in dealing with the question of the personal identity of the individual, attained to this higher level of reflection. For the question of personal identity is one that the ego as a self-conscious being must necessarily raise: it is the question of itself. If the social conditioning of the ego becomes evident in connection with the theme of ego development, then this conditioning can no longer be thrust aside as something extrinsic to the ego.

5

The Problem of Identity

I. The Ego and the Process of Identity Formation
According to Psychoanalysis

Since its beginnings, depth psychology has been characterized by its divergence from the method of classical psychology, which restricted itself to an analysis of conscious acts. Therapeutic involvement with psychic illnesses showed that human behavior and human consciousness are very strongly affected by, among other things, impulses and specific motives which for their part are not conscious. In their opposition to the primacy of consciousness psychoanalysts or depth psychologists were in tune with numerous other trends of the late nineteenth and early twentieth centuries. There was, for example, the emphasis in the philosophy of life, especially in Nietzsche and before him Feuerbach, on the primary role of the body in human behavior; but there was also American behaviorism, existential philosophy, and, not least, Marxist historical materialism. In fact, a contemporary like Paul Tillich thought that opposition to an excessive esteem of consciousness was the common denominator in psychoanalysis and Marxism.[1]

Within this common outlook psychoanalysts directed their special attention to the way in which experiences from the person's own life turn into unconscious motives of behavior; other workers in the broad field of depth psychology adopted other vantage points in studying the unconscious as it extends beyond the realm of the conscious. Yet despite this emphasis on the unconscious, the ego, as the center of consciousness, continued to play a role, and even a central role, in depth psychology and psychoanal-

---

[1] H. Elsässer, *Paul Tillichs Lehre vom Menschen als Gespräch mit der Tiefenpsychologie* (dissertation; Marburg, 1973), 11ff., on "existential protest" in Tillich; see also 54f. for Tillich's recall of the origin of his conception of the demonic. The analogy between psychoanalysis and Marxism touches on an important element common to the two, though D. Wyss rightly points out that "nature as the physiognomy of the unconscious" and therefore the psychic unconscious as a specific theme "is of no interest to Marx"; see his *Marx und Freud. Ihr Verhältnis zur modernen Anthropologie* (1969), 30.

ysis, at least in the more broadly conceived framework of psychoanalytic theory of the person.[2]

In Freud's earliest writings the ego is the agency that represses and turns aside certain representations; it does not permit them to enter consciousness, or, in other words, exercises a "censorship." A first shift in the conception of the ego came in 1904 in Freud's *Three Contributions to the Theory of Sex*. Here Freud placed the instinct of self-preservation alongside, and even ahead of, the sexual instinct or libido; the first pleasurable movements of the infant as it takes nourishment are to be connected with the former of the two. "The ego, which had previously been considered an agency that suppresses instinct, whatever its nature, now came to be regarded as itself an *instinct*" (Wyss 57). In this explanation the ego instincts were contrasted with the libido, and neuroses were explained as an expression of conflicts between instincts, namely, the sexual instinct and the instinct of self-preservation.

The lectures (1916–17) that make up *A General Introduction to Psychoanalysis* brought a second decisive change in Freud's conception of the ego with the introduction of the concept of *narcissism*. This concept presupposes that the opposition between ego instincts and sexual instinct has been removed. Observation of schizophrenics had led Freud to think that the libido can turn back from the object to the ego itself and that the ego can relate to itself in the form of a specifically libidinous "delusion of grandeur."[3] Freud sees an original unity of the instinct of self-preservation and the libido as manifesting itself in early infancy, a still undifferentiated developmental phase in which nursing at the mother's breast serves self-preservation but also represents libido in its first form. This *primary* narcissism is to be distinguished from a *secondary* narcissism which is a neurotic regression to that infantile state and results from avoidance of the task of mastering the social environment; according to Freud, the secondary narcissism has its basis especially in an inadequate resolution of the so-called Oedipus complex.

The conception of the ego as an instinct could not, however, be applied

---

[2]Thus C. G. Jung said in 1937 that with "modern psychology's" discovery of the unconscious, "the position of the ego, till then absolute, became relativized; that is to say, though it retains its quality as the centre of the field of consciousness, it is questionable whether it is the centre of the personality. It is part of the personality but not the whole of it" (*Aion: Researches Into the Phenomenology of the Self*. trans. R. F. C. Hull [*Collected Works* IX/2; London, 1959], 6). This is true, as far as it goes, for all schools of psychoanalysis. For the exposition that follows in the text, which studies Freud in particular, see D. Wyss, *Die tiefenpsychologischen Schulen von den Anfängen bis zur Gegenwart* (1961), 3–98, and H. Hartmann, "The Development of the Ego Concept in Freud's Work" (1956), in his *Essays on Ego Psychology: Selected Problems in Psychoanalytic Theory* (New York, 1964), 268–96.

[3]Wyss, 58f., referring to S. Freud, *A General Introduction to Psychoanalysis*. trans. J. Riviere (New York, 1924; Pocket Books ed., 1952), 422.

without reservations, since the earliest function that Freud had assigned to the ego—that of censoring and controlling the instincts—could not be handed over to another agency, nor could it be fully reformulated according to the model of a conflict of instincts between ego instincts and sexual instincts. In addition, the merging of these two types of instinct in *A General Introduction to Psychoanalysis* raised anew the question of an agency that opposes the instincts, an agency, that is, to which the functions of censorship, control of instinct, and repression could be assigned. The final result was a tendency to look upon the ego once again as an agency opposed to the sphere of instinct in general. This trend was already operative in the period when the narcissism hypothesis was introduced, and it continued to exist alongside the latter development, so that from that point on Freud was working with two concepts of the ego. On the one hand, the ego has its roots in the instinct of self-preservation, in the self-love that characterizes the primary narcissism. On the other hand, the ego functions as a censoring agency, an aspect of the ego that comes into being only in the course of personality development. The starting point for its rise is the "ego ideal" which has its basis in the internalization of the expectations and reproaches of the parents but is established as an internal agency in the child, that is, as an agency of the ego, only through *identification* with the parents.[4]

At this crucial point a comparison between Freud and Mead is especially instructive. To the extent that Freud's ego ideal is based on an internalization of parental expectations and especially of parental criticisms and reproaches, it corresponds in large measure to Mead's concept of the self as a social creation. Mead's explanation of the genesis of the self through a putting of oneself in the place of another and especially through seeing the expectations the other has of me can be applied, without any forcing, to Freud's concept of the ego ideal. Freud concretizes Mead's thesis to the extent that, for Freud, it is primarily in relation to the parents that the ego ideal comes into existence: not just any other person is suitable in this context, but first and foremost the parents.

At this point Mead's analysis lacks a differentiating factor, a principle of selection showing which other human being can best serve as the incentive for a normative representation of my self. In addition, Mead provides no explanation of the fact that the internalized judgment of the other person does not continue to be an alien demand upon me but becomes identical with my self. The concept of *identification* fills both of these needs: Because the child identifies with the picture the parents form of it in their expectations regarding it, this picture ceases to be an alien authority; at the same time, because this process requires a special act of identification, it also

---

[4]Wyss, 59f., referring to the same work of Freud.

provides the desired principle of selection and the explanation of why not any and every other person can equally well determine my self by passing judgment on me.

In Freud's conception of the individual's development the place where this identification occurs is the situation created by the Oedipus complex. Here the male child's jealousy of the father as successful rival for the mother's love is overcome in a positive way through identification with the father as a model. In fact, the child identifies not so much with the real father as with an idealized image of the father, with the father's superego.[5] In such a positive resolution of the Oedipus complex, as seen here in the example of a male child's development, there is a change or, better, a transformation of the narcissistic pleasure ego into the ego as agency for *mastery* of reality through *acceptance* of reality. The ego that emerges from a positive resolution of the Oedipus complex is henceforth the agency of the reality principle within me and the representative of the requirement that I adapt myself to reality in order to master it.

The identification with the father as model gives rise not only to the *real ego* but also to the *superego*. This term, which acquired its fixed place in Freud's analysis of the person only after 1920, had a predecessor in the concept of the ego ideal. On the one hand, then, the internalization of parental criticism gives rise to the real ego which is formed through identification. On the other hand, the norms or idealized father image to which this ego pledges itself also remain, but as something imposed, toward which the ego develops feelings of guilt.

The concept of the ego now has three different aspects. First, there is the narcissistic pleasure ego; then there is the real ego and, third, the superego, both of which acquire their definitive form through the surmounting of the Oedipus complex and therefore through the process of identification. Interestingly enough, Freud emphasizes the ambivalence that marks the process of identification. On the one hand, it can aim at the incorporation and resultant possession of the object of the identification; on the other, it can also contain a phase of self-conquest. One or another of these aspects may prove dominant. In the first case, narcissistic motives gain the upper hand; in the other, motives for self-transcendence and sublimation win out. Here we recognize once more the tension between *amor sui* and exocentricity in human behavior. Of course, the wish to be like the father—or, more exactly, like his ideal image or superego—means that an element of narcissistic *amor sui* remains linked to the self-conquest, so that the ambivalence of the ego becomes apparent once again at each stage of its development, inasmuch as even after a positive resolution of the Oedipus complex all three aspects

5Ibid., 144.

of the ego continue to be intertwined.

Moreover, not only the ego but the superego as well is ambivalent. I mentioned above that the ego ideal contributes to the surmounting of the wishes of the narcissistic pleasure ego and by so doing evokes satisfaction and feelings of triumph or, on the contrary, feelings of guilt and inferiority, depending on the extent to which the ego is able to measure up to the ego ideal. With regard to this second ambivalence, that of the superego, Freud wrote in 1923:

> This double aspect of the ego ideal derives from the fact that the ego ideal had the task of repressing the Oedipus complex; indeed, it is to that revolutionary event that it owes its existence. Clearly the repression of the Oedipus complex was no easy task. The child's parents, and especially his father, were perceived as the obstacle to a realization of his Oedipus wishes; so his infantile ego fortified itself for the carrying out of the repression by erecting this same obstacle within itself. It borrowed strength to do this, so to speak, from the father, and this loan was an extraordinarily momentous act. The super-ego retains the character of the father, while the more powerful the Oedipus complex was and the more rapidly it succumbed to repression (under the influence of authority, religious teaching, schooling and reading), the stricter will be the domination of the super-ego over the ego later on—in the form of conscience or perhaps of an unconscious sense of guilt.[6]

In *The Ego and the Id* (1923), the work just cited, Freud formulated his definitive conception of the place of the ego in the psychic "apparatus." The instincts are now summed up in the concept of the id. The sphere of the id confronts the ego, which must learn to control its instincts and passions. Despite all the criticism that he leveled against the harmful, that is, neurotic consequences of an excessively strict superego, Freud agreed with Milton[7] in regarding this mastery as the lifework of the human person.

In the resolution of the Oedipus complex the superego initially develops in the service of the ego's task of controlling its instincts and passions. But the ego can also be pulverized between two millstones: the demands of the superego and the wishes of the id. "Helpless in both directions, the ego defends itself vainly, alike against the instigations of the murderous id and against the reproaches of the punishing conscience."[8] Psychoanalysis, for its part, serves to strengthen the ego. It is a tool that makes it possible for the ego "to extend its organization so that it can take over new portions of the id." Or, to put it in more

[6]S. Freud, *The Ego and the Id*, trans. J. Strachey (New York, 1960), 49.
[7]According to J. Scharfenberg, *Freud und seine Religionskritik als Herausforderung für den christlichen Glauben* (1968; 1971³), 49.
[8]Freud, *The Ego and the Id*, 72.

lapidary form: "Where id was, there ego shall be."[9]

In order to understand the necessity of this we must take into account the fact that the ego is not completely separated from the id but is itself rooted in the id and thus in the unconscious: "The ego is that part of the id which has been modified by the direct influence of the external world through the medium of the *Pcpt.-Cs* [perceptual consciousness]." Moreover, "the ego seeks to bring the influence of the external world to bear upon the id and its tendencies, and endeavors to substitute the reality principle for the pleasure principle which reigns unrestrictedly in the id."[10] The call of the ego to be master of the id may therefore also be interpreted as the task of bringing the entire person into consciousness and controlling it in the light of perceptual consciousness, inasmuch as perceptual consciousness not only grasps external objects and situations but at the same time relates these to the individual and thus becomes an agency representing the individual.

The last two citations no longer consider the real ego as originating solely in the need of surmounting the Oedipus complex, but look for its genesis farther back, in perceptual consciousness. It was in this direction that the "New York Freudian School" of Heinz Hartmann looked for the further development of psychoanalysis. Freud had raised the question of how the real ego, which is guided by perceptual consciousness, can arise out of the narcissistic pleasure ego. He had initially answered by linking the real ego with the surmounting of the Oedipus complex, but he also went farther back, beyond this crisis which arises in the fourth or fifth year, to the undoubtedly earlier development of perceptual consciousness. According to Hartmann, we must assume that there is from the outset a "primary" ego nucleus that is autonomous in relation to the id; this ego nucleus has the functions of perception, movement, and memory and is determined by the person's interest in self-preservation, which is neglected in the sphere of the id.[11]

---

[9]S. Freud, *New Introductory Lectures on Psycho-Analysis*, trans. W. J. H. Sprott (New York, 1933), 112.

[10]Freud, *The Ego and the Id*, 37.

[11]See H. Hartmann (n. 2, above), 99ff., 130ff., 176ff., etc. According to R. A. Spitz, the concept of an ego nucleus or, rather, of a plurality of ego nuclei as the basis for the subsequent formation of an integrated ego was developed as early as 1932 by E. Glover and then developed further by Spitz himself from 1936 on; see R. A. Spitz, *The First Year of Life* (New York, 1965), 104. But according to Spitz, there is a question here not of the instinct of self-preservation but of a tendency to synthesis that is present in all living things and leads from the realm of the organic into the realm of psychology. Spitz's idea of a plurality of rudimentary ego nuclei is not open to the objection, as Hartmann's views are, that the ego in its function as acting subject is simply reduced to this kind of ego nucleus and that the problem of the genesis of the ego is thus obscured. On the other hand, the problem does arise in Spitz of how ego formation can come about so as to integrate the various ego nuclei.

Erik H. Erikson has developed this approach still farther, while laying the emphasis on social psychology.[12] He conceives the ego as being an "individual way of mastering experience," that is, as an "ego synthesis," which is "a successful variant of a group identity" (22). But this ego synthesis must constantly be constructed anew. There is, therefore, a process, the stages of which are identical with the Freudian phases of development. The latter are no longer interpreted, however, as primarily phases in libido development, but as a sequence of forms of ego synthesis that lead ultimately in adolescence to a process whereby an autonomous ego is fashioned.

The starting point of this entire process of development is childish narcissism (39) with its three components—basic trust, autonomy, and initiative (53)—which become differentiated in that order during the period from the first to the fourth year of life. The three correspond to Freud's oral, anal, and oedipal phases. These are followed by the so-called latency phase, during which the child wins recognition by learning and doing. It learns to develop a sense of industry and thus overcome its feelings of inferiority (82ff.). Then comes puberty, in which the previous childhood identifications with ready-made models yield place for the first time to the task of building an identity of one's own (88ff., 118ff.). Only now do the various identifications turn into a cohesive whole in the sense of an integrative identity. This sense of ego identity is "the accrued confidence that one's ability to maintain inner sameness and continuity (one's ego in the psychological sense) is matched by the sameness and continuity of one's meaning for others" (89). This identity continues to develop during the life of the adult (95ff.), for it must be constantly adapted to the changing experiences of life. Such adaptation is necessary in order to enable the ego to exercise its synthesizing function and thus integrate the experiences of the individual.

Erikson is aware that in speaking of "identity," he is introducing a new term into psychoanalysis (101), and he expressly points out that his concept of identity "covers much" of what is meant by the self in Mead and others (147). He asks, therefore, whether

> it may be wise . . . to reserve the designation "ego" for the subject, and to give the designation "self" to the object [i.e., in consciousness]. The ego, then, as a central organizing agency, is during the course of life faced with a changing self which, in turn, demands to be synthesized with abandoned and anticipated selves (149).

The catchword "integration" provides no basis for representing the constitution of the ego as an acting subject generally.

[12]E. H. Erikson, *Identity and the Life Cycle: Selected Papers* (New York, 1959). The page references that follow in the text are to this book.

Since Erikson follows Hartmann in assuming "a central organizing agency" that is part of the individual from the outset, he inclines in fact to the possibility of locating all change on the side of the self as opposed to the ego. He does say in passing that "identity formation . . . can be said to have a self-aspect, and an ego-aspect" (149), but he does not go any farther into the intimate connection between the two. Instead, he closes with this observation: "Until the matter of ego vs. self is sufficiently defined to permit a terminological decision, I shall use the bare term identity in order to suggest a social function of the ego which results, in adolescence, in a relative psychosocial equilibrium essential to the tasks of young adulhood" (150).

If we examine Erikson's scheme of the psychic life story, we find a singular imbalance: the development of the ego is interpreted as a development not so much of the ego as of the self. In this way, his acceptance, with Hartmann, of an ego that is present from the beginning of psychic development is reconciled with the sequence of diverse ego syntheses which Erikson himself has worked out; at the same time, an answer is given to the question of what the subject is that effects these ego syntheses. But how can ego and self be identical, as the fact of self-consciousness shows them to be, if the self is constantly changing while the ego remains unalterably what it is?

We are back once again with the problem of the unity of ego and self that was raised as a difficulty against G. H. Mead's views. This time, however, the antithesis is not only between the internal aspect and the external social aspect of the individual; it is within the individual as an antithesis between the historical process whereby the individual is formed and the subject of this formative process, a subject that supposedly stands in back of all changes. But here, in a much more pronounced way than in Mead, the process of formation is conceived as one that accounts for the origin and development of the ego as the very agency that must effect the integration of the individual at each new stage. For this reason the contradiction too is all the more pronounced, namely, that the ego, which is presupposed as "a central organizing agency" for the process and each of its phases, is to produce the series of identifications and identity formations of itself, and yet is not to change in the process but is, rather, to keep its changes external to itself, so to speak, as changes occurring in it only insofar as it is the object of self-consciousness, that is, occurring only in the self.

But are not ego and self identical? Am I not my self? And is not my self *my* self only because I am identical with it? But if I and my self are in fact identical, then a change in my self necessarily means a change in my ego as well. At this point, the question does of course arise: Who is it, then, that accomplishes the process of change? That is precisely the problem that is obscured as a problem by the assumption of "a central organizing agency" which underlies the entire process of ego development from the very beginning. Such an assumption seems indeed to answer the question of the subject that produces the entire process of individual development with all its changes. But it is taken too much for granted that this central agency remains always essentially the same and is therefore able to explain the unity of the formative process that goes on in the story of a human life.

The problem is recognizable in Freud, and indeed in a much less camouflaged form. It is the problem of how there can be a passage from the narcissistic pleasure ego to what may be called the exocentric real ego. Freud's answer was to refer to the mechanism of identification. But identification presupposes an ability to stand off from that entanglement with what is its own that characterizes the narcissistic pleasure ego. It is understandable, then, that Hartmann should have traced the roots of the real ego back to an innate predisposition, even though this predisposition acquires independence from the id only in the early postnatal development of the infant.[13] He found a guiding principle in some suggestions of the later Freud that the concern for self-preservation, which is fundamental for the ego, is alien to the instincts of the id. The only ominous thing is that the idea of a primary, independent ego nucleus is accompanied not only by the capacity for exocentricity but also at every point by the idea of a "fixed and abiding" subject. As a result, the problem, left open in Freud, of the origin and development of the ego in the course of a life history, is narrowly focused in a quite specific direction, namely, toward the idea of the further nuancing of an already existing agency. The assumption of an ego nucleus that is present from the beginning could then be developed by Erikson in such a way that the *development* of the ego is entirely on the side of the *self.* The result is the contradiction, already mentioned, between the historicity of the self and the assumption of an ego that is supposedly not affected by the history of the self and yet is identical with this self.

In conclusion, let me sum up the results of this investigation of analytical ego psychology. The superiority of this psychology to Mead's theory of the self consists in the fact that the ego undergoes a process of development or formation that is marked in a decisive way by a processing of the social environment in which the individual develops. Freud was admittedly unable to explain fully the mechanics of this process, because the genetic passage from narcissistic ego to real ego as a censoring agency was not satisfactorily explained. The emergence of the real ego from the id was traced back, on the one hand, to the act of identification with the parental

13H. Hartmann, 176ff.

superego at the time of the resolution of the Oedipus complex and, on the other hand, to the process whereby as a result of perceptual consciousness the ego became, at an even earlier period, an agency independent of the id. But it does not seem that the real ego as an agency with a critical function can be derived from the narcissistic pleasure ego which is constrained by the instincts. Talk of a process whereby ego and id are "differentiated" does not seem relevant unless both factors are present from the beginning, even if only in an undifferentiated unity.

It was for this reason that Hartmann and Erikson assumed human beings to possess an ego agency that exists from the beginning and is fundamentally autonomous in relation to the id. In making this assumption, however, they obscured the real extent of the problem of the origin and development of the ego. The development of the ego is described by Erikson as a process of identity formation in which at each new stage there is an integration of all vital factors in an "ego synthesis," initially through a series of identifications but then, from puberty on, through the development of an autonomous ego identity that also subsumes the earlier forms of ego synthesis. But Erikson's terminology does not steadily reflect this process which in fact describes the development of the ego. The reason is that at the same time he needs the ego to serve as an agency with several functions: it must produce the phases of the process step by step; it must at the same time persist through the various phases of ego formation; and it must make it possible to think of these phases as phases in a single, unified process of which it is from the outset the productive principle. The result of all this is that Erikson can conceive of this process of identity formation only as one of development of understanding of the self, not as a development of the ego as such.

At this point it is impossible to advance farther without a more profound reflection on the relation between ego and self. As we engage in this reflection, the theological or, as the case may be, religious implications of the questions regarding the process of ego formation that have thus far been discussed will also be rendered explicit. It will be seen that behind the difficulties Freud had in deriving the exocentric real ego from the narcissistic pleasure ego stands what is perhaps the most important implicit relation between psychoanalysis and the religious thematic.

II. The Ego and the Self

In both Mead and Erikson (who may have been influenced by Mead here) we found a distinction made between ego and self as subject and object respectively of self-consciousness. The distinction goes back via William James to the idealist philosophy of self-consciousness. It found its classic expression in Fichte's effort to think the unity of ego and self and thus the unity of self-consciousness. For two reasons the attempt has lost none of its relevance for the contemporary discussion of the origin and development of the ego, a discussion that derives its character chiefly from psychology.

The first reason is that the question of the unity of ego and self, which must be posed to Erikson no less than to Mead, continues to be neglected even today. The unity is all too easily taken for granted and presupposed, even though ego and self are for the rest described in completely different ways: the self as a product of society and the ego as preceding any social relations, or the self as object of a development and the ego as productive source of this development. Thinkers see no need of reconciling these differences and showing that ego and self are in fact unified in the self-conscious ego.

There is a second reason for the continued relevance of Fichte's philosophy of the ego. Just as contemporary psychologists take for granted the unity of ego and self, so too they assume almost as readily that this unity originates in the activity of the ego; they assume it even while they also strongly insist that this activity must assimilate and integrate the social relations within which the process of identity formation takes place. Now such an explanation of the unity of ego and self as due to the activity of the ego is also found in Fichte's first model for the unity of self-consciousness as proposed in the first edition of his *Wissenschaftslehre* in 1794. Consequently when present-day thinkers trace the unity of ego and self back to the activity of the ego, they are still accepting the framework of Fichte's first *Wissenschaftslehre*. It is all the more significant, then, that Fichte found it impossible to stay with this model of self-consciousness.[14]

How did Fichte come to the problem of self-consciousness and its unity? Kant in his *The Critique of Pure Reason* (1781) had described self-consciousness as the ground of the unity of all experience.[15] The consciousness that I think the contents of consciousness must be able to accompany all my representations (B 132). For "only because I can connect a variety of given representations in one consciousness, is it possible that I can represent to myself the identity of consciousness in these representations" (B 133; p. 49). The "I think" is, then, the "vehicle of all conceptions in general," as Kant says in another passage (B 399; p. 121).

If self-consciousness is to be the unifying ground of all experience, it must first be unified in itself; in it the ego must be unified with itself. Since

---

[14]In the remarks that follow I am following D. Henrich, *Fichtes ursprüngliche Einsicht* (1967).

[15]I. Kant, *The Critique of Pure Reason.* trans. J. M. D. Meiklejohn, in *Kant* (Great Books of the Western World 42; Chicago, 1952). The references "B 132," "A 345," etc., here and later, are to the sections of the two editions of the German original; the page references are to the English translation.

Fichte's purpose in his *Wissenschaftslehre* was to develop the formal system of knowledge out of self-consciousness as its ultimate ground, he had first to ensure the unity of self-consciousness itself, especially since he was not satisfied with Kant's description of it. According to Kant, the ego produces its self-consciousness by turning back on itself (in reflection).[16] But if this is so, it seems that the self-conscious ego cannot be identical with itself. For, according to Kant, the ego that we grasp through reflection upon it is only the ego as it appears to us, not the ego as it is in itself.[17] Is the self of self-consciousness something, then, that by no means belongs essentially to the ego as such? Yet Kant had also been able to write that "the Ego is but the consciousness of my thought" (B 413; p. 124). This would mean that the ego is essentially conscious of itself, or that self-consciousness is inseparable from it. But if this is true, then self-consciousness cannot first arise through reflection of the ego on itself but must be given from the outset together with the ego.

Now, according to Dieter Henrich, this last sentence expresses what Fichte is saying in the opening sentence of his *Wissenschaftslehre:* "The ego posits itself."[18] This statement means, first of all, that at every point the ego is accompanied by an implicit knowledge of itself. In this sense it "posits" itself. But since in the *Wissenschaftslehre* of 1794 Fichte conceived of this self-positing as an action of the ego, he also understood this self-positing as a production.[19] The question therefore inevitably arises once again: Can the ego that posits itself (in self-consciousness) be the same ego

[16]Henrich, 11. P. Reisinger, "Reflexion und Ichbegriff," *Hegelstudien* 6 (1971), 231–65, has a different view of the thinking of the "I" by the *logical* ego: "It is not possible to determine from Kant whether this operation is reflexive in nature and how it is to be conceived" (235). Reisinger takes as his starting point *Critique* A 345f., where it is said that "we can . . . lay at the foundation of this science nothing but the simple and in itself perfectly contentless representation 'I,' which cannot even be called a conception, but merely a consciousness which accompanies all conceptions" (Meiklejohn, 122). But the fact that this is the case does not itself come into consciousness except through reflection that turns from consciousness of the world to the otherwise simply concomitant consciousness of the ego.

[17]Kant, B 155. It is expressly said here that in its consciousness of itself the ego grasps itself only as an appearance "like other phenomena." Therefore "I have . . . no knowledge of myself as I am, but merely as I appear to myself. The consciousness of self is thus very far from a knowledge of self" (B 158; p. 56).

[18]J. G. Fichte, *Werke* (ed. I. H. Fichte), I, 98. Henrich, 18, insists that this indicates the immediacy with which the ego emerges. The ego is itself the very positing. The fact that the ego posits itself means initially only that it is not something given which, according to Kant, "affects" us (see Reisinger, 237). According to Kant himself in his *Anthropologie in pragmatischer Hinsicht* (in Kant, *Werke,* ed. W. Weischedel, I [1960], 632), the concept of "positing . . . is utterly simple and one with that of being itself." If we add that the being in question is being as object of *thought,* Fichte's language becomes quite clear.

[19]Fichte, *Werke* I, 459. On this, see Reisinger, 236ff., as well as W. Janke, *Fichte. Sein und Reflexion. Grundlagen der kritischen Vernunft* (1970), 7. On the concept of action, see also J. Rohls, "Person und Selbstbewusstsein," *NZST* 21 (1979), 54–70, esp. 60f.

as that of which it is conscious? The thesis that the acting ego is the origin of self-consciousness "follows upon the knowledge the ego has of itself without being reducible to it."[20] That is to say, the idea of action goes beyond what is immediately given in self-consciousness, but, on the other hand, it does not succeed in accounting for the identity, given in self-consciousness, of the two terms, ego and self.

The change made in Fichte's fundamental formula in 1797 was meant to get around this inconvenience. Fichte now said that the ego posits itself *as* self-positing. As a result, the ego known in self-consciousness is grasped as what the ego is meant to be in Fichte's original theory: a positing ego. At the same time, the ego known in self-consciousness is also posited, and posited as knowing itself or in its two aspects as ego and self. Nonetheless the question still remains: Is the positing ego identical with the posited ego? That is, does self-consciousness in its knowledge of itself know itself as at the same time positing, producing this knowledge, and, conversely, does the positing ego know itself at the same time as posited? It seems that the ego which posits itself as self-positing cannot at any point be as yet identical with the ego posited as self-positing.

Fichte seems to have realized, when faced with this situation, that the unity of the ego with itself in self-consciousness cannot be explained as the product of an action of the ego. Rather, the ego finds itself "inserted" (the term is from 1801) into the unity of itself with itself. The henceforth passive formulation—the ego is "an activity endowed with power to see itself"—points back to a prior origin of the ego. This origin cannot be found in the realm of finite objects which the ego itself constitutes as its objects. The issue here is the origin of the freedom of the ego itself, and in order to explain the source of the ego's insertion into unity with itself as experienced in self-consciousness Fichte once again introduces the idea of the absolute. Self-consciousness becomes for him the "manifestation of God,"[21] because the ego cannot posit itself in its unity with itself, but neither does it owe this unity to any of its finite objects.

Fichte's passage from the effort to develop a theory of self-consciousness to the mystical religious philosophy of his late years seems plausible in view of the paradoxes of self-consciousness and especially in view of the impossibility of deriving the unity of ego and self from the ego itself. It is plausible at least if the presupposition made in transcendental philosophy, and shared by Fichte with Kant, is accepted, namely, that the unity of "I think" underlies all experience and therefore cannot be derived from any experiential data. But the objection has legitimately been raised that Fichte's theological grounding of the unity of self-consciousness remains

[20]Henrich, 21.
[21]Ibid., 39.

extrinsic in a way to the set of circumstances whose problematic he is developing; the theological answer "does not contribute to the intelligibility of what is being explained."[22]

Among the philosophers who came after Fichte the basis for the plausibility of his passage from the analysis of self-consciousness to religious philosophy ceased to exist, since these men undertook to understand self-consciousness as mediated through the experience of objects and thus to do away with the autonomy of self-consciousness and its position prior to any and all experience of the world. It now became possible to inquire into and describe the origin of self-consciousness in the context of experience of the world.

Hegel had taken the first step in this direction when he declared Fichte's concept of the ego as "an utterly indeterminate identity" to be the result of an abstraction from all the determinate content of experiential knowledge.[23] Since Fichte simply opposes this abstract ego to the contents of our consciousness of the objects of our experience of the world he does not surmount the dualism of Kant: the contents of objective consciousness remain external to the ego.[24] Hegel finds the true reality of self-consciousness only by doing away with the opposition between self-consciousness and consciousness: the ego is present to itself precisely in what is other than itself.[25]

Yet despite the emphasis on the idea that self-consciousness is mediated to itself through what is other than itself, namely, the consciousness of objects, even Hegel's thinking continues to be based on the starting point of the philosophy of consciousness within transcendental philosophy. In his *Logik* he appeals explicitly to Kant's idea that the unity of the concept is based on the "unity of the *I think* or self-consciousness."[26] Hegel did not take into account the fact that Fichte had moved beyond this starting point in his later philosophy.[27] In this matter, then, that is, in his concept

---

[22]Thus U. Pothast, *Über einige Fragen der Selbstbeziehung* (1971), 45.

[23]G. W. F. Hegel, *Encyclopädie der philosophischen Wissenschaften* (1817), § 45. See Hegel's earlier *Differenz des Fichteschen und Schellingschen Systems der Philosophie* (PhB 62a), 39. In order thus to conceive the ego in its simplicity as beginning and ground of philosophy, abstraction must be made from the empirical ego; see *Wissenschaft der Logik* I (ed. G. Lasson; PhB 56), 61f.

[24]Hegel, *Differenz*, 42f.; *Vorlesungen über die Geschichte der Philosophie* (Suhrkamp Verlag: Theorie Werkausgabe 20), 398f.

[25]Hegel, *Encyclopädie*, § 436; see earlier, § 424.

[26]Hegel, *Wissenschaft der Logik* II (PhB 57), 221.

[27]Compare what Hegel has to say in his lectures on the history of philosophy (n. 24, above), 387f. and 413 on the "popular philosophy" of Fichte's Berlin years. See also Henrich's judgment in his essay "Selbstbewusstsein," in R. Bubner *et al.*, eds., *Hermeneutik und Dialektik (Festschrift H. G. Gadamer)*, I (1970), 281, that Hegel's concept of the ego remains tied to Kant's reflection theory of self-consciousness: "He consistently describes

of the subject, Hegel did not advance as far as Fichte did; on the other hand, he could think of himself as improving on Fichte, because he introduced objective consciousness into the concept of the ego.

In the period that followed, philosophers attempted to think the objective mediation of self-consciousness on the basis of objective reality, and in so doing turned against the conception found in the philosophy of consciousness. I cannot here trace this development in detail. It began with Ludwig Feuerbach and, more generally, with the new turn to naturalism; thus it also continued the tradition of empiricist philosophy and still influences thinking down to the present day. In the process the idealist concept of the subject was opened up in the direction of the self; this is a tendency under which the social psychology of Mead and the analytical philosophy of the ego may be subsumed.

The opposition to the version of the self in the philosophy of consciousness emerges with special clarity in those conceptions which see the *self*, with which "I" know myself to be identical in my self-consciousness, as located in the *body* of the individual. Thus Nietzsche, in his *Thus Spoke Zarathustra* (1883–84), identified the self with the body: "Behind your thoughts and feelings, my brother, there stands a mighty ruler, an unknown sage—whose name is self. In your body he dwells; he is your body."[28] This self, Nietzsche continues, "laughs at your ego and its bold leaps. 'What are these leaps and flights of thought to me?' it says to itself. 'A detour to my end. I am the leading strings of the ego and the prompter of its concepts.' "

The basic idea that Nietzsche expresses here is close not only to the behaviorist interpretation of the way we use the words "I" and "self" but evidently also, and above all, to Freud's psychoanalysis. The instinctual forces of the id, which are connected with our corporeality, exist prior to the development of our ego and seek to determine the behavior of the latter. On the other hand, the Freudian ego is also independent and opposed to the forces of the id as a censoring agency which has the task of controlling these forces in the light of the exigencies of reality and in harmony with the demands of the superego. Therefore despite the general kinship between psychoanalysis and the ideas expressed by Nietzsche, there is also a difference between the two in the conception of ego and self.

William James may well have been even closer than psychoanalysis is to Nietzsche's view. James indeed resisted any materialistic reduction of

---

self-consciousness as the coming to itself of a being that is in itself already self-related—and therefore completely in accordance with the reflection model, which presupposes everything."

[28]F. Nietzsche, *Thus Spoke Zarathustra,* trans. W. Kaufmann (New York, 1954), Part I, no. 4: "On the Despisers of the Body," 34–35.

human behavior to an "automaton theory" and assumed that the key to an understanding even of physiological data was to be found in structures that are accessible only to psychological introspection.[29] Nonetheless, in his psychological analysis of the self he describes the body as not only the innermost part of our material self (as distinct from our social and spiritual self) but even as the nucleus of the self as such: "The nucleus of the 'me' is always the bodily existence felt to be present at the time."[30] James differs from Nietzsche in that only the "feeling" of one's own bodily existence at any moment constitutes the self (but also the ego), and constitutes it in varying ways as material, social, or spiritual self, or also as ego. At every point we are dealing with the concrete bodily actuality of the individual. But this individual that exists in bodily form is thereby thematized in a way that goes beyond what is externally perceptible and observable. For this reason, most later authors have been cool to a terminological identification of self and body. G. H. Mead, who links his own thinking to James's concept of the social self, explicitly rejects the identification of the self with the "physiological organism."[31] In his view, corporeality is an essential presupposition for the self, but the latter must be distinguished from corporeality and seen as "essentially a social structure."

The problems in which Mead's own theory of the self gets entangled showed how easy it is to fall short of the stage of awareness of the problem that was reached in the idealist thematization of self-consciousness, even at the very time when we believe we have passed beyond it by transcending the starting point of the philosophy of consciousness. The same can be said for many of the current attempts to use the tools of linguistic analysis in order to move beyond the idealist theory of the subject. It must also be said, however, that like the emphasis on the body as the indispensable basis for speaking of ego and self and like the doctrine of the social self, linguistic analysis has contributed an important point of view to a new description of self-consciousness.

In its explanation of self-consciousness or, more accurately, of the linguistic utterances in which self-consciousness finds expression, the philosophy of linguistic analysis starts with the way in which the pronoun "I" is used. Ever since Gilbert Ryle—and this was true in substance in Wittgenstein's *Philosophical Investigations*—the pronoun "I" has been regarded as an "indexical term" by which "speakers at any moment describe them-

---

[29]E. Herms, *Radical Empiricism. Studien zur Psychologie, Metaphysik und Religionstheorie William James'* (Gütersloh, 1977), 79f., 71ff.

[30]W. James, *The Principles of Psychology* (1890; repr. in 2 vols., New York, 1950), I, 292 and 400; see 371. In a very similar way, to the "judging thought" which at any given moment effects identity the ego is "nothing but the bodily life which it momentarily feels" (I, 341, n.).

[31]G. H. Mead, *Mind, Self and Society,* ed. C. W. Morris (Chicago, 1934), 139f.

selves."[32] According to Ryle, such indexical terms as "this," "here," and "now" have as their function to make clear to the hearer or reader the precise thing, person, episode, place, or moment of which there is question. So too, "I" is not a "name" for something, but rather points to an individual who may in fact also be named; moreover, "I" points to an individual precisely when that individual uses the term.[33]

Wittgenstein had observed: " 'I' is not the name of a person, nor 'here' of a place, and 'this' is not a name. But they are connected with names. Names are explained by means of them."[34] Ryle makes it clear in addition how this connection between name and indexical sign is created in the specific case of the pronoun "I," namely, through the fact that the speaker of the moment uses it to point to himself or herself. A name stands for the way in which others describe the speaker who speaks of himself or herself with the word "I." Instead of a name, these others can also say "he" or "she" when speaking of that person. In any case, the use and intelligibility of the pronoun "I" are connected in a systematic way with the fact that others may use either "he" or "she" or a name for the person to whom they are referring. It is "a constitutive element in the use of 'I' that the person who says 'I' knows, first of all, that he or she can be addressed by others as 'you' and spoken of as 'he' or 'she,' and, second, that he or she is singling out a particular person from others whom he or she can describe as 'they.' "[35] The use of the word "I" is therefore always conditioned by a field of social communication and therefore indirectly by the body of the speaker as well, since others always speak of him or her with reference to his or her bodily presence (in his or her place, at his or her time).[36]

This description may seem to boil down to the assertion that the use of "I" in speech is to be explained in a purely behavioristic way, inasmuch

---

[32]J. Rohls (n. 19, above), 54–70, esp. 63ff. The term "indexical word" is from E. Tugendhat, *Selbstbewusstsein und Selbstbestimmung* (1979), 73.

[33]G. Ryle, *The Concept of Mind* (London, 1949).

[34]L. Wittgenstein, *Philosophical Investigations,* trans. G. E. M. Anscombe (Oxford, 1968), no. 410.

[35]Tugendhat, 74. See also the earlier work of S. Shoemaker, *Self-Knowledge and Self-Identity* (Ithaca, N.Y., 1963), 12f. Tugendhat rightly regards the correlation of the use of "I" with the description of the same person by others through a name or through "he/she"— designations which at the same time include the bodily existence of the person—as an important insight of Wittgenstein (90).

[36]Shoemaker (15f.) stresses the point that speech about someone in the third person always refers to that person's body, while according to Ryle (189) the use of the first person singular is often but not always equivalent to "my body." The more general thesis that the concept of the individual person is inseparably bound up with the person's corporeal existence is substantiated especially by B. Williams, *Problems of the Self* (New York, 1973), who analyzes various dissenting theses.

as all sentences using "I," including those which refer to states and conditions of the speaker, are reduced to externally observable behavior. Wittgenstein had adverted to this as a possible interpretation and had said that he did not intend to deny "mental processes."[37] By this last term he evidently meant the consciousness of the person's own states and activities. At this point, linguistic analysis places itself on the level of the classical theories of self-consciousness.

Wittgenstein seems to have seen no special difficulty here, because he regarded sentences in which speakers express their own states as equivalent to expressive gestures. Thus he regarded the sentence "I am in pain" as meaning the same thing as a cry or a moan or, as the case might be, a substitute for these. The child who learns to substitute such a sentence for an outcry learns a "new pain-behaviour."[38] E. Tugendhat legitimately asks here whether in adopting this interpretation Wittgenstein has in fact "surmounted the behavioristic reduction."[39] If such a reduction is to be obviated by the fact that speakers have an immediate relation to their own pain, the question nonetheless remains of how the linguistic expression of pain is to be understood semantically.

Probably for comparable reasons, S. Shoemaker finds himself compelled to ask how it is that experiences are mine and known as such.[40] In his discussion of Bertrand Russell he avoids interpreting the knowledge of one's own perceptions as itself a perception that would then require a further perception by which to be conscious of itself (and so on). In the case of sentences dealing with the person's own states, such as feelings of pain, he speaks instead of a knowledge for which there are no criteria and which finds expression in claims not subject to correction.

In thus assuming a "knowledge" of personal states Shoemaker goes beyond Wittgenstein, but he believes that by claiming there is no criterion for such knowledge he remains in agreement with Wittgenstein.[41] At the same time, since the expression of remembering, even without the remembered contents, belongs to the class of claims for which there are no norms and which are not subject to correction, Shoemaker establishes continuity

[37]Wittgenstein, no. 307f.

[38]Ibid., no. 244; see no. 404.

[39]Tugendhat, 125. Rohls, 68ff., does not see the problem that remains here; appealing to Wittgenstein, no. 246, he declares the claim, "I *know* that I am in pain," to be meaningless and therefore describes the verbal expression of pain as a purely performative utterance—without taking into account the fact that performative utterances are certainly linked to objective criteria. Consequently he goes so far as to deny the phenomenon of self-consciousness as such: "There is no such thing as a consciousness of my thinking" (70). But in any rejection of phenomena as such, philosophical dogmas are exerting an influence in the background. Here again, then, Tugendhat proceeds with notably greater caution.

[40]Shoemaker, 81ff. and esp. 215ff.

[41]See Wittgenstein, no. 404.

with the classic empiricist interpretation of self-consciousness which, ever since Locke, has considered this to be closely linked to memory. In Dieter Henrich, moreover, this "normless ascription to the self" seems to make possible a bridge from linguistic analysis to the interpretation of self-consciousness in transcendental philosophy, since, in any case, ascription to the self implies a relation to the self and a normless ascription to the self therefore also includes a normless self-identification of the person.[42] The question of how such a self-identification is intrinsically possible remains open, of course, and at this point linguistic analysis leads to the question asked in transcendental philosophy regarding the constitution of self-consciousness.

The claim of a self-ascription for which there are no criteria has not, however, gone unchallenged. As early as 1968, Michael Woods objected to Shoemaker that a normless self-reference does not exclude "the possibility of uncertainty about *what* it is that is referred to." Thus someone might very well say "I" and nonetheless discover only later on that he or she is a person. In addition, the use of the word "I" involves a self-identification (in the sense of a differentiation of the self from other things) that cannot be without criteria. Woods therefore thinks that self-ascriptions must in principle be open to correction.[43] All that is left, then, of the thesis of a normless self-reference is the vague feeling of familiarity. All actual contents, and even the form of the *self*-ascription as such, are linked to assertions that can be either true or false and that therefore claim to be knowledge in the usual sense and consequently are in principle subject to correction.

Tugendhat has likewise felt compelled to renounce or at least limit the interpretation of self-referential sentences as expressions of a normless knowledge which speakers have of their own states.[44] He admits that I can deceive myself about my "psychic states." Freud's teaching on the unconscious therefore becomes important here for its discussion of self-reference. The problems raised by "epistemic" self-consciousness (in the sense of an immediate knowledge of one's own states) force us to turn to the practical relation of the self to itself (144); only here do these problems find their solution. Tugendhat takes as his guide Heidegger's description

---

[42]D. Henrich, " 'Identität': Begriffe, Probleme, Grenzen," in *Identität,* Poetik und Hermeneutik 8 (1979), 133–86, esp. 176ff.

[43]M. Woods, "Reference and Self-Identification," *Journal of Philosophy* 65 (1968), 568–78, esp. 569, 573f., 576. Woods's point of reference is an immediately preceding essay by S. Shoemaker, "Self-Reference and Self-Awareness" (ibid., 555–67), which repeats the thesis of his book.

[44]Compare 139ff. with 133 of Tugendhat, *Selbstbewusstsein und Selbstbestimmung.* The words cited in the next sentence of the text are from this book, 141, and the further page references in the text are also to it.

of Dasein, which is concerned with the being which it must be (172ff.).
But he relates this explication of the relation to the self solely to "the
existence *in store* at each moment" (177) and to "prospective possibilities
of action" (261). Since, moreover, this relation is mediated through social
interaction, Tugendhat supplements Heidegger with Mead, who, by
adopting the viewpoint of the "generalized other," makes possible a
"critique of the meaning" of present society "in the light of a project for
a better society" and thus, through a process of consensus formation,
provides a criterion, lacking in Heidegger, for determining what is good
for the relation of individuals to their own future.[45]

Tugendhat is certainly correct in pointing out that Heidegger's interpretation of Dasein as "disclosedness" by reason of which "this entity
(Dasein), together with the being-there of the world, is 'there' for itself,"
is to be understood as an explication of Dasein's consciousness of its own
being and therefore as a corrective continuation of classical philosophical
analyses of self-consciousness.[46] But since Tugendhat's interpretation of
Heidegger's thought is applied only to "the existence in store at each
moment" (127), it filters out precisely the elements in Heidegger's reflections that enable these to be read as a theory of self-consciousness. For how
can human beings relate to "the existence in store at each moment" as to
their own future? To what extent is the Dasein concerned with *its own*
being when dealing with the possibilities available to it?

The answer is clear only in the light of the presupposition which Tugendhat describes as the "stronger" and more far-reaching thesis of Heidegger himself as opposed to the "weaker" thesis to which Tugendhat
limits himself in his own interpretation. This "stronger" thesis is that the
future about which the Dasein is concerned and which "it must be" is
decisive for its being as a whole; in other words, that the present being
(Vorhandensein) of the Dasein is based on the future with which it is
concerned in its "to-be" *(Zu-sein).*[47] If we agree with Tugendat that this
thesis must be excised as a "speculative feature" (186), then we have not
simply stripped Heidegger's thinking of superfluous frills and "interfering
eccentricities" (185); we have removed the presupposition that makes it
possible to understand his thought as a contribution to the theme of
self-consciousness. For this requires that in the relation to future activities

[45]According to Tugendhat, the indicated interpretation of Mead's thesis is possible only
"if we introduce into it Heidegger's concept of self-relation to self" (271), the concept being
here understood, of course, along the lines of the interpretation given above of Heidegger's
thought.

[46]Tugendhat, 171 and 165ff. See M. Heidegger, *Being and Time,* trans. J. Macquarrie and
E. Robinson (New York, 1962), 170f. (German text, 132f.).

[47]Tugendhat, 180f., 186f. Tugendhat claims, but does not show, that the "weaker" thesis
as well as the "stronger" is in Heidegger and not simply read into him.

and actions there be the question of a relation to the person's own *selfness* which is in some sense "identical" with the presently existing Dasein (and with its past as well); otherwise there could be no question of *its* selfness.

It is precisely this element of identity which is not thematized in Tugendhat's interpretation. The fact that human beings are "something given, observable" is taken by Tugendhat to represent a fixed reality. But then every relation to the self becomes something supplementary and added on, and it remains a mystery in Tugendhat how this supplement is to affect the persons "themselves." Heidegger's introduction of the time factor into the analysis of self-consciousness yields its meaning only on the basis of his "stronger thesis" that the Dasein is constituted by the future *in the whole of its being.*

In his interpretation of Freud, Tugendhat again fails to adopt the viewpoint of an ego identity that is in a process of becoming. He accuses Freud of reifying the ego and turning it into an "agency that deals with objects" (149), when in fact Freud's concern is with the very origin of this agency to which "objects" are given. The alternative to the theory of self-relation would be the assumption of a self-intimacy that from the outset underlies all experience and is the presupposition for human beings being able to relate to "themselves" in the further course of their development. Such an assumption would, however, presuppose a primordial knowledge by individuals of their "selves," and yet this thesis from the transcendental philosophy of consciousness is also rejected by Tugendhat with the quite unconvincing argument that the only "knowledge" is of *facts,* not of *objects,* and therefore not of the individual's own "ego."[48] In keeping with this position, Tugendhat will allow a self-consciousness that is a knowing of one's own *states* but not a self-consciousness that is a knowing of one's own ego or self.[49]

What, then, is meant by the assertion that my states, intentions, etc., are

---

[48]Ibid., 18f. Even if this claim is accepted for the German verb *wissen* (despite such everyday idioms as "I know [*weiss*] the way"), the close connection between *wissen* and *kennen* must also be kept in mind (English uses "know" to render both of these German verbs). *Kennen* is used primarily in relation to objects or persons, while *erkennen* may refer both to states of affairs and objects. Given this fact, Tugendhat's subsequent statement that the word *kennen* is "in reality always propositional" (57) seems forced. He himself must admit that the sentence "I know [*kenne*] myself" is a "meaningful . . . expression" (57f.; see 33), and when he hastens to add that such a sentence is, however, "elliptical" and calls for the question "What, then, do you know about yourself?" this does not at all change the fact that *kennen* relates to objects (or persons), even if it may also be connected with a knowledge (*wissen*) of particular facts. This means that while the knowledge of objects (or persons) is based on a knowledge of states of affairs, the latter kind of knowledge can also be so conceived that knowledge (*Erkenntnis*) of particular states of affairs reaches its completion only in the knowledge (*Kenntnis*) thereby attained of things and persons.

[49]Ibid., 157f.; see 188ff.

"my own"? Tugendhat rightly says: "It is one and the same being that says 'I' and that relates to itself" (157). The question, however, is what constitutes the identity of this being, and to this Tugendhat gives no answer. He seems to take it for granted that from the very outset the "person" is present as a complete entity which is the subject of the states, activities, and actions that are imputed to it. But then the unavoidable question arises: Is the person from the outset conscious of its states, activities, and actions as being *its own?* If yes, then the self-consciousness which is to be explained is in fact presupposed. If no, then it remains a mystery how the person that later becomes conscious of itself can be identical with the person that lacked such self-consciousness and how it can understand the states and activities of the latter as *its own.*

Tugendhat is evidently far from having gotten beyond the idealist position of the problem in the question of the possibility of self-consciousness. His talk of the "person," whose presence he presupposes as the basis for all relations to the self (and which is not, for example, constituted precisely by the *act* of self-relating), proves to be a variant of the conception which Fichte criticized in starting his own analysis of self-consciousness: the explanation of self-consciousness as a reflection on an already existent ego. Tugendhat does not avoid the difficulties connected with this conception simply by asserting that in statements which persons make about themselves they are claiming a knowledge not of their own ego but "only" of their own states, activities, and actions.

The idealist representation of the ego in transcendental philosophy or, at any rate, a widespread interpretation of the idea of transcendental subject is turned upside down by views that regard the ego or person as not ready-made in advance but as resulting from an originative process; this new approach is present in rudimentary form in Mead and the Freudian school but also in Heidegger. As a result, Heidegger's *Being and Time* displays a tension comparable to that which we saw in Mead and in analytical ego psychology: the Dasein, which according to Heidegger must be thought of in terms of its future being, is also described as that which relates itself to this future. As everyone knows, this ambiguity, which, contrary to Heidegger's own intention, made it possible to read *Being and Time* as a continuation of the philosophy of subjectivity, caused his decision not to write the further volumes of this work. As a result, in his later writings he uses an entirely different language and form of argument in presenting the "turn" in thought at which he is aiming, namely, the turn that is to show the being-there (Dasein) as constituted by being (Sein).

In so doing, Heidegger also renounced, it is true, the completion of the task he had set about in *Being and Time:* to provide the conceptual argument that would apply the viewpoint of temporality (which he had introduced) in order to dissolve the idealist philosophy of the subject. For this reason, the approach he developed remains all the more important. It should give pause, above all, to those who much too quickly judge the attempts of psychology and social psychology at a theory of the genesis of the ego to be purely empirical in value and without relevance to philosophy—especially to the philosophy of subjectivity of transcendental idealism, which asserts the ego and its identity to be the ultimate transcendental basis of all achievements of consciousness. But the fact of distinguishing between a transcendental ego and an empirical ego cannot render the first completely independent and separate from the second, without at the same time causing the loss of the very starting point of transcendental reflection: the consciousness that intuits, represents, and judges.

Heidegger's problematization of the traditional conception of the person as subject[50] was taken farther by Jean Paul Sartre, who for this purpose went back to Husserl's phenomenology of consciousness.[51] In Heidegger (says Sartre), "the *Dasein* has from the start been deprived of the dimension of consciousness." This means that "the ecstatic character of human reality will lapse into a thing-like, blind in-itself."[52] If we are not to do an injustice to the reality of the human, we must take the *cogito* as our starting point, without, however, allowing ourselves to become imprisoned in the immanence of consciousness. In Sartre's opinion, this is the path opened up to us by Husserl's demonstration of the "intentionality" of consciousness, that is, its directedness to something that exists independently of consciousness, something that transcends consciousness. It is the nature of consciousness, then, that it presupposes a being that transcends it; consequently the interpretation of consciousness as constitutive of the being of its object contradicts the very structure of consciousness itself.[53] Consciousness is by its nature "the openness of being."

According to Sartre, however, this consciousness is not connected with an ego as its subject, as it still is in Husserl. Rather, the ego appears only at a secondary stage in the life of consciousness. Sartre had defended this thesis in 1937 in an article on the transcendence of the ego, in which he stated that the concept of the ego includes both sides of self-consciousness,

---

[50]Heidegger, *Being and Time*, 70ff. (German text, 45ff.).

[51]J. P. Sartre, *Das Sein und das Nichts*, German tr. (1962) of *L'être et le néant* (Paris, 1943). [The English translation was published as two books. Part I, ch. 2, and Part IV, ch. 2, appeared as *Existential Psychoanalysis*, trans. H. E. Barnes (New York, 1953). The remainder appeared, in an abridged version, as *Being and Nothingness*, trans. H. E. Barnes (New York, 1956). In the notes that follow I shall give Pannenberg's page references to the German translation, adding references to the ET where I have been able to track down passages being quoted.—Tr.]

[52]Sartre, *Das Sein und das Nichts*, 129; ET 49.

[53]Ibid., 27ff.

that is, the "I" and the self, and that both of these are the product of a reflection.[54] In other words, not only the self-consciousness of the ego (the Kantian view) but even the ego subject itself is seen here as the product of reflection. But does not reflection require a subject that does the reflecting? The answer for Sartre is no. What finds expression in reflection is the subjectivity of consciousness but not a subject.[55] Consciousness is "for itself" and "presence" to itself, but this "itself" precedes all existence as subject and is not captured by any idea of a subject, since in the in-itself of the represented subject the for-itself would disappear. "Presence to self," on the contrary, "supposes that an impalpable fissure has slipped into being," an element of difference, of "not" being identical. The for-itself is characterized by the fact that "it can not coincide with itself."[56]

According to Sartre, then, the reflexive movement of consciousness antecedently excludes anything like identity with self. Nonetheless the "itself" which belongs to consciousness in a prereflective, nonthematic way[57] points to the being from which it thrusts itself away inasmuch as it is present "with" itself, that is, with the human reality of the person.[58] In this sense, consciousness is personal,[59] and out of it there emerges through a second reflection the idea of *selfness*. For Sartre, this selfness is characterized by totality, because it binds together the "contingent in-itself" of human reality and the movement of reflection that advances beyond this in-itself. In the movement of reflection the lack of being on the part of reflective consciousness makes itself manifest, and therefore the movement reaches out once again to being, but to a being that lies beyond the being already at hand: to the self.[60] This self is represented by "impure" reflection as existing in-itself.[61] The impurity of this reflection consists in the "bad faith" which makes it refuse "to cut the bond which unites the reflected-on to the reflective"; instead, it represents the self as existing in itself, thus causing the movement of reflection to disappear. According to Sartre, it is only this impure reflection that brings the representation of the ego which immediately divides into the two aspects of

[54]J. P. Sartre, "La transcendance de l'ego. Esquisse d'une description phénoménologique," *Recherches philosophiques* 6 (1936–37), 85–123.

[55]On the subjectivity of consciousness, see Sartre, *Das Sein und das Nichts*, 23 and 27, as well as 29.

[56]Sartre, *Das Sein und das Nichts*, 129ff.; ET 53f. In the German version, see also 126ff., 139ff., 151, 157, 321.

[57]See Sartre, *Das Sein und das Nichts*, 18.

[58]Ibid., 131; see 65. Later on, Sartre even says: "Reflective consciousness must *be* the consciousness reflected-on" (*Das Sein und das Nichts*, 220f.; ET 127, italics added).

[59]Ibid., 160.

[60]Compare ibid., 160f. with 142ff. and 187f.

[61]Sartre, *Das Sein und das Nichts*, 225ff.; see 159ff.

self and "I" (corresponding to the distinction between reflected-on and reflective).[62]

Sartre's analysis produces an especially radical dissolution of the concept of subject. He is not satisfied to show that the ego as well as the self is the product of a conscious process that has no subject. Rather, he also reproaches this product with being impure, because both aspects of self-consciousness—ego and self—owe their existence to a reification that brings to a halt the still incomplete process of reflection. As a result, the problem of the identity of the ego and self in self-consciousness ceases to be a problem. The phenomenon of the for-itself in the negativity of the movement of reflection excludes identity.

A critique of this analysis must begin with Sartre's description of the ego in its partial aspects as ego and self. According to Sartre, both are aspects of the totality of the process that is human reality: "self" describes the totality of our states and qualities, "ego" the totality of our actions. That, at least, is how Sartre's early essay on the transcendence of the ego explains it. On the other hand, his principal philosophical work leaves undecided the precise nature of the distinction between self and ego. This is probably not accidental, since selfness as totality is now attained in the light of the future and the future possibility of freedom (so that it already includes the element of action). As far as the "self" is concerned, Sartre's description is in general quite plausible. Mead's considerations on the importance of the "generalized other" and especially Erikson's ideas on ego synthesis and ego identity have made it clear that under the heading of "selfness" it is the whole of the individual's existence that is at stake. Heidegger had expressly said as much.

The reproach of reification that is leveled against the idea of the totality of selfness seems to be justified only if this is thought of as existing "in itself" and apart from the process of reflection. But such a view of it arises only if in the concept of the ego the self is connected with the "I" as a totality of action. For then the "I" is supposed to underlie every action as its subject; in other words, it is presupposed as existing "in itself." When the self is joined to this "I" in the concept of the ego, it loses the element of indeterminacy by which it is absent-present.[63] The representation formed of the "I" is therefore decisive in the reproach of reification. The objection is based especially on the aspect of totality that unites "I" and self in the concept of ego. Reification consists in taking a totality that

[62]Ibid., 228; ET 137; see the German text 159f., and the article "La transcendance" (n. 54, above), 28, as well as 20. See also the remarks on the "inclination to independence" in the reflective and the reflected-on (*Das Sein und das Nichts,* 216).

[63]Ibid., 161.

is in fact always still incomplete and representing it as a subject of conscious experiences that exists "in itself."

But in fact Sartre's conception of the ego as a totality is by no means obvious. It reflects the idea, which goes back via Kant to Descartes, of a fixed and permanent ego as a condition for the unity of consciousness. It makes no difference here whether the unity of the ego consists, as in Locke, in the unity of consciousness itself and is therefore bound up with the continuity of memory[64] or whether it is distinguished from consciousness as the subject underlying the latter.[65] It is important, on the other hand, that ever since David Hume there has been another view which links the phenomenon of the ego so closely to individual conscious experiences that the *unity* of the ego through time becomes secondary or even a pure product of the imagination (a product based, according to Hume, on the similarity of the ego element in the individual conscious experiences).[66]

Such a view, which has been proposed even in the present century by philosophers such as Bertrand Russell and (in a modified form) Alfred J. Ayer,[67] avoids Sartre's accusation of a reification of selfness in the representation of the ego. This view is not even discussed by Sartre. It does, of course, have its own problems, which were seen long ago by Hume and in the light of which Kant's very easily misunderstood solution through the idea of a transcendental ego is to be evaluated. But for the moment we should not pass over the observation that the ego is linked first and foremost with the experiences and utterances *of the moment:* "When I turn my reflection on *myself,* I never can perceive this *self* without some one or more perceptions; nor can I ever perceive anything but the perceptions."[68] The ego is primarily *given with* the experiences of the moment. The same holds for linguistic utterances, in which the word "I" functions primarily as an indexical term.

In the light of this observation Sartre's criticism of the concept of ego becomes invalid, since the isolated momentary ego agency, together with the instant of consciousness on which it depends, claims no permanence but is past when reflected on. On the other hand, Sartre's criticism of the idea of an *enduring* ego that underlies the whole of the process of con-

---

[64]J. Locke, *Essay Concerning Human Understanding* II, 27, 16ff. (Dover ed., I, 458ff.).

[65]So G. W. Leibniz ("Theophilus") in his *Nouveaux Essais* II, 27, §9.

[66]D. Hume, *A Treatise of Human Nature,* I, 4, 6 ("Of Personal Identity").

[67]B. Russell, *The Analysis of Mind* (1921), 17f.; idem, *The Problems of Philosophy* (1950), 19 and 51; A. J. Ayer, *Language, Truth and Logic* (1936; 1946²), 126f.

[68]Thus Hume in the appendix to *A Treatise of Human Nature* (ed. L. A. Selby-Bigge, 1888; new edition by P. H. Nidditch, 1978), 634. On this observation Hume bases his thesis that the self is "nothing but a bundle or collection of different perceptions, which succeed each other with an incredible rapidity, and are in a perpetual flux and movement" (ibid., I, 4, 6, p. 252). For this reason, philosophers speak of Hume's "bundle theory" of ego identity.

sciousness is confirmed. And finally it also becomes possible to answer the objection raised to Sartre's destruction of the ego agency, namely, that an ego agency belongs at least implicitly to consciousness as such.[69] This may be admitted; but such an ego agency does not necessarily entail the idea of an ego that *perdures* beyond the isolated act.

But can we do without the idea of an ego that abides permanently in the process of consciousness and through its shifting phases? Even Hume acknowledged that *in fact* we ascribe permanence and identity to our ego. But he declared himself unable to show the factors that make such permanence and identity possible. He saw the weakness of his own attempted explanation, according to which the presence of a comparable ego reference in each of a series of experiences causes us to take likeness for identity.[70]

Hume had assumed that memory not only discovers personal identity but also (co-)produces it, and this "by producing the relation of resemblance among the perceptions."[71] It has been objected to this that memory cannot serve as a criterion of personal identity, nor can it ground such an identity. A *criterion* of a person's identity is needed only by others, but in the eyes of others the sameness of the person is established primarily through *bodily identity*.[72] The latter is reason enough to attribute to the person the memory of his or her earlier experiences or actions, but the lack of such remembering cannot prevent the person from being held responsible for those earlier actions. The ego itself, on the other hand, needs no criteria of identity.[73] The question does arise of the ground in

---

[69]E. Marbach, *Das Problem des Ich in der Phänomenologie Husserls* (The Hague, 1974), 192, observes that even for Husserl the ego as subject that accomplishes acts comes into view only through reflection. But reflection "does not produce this ego; it recognizes it as an ego that lives in 'self-forgetfulness' and functions as agent which unifies acts even *prior* to reflection." See also M. Gisi, *Der Begriff Spiel im Denken J. P. Sartres* (1979), 149, n. 11. Sartre himself agrees with Husserl's view that the reflected-on "gives itself as having been there before reflection" (*Being and Nothingness,* 128). He claims, however, that this pregiven is altered by reflection. But this does not change the fact of the pregivenness, and the claim that it is altered by reflection can itself be demonstrated only by (more precise) reflection, as Sartre in fact undertakes to do when he describes the ego as a materially inadequate representation of selfness.

[70]Appendix to *A Treatise of Human Nature* (n. 68, above), at I, 4, 6 (p. 254 in the edition cited).

[71]Ibid., 261. On this point, Hume was still following Locke's view (see above, n. 64).

[72]Shoemaker, *Self-Knowledge and Self-Identity* (n. 35, above), 15f., 196ff., 243.

[73]Ibid., 124. Here—in the nonnecessity of criteria of identity *for one's own person*—is the element of truth in Shoemaker's assertion of a normless and noncorrigible *knowledge* of one's own states (211ff.; see above, nn. 40ff.). The nonnecessity of criteria of identity for one's own person may be due to the fact that we are continually establishing this identification, as must still be shown in detail. Nonetheless this identification is subject to correction, as is clear from the fact that its concrete content in the life of the person changes.

us for our consciousness of personal identity, but memory is not an adequate ground. The identification of a past with a present self calls for more than memory can provide[74]—unless the past self is already remembered *as* my own self. But then the identification is presupposed and has not been achieved simply through memory.

William James devoted special attention to the process whereby identity is established given the presupposition that reference to the subject is had only at each discrete moment in the sequence of experiences. In the "bundle" theories that go back to Hume, James found no agency that could establish an identification and render intelligible the fact of personal identity. He did find such an agency in the synthetic function of the ego as discovered by Kant, although he leveled sharp criticism at the idea of a transcendental ego, which he understood as the assertion of an unchangeable subject that in reality underlies the stream of consciousness, an "agent whose essence is self-identity and who is out of time."[75] James transferred the synthetic function of the transcendental ego to the successive moments of consciousness which, because of the way in which these are reflexively linked, he called "judging thought." The function of the momentary cross sections in the stream of consciousness is to be a *medium* in which the manifold elements are *linked together* and to which they *belong.* In like manner, Kant had written: "For the manifold representations which are given in an intuition would not all of them be my representations, if they did not all belong to one self-consciousness." Conversely, "all the manifold [intuition]" is "subject to conditions of the originally synthetical unity or apperception" and is brought together only in the unity of consciousness.[76]

[74]Ibid., 130: "My memory can inform me of the existence of a self at t_1 and of its properties and activities at that time, of the existence of a self at t_2 and of its properties and activities at that time, and so on, but it seems that any statement that identifies a past self with a present self, or a past self existing at t_1 with a past self existing at t_2, necessarily goes beyond what can be known solely on the basis of memory."

[75]James, *The Principles of Psychology* (n. 30, above), I, 368; see 361f. But James rates much too low the debt his own thought owes to Kant when he writes: "The only service that transcendental egoism has done to psychology has been by its protest against Hume's 'bundle'-theory of mind" (370).

[76]Kant, *The Critique of Pure Reason* (n. 15, above), B 132 (p. 49) and B 136f. (p. 50). James rightly calls attention to this argument: "No connected consciousness of anything without that of *Self* as its presupposition and 'transcendental' condition" (I, 361). However, Kant's thought is here reported in a one-sided way as speaking only of the establishment of the synthesis through self-consciousness. In fact, Kant can also say, conversely, that only a synthesis of a variety of representations in a single consciousness makes it possible for me to "represent to myself the identity of consciousness in these representations" (B 133, p. 49). D. Henrich, *Identität und Objektivität. Eine Untersuchung über Kants transzendentale Deduktion* (Heidelberg, 1976), makes a detailed examination of this tension between the various statements of Kant.

While James ascribed the unity of consciousness to each individual moment of consciousness as such and not first of all to self-consciousness,[77] he conceived these moments of consciousness as (momentary) ego agencies which at each instant effect an appropriation of the manifold of *preceding* impressions—"a *Thought,* at each moment different from that of the last moment, but *appropriative* of the latter, together with all the latter called its own."[78] But Kant too had been sufficiently influenced by Hume that he did not immediately assume for *empirical* consciousness a continuously identical ego (what James called an "archego"):

> For the empirical consciousness which accompanies different representations is in itself fragmentary and disunited, and without relation to the identity of the subject. This relation, then, does not exist because I accompany every representation with consciousness, but because I join one representation to another, and am conscious of the synthesis of them. Consequently, only because I can connect a variety of given representations *in one consciousness,* is it possible that I can represent to myself the *identity of consciousness in these representations.*[79]

In this Kantian argumentation empirical consciousness appears, first, as primarily a thing of each moment ("fragmentary") and, second, as a synthesis of the representations in consciousness, which synthesis is a condition for self-consciousness. When in the further course of his exposition Kant reverses the relation of founding and founded and explains the unity of consciousness as a condition for continuity in the consciousness of objects, it must be borne in mind that this is a transcendental assertion and does not mean that a unitary ego must be present antecedently to any and every consciousness of objects. A view like the last-named has already fallen victim to a confusion between transcendental and metaphysical statements.[80] The transcendental function that Kant has in mind is already accomplished in the momentary syntheses of consciousness to which the quoted sentences can be referred and which James makes central to his discussion of the concept of the ego. It is true, however, that Kant's

[77]James, I, 363 (against Kant); see 276ff.
[78]Ibid., 401; see 430. *Appropriation* always means *choice* as well (370; see 340), but as a result of this selective appropriation of all preceding impressions the ego of the given moment is at the same time "the *representative* of the entire past stream" (340) and provisional terminus of a series of moments that were likewise marked by integrative appropriation.
[79]Kant, *The Critique of Pure Reason,* B 133 (p. 49).
[80]Kant discusses this confusion in the chapter on the paralogisms of pure reason in *The Critique of Pure Reason,* B 396ff., esp. 406f. and 408: "The proposition of the identity of my Self amidst all the manifold representations of which I am conscious, is . . . analytical. But this identity of the subject . . . cannot . . . enounce the identity of the person, by which is understood the consciousness of the identity of its own substance as a thinking being in all change and variation of circumstance" (p. 123). See also the remarks on self-consciousness at the beginning of the *Anthropologie in pragmatischer Hinsicht* where Kant points out as "noteworthy" the fact that a child "begins only rather late to use 'I' in speaking."

description of the transcendental presupposition as a "unity of consciousness" is questionable and misleading. For it suggests that such a unity must explicitly underlie each moment of consciousness—as asserted in fact in the metaphysical idea of an "archego" as the basis for the stream of consciousness. By speaking in this way, Kant himself fostered the confusion between his transcendental apperception and that kind of metaphysical notion.

Dieter Henrich has argued that while the perception of relations between facts presupposes the unity of *consciousness* (at any given moment), it does not necessarily require an explicit self-consciousness. The possibility of an "egoless consciousness" is suggested by the fact of dream consciousness[81] and furthermore by the consciousness proper to early childhood with its *unthematic* egocentricity. The possibility of reaching an explicit self-consciousness on this basis does indeed presuppose an original, although unthematic, familiarity of consciousness with itself[82] that is subsequently differentiated and articulated in explicit self-consciousness.

But to what is this original familiarity related? What is the content of the "self" in the familiarity of consciousness with itself? Who is it that really appropriates the objects of the consciousness that takes place in the "appropriation" of these? Because of the momentary character of consciousness it cannot be consciousness itself to which these objects are appropriated, as James remarks on one occasion: "Its appropriations are therefore less to itself than to the most intimately felt part of its present Object, the body, and the central adjustments, which accompany the act of thinking, in the head."[83] James assumes here the familiarity—or, to use his word, the "warmth"—that marks the relation to the person's own body.

But we also remember here that the body is, for James, the basic content of the "self," and as a result we are back once more to the question of the relation between ego and self. *The momentary "I" that appears in the form of each momentary unity of consciousness can exercise its synthetic function of appropriating its objects to "itself" only indirectly via the "self."* Consciousness of the "I" as such appears only belatedly. The familiarity of the "I" with 'itself" is a familiarity with a form, diffuse perhaps and rudimentary, of

[81]Henrich, "Selbstbewusstsein" (n. 27, above), 257–84, esp. 275; see 260ff.

[82]Ibid., 269ff., explains the reasons for the acceptance of such an original familiarity that is to be distinguished from reflexive knowledge. This idea is related to Sartre's idea of a "presence" of consciousness to itself. But we must eliminate from the idea at this point the element (emphasized by Sartre) of a *negation* of that which exists and is given in-itself, since this element belongs to the stage of reflection and should therefore not be ascribed to the "prereflective cogito."

[83]James, I, 341. His note on this passage says expressly that for Thought "I" means "nothing but the bodily life which it momentarily feels."

the *self*.[84] This then is the basis on which, or "medium" in which, consciousness grasps the unity of its contents. This rudimentary self is not, however, to be limited to the person's *own* body but at least includes in the "symbiotic" stage of early childhood development the bodily presence of the mother,[85] and later on what James calls the "social" and "spiritual" self. *Familiarity with "oneself" is therefore mediated through trust in a sheltering and supporting context in which I originally awaken to myself.*

There is a reversal here of the usual relationship of ego and self as formulated by the early Fichte and as still taken for granted in the ego psychology of Hartmann and Erikson: the ego does not establish itself through its action by positing itself. The ego is not the continuously existing subject of my individual development, a subject that is always present behind all changes in consciousness and gives ever new definitions of itself in the process of its identity formation, but is not itself changed thereby. Rather, the ego is primarily tied to the moment and receives its continuity and identity only in the mirror of the individual's developing consciousness of itself as the totality of its "states, qualities, and actions." In the initial stages of development the individual's own self must first of all achieve distinction from that of the mother. This distinction comes through the development of object perception and is completed only by the acquisition of speech.[86] Only then can there be the coordination and distinction that are attained through use of the indexical word "I" for the presentation of the person's own self.

In the case of living beings generally and of the higher animals in

---

[84]It would be worth inquiring whether, despite its egolessness, dream consciousness does not give evidence precisely of this kind of familiarity or intimacy with self.

[85]At this stage the child "can distinguish its mother from the environment, but the self is not yet clearly distinguished from the mother. Prior to the end of this period the childish ego can hardly be treated as an independent entity" (J. Loevinger, "Zur Bedeutung und Messung von Ich-Entwicklung," in R. Dobert, J. Habermas, et al., *Entwicklung des Ichs* [Cologne, 1977], 150–68 at 156). See also J. Loevinger and A. Blasi, *Ego Development* (London, 1976), 15f.

[86]Thus Loevinger, "Zur Bedeutung," 156f. Loevinger emphasizes the importance for the child's ego development of the cognitive development studied by Piaget and Inhelder (166). A. Blasi (in Loevinger, *Ego Development*, 41) writes: "The development of the infant's attachment to his mother is explained by the acquisition of the concept of the permanent object." R. A. Spitz, with regard to *Die Entstehung der ersten Objektbeziehungen* (French, 1954; German, 1957), has established that the human face is initially perceived as a gestalt pattern and that only in the second half of the first year of life does the child distinguish the individual face of the mother from other faces; see esp. Spitz, *The First Year of Life*, 86ff. But Spitz still connects with this the assumption, taken from E. Glover, of "ego nuclei" and a "rudimentary ego," which he considers to begin as early as three months (104ff.). Loevinger's thesis that the distinction of the self from the mother is completed only with the acquisition of speech leads to a significantly later starting point. Perhaps this should be assigned to the period when the child learns the use of the indexical word "I."

particular it is legitimate to say that the development of a central nervous system is accompanied by a "tendency toward synthesis" that also characterizes the "organizational function" of the human ego.[87] We may therefore also say that even in the little child there is a quite understandable but still unthematic egocentrism.[88] But we must be aware that the word "I" is being used here in a broad, transferred sense, for this is an "I" without self-consciousness ("unthematic"). The development of self-consciousness evidently begins on the side of the self (the "me") and is only secondarily expanded through the supervention of the ego, which as the speaker of the moment and the one who is experiencing at the moment knows itself to be one with its abiding "self" and yet also distinct from this self. Correspondingly the psychoanalytic description of the earliest ego development should likewise differentiate between id and *self* (not between id and ego), if we want to avoid serious confusion in our understanding of the further development of the individual.

The ego is not as immediately concerned as the self is with the "totality" of its own being. Rather, I am first and foremost the speaker of the moment and the one who at each moment experiences and acts. Only indirectly, insofar as the "I" of the isolated moment is known as identical with "myself," and therefore as the momentarily present manifestation of that totality of states, qualities, and actions that in the eyes of a "generalized other" are to be ascribed to the individual which I am—*only in this way does the "I" as such acquire a continuity that lasts beyond the isolated moment.* It is then, too, that the dialectic specific to self-consciousness arises. When the individual as ego knows itself to be identical with its self, it can know that this identity is based on its self or exercise it as ego. It can distance itself from its bodily, its "social," and even its "spiritual" self and in the course of its identity formation project ever new forms of the self. But it can also, for the sake of its self (especially its social or spiritual self), distance itself from its own ego as well as from the impulses of the id that control the ego. Finally, it can allow the ego to be determined by the self so that the ego gains the stability and the continuity that enable it to master the impulses of the id.

Initially, however, the process of identity formation takes the sameness of the self as its point of departure. Only through this very identity does the life of the individual acquire constancy and stability. Only this identity makes possible the formation of a stable ego that can be not only the subject of behavior generally (the individual, even the prehuman individ-

---

[87]Thus Spitz, *The First Year of Life,* 104ff., in agreement with Glover and Hartmann.

[88]Thus Henrich, "Selbstbewusstsein" (n. 27, above), 276, who appeals to J. Piaget, *The Child's Conception of the World,* trans. J. and A. Tomlinson (New York, 1929).

ual, is already this) but also a *subject of deeds,* a subject which because of its identity is reliable and accountable.

This reversal in the traditional definition of the relation between ego and self enables us to resolve the contradiction that we saw, in the preceding section, in the conceptual foundations of analytical ego psychology. The process of identity formation now becomes intelligible because it is the process whereby not only the self but the ego as well is formed, insofar, that is, as an identity and continuity can be attributed to the ego which enable it, for example, to function as a censoring agency. The cohesion and the unity of the individual's life history are based on the self, not on the ego. Precisely for this reason it is important that each new projected identity should subsume the earlier attempts at identity formation, so that individuals can identify themselves with themselves and thus make it possible for their ego to acquire stability and autonomy.

The insight that the identity and the continuity of the ego are based on the self also makes it possible to resolve the difficulties in G. H. Mead's position. Mead's examination of the sociopsychological meaning of the self led to the question of how far this self can be identical with the ego, as the fact of self-consciousness evidently implies. The understanding of this identity was rendered difficult in Mead by the fact that the self had to be socially conditioned (being the sum total of the expectations and appraisals of the individual by others), while the ego was not thus socially conditioned. Mead had accepted the traditional conception of the ego as subject and had supposed that the ego, being the creative origin of individual behavior, *by its nature* enjoys a continuous existence. It has now become clear that the ego too bears the imprint of social relations in respect of its continuity and identity, since (above and beyond the unity of meaning that comes from the indexical word "I") such continuity and identity belong primarily to the *self,* and to the ego only insofar as it knows itself to be identical with "its self." At this point, the opposition which showed in Mead between ego and self disappears and is replaced by a distinction and coordination which make possible a categorical description of the process of identity formation.

The determination of the individual by society affects both the self and the ego. This holds true, however, only to the extent that the individual is given appropriate consideration as existing in the moment, that is, as ego, in the projected identity of the "social self." Then it is possible for the integrative intention of this project of the self to be fully achieved. It can also happen, however, that the ego does not "accept" the social self and thus falsifies its claim to be integrative. This means that the ego (as existing in the moment) does not regard itself as given appropriate consideration in the classification and expectations assigned it by others. Usually, the acceptance and integration remain partial. The picture of the self that emerges from the classification assigned by others and from their expectations is accepted only in a more or less modified form. Only in the case of their own bodies must individuals make the best of things as they are. As Mead had seen, identification with the social self does not take place in a purely passive way. It always includes more or less extensive modifications, by the individual in question, of the perspectives adopted by others and, above all, a shift of accent within the overall picture.

These modifications carry with them, of course, the claim that the persons who are the relevant points of reference should change their appraisals and expectations accordingly. The result is conflicts between individual and society over the identity of the former. The question of my identity can be a disputed one. The sketch given of a character varies not only in history, as Schiller says, that is, in the memory of posterity, but even during the lifetime of the individual. Moreover, not only are others at odds among themselves about what they are to think of you, but you yourself take part in this dispute, which, when all is said and done, concerns you in a special way. This is the struggle for recognition, for recognition by others of an identity with which individuals can identify, so that they may find their "place" in society and develop a "healthy self-consciousness" instead of having to suffer from a "fragmented self-consciousness."

Even when others do not grant the desired recognition, individuals can assert themselves by taking refuge in privacy (to the extent that this is allowed) or by asserting their spiritual selves against the social appraisal with which they cannot identify. Nonetheless the acquisition of an acceptable measure of social recognition is indispensable as the basis of all life in society, from two-party personal relationships to the institutional structure of society and relations between states.

III. Personality and Its Religious Dimension

The thoughts thus far presented on the interpretation of the unity of ego and self that is attested by self-consciousness have as yet made no appeal to the religious basis for this unity, though the later Fichte found himself obliged to have recourse to it in order to account for the unity of self-consciousness. It may even seem that when the relation of establisher and established is reversed between ego and self, any recourse to a religious basis for the unity of the two has been made superfluous. For, like the self, the ego too (as a continuous, stable agency) now presents itself as the product of a continuous interaction between society and individual consciousness. There is, however, something not accounted for. As Mead realized, the "role" that others assign to an individual can be accepted by the individual or rejected or modified. The same holds for the social self insofar as it includes a "set of roles specifically mine."

Because individuals must *accept* and, in so doing, can *modify* roles and social self, we must speak of a *polarity* between role and individuality.[89] Because the identification of individuals is a *self-identification* that is mediated through their perception of their own being as different from or in harmony with the identification made of them by society, it is not reducible to a matter of the influence exerted by society. At the same time, it is only through such self-identification that individuals accept their social identity in a more or less modified form and ultimately integrate it into their projects for their own identity. Something comparable is true of "identity factors" such as body, name, sex, age, group membership, and life history.[90] These are indeed indispensable "factors" in the personal identity of the individual inasmuch as none of them may be neglected in the formation of an identity without paying the price of pathological ego formations. But *the way in which* they are integrated into the given identity project depends on the latter. To use the vocabulary of Sartre, the for-itself of the individual is not reducible to the in-itself of the conditions affecting the individual's self-realization.

H. Lichtenstein is correct, therefore, when he observes that unlike the beasts the human being "has for ever to struggle with the need to define himself, to create an identity not basically inherent in him by dint of inborn automatisms."[91] While the identity of individuals is not to be conceived as the product of a subject that already exists with its own identity, neither is it to be understood as a simple internalization of social appraisals and expectations. Rather, the opposite is true: "The emergence of social and cultural patterns is possible only because man, in contrast to the animal, must define his identity."[92]

Indispensable, then, for identity formation is the element of self-identification on the part of the momentary ego agency, which in turn achieves

---

[89]Thus D. J. de Levita, *The Concept of Identity,* trans. I. Finlay (New York, 1965), 152; see the reference on 100–101 to the distinction in social psychology between role and identity, since role is here being discussed in the framework of personality structure. According to J. L. Moreno, "The Role Concept," *American Journal of Psychiatry* 118 (1962), 518, every role is a "fusion of private and collective elements" (cited in Levita, 102). But if we begin in this fashion, Levita's concept of identity as a "role set" (141ff.) seems to presuppose what it is meant to explain, namely, the *identification* of the individual with a role or set of roles. In like manner, his definition of the self as a "collective term" for self-perception, self-concept, self-evaluation, etc. (159), supposes the concept of self and therefore cannot contribute to the question of how the self is constituted.

[90]See Levita, 211ff.

[91]H. Lichtenstein, "Identity and Sociality," *Journal of the American Psychoanalytical Association* 9 (1961), 179–261 at 184 (cited in Levita, 110).

[92]Lichtenstein, 202 (in Levita, 111).

perdurance only through this self-identification. But what is it that makes the individual capable of this achievement, especially at the beginning of ego development? If there is to be an identification, there must evidently already be a familiarity with that with which the identification is to be effected. And this familiarity cannot be a familiarity with "itself," even if the latter is thought of as the individual's own body.[93] That would be of no help in the realm of theory, because the argument would be circular. In addition, such an answer does not satisfy the data of the individual's development. This development takes place, rather, in a sphere of familiarity that is more inclusive than the individual and connects the individual with its environment so closely that only secondarily does it manage to delimit its self and its ego *within* this sphere.

Developmental psychology is very much to the point here when it speaks of a symbiotic stage in the development of the child. This stage precedes the formation of the child's own individuality. During it the child's life is not clearly demarcated from the mother's, even though the child distinguishes the mother from the rest of the environment.[94] In this symbiotic relationship we may probably see the ontogenetic point of departure of human exocentricity. A comparable bond between child and mother is admittedly to be found in some primates, but it lasts much longer in the human child; release from complete dependence on the mother comes in the second month for the lower apes, in the fourth or fifth month for the anthropoid apes, but in the human being it occurs only between the ninth and the twelfth month.[95] The foundations are thereby laid for a more intensive experience of the world on the part of human beings as well as for their unique relationship to themselves.

Out of the symbiotic bond with the mother emerges the phenomenon of "basic trust," which Erik H. Erikson introduced into the discussion of identity.[96] The thesis that this comprehensive trust is the permanent basis of all later personality development has been adopted by behavioral scien-

[93]Compare the Stoic idea of familiarity or affinity *(oikeiōsis)* or the "attraction of nature" *(commendatio naturae)* in Cicero, *De fin.* III, 5, 16, and V, 14, 20. On the importance of this idea in early modern times, see D. Henrich, "Die Grundstruktur der modernen Philosophie," in H. Ebeling, ed., *Subjektivität und Selbsterhaltung. Beiträge zur Diagnose der Moderne* (Frankfurt, 1976), 97–121, esp. 105f., and in the Supplement, "Über Selbstbewusstsein und Selbsterhaltung," ibid., 125ff.

[94]Loevinger, "Zur Bedeutung" (n. 85, above), 156.

[95]F. Renggli, *Angst und Geborgenheit. Soziokulturelle Folgen der Mutter–Kind-Beziehung im ersten Lebensjahr* (1974), 77; see 55ff. See also Spitz, *The First Year of Life,* 98ff.

[96]Erikson, *Identity and the Life Cycle,* 55ff. See also his "Growth and Crises of the Healthy Personality," in M. J. E. Senn, ed., *Symposium on the Healthy Personality,* Supplement II: Problems of Infancy and Childhood (New York, 1950), or in C. Kluckhohn and H. Murray, eds., *Personality in Nature, Society and Culture* (New York, 1953), 185–215.

tist I. Eibl-Eibesfeldt.[97] The trust is initially given to the mother as mediator and embodiment of world and life in their totality. Later on, the
mother is joined by the father, whose presence brings protection and
promises security; he is the vital link connecting the family with the
surrounding world, at least according to the traditional division of roles
in the family. But as the child becomes increasingly independent of the
parents, the less do mother and family continue to be the embodiment of
life in its totality for the child. At the same time, the phenomena of family
life that are investigated in psychoanalysis make their appearance, as do
the limitations of parental power and of the family sphere generally in
relation to the surrounding world.

If basic trust is not to be lost, the child must now break its ties to the
mother and to the parents generally. There must be a new direction that
allows the growing child to maintain its trust in an unlimited security
despite all the threats and adversities of life. The task of thus detaching
from its initial connection with the parents the basic trust that nourishes
the courage to face life and of giving this trust a new direction falls
especially to religious formation, for the God of religious faith is able to
ensure an unlimited security as compared with the limited capacity of
human authority, and this even in situations of suffering, distress, and
worldly insecurity.

The fundamental importance of trust is not limited to an initial, infantile
phase of personality development which human beings must leave behind
them in the course of further development. Trust represents, rather, the
first and basic step in introducing a differentiation within the symbiotic
connection between individuals and their world. Individuals must attain
to independence while not destroying that symbiotic connection in the
process. This task is accomplished through the development of basic trust.
The point has correctly been made that the concept of trust includes a
distinction between child and environment.[98] Given this distinction, trust
brings the expectation that the environment (especially the mother) will
remain identically itself in its beneficent attitude toward the child and will
thus make it possible for the child to have continuity and (therefore)
identity. Here is the starting point for the fulfillment of a requirement that
is determinative for the further development of identity, namely, that the
child for its part be identical with itself.

This thesis, that the child's future development into independence is
based on the acquisition of basic trust and that this basic trust remains

[97]I. Eibl-Eibesfeldt, *Love and Hate: The Natural History of Behavior Patterns,* trans. G.
Strachan (New York, 1974), 212ff., 242.
[98]Levita (n. 89, above), 64; see 242.

important for the development of a healthy personality, must not be confused with a narcissistic "omnipotence of wishes" that knows nothing of the resistances offered by the world or else ignores them. Maturing and mature human beings must overcome these resistances by learning to deal with them and take them into account. If instead they take refuge in an imaginary "omnipotence of wishes"—in a fantasy world in which all wishes are fulfilled—their behavior is not simply to be judged, with Freud, a *regression* to an infantile attitude toward reality. Such behavior is also a perversion that is directly opposed to basic trust. For in basic trust, human beings preserve their openness to reality: the reality of other human beings and the world and, via these, the reality of their creator. In narcissistic regression, on the other hand, human beings close themselves against the world and withdraw into their own ego. This represents, in tendency, a destruction of the symbiotic unity of life that makes possible their individual existence; life as a symbiotic whole is replaced by the delusive idea of a world of limitless wish fulfillment.

The perversion we call narcissism is thus the primordial way of substituting the illusion of a limitless power of disposal for trust and a symbiotic wholeness of life into which the individual ego is incorporated for its own good and which is to be preserved only through trust.[99] The ego, which for its part owes its stability to a self, whether developed or rudimentary, here becomes the supposed basis for the whole of life, instead of experiencing itself on the contrary as sheltered within the totality of a trustingly affirmed web of life.

The enduring importance of basic trust for the development of individuals has nothing to do, then, with infantile regression but, on the contrary, helps them to open themselves to the world and its demands instead of taking flight from the real world into an infantile illusory world. The strength given by basic trust enables them to withstand negative experiences of life—the resistances, failures, disappointments, and sufferings—and even to make these part of their consciousness of meaning. This process of maturation is served by the detachment of basic trust from its primitive connection with the parents and by the new direction that religion gives to this trust. Children must learn to perceive and stand firm against the finiteness and limitations of all the authorities and agencies in their familiar world, including even the persons who are their closest points of reference, and yet not let their courage in facing life be turned into anxiety. To the extent that religious faith and religious formation accept the task of helping in this process, they certainly cannot be accused of fostering a regression to an infantile state. They are not in the service

---

[99] On this subject, see ch. 3, "Security Instead of Trust?" in my *What Is Man? Contemporary Anthropology in Theological Perspective,* trans. D. A. Priebe (Philadelphia, 1970), 28–40.

of a flight from reality but, on the contrary, seek to help individuals stand firm in the face even of reality's hostile aspects.

The danger of failure is, of course, undeniable, for, like other elements of social life, religious faith can be put in the service of infantile regression and has in fact contributed in this way to the emergence and promotion of neurotic distortions in ego development. This happens especially when religion directs all attention to the consolations of the world to come and no longer motivates human beings to accomplish their tasks in the present world. This is the same kind of falsification of religion that Marx had in mind when he called religion the opium of the people. But such neurotic forms of the religious outlook do not justify us in interpreting religion as a collective neurosis, as Freud did.[100] Such an interpretation ignores the achievement represented by an active conquest of the world, an achievement that the religions have made possible for human beings, even in the case of life's adversities.

An original, spontaneous trust, then, not only characterizes the initial phase of childhood development which follows upon the symbiotic vital union of mother and child but also remains a "cornerstone of a healthy personality" (Erikson). This claim is confirmed by the fact that every subsequent act of *identification* and independent *identity formation* represents a new actualization of that trustful self-opening to the world which was formed in early childhood. The identifying of oneself with something always requires courage[101] and trust in the soundness of that with which one involves oneself. Thus the child that identifies with the superego of

---

[100]See Scharfenberg (n. 7, above), 133ff. E. Fromm, *Psychoanalysis and Religion* (New Haven, 1950), found that, contrary to Freud (whom, however, he did not openly criticize), he was not prepared to declare religion as such a neurosis: "The study of man shows that this is not so," namely, that the "religious attitude . . . is not an intrinsic part of human nature" (28). Though Fromm had difficulty in accepting the elements in religion that go beyond a humanistic ethics (99ff.), he nonetheless maintained the necessity of religion (24ff.) as a "system of thought and action shared by a group which gives the individual a frame of orientation and an object of devotion" (21). This orientation and devotion are not to be judged neurotic; on the contrary, Fromm judged "neurosis [to be] a private form of religion" (27). This original observation reflects the fact that the failure to acquire an authentically religious orientation leads to neurotic substitutes. Thus Fromm discovered behind the facade of a secular way of life "any number of individualized primitive forms of religion: . . . ancestor worship, totemism, fetishism, ritualism, the cult of cleanliness, and so on" (29).

[101]Tillich's concept of "the courage to be" (*The Courage to Be* [New Haven, 1952]) is closely related to the phenomenon of basic trust which Erikson has brought to light. Just as trust is opposed to mistrust and anxiety, so courage is opposed to anxiety. But while courage is based essentially on self-confidence and can be described with Tillich as ontic "self-affirmation," the range of trust is greater. Trust is directed to a reality that transcends the self and in which the self has its ground. Only in the soil of this kind of comprehensive trust can self-confidence and courage flourish. Therefore the phenomenon of trust is more basic than that of courage, while the "courage to be" is itself a concrete manifestation of basic trust.

father or mother expects safety and security to the extent that it itself meets the demands of the superego. And maturing or matured persons who venture upon a projected identity for themselves as they choose a profession and a partner in marriage and decide to start a family,[102] trust that they will not fail in the venture. Religious formation shows itself successful here when the projected personal identity remains open to future experiences and to the adaptations these will require, without, however, losing its decisive character and without fostering the illusion of being able to begin repeatedly from scratch.

The connection between trust and self-identification makes it clear that in the child's basic trust and in the later actualizations of this the issue is selfhood. This is implicit in the very structure of trust itself, since those who trust abandon themselves to the constancy and reliability of that in which they put their trust. Basic trust is not, however, directed immediately to the self but rather to that agency which is able to protect and promote the self and in fact promises to do so. This last point is important. As a trust that concerns selfhood and not merely secondary issues, basic trust presupposes in those to whom it is given a commitment to the fostering of the selfhood of the trusting persons. Such a commitment characterizes love, for the essence of love is that it fosters the selfhood of those on whom it is bestowed. Basic trust therefore has for its counterpart love received or desired. To this extent, then, the selfhood of human beings has its ground in the love shown them by others, a love to which trust is a response and which trust desires.[103]

---

[102]O. F. Bollnow, *Wesen und Wandel der Tugenden* (1958), 175ff., esp. 178ff., rightly emphasizes the element of risk that is involved in trust. According to Bollnow, "there can be a question of trust only when I relate myself to something that is in principle not within my power" (178). I cannot, however, follow Bollnow when he concludes that trust is therefore limited to relations with other human beings. There is very likely also trust in the construction of a wall and in the "ordinary operation of a machine." Such trust is indispensable in all areas of everyday life, because controls ensuring security are feasible in practice only in exceptional cases, that is, when there is good reason for introducing them. On the other hand, Bollnow's view must be allowed to have an element of truth insofar as everyday trust in the soundness and reliability of things is really trust placed in the stability of their structures and the laws underlying these and thus in the orderliness of the world as a whole and in the ground that supports the world.

[103]But conversely, the selfness of lovers also comes to itself only through the love in which they exist outside themselves for the other. This is something that will have to be discussed in detail elsewhere. The importance of love for the attainment of selfness, that is, for the rectification of the chronic lack of being of the consciousness that exists "for itself," has been set forth by Sartre in *Das Sein und das Nichts* (370ff.; ET 340ff.). Love seeks to make the other —and the other in his or her freedom—my own because "the Other makes me be" (371; ET 343). But the love here is a needy love, not a giving love. In addition, Sartre fails to see that love finds its fulfillment in fidelity, in the case both of a giving love and of a needy love. He barely touches on the real issue when he asks the rhetorical question, "Who would

In the beginning, the love in question is the mother's love. Then, as basic trust detaches itself from the exclusive link with the mother, the real problem of life arises: How can human beings be sure of being loved and affirmed from this point on? Here a further implication of basic trust emerges. Basic trust is directed to an agency that is capable *without limitation* of protecting and promoting the selfhood of those who trust in it. This kind of limitless capacity and readiness manifests itself to the child in the devotion of the mother, but, objectively speaking, it in fact transcends the limits that in every case affect in one way or another the capacity and readiness of a mother. Because of its lack of limitation, basic trust is therefore antecedently a religious phenomenon. In the first phase of her child's life a mother deputizes for and represents to her child the love of God that transcends her love and is directed to the child through her. God is the true object of basic trust even in its beginnings. This fact does not become thematic, of course, until the exclusive ties of basic trust with the mother have been broken. If at this point religious formation is either lacking or is given in a more or less distorted form,[104] the result can be a warping or stunting of the personality structure.

With the aid of Erikson and a full review of research into the phenomenon of basic trust, Hans Küng has discussed the relation between basic trust and religious faith and has turned it into a new justification of the idea of God in opposition to atheism and nihilism.[105] But since basic trust is possible even without explicit religious faith, a distinction must be made between atheist and nihilist. "On the basis of fundamental trust, even an atheist can lead a genuinely human, that is, humane, and in this sense moral, life" (472). According to Küng, this distinguishes atheists from nihilists. But without God a basic trust in reality is, in the final analysis, unjustified (571f.). A yes to God, on the other hand, makes possible a justified basic trust. Küng therefore says that faith in God is also "radical fundamental trust" (572).

Hans Albert has rejected this thesis of Küng. He refuses its "radicalism of alternatives," its "blackmail by means of exclusive alternatives,"

---

be content with a love given as pure loyalty to a sworn oath?" (ibid.). Evidently he cannot see in the obligation that fidelity lays on itself the fulfillment of freedom in love but only its loss.

[104]An example of the latter case is given by T. Moser in his description of the alienating effects of a piety that focuses on guilt feelings; see his *Gottesvergiftung* (1976). See also B. Lauret, *Schulderfahrung und Gottesfrage bei Nietzsche und Freud* (1977). Moser, of course, rejects not only this distorted form of piety but the religious thematic as such. See, to the contrary, Fromm in n. 100, above.

[105]H. Küng, *Does God Exist? An Answer for Today,* trans. E. Quinn (Garden City, N.Y., 1980), 474; see the whole section, 442–77. The page references that follow in the text are to this book.

namely, trust or mistrust.[106] His protest is directed especially against the association of the psychological concept of mistrust with the philosophical position represented by nihilism (65ff.). Albert rightly points out the several meanings of the concept of nihilism (60ff.), although in the heat of polemics he in turn occasionally fails to take into account the distinction between atheism and nihilism, which Küng regards as important (see, e.g., 61f.). His polemic certainly goes too far when he represents the "reality of basic trust," which is certainly a widely accepted psychological datum, as itself the expression of such a "radicalism of alternatives" (140).

Albert would have done well to say how the significance of this phenomenon can be better explained than Küng has (in his opinion) managed to do. There is greater point to Albert's argument against the introduction of the idea of God as "founding" basic trust or, as the case may be, founding the "reality" which proximately supplies the foundation for basic trust but seems itself to be without foundation (Küng, 477). The step from the formulation of the concept of God ("God as a hypothesis") to the assertion of the reality of God leads in Küng (566ff.) to a simple hypothesis (so Albert, 137), in which Küng fails to take into account the human needs that urge the acceptance of God as a reality but at the same time render questionable the claim that this acceptance is based on knowledge (134; see 140).

As a matter of fact, according to Küng only an act of "decision" (570) leads from the simple idea of God (which Küng mistakenly connects with the concept of hypothesis) to the acceptance of God as real. Only the decision to trust opens the way to establishing a relation of founding and founded, an insight into the "condition of the possibility" of reality (572). Even in his presentation of basic trust as such, Küng already introduces the viewpoint of decision, the "alternative" of a yes or a no to reality (442ff.). At this point the interpretation of basic trust that I have been presenting diverges from that of Küng.

In the development of an infant, basic trust is not established by a "decision" but emerges from a process whereby a differentiation is introduced in the original symbiotic unity of life between child and mother. If, instead, mistrust and anxiety gain the upper hand in the behavior of the child, this is, once again, not the result of a decision taken by the child but a deformation of its natural development due to a deficit of the human attention and warmth that the child needs. The element of decision becomes important only in the measure that the individual has reached independence, and therefore there can be no question of a decision at the beginning of its development. The abiding importance of basic trust for

---

[106]H. Albert, *Das Elend der Theologie. Kritische Auseinandersetzung mit Hans Küng* (1979), 76; see 71ff. The page references to Albert in the text are to this book.

the development of the personality shows that our personal life remains encompassed by factors that precede our personal decisions, no matter how much such decisions can contribute to the preservation or destruction of this life.

In relation to the idea of God, then, the element of decision certainly plays a larger part. But here again we must take into account that in the initial phase of their religious socialization children grow up participating in a particular religious tradition that is refracted to them through their parents' participation in it. In this area too, human beings do not find themselves in a situation of decision that lies outside the alternatives in question. When the time for personal decision has come, they have already been involved in the subject matter of the decision. Part of this subject matter is the unique objective link between basic trust and idea of God. In contrast to Küng's presentation of the matter, in my description the objective link does not involve a "foundation,"[107] whether for basic trust itself or for the reality to which the basic trust is first of all directed, but rather an orientation of this trust to its object, to the "in what?" of trust. Even though basic trust is placed first of all in the persons who are the closest points of reference for the child, this trust is, by reason of its lack of limits, *implicitly* directed beyond mother and parents to an agency that can justify the unlimited character of the trust. This agency must be proportionate to the limitlessness that is the unique mark of basic trust.

On the other hand, such considerations cannot by themselves validate the claim that God—and a God who is one—is real. But neither do they inhabit a realm of purely imaginary possibilities, since they are concerned with the *implications* of a fundamental phenomenon in human behavior. They show that the theme of "God" is inseparable from the living of human life, even if for reasons I need not discuss here the theme does not always find expression in monotheistic or even in theistic terms. There is an original and at least implicit reference of human beings to God that is connected with the structural openness of their life form to the world and that is concretized in the limitlessness of basic trust. We may, if we wish, speak of this as a "need" of human beings. If so, it is not an artificially developed need but one that is inherent in their nature and that they cannot

[107]Küng's desire to find a foundation for reality, which is in itself uncertain (see Küng, 477, 564ff.), and therefore also for the basic trust placed in this reality, is rejected by Albert (193; see 146), along the lines of the criticism which critical rationalism levels at the "idea of an absolute justification" (see H. Albert, *Traktat über kritische Vernunft* [1968], 9, 11ff., 34f.); in addition, Albert objects to the lack of clarity in Küng's concept of foundation (Albert, *Das Elend,* 141ff.). Obscurities on this point do in fact exist in Küng, and to Albert's observations I must add that, on the one hand, God is, for Küng, the ground of reality, which is said to be uncertain in itself, and, on the other hand, the trusting acceptance of the existence of God is said to be based on reality (see Küng, 572).

simply evade in one way or another without compensation, that is, without creating substitutes. All this does not prove the reality of God, but it does prove the constitutive link between humanity and the religious thematic.

To the limitlessness of basic trust, which looks beyond the mother to God as its primary object, corresponds its reference to the wholeness of the self. Basic trust in the proper sense is directed to that agency which is able to protect and promote the self in its *wholeness*. For this reason, God and salvation are very closely tied together in the living of basic trust. The salvation looked for from God has to do with the unimpaired wholeness of life, as *Heil,* the German word for "salvation," suggests (*Heil:* "wholeness," "integrity"). In this wholeness, individual life and the life of the community to which the individual belongs are closely intertwined. This kind of wholeness characterizes the symbiotic unity of life which is the point of departure for the individual's development. It is likewise the goal of the individual's development, but by reason of the variations in the formation of a personal self this wholeness is always unattained or at least not attained completely. In this context Sartre has spoken of the experience of a "lack" which characterizes the for-itself in its life movement and which itself is "appearance on the ground of a totality."[108]

This wholeness of personal being, which Heidegger in his *Being and Time* (1927) had recognized as bound up with the question of personal selfness and which seemed to him to be accessible only by anticipating ("running ahead to") the future of one's own death, has rightly been connected by Sartre with the question of God. At the same time, Sartre has exposed the ambiguity of the striving for wholeness that seeks to eliminate the lack: To the extent that human beings try to gain their wholeness and strive to be "in and for themselves," they are always a "desire to be God."[109] Thus the striving for self-realization that is directed toward the wholeness of one's own being is in fact to be understood as an expression of sin, of the will "to be like God."[110] This does not, of course, render the concept of wholeness any less indispensable for psychology or for general anthropology. Nor can it be claimed as the special preserve of theology,[111] although theology may insist that human beings

[108]Sartre, *Das Sein und das Nichts,* 142; ET 62.

[109]Ibid., 712; see 724 and 779f.

[110]Thus G. Schneider, "Überlegungen zur Identität des Sünders," *NZST* 20 (1978), 237–52, esp. 245ff. Schneider's critique of the concept of personal wholeness relates to its connection with the striving for self-realization (see, e.g., 256f.); the critique is understandable from this point of view but is valid only in this limited context. Thus viewed, his criticism of the revaluation of narcissism by Fromm and H. Kohut and of the acceptance of it into theology by Scharfenberg (240f.) is justified.

[111]This point was emphasized by D. Rössler back in 1962 in his inaugural dissertation, *Der "ganze" Mensch. Das Menschenbild der neueren Seelsorgelehre und des modernen medizinischen Denkens im Zusammenhang der allgemeinen Anthropologie.*

can attain their wholeness only in the form of "salvation" that is promised and given by God, and not through any effort at self-realization.

In any case, human beings as such cannot avoid the question of their wholeness; at least from adolescence on, it becomes a theme in the formation of an independent individual identity.[112] But human beings do not themselves produce this wholeness. Rather, it is already present amid the incompleteness of their life which is characterized by a "lack" of being. Lack of being and wholeness of the self may not be related to each other in an extrinsic way, nor may they be simply opposed to each other. Rather, the whole is already present in the fragment. So too from the theological viewpoint "to be like God" describes not only the striving proper to sin but also the divine destiny by which human beings are to participate in God as his images. Sin comes on the scene only when the attempt is made to seize "being like God" as "something to be grasped at" in order to make it part of one's finite existence, instead of putting the latter at the service of God and living it for his glory.

The wholeness of the self, which infinitely transcends the limitations of life at any given moment, finds its present manifestation as personality.[113] "Person" signifies the human being in its wholeness, which transcends the fragmentariness of its reality-at-hand. Therefore, as person, in contrast to a mere thing (W. Stern), the human being is never completely at the disposal of another but is characterized by a hidden "inside" and by freedom.[114] But the consideration in principle of the importance of the wholeness of the self for human personhood forces us to a radical revision of the concept of person.

Boethius' definition of person as rational individuality[115] became normative for the subsequent philosophical tradition. It suppressed the older meaning of the word "person" as role, mask, face,[116] and held its own

[112]According to Erikson, *Identity and the Life Cycle,* the issue is the "wholeness" of the self in the face of the danger of "identity diffusion" (132). Erikson here distinguishes between a "wholeness" that is to be preserved by a constantly renewed integration and a fixed "totality": "Where the human being despairs of an essential wholeness, he restructures himself and the world by taking refuge in totalism" (ibid., n. 9).

[113]Rössler (n. 111, above) has pointed out the connection between person and human wholeness.

[114]On this, see my article "Person," *RGG*³ V (1961), 230–35, esp. 231f.

[115]"A person is an individual substance of a rational nature" *(Est autem persona rationalis naturae individua substantia)* (Boethius, *De duabus naturis,* PL 64:1343C).

[116]On this, see M. Fuhrmann, "Persona, ein römischer Rollenbegriff," in O. Marquard and K. H. Stierle, eds., *Identität,* Poetik und Hermeneutik 7 (1979), 83–106. While in this usage, which was later temporarily revived by humanism and the Renaissance (105ff.), the word means not the individual as such but always simply the bearer of a role (91), the use of *persona* "in the entirely colorless sense of a human individual" as such originated in rhetoric (95) and seems to have passed from there into jurisprudence (96). This latter understanding of the word lies behind the Augustinian and Boethian use of it (102f.); here

against medieval attempts, suggested by the doctrine of the Trinity, at a relational understanding of person.[117] Given the Boethian interpretation of person as rational individuality, it is understandable that the idealist philosophies of the modern age should think of the person as constituted by self-consciousness. Then, since self-consciousness was understood in terms of the ego, ego, subject, and person could become interchangeable concepts.[118]

But the considerations on the structure of self-consciousness that were proposed in the preceding section of this chapter yield a different picture. If self-consciousness is not to be understood primarily in terms of the ego, as the expression of the self-positing of the ego, and if on the contrary the ego acquires its identity only from the self, then the relevance of self-consciousness for the concept of person appears in a different light. Personality is then defined as the presence of the self in the ego.

When this viewpoint is adopted, it is possible to surmount the oppositions between the "absolute" concept of person, which is limited to the individual that exists for itself, and the "relational" concept, which looks rather to the conditioning of the ego by the Thou and by society.[119] The

---

too, *persona,* seen in the light of the Greek *hypostasis,* expresses the individual's peculiar characteristics. For the christological development of the concept of person in connection with the concept of *hypostasis,* see S. Otto, *Person und Subsistenz. Die philosophische Anthropologie des Leontios von Byzanz. Ein Beitrag zur spätantiken Geistesgeschichte* (1968), as well as H. Dörrie, *Hypostasis. Wort- und Bedeutungsgeschichte* (1955).

[117]A. Borst, in his essay "Findung und Spaltung der öffentlichen Persönlichkeit," in *Identität* (n. 116, above), 620–41, has shown that Abelard understood person "as part of dynamic relations" (635). For similar approaches in Richard of St. Victor and Duns Scotus, see H. Mühlen, *Sein und Person nach Johannes Duns Scotus. Beitrag zur Grundlegung einer Metaphysik der Person* (1954), 4ff., 82ff., 90ff., 95ff.

[118]But on the basis of an identification of subject (understood as absolute) and person the ego could be regarded as a secondary phenomenon. Thus M. Scheler was of the opinion that the person as subject of acts cannot be an object of consciousness any more than can the acts themselves, whereas the ego is the object of a reflection, an internal perception; see *Der Formalismus in der Ethik und die materiale Wertethik* (1913–16; 1966⁵), 386ff. The thesis of the nonobjectivity of the person and its acts has been strongly disputed by N. Hartmann, *Ethik* (1926; 1962⁴), 229f. According to Hartmann, the attitude to persons is primarily valuational, but it is also "a thoroughly objective one" (230). This is in keeping with Hartmann's interpretation of the concept of person in relation to the concept of subject: "The person is the subject insofar as in its transcendental acts, i.e., in its behavior, it is the carrier of moral values and disvalues" (227; see 233f.). The word "I" here is associated with the concept of person and the interpersonal sphere and not with mere subjectivity. But the concept of person remains the basis. Thus Hartmann defines personality as a valuational "elevation of existence as pure subject" (*Das Problem des geistigen Seins* [1933; 1962³], 125), instead of giving a new definition of the unity of the subject in the light of his correct insight into the structure of the subject and its wholeness as bound up with time and rooted in the sphere of the "objective spirit" and therefore of interpersonality.

[119]See M. Theunissen's survey, "Skeptische Betrachtungen über den anthropologischen Personbegriff," in H. Rombach, ed., *Die Frage nach dem Menschen. Festschrift für Max Müller*

premise here is the idea of the self, which, on the one hand, is mediated through the dialogically structured social sphere and therefore shows itself to be constituted by the symbiotic exocentricity of the individual, and with which, on the other hand, the ego knows itself to be identical in the for-itselfness of its self-consciousness. Here the peculiarly temporal structure of the person's wholeness is important for its relation both to its social context and to the ego; this temporal structure has been elaborated by thinkers as different as Heidegger and N. Hartmann, and it serves as the positive point of departure for Sartre's polemic against the reification connected with the idea of the ego.

According to N. Hartmann, the unity and wholeness of the person are "not conjoined in the now, but are pulled apart in the life, the duration, the behavior of the person. And identity through it all is something that must always still be established, so that the person must reach beyond its own mode of life in time."[120] The wholeness of the person is "its own integration with itself above and beyond its being pulled apart in time."[121] But Hartmann tells us nothing more about what this "self" really is with which the person integrates "itself," nor about how its identity is to be "established" and who does the establishing, since, after all, it is this process which constitutes the person. If Hartmann thinks that the person constitutes itself in its freedom, as he seems to think since he has it "reaching beyond its own mode of life in time," we would like to know how the person can be thought of as at one and the same time the ground and the result of itself.

Hartmann, then, despite his insight into the temporality of the person, falls back on the scheme of self-positing, even though he can maintain it only as something paradoxical. But six years previously, Heidegger had gone into the question of the wholeness of Dasein and its temporal structure in a much more nuanced way. His analysis begins with an aporia: "As long as Dasein 'is' as an entity, it has never reached its 'wholeness.' But if it gains such 'wholeness,' this gain becomes the utter loss of Being-in-the-world." For "when Dasein reaches its wholeness in death, it simul-

---

(1966), 461–92. But Theunissen's attempt to interpret opposed conceptions of the person as irreducible aspects of "the theatrical origin of the concept of person" (480) is not convincing. As M. Fuhrmann has recently shown, the viewpoint according to which the individual for-itself is isolated "as a neutral quantity" had a different historical origin, namely, in rhetoric (see above, n. 116). On the other hand, I can accept Theunissen's thesis that only with the coming of Christianity was this viewpoint linked to the idea of a self "which is absolute by reason of its self-sufficiency" (497). But the idea of familiarity through dialogue (477f.) probably also came to be linked with the concept of person as a result of the Christian doctrine of the Trinity. Thus the theatrical origin of *persona* accounts only for the role aspect.

[120]N. Hartmann, *Das Problem des geistigen Seins*, 131; see 139f., 146ff.

[121]Ibid., 132.

taneously loses the Being of its 'there.' "[122] Heidegger found a way out of this aporia in the "anticipatory" knowledge of the person's own death, for in anticipation Dasein can "make certain of its ownmost Being in its totality" (310; German 265). More accurately, the anticipatory knowledge of the person's own death only opens the *possibility* of this certainty. The certainty comes concretely through the call of conscience, wherein Dasein calls itself (320; German 275), and through the answering choice of the person's own selfness (330ff.; German 285ff.). But the way in which the self of the call of conscience is connected with the anticipatory knowledge of the person's own death and with the wholeness of being that is reached thereby remains obscure.

Sartre was therefore justified in looking for another access to the wholeness or "totality" of human reality, and he chose to start from the consciousness of the "lack" which allows a human reality to "surpass the given toward the project of the realized totality."[123] In contrast to Heidegger, Sartre does not see the Dasein being brought to its wholeness through death and the knowledge of it. Death makes life absurd rather than meaningful.[124] But Sartre does continue to hold that the self is not present-at-hand.

Heidegger had objected to the traditional anthropology, including Husserl's and Scheler's phenomenology of personality, that by reason of both its Greek and its Christian theological roots it continued to interpret the human reality "in the sense of the *Being-present-at-hand* of other created Things."[125] As far as the Christian doctrine of the image of God in human beings is concerned, this objection failed to consider that the image of God is definitively realized not in the original state but only in Jesus Christ, the Second Adam (a point, admittedly, that theology itself has often neglected), and that modern Evangelical theology has thematized the image of God in human beings as their *destiny.* The passage from Calvin (*Inst.* I.iii.8) which Heidegger cites and according to which the characteristic endowments of reason, intelligence, prudence, and judgment were given to human beings in order that they might transcend *(transcenderet)* their earthly life toward God and eternal blessedness should have made

---

[122]Heidegger, *Being and Time,* 279, 280 (German 236, 237). See 276ff. (German 233ff.) for the approach to the question of Dasein's being-a-whole. The page references that follow in the text are to the English translation and the German original of this work.

[123]Sartre, *Das Sein und das Nichts,* 140; ET 62. See nn. 108ff., above.

[124]Ibid., 670ff., esp. 679f., 687.

[125]Heidegger, *Being and Time,* 71ff., citation at 75 (German 46ff., citation at 49). In Husserl's and Scheler's conceptions of the nonobjectivity of the person (ibid., 72f.; German 47f.; see n. 118, above), Heidegger seems to have found the way prepared for his criticism of traditional anthropology. He goes beyond the thesis of the nonobjectivity of the person to the deeper question of the being of the person as distinct from mere presence-at-hand.

him realize that his own efforts to prove a transcendence of personal existence were fully in harmony with the basic structure of theological anthropology.

Sartre, on the other hand, having adopted the viewpoint that human beings "surpass" the given in the direction of their own totality, has perpetuated the theological approach in his own manner, although in the process he distorts the transcendence toward God into the "desire to be God."[126] He has thus preserved the difference in the being of the person as compared with a mere presence-at-hand or in-itself; this difference emerges from the transcendence proper to the "totality" of the person's being or "selfness" as "the possible which it is," over the given state of "lack."[127] With Heidegger, Sartre also conceives this difference as temporal and defines the possibility, which is constitutive of selfness, as a future that determines the being of the for-itself (185f.).

But in the process the present is canceled out in Sartre. In the light of the "not yet" of the future self (186) the present is defined as nonbeing (182f.) and stands under the sign of the lack. The present does indeed mean presence, specifically the presence of consciousness, which is for-itself, in the in-itself of its world (180), but this presence is not thought of in positive terms as an (even if provisional) manifestation of the wholeness of the self. Rather, it is said of consciousness that it "must be its own wholeness as an un-wholed wholeness" (250). Sartre is therefore unable to do justice to the element of positive identity between the present for-itself and the future it awaits. He does observe that I myself "am" this future (187f.), but he does not draw the conclusion implicit in this statement, namely, that this future is already somehow present in the present of my for-itself, if not definitively, at least proleptically.

Heidegger was able to derive from Dasein's ecstatic being-ahead-of-itself in its future a positive understanding of the present as moment (*Being and Time*, 387; German 338). The present is the moment in which the Dasein returns from its future "in repetition" to its past (ibid., 437; German 385). In Sartre, on the other hand, the negative relation of the for-itself to the in-itself of the present-at-hand world is reified into a perduring opposition that ruptures the unity of the person. Sartre himself says of human reality that it is "by nature an unhappy consciousness with no possibility of surpassing its unhappy state" (*Das Sein und das Nichts*, 145; ET 66). As a result, the relation to God finds expression only in a "desire to be God" and not in an experience by human beings of being given to themselves as creatures, a gift in which they can know themselves

[126]Sartre, *Das Sein und das Nichts*, 712; see above, n. 109.
[127]For the concept of selfness, see Sartre, *Das Sein und das Nichts*, 166, as well as 158 (the "relation of the for-itself to the possible which it is" as a "circuit of selfness").

to be different from God and yet as also affirmed by him.

In the person the whole of the individual's life "appears" in the present.[128] Although in every present moment the life of the human being is partly already past and partly still future, yet in that moment it is at least implicitly present as a whole. This situation may be further defined by turning to the temporal structure of the difference and identity between ego and self.

Each of us is an ego at every moment of our existence. We are still becoming our selves because we are still on the way to our selves in the wholeness of our existence. Yet we are also somehow our selves at the present moment, namely, insofar as we are persons. The word "person" establishes a relation between the mystery—which transcends the present of the ego—of the still incomplete individual life history that is on the way to its special destiny and the present moment of the ego. Person is the presence of the self in the moment of the ego, in the claim laid upon the ego by our true self, and in the anticipatory consciousness of our identity.

This is why we connect the concept of freedom with the person, since freedom means more than the capacity, which is always given with openness to the world, to distance oneself from impressions and objects and therefore also to dwell in them and attend to them. In its deeper sense, freedom is the real possibility of being myself—which is also the true meaning of autonomy in Kant's sense, where autonomy is the expression of my identity as a rational being. In this sense, freedom and personhood belong together, to the extent that personality describes the presence of the self in the ego. This general description does not decide, of course, in what way and to what degree the self is concretely present in the ego, and in what measure, consequently, I have become identical with myself and am therefore free.

The element of for-itselfness that belongs to personality finds its fulfillment in the idea of freedom. At the same time, however, the constitutive meaning of the self for personhood makes clear that personhood is also socially conditioned. Just as the self is given to the individual primarily in the mirror of the appraisals and expectations of others, so too personality is determined by the relation to the Thou and to the social world. In the normal case, persons are immediately related not to their own selves but to other persons and through these to the group, to which in turn they are bound in a we-consciousness. Yet over against the Thou and the group, persons are themselves. The wholeness aspect of the self and the consequent reference to the future enable us to understand also that the personal ego can assert its selfness against the Thou and the group.

---

[128]For the concept of appearance, see my essay "Appearance as the Arrival of the Future," in my *Theology and the Kingdom of God,* ed. R. J. Neuhaus (Philadelphia, 1969), 127–43.

The transcendence of selfness in relation to its social situation corresponds to the reference to God proper to basic trust, which already transcends its initial link to the mother. This reference to God is closely bound up also with the theme of the wholeness of selfness, insofar as this wholeness points not only beyond the fragmentariness of the individual's reality in any given present moment but also beyond earthly life, which will be broken off in death, to a fulfillment in the beyond. Because selfness is ultimately grounded in the relation to God, persons can be free in the face of their social situation. This is true without changing the fact that their selfness is socially mediated. Nor is this social mediation removed by the fact of their relation to God, for the personal identity that is grounded in this relation is destined to community with other human beings.

At the same time, however, the relation of persons to God frees them to be critically independent in reference to the concrete form that social relations may take at any given time.[129] The self-assertion of the individual in relation to other persons and society acquires thereby a deeper justification. This is the case precisely because the relation of the person to others is not basically one of conflict, as Sartre maintains,[130] but instead takes its character from the destination of the individual to community, and this from the symbiotic beginnings of individual life onward. It follows that the self-assertion of the individual against others and society need not be simply an egoistic rebellion of the part against the whole. It can also be the expression of a call to a more perfect fulfillment of the human destination to community.

The openness of persons to their divine destiny, beyond the limits of any finite fulfillment, is the ultimate basis for the inviolability of the person, an inviolability that translates as the "dignity of the person." The person is the ego as a "face" through which the mystery of the still unfinished history of individuals on the way to themselves manifests itself. For this reason, the person is not at the disposition of others, even though others may very well dispose of the present-at-hand, bodily existence of individuals and even, in differing degrees according to the particular case, of their psychic reactions. This kind of disposition may be exercised through physical force but also through seduction and through forms of psychic influence which render the individual pliable and which run from brainwashing to the more subtle forms of persuasion. The personality of the person so abused is not put at the disposal of the other, but it is, as it were, disconnected.

[129]In my essay "A Search for the Authentic Self," I have tried to show that this formulation, which seemingly has its place only in a monotheistic religion, is also valid, with the necessary adaptations, in the interpretation of the Buddhist idea of redemption.

[130]Sartre, *Das Sein und das Nichts,* 547. See also Sartre's *Kritik der dialektischen Vernunft* (1960; German tr., 1967), 610ff.

To these abuses is opposed the demand to respect this inalienable personal dignity of the individual. The demand is based ultimately on the fact that over and above their present-at-hand reality human individuals are related, as persons, to a still open destiny and thereby to God. The Bible uses the concept of image of God to describe this human destiny; in the belongingness to God, which sets human beings apart, it sees that special dignity which makes human beings inviolable and grounds the prohibition against taking their lives (Gen. 9:6). The invocation of God's rights as the divine Majesty makes the inviolability of human dignity immune against human caprice.

6

Identity and Nonidentity as a Theme of the Affective Life

The antagonism between individual and society found its resolution in the phenomena of self-consciousness and personality. It found it, however, only in the sense that the antagonism was seen not to be structurally inevitable and irreconcilable; that is, the resolution operates only at the level of theories that would consolidate and legitimate the antagonism. In the real order it persists because of the many manifestations of human sin, which subordinates the wholeness of the person and its world to the particularity of the ego at any given moment and thus distorts the relation between ego and self. The distortion spoils relations between fellow human beings and consequently every institutional organization of society, whose laws and arrangements it misuses as a mere means to the narrowly individual goals of the ego. It also corrupts any rebellion against social injustice, since the latter becomes a means whereby the one rebelling can pursue selfish interests and self-will unconstrained by the hated social system and its order of law. At this level, conflict and not fellowship proves to be the essence of interhuman relations.

Yet despite and in the midst of such brokenness the wholeness of the Dasein manifests itself in the life of human beings, and this both in the life of the individual person and in the corporate life of individuals. The manifestation does not take the form primarily of knowledge. The discussion of self-consciousness may have given the impression that theoretical adequation in the relation of ego and self is the decisive element in the problem of identity, but the underlying phenomenon of an original familiarity of consciousness not only (or already) with itself but with the symbiotic sphere of the individual's life has already opened up broader horizons via the discussion of basic trust and personality. Only in the context of this original familiarity does the theoretical element in self-consciousness exercise its function. We had to begin with the latter because we are treating the thematic of identity in an explicit manner. But we must still define in greater detail the horizon of original familiarity within which personal life is lived. This is the horizon of feeling. The affective life, which fills the domain of interiority, will once again bring to the fore the social relations in which individuals live their lives. The same holds for the negative modes of self-familiarity as seen in experiences of alienation as well as of shame and guilt. The discussion of these will serve as a transition to the objectivity of communal culture as the provisional locus of the individual's identity.

I. Feeling, Its Moods and Passions

Only by way of exception does the presence of the always as yet incomplete whole of life in the individual moment of life become an object of thematic self-reflection. Nonetheless it is decisive for any living of a normal life. It is present in the form of an immediate familiarity with the self in experience and in the utterances of the affective life. We must speak here of a familiarity with the self and not simply in a general way of a familiarity with the symbiotic life context in which the individual participates. It is true, of course, that the affective life too is determined by an "ecstatic" participation of individuals in their world, but it is at the same time characterized also by a reference to the self. This reference does not take the form of an explicit consciousness of the individual's own self but manifests itself in the feelings of pleasure and displeasure which, as observers noted at an early stage, characterize the affective life. Pleasure and displeasure have to do with the individual's own self, even when they do not appear simply as moods but are referred to objects in which the individual takes pleasure or which cause pain and induce fear. Such an unexpressed relation to the self is also indirectly behind desire, since a living being desires only that which it seems good for it to have and which therefore promises pleasure.[1]

In modern thought the unexpressed relation to the self that makes itself known in sensations of pleasure and displeasure has been described with the concepts of feeling and mood. The two have only recently come into use as philosophical concepts. The concept of feeling first made its appearance as a basic anthropological concept in David Hume's *A Treatise of Human Nature* (1739–40),[2] while it is phenomenology

---

[1]The Stoics in their reflections on the striving for self-preservation noted this point which had already been made in Plato's *Philebus*. On the significance of the idea for modern philosophy, see the essay of D. Henrich mentioned in chapter 5, n. 93.

[2]In an appendix Hume speaks of our belief in the reference of our ideas to reality as a mere "feeling or sentiment" (*A Treatise of Human Nature,* ed. L. A. Selby-Bigge [1888]; new edition by P. H. Nidditch [1978], 623ff.). The preference given to some arguments over others is likewise attributed to a "feeling" (103). A moral judgment too is based on "a feeling or sentiment," not on reason: "It lies in yourself, not in the object" (469). Therefore F. H. Jacobi, in his dialogue "David Hume über den Glauben, oder Idealismus und Realis-

that introduced the concept of mood.[3]

The relation of feeling and mood to each other and to sensation, emotion, and affect cannot be regarded even today as explained. The diversified terminology is matched by very different ways of gaining access to the phenomena themselves.[4]

The independence of feeling as a basic power of the soul, alongside understanding and will, was asserted in 1766 by Moses Mendelssohn, who was following the suggestions of Hume. In 1777, J. N. Tetens stated the grounds for this view in the framework of his systematic psychology.[5] According to Tetens, feeling is closely linked to sensation, but it has for its content not the object of the sensation but the impression made on us by this object (I, 167f.). The close connection with sensation explains his definition of feeling as "susceptibility, receptivity or modifiability," but according to Tetens the soul has also been given a power whereby it is

---

mus," refers to Hume as a precursor of his own philosophy of belief; see Jacobi's *Werke*, ed. Roth and Koppen, II (Leipzig, 1815), 156ff., where he cites Hume's *Inquiry Concerning Human Understanding* V, 2.

[3]E. Husserl was still asking after 1924, "Where does the ego of the moods and states belong?"; see *Ideen einer reinen Phänomenologie und phänomenologischen Philosophie, Husserliana* IV (1952), 311; see 416. Heidegger subsequently made the concept of having-a-mood *(Gestimmtheit)* the key to his analysis of state-of-mind *(Befindlichkeit);* see his *Being and Time,* trans. J. Macquarrie and E. Robinson (New York, 1962), 172ff. (German 134ff.).

[4]In 1956, S. Strasser bemoaned the "indescribable confusion" regarding the concept of emotionality and the relation between feeling or sentiment and emotion; see his *Phenomenology of Feeling: An Essay on the Phenomena of the Heart,* trans. R. E. Wood (Pittsburgh, 1977), 264. D. Rapaport, *Emotions and Memory* (Baltimore, 1942), 266, made the same point. Nor do all authors follow the distinction proposed by H. N. Gardiner, R. C. Metcalf, and J. G. Beebe-Center in their survey of the twentieth-century psychology of affectivity: feeling is, rather, a response to sense impressions, while emotion is a dynamism originating within the organism itself; see their *Feeling and Emotion: A History of Theories* (New York, 1937), 336ff. Thus M. B. Arnold, *Emotion and Personality* (New York, 1960), 80, treats "emotion" ("aroused by an object or situation as a whole") as a subclass of "feelings." S. K. Langer, *Mind: An Essay on Human Feeling* I (Baltimore, 1967), unlike most English-speaking authors, connects the "act" of feeling with the "process" of organic life itself and defines it as a "phase" in the process; she then distinguishes sensitive and emotional feelings as "what is *felt as impact* and what is *felt as autogenic action*" (23). In a far more resolute way, F. Krueger, *Das Wesen des Gefühls. Entwurf einer systematischen Theorie* (1928), 10ff., related the concept of feeling to the "psychic totality" and thus established the pattern for a whole period, at least in Germany. To the related thesis in Krueger that two feelings cannot occur with strict simultaneity (8), Strasser objected (144ff.) that Krueger was confusing feeling and mood, while Ph. Lersch, for his part, distinguishes between movements of feeling and states of feeling; see Lersch's *Aufbau der Person* (1950; 1966[10]), 216f.

[5]J. N. Tetens, *Philosophische Versuche über die menschliche Natur und ihre Entwicklung* (Leipzig, 1777), I, 619f. Elsewhere he says that feelings and the faculties of thought and imagination make up "the entire power of knowing" (238ff.; see 596f.). The page references that follow in the text are to this work.

able "to feel these changes that have been wrought in it" (I, 620f.).

It was probably from Tetens that Kant took the conception of "the feeling of pleasure and displeasure as the middle term between the faculties of cognition and desire,"[6] which was the basis for putting the critique of judgment between the critiques of pure and practical reason. Similarly, Schleiermacher's placing of feeling between knowing and willing as the basis for his theory of religion[7] probably had its origin here.

According to Tetens, feeling grasps the relations and connections of things among themselves and relates these "to our entire present state" (I, 182f.), with a resultant impression of something pleasurable or unpleasurable (185ff.). Kant too emphasizes the reference to the self in feelings of pleasure and displeasure: "Satisfaction is the feeling that life is being fostered, pain the feeling that it is being hindered."[8] Feelings therefore do not belong to objects but are "determinations of the subject." They accompany not only external impressions but also the activity of the imagination, especially in the social intercourse of individuals: "Here the soul feels its freedom in the play of fancies."[9] But Tetens considered assigning to the "feeling of the self" a function that Kant four years later assigned to "transcendental apperception," namely, the function of constituting the unity of the subject, although only with respect to

---

[6] I. Kant, *The Critique of Judgement,* trans. J. C. Meredith, in *Kant* (Great Books of the Western World 42; Chicago, 1952), A VI (p. 461, Preface); see A IX, XXIIf., and LVI; also A 4f.

[7] D. F. Schleiermacher, *On Religion: Addresses in Response to Its Cultured Critics,* trans. T. N. Tice (Richmond, 1969), 81ff. (second address). Here, however, the threefold division still distinguishes between metaphysics, morality, and religion, although in regard to this last it aims at maintaining a "separate province" in the mind for it. In the discussion of religion itself, the concept of intuition ("perspectivity" in Tice's translation) stands alongside that of feeling. The proximate stimulus for this is probably to be found in Fichte's remarks on intuition and feeling in the *Wissenschaftslehre* of 1794 (III, no. 10; *Werke* I, 312ff.). Fichte's derivation of intuition and feeling from the reflection of the ego on itself as determining and determined (I, 312; on the relation of intuition to the determining ego, compare 317ff. with 229ff.; on feeling, 316f.) could easily be connected by Schleiermacher with Jacobi's ideas on the givenness of subject *and* object in the immediate feeling of reality (see below, nn. 17ff.) and in any case, in view of the terminology in the addresses, is hardly to be derived directly from the intellectual self-intuition of the ego; see E. Herms, *Herkunft, Entfaltung und erste Darstellung des Systems der Wissenschaften bei Schleiermacher* (1974), 235f. Schleiermacher's *The Christian Faith* (1821) has the psychological triad of knowing, doing, and feeling (§ 3, 3). The definition of feeling as receptivity, while knowing and doing are conceived as forms of activity (ibid.), likewise echoes Tetens (I, 612ff., esp. 625).

[8] I. Kant, *Anthropologie in pragmatischer Hinsicht,* § 60 (Akad. Ausg. 7, 231 and 230f.). A corresponding reference to the self is already present in Hume's concept of "reflective passion" (Treatise II, 1, 1, in Hume [n. 2, above], 275f.; see II, 1, 6, p. 292), but it is not explicitly applied there to pleasure and displeasure.

[9] Ibid., § 67 (234f. and 240).

the receptivity of the soul.[10] For Kant, on the other hand, feeling cannot correspond to self-consciousness, for the reason that we share feeling with the animals, whereas the representation of our own ego is peculiar to us as human beings.[11]

F. H. Jacobi and Schleiermacher had a still broader concept of feeling. Jacobi could put feeling on the same level as reason, because "the elevation of the mind above sensible representations" initially consists only in a feeling.[12] He could appeal here to Hume, who had made belief—and therefore a feeling—responsible for our conviction of the reality of the objective world (see above, n. 2). This meant, to Jacobi, "that belief is an element in all knowledge and effective action."[13]

Schleiermacher did not go that far. He did not doubt the independence of reason (or "knowing") in relation to feeling and, in describing religious experience as something independent between knowing and doing, even thought it necessary to supplement the concept of feeling with that of the religious intuition of the infinite in the finite and to limit feeling to a subjective result of that experience.[14] In his next period, however, in his effort to distance himself from F. W. J. Schelling's and Hegel's requisitioning of the concept of intuition for their philosophical purposes, Schleiermacher came to connect religious experience even more closely with the concept of feeling. In *The Christian Faith* (1821) the definition of feeling as "immediate self-consciousness" serves as the basis for this closer link. What he means is a prereflective self-consciousness which, with H. Steffens, he can describe as "the immediate presence of whole undivided Being."[15] This immediate self-consciousness is not something purely subjective and disconnected from experience of the world and the consciousness of opposition to it. Rather, it embraces the difference between subject and object that marks the consciousness of objects, so that in the consciousness of its own "dependence" the feeling in question also gives expression to the dependence of nature in its entirety.[16]

---

[10]Tetens, I, 261: "Does not a certain obscure feeling of ourselves accompany all our states, conditions, and changes in the area of the passions?"

[11]Kant, §1 (127).

[12]Jacobi, *Werke* II, 61f. and 74.

[13]Ibid., 163f.

[14]Herms (n. 7, above), 119–63, has shown the importance for Schleiermacher of his exposure to Jacobi's theory of an immediate consciousness of reality. On Schleiermacher's kantianizing correction of Jacobi, see ibid., 139f.; on the influence of Spinoza, 145ff., 152f.

[15]Schleiermacher, *The Christian Faith*, § 3, 2.

[16]The denial of absolute freedom (§ 4, 3) in the consciousness of being "not-self-caused" (§ 4, 1), and therefore the consciousness of absolute dependence, is true, according to Schleiermacher, "of ourselves as individual finite existence in general; so that we do not set ourselves over against any other individual being, but, on the contrary, all antithesis between

It is precisely here that Schleiermacher follows Jacobi, for whom feeling
is the basis of the certainty both of the existence of the world and of one's
own ego.[17] We are reminded of this idea of Jacobi by the reference in the
addresses on religion to that first moment of knowledge prior to the
separation of intuition and feeling.[18] The same idea is also at work in what
The Christian Faith says about the copresence of the world in immediate
self-consciousness. We must regard this idea as the condition for Schleiermacher's being able to interpret this immediate self-consciousness along
religious lines as a consciousness of God, on the grounds that feeling,
precisely as receptivity and therefore in the consciousness of the finiteness
of the world, unites itself to the totality of the finite and therein knows
itself to be related to the infinite as distinct from the world. In this form,
of course, all this cannot be immediately given in feeling but discloses
itself only to reflection, for which the world and the self are already
separate.

In this area Schleiermacher's concept of feeling has by no means been
superseded by the present state of discussion in psychology. The reference
of feelings to life in its totality is, of course, not given its due everywhere
in the literature of psychology. Individual feelings are often studied in
isolation and without reference to life as a whole. For this reason, it is also
difficult to distinguish terminologically what is peculiar to feelings as
distinct from sensations, on the one hand, and emotions, on the other (see
above, n. 4). But the reference to life as a whole that is present in feelings
has not gone unnoticed. F. Krueger in particular has made it central to his
theory of feeling and has won a large measure of agreement.

According to Krueger, we must not simply distinguish "total feelings"
from partially referred feelings, as W. Wundt did.[19] Rather, Krueger sees
every experience as "embedded in a complete whole," and says that "the
experiential qualities of this complete whole are the feelings."[20] In subsequent discussion a sharper distinction has been made between feelings and
moods or between what Ph. Lersch calls feeling arousals and feeling
states,[21] although it is necessary to maintain the connection of individual

one individual and another is in this case done away with" (§ 5, 1; see § 32, 2; § 34, 1 and
3; § 56, 2).

[17]Jacobi, *Werke* II, 175: "In a single indivisible moment I experience that I am and that
there is something outside of me." On this, see Herms, 124f.; on Schleiermacher's use of
this idea, 136ff., 152f.

[18]Schleiermacher, *On Religion*, 85f.

[19]W. Wundt, *Grundzüge der physiologischen Psychologie* II (1910⁶), 351ff., 356ff. Wundt
conceived the self-consciousness of the ego as this kind of complex total feeling (III, 354ff.).

[20]Krueger (n. 4, above), 14.

[21]Lersch (n. 4, above), 216f. Strasser (n. 4, above), 181ff., prefers the concept of mood
(or disposition) to that of feeling-state. But when moods are distinguished from feelings
(186), the feeling aspect of moods is lost sight of.

feeling arousals with life as a whole, which they modify in its "depth."

The simultaneity of momentary feeling arousals and feeling states or moods that are more lasting and touch the person "more deeply" need not lead to the idea of a "stratification" of psychic life.[22] More dynamic and functional models of the life process and its phases[23] can also be used to explain the phenomenon in terms of the effect of feeling arousals on feeling states or moods,[24] just as conversely openness to feeling arousals as well as to perception[25] and to memory[26] is influenced by moods (and

[22]The reasons given in modern discussion for the use of a stratification model in the psychology of the person are summed up in an especially illuminating way by Strasser (56ff.) in his exposition of Scheler's doctrine of levels. The main point to be explained is the simultaneous appearance of various experiences that are "embedded as *distinct* presences in the total experience" (57). This does not seem possible if they are all on the same level; the fact therefore suggests the idea of strata or levels. For a critique of the stratification model —especially Lersch's conception of it which is inspired by N. Hartmann—see A. Wellek, *Die Polarität im Aufbau des Charakters* (1950; 1960³), 67–99. Wellek considers psychoanalysis to be a stratification theory. But the important distinction between, on the one hand, the phenomenologically ascertainable difference between conscious and unconscious (like that between soul and body) and, on the other, the difference of strata—postulated for purely theoretical reasons—between life ground, endothymic ground, and personal superstructure, seems to be neglected in Lersch's model which follows Hartmann. Wellek's criticism is all the more interesting because he himself (having chosen a structural-theoretical model as opposed to a dynamic functional model of personality, 85ff.) retains the idea of a stratification (89ff.; see 78). The most decisive critical viewpoint is probably expressed by Wellek in his remark aimed at E. Rothacker, namely, that the idea of strata brings with it the danger of a "loss of the totality element" (68). His own image of an "onionskin layering" (91ff.) does not do justice to the viewpoint that the integration of the individual life whole must be *accomplished* ever anew and that only in the integration achieved at any given moment do the partial aspects have their present status. While even in humans this process may follow a "program" that is peculiar to the species, though modified in each individual, stratification models, as distinct from, for example, psychoanalysis, are not in a position to give a "structural" description of this process *as such*.

[23]This is the case, in principle, in W. James. L. von Bertalanffy, *Das Gefüge der Persönlichkeit* (1937), has been influential in securing the adoption of this approach. Wellek, 82ff., offers a critique of Bertalanffy that is rather unconvincing, since, in contrast to a fountain which, according to K. Valentin, remains a fountain even when it does not flow (thus Wellek, 83), a living being remains a living being only as long as it lives. While a pure behaviorism does not even envisage the idea of a structure for the life process, because it does not thematize the living individual as *self*-comporting, psychoanalysis on the contrary has projected the most effective model of this structure. See, however, Langer's work mentioned above in n. 4.

[24]This suggests that feeling as such should be assigned a fundamental importance in the integration of the individual life process. In human beings this function is carried further by self-consciousness and the history of identity formation.

[25]U. Neisser, *Cognitive Psychology* (Englewood Cliffs, N.J., 1967), follows E. G. Schachtel in calling attention to the "preattentive processes" that single out an area in the field of perception, to which focal attention is then given (88). In this sense too "the whole comes *before* the parts," even in perception (90).

[26]According to S. Dutta and R. N. Kanungo, *Affect and Memory: A Reformulation* (Oxford, 1975), 27f., the perceived intensity of the affects connected with an impression is decisive

affects). The concept of mood, for its part, points back once again to the concept of feeling, since that which has a mood of one kind or another is precisely feeling as "the immediate presence of whole undivided Being."[27]

It is probable, however, that we should not follow Schleiermacher in giving the name "self-consciousness" to this phenomenon, especially since even according to Schleiermacher it includes more than simply the ego or self as distinct from the world. Feeling in this comprehensive sense relates to the entire area of the individual's original "symbiotic" familiarity with its world, a familiarity within which the differentiation between world and self is first developed. This symbiotic transcendence of the difference between subject and world has been repeatedly emphasized in analyses of moods.[28]

On this important point modern psychological and phenomenological literature has confirmed Schleiermacher. We must even say that only the influence of transcendental idealism and his use of its key concept "self-consciousness" kept him from being aware of the full significance of his insight into the original "symbiotic" solidarity of self and world in feeling.

---

for the ability to remember the impression. The authors add the viewpoint of "contextual interpretation," according to which the insertion of a datum in the individual's "frame of reference" (11) is decisive for the availability of the memory of it (see 28f.).

[27]Thus L. Klages, *Ausdrucksbewegung und Gestaltungskraft* (1923), connects the concept of mood with that of feeling. Similarly, Th. Haecker, *Metaphysik des Fühlens* (1950), 51f. Lersch is likewise close to this view, since with W. Stern he assigns to the "stationary moods" the function of "embedding" not only feeling arousals but experience as such in the "endo-thymic ground" (303f.). I presuppose that Lersch's stereotyped stratum-concept of "endo-thymic ground" corresponds concretely to the unity of feeling.

[28]Thus, according to Heidegger, mood discloses the Dasein's Being-in-the-world and discloses it "as a whole" (*Being and Time,* 176; German 137), and Dasein *is* this disclosedness (171; German 133). This disclosedness constitutes "Dasein's openness to the world" (176; German 137). In this respect there is no material disagreement between O. F. Bollnow, *Das Wesen der Stimmungen* (1941) and Heidegger. According to Bollnow, in moods there is still a unity of human being and world (21), as well as of soul and body (22ff.). Strasser (n. 4, above) likewise writes that "disposition [*Stimmung*] is the feeling of I-and-world together" (188) and that the two are combined without distinction in a feeling for the All" (190). According to L. Spitzer, *Classical and Christian Ideas of World Harmony: Prolegomena to an Interpretation of the Word "Stimmung"* (Baltimore, 1963), the unity of subject and object that is contained in the German word *Stimmung* is lacking in the corresponding word in other languages. This makes the word untranslatable, although as far as its referent is concerned it stands in a long tradition that goes back to antiquity (5ff.). This linguistic peculiarity may account for the fact that in G. Ryle's discussion of moods as "frames of reference" the element of *Stimmung* as transcending the subject-object difference is lacking; see his *The Concept of Mind* (London, 1949), 93ff., 98ff. Lersch, however, speaking of the concept of feeling, calls for a "field theory" of feelings in which these will figure "as performances in a field-occurrence involving psychic subject and field" and not simply as intrasubjective performances (228).

This solidarity has hardly been adequately described even by "being in the world" as an existential of Dasein. Its difficulty resides in the fact of its unavoidable vagueness which it shares, perhaps not accidentally, with the concept of being as the most general and at the same time emptiest (in definiteness) of all concepts. In any case, only with the symbiotic existential certainty that feeling gives is the horizon established within which the separating out of self-consciousness and consciousness of the world (as well as of consciousness of the world and consciousness of God) becomes intelligible even while the two continue to be related to each other.

When we speak of the symbiotic certainty of being that feeling gives, we must immediately add that the certainty and the feeling are not simply identical. Feeling is always defined as pleasurable or unpleasurable,[29] and to this extent, even amid all its openness to the symbiotic unity that precedes the separation of self and world, it is always characterized by an at least implicit reference to the self. This reference distinguishes feeling from "intuition," as the young Schleiermacher used to say, or from perceptual consciousness.

There is another aspect of Schleiermacher's interpretation of the concept of feeling that continues to be relevant: the fact that he discovered the religious significance of feeling as such and thus the condition for the possibility of specifically religious feelings within the wholeness that marks the affective life. Religious feelings are not simply specific feelings that are distinguished from others by their special object or by their reference to such an object. Their peculiar character consists, rather, in the fact that in them the wholeness of human life which is always present in feeling as such becomes thematic.

As I pointed out above, this datum is obscured in Schleiermacher himself by his use of self-consciousness as a key word. Feeling renders us familiar with ourselves in the whole of our being, without our as yet having or needing an *idea* of our self. The reference to the self signals its presence only in the pleasure or displeasure that marks feeling. This

---

[29]Whereas according (e.g.) to Kant (*The Critique of Judgement.* A XXII) feeling is always a feeling of pleasure or displeasure (Hume, Treatise II, 1, 5, had made the same claim for the passions), Schleiermacher accepted this as valid only for the sensible self-consciousness (*The Christian Faith.* § 5, 4; on the concept of "sensible," see § 5, 1). He was evidently of the opinion that a reference to objects (". . . belongs to the realm of reciprocal action," § 5, 1) is constitutive of the difference between pleasure and displeasure. According to Heidegger, however, even moods are always characterized by a "turning towards or a turning away" (*Being and Time.* 174; German 135). In their analysis of feelings contemporary psychologists add the dimensions of intensity (sleep—tension) and attention (attention —rejection) to the qualitative "scale of pleasure and displeasure"; thus H. Schlosberg, "Three Dimensions of Emotion," *Psychological Review* 61 (1954), 81–88. See C. E. Izard et al., "Affect, Awareness and Performance," in S. S. Tomkins and C. E. Izard, eds., *Affect, Cognition and Personality: Empirical Studies* (New York, 1965).

familiarity with self may well be the condition for the understanding and use of the words "I," "self," and "my" and thus provide the basis for the development of self-consciousness in the proper sense of this term. Self-consciousness in this proper sense comes into being only in connection with the *cognitive* development of the child.[30]

Schleiermacher was wrong, therefore, in opposing feeling as "immediate self-consciousness" to the idealist philosophy of consciousness and at the same time making it the point of departure for something like a transcendental deduction of religious experience. Some decades later, R. H. Lotze more correctly described the relation between feeling and self-consciousness when, on the one hand, he made feeling the source of the evidence for the unity of thinker and object of thought in self-consciousness and, on the other, made the cognitive, not the affective, structure of self-consciousness consist in the distinction and unity of ego and self.[31] This shows in an exemplary way that every understanding, including every understanding of the self, must move beyond feeling into the medium of thought. This entails very extensive corrections in Schleiermacher's conception of the relation between thought and religion, philosophy and theology.

The fact remains, however, that in its reaching out to the totality of life, feeling anticipates the distinction and correlation effected by the intellect, even though because of its vagueness feeling depends on thinking for definition. Thought, on the other hand, can never exhaustively transfer to its own sphere what is present in feeling. This is true not only of self-consciousness but of the whole spectrum of experience; it is also, of course, very significant for the relation between religious experience and philosophical or theological reflection as well as for the relation between religious consciousness itself and the objective character of its representations.

Schleiermacher was probably correct when he made the receptivity or stateness (as opposed to activity), which characterizes feeling generally, responsible for the religious mood that is peculiar to feeling in its reference to the *wholeness of life*. This mood can, of course, be concealed by

---

[30]Thus J. Loevinger, "Stages of Ego Development," in J. Loevinger and A. Blasi, *Ego Development* (London, 1976), 13–28, esp. 16.

[31]R. H. Lotze, *Medicinische Psychologie* (Leipzig, 1852), 499: "Direct evidence of the identity between thinking and its object can arise only from the *feelings* that accompany the act of self-consciousness. Not because self-consciousness is simultaneously an object of thought but because the object of thought is at the same time *felt* in the immediate value it has for us, does it ground our self-consciousness. . . . Self-consciousness is therefore to be regarded simply as a theoretical interpretation of the *feeling of self.*" Wundt came to a much less nuanced conclusion later on when he reduced person, ego, and self-consciousness to a "total feeling" (see above, n. 19).

other factors, especially the dominance of rational everyday consciousness that is directed to finite things.[32] But Schleiermacher all too quickly interpreted the element of receptivity and stateness as dependence in contrast to freedom.[33] In addition, when it came to the mediation of the expression of the religious dimension of feeling by the rest of the affective life in its relation not only to the world of perception and the sensations that are ordered to perception but in its relation also to the emotions and affects that arise within human beings themselves, he greatly oversimplified matters in the direction of a specification of the already described religious quality of feeling generally. This specification takes the form in Schleiermacher of a schema of determinations of the relation between the religious consciousness and the "sensible" self-consciousness which is determined by the experience of objects in the world,[34] although Schleiermacher himself says that the religious consciousness (immediate self-consciousness as such) acquires a concrete form only when connected with the perceptual consciousness of objects of worldly experience and with the development of this kind of consciousness.[35]

[32]Thus already in Schleiermacher's third address, "The Cultivation of Religion," in his *On Religion,* esp. 183ff. The basic idea is retained in the reflections in *The Christian Faith* on "sin as an arrestment of the determinative power of the spirit, due to the independence of the sensuous functions" (§ 66, 2). Consciousness of the world and finite things obscures the religious sensitivity in, e.g., the "educated folk" of the third address.

[33]I say "all too quickly," because the concept of dependence has its proper place in the area of "reciprocity between the subject and the corresponding Other" (*The Christian Faith,* § 4, 2) and therefore in the relation of the person to the world. Therefore the assertion of absolute dependence in § 4, 3, is not introduced as "conditioned by some previous knowledge about God" (§ 4, 4), but is based solely on the consciousness of the negation of absolute freedom. Nonetheless the *interpretation* of this negation through the positive idea of a dependence remains an entry of finite relations into the book of "immediate consciousness"; when the latter is also conceived as consciousness of God it can hardly be called "immediate" any longer in view of the extensive effort of reflection required for this. The definition of freedom as spontaneous activity in contrast to receptivity (§ 4, 2), which lies behind the thesis that the denial of absolute freedom forms the meaning-content of immediate self-consciousness, must likewise be judged inadequate, because it does not do justice either to the concept of freedom as the expression of achieved identity with one's own being (this is the nucleus of Kant's idea of autonomy) or to the understanding of freedom (in the later Fichte and in Schelling and Hegel) as grounded in unity with the absolute.

[34]*The Christian Faith,* § 5, links the schema of a development from a confused unity via division to unity made perfect (§ 5, 1) with the opposition between sensible self-consciousness (related to objects) and "immediate" self-consciousness, the second of which thus presents itself as the final stage in the development of consciousness. The sketch, in § 7, of the stages of development in the history of religions corresponds to the picture elaborated in § 5.

[35]The assumption that the "higher" self-consciousness would in itself possess the greatest purity and perfection does not fit in with "our religious consciousness, as we actually find it" (§ 5, 4). According to Schleiermacher, the appearance of the higher self-consciousness in its pure form would even constitute an imperfect state, since it would then "lack the

Should not Schleiermacher really have first of all investigated in detail the process whereby the elements in the consciousness of unity—namely, consciousness of the world, of the self, and of God—are differentiated? He does take a step in this direction in his idea that the religious feeling of dependence is mediated through the experience of dependence on the system of nature.[36] It is possible to think of this idea being developed in terms of a relation of child to mother along the lines, described earlier, of the development of basic trust and its subsequent detachment from its ties to the mother. Had this approach been chosen, representations of the course of religious history might have emerged that were different from those developed in Schleiermacher's scheme of derivation. In addition, other questions might have presented themselves in regard to the relation between the spontaneous development of the individual and the religious thematic and in reference to the reflection in the affective life of the tensions arising at this point.

Schleiermacher correctly treats these tensions as a theme in the theological doctrine of sin. On the other hand, the tensions do not manifest themselves immediately as an "arrestment" of the consciousness of God by the absorption of human beings in their relation to the world, but first and more radically in the emotional forms wherein the self-assertion of the individual finds expression. It is on these that Kierkegaard, unlike Schleiermacher, focuses in his analyses of dread and despair, which may be regarded as paradigmatic for the phenomenological description of moods in our century. Furthermore, affects and passions, like moods, receive no attention from Schleiermacher in his theological interpretation of feeling, although affects and passions had traditionally had a central place in both theological and philosophical anthropology. It is here that we would have to look for the connection between a theology based on the concept of feeling and the deeper levels of Christian teaching on sin. On the other hand, the realm of moods and affects is not of interest solely to the Christian doctrine of sin. On the contrary, positive aspects of human destiny also find expression in them.

Modern discussion of the concept of mood owes its most important impulse to Martin Heidegger, who in his *Being and Time* follows Kierkegaard in regarding the mood of anxiety as key and point of departure in the question of the wholeness of human existence. Anxiety is for Heideg-

---

definiteness and clearness which spring from its being related to the determination of the sensible self-consciousness" (§ 5, 3). Does this mean that the "higher" self-consciousness, when considered in itself, is a mere abstraction? A positive answer is not controverted by the protestation in § 3, 2, that the immediate self-consciousness "is by no means always simply an accomplishment," since the only point being made there is that there are moments in which all thinking and willing "retreat behind self-consciousness in one form or another."
[36]Schleiermacher, *The Christian Faith,* § 46, 2.

ger, as it had been for Kierkegaard, "the most primordial way in which the spirit can relate itself to itself."[37] On the other hand, unlike Kierkegaard, Heidegger relates anxiety only to *finitude* and not to the relation of finitude to infinitude.[38] Therefore, too, freedom, which at the onset of anxiety restricts itself to the finite, is interpreted by Heidegger in a positive way as a decision in favor of authenticity, whereas Kierkegaard saw in it the origin of sin.

Heidegger's special attention to anxiety (and care) elicited the objection that he projects a one-sidedly negative and pessimistic picture of the human being. O. F. Bollnow therefore defended against Heidegger the primacy of elevated and happy moods in an understanding of human existence. He pointed to the "profound cheerfulness" that already fills the awakening being. We may doubt, however, whether this is the case always and without exception. More convincing is Bollnow's reference to the way in which happy moods are marked by an openness to the life of the community, whereas moods of depression lead to isolation. Bollnow also gives a vivid description of the experience of time that accompanies happy moods. In these circumstances the future loses "its challenging urgency," and those in a happy mood feel themselves carried by advancing time; and even though time passes away from them "as though on wings," yet in remembrance time that had represented fulfillment seems to have passed more slowly than periods of boredom and despondence which at the moment had seemed to drag painfully.[39]

Bollnow's criticism of Heidegger has rightly been rejected as a misunderstanding.[40] The primacy of anxiety in Heidegger's analysis of moods has a purely methodological basis, since anxiety is especially adapted to show the relation of moods to the whole of life and since it is exposed to the void (*das Nichts*) and is thereby related to freedom. Bollnow's emphasis on happy moods does not represent a material correction of Heidegger, since according to Heidegger too the mood of joy characterizes the possibility of authentic existence. Joy is the mood in which the freedom of the Dasein finds expression, and Heidegger even says that joy has a liberating effect.[41] For the early Heidegger, joy is based less on the object of the

[37]R. González de Mendoza, *Stimmung und Transzendenz* (1970), 127, on Kierkegaard, *The Concept of Dread*, 39, in relation to Heidegger, *Being and Time*, 231ff. (German 187ff.). For what follows, see 123–38.

[38]Ibid., 142.

[39]Bollnow, *Das Wesen der Stimmungen*, 120ff. and 63ff., 69ff.

[40]González de Mendoza, 152–81, esp. 160f. See also the critique of Bollnow's own analysis of moods in González de Mendoza, 178, and in O. Pöggeler, "Das Wesen der Stimmungen," *Zeitschrift für philosophische Forschung* 14 (1960), 281ff.

[41]Heidegger, *Being and Time*, 358 (German 310). See "What Is Metaphysics?" in Heidegger, *Existence and Being*, ed. W. Brock (Chicago, 1949), 364, and see his *Nietzsche* I (1961), 65.

moment than on "the freedom of decision when a choice has been made," whereas the later Heidegger in the period after the "turn" interprets this mood as an effect of the presence of being. Thus awe, the mood of the holy, "suddenly" seizes the poet.[42] The intoxication of inspiration is the poet's exalted mood "in which the voice of the attuning one is alone heard, in order that the attuned may be decisively given to the utmost other than themselves," that is, be open to being.[43]

In the later Heidegger's statements about moods this phenomenon is connected with what in another terminology would be called the working of the *Spirit,* who elevates human beings above themselves. Thus for Paul, joy is an effect of the Holy Spirit (1 Thess. 1:6) and appears with righteousness and peace as a manifestation of the reign of God (Rom. 14:17).[44] In the Gospel of Luke and in John joy is likewise connected with the appearance of Jesus as the presence of eschatological salvation. In like manner, "joy" was the characteristic mood of the cultic community in the mystery religions, while in the Old Testament (LXX) too "joy" was associated with cultic activity and with the festivals (Deut. 12:7; Isa. 30:29; etc.).

But even in the realm of cult the ecstatic mood of joy is not in and of itself a guarantee of participation in the divine spirit (see Hos. 9:1). In fact, the contrary may be true: joy can be delusive (James 4:10). This is due to its connection with pleasure, whether one says that joy is accompanied by pleasure (Aristotle, *Ethica Nicomachea* 1105b22) or, conversely, that joy flows from pleasure (4 Macc. 1:22). In any case, the connection is so close that Plato still used the two words as synonyms and could speak, on the one hand, of taking pleasure in wisdom (*Republic* 582a10f.) and, on the other, of the reprehensible pleasure felt at the misfortune of friends (*Philebus* 49d7). It was the Stoics who removed the ambiguity from the concept of pleasure by labeling all pleasure as reprehensible and contrasting it with joy as an equally unambiguous good mood of the soul.[45] This contrast evidently influenced early Christian terminology, in which "joy" is almost always a positive value, while "pleasure" is a consistently negative value.[46]

On this point Christian thinking is not materially as far removed from

[42]González de Mendoza, 183ff. The author compares Heidegger's views with the role of moods in Ignatian mysticism, and especially of the basic mood of repose, and with the element of "consolation" (202, 217ff., 237f., 310f.)

[43]M. Heidegger, *Erläuterungen zu Hölderlins Dichtung* (1944), 113.

[44]On this, see R. Bultmann, *Theology of the New Testament,* trans. K. Grobel (2 vols.; New York, 1953, 1955; reprinted in one volume), I, 339f. On this point and on what follows, see H. Conzelmann, "chairō," *TDNT* 9:359–72 (German orig., 1973).

[45]Conzelmann, 361.

[46]Compare the findings in the article on "chairō" with G. Stählin's article on "hēdonē" in *TDNT* 2:909–26 (German orig., 1935). On the antithesis between sensual pleasure and true joy, see ibid., 920.

Platonic thought as it might at first sight seem to be, since in the New Testament "joy" almost always relates to God and his salvation, in contradistinction from earthly goods. This is consistent with the Platonic distinction between authentic and adulterated pleasures (*Republic* 581c6ff.; 585d11ff.). But the Platonic approach based on the ambiguity of the feelings of pleasure and joy is, first of all, more in accord with the phenomenological data than is the terminological distinction inspired by the Stoics. The purpose of Plato's argument was to distinguish, *within* the experience of pleasure and joy, between the wicked, who take their delight in false pleasure, and the good, who long for true pleasure (*Philebus* 40c1ff.). The ambivalence of pleasure as such forces us not to take pleasure as a criterion of the good (ibid., 55a9ff.) and, instead, to take the good as the criterion for distinguishing between true and false pleasures (ibid., 61aff.).

It is a fact that in every happy mood life seems full and complete. And it may be that therein we are experiencing something of cosmic harmony and of the praise of God that is being uttered by creation.[47] But it is also a characteristic of moods that they change and that the criterion of their truth does not reside in themselves. Definitive joy is therefore associated in the Bible with the expectation of the eschatological future of God, and only when this is revealed in the present can human beings live here and now in the *joy* that overcomes the suffering of the present world.[48] This temporal perspective of biblical eschatology may also account for the negative value assigned to pleasure, which takes delight in the goods of this world instead of in the future of God and his salvation. Herein, too, there is a profound difference between the Christian view and the superficially similar Stoic opposition between joy and pleasure. The difference will emerge in full clarity when I turn, as I do now, to the assessment of the affects.

In the Stoics the negative judgment on pleasure is closely connected with its origin in an opposition to the philosophy of Epicurus. The judgment takes systematic form in the Stoic doctrine of affects as disturbances of the logos nature of human beings. Plato, of course, had spoken of a

[47]Spitzer (n. 28, above) has studied the relations between the concept of mood and the ancient idea of cosmic harmony. The discussion is, of course, concerned primarily with positive or "elevated" moods as distinct from "being out of sorts." On the Christian interpretation of cosmic harmony as the song of the angels, see ibid., 19; for its reflection in the liturgy in the form of sung hymns (since the time of Ambrose of Milan), 20ff. Spitzer emphasizes the point that the Christian view of world harmony differs from that of antiquity inasmuch as it does not look to the earthly manifestations of this harmony for their own sake but sees eternity made transparent in them.

[48]Here is the deeper meaning of Augustine's detemporalization of world harmony, described by Spitzer, 28ff.

rebellion (stasis) of the affects against the higher powers of the soul (*Sophist* 228a4ff.) and had described this rebellion as a sickness and a kind of madness of the soul (ibid.; see *Timaeus* 86b1ff.). But he did not regard the *pathē*—among which he here mentions pleasure, displeasure, and desires—as reprehensible in themselves but only in their excess (*Timaeus* 86b6).

In the judgment of Chrysippus, on the other hand, the affects as such are the expression of an impulse that destroys the symmetry of natural striving and because of its lack of moderation is irrational and unnatural.[49] We must understand this view against the background of the conception of order and harmony that permeates the entire Stoic system.[50] This harmony is endangered by the sensations that attack the human senses when reason is not master of them but instead allows itself to be carried away by the intensity with which they present things both good and pernicious to the eyes of the soul and thereby arouse pleasure or pain, or (with reference to future good and evil) desire or fear.[51] The reprehensibleness of the affects is therefore not due to, for example, their self-centeredness[52] but to the way in which they disturb the order and harmony of both the soul and the cosmos. Especially significant in this regard is the fact that Chrysippus' criticism was directed precisely against the ecstatic aspect of the affects.[53] In his thinking he lacked a sense of the fact that life is necessarily lived amid tensions and conflicts and requires that these be overcome. We may also say that he lacked a sense of the historical character of life.

In this respect, Plato's thinking showed a considerably greater comprehensiveness. He realized that the dissolution of a harmonious state (health, for example) necessarily brings pain to a living being, while the restoration of harmony brings pleasure, and similarly that anticipation of these states elicits fear and desire.[54] Plato's criticism was directed only against pleasure and desire that are based on false opinion (*Philebus*

---

[49]See M. Pohlenz, *Die Stoa. Geschichte einer geistigen Bewegung* I (1948), 144–53, esp. 149 (and see II (1949), 81, on Galen's account). According to Cicero, *Acad.* I, 10, 39, Zeno already regarded "inharmoniousness" (*immoderatam quandam intemperantiam*—a certain lack of moderation and sobriety) in the soul as the root of the affects.

[50]See U. Wilckens, *Weisheit und Torheit* (1959), 225–54, esp. 250 and 252.

[51]For the Stoic doctrine of the four principal affects and their relation to present or future good and evil, see Pohlenz, I, 148f. The number four is already in Plato (*Laches* 191d6f.), as is the distinction between pleasure and displeasure as related to the present and as related to the future (*Philebus* 32b9ff.), which yields the number four. On the affects as originating under the force of external impressions, see Pohlenz, I, 145.

[52]This is all the more noteworthy since Zeno had already noted the structural self-centeredness of the affects; Pohlenz, I, 149.

[53]Evidence in Pohlenz, II, 78.

[54]Plato, *Philebus* 31d4ff., 32b9ff. with c2 and 34d2ff.

37c10ff.), as, for example, pleasure derived from false hopes (40b2ff.). Both pleasure and displeasure are part of the *becoming* of the living entity (54c1ff.). To be sure, Plato did not develop this point of view as such, since he was interested less in assessing the necessity of tensions and conflicts in the development of the living being than in the possibility of a pleasure that would be free of all displeasure. His analysis nonetheless offers a positive point of departure for understanding the behavior of a living being as a link between the at-hand and the possible, between lack and whole. Aristotle prepared the way for such an understanding, and his formulation of it is still a subject of discussion today.[55]

Christian thinkers could not accept the Stoic condemnation of the affects for the simple reason that Scripture repeatedly speaks of the sorrows and joys of the devout. Referring to Paul, Augustine explained that even the good could experience sadness.[56] The Gospel reports that even the Lord himself became angry, felt joy, wept over Lazarus, "desired" to celebrate the Passover with his disciples, and was troubled in the face of his own death.[57] The question therefore is not so much *whether* the devout mind can feel anger, but rather *why* it feels anger; not *whether* it grows sad, but *at what* it feels sadness; not *whether* but *why* it is afraid.[58] The impassiveness *(apathia)* which is part of the Stoic ideal of the sage may be good and desirable in itself (provided it does not degenerate into insensibility of spirit, *stupor*), but not in this present life which is ensnared in sin.[59] Augustine was especially incensed that the Stoics should disapprove even of mercy. If the affects that proceed from love are called vices, then one must be on guard lest real vices be passed off as virtues. According to Augustine, on our journey to God the affects are the feet that either lead us closer to God or carry us farther from him; but without them we cannot travel the way at all.[60]

[55] Aristotle, *De anima* III, 10 (433a9ff.). Aristotle conceived desire *(orexis)* as a presupposition even for movement caused by reason (433a21) and reduced the conflict between desires and reason to the fact that desires are directed to the present whereas reason is directed to the future (433b5ff.). In addition, he presupposed that wherever there is desire, there is also a feeling of pleasure or displeasure (434a2f.). For the contemporary discussion, see the disagreement of Strasser (n. 4, above), 129ff., 79ff., with Sartre regarding the latter's conception of emotional behaviors as "magical" reinterpretations of reality (73ff.). Strasser himself, however, does not adequately appreciate the importance which the relation between "lack" and "totality" has in Sartre's phenomenology of human consciousness. Sartre's view is utterly opposed to that of the Stoics, since according to him totality always remains something unattainable by the "unhappy consciousness."

[56] Augustine, *De civ. Dei* XIV, 8, 3. See *Enarr. in Ps.* 76, 14.

[57] Augustine, *De civ. Dei* XIV, 9. 3.

[58] Ibid., IX, 5

[59] Ibid., XIV, 9. 4.

[60] Augustine, *Enarr. in Ps.* 94, 2. Augustine's emphasis on the affective life was continued in medieval Augustinianism by such theologians as Bernard of Clairvaux, Bonaventure, and

The positive value set upon the affective life in Augustine and in the tradition influenced by him must seem surprising to the extent that it was Augustine himself who identified desire (one of the basic affects of the Stoics) with original sin, while early Christianity had passed a negative judgment on pleasure (as distinct from joy). But these negative judgments were directed not against the emotions and excitations, but against the egoism which is hidden in desire and expresses itself in pleasure taken in worldly goods. The longing for God and his reign and the joy found in things as creatures and gifts of God did not fall under the condemnation. In fact, the ecstatic element in the affects, which was so suspect to the Stoics, was assigned a positive value as the impulse that moves human beings along the way to the future of God and of his salvation, but also outward toward their fellow human beings.

Generally speaking, then, the affects have their place in self-transcendence and in the temporal flow of life, as Aristotle had seen (see above, n. 55). Just as through their moods individuals participate in the atmosphere of their world and in the spirit and life of the community to which they belong, so too the life of the affects is related ecstatically to the world and the people around one.[61] As a result, feeling arousals and movements of the mind, which are by their nature "events," are more strongly marked by temporality than are feeling states or moods. Because of their finitude, living beings must look outside themselves for the good that will satisfy their longings. This "outside" is at the same time a "not yet" of possession and enjoyment. But the future can also bring threats and dangers. It is not accidental, therefore, that in the classical doctrine of the affects desire as the anticipation of future pleasure and fear as the anticipation of future danger were regarded as fundamental affects to be set alongside pleasure and displeasure.

But the temporality proper to the affects also includes the continuing effects of past experiences. Plato had emphasized the point that the reference of desire to the future is mediated through memory (*Philebus*

John Gerson. It is also found in Luther, who could accept Augustine's interpretation of the affections as the soul's "foot" or principle of movement and could, like Bonaventure and Gerson, rate the affections higher than reason: "Faith enlightens not the human intellect, which it rather blinds, but the affections; for it leads these that they may be saved, and this through the hearing of the word" (WA 4: 356; also O. Clemen 5, 202, 9f.). Further data are in R. Schwarz, *Fides, Spes und Caritas beim jungen Luther* (1962), 187ff. and 417ff. As E. Mühlenberg has shown, the educational program of Erasmus and its Reformed interpretation by Melanchthon were also based on the priority of the affections over reason as far as the task of human renewal was concerned; see "Humanistisches Bildungsprogramm und reformatorische Lehre beim jungen Melanchthon," *ZTK* 65 (1968), 431–44.

[61]Emotion and affect should not be antecedently judged to be a "derailment," as they are in Strasser, 264. The "boiling" of which he speaks (266) is rather to be taken, along with the temporality inherent in living, as a way of breaking out of a rigidified or sluggish state.

35c12ff.). Thus the presence in feeling of a life totality that transcends the present moment is a presupposition for the behavior of a living being. This fact grounds both the justification and the necessity of a psychology of *experience* and its forms in addition to the simple observation of *behavior*. I said early in this book that the necessary assumption of a *self*-comporting subject for an understanding of behavior forces us to reject the behaviorist reduction of psychology to externally observable behavior.[62] The motivational importance of experience for behavior makes that earlier rejection more intelligible. But the motivational function of experience is concentrated in the feeling arousals, the emotions, and the affects. In this respect human beings share, in their own manner, in what characterizes animal life generally. The only thing specific to human beings is the way in which the whole of their life is present to them, namely, in the explicit distinction and simultaneous interrelatedness of its successive moments.

In human beings, who are in a special way social beings, the self-transcendence of the affective life is largely oriented to the social environment. The positive affects, in which individuals open themselves to their world, are ecstatically inserted into interhuman relations. In these affects individuals are not primarily ego-centered but are ecstatically carried out of themselves in self-surrender. For this reason, Max Scheler could regard "identification" *(Einsfühlung)* as the root of all feelings of sympathy.[63] This thesis is confirmed by the insight gained in modern developmental psychology, according to which the development of the child begins with a "symbiotic" phase in which it does not yet distinguish its own self, or even its body, from the mother (see chapter 5, at nn. 94ff.).

The consciousness of this symbiotic solidarity is not completely lost even after the differentiation of the child's own body, self, and ego from the surroundings, even though Scheler himself admits that it "has atrophied [in humans] more than in most animals" (31), and in modern Western thinking far more than in "primitive" societies (19). In the psychic life of the young child and especially in the absorption of children at play something of this continues to be operative, as it does among adults in sexual union, in certain religious phenomena, and in the behavior of the collective psyche (24ff.). These phenomena may seem exotic and eccentric to a viewer whose sole perspective is that of the everyday world. Nonetheless the original "identification" which continues to exert a subconscious influence finds expression in these phenomena; compared with this "identification," all later differentiation is secondary.

David Hume came to a diametrically opposed conclusion in his philo-

---

[62]See above, chapter 1, at n. 7.

[63]M. Scheler, *The Nature of Sympathy.* trans. P. Heath (London, 1954), 96ff. The page references that follow in the text are to this book.

sophical interpretation of the passions, which occupies a third of his exten-sive treatise on human nature. His understanding of the passions[64] was based on their reference to the ego or self. He began, therefore, with pride and humility as the two basic forms of passion (277ff.), since these have feeling (positive or negative) about the self as their proper content (278). Pride may indeed refer to other objects as well—natural phenomena, possessions, accomplishments, honors achieved—but it does so only because of the importance of these for the feeling that persons have of their own selves (292; see 300ff.). It was from this same angle that Hume dealt with passions relating to other persons; here he considered love and hate to be the basic forms (329ff.). According to Hume, we love others because they belong to us (and therefore love of them is really self-love) or because we feel good in their company (here again the relation to ourselves is decisive) (352f.).

But does not this turn reality upside down? Hume's description of the passions reads like an inversion of Scheler's statement that "a man tends, in the first instance, to live more in *others* than in himself; more in the community than in his own individual self."[65] The truth of this claim is well attested precisely by studies of ego development. Moreover, does not Hume leave completely out of consideration the self-forgetfulness that accompanies passion? On the other hand, Hume's presentation is not based simply on an arbitrary distortion of the facts. The reversal reflected in Hume's description takes place rather in human reality itself and is based on the two-sidedness of human experience. On the one hand, the wholeness of life, which transcends the given moment, is present in feeling and is articulated by means of the object that rouses our affects. On the other hand, all experience is related to the locus of the Dasein at a given moment, to the momentary reality of the ego. If in the development of the individual there has been a successful differentiation of the ego from its surroundings and if this ego has achieved lasting reality in the mirror of its representation of its own self, it is easy also for a hardly passable chasm to open up between the ego and others.

Hume presupposed this rift but did not really describe it. It did not

---

[64]Hume devoted hardly any attention to the relation between affect and passion, while he distinguished the passions from the gentler "emotions" as being "more violent"; see *A Treatise of Human Nature,* 276 (ed. cited in n. 2, above; the page references that follow in the text are to this edition). The concept of "affection," on the other hand, is closely related in Hume to that of "sense impression." Nonetheless Hume did materially accept the distinc-tion between momentary affect and lasting passion (as Chrysippus had; see Pohlenz, I, 147f.), but he did so in his own manner, by distinguishing between "direct passions" ("such as arise immediately from good or evil, from pain or pleasure") and "indirect passions" which depend on reflection (276f.), i.e., reflection on the relation of a given object to the self.

[65]Scheler, 247.

become thematic until Sartre's description of corporeality as the nakedness that is exposed to the gaze of others; of sexual desire as the vain attempt to dominate other persons in the medium of their bodies; and of love as the likewise tragically unattainable longing to possess the freedom of the other precisely as freedom.[66] Here love appears as a defense strategy, as an attempt to escape the clutches of others by identification with them, but an identification that really takes the form of an absorption of them and therefore must inevitably fail. It is inevitable, in particular, that the effort of sexual desire to possess others by way of their corporeality—an effort which, according to Sartre, is a substitute for the failure of love—should be antecedently incapable of reaching others as persons. While this renders intelligible the transition to hate, in which persons seek to rid themselves in a radical way of others and their clutches, hate too proves a failure. For even if hate succeeded in abolishing the Other, "it could not bring it about that the Other had not been." In fact, at this point the relation to the Other becomes an immutable separation and alienation, "since the destroyed Other has carried the key to this alienation along with him to the grave."[67]

Sartre's description, despite all of its shattering realism, is of course no less one-sided than Hume's. Even those human beings who are isolated within themselves remain ordered to the totality of the human community which reaches beyond them on every side. They are never constituted solely by their for-itselfness, but are always determined by the prior fact of the symbiotic connectedness of all life, which provided the framework within which alone they awoke to their for-itselfness. Sartre no less than Hume has neglected this fact and its abiding significance for the constitution of the individual.

It is a merit of C. G. Jung's depth psychology, on the other hand, that it has shown how the prior orientation of the individual to the community is significant for the constitution of the self. According to Jung, the self always includes more than does the ego, which he conceives, along the lines of Sartre's "for-itself," as being "the centre of the field of consciousness."[68] Those components of the self which are not assumed into the consciousness of the ego are regarded as a "shadow" that must be integrated into the ego so that the latter may approximate to the self.[69] The

---

[66]Sartre, *Das Sein und das Nichts*, 454ff., 490, 493ff., 468ff., esp. 471. (See chapter 5, n. 51, above.)

[67]Ibid., 526f.; ET 388.

[68]C. G. Jung, *Aion: Researches Into the Phenomenology of the Self*, trans. R. F. C. Hull (*Collected Works* IX/2; London, 1959), 3. The page references that follow in the text are to this book.

[69]Ibid., 23. This brings the danger of an "inflation" of the ego so that it becomes the all-inclusive reality. In order to obviate this danger, Jung prefers to distinguish the archetypes from the ego (23f.) and to interpret them as a kind of divine agencies (27, 40f.). For the

unintegrated parts of the unconscious find expression in projections; especially important here are the images of *anima* and *animus* (the former for men, the latter for women) (13ff.) which provide positive compensation (see 14) for the limitations of the ego and which overlay factual relations between the sexes (14). The introduction of the viewpoint of "compensation" into the explanation of the unconscious may be regarded as an important addition to the ego psychology of the Freudian school.[70] The social environment of individuals does not make its presence felt in the "psychic apparatus" solely through the agency of the superego. In this environment individuals find not only the point of departure and counterpole for the formation of their own selves, their own identity, but also a complement to their own finiteness.

It must be said, however, that Jung has hypostasized these complementary functions of the unconscious and turned them into archetypes, instead of conceiving of them as expressions of the structure of the psyche.[71] Moreover, he has turned the transcendence of God and the gods into a psychic transcendence of the self over the ego.[72] As a result, it has been possible to level the objection of inflation against Jung himself for "distending" the ego, so to speak, into equality with God (R. Keintzel). This probably also accounts for a tendency on Jung's part to be somewhat indifferent toward the distinction between good and evil when he calls for the integration of the "shadow" into the personality.[73] Finally, the concept of the collective psyche, which betrays a similar inflation, causes Jung to neglect the concrete relations between human beings.[74] Jung's compensation thesis is acceptable when read as expressing the orientedness of individuals to a complementation through such concrete relations between human beings. When, however, compensation through images in the unconscious becomes a substitute for concrete relations or reduces the latter to the level of mere examples of supposed archetypal structures, we are confronted with symptoms of psychic inflation.

The orientation of human beings to a fullness of life that transcends them and manifests itself especially in the community of their fellow

---

concept of "psychic inflation," see R. Keintzel, *Psychische Inflation* (privately printed, 1975), 15ff. Keintzel emphasizes the religious reference of the concept of inflation, in the sense of an imagined equality of the soul with God (17, 19f., etc.).

[70]Despite his criticism of Jung's development of this viewpoint, Keintzel (257ff.) admits its fruitfulness (262), although he would prefer to speak of complementarity rather than compensation (258f., 263ff.).

[71]Keintzel correctly makes this point, 55f.

[72]F. J. Kanne, *Selbstverwirklichung. Eine Konfrontation der Psychologie C. G. Jungs mit der Ethik* (Basel, 1967), 150ff.

[73]On this, see Kanne, 114ff.

[74]H. Trüb, *Heilung aus der Begegnung. Eine Auseinandersetzung mit der Psychologie C. G. Jungs* (1962), 48ff.

human beings finds expression in the positive affects and passions, especially in feelings of sympathy but also in joy and hope. These draw individuals out of their isolation and therefore may not be simply condemned as expressions of human egocentricity. On the other hand, it is characteristic of such affects, moods, and passions as are negatively related to the environment and other people (fear, anxiety, arrogance, sadness, envy, and hate) that they isolate individuals within themselves. The positive affects and passions, on the contrary, must be understood as expressions of an "anticipatory expectation" in which the human being is aware of "the positive or negative termination into which the value of his being necessarily flows."[75]

This latent knowledge is stirred to life by the objects of affect and passion. Thus the feeling of being seized and overpowered becomes intelligible, a feeling that is at the same time accompanied by a letting oneself be seized, by a feeling of being elevated above the everyday, and by the acquisition of hitherto unsuspected powers. There is certainly a danger here that the object of passion may be taken to represent absolute fulfillment, so that obsession and bondage are the result. But passion can also be a response to a call of God (who remains transcendent) in the concrete situations of the world of human life, a response to a call that elevates individuals above the everyday and renders them capable of extraordinary dedication, without causing them to be blinded by false absolutes.

The perversion of passion may be described as a regression to the kind of identification that effaces individuality. As Max Scheler has shown, this makes the person *"more of a hero, and at the same time more of a clod":* "He is simultaneously raised above his physical circumstances *and* despoiled of his spiritual inheritance."[76] The seductive attraction of such regression to identification is due to the fact that isolation and the chasm between ego and world do have to be overcome. But the result must not be achieved at the cost of eliminating the process of individual differentiation. Unity must be sought within differentiation itself. It is love that accomplishes this, for love bridges the chasm between ego and other by acknowledging its existence.

II. Alienation and Sin

The sequence of ideas in this second part of my anthropology took as its point of departure the nonidentity of human beings with their destiny of "openness to the world," a nonidentity thematized in the Christian doctrine of sin. The recognition of this nonidentity gave rise to the ques-

---

[75]Strasser (n. 4, above), 293. On what follows, see Strasser's remarks, 293ff.
[76]Scheler (n. 63, above), 36.

tion of how the nonetheless persisting identity of human life finds its expression in the tension between centrality and exocentricity. The phenomenon of self-consciousness showed that this question is not unconnected with the concrete living of human life. For the study of that phenomenon made it clear that the relation between individual and society has to be taken up along with the question of the identity of ego and self. In addition, self-consciousness proved to be dependent on a more primordial familiarity which does not yet expressly grasp the "self" of the self as its object but rather is at home in the symbiotic vital unity of the individual with the world that makes up its life. We saw that in the individual's life, feeling is the basis of this familiarity that forms the foundation of every self-consciousness.

The investigation of the sphere of the feeling showed, among other things, that in "elevated" moods and positive affects, in which human beings are most at one with themselves, they are not preoccupied with themselves but are "ecstatically" open and surrendered to the reality of their life-world and of the ground that sustains it. In "depressed" moods, on the other hand, and in negative affects they prove to be thrown back upon themselves. We cannot but think here of the Christian vision of sinners as human beings who are curved back upon themselves *(homo incurvatus in seipsum)*. Does this mean that the investigation in this second part of my book, focused as it is entirely on the question of human identity, represents in fact a development of the Christian doctrine of sin?

The human beings who are trying to find their own identity are evidently sinners. Instead of dedicating themselves to service in the objective tasks of the human community and experiencing in this service the meaning of their own lives, their primary concern is with themselves. This by itself is an adequate sign that they lack their authentic identity. This is not to say, of course, that human beings concerned about themselves are always, and without further ado, aware of this lack. They may anesthetize or suppress their feeling of nonidentity. They may think they will attain to their identity by way of identity formation and self-realization. But by this very fact they show that they are alienated from themselves, for if they were aware that in the search for their identity they now lack this identity, they would, in the realization of this lack, have at the same time at least a vague consciousness of their true selves. But when human beings who are concerned about themselves think that they come closest to their own identity through this kind of preoccupation with themselves, then they are really alienated from their true destiny and their true selves.

This appraisal of the situation does not mean that an obscure feeling of this kind of alienation does not accompany individuals on their journey, even amid their cares about themselves. As beings who are familiar with themselves and conscious of themselves, humans must in the final analysis be aware of their situation in some manner or other, however fragmentary. They may even be explicitly conscious of their alienation and of a wish to overcome it. They may make an effort to eliminate it by radically changing the conditions of their individual and social lives. But none of this can alter their condition of real alienation if what they consider to constitute alienation is not the thing that really makes them alienated. And even if in consciousness they correctly understand what it is that objectively alienates them, the alienation itself is, of course, not eliminated thereby. In this case, however, conscience with its exocentricity, though in thrall to the alienation, also looks beyond it. A false identification of the alienation, on the other hand, and a concentration on getting rid of what is erroneously taken to be its cause will perpetuate the actual alienation more surely even than the mere delusion that the individual is not alienated at all.

1. Alienation

The concepts of alienation and self-alienation have been the subject of lively discussion ever since the early writings of Karl Marx, in particular his *Economic and Philosophical Manuscripts* of 1844, became known. The discussion did not, however, reach its full intensity immediately after the first publication of these writings in 1927 (the original German texts were published in 1932), but only after World War II.[77] Marx's thesis that human beings are alienated from themselves by the capitalist system of property and labor provided even Western societies with a diagnosis of the present age and an explanation of the way in which human life is burdened by the anonymous forces at work in advanced industrial and technological society. The "anthropology of the young Marx" gave rise to a new phase in the preoccupation with Marxism.

It was evident, of course, that the concept of alienation in Marx is closely connected with the philosophy of Hegel, and especially with Hegel's use of the same concept in his *Phenomenology of Spirit* (1807). Scholars discussed the differences between Marx and Hegel in their understanding of alienation, and many regarded Hegel as the author of the whole idea of alienation.[78] Since then, we have learned that the idea of alienation has much older roots.[79] In antiquity, "alienation" could mean the theft of

[77]See O. Scholz, "Entfremdung als anthropologisches Problem" (1966–67), in H. H. Schrey, ed., *Entfremdung* (Darmstadt, 1975), 115–79, esp. 116f.

[78]H. Popitz, *Der entfremdete Mensch. Zeitkritik und Geschichtsphilosophie des jungen Marx* (1953), situates Marx's ideas in the broader context of the development of German idealism from the end of the eighteenth century.

[79]See E. Ritz's article on the history of the concept in *HWP* 2 (1972), 509–25. References to usage in antiquity, 510.

property (see Polybius) or the disposal of property and the rights to it (from Aristotle on). But there was another usage that fell outside the realm of ideas associated with property and referred instead to the human community and membership in it. One who is excluded from a person or community is alien to it (Aristotle, *Politics* 1248a40) or alienated from it.

The word "alienation" occurs with this meaning in the Greek translation (LXX, i.e., the Septuagint) of the Old Testament: sinners are from birth "estranged" from God (Ps. 57[58]:3; see Hos. 9:10; Ezek. 14:7). The New Testament too says that the Gentiles are now "alienated from the life of God *(apēllotriōmenoi tēs zōēs tou Theou)* because of the ignorance that is in them, due to their hardness of heart" (Eph. 4:18), just as the present Gentile Christians were formerly alienated (Col. 1:21; Eph. 2:12).

The concept was subsequently used, in the sense of estrangement and alienation from God, both by the gnostics and by the early Christian fathers in order to describe the situation of the sinner. Augustine regards alienation as a consequence of concupiscence, and therefore he can issue this warning in one of his sermons: "If you do not separate yourself from your concupiscence, it will alienate you from God."[80] There is a suggestion here of alienation as a theme in the relation to the self. Augustine is also clearly making use of a Stoic motif. Zeno had applied *oikeiōsis* ("familiarity," "intimacy") and alienation not only to the relation to external things and persons but also to the relation to the self.[81] We should (he maintains) steer clear of giving assent to falsehood and know that it is more alien to us than is anything else that is contrary to our true nature.[82] In like manner, Augustine interprets the psalmist's wish to lie down and sleep in peace as a separating of himself from the transitory things and tribulations of this world.[83]

The ethical use of the term "alienation" in the sense of an "alienating of oneself from . . . ," which was then prolonged into the idea of self-denial, evidently provided a point of contact for the language of the Christian mystics. It is in this latter context that the idea of alienation from one's self first appears. Thus the idea is present, though not in so many

[80]Augustine, *Serm.* 42, 8: "If you do not free yourself from your concupiscence, it will alienate you from God." Further patristic references are in Ritz, 511.

[81]Pohlenz, *Die Stoa* II (n. 49, above), 66. See also I, 330, on Epictetus, *Enchiridion* 2 and 11; according to Pohlenz, the division of things into what is "your own" *(oikios)* and what is to be regarded as alien, constitutes "the foundation of Epictetus' ethics."

[82]Thus Cicero, *De fin.* III, 5, says of the Stoics: "They think that assent to what is false is more alien to us than the other things which are contrary to nature."

[83]Augustine, *Enarr. in Ps.* 4, 9: "He rightly hopes to obtain from these a complete separation of the soul from mortal things and a forgetfulness of the distresses of this world . . . there where supreme peace will not be disturbed by any tumult." See also *Super Gen. ad litt.* 12, 5 (PL 32:632ff.).

words, in Meister Eckhart: "If I am to receive the word of God within me, I must be no less completely alienated from all that is mine, especially in the realm of the temporal, than what is beyond the sea is alien to me."[84] Conversely, the idea of self-alienation as alienation from one's true self is now also connected with the Christian interpretation of sin as an alienation.[85]

The evidence from the history of the concepts justifies Christian theologians in treating the concepts of alienation and self-alienation as part of their heritage; they did not have to wait and borrow them from modern philosophy or social psychology. On the other hand, these concepts played hardly any role in the didactic development of the Christian doctrine of sin, and it was in fact only from outside sources that their use was suggested to modern theologians. As a result, these theologians were not in a position simply to reappropriate their own heritage; they could not indiscriminately adopt the terms as used in philosophy or social psychology. For the modern philosophical use of the concept of alienation is not derived in a direct line from Christian mysticism (although there may be many latent connections between the two[86]) but is based instead on the use of *alienatio* in economics and civil law, where it means the sale or other disposal of a piece of property.[87] Rousseau applied this notion to the relation to the self and thus produced the idea of a disposal or alienation of the self. In his concept of the social contract (as distinct from Hobbes's idea of a contract of submission), Rousseau took the "sale" model and developed it into the idea of the "total alienation" of the individual to the advantage of society, using it to express the "exchange" of natural freedom for the equality of citizens before the law.[88]

The idea, voiced by Wilhelm von Humboldt as early as 1793 and subsequently developed by Hegel, that human beings must go out of

---

[84]Meister Eckhart, *Werke*, ed. H. Pfeiffer (1857), 257, lines 9–11; cited in Ritz, 512. [I have translated from the modern German translation of J. Quint in his *Meister Eckhart. Deutsche Predigten und Traktate* (Munich, n. d.), 340.—Tr.] Ritz gives examples from Christian Scholasticism, especially in the Victorines and Bonaventure, showing how the way was prepared for the mystical use of the term.

[85]Thus in Thomas Campanella, Renaissance philosopher, in whose *Metaphysics* III (1967), 82, it is said that when self-love is placed above the love of God, the soul is as it were alienated from itself *(a seipsa quasi alienata)*.

[86]See E. Topitsch, *Sozialphilosophie zwischen Ideologie und Wissenschaft* (1966), 261f.

[87]Thus Ritz, 512.

[88]Ritz, 513, on *The Social Contract* I, 6. H. Barth, "Über die Idee der Selbstentfremdung des Menschen bei Rousseau" (1959), in Schrey, *Entfremdung* (n. 77, above), 3–26, does not go into Rousseau's own use of the concept of alienation but describes those aspects of his cultural criticism which can be described as "alienation" in the light of the subsequent use of this term in cultural criticism.

themselves in order to gain themselves, is most likely connected with "alienation" in Rousseau's sense of the term.[89] The statement represents a generalization of the idea that human beings give themselves over to society in order to gain themselves back as citizens. In a similar manner, in his *Phenomenology of Spirit,* Hegel describes the appropriation of objective reality by the spirit as a process of self-alienation and subsequent sublimation *(Aufhebung):* The movement of the spirit consists in "becoming something other for itself, i.e., an object for its self, and then to sublimate this otherhood"; in so doing, its immediacy "becomes estranged and then [the spirit] returns to itself from estrangement."[90]

Fichte's *Wissenschaftslehre* of 1794 had prepared the way for the idea of estrangement.[91] Hegel, however, was the first to conceive of such an estrangement or alienation as a phase in the self-consciousness of the spirit: self-consciousness "only has *real existence,* so far as it alienates itself from itself. By doing so, it puts itself in the position of something universal, and this its universality is its validity, establishes it, and is its actuality."[92] While this passage still clearly reflects Rousseau's idea that in giving themselves away to the community, individuals recover themselves as subjects of laws and rights, Hegel finds the same structure also present in the relation between self-consciousness and consciousness of objects. By its self-divestiture the spirit produces its world, although the latter by reason of its externality is so alien to it that "it must now take possession" of it.[93] Finally, in his presentation of the Christian religion Hegel finds the same structure present in the Christian idea of "the Divine Being 'humbling' Itself" in the incarnation.[94]

---

[89]W. von Humboldt, *Werke* I, 236, adds that it is important that "in this separation [or: alienation] human beings not lose themselves" through dispersal in the manifold of reality. See Ritz, 513.

[90]G. W. F. Hegel, *Phänomenologie des Geistes,* ed. J. Hoffmeister (PhB 114), 32; tr. in W. Kaufmann, *Hegel: Reinterpretation, Texts, and Commentary* (Garden City, N.Y., 1965), 412 (only the Preface is translated here). The result of the sublimation is that the spirit, henceforth with its truth and reality, is "the property of consciousness" (ibid.). See *Phänomenologie,* 347f. (the self-alienated spirit; culture) and 350f., but also, much earlier, 20; ET: *The Phenomenology of Mind,* trans. J. Baillie (2d ed.; New York, 1931), 513ff., 80f.

[91]Fichte, *Werke* (ed. F. Medicus), I, 165. In the *Wissenschaftslehre* of 1804 the idea of alienation in the sense of objectification plays a large role (ed. R. Lauth and J. Widmann [1975], 223f.; see 141, 154). Most important, the process of objectification is now called "estrangement" or "alienation" *(Entäusserung)* (265). *Entfremdung* ("alienation," "estrangement") is also used, 10 and 67, as synonymous with objectivity.

[92]Hegel, *Phänomenologie des Geistes,* 351 (Baillie, 514; italics added).

[93]Ibid. See also *Ästhetik* (ed. Moldenhauer and Michel), I (1970), 28.

[94]Hegel, *Phänomenologie des Geistes,* 539ff. (Baillie, 773ff.). Alienation from the divine being through sin is only a phase in this process; ibid., 539f. (Baillie, 773f., 771f.). See also J. Ringleben, *Hegels Theorie der Sünde* (1977), 55ff.

The very fact that Hegel could include the Christian idea of God in his interpretation of estrangement or alienation is enough to show the difference between the modern concept and the traditional Christian idea of alienation. It is true that in the latter tradition alienation could have not only its original negative sense of separation from God through sin but also the positive sense of self-renunciation. But self-alienation of this kind could never be predicated of God. In contrast to the concept of self-divestiture (Phil. 2:7), self-alienation was not used before Hegel to describe the incarnation. The reason is that "alienation" was taken very seriously as a *separation*—whether from God or from the ego of the sinner—and not as a self-preservation and self-acquisition in another than "one's self." It cannot be said of God, even in view of the incarnation and cross of Christ, that he separates himself from himself. Therefore the incarnation cannot be conceived as a self-alienation of God. Sin, on the other hand, does in fact entail a self-alienation—a separation of human beings from their true selves—in the sense described by Campanella (see above, n. 85), namely, that the separation of sinners from God means at the same time their separation from their own destiny, which is communion with God.

The orientation of human consciousness to a world of objects is not, as such, to be interpreted in any way as a "self-alienation." Such a designation would be plausible only if prior to any relation to objects the self were given as a for-itself, so that the relation to objects would have to be thought of as a loss of its original unity with itself. But such a view of the self is consistent only on the basis of a transcendental philosophy of the ego such as is found in Fichte.

Hegel, for his part, defended the thesis that the ego comes to itself only in another than its self. But his idea of self-divestiture and self-alienation suggests that the ego finds itself in the other only insofar as in the other it recognizes an objectification of its own activity. If the unity of the ego were really thought of on the basis of relation to the other, then self-divestiture could not mean self-alienation, since the being-outside-oneself-in-the-other would constitute the ego's proper identity. Given such a perspective, it is those who are enclosed within themselves who would have to be called "self-alienated." In keeping with the considerations on human subjectivity and personal identity that were proposed in the preceding chapter, we must therefore distinguish between self-divestiture and self-alienation. Hegel's idealist concept of the subject as the productive source of its world is at work in his identification of these two concepts.

At this point the Christian understanding of alienation as sin, which is essentially a being closed to God, approximates to the Marxist concept of alienation. The young Marx protested against Hegel's taking the objectivity of human knowledge as a sign of alienation.[95] So too in theology the term "sin" is not correctly applied to the simple turning to the objects of the world as such; it properly describes only the concupiscential focusing of the relation to the world upon one's own ego. There is another point which Christians share with the young Marx in their understanding of alienation: his criticism of the idea that the relation to the world may be reduced completely to the relation of possession.[96] But despite these shared views, there is a profound opposition in the understanding of alienation itself.

Just as according to Marx human beings are naturally related to objects, so too their processing and production of objects is part of their nature: "Their *objective* product simply confirms their *objective* activity, that is, the fact that their activity is the activity of objective, natural beings" (273). Marx saw in this activity the natural "manifestation of life" (239; see 274) for human beings, and in view of the end result of this activity he could at times speak of it as "alienation" in Hegel's sense of the word (229). For the most part, however, alienation in Marx means pretty much the alienation (229) of the active being of the human person (see 239, 289, 299) that occurs because the product of this activity becomes the exclusive property of another. For this reason, Marx could regard private property as the blatant "expression of *alienated human* life" (236). If, as the teaching of Adam Smith claims, human labor is the source of all wealth, then private property signifies the spoliation of those who possess nothing, with the result that "the manifestation of the life" of human beings is "their alienation, and their self-realization is their loss of reality, an *alien* reality"— alien, because now the property of another.

This argument presupposes not only that the activity of human beings is a manifestation of their being but also and above all that in their activity they realize and possess their own being. Only on this condition can the *manifestation* of their being in the products of their activity become an occasion for having their very being taken from them, alienated, along with its products.

Would there, then, be no alienation if active individuals remained in possession of their own activity and its products? Such a view has rightly

[95]K. Marx, *Nationalökonomie und Philosophie* (1844), in *Die Frühschriften,* ed. S. Landshut (Kroner ed.), 226–316, esp. 261f., 270f., 273ff. See G. Lukacs, *Der junge Hegel* (1948; Berlin, 1954), 611–46, esp. 617f., with the objection that when the "pseudo-movement" represented by alienation of the spirit in the world of natural objects is confused with the real alienation represented by the social praxis of history, the latter too is turned into a pseudo-movement.

[96]Ibid., 240; see 258, and the comment of E. Thier, *Das Menschenbild des jungen Marx* (1957), 41ff., on the origin of this idea in Moses Hess. The page references that follow in the text here are from the cited edition of Marx's early writings.

been criticized as betraying a romantic idealization of the kind of work done by preindustrial craftsmen.[97] But the romanticism goes even deeper, for the idea of human activity here is so individualistic that even the exchange of products by individuals becomes suspect. The result is that the concrete mediation between individual and race vanishes, and the individual is regarded as directly identical with society or the human species (238f.).[98] Therefore, too, the active self-realization of the individual can be seen as identical with the human race's engendering of itself (246ff.).

In the background here is Fichte's idea that the ego posits itself; this is the source of the romanticism that characterizes the young Marx's ideas on self-realization and self-alienation. For these ideas presuppose that the active ego already possesses its nature, which finds expression in its activity, and that it is not simply on the way to an as yet unfulfilled destiny. But if the being of humans is connected with their as yet unfulfilled destiny, then alienation will consist in the fact that they close themselves against the future to which they are destined, and not in their being estranged from themselves in the medium of a thing which they already have or which they produce. Furthermore, the relation between individual and species is then mediated through the common sharing of one and the same human destiny.

In the Christian view, the being of humans is bound up, in the way described, with the future to which they are destined. In their activity their being manifests itself as this as yet unrealized future destiny to which they are on the way, and not as an original possession which when manifested is in danger of being stolen or alienated. Herein is to be seen the opposition between the young Marx's idea of alienation and the Christian idea

[97]Thus C. W. Mills, *The Marxists* (New York, 1962), 112, and, following Mills, J. Israel, *Alienation from Marx to Modern Sociology* (Boston, 1971), 188, 318f.

[98]But Marx abandoned and criticized this view only a little later in *The German Ideology*, tr. in L. D. Easton and K. H. Guddat, eds., *Writings of the Young Marx on Philosophy and Society* (Garden City, N.Y., 1967; Anchor Books ed.); see 429, 456f., 469f. It is replaced by the idea that only in community can the division of labor and the resultant one-sidedness of individuals be eliminated: "Only in community is personal freedom possible. . . . In a real community individuals obtained their freedom in and through their association" (457–58). This had already been Rousseau's conception; Marx, however, sums it up no longer in the general notion of "the citizen" but, rather, in the concept of the human essence as "the ensemble of social relationships" (Thesis 6 on Feuerbach; tr. in Easton-Guddat, 402). Given this new definition, there can be no antagonism between individual and society, since the individual is a function of social relations (see above, chapter 4, at nn. 46ff.). Only specific social relations can be superseded, those which restrict the free development of individuals, such as (for Marx) the division of labor (see Israel, 45ff.). The expectation that the division of labor will be done away with seems, however, hardly less romantic than the idea of individual self-realization through work (see Israel, 243ff.). In the later Marx this expectation is replaced by the hope of a lessening of the individual's work time (*Das Kapital* III, 873f.).

of human alienation as a being closed to God and therefore to the future that is one's destiny.

The claim has occasionally been made that alongside the young Marx's original theory of human beings as alienated from themselves through work and production there is another which is not affected by the criticism to which the first is liable by reason of its "romantic" assumptions. This "second theory of alienation" is supposed to be contained in the idea of *reification* which finds expression, above all, in the critical description of the "fetishism of commodities" in the first volume of *Capital.* In the context of the new definition of the human being as a social entity (sixth Thesis on Feuerbach), reification is to be understood as alienation.[99] More accurately, there is a "transition from a theory of alienation to a theory of reification,"[100] and J. Israel gives us to understand that it was really G. Lukacs who, as a student of Max Weber, combined, on the one hand, the tendency (described by Weber) of capitalist industrial society to develop anonymous bureaucratic structures for rational organization and, on the other, Marx's criticism of the fetishism of commodities, and out of the two created the theory of the reification of social processes (280ff.). Israel believes, however, that the theory of reification corresponds to the development in Marx's own thinking and that at the same time it frees his theory of alienation from "erroneous and even metaphysical preconditions" (268), especially the previously mentioned "romantic" assumptions regarding human nature.

In the theory of reification Marxist criticism remains focused on objective sociological structures. On the other hand, more recent sociopsychological discussion of the concept of alienation has to a large extent psychologized the Marxist concept of alienation and reduced it to a subjective feeling of estrangement (or meaninglessness, or anomie).[101] According to Israel, "alienation" has so many meanings and is so freighted with "metaphysical" presuppositions that he would prefer to jettison it altogether (258–68). This is a quite consistent position if one is unwilling to get involved in philosophical questions about the "nature" of the human being (267). For Israel is correct in stressing that "each theory of alienation is dependent on a certain theory or view of man and 'human nature' " (56).

[99]Thus Israel, 57ff., 246, 286ff.

[100]Ibid., 268. The page references that follow in the text are to this book.

[101]For the distinction between the psychological and the objective-sociological meaning of "alienation," see Israel, 5ff. The tendency to psychologize the concept is documented from E. Fromm (151ff.), M. Seemann (207ff.), E. Allardt (226ff.), and others. For L. Srole (according to Israel), "the theoretical difference between the subjective experience of anomie and the subjective experience of alienation is minimal" (234).

But if sociologists and social psychologists shy away from such assumptions and content themselves instead with a "sociological-normative" theory (266), they also limit themselves thereby to an abstract partial aspect of human reality and even of human social reality. In their concrete social reality human beings are concerned with their very humanness, and for this reason it is no accident that the negative findings investigated by sociologists should call for description by the concept of "alienation." Nor can this concept be simply replaced, as Israel suggests, by such seemingly more precise terms as powerlessness, normlessness, and meaninglessness (259). For the term "alienation" not only sums up these phenomena; it also expresses their *relation* to humanness.

The viewpoint of reification, however, cannot by itself justify us in speaking of alienation. The idea of alienation does not follow from the concept of reification with the same clarity as the alienated nature of private property followed (in the young Marx) from the concept of work as self-realization. Nor is the concept of reification specific enough to capture the special character of those modern social processes which have given rise in so many citizens of advanced industrial societies to a state of mind that must be characterized as one of "alienation." The reification of social institutions and processes is not something peculiar to modern industrial societies; according to Emile Durkheim, it is also found in "primitive" societies. Therefore, whatever one may think of reification, it is incapable of explaining the specific phenomena of modern societies which recent social psychology debates under the heading of "alienation." The explanation must be sought in peculiar features of modern societal development.

In their book *The Homeless Mind,* Peter and Brigitte Berger and H. Kellner studied these features and evolved the following thesis: The "homelessness" of human beings in modern industrial societies is due to the fact that the process of modernization, connected as it is with industrialization and bureaucratization, has undermined the public influence of all those agencies and authorities which have in the past established meaning.[102] The privatization of religion, in particular, has created a state of anomie which modern ideologies are incapable of overcoming because they cannot fulfill the social role of "theodicy" by giving meaning to suffering and to the existence of evil. "Because of the religious crisis in modern society, social 'homelessness' has become metaphysical, that is, it has become 'homelessness' in the cosmos. This is very difficult to bear."[103] If this explanation is valid, then the manifestation of alienation in the

---

[102]P. Berger et al., *The Homeless Mind: Modernization and Consciousness* (New York, 1973), 256ff., 184ff.

[103]Ibid., 185.

consciousness of the members of modern societies may be registered by social psychology but its basis is not economic but religious. It is a manifestation of a religious lack, an expression of religious undernourishment. But must not religion itself be regarded as an expression of human alienation, a product of an alienated consciousness?

2. Alienation and Religion

In modern criticism of religion the concept of alienation has played an important role since the time of Ludwig Feuerbach. Feuerbach himself regarded religion as the very epitome of alienation, since in the idea of God human beings separate themselves from their own being (the infinity of the human species and the powers resident in the species) as though it were foreign to them and then worship it. For Marx, on the other hand, religion was no longer the embodiment of alienation but only a reflection of the real—that is, economic—alienation of human beings: "We no longer take religion to the *basis* but only the *manifestation* of secular narrowness."[104] For "it is the *fantastic realization* of the human essence inasmuch as the *human essence* possesses no true reality."[105]

The influence of Feuerbach and Marx in the discussion of the relation between religion and alienation has lasted down to the present time, whether it has been exerted directly or through the medium of Nietzsche and Freud or through Durkheim's concept of reification, which for its part refers back to Feuerbach. As late as 1967, Peter Berger was still describing religion as alienated consciousness; in this context he understood alienation to be an objectivation and reification of the products of human consciousness.[106]

One can, of course, regard all the contents of consciousness as in some sense products of consciousness. This is true of our sense perceptions, our grasp of the structures of nature and society, our representations of past

[104]Marx, "On the Jewish Question" (= review of B. Bauer's *Die Judenfrage,* 1843), in Easton-Guddat, 222.

[105]"Toward the Critique of Hegel's Philosophy of Law," in Easton-Guddat, 250. In contrast to Feuerbach, Marx was here adopting Hegel's treatment of religion in the chapter of the *Phänomenologie* which deals with the alienated world of culture. For according to Hegel too, the alienated world of culture disintegrates into the "actual" (but finite and therefore untrue) "world" of the moral spirit and the "world" of faith understood as a truth to be found only beyond that first world (Baillie, *The Phenomenology of Mind,* 512ff.). But Hegel hastens to say that faith in this form—the form of a "flight from the actual world"—is not the true form of religion (513).

[106]P. Berger, *The Sacred Canopy: Elements of a Sociological Theory of Religion* (Garden City, N.Y., 1967; Anchor Books ed., 1969), 81–101, esp. 85–86. See my review of the German translation (1973) in *Evangelische Kommentare* 7 (1974), 151–54.

and future, our understanding of good and evil, and even our religious experience. But in the case of sense perception or our grasp of structures we do not immediately conclude from the productive character of our consciousness that the objects of consciousness lack a reality of their own that is independent of us. In these matters no one talks of reification. Why, then, should reification enter the picture in the case of religion and socio-cultural data? The distinction between the two realms cannot consist in the fact that we ourselves fashion or cooperate in fashioning these latter objects, since this can also be said of other objects of consciousness.

Of course, if we were to presuppose that only what is perceptible by the senses is real, we would understandably regard as reifications all assertions about the reality of sociocultural or religious phenomena. But the presupposition is not tenable. Our judgments can reach, or fail to reach, meaningful structures and forms just as they can the objects of sense perception. Patterns of meaning are not arbitrary creations of a consciousness that bestows meaning. On the contrary, consciousness and the self-consciousness of the individual are related to continuities of meaning that transcend them, and are constituted by these. However much the shape of these continuities can be transformed by the process of interpretation, it is true of this very interpretation that it in its turn can find the meaning that is given, and allow it to emerge, or can fail to do so.[107] In regard, therefore, to the structures of meaning that are constitutive for the individual self-consciousness, it is legitimate to say that the objectivity of consciousness does not mean an alienation or a reification of consciousness.

Reflection on and interpretation of religious experience and tradition must, of course, take into account the subjective perspective that is operative in each instance; this, however, holds for all experience (including sense perception). In this sense, there is always need of avoiding a false reification that would leave this subjective element out of account. But this is true of all our representations, and not in a special way of the realm of religion. Conversely, this does not make the objective intention of religious claims any more suspect than it does that, let us say, of historical claims. Religions may find it especially difficult to admit the subjective and historical conditionedness of their traditions, because they fear that if they do, the claim of these traditions to mediate divine revelation will be adversely affected. To that extent, religious tradition does betray a tendency to false reification. But there are also other areas of objective consciousness and its communication in which the focus on the object conceals the subjective component. On the other hand, religion in particular is

---

[107]This will become clearer in a later context, when I discuss the understanding of linguistic meaning.

familiar with the struggle, occasioned by its specific objective interest, against confusing human pictures of God with the divine reality itself.[108]

False reification, which uncritically ascribes to the object itself the element of subjectivity in our representations, may be described as "alienation" to the extent that our own contribution appears to us to be something foreign to us, that is, a component of the object. But this phenomenon is not automatically accompanied by a self-alienation in the sense that when we act in this way we are alienated from our selfness. The question of self-alienation enters the picture only to the extent that our subjective participation in the formation of our experience belongs to our human selfness. A failure to recognize this participation does detract from human self-knowledge, but it is an exaggeration to describe this state of affairs as one of self-alienation.

But there is a further element in religious reification. Religious reification, especially in its most advanced form, which is idolatry, confuses a human product with the divine reality and thereby causes human beings to be alienated from God and thus from their own destiny as well. Here, in fact, there is the question of self-alienation, but it is the result less of the general mechanism of reification than of a failure in the relationship to God, a failure that manifests itself, though not primarily, in the form of a reification of this relationship.

In the light of these considerations we must emphasize the point that the concept of alienation ought to be connected less with reification than with the question of whether in the course of their identity formation individuals have found or missed the structures of meaning that are constitutive of selfhood. In other words, the concept of alienation must be connected with that of identity.

Six years after his outline of a sociology of religion Peter Berger developed the concept of alienation further along the lines just indicated. In 1973 he wrote that the ego feels alienated in those aspects of its reality which have not been integrated into its projected identity.[109] Thus individuals can feel alienated in the anonymous world of work if they have focused their identity wholly in the area of private life. This particular case fits in with the traditional notion that human beings are alienated in the world of industrial work. But the converse is also possible: individuals can so identify with their professional role that they feel alienated in their families—or alienation from the family may become the occasion for locating their identity wholly in their professional roles. In any case, the

---

[108]Berger (1967) misrepresents this side of religion as well (93ff.). According to him, religion has power to "de-alienate" (96). Is that possible if the objectivity of religion as such is already a product of alienation?

[109]Berger et al., *The Homeless Mind*, 34ff.

experience of alienation is always relative to the form that personal identity has taken; it is relative to the individual's self-consciousness. There is no such thing as a kind of purely "objective" alienation, because in alienation there is always a question of the identity which individuals make their point of reference in their relation to themselves and, therefore, in their feelings.

For the same reason, however, alienation is not correlative to just any interpretation of the self, as though it were a shadow automatically accompanying it. At this point our description of the phenomenon must go a step beyond Berger's. Subjective identity formation in each case is not something arbitrary, since it ought to correspond to the true meaning of the individual's life, while it can also miss this meaning. The identity that individuals subjectively adopt may itself be an expression of their alienation from their true identity, from the authentic meaning of their lives, from their true selves. Only when this consideration is introduced does the description of the objective state of affairs include the dimension in which alienation and sin coincide. Not every feeling of alienation grasps the real alienation which is sin. The fact, however, that individuals feel alienated in their profession or in their family life can be an expression of a deeper alienation from their true selves. In that case, the feeling of malaise and lack of freedom manifests the real alienation, the separation of the ego from its true self, but it does not manifest the real origin and content of this alienation.

Conversely, the feeling that individuals may have of being at one with themselves and having gotten things straightened out may be delusory and only a symptom of a false security. If the real destiny of human beings refers them to God, then the alienation from God that results from their self-love is the source of their alienation from themselves. This fact may find expression in their inability to integrate the various relationships of life into their own projected identity. It may find expression in a malaise that forms a background accompaniment to the life they lead or in the effort to deaden or suppress the malaise.

The concern of the religions, in the light of their consciousness of meaning, is that human alienation should be overcome by the ground that gives meaning to and supports both reality and the individual's selfhood. This does not mean that religious consciousness itself may not be under the spell of alienation. It will in fact be alienated to the extent that its consciousness of meaning misses the reality of God. As a matter of fact, the religions accuse one another of failing to grasp the divine reality, and in this conflict there are even voices claiming that the very concept of God is already such a failure. In the modern age, moreover, people generally believe that there is no criterion that can give direction and make decision possible in this conflict among the religions. This view betrays the pluralism and indifferentism that mark the modern conception of religion.

In response to this view it is important to realize, first, that such a criterion does exist in principle, in the fact that talk about God or gods is meaningful, because free of internal contradiction, only to the extent that it describes the power that determines all experienced reality. In addition, and more important, this criterion is being applied everywhere in the actual life of the individual religions, where it explains the modifications that actually occur in religious consciousness. We must not expect, of course, that this criterion will be a kind of magic key that can be applied to the disagreements of the religions regarding the reality of God and will lead to easy and indisputed solutions. It does at least enable us to understand that the various claims made regarding God and the gods must be judged by whether and to what extent they illuminate our understanding of experienced reality.[110] If talk about God no longer contributes to our understanding of the experienced reality of the world and, not least, of the reality of the human being, but instead simply opposes another world —a world beyond or a world above—to the real world, then talk about God and even the religious consciousness itself are still in the grip of alienation. This observation retains the element of truth in the criticism made by Feuerbach, Marx, and their followers—and even earlier by Hegel (see above, n. 105)—that the religious consciousness is an alienated consciousness.

That criticism was directed at a form of religion which no longer sheds any light on the *present* world but claims only to speak for *another* world distinct from this. The contrasting of another world to the present one can have a valid meaning when it serves to challenge the self-sufficiency of this world and to offer an alternative in the light which the present world is forced to change. But when the other world of religion no longer represents a challenge to the present world and asks only to coexist with it, then religion truly bears witness to the *powerlessness* of its God in relation to the real world. Then it simply *reflects* the actual disunity, and therefore alienation, of the human being.

As Marx saw, such a religious outlook also expresses the discontent of human beings with the present world. This discontent and the insight that the present world does not contain its meaning in itself can be the first step toward an authentic religious elucidation of the present world. Marx did not take this step, because he thought that if certain changes were made in the present world, it would then have its meaning within itself. Authentic religion issues a more radical challenge to a world that has grown self-sufficient in its secularity, but the criticism of religion offered by Marx

110On this, see my *Theology and the Philosophy of Science,* trans. F. McDonagh (Philadelphia, 1976), 301ff.

and Freud did not penetrate through to this authentic form of religion. Hegel in his phenomenology of the spirit had seen that the criticism of religion touches only the decadent form of religion produced by the Enlightenment.

This kind of criticism, however, easily turns back upon the critics themselves when they in turn claim a religious dignity for authorities in the present world. This happened in Marxism, inasmuch as it assigned the human person, human work, and especially the revolutionary action of the proletariat the objectively religious function of giving meaning to the historical human world. Such a procedure does not come to grips with the real depth of human alienation. Faith in the conquest of alienation by the action of alienated human beings is a faith that is still under the spell of alienation.

3. The Depth of Alienation

Paul Tillich, more than any other modern theologian, adopted the concept of alienation as a means of interpreting the concept of sin. In so doing, he was restoring to theology a concept that had at least one of its roots in biblical and patristic usage. He was not aware of this; in fact, he thought that Hegel had originated the concept and that the expression was not a biblical one.[111] He thought, nonetheless, that the idea of alienation would be helpful to theologians in two ways as they face their present-day task with regard to the doctrine of sin.

First of all, according to Tillich, the concept of alienation makes it possible to safeguard the point of the church's doctrine of original sin in a situation in which the idea of an inherited sin can no longer be maintained. Christianity cannot be satisfied with a restriction of sin to individual actions. "It [Christianity] must simultaneously acknowledge the tragic universality of estrangement and man's personal responsibility for it" (39). We will have to ask whether in fact the concept of alienation as used by Tillich accomplishes this purpose. At least the concern to give expression to an element of tragic or fateful entanglement that goes beyond

---

[111]P. Tillich, *Systematic Theology* II (Chicago, 1957), 45. The page references that follow in the text are to this book. The suggestion that the idea of original (inherited) sin be replaced by that of estrangement or alienation has received little attention. It is not even discussed by K. Rahner and P. Schoonenberg in their treatment of Catholic teaching on sin, although these two theologians, like Tillich, look for something to replace the idea of "original sin" (see earlier, chapter 3, at nn. 123f.). Nor does G. Ebeling go into the concept of alienation in his *Dogmatik des christlichen Glaubens* I (1979). On the other hand, J. Macquarrie did accept Tillich's suggestion in his *The Principles of Christian Theology* (New York, 1966), 65ff., where he uses "alienation" to summarize the "disorder" of existence, primarily in the relation of human beings to themselves and to others (61f.). He finds that this alienation has its deepest roots in sin as a separation from God (237f.).

individual sins as responsible acts is usually acknowledged even by those who are critical of Tillich's implementation of the idea.[112] "Man as he exists is not what he essentially is and ought to be. He is estranged from his true being. The profundity of the term 'estrangement' lies in the implication that one belongs essentially to that from which one is estranged" (45).

In addition to the function of dealing with the problems connected with the doctrine of original sin in the theological tradition, the concept of alienation has another function, according to Tillich: it makes it possible to relate the theological doctrine of sin to human experience of life. "The empirical basis for such a description has become quite extensive in our period" (39). In fact, the basis has become significantly broader in the quarter century since Tillich wrote those words, and this in both of the areas mentioned by Tillich: the relation to the self and social relations. The task, therefore, is to explain the relation between these findings and the Christian doctrine of sin.

The fact that Tillich has elicited more criticism than agreement is due less to his concept of estrangement or alienation as such than to the way in which he relates it to the idea of creation. According to Tillich, creation is good "in its essential character. If actualized, it falls into universal estrangement through freedom and destiny" (44). "Actualized creation and estranged existence are identical" (ibid.). This seems to mean that "the creative activity of God in its pure form is limited to potentiality, while his actual operation is linked to estrangement." And in fact Tillich is here disturbingly close to the idealist "view that the fall was necessary for human self-realization."[113] Insufficient heed is paid to the fact that the preservation of the goodness of creation through resistance to sin and estrangement is itself God's doing.[114]

H. Grass sees the difficulties in which Tillich involves himself as connected with the fact that he "is unwilling fully to demythologize" the temporal element of "fall" in the passage from essence to existence.[115] But the idea of alienation should not be linked to such a construction. In fact, in Tillich himself the intrinsic structure of alienation is independent of the

---

[112]Thus in H. Grass, *Christliche Glaubenslehre* II (1974), 29, and in H. Berkhof, *Christian Faith: An Introduction to the Study of the Faith,* trans. S. Woudstra (Grand Rapids, 1979), 202ff.; see 199. Niebuhr's criticism of Tillich had already taken the same line; see C. W. Kegley and R. W. Bretall, eds., *The Theology of Paul Tillich* (New York, 1952), 258ff., esp. n. 52.

[113]Grass, 29. Tillich does expressly say that "the leap from essence to existence . . . has the character of a leap and not of structural necessity" (44), but this does not alter the fact that the leap into estranged existence is in reality a condition for self-realization.

[114]More justice is done to this aspect in the remarks on spirit and life in the third volume of Tillich's *Systematic Theology.*

[115]Grass, 30. For this notion and criticism of it, see above, chapter 3, at nn. 131ff.

idea of such a passage. Alienation is seen, rather, as a state. It is surprising that in this context Tillich hardly discusses alienation as a social phenomenon.[116] Nor is there any discussion of the Marxist concept of alienation. Instead, Tillich takes the terms "unbelief," "hubris," and "concupiscence" as the motifs of a presentation that is in continuity with the Lutheran reformulation of the Augustinian doctrine of sin and that links this with Freud and Nietzsche.

Does such a version of the concept of alienation make it possible to understand the "tragic universality" of sin in the human world? Only if unbelief, hubris, and concupiscence are presupposed as being universal traits of human behavior. But such an assumption does not require the concept of alienation, nor, conversely, can the concept of alienation justify such an assumption. "Alienation" simply describes a *state,* whatever its origin. In this we have the difference between the concept of alienation and the concept of sin as an act. At the same time, however, both the reason for the state of alienation and the scope of this state still remain undetermined.

The concept of alienation cannot therefore be regarded as the equivalent of the doctrine of original sin in its function of grounding the universality of sin. Alienation looks beyond the act and simply describes the state of separation of what had previously (or even essentially) belonged together. There is no doubt, of course, that the state of separation from the ground of personal identity belongs to the essence of sin. In addition, the use of the concept of alienation in social psychology and sociology opens up the possibility of connecting the brokenness of human life, both in its relation to itself and in its social situatedness, with sin as alienation from God. The concept of alienation allows us to thematize, as a single complex condition, the brokenness of human existence in the relation to the self, in the relation to other human beings, and in the relation to God.

It must be said, however, that Tillich did not fully exploit the potential of the concept of alienation, since he did not deal seriously with the social aspect.[117] He did indeed emphasize the point that alienation from God means at the same time self-alienation (II, 44f.), but this needs to be

[116]The section on "Estrangement Individually and Collectively" (II, 58ff.) contains in substance only a rejection of the idea of collective guilt, a rejection conditioned by contemporary history.

[117]See by contrast the development in P. C. Hodgson, *New Birth of Freedom: A Theology of Bondage and Liberation* (Philadelphia, 1976), on the theme of alienation, which he describes as being, above all, a consequence of the "fragility" of human existence (he is following Ricoeur here; 168ff., see 147) in the conflict between subjectivity and intersubjectivity (see 187ff., 281f., 212ff.). But on human "fallibility" (antecedent to the fact of sin) as Ricoeur's point of departure, see above, chapter 3, at n. 73. "Deception" as passage to actual sin presupposes "alienation from the commandment," as the passage which Hodgson cites (176) from Ricoeur himself makes clear.

supplemented by consideration of alienation from the world of nature and alienation from human society. Both of these emerge in the Yahwist story of paradise. Here, alienation from God entails a rupture between human beings and the natural world which God has created (Gen. 3:17ff.) and a rupture among human beings themselves (Gen. 3:12 and 16).

For this reason, the forms of communal life, on the development of which human beings remain dependent despite their profound alienation from them, will likewise display traces of alienation. Some will feel them to be an oppressive burden and a constricting fetter, while others will be skilled in turning them into a tool of alienated inclinations. But the latter group will at the same time be caught in the maelstrom of the "autonomous laws" of acquisitiveness, envy, domineeringness, and ambition—an autonomy which these modes of behavior acquire through their connection with the structures of the shared life-world. Others, and to some extent even the *very same* individuals, experience these autonomous laws of an alienated world as a system of exploitation and oppression.

In other contexts Tillich has legitimately described these phenomena with the help of the concept of the demonic. The reification of the structures of communal life does display the traits of the demonic insofar as such reification comes about through the interaction of alienated individuals. Alienation at the level of individual life has thus to be presupposed if the reified structures of the shared life-world are in turn to acquire the traits of alienation and the demonic.

Given the alienation of individuals, their shared world inevitably becomes an alienated world, whether or not they experience it as alien. As I pointed out earlier, the subjective experience of alienation depends on what it is that individuals do or do not identify with. Every act of identification is an act of love, even if possibly a perverted love, as is the case with concupiscence. But where love is at work, alienation disappears, although in the case of perverted love (*amor sui* and concupiscence) this is true only in the minds of these lovers themselves, since their behavior objectively disrupts the community and thus intensifies the objectively existing alienation. It is therefore possible for the shared life-world to be far more alienated than the individual realizes.

Indeed, the fact that the state of alienation remains hidden can even be evidence of a demonic seduction that is exercised by the alienated world, as in the case of the seduction of consumer goods in a life-world that is shaped by a capitalist economy, or in the case of the temptation to let oneself be submerged in the moods of the mass psyche. Conversely, the feeling that a social system is exercising an alienating pressure may also be a reflection of the personal alienation of individuals who will not acknowledge themselves bound by any consideration for society.

Feelings of alienation are usually only symptoms of a more deeply rooted, structural state of alienation in personal life. Social structures, on the other hand, are no less ambivalent than individual lives. For, given the alienation in the behavior of individuals, these structures too manifest the traits of objective alienation. This is why Marx's descriptions of the alienating power of private property and the autonomous movements of capital over the hearts of human beings are so vivid and true to life. The same judgment can be passed on other social institutions. Thus Reinhold Niebuhr, true to the Augustinian tradition, sees human sin expressed at the level of social structures especially in the collective egoism and arrogance which manifests itself in structures of political domination.[118] I shall come back to this later on when discussing social institutions.

The social dimension of alienation is present chiefly by association and implication in Tillich's description. Yet this dimension alone enables us to understand how alienation can seem to be a "universal destiny" which is there for individuals and in which their lives are caught. This dimension of alienation corresponds to the modern doctrinal concept of the "kingdom of sin," which I discussed earlier (see chapter 3, at nn. 116ff.). Admittedly, the idea of a "kingdom of sin" cannot adequately justify the Christian doctrine of the universality of sin, any more than the concept of alienation can, but it can nonetheless stand as a symptom of this universality.

III. Guilt and Consciousness of Guilt

The state of alienation makes itself known to human beings in feelings of malaise and discontent or of anxiety and general depression. Alienation does not substantially consist solely in such feelings (anymore than identity consists in feelings of joy and freedom), but it does make its presence known by means of them. Alienated individuals do not feel themselves elevated above their egos but thrown back upon them and reduced to them—and by that very fact removed from their true selves and pushed into questioning their identity. The feeling of being locked into one's own ego can be exacerbated to the point of despair. The imprisonment is probably felt most intensely in the consciousness of guilt, when the tribunal of my own conscience condemns me to exclusion from what at the same time I know to be the content of my own destiny and the condition of my authentic selfhood.

Seen in this light, the consciousness of guilt presents itself as a heightened expression of the alienation of the ego from its own self. On the other hand, the consciousness of guilt is distinguished from feelings of alienation by its determinacy. The distinction between the two does not

---

[118]R. Niebuhr, *The Nature and Destiny of Man* I (New York, 1941), 208ff. (ch. 8).

consist in the element of personal activity (in guilt consciousness) versus entanglement in an anonymous ensnarling net. Alienation too involves a personal turning away and therefore can itself become an object of guilt consciousness. But feelings of alienation are naturally indeterminate. The process of alienation may begin as a separation from a specified counterpart, but it tends to a generalized state of estrangement and apartness in which the ego falls back upon itself. This indeterminacy is essential to the feeling of self-alienation in particular. In the indeterminate feeling of personal nonidentity the identity that is lacking is not grasped clearly, and for this reason the nonidentity too remains vague.

The consciousness of guilt, on the other hand, is, at least in its normal form, related to a quite determinate objective situation, a determinate transgression of a norm. This implies that, to this degree at least, there is a clear knowledge not only of personal identity and the demands this identity makes on personal behavior but also of the person's own failure and the nonidentity this creates. The relation to personal identity and nonidentity as a whole is the special characteristic of the feeling of guilt that accompanies a concrete consciousness of guilt and that is rightly regarded as the normal form of guilt feeling in the psychically healthy individual.[119] This feeling of guilt relates the particular norm and its transgression to the whole of the individual's life as present in feeling, a whole that at this moment is given determinacy by the norm and its transgression, even though at other times this whole is present only in a more or less indeterminate way.

But there can also be an indeterminate feeling of guilt. This arises, to begin with, in relation to heteronomous authority, the representatives of which may catch me in some unwitting offense. The development of an indeterminate feeling of guilt, understood in this way, precedes the reduction of guilt feelings in the adolescent to a function accompanying the consciousness of a determinate guilt; that is how guilt feelings occur in the normal adult.[120] When an adult is seized by an indeterminate feeling of guilt during a simple encounter with a policeman,[121] this must be regarded as close to abnormal or at least as showing that the individual's personal autonomy has not yet fully matured. When, however, indetermi-

---

[119]Thus W. Lauer, *Schuld—das komplexe Phänomen* (1972), 45: "Where consciousness of sin is lacking, the feeling of guilt is not genuine." Following L. Kunz, *Das Schuldbewusstsein des männlichen Jugendlichen* (Lucerne, 1949), Lauer very carefully distinguishes between a consciousness of guilt that is directed to a sin as its object, and feelings of guilt that are indeterminate in their reference but as such are nonetheless always conscious (22ff.; see 29). He finds the needed distinctions to be lacking in Freud, among others (27f.).

[120]Lauer, 24.

[121]Lauer, 30 (see 38f.), following Kunz, says that here authority is exercising a secondary suggestive influence on consciousness.

nate guilt feelings occur more often in adults, influencing their mood or even permeating their entire feeling of life, and when these guilt feelings then find *secondary* expression in all sorts of specific accusations of faults, then we are dealing with neurotic manifestations.

Such neurotic guilt feelings may be, according to Freud, the consequence of an excessively strict superego which has driven the ego into the blind alley of self-aggression.[122] But they may also be a consequence of the decline of a sturdy value orientation in the general cultural consciousness, for then it is not possible to develop a normal consciousness of guilt that would be limited to determinate transgressions of norms, and there is left nothing but an indeterminate feeling of having transgressed against an equally indeterminate ought.[123]

Such a disposition to a neurotic, indeterminate feeling of guilt may have its source in the general cultural situation, but it can be intensified in the churches, where nonspecific calls for the confession of sins and for penance both in the liturgy and in the rest of Christian behavior tend to cultivate this kind of indeterminate and generalized feelings of guilt. But necessary criticism of such phenomena, which play a significant part in the present social and ecclesial situation,[124] must not be allowed to obscure the justification and necessity of a normal consciousness and feeling of guilt in relation to specific transgressions of norms. Admittedly, this function can be ensured and kept distinct from neurotic feelings of guilt only if there is also a renewal of the consciousness of universally binding norms. Such a renewal goes far beyond the subject I am discussing here, but it points up the close connection between guilt feeling, guilt consciousness, guilt and conscience. Where actual guilt is present in the form of a response to

[122]For a good statement, see, for example, S. Freud, *Civilization and Its Discontents,* trans. J. Strachey (New York, 1961), 81ff. On this same point, see B. Lauret, *Schulderfahrung und Gottesfrage bei Nietzsche und Freud* (1977), 298ff. On the various forms of neurotic guilt feelings according to psychoanalysis, see H. Harsch, *Das Schuldproblem in Theologie und Tiefenpsychologie* (1965), 75ff.

[123]There is historically an intermediate stage in which the violation of objective norms is reduced to an interior experience of guilt in the individual (see Lauret, 393). The next stage may be either a critical dissolution of the reality of all sin and guilt or the already mentioned volatilization of their content. The connection between these two aspects was already brought out in Franz Kafka's *The Trial* (1915) in the person of Joseph K. On this, see M. Buber, "Guilt and Guilt Feelings," in his *The Knowledge of Man,* trans. M. Friedman and R. G. Smith (New York, 1966). Buber's interpretation, however, is concerned less with the indeterminacy and ambivalence of the guilt feeling than with that of the accusation, which reflected the collapse of norms at that time. For Buber (and perhaps even for Kafka himself) this became at the same time the background for the challenge to admit "existential guilt" and thus pull aside the veil of secrecy.

[124]J. Scharfenberg, in particular, has leveled this criticism; see "Jenseits der Schuldprinzip?" in his *Religion zwischen Wahn und Wirklichkeit. Gesammelte Beiträge zur Korrelation von Psychoanalyse und Theologie* (1972), 189–208, esp. 196ff.

a particular violation of a norm or as "existential guilt" referring to the whole orientation of one's life, then guilt consciousness and guilt feeling are not only justified but are also a condition for dealing properly with guilt in relation to the break which guilt entails in the personal identity of the culprit.

Guilt always presupposes an authority before which the culprit becomes or is culpable. In the case of legal culpability, the authority is society or, rather, its current order of law which manifests itself in the administration of justice and either wins compliance or takes the side, against the guilty parties, of those whose rights have been violated. But even though they are proved to have done the deed, culprits can reject the accusation of guilt if they do not acknowledge the violated norm as binding on them. Legal guilt therefore takes into account the identity of the culprit as a person and does not concern itself solely with an objectively ascertainable situation. The same holds even more for moral guilt. On the other hand, when dealing with guilt we are dealing not only with a subjective feeling or consciousness but also with an objective factual state that affects the guilty parties, whatever may be the attitude they adopt toward it. A normal consciousness of guilt is only a particular way of encountering the objective fact, though it is one that is appropriate to the situation. The principle that the concept of guilt presupposes a transgression of a norm is also documented in the history of culture, where the perception of this relationship precedes the development of guilt consciousness or at least precedes the internalization of this consciousness.[125]

[125]The idea that culprits should in some way be made legally responsible for their actions is certainly not a late development. In this sense the origin of accusations of guilt and of legal responsibility for guilt goes back probably to the beginnings of human cultural development. In Israel the ancient tradition of Achan's theft shows the culprit being identified and brought to account (Josh. 7:16ff.), despite the idea that the entire community was charged with the deed (7:14) and also despite the fact that punishment fell not only on Achan himself but on his possessions and his entire family as well (7:24ff.). Similarly in 1 Sam. 14:37ff., despite the different outcome of the proceedings inasmuch as Jonathan is "ransomed" by the people. On this subject, see W. Preiser, "Vergeltung und Sühne im altisraelitischen Strafrecht" (1961), now in K. Koch, ed., *Um das Prinzip der Vergeltung in Religion und Recht des Alten Testaments* (1972), 231–77, esp. 254ff. The "guilt" in which the whole people is entangled is removed by the elimination of the culprit (275f.), who is therefore the primary guilty party.

Guilt consciousness can be regarded as a late product of cultural development only if attention is limited to the internalization of the accusation of guilt, so that even apart from the reactions of the community to the deed an identity problem is created for the culprit. E. R. Dodds, *The Greeks and the Irrational* (Berkeley, 1951), has tried to show this for Greek cultural history; see esp. ch. 2, "From Shame-Culture to Guilt-Culture" (28–63), where he discusses the change in moral views from Homer down into the fifth century. But even Dodds, who regards the belief in the contagious effects and hereditability of defilement (a belief that came to the fore in the archaic period after Homer) as an important stage in this

Paul Ricoeur has shown the abiding importance of this origin of the guilt idea for the structure of its material thematic. In his *The Symbolism of Evil*[126] he goes back to the idea of a stain or defilement as "a more archaic conception of fault" (7), which was subsequently "personalized" in the idea of sin, that is, was related to God as a counterpart who is a person (50ff., 69). According to Ricoeur, this also meant an internalization (85) that was completed by the idea of personal guilt (103f.). But the objectivity of the stain is retained in the idea of sin and continues to be presupposed by guilt as well.

Certain aspects of the continuity must be emphasized even more than they are in Ricoeur.[127] In principle, the Old Testament understanding of sin[128] is not as far removed as Ricoeur's presentation suggests from the ideas which he describes with the symbols of defilement and impurity. Despite all the variations of terminology, Old Testament representations of sin and guilt are very much based on the conviction that there is in the nature of things a continuity from act to consequence and especially from crime to disaster and death.[129] Sin as a violation of provisions of the divine law is by no means everywhere as intensely personalized as seems to be the case according to Ricoeur.

Ricoeur gives this impression because he takes as the starting point of his presentation the specialized and relatively late idea of the covenant relationship and of sin as violation of the covenant. Yet in the Hebrew term *ḥaṭṭā't,* which is the closest to the New Testament collective term *hamartia* and like the latter means a missing of a target or norm, the primary viewpoint is that of error. And in fact it was only for transgressions committed in error *(bišgagā)* and therefore unintentionally or through negligence that atonement was possible (Lev. 4:1ff.; Num. 15:22ff., 27ff.).[130] Anyone who, on the contrary, "does anything" against

---

development, sees in it not the *source* of the "archaic sense of guilt" but only the expression of its special character, which leads eventually to the "internalising" of conscience (36f.).

[126]P. Ricoeur, *The Symbolism of Evil,* trans. E. Buchanan (New York, 1967). The page references that follow in the text are to this book.

[127]Especially in regard to the relation between sin and defilement, ibid., 47ff.

[128]In reality there is a series of different concepts that are not summed up in the Old Testament in a collective concept "sin." See R. Knierim, *Die Hauptbegriffe für Sünde im Alten Testament* (1967).

[129]K. Koch, "Gibt es ein Vergeltungsdogma im Alten Testament?" (1965), reprinted in Koch (n. 125, above), 130–80. (There is an abridged translation of this article in J. L. Crenshaw, ed., *Theodicy in the Old Testament* [Philadelphia, 1983], 57–87.) In a later essay (1962), Koch points out (433f.) in particular that all the Hebrew words for "sin" and for upright activity can designate either the act or its consequences.

[130]R. Rendtorff, *Studien zur Geschichte des Opfers im Alten Israel* (1967), 20ff. Knierim (see n. 128, above) has shown that the use of the concept *ḥaṭṭā't* is not limited to faults that are unwitting or due to negligence; nonetheless, while the fault is indeed objective, this term best expresses the element of negligence, as compared with such related concepts as *peša'*

the Lord "with a high hand" (Num. 15:30) "reviles the Lord" and is condemned to death. Here if anywhere there is a directly willed break in the personal relationship with God,[131] an act comparable to the later Christian idea of the sin against the Holy Spirit (Mark 3:29; Luke 12:10).

The decisive and prevailing viewpoint is that a transgression of the norm somehow brings its consequences both for individuals and for the community that is affected by their actions. It is possible, however, in the case of actions done in ignorance or unintentionally (or negligently), to make these consequences less severe, since moral order[132] can be restored in the world in other ways than by a literal kind of retaliation; such other ways would be the payment of a fine or a cultic action. The idea that objective consequences of actions can be repaired, compensated for, and canceled out by cultic acts is one that is now alien to us. Yet the symbolic restoration of moral order in the world by such means is in special accord with the problem of guilt consciousness. I shall return to this point in the concluding part of the present chapter.

For the moment, the important point is that institutions whose purpose is cultic atonement confirm in their own way the impossibility of breaking the connection between events, according to which every action produces its corresponding consequences, both for the culprits themselves and for the communities to which they belong. The fact is that there are actions which promote the well-being not only of the agents but also of their

---

(143ff.) and ʿāwōn (237ff.). This is not rendered less true by the fact that ḥaṭṭāʾt and ʿāwōn are largely used interchangeably (229ff., 242; but see earlier, 182); this signifies only that the areas covered by the concepts overlap.

[131]An older view linked the idea of open "rebellion" with the word pešaʿ in particular. According to G. von Rad, *Old Testament Theology*, trans. D. M. G. Stalker (2 vols.; New York, 1962, 1965), I, 263, pešaʿ is "the gravest word for sin" in the Old Testament. L. Köhler, *Old Testament Theology*, trans. A. S. Todd (Philadelphia, 1957), had earlier expressed the same idea (169ff.). But Knierim (esp. 180ff.) has shown that even the generalized and political use of pešaʿ (meaning "rebellion, separation") can be understood in the light of the word's basic meaning: withdrawal of property. Above all, even here attention is focused primarily on the act, not on a disposition contrary to God; only in the preaching of the prophets does the latter emerge as the root of Israel's transgressions.

[132]H. Gese, *Lehre und Wirklichkeit in der alten Weisheit* (1958), 41ff., has convincingly shown that the act-consequence connection is not to be regarded as simply the expression of a "primitive" or, in a vague sense, "magical" view of life, but is, rather, linked to the "conception of the world as an ordered place" which arose in the ancient Near East as early as Sumer, while peoples like Israel, which entered only later "into the light of history," acquired this outlook only at a correspondingly later date (the Greeks reached it only in the post-Homeric period!). But instead of the excessively abstract idea of Yahweh's free disposition of this order (Gese, 48ff.) I prefer the profound interpretation of Koch (art. cit. in n. 129, above), according to which in Israel's eyes Yahweh's fidelity alone guarantees this order; Yahweh is therefore also able, in a way that spares the culprit's life, to compensate for the consequences of actions through corresponding legal prescriptions or to divert these consequences to cultic sacrifice and so effect forgiveness (154ff.).

families and their people, and there are other actions which do harm to the community and thus also react back upon the culprits. A society that sought to ignore these objective facts and to protect individuals from the consequences of their actions would have to pay for this attitude, sooner or later, with the breakdown of its communal life. This is another way in which the connection between action and consequence can prove its reality in the course of history and overtake those who would like to blind themselves to it.

The connection between act and consequence and therefore the liability of culprits for their actions precede the development of the idea of guilt and create the objective need for such a development. It is only this objective state of affairs that forbids our making no distinction between guilt consciousness generally and the various kinds of neurotic guilt feelings, and deciding that since the latter exist, all guilt consciousness is the manifestation of a disease from which human beings ought to be liberated through a more humane type of education and through instruction of the masses. For if in fact there is a necessary connection between actions and their consequences, so that in the interaction that makes up society the consequences either strike back at the agent or do harm to social life itself, then it shows a lack of realism to shut our eyes to it and to declare that we can do without the idea of guilt, at least in the sense of holding agents responsible for the consequences of their actions.

An assignment of guilt thus understood also precedes the development of guilt consciousness in the sense that over and above their mere liability for consequences culprits also experience an interior conflict. This is the second corrective or addition that Ricoeur's theses call for. Ricoeur lays heavy stress on the fact that consciousness of guilt brought about a "revolution" in the experience of evil (102). Whereas the feeling of guilt originally "issued from the punishment engendered by Vengeance," now, according to Ricoeur, the internalization of guilt consciousness means that "the diminution of the value of existence" which culprits experience calls by its nature for punishment in the sense of penance or, as the case might be, educative expiation (102). Punishment thus acquires a new function: that of restoring the identity of the culprit. As a result, conscience "now becomes the *measure* of evil in a completely solitary experience" (104).

This is correct, but such an experience on the part of conscience does not and cannot of itself become the measure of the punishment to be dealt out. We must continue to take as the point of departure and basis for the formation of guilt consciousness the fact that culprits have to answer for the consequences of their actions. Blame is *attributed* to them independently of whether or not they admit their guilt and acknowledge their actions as faulty. Consequently, guilt in the sense of an attribution of blame exists prior to and independently of the development of a subjective consciousness of guilt.

Ricoeur does not distinguish between these two viewpoints with the needed clarity. Above all, he makes the juridical differentiation of the kinds of subjective blame found in criminal acts directly responsible for the "beginnings" of conscience and its subjective consciousness of guilt (108ff.). He does acknowledge that "the tribunal goes before, psychology follows after" (112). But the conception here presupposed—that "in becoming rationalized, punishment, in turn, caused a like differentiation with regard to guilt" (ibid.)—remains unproved and quite implausible, if we compare the development in Israel which on this point was not so divergent (as Ricoeur claims on 111) but was, rather, in large measure analogous.

In Israel the distinction between deliberate and indeliberate acts is found ever since the oldest document in the history of Israelite law after the settlement in Palestine, namely, the Book of the Covenant (Ex. 21:13ff. and 28ff.); the distinction therefore goes back to the end of the second millennium.[133] But the subjective internalization of the consciousness of guilt as a break in the relation to God came only hundreds of years later as a result of the prophetic preaching. Should we not say that in Greek tragic poetry, which initiated the development leading to the formation of the individual conscience, analogous motives were at work which were not simply reducible to a rationalization of penal law?

The degree of blame that is attributed to culprits according to the deliberateness or nondeliberateness of their actions, and the development of subjective guilt consciousness into an independent theme, are two different things. The *assignment of blame* is for the sake of the community and its purification.[134] That is why the question of individual authorship is asked. *Guilt consciousness,* on the other hand, is based, as Ricoeur rightly says (102), not on the consciousness of being the author of an act, but on the readiness to answer for its consequences. The culprit accepts his guilt. This process begins in fact with his *confessing* his fault. He does not simply accept it willy-nilly but takes it upon himself and in this way becomes to and for himself the author of his act (102).

Among the traditions of ancient Israel the very old story of Achan's theft shows this process at work. When the taking of lots has revealed Achan to be the culprit, Joshua says to him, "My son, give glory to the Lord God of Israel, and render praise to him; and tell me now what you have done" (Josh. 7:19). Achan must have realized that his fate was

---

[133]See F. Horst, *Recht und Religion im Bereich des Alten Testaments* (1956), cited in Koch, *Um das Prinzip der Vergeltung* (n. 125, above), 190ff. The proofs offered by Horst are not invalidated by the unfortunate idea which he introduces of a "de-magification" of law. See also Preiser (1961), in Koch, 240ff. and 265ff., as well as Knierim, 249.

[134]Preiser, 276.

inevitable and that he could no longer save even his family; nonetheless he took his guilt upon him and accepted the consequences of his actions. This occurred in a world of utterly unshakable convictions regarding communal responsibility and the contagious effect of the connection between defilement and suffering. Nor did Achan's response in any way give rise to an autonomous conscience. In fact, the autonomous conscience never became a reality in ancient Israel. Instead, the internalization of guilt consciousness came about only centuries later because of the prophets, and it came then in the relationship with God.

Yet even here it is not possible to say that as compared with the objective nature of stain and sin, guilt "designates the *subjective* moment in fault" (Ricoeur, 101). Rather, it is true of blameworthy fault *('āwōn)* as it is of the other concepts for sin in the Old Testament that the expression covers both the act and its harmful consequences.[135] Precisely for this reason the various words for sin are interchangeable at least partially. On the other hand, we may take it as specific to the concept of guilt that it shows the entire person as modified in a special way by his or her action.[136] This was the objective point of departure for the development in Greek literature of the idea of conscience and therefore of guilt consciousness as well.

IV. Conscience, Self-Consciousness, Consciousness of Meaning

The feeling of guilt which accompanies the consciousness of a concrete fault is an unthematic knowledge of the person's own nonidentity. In feeling, the whole of existence *(Dasein)* is present; in the feeling of guilt of which I am conscious it is present as that from which guilt separates me. In this respect, the feeling of guilt differs profoundly from the feeling of shame, which is also one of the feelings about the self.[137] For the feeling of shame is always based on the "feeling of a positive value attaching to the self." The consciousness of one's own unworthiness "is completely lacking in shame."[138] In fact, the feeling of shame arises precisely from

---

[135]Knierim, 251ff.

[136]This is doubtless the element of truth in the conception criticized by Knierim, 239ff., namely, that *'āwōn* implies subjective involvement in the sense of the act being intentional. On the other hand, it is not legitimate to say that in the concept of guilt the subjective element suppresses the objective element (249). "In this context it is not yet possible to say that the criterion for what is and is not sin, as well as with the sense of the gravity of sin, is made dependent on human insight and conscience" (247).

[137]According to M. Scheler, "Über Scham und Schamgefühl," in his *Schriften aus dem Nachlass* I (1957²), 65–144, there is in all shame a "return to a self," a shift inward of activity previously directed outward.

[138]Ibid., 82 and 100. Herein is to be seen the beauty of modesty; in fact, modesty is "an immediate promise of beauty" (101). On the other hand, Scheler can describe shame as "a feeling protective of individuals and their individual value against the entire sphere of the general" (80).

the contrast between the feeling of the value of the self and the possibility of misunderstanding due to the impression of lesser quality that one conveys to others.

It is true, of course, that according to the biblical story of paradise the first human beings experienced shame as a consequence of sin. Because they wanted "to be like God," their eyes were "opened" to the disproportion between their actual appearance (beginning with their own corporeality) and the magnitude of their pretension. The feeling of self-value that was thereby achieved (a feeling that even in its distorted form is in keeping with the nobility of the human destiny) lay behind their shame. At the same time, guilty persons know from their feeling of shame that they are separated from that which by their destiny they ought to be. Precisely for this reason the feeling of shame is accompanied by a higher degree of explicit self-reference, and this in regard not only to the person's own self and true destiny but also in regard to the individuality of the ego, which is emphasized by the ascription of guilt (and therefore emphasized also in guilt consciousness).[139] This is why the consciousness of guilt could become the place where self-consciousness was born in the form of conscience, however true it may be that the feeling of shame was already a "germ from which conscience as such could emerge."[140]

This is not to say, of course, that self-consciousness arose only when the terminology was at hand by which it could be expressly apprehended as such. Proper names and words such as "I" and "self" were in use in the various languages long before that. A self-consciousness of some kind was always connected with these phenomena, and indeed is part of what it means to be a human being. But insofar as self-consciousness is an object for which the consciousness of it is essential, an express intellectual and linguistic apprehension of it is inseparable from the phenomenon itself. To that extent, self-consciousness becomes actually complete only when there is an explicit apprehension of the self, although this in turn is something whose history is still unfinished. The same can be said of conscience. Conflicts between individuals and social norms are to be found in the primates.[141] Internalized accusations of guilt existed among human beings long before the rise of conscience among the Greeks, and even today conscience develops in the adolescent without any explicit awareness of

---

[139]Shame lacks this reference to the individual which I am as distinct from other. I can therefore also be ashamed for others in virtue of a shared belonging-to. Shame is therefore "a feeling of shame for the *individual self generally* and not necessarily for *my* individual self" (Scheler, 81).

[140]Thus Scheler, 142.

[141]H. Preuschoft, "Angeborene Verhaltensmuster, Konflikt, Norm, Gewissen: Wie frei sind unsere Entschlüsse?" in J. Fuchs, ed., *Das Gewissen. Vorgegebene Norm verantwortlichen Handelns oder Produkt gesellschaftlicher Zwänge?* (Düsseldorf, 1979), 9–18, esp. 15f.

its peculiar nature. Yet conscience as a relation to the self becomes complete precisely through this kind of knowledge and, in the history of cultures, becomes at the same time the origin of explicit self-consciousness. In this context, then, the rise of a terminology for the phenomenon becomes significant in its own right.[142]

The Greek verb *synoida* means first of all a cognizance (a co-knowing). Thus in Sophocles' *Antigone* (442 B.C.) a watchman swears that he and his fellows "know of no one" who has buried the body of Polynices (l. 266). King Oedipus (before 425 B.C.) protests that he will apply to himself the sentence of outlawry which he has pronounced against the murderer of Laius, should this man be found in Oedipus' own house "with his knowledge" (l. 250). Finally, Electra (ca. 418 B.C.) bemoans to the light and the air her cognizance of her mother's affair with her father's murderer (l. 94).

The cognizance in these instances is thought of in quite general terms, yet there is a special reference to deeds or persons that shun the light of publicity.[143] So too when the idea arises that human beings have *within themselves* one who is also aware of their behavior, the idea of cognizance with regard to wrongdoing and guilt is to the fore. In the *Orestes* of Euripides (404 B.C.), when Menelaus asks Orestes what sickness has befallen him (395), the latter replies that the grief which is eating away at him is the result of insight *(synesis)*, because he is conscious *(synoida)* of having done a terrible deed (396).

The turn of phrase here is hardly one that was in common use and merely happens to have been preserved here for the first time; rather, the protagonist is referring to a state of mind which "Euripides was the first to discover; it presupposes a high degree of reflection on the self."[144] The

---

[142]Similar idea in M. Kähler, *Das Gewissen* I/1 (1878), 6ff., against R. Rothe. By contrast, H. G. Stoker, in his *Das Gewissen. Erscheinungsformen und Theorien* (1925), which was long regarded as standard, thought that there was no need of such a differentiation of concepts at various historical stages (12), and he accepted uncritically the views of W. H. S. Jones (cited 13f.), who could without distinction advance such different terms as shame, defilement, and conscience as evidence of the emotional nature of conscience. The result was that Stoker missed the specific problems in the relation between conscience and self-consciousness.

[143]See Kähler, 25 and 52.

[144]B. Snell, *Die Entdeckung des Geistes. Studien zur Entstehung des europäischen Denkens bei den Griechen* (1946; 1955³), 229. [There is an English translation of the 2d ed. of 1948, but I have not been able to find in it the material of the present footnote.—Tr.] There is also a reference in ibid. to the connection with the role of the Erinyes. O. Seel, "Zur Vorgeschichte des Gewissensbegriffes im altgriechischen Denken," in *Festschrift für F. Dornseiff* (1953), 291–319, agrees with Snell (see 295, 298f., 313ff.). But he also indicates a series of older passages, especially three in Aristophanes (299f.) from the years 429–411, which express reflective knowledge in a way that suggests at least an ironic imputation of blame. The earliest instance of *synoida*, which Snell also discusses, is in Sappho, Frag. 37, 11f., and therefore goes back to the period before 600; it seems, however, to express no more than

action of the Erinyes, who will not leave the criminal at peace, is here internalized and becomes an agency within the person's own soul. This means, on the one hand, that the break is transferred within the person;[145] on the other, the externality marking the mythic form is canceled in the process of humanization. Tragic self-knowledge,[146] the essence of which finds expression on the lips of Euripides' Orestes, thus corresponds to the philosophical sublimation of myth and of all purely external authority to the level of the universally human in the age when the Greek state was passing through a crisis.[147]

In this light it seems intelligible and proper that although the concept of conscience[148] had its origin in the experience of guilt, it should not have been limited to this sphere but should have acquired the general meaning of consciousness in the sense of an awareness of one's own behavior and being[149] and thus be able to become as well the preconscious conscience and thereby a normative authority for the way one lives one's life. This idea probably goes back to the Stoics of the middle period, who, in response to the attacks of skeptics on Stoic moral teaching, seem to have based ethical knowledge on the practical certitude of self-consciousness. Panaetius of Rhodes may have been the originator of this development and may have communicated this viewpoint to Roman thinkers during his stays in Rome between 144 and 129 B.C., especially through his influence on the group led by the younger Scipio.[150] It emerges in Cicero[151] and later on in Roman Stoicism in Seneca and especially Epictetus, who iden-

---

a declaration of knowledge (about a state? see Snell, 312f.). See what Orestes says in Aeschylus' *Oresteia* (485 B.C.) to Electra, who is hoping for an avenger: "I know [am conscious] that you grieved bitterly for Orestes" (*Choephorae* 217). Despite this prehistory of the usage in Euripides, it is probable that he was the first to give the word the clear sense of a "split in the ego" (Snell).

[145]Chr. Maurer, *TDNT* 7:900, 904, 906.

[146]See the philosophical assessment of tragedy in Ricoeur, *The Symbolism of Evil*, 211–31, esp. 218ff.

[147]See also Kähler, 74 and 199f.

[148]See the further references in Kähler, 24ff.; Maurer, *TDNT* 7:900ff.; and H. Reiner, in *HWP* 3 (1974), 575ff. Reiner gives Democritus, Frag. 297, as the earliest instance of the substantive *syneidēsis*. On this, see also Maurer, *TDNT* 7:902ff.; also Seel, art. cit. (n. 144, above).

[149]Kähler, 50f. and (on Latin usage) 72f. Kähler also points out, however, that the accusatory function of conscience predominates in the usage. Similarly Maurer, *TDNT* 7:904.

[150]P. Barth and A. Goedeckemeyer, *Die Stoa* (1941), 168. For a different view, see M. Pohlenz, *Die Stoa* I (1948), 317.

[151]Thus especially in Cicero's basing of *recta conscientia* (right conscience) "on *recta ratio* [right reason] which forms a *non scripta sed nata lex* [nonwritten, innate law]" (Reiner, *HWP* 3 (1974), 577, citing *Ep. ad Atticum* XIII, 20, 4; *Pro Milone* 10 and 61; *Resp.* III, 22). Kähler, 63, still maintains, with Jahnel (1862), that "the concept of conscience as a consciousness of a guiding law . . . is not to be found" in Cicero.

tified conscience with the Stoic *hēgemonikon,* or ruling intellectual principle.[152]

Although the trend of that age led to a focusing on the practical questions of life, the whole development represents nothing less than the first philosophy of self-consciousness, wherein self-consciousness is assigned the fundamental systematic function of mediating between the presence of the Logos in the soul and a human activity that takes its direction from the Logos. The break in human identity which the tragedians had discovered and which Euripides had formulated is indeed not healed in this Stoic conception but is simply denied. The movement from the nonidentity experienced in conscience to the identity of a good conscience would, however, find expression in Christian linguistic usage.

If the Old Testament has no concept of conscience,[153] this is probably because it knows nothing of that human independence from the gods of myth which found expression in the tension between the freedom of the tragic hero and the destiny determined by the gods. Hellenistic Judaism, on the other hand, was able to adopt the concept of conscience by turning the latter into a witness to the authority of the laws of God and by justifying this interpretation from the fact that even the non-Jew knows of the legislative will of the true God.[154]

The apostle Paul takes the same approach (Rom. 2:15). Conscience, as witness to the law written in the human heart, is the "representative of God's will in human beings."[155] For this reason, it finds expression in the consciousness of sinners as an indictment that convicts them of their sin,[156] while in Christians who have been set free of sin it expresses itself in testimony to the new identity that comes through the relationship with the Spirit of God (2 Cor. 1:12). And because the consciousness of the individual Christian is so related to the Spirit of God, Paul urges respect for the individual conscience even of the "weak" brother or sister. The acceptance as child of God, which the Spirit assures to each individual believer, "safeguards . . . his or her individuality over against that of the other brothers and sisters and thus grounds an absolute and inviolable freedom

[152]Epictetus, *Discourses* III, 93–95.

[153]Maurer, 907; see Kähler, 19 and 178.

[154]Maurer, 911f., on Philo. According to U. Wilckens, *Der Brief an die Römer* (Evang.-kath. Kommentar zum Neuen Testament VI/1; 1978), 139, the further functions of reprimanding and judging, which conscience has in Philo, have their roots not in the Old Testament but in Neo-Pythagoreanism. In Maurer's dealing with Philo, his limitation of conscience so as to exclude the idea of guidance of behavior seems to be excessive; he is influenced here by Kähler (34–37) (see above, n. 150).

[155]Wilckens, 138.

[156]Maurer, 916f. According to Maurer, in Rom. 2:15 Paul has in view "only the conscience which follows . . . , not the conscience which goes in advance and guides" (917).

of each individual conscience in relation to every other conscience."[157]

The relation that faith establishes between the Christian conscience and the Spirit of faith is reflected in the post-Pauline literature of early Christianity in the expression a "good" [KJV] (1 Tim. 1:5, 19; 1 Peter 3:16, 21) or "pure" [KJV] Christian conscience (1 Tim. 3:9; 2 Tim. 1:3), although the tension between the present and the future of the divine judgment no longer emerges so strongly as it had in Paul (1 Cor. 4:4).[158] The function of conscience continues to be one of judging; conscience does not legislate or give guidance,[159] for the energizing force in the living of a Christian life is not conscience but the Spirit of God. A "good" or "fine" conscience is, however, a testimony to and expression of the newly won identity of the Christian.[160] The fact that this identity, achieved through conquest of the nonidentity experienced in the conscience of the sinner, is that of the human being as such emerges in Paul's appeal to the conscience of all human beings in support of the truth of his message (2 Cor. 4:2).

This appeal presupposes the removal of the heteronomy characteristic of the Jewish law. But does not the linking of the Christian conscience with the message of Christ introduce a new heteronomy? Paul solved this problem with his interpretation of Christ as the new Adam: If the history of Christ is that of the human being as such, then the ties created by faith in Christ do not introduce any heteronomy into the Christian self-consciousness. To its own detriment, the later Christian theology of conscience did not pursue this line of thought but attached the concept of conscience to the doctrine of the law of God, which was interpreted along the lines of natural law teaching. Admittedly, this development took place in the framework of an identification of the Logos at work in the human soul with the Logos incarnated in Christ, so that any heteronomous treatment of Christians as children due to their faith in Christ seemed sufficiently excluded. But the autonomy of the experience of conscience as a manifestation of the identity of self-consciousness was not thematized in its own right, and the result was ultimately a narrowing and displacement of the theme of conscience.

The linking of conscience with the divine law in Hellenistic Judaism and in the writings of the Christian fathers encouraged the tendency, present in the moral philosophy of late antiquity, to neglect the more comprehensive meaning of *syneidēsis* and *conscientia* as self-consciousness and to limit the meaning of the concept to the moral sphere. The trend is especially

[157]Wilckens, 138. The relation of the Christian conscience to the Spirit also allows Paul in Romans (14:1f.) to speak of *pistis* in the same context in which he had spoken in 1 Corinthians (8:7, 10f.) of the "conscience" of the "weak" brother or sister. See Maurer, 914.
[158]Wilckens, 139.
[159]Kähler, 300; see 271.
[160]Maurer, 916.

clear in Cicero, who reinterprets the Stoic doctrine of the basic concepts common to all human beings *(koinai ennoiai)* and turns it into the idea of an innate knowledge of the fundamental norms of morality *(nata lex)*, which was then linked to the doctrine of natural law and especially to the golden rule. Augustine could characteristically describe the golden rule as *scripta conscientia* ("conscience in writing").[161]

This is not the place to trace in detail the subsequent history of the interpretation of the phenomenon of conscience. In view of the present state of discussion in anthropology, the important thing is not so much the Scholastic distinction between *synderesis* and *conscientia*, which was occasioned by a textually corrupt passage in the commentary of Jerome on Ezekiel,[162] nor the discussion of the question whether *synderesis* is to be understood as a special power of the soul (Bonaventure) or simply as a habit *(habitus)*.[163] Much more far-reaching in its importance is the fact that the moral phenomenon of conscience was made independent of the general problematic, including the theoretical, of self-consciousness.

The separation finds expression in the passage in Jerome, inasmuch as

[161]Augustine, *Conf.* I, 18, 29. See J. Stelzenberger, *Conscientia bei Augustin* (Paderborn, 1959), 109ff., esp. 111ff. On what follows, see idem, *Syneidesis, Conscientia, Gewissen* (1963), 81ff.

[162]PL 25:22 = Jerome, *In Ezech.* I, 1 (ed. Glorie [1964], 12). On the relation to Origen, see Reiner, 580f. For the reading given of the passage in the *Glossa Ordinaria* (with *synderesis* for *syneidēsis*), see ibid., 582, and the bibliography given there.

[163]The significance of this controversy for Luther and the modern discussion is overrated by R. Mokrosch, *Das religiöse Gewissen* (1979), 14–31, following E. Hirsch, *Lutherstudien*, vol. I: *Drei Kapitel zu Luthers Lehre vom Gewissen* (1954). Neither in the case of Bonaventure's "conscience of the will" (the "inconsistency" of which in matters of ecclesial instruction of conscience [Mokrosch, 20f.] should really be put to the interpreter's account) nor in Luther is it possible to speak of conscience as independent of norms and to describe conscience itself as "a criticism of all timeless and eternally valid norms" (102; see 28). B. Lohse, "Gewissen und Autorität bei Luther," *KuD* 20 (1974), 1–22, has shown that in Luther's view conscience is indeed free in relation to all human rules and doctrines, but is bound by God's word (in law and in gospel) (see 13f., 16ff.). The difference from the Scholastic doctrine of conscience is to be sought chiefly in the concept of gospel, which according to Luther liberates from the law even the conscience that lives in fear of the law (WA 25: 249, 37ff.), so that the liberated conscience is at one, in the Pauline sense, with faith in Christ (Lohse, 6f.). Luther too (Lohse, 2, 21) speaks of conscience's need of instruction from the church, a point which Mokrosch, with Hirsch, harshly criticizes in the Scholastic theology of conscience (17f., 19f., 21), but without noticing the Scholastic doctrine of the obligation incumbent on even an erroneous conscience (Thomas Aquinas, *De ver.* 17 ad 4). Luther continued to think in the medieval manner even to the extent of not taking into account possible diverse outcomes of such instruction (Lohse, 21); we may leave open the question whether the difference between the "old" and the "young" Luther in this matter is or is not something fundamental. In any case, the decisive difference between Luther and the medieval church was in the area of the norm: Scripture or the teaching of the church. See also Melanchthon's definition of conscience in CR 21:1083 (as well as 686f., and the corresponding statement of 1521, ibid., 116f.).

conscience is there regarded as an independent, fourth power of the soul, along with the Platonic trio of desire, feeling, and rational soul. Even the Scholastic view which was developed by Thomas Aquinas following Albert the Great and which links conscience more closely to the intellect, treats conscience *(synderesis)* as a knowledge of moral principles that is innate in the soul and is coextensive in its content with the principles of natural law. At bottom, this is the idea, originating in Cicero, of conscience as source of the consciousness of moral norms. Conscience stands independently juxtaposed to theoretical reason, although in Aquinas the two are parallel in structure. On the one hand, there is the distinction between a faculty that is independent of all experience and deals with basic theoretical concepts *(intellectus principiorum)* and *ratio,* which applies these basic concepts of theoretical knowledge to the perceptions of the senses. On the other hand, in the realm of practical, moral knowledge there is the distinction between *synderesis* as the sum total of moral principles and *conscientia* which applies these principles.[164]

The idea of an *intellectus principiorum* as developed in Aristotelian Scholasticism was subsequently abandoned in the history of epistemology. The idea of conscience as a consciousness of moral norms that is innate in human beings persisted, however, inert and changeless, through the centuries. Conscience became an isolated and therefore mysterious agency of the soul; its opaque appearance did not give a hint that it had originally been a partial aspect of self-consciousness.

Kant operated within the framework of this "alienation" of the theme of conscience from its original locus in the phenomenon of self-consciousness. Nonetheless, by his interpretation of the moral law as autonomy he recovered an awareness of the fact that conscience deals with the relation of rational beings to themselves.[165] In Hegel's philosophy of right, con-

---

[164]Aquinas describes *synderesis* in *Summa theologiae* I, q. 79, a. 12, in parallel with the *intellectus principiorum* of speculative reason; Article 13 then deals with *conscientia,* which applies the principles of *synderesis* to past or future *acts.* (Aquinas does not regard the *ad aliquid* or relational element in the word *conscientia* as referring to the subject itself.) *Summa theologiae* I-II, q. 94, a. 1 and 2, states the identity of the principles of *synderesis* with those of the natural law.

[165]What Kant calls the "wonderful faculty" of conscience (*The Critique of Practical Reason,* trans. T. K. Abbott, in *Kant* [Great Books of the Western World 42; Chicago, 1952], 333) is described in his science of religion as a relation to itself: "Conscience does not pass judgment upon actions as cases which fall under the law; for this is what reason does so far as it is subjectively practical. . . . Rather, reason here judges itself, as to whether it has really undertaken that appraisal of actions (as to whether they are right or wrong) with all diligence, and it calls the man himself to witness *for* or *against* himself whether this diligent appraisal did or did not take place" (*Religion Within the Limits of Reason Alone,* trans. T. M. Greene and H. H. Hudson [Chicago, 1934], 174). In the *Metaphysics of Morals,* on the other

science is then explicitly conceived once again as a facet of self-consciousness.[166] The viewpoint of relation to the self continued to be decisive in the ensuing period. Purified of any doubts that conscience may perhaps after all be the voice of God in human beings,[167] the relation to the self is central especially in Heidegger's analysis of the phenomenon of conscience in *Being and Time;* this analysis, along with those of Nietzsche and Freud, has become the most influential one in our day.

Heidegger defines conscience as the call that the Dasein issues to itself. It calls itself—in the mode of keeping silent—from fallenness into the "they" to "its ownmost potentiality-for-Being."[168] The element of accusation of fault, which M. Kähler and H. G. Stoker had determined to be both historically and objectively fundamental to the experience of conscience, is here subordinated to the call aspect of conscience. Heidegger manages this shift by dissociating the idea of guilt from any "Being with Others" and even from "relationship to any law or 'ought.' "[169] All that is then left

---

hand, Kant regards it as necessary to relate the voice of conscience to the idea of a divine judgment, since otherwise one and the same person would be both the accused and the judge (Akad. Ausg. 6, 498f.).

[166]As "formal subjectivity" independent of all content (*Hegel's Philosophy of Right,* trans. T. M. Knox [Oxford, 1942], § 139; see § 137), conscience according to Hegel is a source of both good and evil, since "in independent self-certainty, with its independence of knowledge and decision, both morality and evil have their common root" (§ 139). Whether what the individual conscience "takes or declares to be good is actually so, is ascertainable only from the content of the good it seeks to realize" (§ 137).

[167]H. G. Stoker, a disciple of Scheler, still saw in conscience's experience of guilt a reference to a personal power or order, because only to such could a human being be answerable; see his *Das Gewissen* (n. 142, above), 147f.; see 158ff. Heidegger regarded this view as "blurring the boundaries between phenomenology and theology, with damage to both" (*Being and Time,* 495, n. VI; German 272, n. VI). This is true, however, only if one supposes as extrinsicist a relation as Heidegger does between divine revelation and created reality. Working in the tradition of a philosophy that culminates in a "natural theology," H. Kuhn, *Die Begegnung mit dem Sein. Meditationen zur Metaphysik des Gewissens* (1954), once again asserts against Heidegger the openness of conscience to God (45, 53ff., 19, 172ff.).

Most contemporary theologians, too, no longer regard conscience as the direct voice of God. See H. Thielicke, *Theologische Ethik* I (1951), 492 (only in the justified person is conscience the voice of God, 523); P. Trillhaas, *Ethik* (1959), 93 (expanded in 1970³, 108ff.); G. Ebeling, "Theological Reflections on Conscience," in his *Word and Faith,* trans. J. W. Leitch (Philadelphia, 1963), 418. In Catholic theology, conscience as a disposition innate in human nature is not looked upon as already the voice of God in the human person; it becomes this by being brought into accord with the law of God; see J. G. Ziegler, *Vom Gesetz zum Gewissen* (1968), 40; R. Barenz, *Das Gewissen* (1978), 235. J. Stelzenberger, in *Handbuch theologischer Grundbegriffe* I (Munich, 1962), 528, insists, however, that conscience cannot simply be called the voice of God.

[168]Heidegger, *Being and Time,* 320 and 318 (German 275 and 273).

[169]Ibid., 328 (German 283). As an argument for this view, Heidegger uses here, as he does earlier in rejecting the interpretation of conscience as a call of God (320; German 275),

is the "Being-guilty" which the call of conscience itself gives Dasein to understand, namely, that Dasein must "bring itself back to itself from its lostness in the 'they.' "[170] Being-guilty is therefore not primarily a consciousness of a moral fault but rather the expression of an "ought," the content of which, however, is the authenticity of the Dasein itself. According to Heidegger, it is only in this light that guilt as involving a transgression becomes intelligible.

The difference between the Heideggerian concept of guilt and the ordinary use of the word "guilt" is obvious, although the former has given rise to many misunderstandings.[171] On the one hand, Heidegger recovered for the concept of guilt a dimension that has been preserved in colloquial speech in such phrases as "to owe *(schuldig sein)* someone (or oneself) something." In other words, guilt involves not only an accusation of blame relative to a transgression *(reatus)* but, even before this, an obligation *(debitum)*. And transgression as blameworthy is understandable only in the light of obligation. For responsibility is grounded in the consciousness of obligation and not in the mere fact of having been a cause. In fact, as Paul Ricoeur has rightly emphasized, it is the acceptance of responsibility that is the basis of the consciousness "of being cause, agent, author."[172] This means, however, that the concept of action—in the sense of authorship—presupposes the concept of responsibility. And the capacity for action is, along with responsibility, grounded in the call to authentic selfhood. This is the new dimension of the concept of guilt that Heidegger's analysis has brought to light.

Heidegger has, however, paid for this achievement with an obscuring of the real phenomenon of consciousness,[173] which has for its starting

---

the difference between conscience and all that is present-at-hand (329; German 283). But it seems somewhat forced in this case, since Heidegger describes the lack contained in guilt (as a failure to achieve an ought) as a (negative) "definite sort of Being which goes with the present-at-hand" (ibid.). This is questionable not only in view of the function of "lack" in Sartre where it precisely points beyond what is present-at-hand (see earlier, chapter 5, at n. 60) but especially in view of the fact that Heidegger himself defines Being-guilty as an ought (333; German 287), even if it is an ought that has for its sole content the authenticity of the Dasein itself. Evidently, then, the ought which is excluded on 328 (German 283) is only an ought that is *distinct* from the Dasein itself.

[170]Ibid., 332f. (German 286f.). Therefore even according to Heidegger the call of conscience articulates an ought.

[171]See the positions and statements presented by Lauer, *Schuld—das komplexe Phänomen,* 127–213. Lauer himself objects, above all, to Heidegger's demand that guilt be detached "from relationship to any law or 'ought' " (143). But he fails to see that this is a criticism that is to be raised on internal grounds of Heidegger's own usage.

[172]Ricoeur, *The Symbolism of Evil,* 102.

[173]According to Kuhn (n. 167, above), 90ff., Heidegger opposes to the traditional view of conscience another "revolutionary, modern view" which is utterly "irreconcilable" with the first and in which "familiar words" take on a different meaning. Heidegger himself

point the consciousness of guilt in the sense of having already violated an obligation and done a wrong that cannot be undone. Heidegger's analysis fails to penetrate the depth of the nonidentity that makes itself known in the consciousness of guilt, for this nonidentity does not consist simply in the inauthenticity of being lost in the "they," but, as can be seen in Orestes' pangs of conscience, points to a rupture of communal order[174] by a rending of the ties uniting individuals to their fellow human beings. This implies that the authentic self of the Dasein, which makes its appearance in conscience as accuser, speaks not simply as the isolated self of the Dasein but as a member of the human order to which it belongs. Moreover, not only has Heidegger not seen, first, the depth of the nonidentity that is experienced in the consciousness of guilt and, second, the constitutive meaning of human order for selfhood. He has also failed to see, third, that the nonidentity experienced in conscience is overcome through expiation which is to be accomplished in the life of the injured community.

Criticism of Heidegger's analysis of conscience has justly focused, above all, on the abstraction, which he calls for and accomplishes, from the human community and its ethos.[175] We must, however, view this theme in the context of the other two—the nonidentity specific to guilt and the overcoming of this nonidentity—if we are to see that the criticism is not simply one imported into Heidegger's analysis from outside. In the psychoanalytic theory of conscience, on the other hand, the human community is recognized as having, in itself, a central importance. This theory therefore presents itself precisely as supplying the lack in Heidegger's theory of conscience. It is another question whether the psychoanalytic theory in turn does full justice to the complex phenomenon of conscience.

Freud identified conscience with the superego, an agency which he himself introduced and which represents an internalization of parental authority (and, more broadly, the authority of society) over the individual. This agency shapes the child from its fifth year on, after the Oedipus complex has been mastered. The superego "observes the ego, gives it orders, corrects it and threatens it with punishments, exactly like the

---

acknowledges, says Kuhn, that "the everyday experience of conscience may not be simply set aside" (90); yet in fact he largely fails to do justice to it, especially when he abstracts from any "relation to failures and omissions which have already befallen or which we still have before us" (citing *Being and Time,* 324; German 279). "To remove from conscience the determinacy of its judgments and attribute it to the 'popular concept' of conscience is to play conscience down by penetrating it more deeply" (180f.).

[174]Kuhn, 145ff., 166ff., 171, rightly emphasizes the importance, for the experience of conscience, of the order of common life that is injured in injuring a fellow human being.

[175]On this, see, in addition to Lauer (n. 171, above), L. Binswanger, *Grundformen und Erkenntnis menschlichen Daseins* (1953²), 65ff., and H. Harsch, *Das Schuldproblem in Theologie und Tiefenpsychologie* (1965), 145, 146ff., 152ff.

parents whose place it has taken."[176] According to Freud, the superego plays an important role not only in the development of the individual but also in the history of human culture, where its function is to curb the human inclination to aggression. Aggressive energy is turned inward, and

> there it is taken over by a portion of the ego, which sets itself over against the rest of the ego as a super-ego, and which now, in the form of "conscience," is ready to put into action against the ego the same harsh aggressiveness that the ego would have liked to satisfy upon other, extraneous individuals. The tension between the harsh super-ego and the ego that is subjected to it, is called by us the sense of guilt; it expresses itself as a need for punishment.[177]

In Freud's view the formation of this guilt consciousness is the price we pay for the evolution of culture, which has for its task "the creation of a unified group out of many individuals." For if this goal is to be achieved, restrictions must be placed on the claims of individuals to happiness; the effect is to unleash aggressivities which are then turned inward upon the individual ego in the form of feelings of guilt.[178] Confronted with the resultant neuroses, Freud the doctor has this complaint:

> In the severity of its commands and prohibitions it [the superego] troubles itself too little about the happiness of the ego, in that it takes insufficient account of the resistances against obeying them—of the instinctual strength of the id [in the first place], and of the difficulties presented by the real external environment [in the second].

The result is, on the one hand, neuroses and, on the other, the inefficacy of ethical norms.[179]

This reduction of the function of conscience to the authority of society and its approved norms, and the connected historical relativization of the

---

[176]S. Freud, *An Outline of Psychoanalysis,* trans. J. Strachey (New York, 1949), 121. See P. Ricoeur, *Freud and Philosophy: An Essay on Interpretation,* trans. D. Savage (New Haven, 1970), 211–30; also 204. In addition, see E. Spengler, *Das Gewissen bei Freud und Jung* (1964), and E. Stadter, *Psychoanalyse und Gewissen* (1970).

[177]S. Freud, *Civilization and Its Discontents* (n. 122, above), 70.

[178]Ibid., 86ff., 85. The striking analogy with Nietzsche's critique of morality and especially with his description of conscience in *On the Genealogy of Morals,* Essay II, no. 16, has often been remarked, but Freud's relation to Nietzsche has still not been fully clarified. H. Spencer's description of the function of conscience in his *Principles of Ethics* (2 vols.; 1879–93) had already taken a similar approach.

[179]Ibid., 90. Freud's criticism was directed especially toward the Christian commandment of love, "the strongest defence against human aggressiveness and an excellent example of the unpsychological proceedings of the cultural super-ego. The commandment is impossible to fulfil; such an enormous inflation of love can only lower its value, not get rid of the difficulty" (ibid.). This criticism of Christian morality is very worth taking to heart; it should cause us to think of love once again more as a grace, as a participation in the life of God himself in its movement toward the world.

contents of conscience, undermined the traditional conviction that the voice of conscience possesses an unqualified authority. Yet precisely on this point Freud's theory of conscience as superego has met with mounting criticism. Jean Piaget, in his studies of the moral judgment of the child,[180] found that in about the tenth or eleventh year of children's lives the heteronomous morality based on a one-sided respect for the authority of adults is replaced by forms of collaboration in which these children develop a consciousness of rules based on mutual consent. This development leads ultimately to moral autonomy. Though Piaget did not expressly come out against Freud, his results make it necessary to revise the Freudian theory of the superego.

H. Häfner therefore limits the activity of a heteronomous morality, which when internalized takes the form of the superego according to Freud, to a transitional phase of childhood, before the development of a conscience in the proper sense of the term.[181] D. Eicke reaches comparable conclusions in his study of the relation between conscience and superego.[182] According to Eicke, the superego is simply a provisional representative of conscience, while the childish ego is still weak and not yet capable of dealing autonomously with its world, or else a surrogate of conscience in the neurotic who has regressed to infantile forms of behavior. Eicke classifies conscience itself, which in the adult regulates suitable ego behavior in relations of mutual recognition, as an ego function. In contrast to Freud, conscience is here again not a heteronomous agency. Finally, Erich Fromm's distinction between a humanistic conscience and an authoritarian conscience points in the same direction.[183]

C. E. Benda is therefore able to claim (1970) that Freud's theory of the formation of conscience is "of purely historical interest" today. Conscience, he says, is not a heteronomous agency, but represents "the moral principles which individuals have made their own and which determine their actions." The development of conscience derives "from the experience of mutual dependence and reciprocity," whereas the neurotic is no longer capable of this reciprocity.[184]

[180]J. Piaget et al., *The Moral Judgment of the Child,* trans. M. Gabain (London, 1957; New York, 1965), 65ff.; see 70, 199ff.

[181]H. Häfner, *Schulderleben und Gewissen* (1950). For a comparison with Freud, see also Harsch (n. 175, above), 154f.

[182]D. Eicke, "Das Gewissen und das Über-Ich," *Wege zum Menschen* 16 (1964), 109–26 = N. Petrilowitsch, ed., *Das Gewissen als Problem* (1966), 65–91.

[183]E. Fromm, *Man for Himself* (New York, 1947), 141ff.; idem, *Psychoanalysis and Religion* (New Haven, 1950), 88ff.

[184]C. E. Benda, *Gewissen und Schuld* (1970), 52, 117f., 269, 73. In Catholic moral theology the passage, in the course of an individual's life, from a formation of conscience that is determined from outside to a formation for which the individual is responsible was already taken into account in Ziegler (n. 167, above), 45f.

All this criticism of Freud, however, leaves untouched the basic thesis that conscience has a social matrix and that it develops in the context of social relations. This is a truth that ought to receive more attention than it usually does in the theological interpretation of conscience. But neither is it enough to exchange the primary socialization that takes place in the family and the larger social world for the ecclesial community as a new social framework for the formation of conscience. Suggestions such as these can only amount to a new imposition of heteronomy.[185] The ecclesial community can exercise a liberating function in the formation of conscience only by way of its specific relevance to the social world to which individuals belong.

The authority with which the social context confronts the self-consciousness of the individual is not necessarily heteronomous, since the self for its part is socially constituted. On the other hand, individuals are not simply functions of the social world; they are independent beings. They preserve their independence within the social world only if their integration into their vital context is accomplished not through the threat of sanctions for violations of externally imposed norms but through participation in the cultural consciousness of meaning, out of which flow rules of behavior that individuals understand and accept. In this sense, conscience in fact needs a formation that not only protects it against mistaken judgments regarding particular situations but that also has to do, above all, with its overall orientation regarding the meaningful foundations of the shared world, thus enabling it to set norms for its own behavior.

This kind of formation of conscience need not mean an authoritarian exercise of guardianship.[186] That is what it becomes when it is no longer an admission of individuals into the shared world as a context of meaning which they understand and make their own, but takes the form rather of

----

[185]P. Lehmann, *Ethics in a Christian Context* (New York, 1963), 285–367, has the merit of looking upon the proof of the social conditioning of conscience as a positive contribution to a Christian ethics. But he has not avoided the danger of introducing the theonomous *koinōnia* of the church as a new "environment of decision" (346f.), as though this could without further ado replace the existing social life-world.

[186]Because Mokrosch (n. 163, above) limits the relevance of the proof of social dependence to the conscience that is unfree and tied to norms (105), he does not do justice to the need of conscience for instruction or formation, and he therefore reaches exaggerated conclusions about the supposed ecclesiastical "tutelage" (102) of conscience in the Middle Ages, the "church's position of power in matters of conscience" (20), and its "monopoly of control over the consciences of the faithful" (18), this control being described as virtually a "right to treat the faithful as children" (25). In the process he ignores both the connection of the synderesis with natural law and the explicit teaching that the individual is bound by even an erroneous conscience (see above, nn. 163f.). For the present-day treatment of the formation of conscience in Catholic moral theology, see, e.g., Ziegler (n. 167, above), 46ff., 138ff.

a simple announcement of norms and sanctions. The judgment of conscience does indeed always have the function of ascertaining any violation of norms that has occurred or (in the case of the "warning" conscience) threatens to occur.[187] But for the conscience that judges autonomously, these norms are based in the context of a social world whose meaning is understood and affirmed. In this case, self-consciousness is in possession of the freedom that distinguishes the autonomous from the heteronomous conscience.[188]

It is in this context that the relation of conscience to God must also be assessed. Although this relation may make itself directly known—as the voice of God—in the consciousness of the individual, it is nonetheless not given in an unmediated way as an inherently certain and private relation of the individual to God. It is mediated through the social life-world, and it manifests itself only to the extent that the human understanding affirms God to be the ultimate ground and fulfiller of the shared world and of the rules governing human life in society. From this point of view, Gerhard Ebeling is right in insisting that in conscience God, human beings, and world belong together.[189]

[187]M. Kähler, in particular, urged that conscience be understood in the light of this function: "One should . . . never forget that according to the historical evidence conscience has shown its originality solely in its judgmental role" (*Realencyklopädie für protestantische Theologie und Kirche* 6 [1899³], 563). See also his book on conscience (1878), 300f. Conscience is not a legislative faculty, Kähler says—but this is an assertion that must be greeted with reserve when we think of the Stoics (see above, at nn. 150ff.). Stoker too (204ff.) insists that not only the "bad" conscience but the "warning" conscience as well is to be understood as a judgmental function following upon an action. The "warning" conscience, too, "always tells us what we ought not to do, never what we ought to do" (206). See also the remarks of Wilckens (n. 154, above), 138, on the difference in Paul between the testimony of the Spirit and the testimony of conscience: Conscience always judges works alone, while the positive impulse to a new life comes from the Spirit and from the freedom from the law which the Spirit makes available to us. For the sake of freedom it is important to limit conscience to its judgmental function and not to assign it a legislative function as well. This is probably the intention behind Mokrosch's plea for a transmoral and nonnormative conscience (101, 103). Whether this expression from Tillich does justice to Luther's conception, as Mokrosch believes, seems doubtful. But Mokrosch is one of the few authors who have noted in Luther the passage, within conscience itself, from an unfree to a liberated conscience (49ff.), a passage that corresponds to the situation observable in Paul.

[188]B. Lauret, *Schulderfahrung und Gottesfrage bei Nietzsche und Freud* (1977), points out that the passage from the nonidentity of guilt to identity "is mediated through the experience of meaning (between meaninglessness and totality of meaning)" (16). He is able to show this particularly in Nietzsche, for whom "affective wholeness, innocence, and completed fullness of meaning" coincide (383; see 109f., 111ff., 127). But Lauret (following Ricoeur) also understands psychoanalysis as a "linguistic process" between meaning and power; it leads from the dynamism of instinctual life to the identity, mediated through meaning, of the ego (373; see 375ff. on Freud's criticism of religion as an illusionary way of bestowing meaning).

[189]Ebeling, "Theological Reflections on Conscience" (n. 167, above), 407ff., esp. 410.

The situation will become clearer if we take into account the fact that conscience belongs to the realm of the feelings.[190] Every feeling, as we saw in the first part of this chapter, is related to the whole of the individual's life. This relation, however, is not thematic in every feeling but only in the group of feelings that refer to the self. Among the latter, conscience has a special place because in it not only is the whole of life vaguely present in the form of a positive or a depressed mood, but at the same time the individual's own ego becomes an object of consciousness as subject of deeds or omissions in regard to which the judgment of conscience declares it to be blameworthy. In this negative judgment there is at the same time a positive reference to the identity that is forfeited by the action and to the social order that is injured by it.

By its negative content, conscience thus forms a bridge from the feeling of the self to self-consciousness in the narrower sense of an explicit apprehension and knowledge of the self. But at the same time, as a feeling it precedes the always incomplete retrieval by rational reflection of the meaningful interrelationships that ground the judgment of conscience. The reason is that, for feeling, the whole is not incomplete but is present as a whole. It is this which gives feeling its immediacy and grounds the certainty that is peculiar to feeling.[191] Yet conscience is not to be opposed to reason (and theoretical self-consciousness),[192] since if such an opposition is erected, the connectedness of the world, which as a context of meaning grounds the structure of conscience, is disrupted or at least rendered opaque, and conscience succumbs either to an irrational subjectivism or to heteronomy.

This brings us back once more to the question of the relation between human being and world in conscience. Under the influence of Heidegger, Ebeling has described this relationship as constituted from the human point of view: "It is only in relation to man as conscience that the world comes into view as world, i.e. not as something that is merely there, but as a thing to be answered for."[193] But is this opposition between what is there and what is to be answered for an adequate one? It eliminates the

---

[190]On the primarily but not exclusively emotional character of conscience, see Stoker, 75ff., 167ff. In conscience the knowledge of guilt deepens to become an experience and is related to "our whole being" (163).

[191]There is more on the relation between conscience and certainty in my essay "Wahrheit, Gewissheit und Glaube," in my *Grundfragen systematischer Theologie* II (1980), 248ff., esp. 261ff.

[192]Thus Ebeling, "Theologie und Philosophie," *RGG*³ VI (1962), 822f. Similarly in his contrast between Luther and Descartes on the foundation of certainty, in his *Wort und Glaube* II (1969), 163. Such an opposition between reason and conscience seems improper even in the light of the original meaning of the word "conscience," namely, self-consciousness (see my essay "Wahrheit," 259f.).

[193]Ebeling, "Theological Reflections on Conscience" (n. 167, above), 418.

entire dimension in which the relationship of a child to the world takes shape and in which the child grows to responsibility for itself, the dimension in which human social life finds supportive security and which also makes possible a responsible life on the part of adults. The world is given first and foremost in the form of a social life-world, in which "the givenness of life and the giving of life are bound together in a fundamental way." This reciprocity constitutes the human being as a conscience. Conscience is the "place" in which this unity manifests itself.[194]

Because Ebeling does not thematize the world, in its relation to conscience, as a *social* world, the "word," which is asserted to be the "mode of encounter" between human beings and God, remains related to these human beings in an excessively extrinsic and supernaturally authoritative way, instead of being mediated through an understanding and appropriation of the world as a unified context of meaning.[195] As a result, and contrary to Ebeling's intention, the call of conscience that is linked with this concept of the "word" still has at this point an authoritarian cast that diminishes only in a later study of Ebeling on the concept of the word.[196]

It is true, of course, that when the relation to the social life-world alone determines conscience, heteronomy likewise threatens. Only through the understanding appropriation of the foundations of the world's meaning does conscience become independent. The relation to God in particular enables it to adopt a critical attitude to social institutions and norms. This is possible because divine reality is absolute, in contrast to purely human constructions and rules. The relation to God therefore renders human beings solitary within conscience and over against the world.[197]

This immediate relation to God should not be confused with Heidegger's "call of conscience." The latter has to do in fact with a special case of the judgment of conscience showing a nonidentity; the judgment is pronounced, in this case, not because of specific transgressions against other people, but because of a failure in regard to one's own selfhood. I become conscious of this last as something I lack and at the same time as

---

[194]T. Rendtorff, *Ethik* I (1980), 112.

[195]Ebeling, "Theological Reflections on Conscience," 411. The relation to the world calls for attention only as a consequence, that is, as an object of the human "answering-for" that is based on the word event. Ideas from F. Gogarten are clearly in the background here; see Gogarten, *Der Mensch zwischen Gott und Welt* (1952), 251ff., 360f.; see earlier 27ff. On Ebeling's acceptance of Heidegger's interpretation of conscience in terms of the "call of conscience" ("Theological Reflections on Conscience," 420), see the critical remarks of Mokrosch (n. 163, above), 88, especially on the point that Ebeling disregards the opposition between Heidegger's understanding of conscience and Luther's. But in my opinion this criticism does not affect the originality of the way in which Ebeling bases his interpretation of conscience (see above at n. 189).

[196]G. Ebeling, *God and Word,* trans. J. W. Leitch (Philadelphia, 1967), 33ff.

[197]Rendtorff, *Ethik* I, 112.

something I need. To the extent that in all concrete transgressions against others one's own selfhood is forfeited at the same time, the judgment of nonidentity may be taken as the *universal form* of all judgments of conscience. But it is only the *subjective* form of these judgments, since it abstracts from all reference to the order of the social world.

In addition, Heidegger's description has to do with a specifically modern experience: the advent of consciousness of an actual alienation. But in fact the isolation of the relation to the self in Heidegger's "call of conscience" serves to fix the consciousness in its alienation. The violence exercised in "choice" does not bring consciousness out of its isolation, but at best leads it (with Kierkegaard) into despair.

It is, rather, through repentance that the nonidentity asserted in the judgment of conscience is to be overcome. In repentance, culprits distance themselves from their acts and identify themselves with the agency that passes judgment on these acts. At the same time, however, repentance alone cannot strip guilt of its power, as Max Scheler thought.[198] The reason is that guilt is not entirely an inner state of the culprit. To the extent that subjective guilt is connected with an objective injury to others and to the social order, its removal requires that this order be restored. That is the point of expiation.

The call for expiation does not reflect the objectively superfluous severity of primitive societies toward their culprits.[199] This would be the case

[198]According to Scheler, repentance "kills the life-nerve of guilt's action and continuance" and sets the past to which it refers in a "new relation" to our life as a whole; see *On the Eternal in Man,* trans. B. Noble (New York, 1960), 42. When Scheler says that "an indwelling [i.e., in repentance] force of regeneration builds up a 'new heart' and a 'new man' " (48), it is impossible not to think of Luther's criticism of the role of repentance in the Late Scholastic theology of penance (though Scheler rightly intends, 48f., to keep repentance free of the motive of fear, which he mistakenly attributes to Protestantism). In Christianity our guilt is overcome not by the power of repentance but by the word of forgiveness that is based on the message and sacrificial death of Jesus. H. G. Stoker, a disciple of Scheler, soon departed from his teacher on this point: repentance cannot "by itself" remove guilt; this "requires an action of a judge" who acts in the name of the injured community (*Das Gewissen* [n. 142, above], 180).

[199]In his discussion of Durkheim and Fauconnet, J. Piaget, *The Moral Judgment of the Child* (n. 180, above), 327ff., esp. 341ff., condemns the ideas of punishment and expiation as manifestations of the heteronomous morality of primitive societies, which has been superseded by the individualism of civilized society, just as the heteronomy characteristic of the morality of early childhood is superseded by the autonomy of the adolescent. But this parallelism between the development of individuals and cultures is already undermined by the fact that Piaget has not prolonged his investigation of individual moral development to include a study of the way in which adults develop a responsibility for the injuries their actions do to other human beings and to the order of society. Piaget stops short of puberty in his study and therefore does not take into account the fact that the problem of expiation does not arise only in the context of a heteronomous morality but presents itself anew in connection with the full responsibility of adults for the consequences of their behavior.

only if the culprit's acts caused no objective injury to society and other human beings. If such an injury has in fact been caused, then order must be restored. Expiation is not the application of a principle calling for vengeance; it is concerned with the restoration of the social order of meaning that has been harmed by the action, and therefore also with the restoration of the culprit's own identity.

Nor is the idea of expiation tied to the cruel punishments imposed and inflicted in early cultures; these were forms of expiation that were based on the legal principle of reciprocity, which we must discuss later on. On the other hand, the humanization of expiation does not call for the restriction of punishment to an ever more narrowly conceived subjective responsibility and to minimal requirements of public security. It is, rather, the case that this development in the direction of the humanization of the penal code has its counterpart—and perhaps its condition—in the shifting of expiation in the proper sense into the realm of symbolic cultic action. The symbolism of ritual restores the culture's religiously based order of meaning and restores to the culprit his or her identity as a member of the community.

At the same time, however, the symbolism of expiatory rituals is also their weakness.

> How can guilt be atoned by the killing and eating of an animal? It can make sense only if the guilt itself consists in the fact that the internalization and commemoration [of the primordial establishment of the world by sacrifice] have not taken place on some occasion which should properly have evoked it, so that guilt must be consciously revived.[200]

In the eucharistic anamnesis, the Christian churches likewise commemorate and render present the restoration of communion between human beings and God and among human beings through the sacrifice of Christ, which was offered to God in order to "purify your [or: our] conscience from dead works to serve the living God" (Heb. 9:14). Here too the goal is the restoration of community, the reintegration of the individual into the community, the removal of alienation, the "purification" of conscience

---

Educators may disregard the consequences of children's actions: partly because the adult community is seldom seriously injured by them, partly because a child still lacks a full prevision of the consequences of its actions, so that the penal law governing the young assigns a lesser degree of responsibility to the adolescent. But adults must assume responsibility for the consequences of their actions. If the law here does not apply responsibility for consequences with the full rigor of "an eye for an eye and a tooth for a tooth," this is because it supposes that the restoration of social order and the reintegration of the culprit into it can be achieved in other ways than by establishing the principle of reciprocity through retribution.

[200]A. E. Jensen, *Myth and Cult Among Primitive Peoples,* trans. M. T. Choldin and W. Weissleder (Chicago, 1963), 173; see 210f.

from the judgment that condemns our works and keeps us imprisoned in nonidentity. Such a restoration can only be a communal event, since the deeds of individuals affect not only themselves in isolation but also the community (and precisely thereby "themselves"). Individuals recover their identity through reintegration into the community; they recover a freedom which they neither possess nor can exercise for themselves in isolation, but which they possess only as recognized members of the shared world.

Part Three
THE SHARED WORLD

7

Foundations of Culture

I. Aporias in the Concept of Culture

The world that human beings share has never been a natural world. It is nature as they have interpreted and shaped it and subjected it to their own service, but also as it limits and, in many instances, frustrates their efforts. It is, above all, the world of human relations. Moreover, when we speak of the shared world of human beings we are not referring simply to human beings as gathered in society within a natural environment. A social way of life and the formation of groups are not specifically human realities but are widespread among the higher animals. The specifically human form of common life is constituted by the concept of a shared world, which we call "culture."[1]

But what is culture? Very diverse answers have been given to this question. In 1952, two American cultural anthropologists, Alfred L. Kroeber and Clyde Kluckhohn, gathered and critically reviewed over a hundred different definitions of culture. Yet the end result was less a positive explanation of the concept than "to demonstrate the complexity of the problem and the incompleteness of the solutions proposed thus far."[2] Agreement is most easily achieved on a list of the elements that must go into the concept of culture. These include subjective factors such as convictions, attitudes, types of knowledge, and values as well as modes of behavior, habits, and customs; in addition, language and tradition, skills such as the use of tools, specific types of dwellings and clothing; and, finally, art and other products of human activity as well as social institutions.

[1] D. Kaplan and R. A. Manners, *Culture Theory* (Englewood Cliffs, N.J., 1972), 4, rightly insist that what is specifically human is not the fact that the shared life of individuals has a "social structure" but rather the cultural character of this life.

[2] E. Vermeersch, "An Analysis of the Concept of Culture," in B. Bernardi, ed., *The Concept and Dynamism of Culture* (The Hague, 1977), 9–74 at 26. See A. L. Kroeber and C. Kluckhohn, *Culture: A Critical Review of Concepts and Definitions* (Harvard University Papers of the Peabody Museum of American Archaeology and Ethnology 47; Cambridge, Mass., 1952).

316 Anthropology in Theological Perspective

As soon, however, as we go farther and ask what the criteria are that allow all these phenomena to be described as "cultural," considerable difficulties arise.[3] Neither the social character of these phenomena nor the element of adaptation and transformation of natural conditions seems adequately to define what is specific to culture. Yet if these points of view are still too partial, others are too general. The capacity for learning and the creative character of human activity need not be accompanied by the development of a culture. The widespread inclination to take the word "culture" simply as the common quality found in the various phenomena described as "cultural" seems particularly inappropriate.[4] Human habits, convictions, products, and systems of learning become "cultural" only because they are the expression of a particular culture. The key question, therefore, is, What is it that grounds the unity of a culture, a unity that manifests itself in the specific "style" of its various forms of life and distinguishes this culture from others?[5]

This point has been missed even in so important and influential a theory of culture as that of Bronislaw Malinowski. Malinowski sought to understand a culture as a whole in terms of its social institutions. "Culture is an integral composed of partly autonomous, partly coordinated institutions."[6] The statement is an accurate one, but it is inadequate as a definition, because it leaves unanswered the question of what it is that actually integrates the plurality of institutions into a single whole. Malinowski did go on to list "a series of principles" that will integrate a culture: for example, "the community of blood through procreation; the contiguity in space related to cooperation; the specialization in activities; and last but not least, the use of power in political organization." But while "principles" may indeed consolidate the cohesion of an already existing culture

---

[3]Vermeersch, 15ff., finds different difficulties than those raised in what follows here, because he tries to define culture as a generic concept that includes a plurality of cultural objects.

[4]Among the definitions of culture that Vermeersch discusses, 26ff., 31ff., is his own: "The class of cultural objects is the class of forms determined by man" (47).

[5]E. Rothacker, *Probleme der Kulturanthropologie* (1942; 1948), sees "life-style" as such as the essential factor in cultural unity. See also idem, *Philosophische Anthropologie* (1964; 1966[2]), 87, and *Zur Genealogie des menschlichen Bewusstseins* (ed. Perpeet, 1966), 35f. These views must face not only the difficulty that life-styles change even within a culture, as Rothacker himself sees, but, above all, the question of what it is that grounds the unity of a life-style itself. In reflecting subsequently on his thesis, Rothacker saw reason for "self-criticism" to the extent that the "convictions" of a society, which are subordinated to the unity of life-style, refer to the community's gods, of whom the community feels itself to be the "incarnation"; see *Zur Genealogie*. 35. In these remarks Rothacker seems to assign religion a more fundamental role in unifying a culture than his original thesis allowed.

[6]B. Malinowski, *A Scientific Theory of Culture, and Other Essays* (Chapel Hill, 1944), 40. The next citation in the text is from the same page.

and society, they are unable to explain what it is that actually creates the unity.[7]

Hardly any other explanation of culture is so opposed to the explanation in terms of institutions than the one that takes as its starting point the symbol-creating activity of human beings. Various approaches have been used in developing this conception. Thus Ernst Cassirer in his *The Philosophy of Symbolic Forms* (1923–29; ET: 1953–57) and in his philosophical version of cultural anthropology traces the various sectors of culture—language, art, myth, religion, science, and history—back to the specifically human "basic function" of symbol formation.[8] In like manner, L. A. White (1959) and Clifford Geertz (1973) have taken the symbolizing activity of the human being and the function of symbols in the mechanisms of social control as the criteria for the concept of culture.[9] Claude Lévi-Strauss too has described a culture as "a set of symbolic systems" that includes first and foremost language, regulations governing marriage, economic relations, art, science, and religion and that in each case takes into account the connections between society and the natural world.[10]

The symbolism theory of culture calls attention to one of the most important factors in cultural life, perhaps the most important next to the organization of social life by means of institutions and the social control of the world by means of technology. As a matter of fact, "no longer in a merely physical universe, man lives in a symbolic universe. Language,

[7]Therefore T. Parsons, "Malinowski and the Theory of the Social System," in R. W. Firth, ed., *Man and Culture* (London, 1957), rightly complains about Malinowski's failure to distinguish between the order of values on which a culture is founded and the system of social organization (against E. S. Makarian, "The Concept of Culture in the System of Modern Sciences," in Bernardi [n. 2, above], 113). Malinowski himself occasionally expressed insights in this area which, however, he did not develop in his theory of culture. Thus, for example, he wrote in his *Myth in Primitive Psychology* (1926) that myths form "the dogmatic backbone of primitive civilization."

[8]E. Cassirer, *An Essay on Man: An Introduction to a Philosophy of Human Culture* (New Haven, 1944; Anchor Books ed.: Garden City, N.Y., 1953), 93; see 43f., 45. See also S. K. Langer, *Philosophy in a New Key: A Study of the Symbolism of Reason, Rite and Art* (Cambridge, Mass., 1942; Pelican Book 20, 1948), 20ff., 32ff. (without reference to the concept of culture).

[9]L. A. White, "The Concept of Culture," *American Anthropologist* 61 (1959), 227–51; C. Geertz, *The Interpretation of Cultures* (New York, 1973), 46. Geertz's view—that the human being as "an incomplete, an unfinished animal" (46) needs controlling mechanisms to stabilize behavior ("the governing of behavior," 44) and that he creates these for himself by developing a culture—is reminiscent of A. Gehlen's theory of institutions. See, e.g., A. Gehlen, *Anthropologische Forschung* (rde 138, 1961), 21ff.

[10]Thus C. Lévi-Strauss in his introduction to M. Mauss, *Soziologie und Anthropologie* I (1974), 7–41 at 15; see earlier, 13.

myth, art, and religion are parts of this universe."[11] We may add (with Lévi-Strauss) that the economy and the legal system as well as the kinship system are also parts of this universe. We may also point out that the functions of technological control of the world are mediated through symbols and, in any case, only thereby acquire their cultural character, for the areas sometimes distinguished as culture and civilization belong together in actual life.

Yet the explanation of culture in terms of the symbol-creating function of the human spirit is inadequate. The reason is that when we speak of the capacity for symbolic representation and of its implementation we are always speaking first and foremost about a capacity of individuals and about the behavior of individuals. The cultural world, however, is one that is shared by individuals and, somewhat like the cosmic order, is experienced as given prior to individual behavior, even though individuals are constantly contributing to change its appearance. This priority of the cultural organization of the life-world, which is connected with the priority of institutions (although it is definitely not reducible to the needs that are the ground of institutions), cannot be explained in terms of human symbolizing activity. If we explain it as a reified version of the symbols created by human beings, we must still specify the objective ground of this reification.

If, on the other hand, we were to look upon a culture simply as the expression of a false consciousness, such an elimination of the objectivity of culture would contradict not only the self-understanding of all ancient cultures but also the social nature of culture. This point makes clear the opposition between a description of culture in terms of human symbol-creating activity and an explanation of it in terms of social institutions.

The concept of culture must in fact combine both of these aspects. Society as such is not culture. A human social formation acquires its special character only through its cultural form. On the other hand, an explanation of the concept of culture may not overlook the fact that cultures always take shape within socially organized reality. And the social nature of the cultural world makes it impossible to reduce the contents of this world to the symbolizing activity of the individual consciousness. That which is grasped by means of this activity must precede it. Nor may the supraindividual meaning of cultural contents be understood with Emile Durkheim as an expression of the superiority of society over its individual members. For, as I have pointed out, the unity of society needs for its establishment the foundational order of values that is supplied by the cultural system. It is for this reason that Talcott Parsons distinguishes the cultural system from the social system and gives the former priority over

[11]Cassirer (n. 8, above), 43.

the latter.[12] There is need, therefore, of a third level which is distinct from individual and society and on which the symbolizing activity of the individual is related to the foundations of social life.

In the self-understanding of most societies this third level is thematized as the level of the myth which recounts the establishment of the social order and the order of the natural cosmos and to which both individual self-consciousness and religious practice are related. The difficulties in the modern concept of culture that I have touched on are probably due to the fact that the modern consciousness no longer regards this level of myth as independent in relation to the individual, on the one hand, and the social order, on the other; instead, it either reduces it to creative human activity (and therefore to individuals) or takes it to reflect the superiority of the social nature of the human person (and therefore concretely of society) to individuals. But this method of dealing with myth in a modern, secularistic way inevitably gets involved in aporias that cannot be resolved on these premises. As the preceding survey of the various approaches to a theory of culture has shown, the establishment of a culture as a shared world cannot be conceived in terms either of the symbolizing activity of individuals or of the organization of society.

M. Landmann's statement that human beings are both the creators and the creatures of culture expresses this aporia in a pregnant way, though the writer does not seem to have been aware of it.[13] According to Landmann, in individuals "a passive being-produced takes priority. . . . All human individuals become themselves only through participation in a cultural medium which is supraindividual in character, transcends them, and is common to an entire group."[14] On the other hand, if we "are to be able to make a culture part of us, it must first have been created."[15] Since, according to Landmann, only the human person can be involved in this creative process (even though any given individual "can add but little" to the inherited culture "and change but little in it"), he regards human beings as also the creators of culture, and, more specifically, human beings in the form of the preceding generations whose accumulated heritage is responsible for the cultural shaping of present-day individuals.

[12]T. Parsons, *Societies: Evolutionary and Comparative Perspectives* (1966), 10f.; see 6f., as well as idem, *The Social System* (Glencoe, Ill., 1951, 1964), 34. Parsons himself likewise makes the concept of cultural system relative to the concept of human activity, which, he says, is cultural to the extent that it produces symbolic systems (*Societies,* 5). On the other hand, he says that "no individual can create a social system" (6). Parsons does not seem to have fully realized the problem raised by the fact that the concept of culture cannot be based either on the individual or on society.

[13]See M. Landmann, *Der Mensch als Schöpfer und Geschöpf der Kultur* (1961). See earlier his *Philosophische Anthropologie* (1955), 222f., 242f.

[14]Landmann, *Philosophische Anthropologie,* 242, 244.

[15]Landmann, *Pluralität und Autonomie* (1963), 16. The next citation in the text is from 17.

But how is it possible to attribute to the mere sum total of individual accomplishments that which is rightly said not to be the work of the individual? As Landmann himself observes, the peoples of older cultures looked upon their cultural order "as a divine gift or an endowment accompanying nature." Should their view be set aside as a simple error regarding the real state of affairs? Is it enough to say, "The creative element, though objectively already at work, was not subjectively discovered"?[16]

The idea of an unconscious productivity must, of course, be allowed a partial truth, unless one is willing to suppose that only as a result of the modern *consciousness* of their creative activity have human beings been made capable of such activity. In Landmann, however, this idea becomes the modern version of a notion that the early modern age still regarded as acceptable, at least in the doctrine of God: the notion of *causa sui.* But there is no empirical evidence that human beings, regarded as cultural beings, can take the place of God to this extent. They do contribute by their creative activity to the shaping and revision of their cultural world, but there is no question in this activity, even in art and technology, of a creation out of nothing. Human creative activity serves predominantly to apprehend and represent facts that can be apprehended and represented only in this medium but that do not owe their reality to an arbitrary human productivity. The treasure accumulated in the process of cultural transmission is made up of disclosures of reality, and only what promises further to broaden and deepen human dealings with experiential reality is preserved in this transmission. In speaking of human creativity, we must not lose sight of the fact that in human creative activity reality is in the process of manifesting itself.

With its gaze focused on the order of society as a whole and on the cosmic order, myth formulates the reality that manifests itself therein and that grounds the order. This, however, does not automatically mean that myth and religion are to be considered the factors that establish the unity of a culture—that is, myth and religion regarded not as human products but as expressions of divine revelation.[17] In its doctrinal statements the

[16]Landmann, *Philosophische Anthropologie,* 241. See on this point the remark made by Rothacker in self-criticism (n. 5, above).

[17]Thus T. S. Eliot, *Notes Toward the Definition of Culture* (New York, 1949), 27: "We may go further and ask whether what we call the culture, and what we call the religion, of a people are not different aspects of the same thing: the culture being, essentially, the incarnation (so to speak) of the religion of a people." How explain, then, that the "life-style" of a culture may be in tension with and, at times, even openly opposed to its official religion, as it clearly was, for example, in the European Renaissance and during the Enlightenment? Eliot himself elsewhere (32) protests against the identification of religion and culture which the passage just quoted suggests. I myself am trying to make my own, in a modified form, Eliot's real intention.

normative consciousness of many cultures has indeed thought of myth as narrating the establishment of the shared world and its order and of the cultic life of religion as responsible for the maintenance and renewal of this original order. On the other hand, Malinowski was able to show, against Durkheim and Lucien Lévy-Bruhl, that even in early cultures that did not yet have writing the profane sectors of life enjoyed a relative independence over against mythical and religious tradition and practice.[18] The high cultures, of course, are characterized by a greater differentiation of their institutions and by the independence of these from one another; among these institutions, even religion, despite its responsibility for social life in its entirety, is at the same time only a partial system alongside others.

It is not possible, therefore, simply to derive the unity of culture from myth and religion alone, no matter what claims myth and religion may make along these lines. Rather, it is the tension between the claims of the mythical and religious tradition, on the one side, and the changing life experience of individuals and community, on the other, that provides the field in which the life-style of a culture is formed and renewed. Here even religion and myth undergo change, since reality itself, the fundamental order of which is described and actualized by myth and religion, presents itself in ever new ways to the experience of the society.

The question of what it is that grounds the unity of a culture may not be answered, then, simply on the lines of what might be called the culture's official self-understanding as expressed in its myths. Attention must also be paid to the actual experience of reality in the various areas of the culture's life and to the relation of this experience to the official self-interpretation of the culture. On the other hand, this self-interpretation may not simply be set aside in favor of a modern secularistic prejudgment, as happens in the thesis that culture is a human creation and nothing more. The importance of the human creative subjectivity for the process whereby cultures come into existence and change must be maintained, but in such a way that the mythical self-understanding of the agents of that culture is not simply rejected as a false consciousness. Rather, account must be taken of the importance of this self-understanding for the social character of cultural life.

Among the theories of culture that are current today, Johan Huizinga's interpretation of culture in terms of the phenomenon of play seems to satisfy these requirements best. Playing together, in its various forms, is to be seen in all modes of communal life, including even cult. On the other hand, playing also forms the biological basis of all the free and creative

---

[18]B. Malinowski, *Magic, Science and Religion* (1925), cited from the collection of the same title, ed. R. Redfield (New York, 1954; Anchor Book A23), 17–92, esp. 25ff., 59ff.

activity of individuals. Thus the theme of play links together the question of the identity of the individual, which provided the guiding thread for the second part of the present book, with the further question, arising out of the previous one, regarding the shared world in which individuals are given the opportunity for achieving their personal identity.

II. Freedom in Play

For Nietzsche the child at play is a symbol of innocence and a sign of the conquest of the nonidentity that finds expression in guilt consciousness. "The child is innocence and forgetting, a new beginning, a game, a self-propelled wheel, a first movement, a sacred 'Yes.' "[19] The image of the self-propelled wheel suggests the self-contained world of meaningful play that forgets everything outside it and is free from extrinsic goals, free to be itself.

After Nietzsche no one has given a more penetrating formulation of the connection between play and freedom than Jean Paul Sartre. According to Sartre, "play in fact sets subjectivity free." And the converse is true: "As soon as individuals understand themselves to be free and are determined to use their freedom, their activity turns into play, no matter what anxiety may otherwise weigh them down."[20] We will have to concern ourselves further on with the sense in which, according to Sartre, play initiates freedom and how play is to be understood in this context. For the moment I shall consider only the thesis that play and freedom are connected. It is a thesis that is confirmed by the anthropology of play.

The play impulse is something that the human child has in common with the young of many higher species of mammals, who can be observed playing. What is the basis for this connection between play activity and youth?

Play enters the picture only when behavior is not rigorously directed to a goal, as it is in instinctual movements. For "the limitation of the possibilities of movement in the field [of goal-oriented actions] means that any actions which are not directed to the goal by the shortest possible route must make way for those which are directly goal-oriented."[21] This

---

[19]F. Nietzsche, *Thus Spoke Zarathustra*, trans. W. Kaufmann (New York, 1954), Part I, no. 1: "On the Three Metamorphoses" (Kaufmann, 27).

[20]J. P. Sartre, *Das Sein und das Nichts* (1943; German tr., 1962), 729f. See M. Gisi, *Der Begriff Spiel im Denken J. P. Sartres* (1979), 157f. Sartre distinguishes between genuine play, which alone can be an expression of freedom, and unauthentic play, which is inspired by an insincerity that, for example, apes compassion or is indifferent and in which in Sartre's view those are still involved who only play their professional role (like the café waiter, ibid., 106f.; see Gisi, 100ff.) and are unable fully to identify with it.

[21]G. Bally, *Vom Ursprung und von den Grenzen der Freiheit. Eine Deutung des Spiels bei Mensch und Tier* (Basel, 1945), 22.

is true even of what is called appetitive behavior, in which an animal seeks restlessly until it finds a suitable object, so that instinctive activity may then run its course. Only when the tension toward a goal has been relaxed do otherwise overlooked characteristics of objects become visible. "Distance from the goal leads to an enriched grasp of individual details" in perception.[22] It is then possible, for species capable of it, to develop what Konrad Lorenz calls exploratory behavior or behavior inspired by curiosity.

Here, unlike the case of appetitive behavior, "it is not *one* fixed motor pattern that is tried in various situations and on various objects but virtually all the patterns in the repertoire of the species are exercised successively on one and the same object."[23] The presuppositions for this kind of curiosity-inspired behavior are verified especially in the young animal because the presence of its parents guarantees it nourishment and protection from enemies. Here once again it is especially in the phase of transition from the behavior characteristic of the young animal (e.g., the opening of the beaks of birds) to the adult behavior characteristic of the species (e.g., pecking for grain) that playful movements occur.[24] For in this period of transition not only is the young animal still unencumbered by the task of looking for food and warding off enemies, but it is also characterized by an especially high degree of plasticity in its behavior.

By reason of its open-endedness and freedom of movement the play of young animals is comparable in principle to human openness to the world, as Lorenz emphasizes. The difference is that the openness and plasticity of the behavior of young animals disappear as soon as they mature, whereas in this respect human beings remain at a stage of youthful development (neoteny) and retain this kind of openness to the world as a behavioral characteristic throughout their lives[25] In play behavior, then, we have before us the concrete process whereby that human openness to the world is developed which we have hitherto treated more as an abstract behavioral characteristic that distinguishes human beings from all the other animals. Through play, human beings develop their capacities for behavior that is not goal-directed but can secondarily be used for any goal chosen. In this sense, play is, first of all, the "beginning of freedom": "The freely exercised distance from goal-oriented instinct and the sovereign playfulness in the field [of behavior]—things only hinted at in the highest animals and even then only for rare moments within a short period of adolescence—become the basic posture of human

[22]Ibid., 30; see, on what has just been said, 19 and 23f.
[23]K. Lorenz, *Behind the Mirror: A Search for a Natural History of Human Knowledge,* trans. R. Taylor (New York, 1977), 145.
[24]See Bally, 46.
[25]Lorenz, 149 and 151.

beings."[26] This release from the ties of instinct is, of course, only one side of freedom. Freedom reaches completion only when individuals impose ties on themselves that are interwoven with their social relations. This side of freedom, too, is developed through play.

According to Jean Piaget, in the development of the human child all play has its origin in imitation. The movements made available through imitation (including self-imitation) are "ritualized," that is, released from their function in the process of adaptation and accomplished purely for "functional pleasure."[27] The second year of life brings not only the internalization of imitation through imagination but also memory images as symbolic "evocations of absent realities."[28] In "symbolic games" this symbolism is connected with objects which by reason of quite remote similarities give the child an opportunity to penetrate more fully into the absent "realities" hinted at by these similarities. The object with which the child is playing is only a "representative" of the reality with which the playing is really concerned. The real object of the game is different from the object at hand: the child rides a horse with the help of a broomstick.

Although playing develops initially by way of liberation from the imitation of immediately given objects and although in symbolic games the things directly used are simply occasions, the fullest form of symbolic play, which occurs in the fourth to the sixth year, brings the child back to

[26]Bally, 74. According to J. Piaget, *Nachahmung, Spiel und Traum. Die Entwicklung der Symbolfunktion beim Kinde* (1945; German tr., 1975), "all the games of animals (except for the rare examples of symbolic games among chimpanzees)" correspond to the sensorimotor practice games of human children during the first sixteen months of their lives; the more developed symbolic games of the child must be regarded as specifically human (141; see 147f.). [There is an English translation of Piaget's book: *Play, Dreams and Imitation in Childhood,* trans. C. Gattengo and F. M. Hodgson (New York, n.d.).]

[27]Piaget, 121; see 119. On ritualization, 125, 127. On imitation, see also the observations of Lorenz, 204ff., 265ff., with his surprising remark that the capacity for imitation "in the proper sense is found . . . in the animal world, apart from human beings, only in certain birds," and in these it is limited to the imitation of sounds; in the apes there are only "weak hints" of it.

[28]Piaget, 90; on what follows here, see 127ff., 153. On the role of the toy as a "representative" of the symbolized reality, 216. See also the comment of F. J. J. Buytendijk that in symbolic games or games of pretense "the comings and goings" characteristic of games acquire their properly human meaning from the coming and going between the present object and the reality it signifies; see his "Das menschliche Spielen," in H. G. Gadamer and P. Vogler, eds., *Kulturanthropologie,* Neue Anthropologie 4 (1973), 106: "An existence in *two* worlds: the sensible and the nonsensible." See in addition the remarks of E. Fink on the "magical character" of toys as representatives not only of a particular thing but "of all things as such. . . . A toy is a concentration of the universe in a single thing"; see his *Oase des Glücks. Gedanken zu einer Ontologie des Spiels* (1957), 34.

imitation once again, but to "a striving for an exact imitation of reality."[29] Now, however, it is the *absent* reality as such which is imitated or, more accurately, reconstructed. As a result, the empathetic identification with the (symbolized) object of the game or, rather, the seizure by the absent object takes on a new intensity: the absent object becomes increasingly present in the game.

Lorenz aptly observes that even in its initial form imitation is based on a kind of inspiration.[30] The element of inspired transport is found especially in symbolic games and their most important subspecies, role-playing, in which children play the parts of adults as engine driver, trades person, automobile driver, etc. The symbolico-imaginative transport that occurs in games prepares the way for the future free identification of the child's real self. "The role a child chooses to act depends on what impresses him, and the pleasure he feels derives from the lift that the acting gives to his self-esteem."[31] The connection between play and the process of identity formation becomes evident here, and with it an aspect that is important for an understanding of the "seizure" that occurs in play. At the same time, however, it is not only the child's own self that is involved. The fascination of symbolic games is due to the presence of (absent) reality generally, insofar as this "impresses itself," and thus also becomes a model for the definition of the self.

The fascination of playing contains the element of a self-binding by the player. The experience of seizure gives rise to the urge to an increasingly realistic representation. Following J. Henriot, F. J. J. Buytendijk has pointed out that playing is always accompanied by a desire to *succeed* and therefore by an element of self-discipline and self-commitment.[32] Thus the

[29]Piaget, 167. The passage to role-playing with its increasing differentiation of roles and ever greater attention to the details of them is connected with this imitation.

[30]Lorenz, 155, insists that one cannot produce an impersonation at will but "has somehow to be 'inspired,' as with the functions of higher gestalt perception." This is a point of view which is lacking in Piaget not only in connection with imitation but also in his description of play, probably because he describes play only in terms of assimilation that is stimulated by accommodation to the environment (Piaget, 207ff.; see 116, etc.). Yet L. Frobenius, *Kulturgeschichte Afrikas* (1933), 147, had already emphasized the "seizure" *(Ergriffenheit)* that is characteristic of children's play.

[31]Lorenz, 202.

[32]Buytendijk (n. 28, above), 88–122, esp. 102ff., 107f. But Buytendijk does not take into account that this commitment springs from the fascination exerted by the reality present in the game. Gadamer, on the other hand, stresses this element in connection with an earlier publication of Buytendijk, although in the narrower form of a fascination exerted by the game itself: "The attraction of a game, the fascination it exerts, consists precisely in the fact that the game tends to master the players" (Gadamer, *Truth and Method*, trans. G. Barden and J. Cumming [New York, 1975], 95; see 98; cited, pretty much in passing, in Buytendijk, 114f.). The fascination exerted by the playing of the game probably applies most to games

aim in role-playing is to play the adopted role as well as possible. This commitment to which fascination gives rise ensures the unity and internal completeness of the game, and the keeping of the commitment is the basis for satisfaction at the success of the game.

In playing that involves others the commitment takes the form of an agreement about a subject or work to be represented jointly (as a direction governing the game) or, as the case may be, the form of an obligation to observe the rules of the game. The object being represented in the game may in the process more or less fade from view behind the rules of the game and the reciprocity among the players that is established by these rules. In fact, this reciprocity may become the real object of the game. The players oblige themselves only to observe the rules, and this obligation gives their game its unity. The representational function can fade into the background. The game becomes a pure contest.

In a book that is a classic of cultural anthropology Johan Huizinga developed the thesis that all forms of cultural life can be traced back to the main types of communal play: to representational playing, on the one hand, and to contests according to rules, on the other.[33] But Huizinga himself conceded that the two types of game may interact with each other in the forms of cultural life. Representational playing comes first genetically and objectively, but in all playing with others an element of competition is always present.

Representational play finds its fullest embodiment in ritual that represents the mythical order of the cosmos. Just as every fully developed game is self-contained and complete, so in ritual a world that is complete in itself stands over against the profane world (9). This setting apart is achieved by the spatial separation of the cultic area (the separation of playground and playing field from the everyday world is still a reminder of this, 10) and by the removal of the time of a feast from ordinary time (21). In addition, just as players are seized by the fascination of the game, so too, and even more so, are they raised above their ordinary state when they engage in ritual. In cult it is not only the agents of the ritual drama that experience this exaltation; as in many other forms of representational playing, the community that attends the performance of the representation has the same experience. An analogous claim may be made not only for the theater, which only since the days of Greek tragedy has detached itself increasingly from the religious context of cult. It also applies to the performance of musical compositions, as well as (in some degree, at least) to

---

with others, but it can also be found in the early symbolic games and role-playing of the child, in which the playing of the game serves, rather, to represent the reality that is symbolized by the toy and is present in the game. It is this reality that the game is really all about.

[33] J. Huizinga, *Homo Ludens: A Study of the Play-Element in Culture,* trans. R. F. C. Hull (London, 1949), 13. The page references that follow in the text are to this book.

solemn social and political functions. Hans Georg Gadamer has correctly observed that the performance of a dramatic or musical composition is completed only within the viewer or hearer.[34]

Here, then, we see the full flowering of what was said above about the symbolic games of children, namely, that in play the (absent, but) symbolized reality becomes present, is represented. The difference between work or composition and performance shows that the state of being seized which occurs in play is attributable not only to the actual playing but also to the object represented in the playing.[35] The performance achieves its purpose when the object throws its spell not only over those directly involved in the playing but also, through their activity, over the community of participants, who for their part represent the public formed by the whole society. The work being performed holds the place that myth occupies in ritual; ritual renders effective in the present moment the mythic truth that is at the foundation of the world, and it does so through the action of the priest on behalf of the entire cultic community. The fascination exercised by theater and concert becomes fully intelligible only in the light of their cultic origins; at the same time, we realize also the ambiguity that attaches to them, since they can be misused as aesthetic substitutes for religion.

In a certain sense, the motive behind the representation finds its full satisfaction when that which is represented acquires permanent form in an image.[36] Thus we see the rock painters of the Paleolithic Age making permanent representations of the numinous power they had experienced in animals.[37] In images, especially in such perduring material as stone, the eternity of what is represented becomes present in time, whether in the form of a relief or a statue or a building. Such gains exact their price, however. The price is that the image stands outside the temporal life stream of human beings. Statues and temples may still be standing when

---

[34]Gadamer, *Truth and Method,* 97f. See 111 on the "self-forgetfulness" of "being present," and 117 on tragic catharsis as "a genuine communion."

[35]Gadamer places the stresses differently when he writes that play "has its own essence, independent of the consciousness of those who play" and "merely reaches presentation through the players" (82; see 93, 94f.). Gadamer does not distinguish here between the game and the represented object, whereas at a later point he correctly emphasizes the priority of the work (composition) over its rendition or performance (96, 109).

[36]On this, see Gadamer, 119ff., esp. the contrast between representation and mere copy: "In representation, the presence of what is represented is completed" (122). In this case, therefore, "the picture itself is what is meant" (123), and not simply what is being represented, for the latter achieves representation only in the picture (ibid.). See also G. van der Leeuw, *Sacred and Profane Beauty: The Holy in Art,* trans. D. E. Green (New York, 1963), Part 7.

[37]K. J. Narr, "Beiträge der Urgeschichte zur Kenntnis der Menschennatur," in Gadamer and Vogler (n. 28, above), 43.

human beings have long since lost any receptivity to their claims. Consequently, the meaning of the representation, namely, that it causes what is represented to become present to temporal human existence, finds a more appropriate expression (as far as the recipient is concerned) in the performance, within time, that we experience in theater or concert hall.

Cult combines the two elements: permanent image and the ever repeated rendering-present of what is represented, though the details of its form are here only hinted at. Even such works of fine art as are removed from their vital context in cult continue to be oriented to the act in which they are contemplated; as they continue to live on in time, the claim they implicitly make is met through the medium of the space in which the work is located and by means of which it places resident and visitor under its spell.

These reflections are not unimportant for a Christian interpretation of art. Inasmuch as they limit the power of permanent images in comparison with human reality as lived within time, they make it possible to do justice to the argument in behalf of images that was developed in the Byzantine iconoclastic controversy of the seventh and eighth centuries, while at the same time not allowing the special character of Christian faith in the incarnation to be lost from sight in the profundity of the ancient belief in images. In the face of the biblical prohibition against making an image of God (Ex. 20:2ff.)[38] the classical Christian justification of images has been the appeal to the incarnation: "If, indeed, it is true that God became man in order to be 'humanly' near to us, then it is obviously no longer blasphemous to contemplate him in the image of this one man."[39] When, therefore, after an initial rejection of representational images, Christian theologians accepted such images from the fourth century on as reminders of the biblical story and as lessons about its meaning, their acceptance was doubtless based on the understanding that what is imitated is not God but the human and historical reality in which he has revealed himself.

But even in images the divine and the human in Christ remain inseparable. The warning on this point by Epiphanius of Salamis was unwittingly validated, centuries later, by the iconophiles when they extended to icons the dogma of the union of God and man in the person of Christ.[40] Admittedly, the image does make us conscious of the divinity of Christ as well as of his human nature. But the hypostatic union refers to the historically unique, corporeal existence of Jesus and not to the pictorial representation of his outward form. It is only through an act of faith that a pictorial

[38]See the detailed study by K. H. Bernhardt, *Gott und Bild* (1956).

[39]H. von Campenhausen, "The Theological Problem of Images in the Early Church," in his *Tradition and Life in the Church: Essays and Lectures on Church History*, trans. A. V. Littledale (Philadelphia, 1968), 171–200 at 199.

[40]Ibid., 193ff.

"representation" of Christ leads, as does the proclaimed word, to an indwelling of Christ in believers through the Spirit. Jesus Christ by his promise linked his bodily presence with the sharing of a meal of bread and wine; he linked it, that is, with the performance of an action, not with an image.[41] Only through the historical action of the community in union with him is his body, the church, built up in the world; and in this action he himself is the "image of God" and makes us share in it as our destiny. An image shaped by a human being is, on the contrary, precisely by reason of its timelessness, only a symbol, a pointer to the eternal God, who manifests himself in the humanity of Jesus.[42] As a symbol it also represents his presence, but it is not the actuation of that presence. In Christianity the element of representation, which had seemed to find its highest expression in the perduring image because it there conquered the transiency of representational play, has once again been linked to action in time.

The representational function of games gives us special insight into the cultural realms of cult and the arts. It can also be seen at work in all forms of political and social representation. But it is not enough by itself to prove Huizinga's thesis that culture as a whole and in all its forms has its origin in play. Such a claim becomes plausible only when the representational element is combined with the other main element in social play: the element of competition or contest. But this element of competition is always present, at least potentially, when the representational element takes on a social dimension, although it may be of secondary importance as compared with the task of representation.

The element of competition comes into its own as an independent reality in games that take the form of contests. Nonetheless in contests the element of individual apartness and distinction remains subordinated to the rules of the game. Here again these rules represent the order that constitutes social play as it does the social world generally and that is represented as such in representational play. Thus the very ritualization of antagonisms among individuals and groups that occurs in contests represents something further: the integration of these antagonisms into the cultural order.

[41]In contrast to P. Brunner's remarks on a theology of art, in "Zur Lehre vom Gottesdienst," in K. F. Müller and W. Blankenburg, eds., *Leitourgia. Handbuch des evangelischen Gottesdienstes* I (1954), 83–361, esp. 291–332, I prefer to ascribe to the image, as understood in the Western Christian idea of the *biblia pauperum,* a greater affinity to the proclamation of the word. I do, however, agree with Brunner that neither the image of Christ nor the sign of the cross and other Christian symbols may be "said to have the power *effectively* to render present what is described in the symbol" (330).

[42]Precisely the linking of the eternal with the temporal and the illustration of it by the temporal make an image more than a simple copy of the finite; it becomes a symbol of the latter's transfiguration through participation in the eschatological glory of God.

In the life of society, contest motifs are to be found in all ritualized interactions among individuals and interest groups; this is true especially in the legal sphere (Huizinga, 76ff.) but also in the economic. War too has been ritualized, at least inchoatively, by means of the rules of war (95ff.). In addition, Huizinga points to the antagonistic or dualistic structure of exogamous societies (53)[43] and to the dualistic but complementary specification and assignment of the roles of the sexes.

Representational games and contests, as I noted earlier, are not out-and-out contraries in cultural life, but rather intermingle. Thus cult drama also has elements of contest in it. Conversely, sporting contests may at the same time have cultic meaning; think, for example, of the ballplaying of the ancient Indian cultures of America or of the original form of the Olympic games. The legal process as ritual antagonism both represents and renews the unity of the legal order.

Huizinga's thesis that "culture arises in the form of play; . . . it is played from the very beginning" (46) has met with a great deal of criticism ever since his book was published (1938). Especially obvious and weighty is the criticism that Huizinga fails to recognize the seriousness of both the sacral and the legal spheres. Thus, according to Buytendijk, between the "rules of life and the norms that condition human existence" there is a difference in principle that forbids any reduction of the law's claim to validity to that of rules for a game. Huizinga also fails to do justice to the seriousness of the sacred: "The sacred is permeated by reverence and dread; play is a lighthearted form of liberation." Play is even "essentially desacralizing."[44]

What elements of this criticism deserve to be retained? As far as law is concerned, Piaget has shown that in the moral development of children the rules of games are the origin of a consciousness of norms that are grounded in autonomy and are therefore freely accepted and not unilaterally imposed.[45] In his polemic against Huizinga, Buytendijk seems to have forgotten his own remarks about the element of self-commitment in games (see above, at n. 32). Otherwise he could not have contrasted games as

---

[43]The view that the exogamic structure of so-called totem cultures is based on a "dual organization" which is in turn based on, among other things, the difference between the sexes (but also on a number of other two-membered oppositions) has been adopted in modern ethnology by, e.g., A. E. Jensen, *Myth and Cult Among Primitive Peoples* (1951), trans. M. T. Choldin and W. Weissleder (Chicago, 1963), 151ff. For a critique, see C. Lévi-Strauss, *Structural Anthropology,* trans. C. Jacobson and B. G. Schoepf (New York, 1963), 132–63; see 120ff.; Lévi-Strauss follows the tradition of Mauss and Malinowski and prefers to speak of structures of opposition.

[44]Buytendijk (n. 28, above), 101f.

[45]J. Piaget et al., *The Moral Judgment of the Child,* trans. M. Gabain (London, 1957; New York, 1965), 50ff., esp. 64ff.

a "lighthearted form of liberation" with the holy and the reverence it elicits.[46]

It is true, of course, that play can be detached from its orientation to an order that achieves representation in it. But this degeneration of play into pretense should not, any more than its reduction to a mere way of passing time, be allowed to make us lose sight of its original meaningful structure that is evident in the symbolic games of children. In the representational urge that is at work in children's games we should, rather, see an anticipation of that "seizure" *(Ergriffenheit)* which has its most appropriate locus in the context of a cultic celebration. In a cultic celebration the structure of meaning that marks the representational function of play becomes fully explicit. Therefore representational play finds its perfect form in cult.

If, then, Huizinga's observations on the relation between representational play and cult call for any criticism, it is along the lines that his idea of play is still too subject to the prejudicial view of play as pretense without commitment, and that for this reason he conceives of what is special about cult as being extrinsically added to play, as being "more of a mental element" (14). Then the element of play, but of play conceived as pretense without commitment, suddenly becomes the very substance of cult: "Ritual grafts itself upon it [play]; but the primary thing is and remains play" (18).

Adolf E. Jensen, who appeals to Karl Kerenyi, has raised "serious objections" against this view.[47] His objections are directed both against Huizinga's definition of the relation of cult to profane play and against the claimed primacy of profane games in gaining an understanding of play as such. According to Jensen, the fact that in cultic play human beings experience "primeval times . . . [as] the true order of the world" (53) is not only the special characteristic that turns cultic play into a festive occasion (54); at the same time, it gives this play its originality over against other forms of play. For whereas the function of myth and cult is to establish the world, children in their games simply appropriate "an order of things which has already been actualized" (58). Communal games, which are to be distinguished as a separate type and have been handed down in the community

[46]But Huizinga's description of play does contain turns of phrase that suggest such an erroneous interpretation. When, for example, he describes play as "a free activity standing quite consciously outside 'ordinary' life as being 'not serious,' but at the same time absorbing the player intensely and utterly" (13), the description does not, of course, apply to the legal sphere or to cult.

[47]Jensen (n. 43, above), 39–59 at 57. The page references that follow in the text are to this book. Jensen cites K. Kerenyi, "Vom Wesen des Festes," *Paideuma* I, Part 2 (December 1938), 59ff. Huizinga agrees with Kerenyi (21–22) but follows him only in part.

of playing children, are to be taken, according to Jensen, as "survivals" which a loss of function and a "process of semantic depletion" have turned into children's games.[48]

In these remarks Jensen has probably underestimated the independent meaning of children's games and the importance of the part they play in the genesis of cultic behavior itself. In their symbolic games and role-playing children are not simply copying the world created by adults; they are also preparing themselves for independent and productive participation in that world. The development of play behavior in children may be culturally determined in its content, but it develops out of roots in human biology and as such precedes any participation in sacred cultic games in the life of every member of a cultic community. It is therefore important that the relation to cult can be shown to be an intrinsic element in the structure of human play, to the extent that cult shows itself to be the fully developed form of that representational playing, the structure of which already determines the symbolic games of children. It may be true to say, from the viewpoint of adults, that in their symbolic games and role-playing children "play an order of things which has already been actualized" (Jensen, 58). But in the minds of children themselves their playing is concerned with an intuition and representation of the "true order" of things, and this intuition and representation are very comparable to the sacred play of cult. Precisely this structure of children's symbolic games makes it possible to assert that all human playing is to be understood, as regards its representational function, in the light of cult.[49]

---

[48]Jensen, 58, 59ff. and 76ff. See also E. Fink, *Spiel als Weltsymbol* (1960), 202ff.

[49]Fink (157) speaks somewhat misleadingly of a "cultic derivation" of all human play, but at the same time he defends himself against a misunderstanding of this formula, lest it be taken as implying that "all play springs from the root which is cult." In speaking of "cultic derivation," he means, rather, to call attention to the fact that "the 'unreality' that marks play as a world apart is to be understood as carrying the mind to a mode of being which is superior, not inferior, to the being of the things of everyday experience" (ibid.). This point of view, which does illuminate the nature of play as such, is in fact justified and made accessible only by the function of cult as constitutive of the world. Therefore Fink's effort to "counteract" such a cultic "derivation" for play and to show play to be purely "worldly" (218ff.) seems rather forced. He believes that as a philosopher he is bound to make such an effort (145ff.), even though the relation to cult is at the center of his study and even though he himself admits that "when the theological question is bracketed," the view taken of "cultic playing is already too narrowly conceived" (195). Why the bracketing, then? Is it due simply to a now traditional prejudice regarding the object reserved to theology? Is phenomenological analysis not to look at the phenomena in their full range, even if this means shaking the rigidified barriers between academic disciplines? Fink's description of the "worldliness" of play continues to be quite theological in its substance: "In human play the world as a totality is reflected back to itself; it allows traces of infinity to shine in and through intraworldly and finite reality" (230). Why not give the thing its true name instead of using the second-rate lingo of pantheism?

Jensen's correction of Huizinga must, then, be made more precise. Contrary to the asserted primacy of a profane concept of play, play as such, beginning with the symbolic games of children, already has a dimension that will be appropriately perceived in the sacred play of cult. In the content of their play children look to "the true order of things," but they are unable to thematize it in its authentic form.[50]

Play and seriousness seem to have been less divided in the consciousness and feeling about life of the peoples of the premodern cultures than they are in the members of the modern industrial societies. Certainly toil brought greater tribulation in many spheres than it does today. At the same time, however, the normative role of religion and cult in public life and the resultant division of time through the sequence of religiously oriented festivals prevented any separation in principle between everyday life and play. On the contrary, motifs and rituals conveying religiously grounded meaning gave structure even to the institutions of everyday life.

The element of play has, however, largely disappeared from the modern world of industrial labor.[51] Above all, the representational function of play has atrophied. Conversely, play is limited to the area of leisure activities and as a result, like the entire content of a culture based on leisure (this includes art and religion), stands under the sign of arbitrariness and of the depletion of meaning to which arbitrariness leads. This is why it has become so difficult today to grasp the seriousness of human play and the difference between play and the pretense that involves no commitment. This kind of pretense used to be simply a precondition for play (it gave expression to the release from the goals and compulsions of self-preservation) or else a concomitant phenomenon or, finally, a degenerate form of play. Now the limitation of play to an arbitrarily ordered leisure time has largely reduced it to a matter of pretense. The heritage of one's own cultural tradition and the records of alien cultures have become interchangeable consumer goods.

Even in this reduced form, play, art, and consumer goods in the broadest sense (including religion) do, of course, have an important social function, that of compensating for the meaninglessness of the public world of politics and the economy.[52] The use of games and other entertainments as compensations for the privations of life has from time immemorial been part of the prudential wisdom of rulers. Thus in Rome, as everyone knows, "bread and circuses" were the means the authorities used to pacify

---

[50]These last two sentences reflect the element of truth in Buytendijk's critique of Huizinga. His criticism does not touch the category of play as such but, rather, the inadequacy of Huizinga's concept of it.

[51]H. Cox makes this point in his *The Feast of Fools: A Theological Essay on Festivity and Fancy* (Cambridge, Mass., 1969), 9ff.

[52]See J. Moltmann, *Theology and Joy,* trans. R. Ulrich (London, 1973), 29ff.

the people. Games can be misused simply to entertain and distract the populace and thereby to consolidate a rule by drawing attention away from the question of the legitimacy of the power and its exercise. When looked upon simply as a leisure occupation, games become a compensation for the meaninglessness of life in the modern world of labor and professional work. This separation of work and play makes it especially clear that life in the modern industrial societies is alienating.

In contrast, the young Marx in *The German Ideology* (1845–46) depicted the communist society of the future as a state in which individuals may freely choose their activities: "Society regulates the general production, making it possible for me to be one thing today and another tomorrow, to hunt in the morning, fish in the afternoon, breed cattle in the evening, criticize after dinner, just as I like."[53] But in later years Marx was forced to recognize: "Labour cannot become a form of play." It would therefore be necessary to limit the time spent in working and to increase leisure time; for only beyond the world of work does "the true realm of freedom begin." But Jürgen Moltmann rightly comments: "Since Marx we have become considerably more resigned at this point, because the history of industrialization—even of socialist industrialization—has shown that an increase in leisure time does not automatically assure an increase in human freedom or better opportunities for self-realization." For this reason (says Moltmann), Herbert Marcuse and other neo-Marxists have returned to the demand of Fourier (rejected by Marx) that the realm of freedom become a reality not alongside but in the realm of necessity, "*in* labour and not merely *beyond* it."[54]

We may not expect, of course, that work will ever become play in the sense of being an activity that may be taken up and set aside at will. But the concept of play reflected in this assertion is no less extreme than the concept of a work world that is stripped of all elements of play. Both concepts have come into existence because the world of modern life has been emptied of meaning. A combination of economic and bureaucratic rationality has gained the upper hand, with the result that religion, along with all the other functions of life that are meaningful in the narrower sense of the term and not simply ordered to rational goals, has been forced into the private sphere and subjected to the principle of arbitrary choice. In consequence, the concept of play too had been emptied.

But a reduction to arbitrary play-acting misses the real nature and point of play. Every developed form of play (beginning with the symbolic games

[53]K. Marx, *The German Ideology*. tr. in L. D. Easton and K. H. Guddat, eds., *Writings of the Young Marx on Philosophy and Society* (Garden City, N.Y., 1967; Anchor Books ed.), 425.
[54]Moltmann, 72, citing Marx, *Das Kapital* III, 873f., and H. Marcuse, *Versuche über die Befreiung* (1969), 40f.

and role-playing of children), and especially every form of regulated communal play, requires a self-commitment from the players so that the game can develop and display its inner *telos*. As a result, the capacity for play that is engendered by liberation from the compulsions of nature is put in the service of a higher necessity. It is thence that play derives its own peculiar seriousness, its order and discipline. This order and discipline are distinguished from those required by the modern world of work, in that their object is experienced as meaningful in itself, so that the time devoted to play is a time of fulfillment for the players. For this reason, even though play requires effort and discipline it is experienced as being an end in itself, whereas work and its object are often felt to be only a means to an end, and in particular a means of earning a livelihood.

If, however, work can be conceived and carried out as an end in itself, it ceases to be an imposed and oppressive compulsion and becomes a form of play. In order for this to happen, it is not necessary that the object of the activity have its end completely in itself. It is enough that the activity and its object be seen as a manifestation of a goal that carries its own justification and gives human existence its content. Then human beings will feel free in their activity, and the activity, exercised in the consciousness of freedom, will become a game, as Sartre says (above, at n. 20).

In adults, unlike children, this state of freedom can be realized only to a limited degree in activities that individuals carry on by themselves. A child, absorbed in its symbolic games or role-playing, can play entirely by itself; precisely then the perfection of its play world remains undisturbed. But even in older children, priority is given to team play, which is successful only where there is mutual agreement and mutual observance of the rules. In the case of adults, only the meaning that flows from personal activities performed together with others can mediate the full consciousness of freedom. Therefore the roles undertaken in communal play can be played with a role distance that is mutually guaranteed and claimed, because, after all, the toy played with and the real object of the game—life itself—are not identical. On the other hand, the consciousness of freedom is not given by role distance as such.[55] In the case of a successful

---

[55]Sartre's concept of freedom in his *Kritik der dialektischen Vernunft* (1960; German tr., 1967), 485ff., where he develops it by using the example of the collaboration between members of a football team (on this see Gisi [n. 20, above], 160ff.), is interpreted by Gisi in a one-sided way as referring to the distance maintained from the role being played (Gisi, 187f., with D. Claessens). The game, Gisi says, is "a symbol of freedom because the result is still open in the form of a future to be shaped" (194). But in fact Sartre bases the freedom made accessible to individuals in their interaction with the group on the common *goal* being sought (*Kritik*, 487f.; see 491, 540ff., 580). Gisi has probably failed to take this into account, because this interaction is also the basis for conflict between the group and the individual's perception of the group's goal (Sartre, 617ff.) and for the ultimate loss of freedom through an institutional reification of the group's unity (Gisi, 167f., on Sartre, 641). But this dialectic

communal game, this consciousness is, rather, based on an agreement that finds expression both in the identification with the roles in question (it is in their collaboration that the agreement manifests itself) and in the distance from them (since what is at issue is the game in its entirety).

In the real life of society, interaction with others is usually disturbed by conflict and compulsion. This is the more profound reason why work cannot easily turn into play and why there must be scope, outside the everyday world, for interaction that is free of care. At the same time, however, communal play need not have a place only alongside the world of work, as compensation for the privations the latter brings. It can also become a model for a more authentic form of everyday communal life. This may be the deeper reason why games have been held in connection . with the high points of public life, as in the case of the medieval tourneys, the Olympic games in their original form, and the sporting and musical competitions held in connection with the Panathenaeas. In particular, however, the function of games as model determines the cultic representation of the mythical order that is the foundation of cosmos and society. Cultic drama is not, of course, a game in the sense of a bit of arbitrary pretense. It is a game in the sense of a ritual representation and symbol of a world of meaning which is complete in itself and in which everyday life participates through the cultic drama.

The cultic realm of ritual play that represents the mythical order stands apart, with its feasts and festivals, from the world of the everyday.[56] Only

---

cannot be avoided by a formalistic theory of the collaboration of individuals that neglects the consciousness of meaning which unites them. The limitation of Sartre's analysis consists in the fact that the unity of the consciousness of meaning is thematized only in the form of a shared *goal;* in itself the sharing of a goal makes unavoidable a conflict between individuals (attainment of the goal through individual praxis) and the unity of the group, because the category of goal must constantly be reduced to the praxis of individuals. It must, rather, be said, therefore, that the shared world is based on a shared consciousness of meaning by which determinate goals must in turn be justified. It is possible for individual players on the team to adopt their own perspective in cooperating for the purpose of the common game. But the community that results from the merger (via Sartre's "oath") is on another level: that of the consciousness of meaning as an end in itself, and of the game as its representation.

[56]To that extent a festivity is in "contrast" to the everyday world, as Cox insists (23). But this contrast is not to be interpreted as meaning excess, as Cox claims (22f.). For then a festivity would simply be a compensatory reaction against the everyday world. Excesses may appear as concomitant phenomena in a festivity, and especially in festal joy, but if they gain the upper hand, they will eventually destroy the festivity. Festal joy has its true basis, not in a temporary suspension of the order of everyday life (see Moltmann, *Theology and Joy,* 32), but in the elevating feeling of living a moment of life that is exceptional in its meaning and of being in the presence of festally celebrated meaning that cannot be indifferently reduced to a mere "occasion" for celebration without stripping of its depth the affirmation of life which Cox, following J. Pieper, rightly regards as the decisive characteristic of a festivity (see Cox, 47; J. Pieper, *In Tune with the World: A Theory of Festivity,* trans. R. and C. Winston [New York, 1965]).

through this apartness can cult portray the order of the cosmos as a world complete in itself in which evil and suffering have been overcome. Everyday life never presents itself as this kind of completely meaningful world. Cultic drama ignores the proportions found in everyday human reality both on the side of terror and in the bright tones of goodness and justice. This is not due solely to the fact that the myth which cult represents and renders present tells of the activity and fortunes of God and the gods. It is also true that the passions and fortunes of the personages of tragic drama far exceed the limited proportions of everyday human reality. Precisely for this reason drama can turn into a theater depicting the world, and cult can provide the framework within which to interpret the meaning of everyday life.

The totality of meaning that is rendered present in religious feasts and that grounds the order of the cosmos and society gives meaning to the everyday routines and fortunes of individuals as well as to the order of the everyday world. In the light of that totality of meaning these other things are given solidity and also put right. By means of ritual celebrations and feasts the administration of law, important political events, but also the various phases of the activity of farmers and craftsmen, as well as the segments of individuals' lives, are linked to the universal order that sustains society and, in the final analysis, has a religious basis and is celebrated in cult. Thus a reflection of the perfection proper to sacred play falls upon the everyday world. How different from the modern work world with its secularity that has been stripped of any presence of complete meaning!

Given the inevitable generality of anthropological reflection, the picture just drawn of the significance of cultic play for the world of culture as a whole applies first and foremost to the prebiblical religions and cultures. But despite the special character of the biblical religions and, above all, despite the experience, so fundamental to them, of the historical action of God, which also determines the special character of their liturgies, what I have said applies in its generality even to them. The basic structures of mythical consciousness are not simply eliminated and suppressed by the historical experience proper to faith; rather, they are transformed and retained.[57] Even the Christian liturgy is still a sacred play[58] at the center of which is the supper that sums up the ministry and destiny

[57]See my essay "Christentum und Mythos" (1972), now in *Grundfragen systematischer Theologie* II (1980), 13–65, esp. 60ff.

[58]See R. Guardini, *The Spirit of the Liturgy*, trans. A. Lane (London, 1930), 85ff., as well as H. Rahner's remarks on the context of this theme in the patristic vision of the "playing of the Church," in his *Man at Play*, trans. B. Battershaw and E. Quinn (London, 1965), 46ff. On the Evangelical side, however, only hesitatingly and rather in passing does P. Brunner (n. 41, above) raise the question of whether the liturgy with its "combination of constraint and freedom," which is analogous to that found in art, can perhaps also be "understood from the vantage point of play." "Or ought the way in which the liturgy is performed be thought

of Jesus and links the created reality of human beings and their social life with their eschatological destiny. For the community that remembers Jesus and awaits his future, that supper becomes here and now a meal shared with him; by means of it, Christians' lives and their world are made part of the history of Jesus Christ. For this reason the celebration of the supper of Jesus includes the praise of the community. In this they anticipate the song of the angels who praise and glorify God and the song of the eschatological community of those who have reached the goal. Undismayed by present appearances, they also glorify God's righteousness as manifested in his conquest—still incomplete here on earth—of sin and death.

The subject of play has turned us from individuals and their concern with identity (although this theme itself is located within the horizon of the social relations of individuals) to the life-world which individuals share. In play, human beings put into practice that being-outside-themselves to which their exocentricity destines them. The process begins with the symbolic games of children and finds its completion in worship.

I should not fail to mention here that the ecstasy characteristic of play also conceals demonic possibilities;[59] this is a point to which I must return later. The world of the religions offers abundant examples of this truth. Yet in this area as in others demonic distortion does not simply ruin God's creation. When judged in the light of God's revelation in Jesus Christ, the cultic life of the religions is not marked exclusively by idolatry; it also expresses, even if in sometimes extremely alien forms, a praise of the divine creative power and of the divine conquest of evil which, according to Christians, is accomplished by the cross of Christ.

It can be said, then, that cultic play is the organizing center of the shared human world and of its unity. Such a statement presupposes a perception of the mythical meaning in which the order of the everyday world

---

of as akin to the childlike play in which Wisdom engages on earth and in the presence of God (Prov. 8:29–31)?" (295). See at an earlier date Guardini, 98, on the same passage from Proverbs. If we pursue this thought which Brunner only suggests and does not follow up, the salvation-historical activity of the divine Logos (the Wisdom of God) from creation on via reconciliation to the future consummation of the world will be seen as a divine game which is symbolically replayed in the liturgy. On this point, see the patristic interpretations of the biblical passage as discussed in Rahner, 19ff. See also H. E. Bahr, *Poiesis* (n. 59, below), 92f.; in addition, see O. Seydel, "Spiel und Ritual. Überlegungen zur Reform des Gottesdienstes," *Wissenschaft und Praxis in Kirche und Gesellschaft* 60 (1971), 507–15. According to Moltmann, 47ff., however, "the cross of Christ does not belong to the game itself, but it makes possible the new game of freedom" (53). Does not this observation rest on an all too innocuous conception of play? It is not without reason that the roots of tragic drama are to be found in the fate of Dionysus!

[59]H. E. Bahr, *Poiesis. Theologische Untersuchung der Kunst* (1961; pocket-book ed., 1965), 93ff.

is grounded,[60] although at the same time this meaning needs further clarification and correction. This means that in its function as a basis for culture, play is closely connected with specifically human intelligence and with language. Together these lay the foundations of the shared human world.

III. Language as Medium of the Spirit

The meaning of reality is the common theme of language and reason. In language, meaning achieves presentation, and by means of its expression in language it is communicated. Reason, on the other hand, detaches the content of meaning from its linguistic form. It is able to do this because it precedes language and speech, even though it remains dependent on language as the medium for presenting meaning.

Language and reason are so fundamental for human beings that they might claim the right to be discussed early on in a study of anthropology and not only now in the framework of cultural anthropology. Language and reason are specific to the human being as a biological entity. But in the final analysis the same can be said of culture, if it is correct to say that humans are by nature cultural beings,[61] since human drives with their nonspecialized openness to the world and their exceptional dependence on the security given by society need direction from a cultural order that transcends the world of nature. It is precisely in this respect that language and reason are closely involved in the development of culture; for both transcend the naturally given inasmuch as they grasp and name its essence. The adaptation of human beings to nature and the appropriation of nature for human use mean the reorganization of nature that we call culture. The transformative processing of nature is, of course, only one aspect of culture, not the whole of it, for the concept of culture also includes the purpose of this processing, namely, the integration of nature into the order of the shared world.

The early cultures took the opposite view of the situation. Their myths see the order of the natural cosmos as the model for the world of society. As a matter of fact, however, in their unified vision of the cosmic and social orders they have moved beyond the natural realities of their world into the realm of culture.

Language and reason, which operates in the medium of language, are fundamental in this advance into culture. Scholars have disagreed on whether language itself is to be regarded as a component of culture or is,

---

[60]On the much-discussed question of the relation between myth and ritual, see my essay "Christentum und Mythos" (n. 57, above), 16f.

[61]See the statement of M. Sahlins, above, in chapter 4, at n. 11.

rather, to be taken as a presupposition for the formation of culture.[62] In any case, language is fundamental in all areas of cultural life. Any discussion of the foundations of culture must therefore devote special attention to language. But the question of the cultural importance of thought and reason is inseparable from the question of language. This is clear from, if nothing else, the claims of linguistic relativism, according to which the language of a given culture already implies its determinate view of the world and thereby simultaneously supplies and limits the horizon of the thinking that develops in that culture.

1. Language and Thought

In his *Einführung in die Sprachphilosophie* (Introduction to the philosophy of language), E. Heintel correctly observes that in our time philosophy "has concerned itself with language as never before in its history."[63] In fact, the philosophy of language today may claim the foundational philosophical role which an earlier age assigned to the theory of knowledge. In a sense this represents a reversal of the development that began with what the Platonic Socrates says at the end of the *Cratylus* about the philosophical knowledge of essences being independent of the ambiguities and contentiousness of words (*Cratylus* 438d-g; 439a), and that by way of Aristotle and the Stoics determined the course of Western thought.

This reversal was begun by Ernst Cassirer. In his philosophy of symbolic forms, which was presented as a critical "phenomenology of the spirit,"[64] Cassirer traced the development of consciousness which by its nature (contrary to what Henri Bergson claimed, ET III, 36ff.) objectivizes itself and only in its objectification achieves self-awareness. Consequently, the intuition of the human person as an individual being comes only at the end of this journey as "the mature fruit of a creative process in which all the diverse energies of the spirit are at work and acting reciprocally on one another" (ET 91). Since only by way of language and myth does the

---

[62]For E. Voegelin's criticism of the introduction of language into the concept of culture and for the discussion this criticism launched, see Kroeber and Kluckhohn (n. 2, above), 115ff.

[63]E. Heintel, *Einführung in die Sprachphilosophie* (1972), 7.

[64]In describing his philosophy of symbolic forms, Cassirer expressly claims to adopt "the standpoint of a universal phenomenology of the spirit": *Philosophie der symbolischen Formen* (3 vols.; Berlin, 1923, 1925, 1929; 3d ed., 1958), III, 92, see 64; ET: *The Philosophy of Symbolic Forms*, trans. R. Manheim (New Haven, 1953, 1955, 1957), citation from III, 78. [I shall give the references to the German text, adding the page in the ET for quotations that I have been able to track down.—Tr.] The page references that follow in the text are to this work (German page reference, followed by English page reference).

process lead to a scientific consciousness of the world, conceptual and exact knowledge proves to be dependent on those original "basic forms of symbolic perception"[65]—and dependent on language in particular, although in Cassirer's view the dependence cannot affect the validity of conceptual thought but refers only to its genesis.

The philosophy of Heidegger shows a more radical shift from the primacy of independent thought to a primacy of language. In his *Being and Time,* Heidegger still presented language as the expression of prior thought.[66] Accordingly, "discourse is the Articulation of [the] intelligibility" (203–4; German 161) of previously understood meanings and contexts of meaning: "To signification, words accrue" (204; German 161). But in his later writings Heidegger reverses his position on this question: now it is language that makes thinking possible. Human beings are "admitted to the essence of language."[67] Language "signals" to us "the essence of a thing." The "claim to accede to the essence of a thing" can (Heidegger now writes) "be derived only from where it is received, and human beings receive it from the address of language." Human beings are not to act "as though they were the creators and masters of language, since in fact she remains the mistress of human beings. . . . For in truth it is language that speaks. Human beings speak only when and to the extent that they co-respond to language by listening to her call."[68]

Expressions such as these are reminiscent of J. G. Hamann's idea of the language of God as spoken in all things. Hamann derived this idea from the biblical belief that the essences of all things have their ground in the divine word: "Every manifestation of nature was a word—the sign, symbol and pledge of a new, secret, and therefore all the more intimate and profound union, sharing, and communion in the divine energies and

---

[65]Cassirer, *Philosophie* III, 55ff.; see 137ff., 238ff., 383ff., on the relation between language and thought. But Cassirer is at every point concerned that thought should "free itself from the constraint of the word" and "become independent of it" (384; ET 329). It is, above all, in its presentation in mathematical form that thought "detach[es] itself from the native soil . . . of language" (398; ET 341). Cassirer should therefore not be lumped together with L. Weisgerber and B. L. Whorf as advocates of a dependence of thought on language. See G. Seebass, *Das Problem von Sprache und Denken* (1981), 200ff.; the citation from the Preface (p. IX) of vol. I of *Philosophie* which Seebass gives on 202, n. 202, does not justify such an objection and classification. Weisgerber admittedly puts himself with Cassirer in his *Muttersprache und Geistesbildung* (1929), 109ff., but he also queries Cassirer's statements with regard precisely to the critical independence of science from language (111).

[66]M. Heidegger, *Being and Time,* trans. J. Macquarrie and E. Robinson (New York, 1962), sect. 31ff. (188–211; German 142–67). The two page references that follow in the text are to this book.

[67]M. Heidegger, *Unterwegs zur Sprache* (1959), 266.

[68]M. Heidegger, *Vorträge und Aufsätze* (1954), 190.

ideas."[69] Heidegger differs from Hamann, however, in that language comes to human beings not through the incarnate Word but through the inspiration of the poets. The hiddenness of being, as understood by Heidegger, is not due to sin, as is the hiddenness of God's presence in creation according to Christian teaching. According to this teaching, God's presence is hidden only from sinners, and this in such a way that the hiddenness cannot be removed by the discourse of the poets but only by the expiatory death of Christ, who atones for sin so that human beings may once again be able to hear God's discourse in creation. But despite this profound difference Heidegger's understanding of language is at one with Hamann's to the extent that both men regard language as a more than human reality and not simply as a human product.

This conception of language makes it difficult to accept Heidegger's views as it does those of Hamann. Herder, in his prize essay on the origin of language (1772), which initiated the development of the modern German philosophy of language, was already turning against, above all, a supernaturalist interpretation of the origin of language and was endeavoring instead to render plausible the idea that human beings themselves had invented language. He even appealed to the Bible, which "evidently assigns language a human beginning in the naming of the animals" (see Gen. 2:19f.). The claim that language originated immediately in God actually belittles God, whose greatness really emerges precisely in the human creation of language, since the human soul "acts as a creator and an image of God's being when it forms for itself this activity of reason."[70] At the same time, however, Herder maintained the view that "not even the least use of reason is possible without a distinguishing mark," so that while language originates in the disposition to reason, it "follows quite naturally from the initial act of reason" and is at the basis of all further activity of reason.[71]

[69]*Hamanns Schriften,* ed. F. Roth, IV, 33. Only as a consequence of sin has God's creation become a dead mechanical world for human beings, so that the incarnation of the Word became, in the crucified Jesus, a self-emptying in the form of a slave. See W. Leibrecht, "*Philologia crucis.* Joh. Georg Hamanns Gedanken über die Sprache Gottes," *KuD* 1 (1955), 226–42.

[70]J. G. Herder, *Sprachphilosophische Schriften,* ed. E. Heintel (PhB 248; 1964²), 86f. [I have not been able to find these two short passages in the English translation (next note); Gen. 2:19 is cited, however, on p. 131.—Tr.]

[71]Herder, *Essay on the Origin of Language,* in J. J. Rousseau and J. G. Herder, *On the Origin of Language,* trans. J. H. Moran and A. Gode (New York, 1967), 120. See 116f. (on the invention of language through the discovery of the distinguishing mark) and 112f. (on the conception of reason as a disposition to be developed). It is along these lines that most of Herder's statements on the question of the priority between language and thought—which Seebass, 40f., describes as "contradictory"—are to be explained.

The conception of language as a human invention instead of a supernatural gift of God thus did not exclude the priority of language over thinking. As the most primordial product of reason, language does not precede reason absolutely, but it does precede all further acts of thought. Wilhelm von Humboldt expressed himself along similar lines. As the "creative organ of thought," language presupposes the "intellectual activity" which finds "external" expression by means of it. On the other hand, language is "a necessary condition of thinking" for the individual, and this even when the individual is "completely isolated."[72] Just as no concept is possible without language, so too "the whole range of subjective perception of objects" finds expression in language; consequently, "every language contains a characteristic view of the world."[73]

This famous statement of Humboldt became the point of departure for what is called linguistic relativity, which sees a culture's characteristic conception of the world as already mapped out for it by the special character of its language. As a result, this characteristic conception is simply rendered explicit by thought, or at least the conception "channels" thought. L. Weisgerber and his school have been the chief proponents of this thesis in Germany; in America it has been developed in the ethnolinguistics of Edward Sapir and his disciple Benjamin L. Whorf.[74] Bruno Snell's interpretation of the development of Greek thought comes close to it,[75] as does Thorlief Boman's contrast between Hebrew thought and Greek thought, since this is based at every point on peculiarities of the Hebrew language.[76]

Admittedly, Boman does regard the Hebrew language as an "expression" of the specifically Hebrew way of thinking, rather than explain the

---

[72]W. von Humboldt, *Über die Verschiedenheiten des menschlichen Sprachbaues* (1827–29), *Werke* III (Schriften zur Sprachphilosophie), ed. A. Flitner and K. Giel, 191 (see 223, 426) and 195f.

[73]Ibid., 223 and 224.

[74]L. Weisgerber, *Muttersprache und Geistesbildung* (1929). B. L. Whorf, *Language, Thought, and Reality,* ed. J. B. Carroll (New York, 1956). For more recent developments, see H. Gipper, *Gibt es ein sprachliches Relativitätsprinzip? Untersuchungen zur Sapir-Whorf-Hypothese* (1972). See also Gipper's *Denken ohne Sprache?* (1971). Among the philosophers, K. O. Apel (e.g., *Die Idee der Sprache in der Tradition des Humanismus von Dante bis Vico,* 1963) and J. Lohmann (*Philosophie und Sprachwissenschaft,* 1965) have proposed similar views, while F. von Kutschera (*Sprachphilosophie,* 1971, 1975², 289–344) inclines to this position in the limited sense of claiming that there is "no priority of language over thought" (339).

[75]B. Snell, *Die Entdeckung des Geistes. Studien zur Entstehung des europäischen Denkens bei den Griechen* (1946; 1955³), especially the essay on "Die naturwissenschaftliche Begriffsbildung im Griechischen" (299ff.). (In the ET of the 2d ed. of 1948: *The Discovery of the Mind: The Greek Origins of European Thought,* trans. T. G. Rosenmeyer [Cambridge, Mass., 1953], ch. 10, "The Origin of Scientific Thought.")

[76]Th. Boman, *Hebrew Thought Compared with Greek,* trans. J. L. Moreau (London, 1960).

thinking as a function of the language. Nonetheless, in responding to the criticism of James Barr he appeals especially to the support of the linguistic relativists.[77] Barr, for his part, doubts that the formal peculiarities of a language, its special grammatical structures, and its lexical resources express, much less determine, the thinking peculiar to a culture, because he considers that ideas are expressed not in grammatical forms nor in vocabulary but only in sentences. It is this which allows a statement to be translated into another language.[78]

The fact that translation is possible does indeed militate against the rigid form of linguistic relativity. The mother tongue of individuals does not impose a certain direction on their thinking in the sense of channeling it, although it must be admitted that the structure and vocabulary of a language do embody certain emphases in the linguistic community's experience of the world and that these suggest certain modes of representation rather than others to the individuals using the language.[79] But a much greater influence along these lines is exerted by the convictions that dominate in certain phases of a culture's development. These convictions are not explicable in the light of the structure and vocabulary of the language; they do, however, themselves lead to shifts in the meanings of words and thus in the associations linked with such words. The linguistic relativists greatly underestimate this influence of ideas on the development of a language.

The thesis that thought depends on language has also been ascribed to Noam Chomsky's idea of a universal generative transformational gram-

---

[77]Th. Boman, *Sprache und Denken. Eine Auseinandersetzung* (1968) = 5th ed. of *Hebrew Thought* (n. 76, above), 194–231, esp. 197, 203f. On the basic relation between thought and language, see 200. The response to the critics is addressed chiefly to J. Barr, *The Semantics of Biblical Language* (Oxford, 1961).

[78]Barr, 263f., see 268f. This essentially correct judgment of the situation is also the basis of Barr's criticism of the theological conception behind the *Theologisches Wörterbuch zum Neuen Testament* (ET: *Theological Dictionary of the New Testament*), in which he likewise sees an attempt to represent the vocabulary of the New Testament (and not, rather, the sentences formulated with the aid of it) as the vessel of revelation (206–61). According to M. Black too, the possibility of translation from one language to another renders the thesis of linguistic relativity "highly dubious": "Linguistic Relativity: The Views of Benjamin Lee Whorf" (1958), reprinted in his *Models and Metaphors: Studies in Language and Philosophy* (Ithaca, N.Y., 1962), 244–57 at 249. H. Gipper, *Gibt es ein sprachliches Relativitätsprinzip?* (n. 74, above), is able to meet this objection only by greatly weakening the linguistic relativity position (88ff.). There is, of course, no denying that translation does become more difficult as the languages in question are farther apart.

[79]Same idea in Seebass (n. 65, above), 235f., 240. But, according to Seebass, even Whorf, despite his exaggerated statements about the thinking of individuals being "controlled by inexorable laws of pattern" embodied in a language, does not regard the limits thereby imposed on thought as insuperable. Rather, says Seebass, he saw linguistics as helping "to think straight" so that we might avoid the errors into which "an unconscious acceptance of our linguistic background will otherwise lead us" (21f.; the words of Whorf in the previous sentence are from *Language, Thought, and Reality,* 252).

mar that transcends the differences between the individual languages. What is meant is, of course, not that he correlates thinking with the historical language of the given culture, but rather that he links it with the most universal structures that control the formation of human languages, structures which according to Chomsky must be innate.[80]

But Chomsky's reversion to a Cartesian model according to which the capacity for language is given in innate structures of the human mind is probably to be described more objectively as an intellectualist position that reduces language to the structures of the intellect.[81] In any case, in responding to John R. Searle's critique of his view, Chomsky has expressly accepted the view that we also think without words; introspection makes this clear. Another evidence that Chomsky should not be ranked with the linguistic relativists is the close relation, which he emphasizes, between his own work and Eric H. Lenneberg's study of the biological bases of language. Lenneberg quite explicitly defends a position the direct contrary of linguistic relativity: "that cognitive function is a more basic and primary process than language, and that the dependence-relationship of language on cognition is incomparably stronger than vice versa."[82]

Here we have the thesis, defended by the critics of linguistic relativism, that thinking is independent of language. They regard language as a product and expression of thought. But this view, which is closer to the perspective that has been traditional in the history of Western philosophy, must answer a fundamental objection, namely, that thought, supposedly distinct from and independent of language, can nonetheless be grasped as such only by means of language. For this reason, the argument in particular that introspective consciousness shows the priority of our thinking over its linguistic expression is not conclusive.[83] Other attempts at a direct

[80]The placement of Chomsky among the linguistic relativists—a placement I am here denying—is found in Seebass, 140f. Seebass' judgment seems prompted by the fact that Chomsky's views are linked too closely to those of Kuno Lorenz, *Elemente der Sprachkritik* (1970), 105, 161, and K. Lorenz and J. Mittelstrass, "Die Hintergehbarkeit der Sprache," *Kantstudien* 58 (1967), 204 (see Seebass, 141, n. 145). On the thesis of innateness, see also N. Chomsky, *Reflections on Language* (New York, 1975), 12ff., 29f.

[81]Thus Chomsky asks, "What initial structure must be attributed to the mind that enables it to construct such a grammar from the data of sense?" in his *Language and Mind* (enlarged ed., New York, 1972), 79. According to J. Piaget, *Einführung in die genetische Erkenntnistheorie* (1970; German tr., 1973), 16, "Chomsky claims that logic does not depend on language and is not derived from it and that, on the contrary, language depends on logic and reason. He regards reason in this case as even innate. Perhaps the claim that it is innate goes too far." On the last sentence, see also ibid., 57, and n. 90, below.

[82]E. Lenneberg, *Biological Foundations of Language* (New York, 1967), 374. Lenneberg invokes Chomsky (393), and Chomsky in turn (*Language and Mind*, 93) speaks of his ideas as "closely related" to those of Lenneberg. The remark on thinking without words is in Chomsky's *Reflections on Language*, 57.

[83]See also Seebass, 311ff.

demonstration of thinking as independent of language are likewise more or less dubious, at least to the extent that they seek to exclude any and every connection with language.[84]

On the other hand, the behaviorist reduction of all mental processes to linguistic behavior—a view that even determined the linguistic philosophy of the later Wittgenstein—likewise appears untenable.[85] If, then, it seems at least possible that thinking enjoys a priority over its linguistic expression, the proof that this priority actually exists is most likely to be gained through a study of the origin of language. Such a study must deal, on the one hand, with the ontogenetic conditions required if a child is to learn a language and, on the other, with the phylogenetic conditions required for human language to come into existence at all. In this second area, it is the differences between communication among primates and the formation of language among human beings that must be the point of departure for efforts to retrace the genesis of human language.

I shall restrict myself here to the work of Jean Piaget as an example of how a psychologist analyzes and retraces the steps by which a child acquires a language. I shall also hark back to points made earlier (chapter 5, sec. III, p. 226) and cast my presentation of Piaget's construction in the form of a theological "rereading" that makes explicit, or at least suggests, the religious implications of what I am explaining. The reason for this is that Piaget takes as his starting point the phenomenon described earlier

---

[84]See on this point the detailed critical discussion in Seebass, 371–73. The evidence that thinking is unassociated with language in the case of speech defects does not prove the universal truth (373ff.) any more than efforts to show the dependence of thought on speech by investigation of speech disturbances prove the opposite (240–303).

[85]Seebass, 380–439, is doubtless correct in counting Wittgenstein among the behaviorists (esp. 429; see 384, 126f., 387). The later Wittgenstein (Seebass says) was unable to adopt "a reflective approach to language," because he wanted "to answer philosophical questions by recourse to colloquial speech" and therefore could "not turn this kind of speech itself into a problem" (438). Seebass' decisive argument for the claim that Wittgenstein presents a reduced picture of language (436) is that "the grasp of the complete meaning of sentences" in linguistic communication "cannot be understood in processual terms" (406; see 326 and 408). This necessarily entails the acceptance, disputed by Wittgenstein, of thinking that is distinct from its linguistic expression (408).

On the other hand, the concept of behavior that Wittgenstein presupposes is to be described, with G. H. Mead, as a self-comporting and not simply as behavior that is stimulated solely from outside and does not reach the level of subjectivity (see above, chapter 1, at n. 11, for J. Habermas' critique of the behaviorist explanation of language). E. Tugendhat, *Vorlesungen zur Einführung in die sprachanalytische Philosophie* (1976), 212ff., likewise seeks to distinguish Wittgenstein's understanding of language from that of the behaviorists by appealing to G. H. Mead, that is, by introducing the viewpoint of intersubjective agreement on the meaning of words (257ff.). But does this not presuppose that each partner in communication is already conscious of the constancy of objects and grasps the gestalt of the object in question?

as the symbiotic vital unity between child and mother (organism and environment). In doing so, he does not, however, consistently keep in view the field aspect of this phenomenon. This will be the main criticism I have of Piaget's exposition.

Nonetheless Piaget does consider both the starting point and the goal of child behavior to be the state of "totality" in the relation between organism and environment, a state that is to be described, with Scheler, as one of ecstatic identification, and whose religious significance has already been brought out (pp. 226, 233).[86] The development of the child is thus a process of differentiation in which the totality must be restored at every stage; the totality thus reappears in a constantly new and enriched form—as an element in the joy the child takes in life. It makes its appearance in the repetition of the sucking reflex and in the resultant need of repetition—of a first "generalizing assimilation" that aims at "incorporation" and is soon connected with motor recognition.[87]

The restoration of totality through repetition and assimilation draws the child's attention to itself,[88] and as the child develops, its assimilation is continually enriched and broadened in cumulative steps. In the process each assimilative behavior pattern is again implemented as a totality in which the original totality is renewed and which shows itself in play.[89]

---

[86]Piaget, in his book *The Origin of Intelligence in Children*, trans. M. Cook (New York, 1952; Norton Library paperback, 1963), 9ff., introduces "totality" as a basic category which is to be supplemented and differentiated by the concept of "relationship." Totality functions as both the "ideal" and the "goal" of behavior. On the other hand, totality is also the starting point of development, in the form of the initial nondistinction between subject and object. See also his *The Construction of Reality in the Child*, trans. M. Cook (New York, 1954), and *Nachahmung, Spiel und Traum* (n. 26, above), 31.

[87]Piaget, *The Origin of Intelligence in Children*, 34ff.

[88]E. G. Schachtel, *Metamorphosis: On the Development of Affect, Perception, Attention and Memory* (London, 1963), 251–78: "The Development of Focal Attention and the Emergence of Reality." Schachtel has supplemented Piaget's presentation, to which he refers (257), by pointing out the role of attention, which sets off a part of the field of perception and lets the rest of the field fade out (253). In this context U. Neisser speaks of preattentive processes; see his *Cognitive Psychology* (Englewood Cliffs, N.J., 1967), 86–104: "Focal Attention and Figural Synthesis" (esp. 89ff.). Attention is directed to the whole of the figural unity that is its focal point (160ff.; see also Schachtel, 259ff.). I connect this observation with Piaget's thesis on the significance of the (symbiotic) organism-transcending total experience of life for the development of the child, and I therefore raise the question, not raised by Schachtel and Neisser, of the motives for attention. If we (correctly) find these initially in the child's affective life, our attention is turned once again to the totality of life as present in feeling (see earlier, chapter 5, pp. 220ff.).

[89]Piaget, *The Origin of Intelligence in Children*, chs. 3 and 4. I pass over what Piaget explicitly says, since I am relating his remarks on the fundamental importance of assimilation and accommodation, as functional invariants in the development of the child's intelligence (3ff.), both to the totality motif generally (9) and to its concrete form at any point in the successive phases of development. If this relationship is not made clear, assimilation and accommoda-

Piaget sees the interplay of assimilation and accommodation as developing the potential of an innate intelligence, which, however, acquires its structure only as it is developed.[90]

The beginnings of object constancy also depend on sensorimotor repetition and recognition. This constancy is consolidated from the eighth or ninth month on by coordination of the various schemata of sight, hearing, and touch.[91] This provides a point of attachment for the start of symbolic play at the beginning of the second year of life, for this kind of play depends on the association of properties not directly perceptible in the object but accessible through the activity of the other senses, and thus on what Arnold Gehlen calls "the symbolism of sense perception."[92]

Symbolic play reaches its full development, however, only when "representations" that go beyond the immediate object being played with are attached to this object. Piaget sees representations too as originating in sensorimotor repetition and recognition, insofar as these display a rudi-

---

tion will appear to be simply manifestations of an organism that is *separated* from its environment. This is an interpretation which Piaget not only does not exclude but even suggests by his talk—to be mentioned later—of an "action" even of the childish organism on the environment. Yet such an interpretation is opposed to the viewpoint of totality insofar as at every stage this unites organism and environment in a single experience of life.

[90]Piaget thus distances himself from an interpretation that would introduce an a priori along the lines of "innate ideas," as in transcendental philosophy. This is also what differentiates him from Chomsky (see Chomsky, *Language and Mind,* 93), and Piaget calls it a "mistake" to regard "the *a priori* as consisting in structures existing ready-made from the beginning of development" (*The Origin of Intelligence in Children,* 3). The structures that govern experience must, rather, themselves be developed. "This *a priori* only appears in the form of essential structures at the end of the evolution of concepts and not at their beginning" (ibid.).

[91]Piaget, ibid., chs. 3 and 4. See also *The Construction of Reality in the Child,* ch. 1, sec. 1 (3ff.). The coordination of the sense schemata consolidates object constancy, which starts when the child follows moving objects with its eyes (9). Since this action presupposes the focusing of attention on the object (Schachtel, 256f.), a connection is made in the behavior of the organism between the totality motif and object constancy in the form of a total and abiding objective world; this connection in turn grounds the individual's feeling that the world is trustworthy (Schachtel, 263ff.). According to Piaget, object constancy is fully developed only when the child *looks for* objects that are no longer present in its field of perception (*The Origin of Intelligence in Children,* 210ff.), because at this point it manifests its persuasion that the object, though not perceived, continues to exist (for a different view, see T. G. R. Bower, *Development in Infancy* [San Francisco, 1974]). But this does not yet mean a strictly numerical identity (Seebass, 309f.).

[92]A. Gehlen, *Der Mensch* (1950), 183ff., whose description of how the sensorimotor behavior of the infant prepares the way for language (140ff.), anticipates in many respects the approach and findings of Piaget (see Gehlen, 147, on the "objectivity" of the world of things). See also Piaget, *The Origin of Intelligence in Children,* 190ff.; Piaget also notes, however, that there can be no question of symbols in the proper sense of the term before the appearance of mental representations in the second year of life (191). See his *Nachahmung, Spiel und Traum,* 90ff., 131.

mentary form of imitation that ultimately leads, via the repetition of the movements of others (made possible by coordination of the various sense schemata from the eighth or ninth month on), to deferred imitation which Piaget finds operative at the age of sixteen months. This deferred imitation is intelligible only on the supposition that memory images are present in the form of representations.[93]

The child then also associates these images with the object of its play; they become bound up with this object, so that they are now represented by it. With it are then linked sounds as well, which initially are as much commands as names. Only later on is the command element in the sound directed principally to the child's own memory, so that henceforth the sound replaces the object being played with, evokes the associated meaning, and represents for the individual the objectivity of objects (an objectivity that has meanwhile been placed on a sure footing). This development is promoted by the social character of language; this social character makes central the representational function of words, since the shared "objective" world, to which words refer, becomes the medium of communication through speech.[94]

[93]Piaget, *Nachahmung. Spiel und Traum.* 84f. The fact that representations are a postulate is missed in H. G. Furth's presentation of Piaget's argument in his *Denkprozesse ohne Sprache* (1966), 187f. The result is an inadequate behaviorist interpretation of Piaget which eliminates representations (202ff.) or at least reduces them to deferred imitation (188), instead of accepting them as presuppositions. See Piaget, *Einführung in die genetische Erkenntnistheorie.* 55 ("interior pictures" as "internalized imitation").

An especially penetrating and nuanced critique of the assumption of representations in the context of object-knowledge is given by Tugendhat, *Vorlesungen* (n. 85, above), 86ff., 184ff. As far as the linguistic reference to objects is concerned, Tugendhat rightly says that the reference is to objects, not to representations of objects, and this in the sense that we *intend* the objects. One may, of course, try also to represent to oneself in a concrete way an object that one intends (88), but then the intention of the object is presupposed by the representation of it, and not vice versa.

Nonetheless the intention, in language, of an *absent* object could require as a condition that we be able to connect a representation of the object with the word referring to it. How otherwise could a word or sentence be anything more for us than a series of sounds or sound sequences? Tugendhat has not succeeded in showing (184ff., 201ff.) that the possibility of linking words with representations is irrelevant. An explanation of words by examples instead of by the assumption of something which retains its identical form and for which the words "stand" (206) can itself be successful only if I can in each instance "connect a representation" with that which is intended in the examples. Moreover, it is indeed correct to say that the assumption of representations cannot explain the intersubjective validity of the meanings of words (356), since only the one doing the representing has the representations. Nonetheless the analogous development of object constancy in particular individuals (along the lines described by Piaget) may be a condition required if individuals are to turn the words of a language into representations in a correspondingly analogous way.

[94]Piaget, *Nachahmung. Spiel und Traum.* 116f., 127ff. On socialization through language, 131ff.; on the change of words from commands to representative meanings in the context of play, 283f.

According to Piaget, then, a child develops its thought processes through its sensorimotor interaction with the environment and this development clearly precedes the acquisition of language.[95] The evidence he offers merits our assent.[96] This signifies to me that the development of the religious thematic also precedes the acquisition of language and plays a constitutive role in this acquisition. The religious thematic in the development described by Piaget is latent in the totality motif. Piaget himself has not thematized the religious implications of this motif, because he has not paid attention to the totality thematic as a field. The result of this neglect is certain distortions in the overall picture drawn of the child's development. One distortion that has particularly serious consequences is that in his very first view of the developmental stage in which the child is still a suckling he speaks not only (with justification) of "behavior," but in the same breath also of "actions,"[97] as though the suckling were already an independent entity in facing its environment. But such an interpretation of the child is contradicted by what developmental psychology has to tell us about the initial "symbiotic" phase in the development of children.

Piaget is also unclear when, in speaking of the totality aspect of childish behavioral schemata, he says that there is a question in these of modifications of the unity of organism and environment and not simply of vital action that is detached from its environment. The problem seems to be also connected with the use of the categories of assimilation and accommodation, which seem unconsciously to presuppose that the childish organism is more independent, and the environment more external to the organism, than can be assumed on the basis of the other knowledge we have from developmental psychology regarding the experience of the child. The same holds, finally, for the idea (queried by Chr. Bühler) of a childish "egocentricity," since it is hardly possible to speak of egocentricity in the psychological sense (i.e., with reference to the child's own experience) as long as there is not yet present an ego that is clearly distinct from the environment.[98]

<hr/>

[95]Piaget, *Einführung in die genetische Erkenntnistheorie,* 50f.; see 28f.

[96]When Seebass writes this off as a mere "pseudo-proof" for the independence of language from the identification of objects (307ff.), he does so as a result of exaggerated expectations of what a proof should be. He (correctly) gives a negative answer to the question whether the researches of Piaget and Bower have shown that the children they tested had the concept not only of qualitative sameness but that of numerical identity as well, "without which there can be no talk of a concept of object" (309). However, he overlooks the fact that even in the early forms of speech the distinction between individual and generality is at least uncertain; see Piaget, *Nachahmung, Spiel und Traum,* 287f. See also Cassirer, *Philosophie der symbolischen Formen* (n. 64, above), I, 253ff.

[97]Piaget, *The Origin of Intelligence in Children,* 41, 43f., etc. The applicability of the concept of behavior is discussed on 40f.

If Piaget had taken more careful account of these problems, he would not have felt obliged to regard as something so utterly new the initial integration of the child's behavior and its own body (beginning with the hand, which the child observes in the act of grasping) into a world stabilized by the development of object constancy.[99] Nor would he have regarded as utterly new the socialization that starts with the development of language, since in fact the initial symbiotic integration into the surrounding human world simply acquires a new and more differentiated form thereby.

Attention to the religious implications of the theme of symbiotic totality in early childhood development also makes possible a more profound understanding of children's symbolic play and of symbols generally (including the symbol that is the human word) as the presence of reality and its order; it is the same presence that finds a different expression in myth and cult (see above, this chapter, at n. 30). For this reason too, the "mythical" and "animistic" traits seen as children develop language during the period of intuitive thinking (fourth to seventh year) need not be interpreted simply as the expression of a lack, that is, of the still lacking distinction between subjective and objective reality.[100] It can also be interpreted as the expression, admittedly still not clarified, of a sense of

---

[98]Piaget in *Nachahmung, Spiel und Traum*, 285, rejects Chr. Bühler's criticism (in *Kindheit und Jugend* [1928³] 163) of his concept of the child's egocentrism, with the remark that she understands this concept differently than he does. But he owes an explanation of the objective situation represented by the word. Although it can be said that human behavior is in fact (therefore for the impartial observer) related to the center which is the self and takes its direction from this, there is still need of explaining what this really means in relation, on the one hand, to the child's early symbiotic union with its mother and, on the other, to the development, which comes only later, of the child's own ego as distinct from its surroundings. I spoke earlier (chapter 3, sec. III, pp. 106ff.) of the human being as characterized by egocentricity and a centralist organization which find their expression in the perspectivity given by the experience of space and time. But these attributes are at every point already in tension with the other basic attribute that must be predicated of human life: its exocentricity. By contrast, Piaget seems to acknowledge only egocentricity at the beginning of human development, and he has this being suppressed, at the point when language is acquired, by an integration into the objective and social world. Christian anthropology must, on the contrary, assert the persistence of the tension between exocentricity and centrality.

[99]Piaget, *The Construction of Reality in the Child*, 86. By learning to integrate its own body into the solid world of objects, "the child ends by completely reversing his initial universe, whose moving images were centered on an activity unconscious of itself." But is it possible to speak of a reversal if the child was unconscious of this initial centering on its own activity and if even now it is as yet by no means conscious? And is the experienced integration of its own body into the environing world—made up of the persons and objects to which it relates—comparable to the preceding unconscious centeredness of its behavior? Are not the levels described too diverse to permit of direct comparison?

[100]Piaget, *Nachahmung, Spiel und Traum*, 310ff., 316ff., esp. 323. See also *The Construction of Reality in the Child*, ch. 2, *passim*.

the religious depth dimension of reality as a spiritual field that takes concrete form in the child's own experience. Sensitivity to this dimension is not merely a sign of incompleteness and of a defect in the child's development. It is also the manifestation of a sense of reality that unfortunately often atrophies in the later phases of development, not least because of a deficient religious education, and yields its place to a rationality that admits no mystery.

The phylogenetic problem of the origins of language makes clear the extent to which the emergence of language from initial intelligent contacts with the environment leads us to the relation between language and religion. A discussion of this theme must start with the question of the peculiar nature of linguistic communication among human beings as compared with prelinguistic forms of communication in the animal world and especially among the primates.

Until a few years ago the difference that the ability to speak made between human beings and their closest relatives in the animal world still seemed far more radical than can be claimed today. It is true that ever since Wolfgang Köhler's report on the intelligence tests given to anthropoids (1921) we have been aware that these, and especially the chimpanzees, were capable of lofty feats of practical intelligence, including even the use of tools. But human conceptual thought, and therefore human conceptual language, seemed to be a closed world to them. The "animal languages"—as, for example, the famous "dance language" of the bees and in fact the whole realm of communication through gestures—were rightly regarded as languages made up of signals, which, despite the inchoative presence of symbolic functions, are fundamentally different from human language with its predicative structure. Signals are directed to eliciting a behavioral response; human language refers to objects which it names by means of words and of which it "predicates" properties or activities. Thus as late as 1961, F. Kainz could conclude that the term "language" means "something radically different" as applied to the forms of communication among various species of animals and to the language of human beings.[101] Any talk of animal languages is a metaphor and nothing more.

The situation has, however, changed radically since the astonishingly successful efforts of Allen and Beatrice Gardner (1969) to teach young chimpanzees the system of signs used in the American language of the deaf and to communicate with them thereby.[102] In particular, the experiments

---

[101]F. Kainz, *Die "Sprache" der Tiere* (1961), 279. See the detailed discussion of Kainz's views in Heintel, *Einführung in die Sprachphilosophie* (n. 63, above), 185ff., esp. 194ff.

[102]On this, see D. Ploog, "Kommunikation in Affengesellschaften und deren Bedeutung für die Verständigungsweisen der Menschen," in H. G. Gadamer and P. Vogler, eds., in vol. 2 (1972) of Neue Anthropologie, 98–178, esp. 157–67; also H. Autrum, "Sprechen,

of David Premack (1971) with his young female chimpanzee Sarah seem to show that there is present at least in an inchoative form the capacity for using a sign language in a predicative way.[103] The specifically human element in language is therefore not to be sought in its intellectual basis but rather in the human capacity for forming sounds or, more accurately, the human capacity for controlling the formation of sounds and thus achieving articulation.[104] It may not be asserted, however, that the further step from sign language to the formation of a culture is impossible in principle.[105] It is simply the case that in fact this step does not seem to have been taken by societies of apes living in the wild, although at least chimpanzees have at their disposal intellectual abilities of which (as far as we know at the present time) they make no use in communicating among themselves. Neither vocal signals nor gestures seem to be used by them for purposes of naming. But what is lacking seems to be less the capacity than the need to apply it. One scholar has therefore rightly urged us "not to treat even human language as an isolated feat but rather to investigate the psychobiological connections of this supreme means of communication."[106]

It follows from all of this that the development of intelligence and thought is phylogenetically prior to the acquisition of language and even today is inchoatively present in the primates, where it is unaccompanied by language. It is also true, of course, that the passage to the use of predicative language must have promoted the further development of the

---

Sprache und Verstehen," *Jahrbuch der Bayerischen Akademie der Wissenschaften* (1978), 83–110, esp. 88ff., and the report, of which an account is given there (97ff.), of R. S. Fouts, "Communication and Chimpanzees," in G. Kurth and I. Eibl-Eibesfeldt, eds., *Hominisation und Verhalten* (1975), 137–58.

[103]Ploog, 159ff. In his contribution to the Congress on the Origin and Evolution of Languages (1975), D. Premack emphasized, on the one hand, the purely quantitative nature of the difference between apes and humans in feats of linguistic intelligence ("Mechanisms of Intelligence: Preconditions for Language?" in S. R. Harnad et al., *Origins and Evolution of Language* [Annals of the New York Academy of Sciences 280; New York, 1976], 544–61 at 560), but on the other hand, in agreement with S. Chevalier-Skolnikoff (in ibid., 206f.), the superiority of human beings in regard to the mastery of all the sensorimotor systems required for the development of language and, in particular, of the system of relations of identical qualities (second-order relations) that is the basis of predication.

[104]Autrum (n. 102, above), 85; see 99ff., 107. See especially R. E. Myers, "Comparative Neurology of Vocalization and Speech," in Harnad, 754ff.: Apes have voluntary control of their hand movements; they do not have such control of their voices and hardly any power to mimic facial expressions.

[105]Autrum, 99.

[106]Ploog, 169; see 167ff. M. Midgley, *Beast and Man: The Roots of Human Nature* (Ithaca, N.Y., 1978), also emphasizes, as being decisive for the development of human language, not only the control of the formation of sounds but in addition an *interest* in naming and in communicating through predicative language instead of through other modes of communication (249f.; earlier, 214f., 226f.).

capacity for thought, as can be seen in the development of the individual child. But how are we to understand this transition from the capacities that precede language to the actual rise of language?

Konrad Lorenz (1974) has summarized the various biological presuppositions for the development of conceptual thinking and verbal language in human beings. He puts in first place the "abstracting functions of perception," which, in the form of gestalt perception, are not limited to the higher animals but are a "basic process of cognition."[107] Connected with this abstractive function are the capacity for insightful (i.e., situation-oriented) behavior (a capacity seen in a preliminary form in the higher animals) and the capacity for voluntary movement, which makes possible a control of the individual's own movements and therefore a freedom to repeat movements.[108]

The last-named capacity is necessary for the formation and free use of articulated sounds as well as for communication through gestures that are not species-predetermined. A prerequisite for the development of this kind of freely available movements is a phase of curiosity-inspired exploratory behavior that is free of the pull of instinct.[109] This exploratory behavior is found in the young of many of the higher animals, but especially in human beings. The social nature of human verbal language, which makes it possible for this language to become the basis for a shared cultural world, requires in addition the ability to imitate others and the resultant phenomenon of tradition.[110] Human verbal language integrates all these

[107]Lorenz (n. 23, above), 113ff. This is not to deny, of course, that gestalt perception in human beings is no longer simply correlative to an instinctual behavior that is peculiar to the species nor a manifestation of an innate specialization to schemata that are adapted to a world limited to certain features. Rather, human gestalt perception is acquired in a productive way through sensorimotor involvement with the environment. See Piaget's remarks on gestalt psychology and its (supposed?) apriorism in *The Origin of Intelligence in Children,* 376–95. A behavioral pattern is (at least in human beings) "a 'Gestalt' made dynamic" (379), "a Gestalt which has a history" (384).

[108]Lorenz, 120ff. and 132ff. The significance, for communication, of the (inherited and acquired) ritualization of utterances is emphasized by Lorenz in his lecture "Kommunikation bei Tieren," in A. Peisl and A. Mohler, eds., *Der Mensch und seine Sprache* (1979), 167–80 (at 169ff.).

[109]Lorenz, 144ff. In the teaching of A. Gehlen, curiosity, a behavior freed from the pressure of instinct, was, along with the formation of sounds, the point of departure for the "roots of language" in the sensorimotor behavior of children. See Gehlen, *Der Mensch,* 19–21.

[110]Lorenz, 151ff. (see 161ff.), 156ff. Lorenz' view of imitation as a highly specific behavioral characteristic of human beings, and not one proper to the primates generally, is probably to be explained by the fact that he defines imitation in a narrow way as imitation of others, whereas Piaget adopts a broader concept of imitation. According to Piaget, too, imitation of others is reserved to a later stage of development; see his *Nachahmung. Spiel und Traum,* 72ff.

presuppositions. But Lorenz has nothing to say about how such an integration might have come about.

Some years earlier Lenneberg had attempted to describe the passage from the "cognitive function" presupposed by language to verbal language itself.[111] According to Lenneberg, the cognitive function consists in the ability to put impressions in categories. This is very like the abstractive function of perception which Lorenz places at the head of his list. It has for its basis the limited capacity for reaction that characterizes all animals as compared with the far greater range of stimuli (325).

What is specifically human, according to Lenneberg, is the naming of these conceptual schemata by means of words. In this context, however, he does not think of words as names for individual objects or even for classes of objects established by convention. They are, rather, "labels for categorization processes" and point to "a creative process of cognitive organization" (333). Lenneberg thus arrives at an understanding of the dynamic way in which language is formed by a process in which the meanings of words are changed, broadened or narrowed. This is what makes his suggestion so fascinating. The capacity for such "categorization processes" (374) also includes the ability to subsume *words* under other words that are more comprehensive and, conversely, the ability to divide them into more specific categories—and consequently the ability to predicate (as Lenneberg understands this), which may also be described as the placing of objects in categories.[112]

The capacity for such processes of categorization is peculiar to the human species, according to Lenneberg, and can develop, via processes of communication, into the most diverse historical languages. It functions as a universal generative grammar, in Chomsky's sense of the phrase (407), so that out of the "raw material" of the languages spoken by others individuals can spontaneously form their own languages, that is, can synthesize (or create anew) the entire mechanism of language (375).

It is true that Lenneberg does not, any more than Chomsky, answer the question of how this structural capacity itself came into existence—unless one is willing to accept as an answer a reference to a specific (and therefore innate) capacity of human beings. But to such a supposition there are objections similar to those which Piaget raised against the assumption of innate concepts as structures ready for use in dealing with the environ-

[111]Lenneberg (n. 82, above). The page references that follow in the text are to this book.

[112]See B. von Freytag-Löringhoff, *Logik. Ihr System und ihr Verhältnis zur Logistik* (1955), 58ff. Just as the application of Lenneberg's categorization schema to words has the character of an automatic application, so according to Freytag-Löringhoff judgments, "opinions on what is subject to opinion" (i.e., on concepts), are the manifestation of an automatic application of opinion and, like this last, are reducible to the categories of identity and difference (14ff.).

ment. As Piaget says, such an assumption is "superfluous"[113] if it is possible to describe the manner in which these capacities arose. Furthermore, the assumption abstracts from the concrete conditions without which, according to Lorenz, there can be no development of language and speech. Lenneberg accepts as a foundation only the abstractive function of perception, although he does regard this as dynamic, that is, accompanied as it were by the ability to control and make voluntary use of the function.

In addition, a categorization function that is assumed to be specific to human beings would have had to make its appearance in the evolutionary process as the result of a qualitative "evolutionary leap."[114] Moreover, it seems questionable whether the schema of the categorization process is really adequate to explain the function ascribed to it: How explain the differentiation of mental contents, a process which, according to Cassirer, is even more fundamental for the formation of concepts than is the synthetizing function which only follows upon the differentiating function?[115] This question is to some extent answered, as far as individual development is concerned, in Piaget's demonstration of the development of object constancy. He could therefore claim that his "genetic theory of knowledge" explains, in the case of the individual, the development of the competence which Chomsky describes and that it renders superfluous the assumption of a ready-made innate structure. Can something similar be shown to be plausible for the phylogenetic origin of language?

The Congress of the New York Academy of Sciences (1975) on the origin and evolution of language and speech saw a number of efforts to shed light on this question. One group of participants tried to relate the development of language to the invention and use of tools. Thus Ashley Montagu would understand language as originating in close relation to the use of tools and to hunting. He regards ideas and words as conceptual tools, mental analogues of material tools; just as human beings had to learn the use of material tools, so they had to learn the use of these mental tools.[116] To this view it was objected that hunting and the use of tools

[113]Piaget, *Einführung in die genetische Erkenntnistheorie*, 57.

[114]See the critique by M. Eigen, "Sprache und Lernen," in Peisl and Mohler (n. 108, above), 181–218, esp. 211.

[115]Cassirer, *Philosophie der symbolischen Formen* (n. 64, above), I, 252 (ET 281): "The original and decisive achievement of the concept is not to compare representations and group them according to genera and species but rather to form impressions into representations."

[116]A. Montagu, "Toolmaking, Hunting and Language," in Harnad (n. 103, above), 266–74: "Man's ideas, his words are conceptual tools, mental analogs of material tools. Man has to learn how to 'handle' these conceptual tools, just as he does other implements" (268). See E. von Glasersfeld, in Harnad, 212ff., who likewise explains language as a tool (218) and social communication as "reciprocal instrumentality" (223).

cannot explain the origin of language, because the latter must have been acquired in youth.[117]

Because of the impression that had been made by the chimpanzee experiments of the Gardners and Premack, the old notion that human verbal language had developed out of gestural language met with far greater interest than the theory just described.[118] It was objected, however, that the explanatory value of such an assumption is small, since the passage from a gestural language to communication through sounds and sequences of sounds would still be an unresolved problem. What we would have expected would be a further perfecting of gestural language rather than a shift to another medium of communication.[119] The really decisive step was the shift from *signals,* which aim to elicit a certain behavior from the partner, to *naming,* which depends on objects, whether the naming is done by gestures or by sounds.[120] But how is this shift to be explained?

The question is partially answered, but at the same time also rendered more acute, by the widespread assumption that, apart from the interjection, the imperative was the original form of linguistic utterance[121] and that, initially at least, it was not distinct from naming. In the beginning, names themselves were still a form of incantation, and the appearance of magic in the history of culture may have had its basis here in the conditions in which language originated. The assumption that the imperative came

[117]A. Marshack, "Some Implications of the Paleolithic Symbolic Evidence for the Origin of Language," in Harnad, 289–310 at 309.

[118]G. W. Hewes, "The Current State of the Gestural Theory of Language," in Harnad, 482–99, presented the history of the idea from Rambosson (1880) and W. Wundt (1900) down to G. H. Mead, G. Revesz, and F. Kainz. H. D. Steklis and S. R. Harnad, "From Hand to Mouth: Some Cultural Steps in the Evolution of Language," in Harnad, 445–55 (esp. 450), also argued for the origin of language in gestures. So too did J. Jaynes in a communication which I shall be mentioning again (Harnad, 316). F. R. H. Englefield, *Language: Its Origin and Relation to Thought* (London, 1977), has called attention to the fact that communication through signs (of whatever kind these may be) can come about only if the signs are either peculiar to the species or are based on natural signs (as clouds are signs of a coming storm) and are therefore "self-explanatory." Conventional signs must have been developed by abbreviation of such natural signs (19f.). This view provides an answer to the question rightly raised by B. Rosenkranz in his *Der Ursprung der Sprache. Ein linguistisch-anthropologischer Versuch* (1961): How is "communication possible unless there are universal human gestures"? (63).

[119]M. J. Raleigh and Frank R. Evin, "Human Language and Primate Communication," in Harnad, 539–41, esp. 540.

[120]P. Kiparski, "Historical Linguistics and the Origin of Language," in Harnad, 97–103, esp. 102.

[121]See, e.g., G. Höpp, *Evolution der Sprache und Vernunft* (1970), 7ff., as well as Englefield (n. 118, above), 33. The same conclusion follows from the assumption by Jaynes of a shift from an "accidental" to an "intentional" signaling effect of gesture or sound; see "The Evolution of Language in the Late Pleistocene," in Harnad, 312–24 at 315f.

first in the development of languages seems to find a confirmation in developmental psychology: "In the beginning language is the expression primarily of commands and wishes."[122] Nouns and action words (verbs) alike have their origin in the sensorimotor context in which language is developed.

Such a view, however, renders all the more urgent the question of how the element of naming and the element of activity become distinct or, if you will, how the naming which is originally inspired by activity acquires a priority over activity, so that the latter ultimately becomes the activity of the named and "objectified" object itself. There is no doubt that the prelinguistic development and consolidation of object constancy is an indispensable condition for this. But the real transition to naming as an independent activity seems to be connected with the symbolic playing of children as a representing of an object that is suggested by the object being played with and is linked to the latter by words.[123]

The prehistoric transition from signal to symbol and therefore the discovery of the symbolic meaning of words as names have correspondingly been connected with play and, more specifically, with the festal play that is also the origin of cult.[124] And in fact the experience of being "seized"

---

[122]Piaget, *Nachahmung, Spiel und Traum,* 283; see 176ff. on the "first verbal schemata," all of which (including even "mama" and "dada") describe first of all "particular actions which interest the child or affect it in some way" (280).

[123]See Piaget, *Nachahmung, Spiel und Traum,* 285ff., on the relations between ludic symbol, imitative image, and preconcept. On the whole, however, because of a one-sided emphasis on the assimilative function of play (207ff., despite the remarks, 209, on the special character of symbolic play as an expression of the transition to "representational intelligence"), Piaget probably underestimates the significance of play in the development of the representational function of language. The idea that the transition from the function of the vocal utterance as an *accompaniment* of an unfolding activity to its function as a *representation* of this activity is mediated solely through memory and the memorative repetition of words (284) is not really convincing. An intermediate link in the chain is missing and is to be found precisely in symbolic play, provided that, unlike Piaget, we regard the "seizure" by the object of play (see above, this chapter, sec. II, pp. 325ff., 331f.) as a constitutive element in symbolic play.

[124]The remarks of O. Jespersen, in *Language: Its Nature, Development and Origin* (London, 1922; Norton Library 229, 1964), 418ff., on the original unity of speech and song, reminded S. K. Langer, *Philosophy in a New Key* (n. 8, above), 105ff., of the observations of J. Donovan in *Mind* 16 (1891), 478–506, and 17 (1892), 325–33 on the "festal origin of human speech." According to Donovan, song, which was nonutilitarian, led, together with dance, to rhythmic noises which were connected with the particular object of the moment and out of which eventually came the word suited to that object. Langer, in her great work *Mind: An Essay on Human Feeling* II (Baltimore, 1972), 303ff., has laid greater emphasis on the religious character of those communal celebrations from which the profane use of language emerged (307f.).

Following Langer and Donovan, B. Rosenkranz (n. 118, above), has likewise concluded that the most plausible context for the passage from signal to symbol is supplied by ritual

in play explains best the origin of the representational schema in which sounds and (rhythmic) sequences of sounds[125] become the medium in which the object is present, this presence taking the form of a self-representation of the object by itself. The word is constituted a symbol by the fact that in it the absent object becomes present. The word originally makes its appearance as mythical word, for in the word of myth[126] the object is not simply present in a general way but is present as acting. The vocal utterances that accompany and express sensorimotor activity now appear as the activity of the very object that is present in the word.[127] This is mythical causality,[128] and it is at the same time the form of the verbal sentence which ascribes to the named object the activity being experienced. The seizure of the player by the object of play renders intelligible both of these claims. This means that language emerged from a "sei-

---

play (114ff.) and not by the use of tools, which here explains nothing (112f.). The ritual play of Stone Age hunters may also (he says) be thought to be the place where the imitation of animal sounds developed and then turned into naming (118). Such considerations shed a new light on the naming of the animals in the biblical story of paradise (Gen. 2:19ff.); for it has always been maintained that this name-giving represents the origin of all language. But if we are to assume an originally ritual and cultic context for such naming, then the biblical story represents a secularization of the origin of language. Words no longer come through inspiration from theomorphic divinities; rather, human beings themselves are the creators of language—but human beings into whom the one God has breathed his spirit which leads them to the creatures they are to name.

[125]The importance of rhythm for the organization of linguistic expression has been emphasized by Langer (see n. 124, above; esp. *Mind* II, 294f.) and earlier by J. Stenzel, *Philosophie der Sprache* (1934, 1964), 29ff. Even in the developed languages with their grammatical differentiations it is the rhythmical organization of the spoken sentence that makes the utterance "comprehensible" as a totality (17); rhythm is to speech what punctuation is to writing.

[126]It is a merit of Cassirer to have emphasized the close relationship of language and myth in regard to the symbolic structure governing the presence of the spiritual in the sensible (*Philosophie der symbolischen Formen* I, 17). He sees as the "prototype and model" of this relationship that of the soul to the body as its "manifestation" (III, 117). According to Cassirer, the only distinction between language and myth is that in the word of myth the object is not only represented but is itself present (II, 53). Linguistic expression, understood as *only* a representation, thus becomes a reduced version of the mythical word. On the lack of distinction between word and thing in the mythical understanding of the word, see also I, 56f.

[127]See in this connection the remarks of Piaget, *The Construction of Reality in the Child,* 86ff., on the attribution of experienced or imagined activity to objects that were hitherto conceived as unchanging but that now, as a result of this attribution, become acting subjects.

[128]Cassirer, in his description of mythical causality (II, 57f.), passes over the decisive point, namely, the *activity* ascribed to the object; this element of activity constitutes the most important difference between mythical causality and the modern scientific concept of causality as the operation of a set of laws. But in III, 84, he himself describes the mode of experience that grasps manifestations and processes as activities: The indefinite formulations used in such phrases as "It is windy," "It is raining," "It is cold," point to a hidden subject that is acting in these manifestations.

zure" that was religious in origin. This does not make language any less a human creation; it means, however, that language, like every human creative activity, owes its existence to an inspiration that raises human beings above themselves.

The original unity of language and myth in play (together with song and dance) renders it plausible that the earliest Stone Age representations of animals were connected with the acquisition of speech by the human race; this was the suggestion of J. Jaynes in a lecture at the Congress of the New York Academy of Sciences in 1975 that was among the most speculative and stimulating contributions to this congress. Jaynes thinks that it was possible to ascribe a continuous existence to animals (and especially to game animals) only when they were connected with word symbols—that is, names—for then hunters could, as it were, take the animals with them when they returned to their caves and could paint them on the walls. Jaynes ascribes similarly wide-ranging consequences to the development of proper names for human individuals, for the individual could now continue to be present even when absent. It was out of this, according to Jaynes, that belief in souls and ceremonial burial arose.[129]

Since traces of burial and cave paintings both go back to approximately the same time (ca. 35,000 B.C.), Jaynes assumes that language was first acquired at about that time; the appearance of language must, after all, have caused a significant change in behavior and this change must have been reflected in artifacts. Jaynes therefore conjectures that language originated during the final ice age, which ended ca. 35,000 B.C.; this was a period which in other respects too is recognized as being a time of profound transition within more recent prehistory.[130] If we accept the period suggested by Jaynes for the origin of language, there are many reasons for thinking that only in this period did the transition between animal and human reach its final stage.[131] If, however, the full development of the human frontal lobe is to be understood not as a condition but as a consequence of the acquisition of language, then we would have to reckon with a significantly earlier development of lan-

[129]Jaynes, "The Evolution of Language in the Late Pleistocene," in Harnad (n. 103, above), 312–25 at 319.

[130]Narr, "Beiträge der Urgeschichte zur Kenntnis der Menschennatur" (n. 37, above), speaks, with reference to the period around 30,000 B.C., of an "epochal landmark" that from both the anthropological and the historical standpoints justifies a "division of prehistory" into an earlier and a later prehistory.

[131]See on this point the reflections of Narr, 37. But (without discussing the question of the origin of language) Narr rejects this possibility because—even prescinding from the findings connected with Peking Man, which are difficult to interpret—before the beginning of the period named, there were already "burials of a kind which allow us to conclude to the idea of some kind of survival after death." Such ideas are, once again, hardly thinkable without language.

guage.[132] But the lack of archaeologically verifiable clues to the effects to be expected from such a radical change is an argument for the later date.[133]

Whatever is thought on this point, the development of language seems in any case to have been originally connected with the religious consciousness. But there was a tension between, on the one hand, the magical possibility of controlling reality by means of names and, on the other, the mythical consciousness of the active presence of hidden realities themselves. That tension would run through the subsequent history of the religious consciousness, as can still be seen in the biblical prohibition against using the name of God "improperly" (Ex. 20:7). But in the understanding of language there is a comparable tension between the representational function and the act of utterance. An investigation of this tension would seem helpful in penetrating more deeply into the anthropological nature of language and into its religious dimension.

2. Speech Act and Conversation

The discussion of the relation between language and thought has led to the conclusion that language, especially in its origin, can be understood only in the light of a prior development of thought. Language is, however, the "creative organ" (Wilhelm von Humboldt) which thought needs if it is to take abiding form and achieve sophisticated development. Since control of language in large measure determines whether the contents of memory are to be accessible and retrievable, any thinking marked by a high level of discrimination is possible only on the terrain of language.

On the other hand, the possibilities inherent in every linguistic utterance can be activated in one direction or another only by means of selective thought. "Thinking learns in and from language, achieves clarity and stability in language, uses language, creates its language for itself." In all of this, nonetheless, thought is "more than language. Only because of this is it possible for us to translate from one language into another, for it is thinking that does the translating."[134]

[132]See the doubts raised by H. Jerrison regarding Jaynes's chronology, in his discussion of the latter's lecture (in Harnad, 326f.).

[133]Thus also G. L. Isaac, "Stages of Cultural Elaboration in the Pleistocene: Possible Archaeological Indicators of the Development of Language Capabilities," in Harnad, 275–88 at 286. According to Isaac, this thesis was first proposed by K. Oakley, *A Definition of Man* (Chicago, 1971). G. W. Hewes (in Harnad, 491) mentions that Washburn and J. D. Clark, "Africa in Prehistory," *Man* 10 (1975), 175–98, are also inclined to suppose a discovery of language forty to fifty thousand years ago.

[134]M. Wandruszka, "Sprache und Sprachen," in Peisl and Mohler (n. 108, above), 7–47; citation from 45.

But this view of the relation between language and thought does not automatically mean that language is a product of the thinking subject and that speech is therefore an action. True enough, such a step seems natural whenever thought itself is regarded as the product of a subject that is presupposed. Conversely, Heidegger's reversal of the relation between thought and language is evidently connected with his criticism of the foundational function of the subject in modern metaphysics. Our investigation of self-consciousness and ego identity (chapter 5) has shown that the human ego and its subjectivity are themselves the products of a genetic process in every individual life and do not exist fully formed at the start of all consciousness and thought. Therefore the priority of thought over language does not justify the conclusion that language is a product of human beings as subjects of their behavior, a product of an action. On the contrary, such an interpretation even of thinking itself must be regarded as questionable.

Among the various philosophical anthropologies of the present century, Arnold Gehlen's is characterized by the fact that he places human beings as "acting beings" at the center of the picture he projects. In so doing, he has developed the approach not so much of his model, Herder, but of the early Fichte and of Nietzsche, as well as of American pragmatism. His treatment of language is set within that same framework. Language plays a large part in his anthropology, for he justifiably regards it as fundamental for the entire human relationship to the world.

At the same time, however, the relation of language to the basic concept of action remains oddly ambivalent. On the one hand, Gehlen considers language to be constitutive for the structure of action: only the "overview"—a term he takes from Schopenhauer—that is mediated through language renders human beings capable of acting. On the other hand, the sensorimotor roots of language are themselves described as "actions," while the word is called a "complete action."[135]

In thus speaking of actions, Gehlen is not concerned to assert a priority of the thinking subject. It is, rather, that he understands thinking to be "soundless speech" and the "illustrated interior world" of consciousness to be a function of language. But all of it is an "accomplishment" of acting human beings who seek to form a network of symbolic meanings and thereby to control the multiplicity of stimuli in which they are immersed. B. Liebrucks in his critique of Gehlen has doubtless oversimplified Gehlen's position by reducing it to the thesis of human beings as acting beings, with the result that the ambivalence I have described does not receive adequate attention. But Liebrucks is right when he objects to Gehlen "that human linguisticality is never based on action, but on the

[135]See Gehlen, *Der Mensch* (n. 109, above), 53 (and 253f.); on the other side, 257, 270.

contrary action is always based on linguisticality."[136] It is possible to speak of an action only—as Gehlen himself notes on one occasion—if there is an "overview" of the field of action, and this overview is in turn acquired only through language-mediated thought.

The labeling of speech as an action is widespread and usually taken for granted. The philosophy at work in the background may be pragmatism or a behaviorism interpreted along pragmatist lines, but it may also be idealism.[137] The conception has also acquired the status of a theoretical position because of the theory of speech acts which emerged in turn from the philosophy of linguistic analysis. In contrast to structuralism, the speech act theory focuses not on the universal structures of language but on concrete speech, which it defines precisely as an action.

In a series of lectures at Harvard University in 1955, Oxford philosopher John L. Austin set up a contrast between statements or assertions—the type of sentences that logical positivism regarded as the model of all meaningful speech—and "performative" utterances, which do not express a pregiven content but, rather, by their very use establish the content to which they refer. What is meant are such utterances as "I christen this ship the 'Queen Elizabeth' " or "I promise to visit you tomorrow." Austin says of such utterances as these that "the uttering of the sentence is, or is part of, the doing of an action."[138] Austin himself extended this observation into a description of all linguistic utterances as "illocutionary" acts and therefore as actions.[139]

John R. Searle then developed the speech act theory still further and linked it to the theory of play by introducing the idea of rules which, in

[136]B. Liebrucks, *Sprache und Bewusstsein* I (1964), 83.

[137]Thus according to Von Kutschera (n. 74, above), 17, a "linguistic utterance" as such is already an "action." Similarly A. Schütz, *The Phenomenology of the Social World* (1932), trans. G. Walsh and F. Lehnert (Evanston, Ill., 1967), 116ff., simply describes a linguistic utterance as an "expressive act" (116) or a "communicative act" (117); see 122. Höpp (n. 121, above), 3ff., introduces the idea of goal-oriented action as a self-evident element in the description of the development of language. I pointed out earlier, at n. 97, above, that Piaget feels able, without discussion, to substitute the concept of *action* for that of *behavior*. M. Black, *The Labyrinth of Language* (New York, 1968), 91, describes speech as a "purposive activity" and writes: "Normally, we speak in order to achieve some purpose; and that is why we can appraise the success or failure of acts of speech, judging them by reference to what we try to accomplish when we speak." Examples might be multiplied almost at random (see also n. 116, above).

[138]J. L. Austin, *How to Do Things with Words.* ed. J. O. Urmson (London, 1962), 5.

[139]Ibid., 98ff. According to Austin, every "locutionary act," i.e., the utterance of a content ("saying something"), is at the same time an "illocutionary act," i.e., the performance of an action, in the form of an answer to a question, a giving of information, assurance, or warning, and so on. Even an assertion is an action (103). An illocutionary act differs from a perlocutionary act in that in the former the effect of the act on the addressee is not named (though it may be intended) (see 108ff.).

a manner comparable to the rules for games, determine the performance of speech acts. Austin still thought that his theory of speech needed a foundation in a general theory of action. Searle believes he has satisfied this requirement by showing that the conformity or nonconformity of speech acts to rules (explicit or implicit in, e.g., the institutional context of an utterance) serves as a criterion for their success or failure. He can say, therefore, that "a theory of language is part of a theory of action, simply because speaking is a rule-governed form of behavior."[140]

But is this enough to justify the application of the concept of action to all linguistic utterances? When a piece of behavior unwittingly follows rules, the identification of which is left to others, it is not possible as yet to speak of an action. It is only when observance of a rule is *intended* that there is undoubtedly question of an action. For the behavior is then behavior directed to the attainment of a goal, and behavior of that kind satisfies the definition of an action. D. Wunderlich, who refers to the theory of action formulated by A. I. Goldmann, has correctly seen the speech act theory to have its valid basis in the concept of action as behavior intentionally ordered to a goal, and he has reformulated the theory in this light.[141]

There is widespread agreement today that the concept of "action in the narrow sense" includes a relation to goals that are to be attained through the action.[142] Action is thus distinguished, on the one hand, from the more

[140]J. R. Searle, *Speech Acts: An Essay in the Philosophy of Language* (Cambridge, 1969), 17. On the concept of rule, see 33ff.; on the embedment of rules in institutions, 50ff. See also Austin, 106. As a description of the "pragmatic dimension of the use of language" the speech act theory has meanwhile become influential in linguistics and literary theory; for example, W. Iser, *Der Akt des Lesens* (1956), 89ff., makes it the basis for the interpretation of fictional texts. See especially D. Wunderlich, *Studien zur Sprechakttheorie* (1976), 119ff.

[141]Wunderlich, 30–50: "Handlungstheorie und Sprache" (esp. 37). Wunderlich refers to A. I. Goldmann, *A Theory of Human Action* (Englewood Cliffs, N.J., 1970). According to Goldmann, actions are structured teleologically by wishes (49ff., 114), but the latter are themselves not acts (92f.).

[142]See, e.g., T. Parsons and E. A. Shils, *Toward a General Theory of Action* (Chicago, 1967), 53ff. (see also 5); Schütz, (n. 137, above), 57ff. M. Weber, *Wirtschaft und Gesellschaft* (1922; 1972⁵), 12f., apparently deviates from this "teleological" concept of action by distinguishing action in which means are adapted to ends *(zweckrational)* as but one type of action alongside others, namely, action based on values *(wertrational)*, affective action, and traditional action. But these distinctions have to do more with motivation than with the structure of action. Even value-based and traditional action are goal-oriented in their structure: their purpose is to realize values or maintain tradition. In the concept of affective action it is not always clear (if we take Weber's examples) where the dividing line is to be drawn between affectively motivated but rationally structured action and mere instinctual behavior. J. Habermas, *Theorie des kommunikativen Handelns* I (1981), 126ff., distinguishes various types of action, but according to his own explanation all of them retain the teleological structure which is "fundamental to *all* concepts of action" (151). Habermas appeals for support to R. Bubner,

general concept of behavior,[143] and, on the other, from the concept of activity (praxis).[144] The latter distinction goes back to Aristotle, who distinguished between action that has its goal outside itself (as something still to be attained) and is therefore imperfect praxis, and the perfect activity which has its goal within itself and therefore does not come to an end as a result of reaching this goal but is intrinsically capable of being continued indefinitely (*Metaphysica* 1048b21ff.). Seeing and thinking, for example, are activities in this sense, but so is living or existing.

Activity thus understood would differ from the modern concept of behavior because the former has its *telos* in itself, and this is something that cannot be said of all forms of behavior—not of action, nor (for example) of weeping, being cold, or being hungry. Rather, it is necessary to distinguish, under the generic concept of behavior, between, on the one hand, instinctual behavior and reactive behavior and action and, on the other, the realm of the states of mind, of experience, and of nonutilitarian activities. Is not speech to be accounted among the last-named forms of behavior rather than among the goal-oriented actions? But before this question can be answered, we must look more carefully at the structure of action.

In his phenomenological analysis of the structure of action Hans Reiner distinguishes between the "attitude" toward the goal or purpose to which

---

Handlung, Sprache und Vernunft. Grundbegriffe praktischer Philosophie (1976; 1982), 168ff.; see also 128ff. and 307ff.

[143]On the distinction of "intentional action" from behavior elicited by stimuli, see J. Habermas, *Zur Logik der Sozialwissenschaften* (*Philosophische Rundschau*, Beiheft 5; 1967), 58–79, esp. 76. But the concept of action must also be distinguished from a broader concept of behavior which is not restrictively defined by reference to external stimuli. Thus Schütz (n. 137, above), 59, distinguishes action characterized by a "plan more or less preconceived" and having the "nature of a project" from a behavior directed to the future in another manner (behavior that is thus thought of as definitely a self-comporting). W. Kamlah, *Philosophische Anthropologie. Sprachliche Grundlegung und Ethik* (1973), 49, conceives of action as a "special case" of "self-comporting," because even self-abandonment and suffering are forms of behavior, while it is difficult to describe weeping or being cold, for example, as actions. Goldmann (n. 141, above) likewise distinguishes actions from states and from "things that *happen* to persons, things which they *suffer* or undergo" (46f.), but not from activities which are not goal-oriented.

[144]See E. Tugendhat, *Selbstbewusstsein und Selbstbestimmung* (1979), 211ff. See also Hegel's distinction between *Tat* (deed) and *Handlung* (action) on the basis of deliberation. E. M. Lange's criticism that this distinction "is unsuited for distinguishing between actions and mere happenings" (*Das Prinzip Arbeit* [1980], 38ff. at 40), is not convincing. Nor does this thesis really presuppose the "alienation model" of action which Lange criticizes (32ff. at 41), for it points back rather to Aristotle, whose distinctions, incidentally, are suppressed in Hegel because the latter adopts the viewpoint of the productivity of action; see M. Riedel, *Theorie und Praxis im Denken Hegels* (1965), 105ff., and idem, *Studien zu Hegels Rechtsphilosophie* (1969), 30ff.

the action is ordered and the actual intention of the action.[145] As Reiner explains (following D. von Hildebrand), the attitude toward the goal of action is a question of disposition. It is a matter of feeling and therefore (to interpret Reiner's description in terms of what I said earlier) of the congruence between the content of the goal in question and the whole of our personal being with its "identity." Because of the totality that thus characterizes the attunement to a goal or purpose, the individual purpose is at every point located within a comprehensive set of interrelated purposes (this is a point that goes unmentioned in Reiner). This does not mean, however, that the whole of the ongoing life must be rationalized so that all behavior is related to a single ultimate purpose.

In contrast to this emotional identification with the goal, the actual intention in acting has to do with the means that will lead to the accomplishment of the purpose envisaged. It is true, of course, that intention and approval of the goal are often tied together in an inclusive act of decision (74f.). Nonetheless the relation, emphasized by Hildebrand, of the intention to the means used in action seems to me important with regard to the distinction between action and activity or praxis.

The intention of an action and the execution to which the intention leads must be directed to the means as to the initial steps that will lead to the attainment of the goal. It is this very fact that gives rise to the temporary separation between means and goal which is characteristic of action. Thus in the production of an object attention must be focused on the movements to be performed at each step, lest the material be spoiled or some even greater harm be caused. On the other hand, activity in the sense of Aristotle's praxis is not separated from its goal, so that the difference between means and end does not arise in connection with it.

It must be pointed out, however, that human action is not separated from its goal in every respect, since the goal is present in consciousness by anticipation. To that extent an element of praxis plays a vital part in action. The greater the mastery a person has of the individual phases of an action (e.g., the playing of a piece of music), the closer the action approximates to praxis in its character; its nature as action is sublimated and it thus turns into play or pure presentation. Those who are active in play are immediately present to themselves, while at the same time they are momentarily absorbed in their playing.

In action, on the contrary, agents are one with themselves only through anticipation of the goal. The necessary concentration on the means is accompanied by the danger of an alienation that is obviated only through

---

[145]H. Reiner, *Freiheit, Wollen und Aktivität. Phänomenologische Untersuchungen in Richtung auf das Problem der Willensfreiheit* (1927), 69ff. The page references that follow in the text are to this book.

attainment of the goal. This is why the ego achieves identification with itself through the performance of actions.[146] At the same time, however, the unity which the ego achieves through anticipation of the goal and by which it bridges the temporal flow is not only presupposed but must be maintained throughout the entire course of an action. The ego must dominate and control this course in advance; otherwise the goal slips from view, and the acting ego loses itself in the unanticipated dynamism proper to the means, which can then sweep it off to far different shores than it desired to reach.

The unity of the ego as subject is thus fundamental to action. In fact, action is the only area of life in which the concept of the subject is both appropriate and indispensable. The hypertrophy of the concept of subject in modern thought was connected with the tendency to elevate every fact to the rank of an action. But, as we saw in an earlier context, the unity and selfness of the ego (and therefore also its function as subject of sequential actions) are established only through processes of identity formation. For this reason, the world of life and experience includes far more than the area in which the subject is dominant; it includes far more than the sphere of action. Consequently, it is presumptuous for individuals to want to produce the whole of life by their own action. The adoption of such a presumptuous strategy can only undermine the wholeness of life in the specific areas of life. It is here that the Pauline and Reformed doctrine of justification is critically relevant for anthropology.

The positive potentialities of action are to be found in specific details within a life totality that derives its validity from some other source. Identity formation, however, and identification (which is therefore a matter of feeling) with the goal of any given action are at every point concerned with the whole of the individual's life (this is also why a number of individuals can work together for common goals: because individuals secure the totality of their life only in community). Therefore the overview required for the identity of action looks, via the means-end connection, beyond the field of action itself. The prevision of the consequences and side effects of one's own action is part of the very concept of action, for without such an overview the plurality of means used in carrying out the intention could not be ordered to the goal, nor would agents be responsible for their actions. Conversely, in expecting individuals to accept responsibility and blame for their deeds and omissions, society supposes that individuals have an identity that embraces the whole of their individual existence and therefore also of their social life-world.

We may now return to the question: Is speaking an action? Or is it,

---

[146]See D. Wyss, *Strukturen der Moral. Untersuchungen zur Anthropologie und Genealogie moralischer Verhaltensweisen* (1968), 59.

rather, an activity in the sense described above? In answering, we must avoid oversimplification. There are, after all, forms of speech that undoubtedly display the structure proper to action. This is true at least of the performative utterances to which Austin calls attention. The christening of a ship or a child is as much an action as the opening of an assembly and the sentence of a judge. At the same time, however, the formulas used on such occasions are only partial actions. That is why their use must be marked by the care that agents must display in regard to the means that are to secure the end. The same holds for the example of a promise, with which Searle begins the detailed exposition of his speech act theory. A promise is an action, but it is also only part of the total action that leads to the goal, namely, the keeping of the promise, provided the promise is sincere and real. The unity and selfness of the ego, which we have seen to be fundamental for the unity of the "arc" of action that links together intention, means, and end, are also fundamental here, since those who make promises present themselves as guarantors that the promises will be fulfilled, and for this reason must consider carefully whether it is in their power to do as they say they will.

At first glance it may seem that a promise does not in every respect satisfy the criteria for an action. In particular, it seems doubtful that the promise really functions as a means. Is the coming of the promised future dependent on the promise given here and now? Is the future fulfillment really the goal of the promise? Is its goal not, rather, the present happiness of the person to whom the promise is given? But while this function of a promise is surely an important one, it is also clear that the promise would be insincere if the one promising were to look only to this here-and-now effect. After all, the happiness of the recipient of the promise depends precisely on the auspicious future thus opened up. This future, the object of the promise, is to be made real for the recipient. To that extent the promise itself is also a means to this end, since it draws the recipient to the promised future or encourages and maintains hope that this future will come to pass.

Performative utterances are thus actions in the proper sense. The difficulty with the speech act theory is that with the aid of the concept of illocutionary act it generalizes from this initial discovery. But it is not correct to say that an assertion or statement of fact, to take but one example, is no less a speech act than is a promise. For everyday assertions do not usually take the form of explicit assertions which can by their structure be true or false. People simply state how things seem to them. To say that such a statement amounts to a mere assertion is to adopt a third-party standpoint or to engage in reflection on the content of the statement. For this reason, an assertion or statement of fact is essentially different from a promise.

In a promise the element of action is present in the consciousness of the person who makes the (explicit) promise. In a statement, on the other hand, the element of action has to be presupposed, and presupposed by someone else, who doubts the truth of what has been said or who ignores the element of truth, like the theoretician of speech acts who is interested in something other than the subject matter of what has been said. In other words, the reflection that focuses on the act of making a statement passes over the intention of the one making the statement.[147] This very fact shows that a statement cannot be an action, since in an action the intention that is directed to the goal embraces at the same time the entire course of action leading to the goal; otherwise the focus on the goal would not be an action but a simple wish.

In its interpretation therefore of utterances about facts, and of emotional utterances as well, the speech act theory replaces the linguistic event by something else which it assumes to be there. It supposes that the utterance is a means to the end of communication and, to that extent, an action. It is to this point that Chomsky's criticism of Searle is directed. According to Chomsky, linguistic utterances are primarily expressions, and therefore representations, of meanings. Any intentions that speakers may additionally attach to their utterances are by comparison secondary. "The 'instrumental' analysis of language as a device for achieving some end is seriously inadequate."[148] And, more incisively: "The point is, I

[147]Seebass (n. 65, above), also objects to the speech act theory on the grounds that in several respects it is open to the danger of "improperly generalizing from the 'paradigms' postulated as basic" and consequently of "distorting" important aspects of language as it is actually used. This has led in particular (Seebass says) "to a failure to realize the special role of the claim to truth and (in consequence) to an inadequate treatment of 'propositional content' as well" (450).

[148]N. Chomsky, *Reflections on Language* (1975), 69. This pithy formulation is hardly meant to deny the communicative function of language generally. It says only that this function is not to be regarded as primary for the understanding of language. In this sense, J. M. Edie, *Speaking and Meaning: The Phenomenology of Language* (Bloomington, Ind., 1976), admits the partial truth of the view that the inherited and acquired mother tongue is an instrument of communication, "but it is not the whole truth. Language is more than an instrument" (145).
A further problematic element in the instrumental view of language is the interpretation of words as *signs,* especially in behaviorism (C. W. Morris, *Signs, Language and Behavior* [New York, 1955]). In contrast, Langer, *Philosophy in a New Key* (n. 8, above), had urged the view that speech be not conceived primarily as "communication by sound" but as a symbolic apprehension of reality that, unlike a mere sign, does not elicit an action from an addressee (48) but stimulates the other to conceive the object (49). It seems better, however, to depart somewhat from Langer, who separates not only signs but symbols from objects, inasmuch as she relates symbols to "conceptions" (ibid.), and to say with H. G. Gadamer that a symbol differs from a sign in that it does not simply point to something else but "makes something immediately present" by representing it (*Truth and Method* [n. 32, above], 136).
In this light it is understandable that in speaking we are not concerned with language as an instrument but with the object that language makes present. A word is, of course, *also*

think, that the 'communication theorists' are not analyzing 'meaning,' but rather something else: perhaps 'successful communication.' "[149]

James M. Edie has correctly pointed out that when we speak, our attention is normally directed not to the linguistic form of our utterance but to the object with which we are dealing. This "object" may be the person to whom we are speaking, or the subject matter of our conversation, or, finally, simply the common goal we are pursuing with our partner.[150] In making this point, Edie turns our attention to an area of speaking-together that cannot but be inaccessible to the speech act theory: I refer to the phenomenon of conversation.

In conversation it is an object of shared interest that creates a common ground and therefore communication. Of the three basic functions of linguistic utterance that K. Bühler has distinguished—namely, expression, representation, and communication—representation is dominant in conversation,[151] since it mediates between expression and communication. The expression of subjectivity can reach the other and be communicated to the other only through the medium of representation. This is true even of performative utterances. The baptismal formula, for example, represents what is happening to the candidate; a promise represents its content as a benefit intended for the recipient. To its own disadvantage the speech act theory fails to take into account the representational aspect of play when it interprets language with the aid of play theory.[152] There may

---

a sign, but it is such primarily for those who do not (yet) understand it and who hope to achieve an understanding of the object by means of the word. As soon as they do understand it, the word has become a symbol in which the object is present. Word and sentence differ from a signpost which we leave behind when we follow in the direction in which it points. See also the remark of Heintel (n. 63, above), 40ff., on the "more-than-sign" character of language.

[149]Chomsky, *Reflections on Language,* 68. Chomsky is here opposing in particular P. F. Strawson, who in his Oxford inaugural lecture, *Meaning and Truth* (London, 1970), asserted a basic opposition between the "formal semanticists" who focus on the expressive function of language and the "theorists of communication intention." But see also Searle (n. 140, above), 141ff.

[150]Edie (n. 148, above), 144.

[151]F. Kainz, *Psychologie der Sprache* I (1941), 174f., even says that representation "is not a limited linguistic achievement alongside others but is the fundamental and essential element of language; it stands behind all the achievements of language and alone makes them possible." See 70ff.

[152]Tugendhat, *Vorlesungen* (n. 85, above), 258, likewise complains that Searle does not fully carry out his intended interpretation of language in the light of game theory: Searle's suggested system of rules "ends where it ought to begin, namely, with the simple naming of the move that begins the game." But Tugendhat's criticism stays within the framework of the contest model of play. The phenomenon of language becomes accessible at a significantly deeper level when the play model is looked at also, and especially, in its representational function, as Gadamer indicates (*Truth and Method,* 446) with reference back to his own interpretation of play (91ff.).

indeed be elements of contest or competition in a conversation, but in a successful conversation they remain subordinate to the object with which the conversation is concerned and which achieves representation in it.

In 1967, Erving Goffman published an analysis of the phenomenon of conversation as seen from the standpoint of the interaction among the participants.[153] One result of this analysis was to show very clearly the limited value of the element of action for a description of the real situation in a conversation. Goffman begins with what must be presupposed in the participants. In addition to the requirements of linguistic competence the primary condition to be met is that of "spontaneous involvement": each participant "must maintain proper involvement" but also "act so as to insure that others maintain theirs" (116). For this reason, Goffman characterizes conversation as "interaction."

It is possible even at this early point to ask whether "spontaneous involvement" can be described, in an objectively appropriate way, as an accomplishment or action of the participant in question. For, if such involvement is indeed an action and therefore compels the participants in the conversation to be attentive, the conversation will never get under way, since it will by its nature have something forced about it. Yet Goffman himself says that a shared spontaneous involvement produces something like an *unio mystica,* a "socialized trance," in which "a conversation has a life of its own" (113). This describes very accurately the atmosphere of a conversation, but it also completely destroys the conceptual framework derived from the pattern of action and interaction. The phenomenon described by Goffman belongs, rather, in the realm of experiences to which the person "surrenders."[154] Yet even "surrender" does not capture the "density" of the atmosphere in a successful conversation, which is characterized by both "ecstasy" and mutuality. It is no accident that Goffman speaks here of a state of "trance."

In an earlier age the energy resident in such a state of crackling tension was called "spirit." Is there any real reason why we should not speak of the "spirit" of a conversation? The term is an accurate one for what we are dealing with here and cannot, by any accounting, be replaced by "interaction." The widespread reserve shown today toward the concept of spirit is indeed understandable and justified: it carries an excessive metaphysical freight and, more especially, is bound up with a dualistic anthropology that is no longer able to take a natural view of human beings in the corporeal unity in which they live out their lives.[155] But this is not

[153]E. Goffman, *Interaction Ritual: Essays on Face-to-Face Behavior* (Garden City, N.Y., 1967). The page references that follow in the text are to this book.
[154]See again Kamlah (n. 143, above), 49.
[155]See above, chapter 1. On what follows, see also B. Liebrucks, *Sprache und Bewusstsein* II (1965), 57ff.

a sufficient reason for completely avoiding the term and thus condemning ourselves to be mute in the face of a phenomenon like conversation.

We must, of course, define clearly what the word "spirit" says, and, above all, what it does not say, if we are to avoid undesirable broad associations that, unnoticed, make their way in and then suddenly and without justification direct our thinking along traditional lines. This is not to say that the statements made in the traditional philosophy of spirit are to be completely rejected from the outset. The element of truth in them can, however, be recovered only step by step. In the process it is necessary to eliminate any connotation of a dualism of spirit and matter that may be associated with the relation between consciousness and bodily existence.

I shall use the word "spirit" initially only to indicate that the peculiar phenomenon of conversation, which Goffman is describing, is a state of "seizure" or "being gripped" *(Ergriffenheit)*, in which the "conversation has a life of its own." We cannot, of course, help being reminded here of the seizure experienced in play and, more generally, of the ecstatic character of human living that only finds especially intense expression in such moments of seizure. The phenomenon here being described as "spiritual" is not exclusively social; it is also present in the life of individuals. This does not, however, alter the fact that in speaking of "spirit" we are not speaking of a "faculty" of human beings nor of a "part" of their anthropological structure. Far more to the point is Goffman's description of a conversation as a condition of "trance," since this also pinpoints the difference from what people usually understand by "consciousness."

In saying this I am not excluding the possibility that the individual consciousness may itself be perhaps understood as such a condition of "trance"; this, however, is not a possibility on which we must decide here. More important at the moment is the observation that the image of a state of trance and the experience of a special "atmosphere" bring us closer to the meaning of the words used for "spirit" at the beginning of our cultural traditions than do the ideas associated with the word as a result of subsequent developments in metaphysics.

In the Old Testament, *rūaḥ* means, first of all, breeze, breath, wind; only then, and on this basis, does it mean the life-giving power that God blows into the nostrils of the human person at creation (Gen. 2:7). This power never passes completely into the possession of human beings, however, and at death it leaves them "with their final breath" (a phrase we still use) and returns to God.[156] Notions not totally dissimilar were originally as-

---

[156]Eccl. 12:7. See the detailed discussion of the Old Testament understanding of "spirit" in H. W. Wolff, *Anthropology of the Old Testament,* trans. M. Kohl (Philadelphia, 1974), 32–40. It seems to me, however, that the close connection between the spirit at work in human beings and the Spirit of God should be more strongly emphasized. The human spirit is a participation in the Spirit of God, even though it is true that this participation plays its

sociated with the word *pneuma* in Greek thought, although the meaning of the word then developed in a different direction than in the Bible.[157] In any case, John the Evangelist still seems to have been counting on his readers to understand him when he has Christ say to Nicodemus: "The *pneuma* (wind) blows where it wills, and you hear the sound of it, but you do not know whence it comes or whither it goes" (John 3:8).

The spirit of a conversation, then, or—to use the words of Goffman— the "socialized trance" in which the participants in a conversation are caught up, causes them "to be spontaneously carried away by the topic of conversation."[158] How does this happen? It happens because, as we say, one subject leads to another. The course of the conversation is not established in advance. The freedom that characterizes it leaves room for ever new and surprising twists and turns and therefore also for the contribution of each new interlocutor. Nonetheless a successful conversation does not run along in a disconnected way. If the utterances are simply disconnected, the atmosphere conducive to conversation is quickly dissipated. But how is a connection established when the course of the conversation is not itself

---

part in the assertion of human independence and the turning away from God. On this, see my essay "The Spirit of Life" in my *Faith and Reality,* trans. J. Maxwell (Philadelphia, 1977), 20–39.

[157]See G. Verbeke, "Geist (Pneuma)," *HWP* 3 (1974), 157–62 (with bibliography).

[158]Goffman (n. 153, above), 134. But in an unwitting paradox Goffman presents this being carried away as a duty of the participants. The heterogeneity between the phenomenon described and the interpretative model set up for the description is projected into the behavior of the participants in the conversation: "On the one hand, the participants are required to be spontaneously carried away by the topic of conversation; on the other, they are obliged to control themselves so that they will be always ready to stay within the role of communicator and stay alive to the touchy issues that might cause the others to become ill at ease" (134; see earlier 115f.). Goffman seeks to resolve the difficulty by appealing to the help that the participants give to one another, instead of appealing to the fact that even within behavior to one another they let themselves be led by the spirit of the conversation (in which case the alleged conflict disappears).

A successful conversation can only "take place"; the participants cannot bring it about by force, but can only avoid what will disrupt it. If the element of action in the behavior of the partners makes its way into the foreground, the conversation comes to an end. This explains why even though—and even because—the participants may follow all the rules of correct social behavior, "the interaction may become flaccid, stale, and flat" (130, n. 9). The participant in a conversation who, according to Goffman, is obliged to involve himself "cannot do so *in order* to satisfy these obligations, for such an effort would oblige him to shift his attention from the topic of conversation to the problem of being spontaneously involved" (115). Here we see the difference between interaction and conversation.

In a discussion, on the other hand, or in an argument the contributions of the participants do in fact have the character of actions. Here carefully considered formulations are advanced like actions in a tournament. In a discussion it is not the relaxed atmosphere of a conversation that dominates, and it is a happy accident when a concern for the true meaning of the subject under discussion gains the upper hand and allows an atmosphere of mutuality, comparable to that of a conversation, to be created.

established in advance? How is the description "One subject leads to another" to be properly understood? How does this "leading" come about? Some light may be thrown on this point if we look at the indeterminacy of words and the multiplicity of meanings that can attach to them.

The words of natural languages do not signify sharply delimited classes of objects, activities, qualities, and relationships. The meaning of a word is not completely restricted to the spectrum of possible uses listed in a dictionary. The meaning is susceptible of expansion and as a matter of fact it changes during the history of the language—not arbitrarily, indeed, but only while retaining its ties with a meaning that finds expression precisely in the choice and use of this particular word. Words are therefore always characterized by a combination of determinacy and indeterminacy. They acquire their determinate character in the context of a given sentence.[159] Moreover, they owe the possibility of being thus determined precisely to the indeterminacy of words, for it is this which allows the same words to be used in an incalculable number of diverse sentences.

Even within a sentence, however, words do not completely lose their indeterminacy. For this reason, the meaning of the individual sentence is in turn fully established only by the context of the discourse or situation in which it is spoken. Correspondingly, the interpretation of a sentence must look to its context in the discourse; the "context" here is both the narrow and the broader, and even broadest, context.[160]

The combination of determinacy and indeterminacy in the use of words entails this consequence for the ongoing discourse: that as we continue to speak, new determinate meanings are continually being articulated, but that at the same time these are in turn surrounded by "an indeterminate penumbra of obscure possible meaning."[161] The connotations of what is

[159]On the relative indeterminacy of individual words and on the way in which they achieve definition in the context of the sentence, see J. Stenzel, *Philosophie der Sprache* (1934; 1964), 48 and, earlier, 16. On the indeterminacy of words, see also W. V. O. Quine, *Word and Object* (Cambridge, Mass., 1960, 1964), 125ff., where, however, indeterminacy is not ascribed to every isolated word as such. According to Von Kutschera (n. 74, above), 125ff., Quine, like Wittgenstein, links the meaning of a word to its use (129) but also emphasizes its indeterminacy. The result of this indeterminacy is both the lack of distinction between analytic and synthetic judgment and the plurality of possible translations of one and the same sentence.

[160]Stenzel, 16. W. V. O. Quine, *From a Logical Point of View* (Cambridge, Mass., 1952; 1963²), 85ff., argues for a contextual theory of verbal meaning (166), which, in contrast to a field theory (see H. Geckeler, *Strukturelle Semantik und Wortfeldtheorie* [1971], 49ff.; see 100ff. on J. Trier), takes into consideration not only the lexematic context (Geckeler, 85f.) but also the actual context in speaking. See also Von Kutschera (n. 74, above), 112ff. Von Kutschera attributes to Quine the view that "the meaning of a term changes with our views of the world" (108); on this, see Quine, *Word and Object*, 12f., and idem, *From a Logical Point of View*, 41f.

[161]Liebrucks, *Sprache und Bewusstsein* II, 242. See also Gadamer's remark, in *Truth and Method*, 426, that a linguistic utterance "means to hold what is said together with an infinity

actually said form the bases for possible continuations which, in view of the multiplicity of connotations and the associations linked to these, can turn off in various directions at any point in the conversation. To that extent, one subject leads to another, and an essential element in the charm of conversation is that throughout its constant twists and turns there is a single thread of discourse.[162]

In addition, from the start and in its every phase the course of a conversation is located within the horizon of a totality. Every utterance is a temporal process, and during its course the hearer anticipates the whole of each sentence and the total context of unfolding meaning.[163] Conversely, in formulating what is to be said in each succeeding utterance the speaker anticipates the whole of what he or she intends to say. The anticipation that is continually being corrected in the course of listening gives rise in turn to what the hearer, now turned speaker, says; from this the former speaker, now turned listener, can judge how successfully he or she managed to communicate the intended meaning. In this process, elements of action are introduced into the course of the conversation in the form of carefully considered communications or explanations of something said earlier. Such actions may interrupt and break the thread of the conversation, but they can also introduce order into the ongoing discourse.

The alternation of speaking and listening unites the conversing partners in an encompassing community, and it is this which gives the conversation a "life of its own."[164] This common bond may arise out of the topic of

---

of what is not said in the unity of one meaning and to ensure that it will be understood in this way. Someone who speaks in this way may well use only the most ordinary and common words and still be able to express what is unsaid and to be said."

[162]The viewpoint of a gradual accumulation of meaning in the process of speaking also offers an access to the understanding of the way in which words change their meaning in the history of a language. See Liebrucks II, 243. Ricoeur, in his essay "Structure, Word, Event," trans. R. Sweeney, in his *The Conflict of Interpretations: Essays in Hermeneutics,* ed. D. Ihde (Evanston, Ill., 1974), 93f., emphasizes the metaphorical structure of this process in which the polysemy of words at any given moment has its basis. In developing his generative transformational grammar into a "theory of traces," Chomsky has increasingly attempted to do justice to the phenomenon of polysemy. Wandruszka, on the other hand, emphasizes the accidental character of the polysemies and polymorphies found in the development of a language; these, he says, are not reducible to general structural conditions; see his "Sprache und Sprachen," in Peisl and Mohler (n. 108, above), 7–47.

[163]Seebass (n. 65, above), 352ff., 334ff. The anticipation of a totality of meaning shows that there is an analogy between speaking and acting. But whereas the right word "comes" to a speaker who is concentrating on the "whole" of the topic, an agent must, on the basis of past experience, determine what means will lead to the chosen goal and are suited for achieving it.

[164]Goffman, 113. I should point out that when in this section I bring in the concept of spirit as a way of explaining the peculiarity of conversation I am saying something essentially

the conversation, which develops in various directions because of the successive utterances of the participants and which each participant anticipates in its totality during the utterance by the speaker of the moment. But the unity of a conversation may also arise simply from the reciprocal feeling of emotional solidarity. This solidarity, already present as a whole in feeling, can then take concrete form in a casual series of utterances on various topics; these utterances in turn assure the partners that their mutual solidarity is real. In any case, a successful conversation leads to "a transformation into a communion, in which we do not remain what we were."[165]

At the same time, however, while the conversation is still progressing, the "object" is fully present as a spiritual unity; it produces its own atmosphere and is reciprocally anticipated by the partners as it becomes increasingly concrete in the course of the conversation. Any contribution that promotes the ongoing conversation owes its existence to attentiveness to the object as it manifests itself in outline and through intimations. It is due to a concentration on the conversation as a totality that the speaker of the moment finds the right thing to say. The choice of what to say is in this situation not really a choice made after deliberation—unless, of course, we are to say that every choice is "accidental" in the sense that it is made in virtue of the feeling of the totality of life as present here and now.[166]

In the final analysis, the object of any particular conversation is likewise integrated into the totality of life, which is represented and made present by that object. Within this common horizon it is clear that the two types of conversation previously distinguished belong together as variations on the basic topic that ultimately grounds any interest in a conversation, in its particular topics, and in the communication event: I mean the presence of life itself. In the "trance" into which the participants in a successful conversation fall, the spirit of life as a totality finds expression. This is the religious dimension of language or—to use the terminology of Schleiermacher's theory of religion—the universe of meaning that is apprehensible in the particular theme and its articulation or that is simply experienced as present in the feeling of agreement with the partner which is then articulated in the exchange of almost any kind of utterance whatever.

---

different from what L. Weisgerber says about *Die geistige Seite der Sprache und ihre Erforschung* (1971), 14f., 28ff. Admittedly, Weisgerber too makes language as a social phenomenon his starting point, but he does not base his observations on the actual process of speaking. What he calls the "spirit of a language" is in fact only the sediment left by a vital process of communication that finds its purest form in conversation.

[165]Gadamer, *Truth and Method.* 341. The "object" of the conversation, which is the basis of the common bond (330), need not, however, always take the form of a common topic. My last few remarks in the text attempt to show this.

[166]See above, at n. 145. On the "choice of words," see Stenzel (n. 125, above), 45ff.

3. *Imagination and Reason*

The appearance of the right word, which cannot be forced to show itself but (not unlike an inspiration) comes unbidden to one who is attentive to the object of the conversation, is an example of the operation of the imagination. In the life of the imagination human beings experience themselves as simultaneously creative and dependent. Not without reason do we speak of "unexpected flights" of imagination: these cannot be induced by force. Only in a state of relaxation do images begin to "flood" the imagination.[167] Imagination and freedom thus go together. It is worth noting that individuals who are especially creative intellectually have emphasized the inspiration aspect of their insights.[168] This state of affairs recalls Hamann's notion of the divine origin of language. Contrary to Hamann's view, however, as far as imagination is concerned, divine inspiration and human creativity are not in competition but, rather, work together in such a way that inspiration is the condition for human creativity.

The radical importance of imagination in human intellectual life has been a concern of philosophical anthropology and epistemology ever since Aristotle. But the philosophers have never grasped with full clarity the unique interaction of creative freedom and receptivity that characterizes the life of the imagination. In Aristotle's view, imagination belongs with memory: it serves to make the content of memory present in images, although there can be mistakes in the process.[169] It was not until the

---

[167]H. Kunz, *Die anthropologische Bedeutung der Phantasie* I (1946), 7f., 16, expressly calls attention to the element of dependence in the life of the imagination (see also 175ff. on the passive character of spiritual acts). Back in 1962, following Kunz, I pointed out the theological significance of this trait in the phenomenon of imagination; see my *What Is Man? Contemporary Anthropology in Theological Perspective,* trans. D. A. Priebe (Philadelphia, 1970), 26. R. L. Hart, *Unfinished Man and the Imagination* (New York, 1968), gives a voluntaristic interpretation of the imagination (219–28); he therefore neglects the unique merging of creativity and dependence in the life of the imagination and consequently the real problem that must be faced in a phenomenological elucidation of the imagination (228ff.). The point I emphasized in my 1962 book, namely, "the ability to detach oneself from one's own situation and to transpose oneself into any other position one might choose" (*What Is Man?* 25), will be discussed later in this chapter in connection with the importance of attention (see below, at nn. 179ff.).

[168]M. Polanyi, "Schöpferische Einbildungskraft," *Zeitschrift für philosophische Forschung* 22 (1968), 53–70, speaks explicitly of the "inspiration" *(Eingebung)* that guides the imagination, which "in turn sets free the powers of inspiration" (66). Polanyi thus sees inspiration and imagination, receptivity and productive activity, as working in harmony. This is a point to which I must return farther on.

[169]Therefore, according to Aristotle, representations—which, like the faculty of the soul that produces them, are called "imagination"—are "usually false," in contradistinction to

modern age, and especially the eighteenth century, that there was a shift to a positive appraisal of this power of free combination.[170] Thus Kant made the "productive" or "constructive" function of imagination, as distinct from the function of simply reproducing what is present in memory, the source of all the synthetic accomplishments of reason in its application to the objects of experience.[171]

In Kant, however, this idea remained of limited application. Despite further advances that are ultimately reflected in the second edition of *The Critique of Pure Reason,* the synthetic achievement of the productive imagination was restricted to the sensible "schematization" and illustration of the functions of the understanding. Kant was here holding to the voluntary character of imagination. Aristotle had said long ago that it is in our power to produce images in the imagination "whenever we wish" (*De anima* 427b18), as is evident from the ability of those who produce works of art from memory. In Kant, the voluntary control of the imagination was the basis for a distinction between productive imagination and fantasy;[172] this indicates that Kant's attention was not focused on the connection between uncontrollable inspiration and creative intellectual activity.

As long as the activity of the imagination was limited to the reproduction of what is stored up in memory, it was possible to conceive of its activity as subject to the will. But once the creative function of the imagination began to be emphasized, difficulties inevitably arose. I can, of course, deliberately reflect and recall something that has for the moment

---

perceptions (*De anima* 428a12). For the connection between imagination and memory, see *De memoria* 450a22, as well as the discussion of this point in H. Cassirer, *Aristoteles' Schrift "Von der Seele" und ihre Stellung innerhalb der aristotelischen Philosophie* (1932; repr. 1968), 108ff., esp. 114f.

[170]J. H. Trede, in *HWP* 2 (1972), 347. H. Langendörfer, *Zur Theorie der produktiven Einbildungskraft* (1940), plays down too much (24, 32) the difference that exists here between the modern age and, for example, Thomas Aquinas (18, 20f.). It is true, however, that Aquinas does describe the activity of imagination as a *formatio* (a "forming" or "formulating") (*Summa theologiae* I, q. 85, a. 2 ad 3).

[171]I. Kant, *The Critique of Pure Reason,* trans. J. M. D. Meiklejohn, in *Kant* (Great Books of the Western World 42; Chicago, 1952), A 115ff., B 150ff. The fundamental importance of imagination for knowledge emerges from the fact that, according to Kant, all synthesis depends on the imagination (B 103). According to H. Mörchen, "Die Einbildungskraft bei Kant," *Jahrbuch für Philosophie und phänomenologische Forschung* 11 (1930), 311–493, in the works that paved the way for *The Critique of Pure Reason* the categories themselves were still "functions of the imagination in the abstract" (392). But even in the first edition of the *Critique* a tendency to restrict this role is discernible (A 97; see Mörchen, 370 and 385).

[172]I. Kant, *Anthropologie in pragmatischer Hinsicht* (1798), § 28: "The imagination, insofar as it also brings forth spontaneous images *(Einbildungen),* is also called the fantasy *(Phantasie).* See no. 340 in the reflections on anthropology (Akad. Ausg. 15 [1923], 134). See also Mörchen, 332.

escaped my memory, but I cannot simply decide to get a new inspiration; at the very least, the decision does not guarantee success. There is admittedly a distinction between the unregulated activity of imagination in the dreaming consciousness and its disciplined activity in the waking state, where it is combined with reflection.[173] But justice is not done to this distinction by asserting a voluntary control in the waking state. Voluntary control may aptly describe the ability to visualize already existent structural facts and states, but it is not relevant to the properly "compositional" nature of the imagination that is connected with creative inspiration.[174]

Even in post-Kantian thinking the creative imagination was conceived in a one-sided manner as an activity subject to the free disposition of the will. This development reached its provisional high point in F. W. J. Schelling, for whom the productive imagination is no longer limited to the illustration of already established functions of the understanding but springs directly from the activity of the ego: "What is generally called theoretical reason is nothing but the imagination in the service of freedom."[175]

This critical thesis becomes intelligible in the light of Schelling's explanation that the ego's active knowledge of itself implies the difference between this activity as conscious and finite, and the infinite, whereas imagination "is suspended in between infinity and finitude" and—as Schelling will say later on—"gives shape" *(einbildet)* to the infinite in the finite and "represents" the finite to the infinite. Here too, then, the imagination is entirely at the service of the acting ego and its arbitrary control. In his discussion of the philosophy of art, Schelling does indeed try to render account of the fact that the artistic genius experiences the operation of imagination as taking the form of inspirations that befall him. But Schelling characteristically interprets this experience as a natural illusion which supposedly arises because the ego as productive cannot know

---

[173]Kant, *Anthropologie,* §§ 28 and 31.

[174]Thus Kant describes the productive imagination as "constructive" (ibid., § 28), but calls it "noncreative" because it must "derive the *material* for its images from the senses" (ibid.). In contrast, he says of the genius, who is distinguished by "originality . . . of imagination" (§ 30), that his proper field of activity is precisely the imagination "because this is creative" (§ 52). This one-sided interpretation of the imagination as spontaneity has been criticized by Mörchen, 316, 379, 401. According to Mörchen, Kant was unable to grasp the unity of receptivity and spontaneity which marks the imagination, because for him " 'I think' is outside of time" (406), so that the subject is conceived as pure spontaneity and, at the same time, as substantial (412, 145f.), while its being given to itself in the course of time is not thematized.

[175]F. W. J. Schelling, *System der transzendentalen Idealismus* (1800), in *Werke* III, 559. The next citation is from ibid., 558. R. Hablützel, *Dialektik und Einbildungskraft. F. W. J. Schellings Lehre von der menschlichen Erkenntnis* (1954), 78ff., is unfortunately vague and unproductive.

itself as immediately one with its product.[176]

In the ensuing years Schelling qualified this view insofar as in his lectures on the philosophy of art (1802–5) he defined the artist's genius as "the idea of man in God" or, as the case might be, "the divine that indwells in the human," so that the poetic "imagination of the infinite in the finite" could now also be looked upon as "inspiration."[177] But the foundations of his overall approach remained unchanged. The only result of the thesis on the participation of the genius in the absolute was that the problem of the opposition between creative activity and inspiration no longer arose, although the price paid for not having to face it was that human freedom lost its finite character.

The problem does not seem to have emerged with full clarity even in the postidealist development of philosophy. In Sartre's book on the imagination the latter is equated with consciousness as an embodiment of its freedom. The movement of consciousness that transcends what is at hand and by this act of "nihilation" first establishes it as "world" makes imagination possible by transcending the world, while at the same time it is able to express itself only in the act of the imagination.[178] The element of inspiration vanishes here. It would be natural indeed to understand the transcendence which marks openness to the world, and to which alone the world shows itself to be a unity, as an openness to the absolute and thus to understand imagination as inspiration from the absolute. But such a view would be incompatible with Sartre's understanding of the freedom that finds expression in the imagination. In view of this, the question of whether and how the two aspects brought out by the phenomenology of the imagination can be combined becomes all the more urgent for us.

The key to a solution of this problem may be found in the role played by attention, which directs the activity of imagination in the waking state. The reader will recall that in a conversation the attention paid by the participants to the object of the conversation is a condition required if suitable formulations are to present themselves and if the partners in the conversation are to keep one and the same object in view as they alternate listening and speaking. Attention, or rather the preattentive turning that delimits the field within which focal attention can move hither and yon

---

[176]Ibid., III, 615.

[177]Ibid., V, 439f. (§§ 62 and 63). The cited definition of poetry (as distinct from the fine arts) is given ibid., 461 (§ 64). The creative activity of the poet, here described as "invention," is subsequently—in connection with the discussion of language (634ff.)—occasionally also called "inspiration" (681).

[178]J. P. Sartre, *The Psychology of Imagination,* trans. B. Frechtman (New York, 1948), 233ff., esp. 235f.

among changing objects,[179] defines the horizon within which we are open to the inspirations of the imagination.

The focusing of attention, however, is not simply a matter of willing; rather, like the choice of a goal in the context of action (see above, at n. 145), the focusing of attention is a matter of a total attitude that has its basis in feeling and thus in an anticipation of the whole of the individual's own life. This enables us to understand how attention to an object can, on the one hand, be accompanied by a state of fascination and "seizure," and yet can, on the other hand, also "slacken off" and turn away. The perceptions *or* the imaginative representations that emerge within the preattentive field then become the object of focal attention; in the light shed by the latter, they can then be constructively grasped in their particular gestalt through reflection on the horizon of the field as a whole.

In this way the element of inspiration is combined with that of creative activity. The inspirations of the imagination set in motion the constructive imaginative activity that is connected with reflection (see above, chapter 3, n. 75); as a result of this activity, the objective thematic horizon that is anticipated by the attention acquires concrete form or, as the case may be, is enriched by this or that particular trait. In the light of the role of attention, it becomes understandable that, on the one hand, we cannot force the inspirations of the imagination to appear and that, on the other, such inspirations do not exclude human activity but, rather, energize it to a productive concretization, in the medium of the objective theme on which attention is focused, of that totality of the person's own life which has been anticipated in feeling.

The power of imagination is thus in fact the vital element at work in freedom as the latter takes concrete form. At the same time it can manifest itself to the eyes of the theologian as a paradigm of the relation between grace and freedom. But the role played by attention in combination with imagination makes it clear that the inspirations of the imagination do not by any means always present the word of God in its pure form to human beings in their concrete situation. God can speak to human beings through the inspirations of the imagination, if these beings have pure hearts that are open to the whole of the world in which they live and to God as their origin and goal. But if their attention to their lives as a whole is bound up with attention to other thematic areas in such a way that these no longer bear witness to God as the ground and fulfillment of all things but ignore

[179]Neisser (n. 88, above), 89f. Neisser emphasizes the importance of attention for imagination as well as for perception (94f.). Both the perceived and the imagined gestalts are grasped by constructive processes which depend on attention. Neisser comments in passing that no contemporary psychological theory "deals satisfactorily with the constructive nature of the higher mental processes" (300).

him as they claim the total attention of the human being, then this human distortedness also corrupts the life of the imagination.

Sinners, whose attention is limited to the object of their self-seeking desires or is even sucked down into the whirlpool of envy and hatred, encounter in the images of their imaginations not the voice of God but the whisperings of the devil. In either case, it is clear that the creative freedom of the human consciousness depends on the inspirations of the imagination. And because the life of language is so continuously determined by the imagination, it is not surprising that human language can likewise be warped by a corrupt imagination.[180]

The part played by attention in the activity of the imagination[181] also throws new light on the relation between imagination and reason. The reason for saying this is that, through their relation to the preattentive turning, the inspirations of the imagination are provided with a framework within which their significance manifests itself. This is to say that these inspirations do not emerge in isolation, nor in the shapeless flow of a "stream of consciousness," but in the setting of the momentary field of attention, which in turn is related to the thematic of life as a totality and its identity and which consequently shifts with the progress of inner and outer experience. This means, however, that in the life of the imagination, at least in the waking state, there exists at every point the tension between particular and universal which shows itself in perceptual consciousness as

[180]This aspect of the problem is discussed by I. Illich, "Sprachgefangenschaft. Warenbezogene Sprachlähmungen im Gespräch über die Umwelt," in Peisl and Mohler (n. 108, above), 320–37. In any case, not every "personal language" of an individual is superior from the standpoint of self-realization to the language of a cultural community—if there is any such thing; rather, a rich individual linguistic competence becomes possible only as a result of the wealth of the cultural heritage that is compresent by connotation in the words of the language. Connections between linguistic deformation and neurosis have been discussed especially by J. Lacan and, from a Marxist standpoint, by A. Lorenzer, *Sprachzerstörung und Rekonstruktion* (1970). A theological counterpart to these discussions is to be found in Ebeling's remarks on the therapeutic function of hermeneutics in curing "the disorders of language"; see his *Introduction to a Theological Theory of Language,* trans. R. A. Wilson (Philadelphia, 1973), 162; see 162ff.

[181]Attention ceases only in sleep, in which, according to Schachtel, *Metamorphosis* (n. 88, above), 72, we return to that original "embeddedness" in a preconscious, symbiotic web of life from which the ego has subsequently separated itself in the course of its development. In the dream phases of sleep the images of the imagination stream without guidance from the attention of the ego and for that reason are all the more easily evoked by affective excitations and anxieties. See in this context the disagreement with Freud's interpretation of dreams in Piaget's *Nachahmung, Spiel und Traum* (n. 26, above), 234–47. Piaget disputes a (supposed) memory of the earliest events in the history of the child, since memory itself comes into existence only in the course of the individual's development. In addition, unconscious symbolism extends far beyond the realm of repressed phenomena.

the relation of objects to space and which forms the framework for the activity of reason.

Reason does not produce the universal only through abstraction or—in the nominalist explanation—through the generalization effected by linguistic labeling. Since rational reflection presupposes both the sensorimotor life of perception and the life of language and imagination, it already operates at every point within the tension of gestalt and field, part and whole, particular and universal. It is true, of course, that both sides acquire their clear contours only in rational reflection. Following Lotze and Sigwart's criticism of the theory of abstraction, Ernst Cassirer correctly emphasized the point that "the original and decisive achievement of the concept" is not to compare and group representations already at hand but, rather, "to form impressions into representations."[182] This operation is one that at every point has already been carried out by language, which identifies representations by means of words, thus rendering them repeatable and therefore available in an identical form and also making it possible to raise the question of their interrelationships, the distinctions between them, and the traits they have in common.

But the universal is also at every point simply given to reflection as symbiotic unity of life and as field of movement, objective space, and world. It thus forms the unexpressed, unthematic horizon[183] within which phenomena, whether of perception or of imagination, make their appearance. Through the activity of reflection these phenomena are related to and distinguished from one another in accordance with the viewpoints of unity and difference that are made available by the identificatory work of language. Lenneberg's "categorization processes" describe this activity from only one standpoint, that of the identification of the particular as a "gestalt" and its classification in (changeable) general schemata. But identification of the particular supposes reflection on the field in which the particular emerges as this particular. The question of the totality achieved by the categorization processes pertains to the same type of reflection. It may be that human attention is directed primarily to the particular objects in the environment. But the horizon that contains these objects is also already given at every point, at least in an unthematic way. It is only through reflection on this horizon that the theme of subsumption under

[182]Cassirer, *Philosophie der symbolischen Formen* (n. 64, above), I, 252 (ET 281).

[183]There are points of contact between the reflections offered here and the fundamental-theological explanation of the structure of consciousness that is developed by K. Rahner in his transcendental philosophical interpretation of Thomist epistemology; see his *Spirit in the World,* trans. W. V. Dych (New York, 1967). However, I substitute for Rahner's transcendental mode of reflection a more phenomenological approach that links the themes of consciousness and self-consciousness to wider anthropological contexts.

a universal, which is the structure of the categorization process, becomes at all intelligible.

Human beings are indeed turned primarily to the objects of their environment. Nonetheless, as exocentric beings they develop at an early stage (to wit, at the transition from the first to the second year of life when their bodies become integrated into the space containing objects) a reflective relation to themselves and thus also to the ultimate comprehensive unity that renders possible their conceptual categorization of things. This horizon of their individual existence is initially coextensive with the horizon of the world of which they learn to understand themselves as members. Materially, however, as they thematize a divine reality that grounds the unity of the world, they already have at every point a knowledge of a mystery which transcends the world in its entirety and with which their own existence, itself transcending and therefore encompassing the world, is mysteriously interwoven. Only much later do they discover that this mystery is the ground and essence of their own freedom. On the other hand, human beings learned at a very early stage, through the divine word that establishes the world, that the divine mystery behind the world is not simply a dark abyss containing the world but addresses them in the midst of the world and exalts their lives into itself.[184]

4. Theology and the Religious Implications of Language

Admittedly, the divine word that establishes the world originally took the form of a mythical word. The word of myth is a word in which the reality itself is present, and present in such a way that the reality automatically makes itself known in this word and at the same time establishes the context in which it makes itself known.[185] The characteristic mythical

---

[184]Justifiably appealing to the New Testament concept of *mystērion* as the divine plan of salvation, and also in harmony with the human phenomenon, E. Jüngel, *Gott als Geheimnis der Welt* (1977), 340ff., stresses the point that the self-withholding of the divine mystery cannot be the final word in Christian theology. But he is doubtless wrong (despite his valid criticism of the idea of "self-possession" as the basic statement of the doctrine of God, 302) in attributing to Rahner such a theology of the divine silence. For Rahner too, the loving self-manifestation of God is evidently the specific element in the Christian doctrine of God, and the self-withholding by which God separates himself from the world is in the service of that self-manifestation; see K. Rahner, *Foundations of Christian Faith*, trans. W. V. Dych (New York, 1978), 35, 53f., 57f., 65f., 119ff., 224f.

[185]Cassirer, II, 33, was probably right in considering the original lack of differentiation between word and thing to be the root of both linguistic symbol and myth. But the distinguishing element—the necessity of which he also rightly emphasized (28ff.)—emerged less clearly from his presentation, except for the point that in its "signifying" function language moves away from the immediate unity of word and object. Myth then becomes simply an expression of a symbolic consciousness that is not aware of its independent, formative activity. But there seems to be a further peculiarity of mythical consciousness that Cassirer

representation of a primordial time in which the world came into existence as an ordered place is probably connected with this structural peculiarity of the mythical understanding of words. I need not concern myself here in detail with the material form this representation took in particular experiential contexts or, in other words, with the kinds of divinities associated with the establishment of the world.

I may not, however, leave unmentioned the similarities and differences between the mythical and the magical use of words.[186] In the magical view, the real connection between word and thing makes it possible, by means of the name, to control the thing or person thus named. This kind of magical use of words is in contrast to the mythical experience of things as making themselves present through words. On the other hand, in myth the magical use of words is attributed to the divinity itself, especially in connection with the creation of the ordered world. Human beings too are regarded as able, at exalted moments of their lives, to speak words of power in the form of blessing and curse; for example, at the birth of a child or the approach of death.

This entire complex mythicomagical understanding of words is doubtless also present in the background of biblical talk about the word of God.[187] Theologians should not be embarrassed to regard as mythical in origin the idea of creation through the word and the more comprehensive idea of words as having the power to produce the objects directly designated by them, as well the vision, underlying both of these ideas, of the unity of word and thing. Anyone who is ready to accept the presence of mythical elements in the biblical documents should also be able to acknowledge that in few areas is the connection with mythical thinking so close as in the understanding of the word.

This does not mean that one must immediately become a radical demythologizer and reduce all talk about the word of God to a manner of

---

does not take into account and that is grounded in the very nature of myth and also remains normative in the development of religion beyond the mythical forms of consciousness. I refer to the function, linked to the mythical word, of establishing the world.

[186]On the concept of magic and its relation to religion, see the criticism by Jensen, *Myth and Cult Among Primitive Peoples* (n. 43, above), 209–62, of those who assert a "pre-animistic" phase of magic prior to the rise of religion properly so called. See especially 212ff., against C. H. Ratschow, *Magie und Religion* (1947). According to Jensen, it was the loss of their original meaning that allowed religious formulas to become spells (247f.), while it remains unproved that profane purposes were ever essential and temporally prior elements of cults (211).

[187]L. Dürr, *Die Wertung des göttlichen Wortes im Alten Testament und im antiken Orient* (1938), is still a fundamental treatment of this subject. On Ptah of Memphis as creator of the world by his word, see ibid., 23ff.; on corresponding ideas in Sumer and Babylon, 17f. The idea, found in Jeremiah (23:29), of the divine word as exercising a destructive power recalls the power of magically operative speech that was ascribed to the Sumerian Enlil (ibid., 9ff.).

expressing human self-understanding. It is indeed possible to ask what the truth is that is contained in the mythical understanding of the word and in myths generally in regard to the reality, distinct from human beings, that is therein intended. It is possible to inquire what modifications the mythical understanding of the word has undergone in biblical thinking. But we should not try to locate the uniqueness of biblical revelation in representations where it is not to be found. Yet the idea of the word of God and its authority have traditionally been regarded as of such fundamental importance in Christian theology (especially in Protestantism) that, right down to the present time, theologians whose critical consciousness in other matters has often been quite untroubled by any anxiety have here been immobilized and subject to breakdowns. Thus Rudolf Bultmann's program of demythologization and the discussion it elicited remained strangely silent about the mythical structure of the idea of the divine word.

Yet it is only when this structure has been acknowledged in principle that questions can be raised regarding the specific traits in biblical conceptions of the divine word that take them beyond the mythical understanding of words. Such traits are probably to be found, for example, where a distinction is made between the word of God and its human formulation. Or again, where the relation of the prophetic word to the future is thought of not as automatically verified through the magical operation of the word of God but as fulfilled in such a way that God remains master of the word spoken in his name. Or, finally, where the word is thought of in conjunction with the idea of divine wisdom as the source of intelligible order in the world, so that the idea of the divine Logos replaces myth.[188]

The opposition between the Logos—the Logos at work not only in human beings but also and above all in the cosmos—and myth is admittedly not complete. Indeed, the Christian idea of the incarnation of the divine Logos may even be described as a resumption of the basic notion of the mythical word as a symbolic manifestation of the named object in the sensible medium of sound[189]—although on a more sophisticated level at which a distinction is first made between the content of the word and its sensible manifestation.

All this need not disturb theologians, provided a foolish purism does not lead them to claim that the biblical word of God is free of all human (and, specially, all mythical) additions. After all, the biblical word of God —and, above all, the Logos of the New Testament—may well have absorbed into itself the element of truth in the mythical understanding of the

[188]On the relation between myth and word, see W. F. Otto, *Die Gestalt und das Sein. Gesammelte Abhandlungen über den Mythos und seine Bedeutung für die Menschheit* (1955).

[189]According to Gadamer, *Truth and Method* (n. 32, above), 378, the Christian idea of the incarnation does most justice to the "nature of language," that is, the presence of the reality in the verbal symbol. See 136f. on the concept of symbol.

word. On the other hand, a purist theology of the authoritative word of God may, ironically enough, very easily succumb to the tendency to pass off the mythical and especially the magical characteristics in the idea of God's powerful word as uniquely biblical and, at the same time, leave in the background the specifically biblical characteristics of that word.

A theology that, precisely in the interests of its claim to truth, does not close itself to the need of critical reflection on the biblical traditions in the light of modern experience of the world, may not, of course, simply offer the structure of the mythical understanding of the word as authoritative truth for its own time. Theological apologetics has always been open to the temptation of using modern categories with a seemingly analogous structure in order to effect an outward modernization that leaves everything just where it was, not only materially but even in the customary form of presenting it. That kind of superficial modernization does little service to the truth.

At the present time, theologians dealing with the concept of God's word and with the faith character of Christian discourse yield to this kind of temptation when they rashly take over the speech act theory. The gospel, for example, is then presented as a performative linguistic act which by its nature establishes the truth of what it says in the area that is opened up only by these words. In this approach the truth of the propositions proclaimed is supposedly not bound to answer the human question of verification or falsification.[190] The apologetic concern to render the proclamation immune against critical reflection is understandable, but the price paid for the immunity is a high one. We are supposedly dealing with a linguistic action of God, and yet this evidently comes to us in the form of human proclamation. If the latter is interpreted as a linguistic action, there is simply no way of distinguishing it from the object to which it is related and then, possibly, to understand it as also legitimated by that object. As a result, the claim that the words embody a divine linguistic action collapses into an anthropomorphic projection on the part of a linguistically active human being.

---

[190]Thus O. Bayer, *Was ist das: Theologie? Eine Skizze* (1973), 24ff. ("Performatives Wort als Sache der Theologie") and 52f. In the case of the "elementary speech acts in which gospel and law—the one setting free, the other imposing obligations—make themselves known" (80, 83), we are evidently meant to think (in contrast to 31f.) of human speech acts (in the form of proclamation). But, characteristically, any clear distinction between the two is lacking, as is the consciousness (present in Austin) of the interweaving of performative and constative elements in concrete speech. Along with the distinction between the human side of the proclamation and the latter's cognitive content the question of the *competence* of the linguistic act of proclamation and its justification is also missing; had the author raised this question, he could not have failed to attend in a constative way to what is cognitively relevant. On the concept of promise, which is not reducible to a simple act of encouragement, see above, p. 369.

In another application of the speech act theory the interpretation of statements of faith as performative utterances immediately appears as likewise a description of human speech actions, on the grounds that belief statements are usually performative utterances.[191] But this makes the acting human being so exclusively central to the understanding of religious speech that a distinct divine reality slips completely out of sight.[192]

In this context the task facing the understanding of language becomes analogous to that facing the doctrine of justification: the need to limit the claims of human action. A theoretical reflection on the understanding of language must break out of the narrow alley of the speech act theory in order to reach a vision of the dimension in which language and the religious thematic come together. This does not mean that we must also move beyond the phenomenon of linguistic communication within the world in which we live, to a formalized theory of language which is purified of the indeterminacies of everyday speech and which supposedly would alone ensure the intelligibility of everyday language.

The fact is, rather, that by reason of the combination of determinacy and indeterminacy in its linguistic utterances everyday language makes possible a living process of understanding, in which the "unspoken horizon of meaning" (Hans Georg Gadamer) is open to the religious dimension of reality. If, on the contrary, we reduce the wide realm, reaching into indefiniteness, of linguistically articulated meaning to the univocal meaning of words that have hardened into defined terms, the reduction will eliminate not only the vital and productive process of linguistic utterance and communication but also the religious depth dimension of this process.[193] Any talk of God must then be judged to be simply a transposition

---

[191]Thus, according to W. D. Just, *Religiöse Sprache und analytische Philosophie. Sinn und Unsinn religiöser Aussagen* (1975), statements of faith "are defined principally by their illocutionary function . . . by their character as actions" (148; see 141ff.). Just's assertion that the meaning of statements of faith is "completely missed when they are taken as statements about the being of God" (151)—although at least "at a superficial grammatical level" they resemble such statements (150)—is based on a distinction (144ff.) between a "parenthetical" and a "nonparenthetical" use of the expression "I believe." On the unity of these aspects, see my remarks in *Grundfragen systematischer Theologie* II, 226ff., esp. 247ff.

[192]W. Trillhaas, *Religionsphilosophie* (1972), has likewise failed to take this explicitly into account when, following the speech act theory, he gives a general definition of "religious language as action" (237ff.). As a result, religious language as a whole is assigned to the realm of magic, in the sense of being "linguistic spells" (see the article, cited 239, of H. Schweppenheimer in the *Philosophie* volume of Fischer-Lexikon [1958], 314). Trillhaas simply ignores the difference between a mythical and a magical understanding of language. In the life of religion, linguistic actions in the proper sense of this term certainly do occur, as I said earlier, but they are embedded in a linguistic context that cannot be qualified as "action."

[193]This is what happens when, in the service of an enlightened intention of "criticizing metaphysics," logical positivism demands that current speech be replaced by a formalized

of meanings that are defined primarily in secular terms.[194] But *to what* are the words being transferred if not to an empty horizon, so that the metaphor proves to be in fact only a projection?[195]

There is no doubt that theologians must engage in theoretical reflection on language, because, as Gerhard Ebeling has aptly said, "*That which* the gospel contains cannot come to us except in the form of a linguistic

scientific language, at least for scientific use. The Erlangen "Constructivists" (W. Kamlah and P. Lorenzen, *Logische Propädeutik* [1967]; K. Lorenz, *Elemente der Sprachkritik* [1970]) seem to be struggling with similar problems when they maintain that only by reconstructing the situation into which a discourse is introduced and to which it applies can they establish the basis for the intelligibility of language, an intelligibility which, despite the partial indeterminacy of everyday language, is present in it at every point. To reach a higher degree of accuracy is the task of intellectual apprehension of the subject matters in question but not of the philosophy of language. The latter aims, rather, at making available, in its significance even for science, the power which colloquial language possesses of giving access to things and which is due to the public character of its structures of meaning (as opposed to a reduction to explicit definitions of terms).

This holds true especially in theology. Unfortunately, this fact is overlooked in J. Track's *Sprachkritische Untersuchungen zum christlichen Reden von Gott* (1977), which is otherwise instructive in many respects. The difficulty is that Track makes his own (126ff.; see 142, n. 75, etc.) the methodological requirements of constructivism (103ff.), even though he adopts a critical attitude to its ideal of an "ortholanguage" (140, n. 70).

[194]Track, 168ff., 189. In earlier essays on the concept of analogy I too presupposed that any discourse about God must involve a *transfer* or transposition of secular language. Observations suggesting the primarily religious origin of certain meanings of words (e.g., "life"), as well as my attempt to come to grips with the word-of-God theology, have led me to a more thorough study of the importance of religious themes in the origin of language; I am presenting the results of this study here. The theory, based on Aristotelian empiricism, of a unilateral transposition, by analogy, from experience of the world to God, must presuppose at least the word "God" itself and its basic meaning. In medieval theology this presupposition was ensured by the idea of a first cause. The same problem arises in an analogous manner in Tillich's theory of religious language as symbolic (see G. Wenz, *Subjekt und Sein. Die Entwicklung der Theologie Paul Tillichs* [1979], 161ff., esp. 171ff.), and it makes its presence felt in Track as well (see the next note).

[195]F. Kambartel's conception of the word "God" as a "syncategorematic" expression (a synsemantikon) similar to conjunctions or prepositions—see "Theo-logisches," *ZEE* 15 (1971), 32–35—shows the awkward situation that arises here. Track recognizes the problems raised by this suggestion when he rejects the "superficial grammatical" use of the word as a proper name or label (228f.; see 251), so that he can allow any use of it only a limited importance (261ff.). In itself a syncategorematic interpretation of "God" must lead to a denial of the divine transcendence and independence (aseity) that is the basis of any talk of grace. It is surprising, therefore, that G. Ebeling, in his *God and Word,* trans. J. W. Leitch (Philadelphia, 1967), should, on the basis of an "allusion" by P. Lorenzen, be prepared to accept this view which would fit better with the theology of H. Braun. Anyone who wants to maintain that God's relation to the world is determined by his free gracious action may not renounce the interpretation of the word "God" as "Nominator," an interpretation certainly not suggested solely by a "superficial grammatical" approach. The use of the word "God" as "Nominator" (Track, 280ff.) presupposes that the word has a basic meaning which is nonmetaphorical.

communication." Recourse, therefore, to approaches based on the philosophy of language and on linguistics should not be condemned as sacrilegious attacks on the inviolable authority of the word of God. We have seen how questionable such a position is when critically judged by theological standards. E. Güttgemanns is therefore fully justified in arguing that consideration must be given in theology to the formation of theory as this is done in the linguistic sciences.[196] His transposition of the concept and tools of Chomsky's generative transformational grammar into theology where it functions as a "generative poetics" has proved fruitful in many respects and has opened up new perspectives for hermeneutics[197] and in particular for the productive interpretation of texts in preaching.

The theoretical framework of transformational grammar does, however, need to be thoroughly revised if the necessary room is to be made for, on the one hand, the objections raised in the discussion of it by linguists and philosophers of language and, on the other hand, the concerns of theology. Linguistic competence in Chomsky's sense of the term is based on innate grammatical structures. Either, then, the use of this concept in theology will subordinate the biblical revelation of God to the a priori structures of human reason, as happened in, for example, Kant's *Religion Within the Limits of Reason Alone,* or else the grammatical structures themselves must (along the lines, e.g., of Piaget's earlier cited position in regard to Chomsky) be thought of as formed through experience and as historically mutable. This means that the foundations of our understanding of language in general must be more deeply laid; it is at that deeper level that the basis of the relation between God and language would have also to be sought.

Theologians cannot, without prejudicing their own subject, simply attach themselves to this or that methodological approach that has been conceived for secular use. The secular understanding of a method must

---

[196]E. Güttgemanns, "Theologie als sprachbezogene Wissenschaft," in his *Studia Linguistica Neotestamentica. Gesammelte Aufsätze zur linguistischen Grundlage einer neutestamentlichen Theologie* (1971), 184–230, esp. 196ff., against E. Grässer, "Von der Exegese zur Predigt," *Wissenschaft und Praxis in Kirche und Gesellschaft* 60 (1971), 27–39, and idem, "Die falsch programmierte Theologie," *Evangelische Kommentare* 1 (1968), 694–99. Güttgemanns objects to Grässer's "hypostatizing" talk of "the" word of God (201); he correctly describes this as "mythological talk" (203; see 208).

[197]This is especially the case with Güttgemann's discussion of the "transcendentality" of what is meant in a text and therefore of its intention as well (see 213: "The literal sense as apriori open to the fuller sense"). In this discussion he presupposes a linguistics of contexts along with R. Jauss's aesthetics of receptivity (204). This makes intelligible Güttgemann's claim that his linguistic theology is the "legitimate heir" of the modern theological hermeneutics established by Schleiermacher; see O. Gerber and E. Güttgemanns, eds., *Glaube und Grammatik. Theologisches Verstehen als grammatischer Textprozess* (1973; 1974²), 5. But it need not therefore be "the only legitimate heir" (as is claimed ibid.).

be subjected to scrutiny in relation to the (usually omitted) religious dimension of the realm of phenomena under discussion and must be revised in the light of this scrutiny. Moreover, when it comes to linguistics, theologians are not faced solely, as Güttgemanns thought at one time,[198] with a choice between Chomsky's generative transformational grammar (or its semantic expansion by J. J. Katz), on the one side, and a behaviorist linguistics, on the other. At least the speech act theory and the theory of linguistic relativity must now be added.

Linguistic relativity has likewise been applied to theology in an original way. According to H. Fischer, the syntax of languages "compels thinking" in a special way. Since in many languages and in the Indo-European languages in particular the sentence is structured as a linking of subject and predicate, events are represented as actions of an acting subject. Asiatic languages like Chinese and Japanese, on the other hand, know no such "compulsion by the (grammatical) subject." In the light, therefore, of his assumption that language determines thought, Fischer concludes that the idea of the world as originating in the action of a subject—that is, the idea of creation—is simply the result of the "subject compulsion" which syntax exercises on thinking. At the same time, the whole theistic idea of God falls by the wayside. According to Fischer, the word "God" should simply be interpreted "in operational terms" as standing for a "happening."[199]

Whatever may be one's reaction to these views, which are convergent with those of H. Braun and M. Mezger, an argument based on the idea of linguistic structure as exercising a compulsion on thought will not convince anyone familiar with the objections against linguistic relativity (see above, at nn. 76f.). For that matter, neither Weisgerber nor Whorf proposed the relativity position in as one-sided and deterministic a fashion as Fischer does, to say nothing of the much qualified form in which the

---

[198]Güttgemanns, "Theologie als sprachbezogene Wissenschaft," 215. For criticism of Chomsky, see above, n. 90 (Piaget), n. 114 (M. Eigen), and n. 162 (M. Wandruszka), as well as Seebass (n. 65), 44, n. 28.

[199]H. Fischer, *Glaubensaussage und Sprachstruktur* (1972), 222ff., 232ff. (doctrine of creation), 236ff., 244ff. (idea of God). For the rest, Fischer's book gives a nuanced and readable account of the present state of discussion in language theory. His acceptance of the effectiveness of a subject schema as a source of projection in the religious consciousness is close to the position of G. Dux, *Die Logik der Weltbilder. Sinnstrukturen im Wandel der Geschichte* (1982), 93ff., 107ff. (see idem, *Strukturwandel der Legitimation* [1976], 69–88). Dux, however, traces the "subject schema" back, not to linguistic form, but to the ontogenesis of the cognitive system. Here "the primary and utterly dominant object with which a child must learn to cope is the caring person to whom it is related." It is understandable, therefore (says Dux), that "the primordial object schema is that of the subject, and the primordial schema for events, that of action" (*Die Logik der Weltbilder*, 94). But this approach does not tell us how the child itself, whose subjectivity, according to Dux, is only beginning to form, attains to the concept of subject.

position is presented today by H. Gipper after careful consideration of the criticisms raised against it.

Fischer completely fails to recognize the independence of thought from language. Were we to follow him, we could not but marvel that even the Chinese and the Japanese are familiar with acting subjects and that, on the other hand, Greco-European thinking could have produced pantheistic and atheistic systems of thought. In addition, as we saw earlier, the idea of a causality in the form of action is already present in the structure of meaning which myth assigns to linguistic symbols prior to any diverging development of syntactical forms. The predicational sentence structure that predominates in some languages has indeed articulated this primordial linguistic experience with greater clarity than other languages have. But thinking is not restricted to limits set by this structure, nor does the acceptance of this structure determine in a positive or negative way the truth of the thought expressed by means of it.

These various theological applications of the theoretical models produced by linguistics and the philosophy of language are all characterized more or less by a one-sided attachment to a particular model. The authors involved have not sufficiently heeded the critical discussion of the model's foundations and then made this discussion the starting point for a radical reformulation of it in a theological perspective. From the viewpoint of a critical theological reception of proposed models, Ebeling's hermeneutical analysis of language is still superior to most of the recent essays in this area. The reason is that despite all the limitations of his hermeneutical approach to the phenomenon of language—an approach that neglected many aspects rightly introduced in more recent contributions—he nonetheless made the concerns of theology serve as the guiding thread for a deeper understanding of language and did not simply apply a secular theory of language to theology.

Ebeling's starting point for his theology of language was the theology of the word of God. Bultmann had not utterly dissociated the latter from generally accessible human experience, as Barth had; he did, however, establish no less sharp an opposition between the two. Ebeling, on the contrary, attempted even in his earliest contributions to the discussion to relate any talk about the word of God to human linguisticality. Thus in a programmatic essay published in 1959 he says that the word of God is "not . . . any separate, special Reality" alongside human speech; it is nothing else than "true, proper, finally valid" word.[200] The essence, therefore, of human language itself can be understood only in the light of God.

---

[200]G. Ebeling, "Word of God and Hermeneutics," in his *Word and Faith* (1960), trans. J. W. Leitch (Philadelphia, 1963), 305–32 at 324.

As Ebeling says in a later work, "man precisely in his linguisticality is not master of himself."[201]

In the beginning, Ebeling developed his theological interpretation of language along narrow lines inspired by Heidegger, although he treated the latter's thought in an independent way. He went behind the objectivizing *statement* to the linguistic event itself and sought to understand language as essentially *communication.* This position immediately yielded the theological meaning of language. For communications that disclose existence are promises in which speakers pledge themselves and thereby disclose the future to others. Ebeling can therefore see the proper meaning of word and language as fulfilled in the gospel insofar as the latter is a *promissio Dei.* The gospel is the word that in an unqualified way opens up the future and discloses existence; it is therefore word in the full sense. As this kind of word the gospel stands in contrast to the word of the law, which blocks off the future. What Ebeling here asserts to be the essence of human language proves to be identical with the distinction of the Reformers between the word of God as gospel and the word of God as law.[202] Ebeling's thesis that the word of God is the true essence of word as such thus becomes intelligible.

This thesis does violence to the facts, however, inasmuch as it does not integrate the full range of anthropological phenomena associated with linguistic structures but antecedently excludes much of it as secondary. The so-called "three strands" of semantic structure found in linguistic utterances (K. Bühler, 1934) are reduced to one: the aspect of "communication" between persons. This reduction, which is hinted at in Heidegger, is transferred by Ebeling to the theological order in the form of a personalist interpretation of language that prescinds from the expressive structure and representational function of language. As a result, during the period of logical positivism it was diametrically opposed to the analytical philosophy of language, since the latter focused on the expressive structure of assertions.

In later publications Ebeling has moved beyond the narrowly existen-

---

[201]Ebeling, *God and Word* (n. 195, above), 29.

[202]Ebeling, *Word and Faith,* 327f. For his distinction between the "basic structure" of the word as "communication" that aims at "what it effects," and that of the "statement" that aims at "information," Ebeling appeals to the ancient Israelite understanding of word, for which "the questions as to the content and the power of words are identical" (326). In practice, however, in his rejection of the mythical understanding of words (323) that doubtless lies behind these Old Testament ideas, Ebeling follows rather Heidegger's contrast between communication that discloses existence, and objectivizing statement *(Being and Time).* The connection with the distinction between law and gospel is retained in Ebeling's later writings; see his *Introduction to a Theological Theory of Language* (n. 180, above).

tialist and personalist approach that marked his early interpretation of language and has attempted to do greater justice to the full range of linguistic phenomena. It is true that he still refuses to understand language in terms of its "significatory" function, because in his view to do so is to prescind from "the humanity of language" and especially from the element of time.[203] This viewpoint leads him, via the observation that language makes past and future present, to the generalization that the word "make[s] present what is not at hand, what is absent."[204] For this reason, even the hidden "mystery" of the divine reality can be accessible to human beings only through the word. On the other hand, "in every word event" this mystery is "present [as] a depth dimension" "to which every word owes its existence."[205]

In thus bringing out the symbolic function of the word as rendering present what is not at hand, these statements of Ebeling lead us into the religious dimension of language. What I said earlier about the interweaving of determinacy and indeterminacy in linguistic utterances and in the registration of them by listeners in a conversation can supply the argument needed as the basis for the remark of Ebeling, just quoted, about the "depth dimension" of the divine mystery to which every word owes its existence. It is not possible, however, to show this connection between the symbolic function of the word and the idea of God unless we introduce as a link the idea of the indeterminate totality of meaning that is implicitly present in the spoken word, above and beyond its linguistic context, and that is articulated in a particular way by this word.

It is another question whether such considerations serve, as Ebeling believes, to justify the concept "word of God" on the basis of the reality of language. If every human word owes its existence in the final analysis to an unthematic, hidden presence of God in the depth dimension of linguistic consciousness (somewhat as for Augustine the light of truth is

[203]Ebeling, *God and Word.* 16–17. In opposition to this view, Ebeling in his subsequent remarks develops the temporality of the statement as the basic unit of language.

[204]Ibid., 24. The idea that language makes present what is absent had been put forth in the 1959 book but only as an explanation of the concept of promise. In the 1966 book the view has changed. Here the rendering present of what is not at hand is rightly asserted to be a characteristic of language generally. A similar remark occurs in H. Ammann, *Die menschliche Rede* (1925–28; 1974⁴): when the *meaning* of a fact "forms the content of a communication, the realm of the purely factual is already transcended" (149). Therefore in every instance, even when the *object* of a communication is present to the senses, its *content* is not something present (146ff.). According to Ammann, this temporal mode of nonpresence (in contrast to spatial or, as the case may be, nonsensible nonpresence) is *pastness,* whereas Ebeling, a Christian theologian, gives priority to the future (44ff.).

[205]Ibid., 29. With regard to speaking of God as the "mystery of the reality" that is present in the word (31), see the development of this idea in Jüngel (n. 184, above), 340ff. and esp. 393ff: the man Jesus is the parable of God in which the absent God becomes present (400ff.).

a condition for human knowledge), it is possible to conclude that human speech is somehow inspired to the extent that it is open to this depth dimension. But even if this is so, the speech remains human speech and, in addition, its inspirations are exposed to the distortions of the human imagination.

A mythical understanding of words could indeed conceive of the inspired utterances of seer or poet as the word of the godhead itself, and even the church's doctrine of inspiration regarded the inspired origin of the biblical writings as the basis for their status as word of God. We, however, differentiate more sharply between the human word and its divine origin, and even a recollection of this depth dimension of language cannot restore the mythical unity between divine word and human word.

In addition, the mythical understanding of language did not consider every word as alike divinely inspired. Even for Ebeling only those words are the word of God which, in addition to announcing something that is hidden, give expression to that which "—as the truth—renders a decision concerning the humanity of man."[206] But, as Ebeling himself had shown in his essay on the concept of conscience, this is possible only in combination with the truth regarding the world as a totality. Divine truth would thus make itself known only in such human words as express the truth about the totality of the world and of human existence. These human words could be called word of God insofar as at the same time they locate human existence in its truth as seen in the light of God. "Word of God" is therefore another way of speaking of the self-revelation of God insofar as this requires linguistic form in order to be communicable as something hidden.[207]

Every statement about the meaning and nature of a present reality looks beyond what is presently at hand to its context, in which alone the particular thing acquires its due meaning. In this sense, every word that names the nature of a thing by assigning it its meaning gives expression to something "hidden." This phenomenon, then, is not something peculiar to talk about God. The peculiarity of the latter is, rather, that it expresses the decisive truth about the whole of the world and of the human person. According to the biblical traditions, as opposed to the mythical conception

---

[206]Ibid., 44.

[207]I cannot, however, share Ebeling's view that because the word of God "serves to render more precise our understanding of revelation" it therefore "takes dogmatic priority" over the concept of revelation (*Dogmatik des christlichen Glaubens* [1979], I, 257f.). In the history of modern theology it is, rather, the concept of the word of God—a concept linked to the dogma of biblical inspiration—that has proved to be at the very least in need of reinterpretation and that even today remains dependent for its interpretation on the concept of revelation. Only along these lines is it possible to show that the expression "word of God" represents more than a mythicomagical notion.

of the world, this truth about humanity and world will achieve completeness only in their future. Consequently, only that human word may be called "word of God" which announces the definitive future that is still hidden from every historical present and which does so in such a way that in this communication the future of God is present by its own choice. According to Christian teaching, this has already taken place in the preaching and history of Jesus; Christian faith is therefore able to understand Jesus as being the revelation of the divine Logos and thus himself the Word of God.

Yet even in Jesus the distinction between human speech and the self-proclamation of God that takes place through this freely posited speech is not removed. The difference within the history of Jesus between his journey to the cross and his proclamation of the coming reign of God represents the explication of this difference between the word of God and the word of Jesus. Only the end of the story, that is, the Easter event, makes it clear that God himself was speaking through Jesus, and this in such a definitive way that henceforth the word of God can only be understood as being a report of what was done in Jesus.

This means in turn that for Christian faith human language loses the kind of power assigned to it in myth. In so doing, it loses, however, not its religious depth dimension but only its immediate, inspired oneness with the divine truth. If even the message of Jesus insofar as it was human speech did not immediately contain the truth of God within itself but had to have its divine authority confirmed by the history of Jesus, then Christian speech too remains distinct from the divine word that is its content. This word makes its truth known not immediately through what Christians say but through the future of God's reign and through the signs that precede this.

8

The Cultural Meaning
of Social Institutions

In the preceding chapter we saw that the unity of a culture is based on a communal consciousness of meaning which establishes the social world as an orderly place, permeates it, and, in the beginning, is represented in communal play. Language was seen to be the universal medium for this communal consciousness of meaning that forms the basis for the exocentric identity of individuals. Language itself takes the form of play, as can be seen not only from its obedience to rules but also and above all from its representational function. It is this representational aspect that makes language, in its original closeness to myth, essentially symbolic and distinguishes it from a set of mere signs. The presence of meaning in the life of language is not left wholly to the arbitrary choice of individuals, although the articulation of the meaning that is present in the experiential situation is indeed dependent on the development of language in individuals.

Similar statements can be made about the unity of the consciousness of meaning that constitutes a culture. This consciousness, too, is not adequately defined when it is presented as simply a human creation. Just as in the case of the individual's apprehension of meaning, so too in the consciousness of meaning that grounds the unity of a culture we are dealing with a meaning that imposes itself and manifests itself in linguistic articulation. This is true even though the linguistic signs in which this meaning finds expression may in large measure be the result of arbitrary decision, and even though the linguistic articulation may take any number of forms. Linguistic articulation and individual interpretations of meaning need to be examined for their correspondence to the objective order of meaning and must show themselves as related to an already existing body of meaning. The very plurality of interpretations of meaning shows, too, that linguistically articulated meaning is not indistinguishable from the linguistic form in which that meaning originally manifests itself.

At this point the kind of reflection that distinguishes and identifies comes into play. It examines the consciousness of meaning that grounds the social order and explains it in relation to this grounding function; in

397

the process it distinguishes mythical language from everyday language. If, however, in the course of this reflection the mythical consciousness of meaning is wholly cut off from the world of everyday life, it no longer serves as the basis for the unity of culture. The mythical consciousness of meaning serves this purpose only to the extent that, in one form or another, it actually permeates and determines the order of the shared world, an order comprising the methodical ways in which individuals live together. These ways or forms are called "institutions."

According to Bronislaw Malinowski, institutions are the component parts of a culture; a culture is a whole composed of "partly autonomous, partly coordinated institutions." As a definition of culture this description proved to be incomplete, because it does not indicate that the consciousness of meaning which turns the various component parts into a single whole is constitutive of the unity of a culture.[1] It is undeniable, however, that the unified communal consciousness of meaning, which in its mythical form has for its content the meaning that grounds the order of the shared life-world, needs to be made concrete in this order; in other words, the unified meaning must take concrete shape in institutions that regulate the communal life of individuals. Only by means of these regulatory institutions does the shared consciousness of meaning produce the communal life-style which E. Rothacker rightly considers to be characteristic of the unity of a particular culture at any given moment in its development.

Life-style and institutional organization of communal life are both characterized by permanence. It is clear from this that the meaning which grounds the unity of communal life does not find its complete expression in the enthusiasm of any given moment but, rather, extends to the whole of life, thereby giving individuals the opportunity to achieve their identity. Institutions may, however, even though permanent, degenerate into empty forms if they lose their meaning. They may then be seen as imposing on the behavior of individuals meaningless constraints from which these individuals will endeavor to free themselves. But it is not enough simply to destroy empty forms. The tasks of communal life constantly demand the development of institutional forms of interaction that can be affirmed as meaningful only on the basis of a shared consciousness of meaning.

I. The Concept of Social Institution

Since the time of Emile Durkheim, "institution" has meant to sociologists the modes of behavior that are established by society and introduced

---

[1]B. Malinowski, *A Scientific Theory of Culture, and Other Essays* (Chapel Hill, 1944), 40; cited above, chapter 7, at n. 6.

into communal life[2] and that confront individuals as reified structures or arrangements controlling the way they are to live. Among these pregiven structures are the six areas that Herbert Spencer had earlier listed in his *Principles of Sociology* (1876): (1) marriage and family; (2) state and forms of political organization; (3) forms of economic organization; (4) law; (5) educational institutions; and (6) religious organizations or churches.

On these fundamental points there is a large measure of agreement. Even today, however, there is disagreement on how institutions are related to the overall social system and on the question of whether institutions have their origin in the behavior of individuals. The two questions are interconnected. The second of them—whether the development of specific institutional areas springs from correlative specific needs or whether it is to be seen rather as a function of the self-preservation of the total social system in its environment and as due to the tasks set a society by the need to "control contingency" (Niklaus Luhmann)—is primarily a matter of sociological theory. There is no need to discuss it directly and in detail in a book on anthropology.

On the other hand, an anthropology must definitely respond to the first of the above two questions. To what extent do the many and varied institutions precede all individual action as "social facts" in Durkheim's sense (because, according to Durkheim, these institutions give expression to the superiority of universal human nature over individuals)? To what extent, on the contrary, are they to be conceived as themselves the products of individuals' actions? The answer to this question will contain a response to a further question: Is the social system, together with its partial systems (institutions), to be understood ultimately in the light of the behavior of individuals? Or, on the other hand, are individuals simply interchangeable as component parts whose individuality is irrelevant for an understanding of the social system, even though, of course, the social system must, if it is to be a reality, presuppose the presence of individuals generally?[3]

If in fact the peculiar features of individuals and their behavior are not a matter of indifference for the social system and for its shape and development, then the generality of systematic sociological theory is obtained at the cost of abstracting from the actual behavior of individuals which is at every point already constitutive of the social system in its concrete historical form. The same applies to the theory of institutions. Both must answer the challenge: Is not the asserted priority in principle of institutions or, as

[2]E. Durkheim, *The Rules of Sociological Method,* trans. S. A. Solovay and J. H. Mueller, and ed. G. E. G. Catlin (Chicago, 1938), ch. 4.

[3]This is the critical viewpoint adopted in the debate between T. Rendtorff and N. Luhmann, especially with reference to the latter's controversy with J. Habermas, *Gesellschaft ohne Religion? Theologische Aspekte einer sozialtheoretischen Kontroverse* (1975), 71ff.

the case may be, social systems over individual behavior really a pseudo-theological assertion, inasmuch as this priority replaces the primacy of God (or, in the case of Durkheim, of universal human nature) over the concrete reality of individual and communal human life?

There is, of course, no denying the fact that social institutions and the social system as a whole outlast the life of the individual and thus also antecede each individual. At the same time, however, they are also subject to alteration and reformulation through the behavior of individuals. Individuals and their behavior are not mere functions of society in the way that the organs of the individual organism are nonindependent functions of the unity of the living being. To the consciousness of archaic cultures society and its institutions do indeed seem to have enjoyed such a priority in principle over individuals. That is understandable, since in these cultures the religious consciousness of the meaning that sustained the community found concrete expression in social institutions. But to the observer of a later time this identification must appear to be a simple hypostatization.

The hypostatization did not consist, as has often been asserted, in making divine reality independent of social institutions; on the contrary, it consisted in taking the independence that by nature belongs solely to the divine and attributing it to the "great Leviathan" and its institutional parts. Modern sociologists are in danger of unconsciously yielding to this kind of hypostatization, against which the Jewish prophets and Christian thinkers with their distinction between the kingdom of this world and the kingdom of God raised their voices in criticism. The sociologists are subject to this danger in the very measure that the constitutive significance of religion for the social system and its institutions has been eliminated as a theme for sociological discussion. Durkheim's thesis of the superiority of universal human nature over individuals—a superiority that according to him finds expression in the priority of society as a whole over individuals—was a kind of political theology.

Malinowski proposed a modified variant of Durkheim's position and at the same time gave it a naturalistic bent when he conceived the variety of institutions as an expression of basic human needs which precede the behavior of individuals and "impose" a certain determinism on it.[4] According to Malinowski, every society must in one fashion or another take into account certain basic needs: metabolism, reproduction, bodily comforts, safety, movement, growth, and health. This can be done in various ways. But the criterion for the success of the particular "cultural responses"—commissariat, kinship system, shelter, measures for collective security, training, and hygiene—is to be found (he says) in the "function"

---

[4]Malinowski, 85.

which these arrangements fulfill by satisfying the various needs. In other words, institutions are developed in order to make it possible to satisfy the basic human needs.

As these institutions arise and are developed, new, derived needs also arise (111ff., 120ff.), as, for example, the need of education for the carrying out of specialized individual roles in the service of such institutions. Furthermore, each institution is not ordered solely to the satisfaction of a single need. Rather, says Malinowski, "the production of certain comprehensive instrumentalities and their maintenance [is] best suited to the integral satisfaction of a series of needs," as is especially clear from the example of the family (112f.).

At this point, however, the question arises whether needs can play such a decisive role in explaining institutions. If individual institutions cannot be correlated in an exclusive way with particular needs, then the existence of such institutions must evidently still be traced back to other causes. For this reason, Talcott Parsons' systematic theory of society takes as its point of departure not particular needs but the social system as a whole. Only in the framework of the social system as a whole is it possible to understand the development of institutions as partial systems that (according to Parsons) are based on the values and norms fundamental to the social system as a whole and that fulfill specific "functions" in the life of society with its division of labor.[5]

Another aspect of Parsons' theory of the social system, namely, his conception of the social system as a structure of interactions between individual modes of behavior, brings us to the idea of institutions as originating in the behavior of individuals. Let us consider first the function of individuals in already existing institutions.

At any particular time individuals play a determinate "role" that is assigned to them and is distinct from the roles filled by others; as a result, they enjoy a precise "status" or, if they fail to meet their "role expectations," they are subject to precise "sanctions."[6] Since any institution represents only one sector of the social life in which individuals participate, each individual must fill not just one, but various roles: for example, wife and mother, woman working in a factory, member of a sports club or a church choir, member of a district council and a political party. This situation gives rise to the question of the relation between, on the one hand, persons and their identity and, on the other, the multiple roles they play. In modern industrial society, institutions, and therefore the roles of in-

[5]T. Parsons, *The Social System* (Glencoe, Ill., 1951), ch. 1. See also the remarks of Luhmann in H. Schelsky, ed., *Zur Theorie der Institutionen* (1970), 28.

[6]On this, see R. Dahrendorf, *Homo Sociologicus. Ein Versuch zur Geschichte, Bedeutung und Kritik der Kategorie der sozialen Rolle* (Cologne, 1959).

dividuals, have become so independent of one another that the unity of the person amid the various roles becomes problematic.

This modern problem, of which Robert Musil has given a now classic description,[7] results from the fact that in modern society the various institutions no longer represent univocally clear divisions of labor within a unitary order of life that includes them all. Instead, the unity of life seems to fade from sight behind the variety of institutions that operate each according to its own laws.

In the light of these remarks, what is to be said about the possibility of institutions originating in the interaction of individuals? This response to the question of the origin of institutions is, of course, contrary to the explanation according to which institutions are produced by a process of differentiation within the social system as a whole. In this alternate response the key issue is evidently the passage, in the interaction of individuals, to role behavior. Is this transition to be understood in the light of the peculiar character and needs of individual behavior as such? Arnold Gehlen has interpreted the formation of social institutions as the solution of a problem that arises in principle in the life of human beings as individuals.

Gehlen became interested in the concept of institution because institutions, as objectively existing over against individuals, help the latter, who are biologically unstable because of their openness to the world and who are not strongly oriented in a particular direction, to stabilize their behavior. On the other hand, in keeping with the approach he had adopted in his anthropology, Gehlen had to derive institutions from the action of individuals. He managed to connect these two aspects of his thought with the aid of the phenomenon of play. That is, following G. H. Mead, Gehlen describes the functioning of institutions as a matter of individuals cooperating after the model of a group game that proceeds according to rules. A group game is

> a system of interrelated actions, all directed to the execution of a specific task, in which each action anticipates certain responses on the part of specific others. This ordered system of potential reactions from partners and adversaries is sublimated in the form of "rules of the game." It is these that organize the network of possible behaviors; only within this network does the free exploitation of chance occurrences become a source of delight.[8]

According to Gehlen too, culture or, as the case may be, the institutional structure of human communal life arises out of play, although not from the representational play found in cult but—to use Huizinga's distinction —from the element of contest or competition. Gehlen does not, however,

---

[7]See the lengthy citation from R. Musil's *A Man Without Qualities* in Dahrendorf, 58f.
[8]A. Gehlen, *Urmensch und Spätkultur* (1956; 1964²), 37ff.

discuss in detail the various forms of play and their structures, but, like Mead, simply speaks in vague terms of "group play." Because of this lack of clarity he is unable to take advantage of the possibilities that the concept of play in fact offers for explaining the independence of institutions over against individuals. Instead, he appeals to the concept of purpose as a way of explaining this phenomenon.

He does so because the concept of purpose seems to provide a link between the structure of individual action and the unity found in play. More particularly, the link is the idea of end in itself. To one who shares in a game the game becomes an end in itself and thus acquires an existence that is independent of the individual players. But because Gehlen thus seeks to understand the independence of games in the light of the category of purpose, his ensuing analysis of the independence of institutions is caught in the problem of alienation. For the purposefulness of play as an end in itself is independent of the ends sought in the actions of individuals and must therefore appear as imposing a set of autonomous and alienating laws.

This alienating character finds expression in the fact that, according to Gehlen, the cooperation of individuals, precisely because it is an end in itself, can be put into the service of secondary purposes: "Certain games turn into mass performances, national demonstrations with banners, great commercial enterprises and opportunities for profit, or even genuine sociological necessities of industrial society, because leisure time has to be filled."[9] In Gehlen's description, then, the independence of institutions is at the mercy of such secondary purposes because it is not based on the independence of the meaning that they are to represent.

Peter Berger and Thomas Luckmann have formulated a more general description of institutions in terms of the actions of individuals. Unlike Gehlen, Berger and Luckmann do not make the social division of labor the basis of their concept of institution. According to them, the division of labor is itself a secondary consequence of a reciprocal stabilization of behaviors that precedes any such division of labor. In this view, institutionalization occurs whenever the habitual behaviors of a plurality of individuals are interordered in a typical and constant way.[10] The starting point of institutionalization is thus the fact, which Gehlen too had noted, of the development of custom, the habitual performance of certain actions. In this context Gehlen remarks that "all cultures . . . have at their base systems of stereotyped and stable habits."

[9]Ibid., 38. On Gehlen's concept of an institution, see also F. Jonas, *Die Institutionenlehre Arnold Gehlens* (1966).

[10]P. Berger and T. Luckmann, *The Social Construction of Reality* (Garden City, N.Y., 1966), 51: "Institutionalization occurs whenever there is a *reciprocal typification of habitualized actions by types of actors*" (italics added).

Characteristically, however, Gehlen immediately links this viewpoint with that of the specialized division of labor. Thus he continues: these habits "are in every case *limited in scope,* because unambiguous courses of action are needed to deal with circumscribed situations." In the background here are those basic needs which, according to Malinowski, are the basis for the formation of institutions. Because of these basic needs, when actions become habitual they are immediately put in the service of a division of labor and thus of cooperation for the purpose of satisfying the needs. The result, according to Gehlen, is the solidifying of interaction into institutions, and he remarks in conclusion: "Any and every permanence of social creations, any resistance they offer to time, is connected with the one-sidedness—the specialization—of courses of action and thus with the limitation of objective aspects. Conversely, to stabilize a society means to give it permanent institutions."[11] And by "permanent institutions" Gehlen means "a selection of modes of behavior and situations that is inseparable from their limited scope."

Berger and Luckmann, on the contrary, move beyond the phenomenon of specialization and give a general description of the interaction of individuals. "*A* watches *B* perform. He attributes motives to *B*'s actions and, seeing the actions recur, typifies the motives as recurrent. As *B* goes on performing, *A* is soon able to say to himself, 'Aha, there he goes again.'" In this way, reciprocal specific patterns of conduct develop. "That is, *A* and *B* will begin to play roles *vis-à-vis* each other." Their actions become predictable, and they become aware of how they condition one another.[12]

In this description the division of labor becomes a derivate phase in the process by which stereotyped interaction is developed. Gehlen himself gives a delightful and vivid example of this process of institutionalization that takes place as individuals deal with one another: "The correspondence a person carries on with various others is already such an institution."[13] This example also shows how the stereotyped reciprocity of behavior becomes "obligatory" for the individual: "With varying degrees of urgency letters queue up to be answered, and if one delays replying for a long time, one has a 'bad conscience.'"

This aspect of obligation that accrues to ascriptions of typified behavior shows with particular clarity how institutions get "detached," become independent, and even take priority over individuals. The chief problem confronting the general sociological theory of institutions is to explain precisely this independence of institutions. Durkheim answered by invoking the concept of objectification. Just as objects appear independent in

[11]Gehlen, 19.
[12]Berger and Luckmann, 53 and 54.
[13]Gehlen, 60.

relation to us as the subjects who nonetheless ourselves produce the representations of the objects, so too do institutions. According to Durkheim, this objectivity of social relations also manifests, in the final analysis, the superiority of the social nature of the human being in relation to the individual.

Gehlen, like Malinowski, avoided such quasi-metaphysical assumptions regarding human nature. Because Malinowski adopted the viewpoint of the functions that institutions exercise for human beings, his grounding of institutions in the already existing basic needs of human nature makes clear not so much the independence of institutions as the way in which they come into existence on the basis of individual behavior. Gehlen, however, could not be satisfied with the assumption of a fixed system of needs. He therefore attempted to deduce the independence of institutions from the concept of action and specifically from the dialectic of the goals of action. "Rational, goal-oriented action can in a characteristic manner undergo a change of meaning, namely, when it becomes *an end in itself.*"[14]

Berger and Luckmann begin by tracing the seemingly superhuman objectivity of institutions back to a reification (along the lines of Durkheim). This reification is closely connected with the process of alienation as understood by Marx, that is, with a self-divesting and self-alienation on the part of human activity. In the background here, as in Gehlen, is the view that institutions are the product of human action.[15] Berger and Luckmann do not, however, accept either Durkheim's or Gehlen's explanation for this process. Their application of the alienation concept is to some extent inappropriate to the state of affairs that they are attempting to explain, since they do not wish to maintain that the opposition of institutions to individuals, the independence of institutions, and the claim they make on individuals have no basis in objective reality.

As a result, we see emerging at another point in their argument a different answer to the question of the conditions for the independence of institutions. In its inner logic this answer challenges the view that the theory of institutions should take as its starting point the concept of action. The authors call attention to the way in which individuals are linked to

[14]Ibid., 29. F. H. Allport, *Institutional Behavior: Essays Toward a Reinterpreting of Contemporary Social Organization* (Chapel Hill, 1933), had attempted to use the concept of purpose as a way of apprehending the nature of institutional behavior, inasmuch as he reduced institutions to the behavior of individuals. But he was unable to explain convincingly how the seemingly independent objective existence of institutions (an objectivation that he denied, 13) could arise through purposes taking on an independent life of their own (see 21, 26f., 120ff.).

[15]Berger and Luckmann, 57: "The institutional world is objectivated human activity, and so is every single institution."

one another in the consciousness of each of them. This linkage and the corresponding tendency of institutions themselves to interlock with one another are explained by Berger and Luckmann as due to the human need of meaning: "While performances can be segregated, meanings tend toward at least minimal consistency" (60). As a result, the consciousness of meaning leads to the integration of institutions in the context of the shared life-world:

> Individuals perform discrete institutionalized actions within the context of their biography. This biography is a reflected-on whole in which the discrete actions are thought of not as isolated events, but as related parts in a subjectively meaningful universe whose meanings are not specific to the individual, but socially articulated and shared. Only by way of this detour of socially shared universes of meaning do we arrive at the need for institutional integration.[16]

But should not this point of view be applied to the question of the rise of institutions as such? When individuals see recurring patterns of behavior in others, explain this fact in terms of recurring motivations, and order their own behavior accordingly, they are creating a web of meaning that links the behavior of the individuals involved. However, only when they grasp this web of meaning within which each of them plays his or her role, and when they are in agreement on this common consciousness of meaning and order their own behavior in accordance with it, is there present the nucleus of an institutionalized reciprocal relationship, along with the element of obligation that is specific to this relationship.

The precedence of institutions over the individual thus depends on the prior existence of experienced and linguistically articulated webs or coherences of meaning. But what webs of meaning are we dealing with here? Evidently with such as have to do with the reciprocity of human behavior in concrete recurring real-life situations or in continuous and permanent relationships. Institutions are thus abiding, meaningful forms of human coexistence. This point of view does justice to Malinowski's idea that the function of institutions is to regulate basic human needs. For only the existence of such basic needs makes it understandable that (to take but one example) structures for the family have been developed in all cultures, even if they take quite different forms. At the same time, however, the structures of meaning embodied in institutions normally extend far beyond the natural foundations supplied by the basic needs and integrate the satisfaction of the latter into a structure of meaning that embraces the whole of communal life.

As structures of meaning, institutions impose themselves at every point

[16]Ibid., 61.

on the action of individuals,[17] and this prior existence is not simply a reification in the sense of an alienation. Nor are institutions originally ends in themselves as understood by Gehlen. An institution that is an end in itself, independent of any grounding or justification, and can therefore be placed in the service of any end whatever, would be an institution that is degenerating by becoming isolated, formalized, and emptied of meaning.

Berger and Luckmann have correctly pointed out that in the consciousness of individuals particular institutions are normally dependent on the universe of meaning which is the social life-world. But the priority of the jointly experienced structures of meaning of the life-world is not simply an expression of the social "nature" of human beings, as Durkheim thought. All that is given in the social "nature" of the human person is a need of socialization; the concrete form this socialization is to take is not yet determined. There may be a failure of socialization, and when socialization does occur, it comes about on the basis of a consciousness of the cultural significance of the order of human life together, while the precedence of the latter over the individual has its roots in the realm of myth and belief.

In order to see clearly the foundational role that the consciousness of meaning plays in the development of institutions out of the interaction of individuals, let us turn to language. It has justly been said that language is a "primordial institution." In fact, a language spoken in common shows all the characteristics of a habitualized and reciprocally stereotyped pattern of behavior. At the same time, the use of a common tongue is one of the bases for any further development of institutions. Language is distinguished from other institutions most of all by its lack of any fixed distribution of roles (or division of labor), since all can construct sentences for themselves by following the grammatical rules of the language. Only when reference to a concrete life situation is introduced does the content of the sentences cease to be arbitrary; everyone is not entitled to speak the same way in any and every situation. At this point linguistic competence becomes interwoven with other forms of institutionalization in reciprocal human behavior.

A common speech has its basis in the shared meaning that the partners in the communication process connect with words and combinations of words. This phenomenon is both fundamental and in many respects obscure. G. H. Mead thought that the ability of different individuals to grasp

---

[17]That the consciousness of meaning is constitutive of the concept of action, and not the converse, is a point that emerges from the discussion between N. Luhmann and J. Habermas on the foundations of sociology in their *Theorie der Gesellschaft oder Sozialtechnologie* (1971), 25–100 (N. Luhmann, "Sinn als Grundbegriff der Soziologie") and 142–290 (J. Habermas, "Theorie der Gesellschaft oder Sozialtechnologie"), esp. 171. See my remarks in *Theology and the Philosophy of Science*, trans. F. McDonagh (Philadelphia, 1976), 96ff.

the same meaning was due to their ability to put themselves in the place of others. But this latter ability must itself spring from the specifically human capacity for grasping the objectivity of the relation to the world, while this last-named capacity must in turn, and finally, have its root in the exocentricity of the human form of life. As beings who are characterized by a reduction of instinct and a need of direction for their drives, humans, despite all the egocentricity of their behavior, do not have within themselves the unity of their being. They must look outside themselves for what will give unity and identity to their lives.

This quest is present at every point in the process of object perception with its gradual differentiation. It reaches a first high point in the symbolic play of children. The ability to put oneself in the place of others (something quite different from the capacity for undifferentiated symbiotic identification) is mediated through the perception of objects: others, like the perceiver's own body, are located in the world of objects and understood in terms of their context. It is therefore possible to assume that just as one understands one's own experience in terms of the world of objects, so others understand themselves and their experience in the same way. Only thus is it possible for individuals to put themselves in the place of others and to assume that when they use the same words they are conveying the same meaning.

On the other hand, the meaning of words embraces more than what is identifiable by the senses. A common tongue can therefore serve to conjure up the identity of objects and the unity of the shared world. The world in which individuals seek outside themselves the basis for the unity of their lives is a social world as well as a world of objects. Thus while the understanding of others is mediated through a common relation to the world, the converse is also true: through its shared language the social community vouches for the unity of the world of objects. In the we-consciousness springing from consciousness of a meaning that is conceived in common and founds the unity of a life-world[18] individuals find outside

[18]M. Scheler defended the thesis that the "we" precedes the "I" and "with a genetic priority is always the first of the two to be filled with content" (*Die Wissensformen und die Gesellschaft* [1925], *Werke* 8:52; see *The Nature of Sympathy,* trans. P. Heath [New Haven, 1954], 213ff.). To this A. Schütz has objected that there can be a "we" only in relation to an "I" and that the "I" is presupposed by the "we" in the same way that a "they" (those others) can come into existence only by distinction from the "we" of our own group; see *Collected Papers,* vol. I: *The Problem of Social Reality,* ed. M. Natanson (The Hague, 1962), 175. Schütz agrees with Scheler to the extent that an I-consciousness presupposes a "mundane sphere" (ibid.), in which the reality of the alter ego is also given to me with equal simultaneity (173; see 220). But, says Schütz, Scheler does not distinguish adequately between this naïve view and reflection as the basis on which I first grasp the contents of my consciousness as my own.

This criticism seems justified especially in view of the fact that Scheler gives the sphere

themselves the ground that allows each life to develop its own special identity and unity. The roots of individual identity are to be found, however, not in the we-consciousness as such, but in the jointly affirmed meanings from which the very consciousness of unity derives its strength but which can also enable individuals to resist the thinking and behavior of the group and can motivate them to do so.

The ordered meaning that attaches to the institutions of communal life and to their interconnection in the political order of society with its religious or quasi-religious foundations has enabled the human beings of every age to experience as present their common destiny, namely, a life springing from a shared center that transcends the limitations of individuals. To use the language of the Bible: in a sense they have experienced the kingdom of God—the common human destiny in the face of the divine reality—as already present at every point. This experience has, of course,

---

of the "we" priority even over consciousness of the world of natural objects and thus rejects the view that I am defending here: that our knowledge of others is mediated through the development of our object perception as such. Here again, a grasp of the sphere of the "we" *as distinct from* the world of objects comes only as the result of a secondary reflection. In the symbiotic web of life, in which early childhood development takes place, the reality of the "we" precedes individual development, but it is not reflectively grasped as distinct from either the individual ego or the world of objects. These dimensions are not yet separated out but, rather, exist together in the symbiotic web of life. Then, as they are thematically grasped in the process of individual development, the apprehension that grasps and distinguishes the other is always mediated through the process of object perception as such; the we-consciousness is thus mediated through experience of the world and experience of the self.

Even the reality of the alter ego is not given to me *as such* (that is, as distinct from the other contents of experience) independently of the general process of experience of the world (contrary to Schütz). We must speak, rather, of a progressive differentiation of the initially indeterminate symbiotic web of life (Schütz's "mundane sphere") in the course of experience. In the process the symbiotic web of life reveals itself progressively as an increasingly differentiated meaningful whole. This fits in with the concept of the life-world which Schütz has taken over from Husserl and which he equates with "world of culture": it is for us a "universe of significations," a "framework of meaning" (*Collected Papers* I, 133), which is given to us in advance as objective meaning (as distinct from subjectively intended meaning). (For the concept of objective meaning, see Schütz, *The Phenomenology of the Social World*, trans. G. Walsh and F. Lehnert (Evanston, Ill., 1967), 31ff.

For Schütz, however, as for Husserl, and contrary to my own view, meaning is a product of consciousness (*Phenomenology*, 33f.), but because of our natural orientation to objective meaning we simply do not reflectively grasp the fact (34). Schütz, unlike Dilthey, does not regard "sense experiences" as meaningfully structured in themselves (as parts or moments in a whole); rather, they must first be "animated" (35) by means of an act of attention (51ff.; see *Collected Papers* I, 210). With this, Schütz joins a dualism inspired by Bergson (*Phenomenology*, 45): "Only the already experienced is meaningful, not that which is being experienced" (52), and only to the "retrospective glance" of reflection does what has been experienced show itself to be meaningful (ibid.; see 75). Therefore, according to Schütz, our own present, in which the naïve attitude exists, has no meaning, because it is inaccessible

been repeatedly associated with the tendency to take the given state of society as representing the fully achieved human destiny and to look upon it as being the kingdom of God in its definitive form. The outbreak of social conflicts has been enough to show the falsity of such claims.

When such conflicts arise, critics of the existing state of society may in their turn appeal to the shared consciousness of meaning and show how it is contradicted by the actual reality of society. Alternatively, the fact that the reality of society is so open to criticism may become the occasion for casting doubt on the undergirding consciousness of meaning. On the other hand, the institutional forms of communal life in the most diverse cultures have proved to be astonishingly durable even after the spirit that once established and animated them has departed. The durability of institutional forms even after the convictions that originally gave birth to them have lost their power can in all likelihood be explained solely by what these institutions still do to satisfy the basic needs of individuals and to integrate the latter into the life of society.

It is here, in this functional context, that the viewpoint of Malinowski in his doctrine of institutions is most fully validated; characteristically enough, it shows its value precisely in enabling us to understand the operation of social mechanisms when they have become defective. Evidently, once institutions have settled into place, the fact that they are connected with the satisfaction of basic needs will enable them to go on regulating individual behavior for a certain period, and to a certain degree, even when the consciousness of meaning that originally determined their configuration has dissolved. Conversely, any renewal in the forms of

---

to reflection (*Collected Papers* I, 172f.). Action too becomes an object of consciousness only after the deed is completed (*Phenomenology,* 69; see 74f.), although consciousness of a projected action does precede the action itself.

But does not the category of anticipation (on this, see Schütz, *Phenomenology,* 57ff., as well as *Collected Papers* I, 218ff.) make possible a consciousness of the action (as it does of my own ego) in the course of the action itself? This seems excluded for Schütz because of the dualism he maintains between life and reflection and because he limits the concept of meaning to reflection. But does not the phenomenon itself declare such theoretical assumptions to be untenable? The anticipated action (like the anticipated unity of the world) and the real action will be separated unless the anticipation of meaning is not based on a mere extrapolation from past experiences but stands within a continuity of references which shades off into vagueness and in which we are always aware of reality as a whole, while the latter possesses in itself structures of meaning that disclose themselves in fragmentary fashion to human anticipation and experience.

Thus the consciousness of meaning (a consciousness constitutive of the unity of a culture: *Collected Papers* I, 133ff.) by which a web of meaning is grasped that embraces the whole life-world and precedes the consciousness of the individual becomes intelligible without any forcing, whereas in Schütz's view, the "pregivenness" of objective meaning, if the term be taken strictly, is due to a self-deception fostered by the natural attitude that human beings adopt.

a society's institutional life due to a shared consciousness of cultural meaning must, of course, ensure the satisfaction of the basic needs insofar as institutional regulation is required for this purpose.

One might be inclined to derive from this minimal function of social institutions criteria that must be met by every historical establishment of such institutions as "cultural responses" to the "demands" of the basic needs. We have already seen, however, that Malinowski's own application of this point of view is unable adequately to explain the differentiation and special character of the forms of institutional life, inasmuch as at least some institutions (e.g., the family) refer to more than one basic need. The family, like the state and like patriarchally governed economic enterprises, readily tends to meet the needs of individuals in a comprehensive way in order to bind these individuals to themselves as fully as possible. The peculiar character of such institutions cannot therefore be understood in terms of any one particular need. On the other hand, when society is in an abnormal phase, it is possible, should the necessity arise, to satisfy individual needs even without the aid of such institutions, at least in isolated cases.

Institutions do therefore play a part in the satisfaction of needs, but this part must be more exactly defined and, in any event, must not be so defined as to say that without such institutions no satisfaction of needs is possible. If, then, we are to explain the similarities among the most important institutions in otherwise widely varying cultural systems, we need some other viewpoint, some other anthropological constant, than the common presence of the basic needs.

What is it that institutions such as marriage and the family, property, the organization of work, and law really do for the satisfaction of basic human needs? In case of necessity, human beings seek and find the satisfaction of their need for food, shelter, and sexual union even without such institutions. What, then, is the special contribution of these institutions? It does not seem to be directly the satisfaction of basic needs as such. The purpose of institutions seems to be, rather, to regulate *relations among individuals* in connection with the satisfaction of their basic human needs but also in connection with the secondary needs that attach themselves to the basic needs. This view is in keeping with the general concept of an institution as this has emerged here, especially from the discussion of the views of Berger and Luckmann. It is therefore in the reciprocity of relations between individuals that the key to the basic forms of institutionalization must be sought.

The requirement that the basic forms of institutionalization be understood in terms of the reciprocity of relations between individuals need not contradict the insight that institutions, at least in their origin, spring from a religious (or quasi-religious) shared consciousness of meaning that has for its content the situation of human beings in the natural world and in society. One can indeed use universal structural motifs from anthropology to show that certain forms of behavior—and therefore (in this context) certain fixed stereotyped forms of communal life—constantly make their appearance in a similar manner under the most varied conditions. But this does not mean that this kind of institutional bond need in fact make its appearance, for in particular cases it may not. The actual rise of the forms of institutional life always requires still other impulses and bases that are to be found precisely in the consciousness of meaning that grounds the particular and historically unique culture.

On the other hand, the historical variety manifested by the cultural and especially the religious consciousness of meaning cannot by itself explain why the forms of the institutionalization of human behavior that have repeatedly arisen throughout history have been relatively few and have resembled one another despite widely varying conditions of life. It seems, then, that we should look for constants in human nature which might explain this astonishing uniformity in institutionalization despite the otherwise vast differences between cultural worlds.

We may return in this context to a viewpoint already examined: that of the reciprocity of relations between individuals, the regulation of which is the theme of all institutionalization. Here we do see in fact the starting point for the development of the most varied kinds of institution. Reciprocity (correspondence) in the behavior of individuals (a phenomenon rendered permanent by being institutionalized) binds together the formal structural elements of particularism and mutuality that are found in this behavior. For, on the one hand, individuals seek to assert themselves against others. This is the element of particularism; it cannot by itself be the basis of a lasting relationship. Permanence arises only when to particularism is added the element of mutuality, which motivates individuals to adapt themselves to others.

We are dealing here with an aspect of the exocentricity of human behavior, due to which the relation to the objects of the perceived world is connected with the relation to other human beings in the manner described earlier. A first condition for the institutional stabilization of human behavior is that interaction should take the form of reciprocity (correspondence), that is, that the element of mutuality, of adaptation to others, be operative on both sides. Institutionalization is accomplished as soon as a *measure* of correspondence determines the behavior of human beings toward one another; behavior then becomes reciprocal. Reciprocity is the basic form of mutuality on the foundation of the particular existence of independent individuals.

Not all human relations, however, can be described as interactions of independent individuals. In addition to relations based on individual uniqueness there are others in which the element of community takes priority, even though, within the framework this creates, room is also made for the unique qualities of the individual. The basic form of this new type of relationship is the family. Here the community as a whole takes precedence over its individual members. The behavior of individuals toward one another is defined primarily in terms not of reciprocity but of membership in the community and of the contribution each makes to it, a contribution that then grounds relations of mutual acknowledgment within the community and solidarity in the face of the outside world.

In some of the forms, then, that the institutionalization of human behavior takes, the aspect of particularism is to the fore, while in others that of mutuality is emphasized; in all cases, however, the contrasting aspect is also taken into account. This consideration yields two (and only two) primordial areas of institutionalization: on the one hand, the *family* as the most basic area of mutuality, but one that also allows the individual members of the family to have their special place within it; on the other hand, *property* and the economy (i.e., the production and exchange of property), although these are subject to conditions of reciprocity.

In the family the aspect of individual uniqueness is subordinated to that of community; in the area of property and of private economy, on the other hand, the formation of community is subordinated to particularist self-assertion. In both areas, however, the essential nature of the institution is destroyed if the subordinate aspect is completely neglected. Thus if the independence of the members is suppressed in a family, the destruction of the familial community inevitably follows. Remarkably enough, this can happen when the familial relations of one or another member are confused with property relations. Conversely, the institution of property is undermined when the communal dimension of property and therefore the element of reciprocity is neglected; property may then easily come to be seen as theft.

All other institutions can, without prejudice to the thematic peculiar to each, be seen as variants, further developments, or combinations of the two basic formal types that find their purest and most original embodiments in the institutions of property and family. One of these types takes the form of a social association. In addition to the family, this type includes tribe, people, and state, but also other forms of community, such as religious communities. The second basic type of institution comprises forms of communication in which individuals relate to one another as they assert their independence.[19] This type includes, above all, the institutions of

---

[19] According to C. Schmitt, *Über die drei Arten rechtswissenschaftlichen Denkens* (Hamburg, 1934), 55ff., this distinction corresponds to the two types of institution distinguished by M. Hauriot in his *La théorie de l'institution et de la fondation* (1925): personal institutions (corpo-

economic life as well as the broad area of the juridical sphere; the juridical order, however, especially when it develops into civil law that is authorized and enforced by the state, also embodies a concern for those interests which the community insists on in opposition to individual interests.

Mixed forms are to be seen in economic life. Thus agricultural businesses but also industrial enterprises may be run in a patriarchal way as extended families. The educational system and the health system are also to be reckoned among the mixed forms. The educational system plays a special role, since in it the goal of individual independence (which is the special concern of education) is accompanied by the intention of integrating individuals into the life of society and into the shared consciousness that sustains this life.

The individual areas of social behavior have been developed in very varying degrees in different cultures. Even more important, however, is the fact that the areas of behavior have not received separate institutionalization in all cultures. Thus education may be cared for partly in the family and partly in institutions of the state. In any case, state and religion are usually more closely intertwined than they are in modern Western civilization. Frequently the religious system is also linked to the care of health. Generally speaking, in archaic cultures the individual subsystems of a society are more closely connected with one another and especially with religion than is the case in modern Western society. Durkheim and, following him, Luhmann could therefore describe the development of society as, by and large, a process of differentiation in the course of which partial systems become increasingly independent of one another, and in consequence there is greater room for individual freedom of movement.[20]

We may leave aside here the question whether this view of societal development does not in a rather unbalanced way turn the modern pluralistic society of Western secular culture into the goal of history. In any case, it can hardly be denied that there is a trend toward an increasing differentiation within the overall institutional structure. The point of entry for this movement is the varied objective tasks performed by the different institutions. At the same time, however, the viewpoints of particularism and mutuality are always at work in the institutionalization of these objective

---

rate bodies) and objectified institutions *(institutions choses)*. See also the survey in R.-P. Callies, *Eigentum als Institution. Eine Untersuchung zur theologisch-anthropologischen Begründung des Rechtes* (1962), 29–38, on the development of the idea of institution in jurisprudence.

[20]E. Durkheim, *The Division of Labor in Society,* trans. G. Simpson (New York, 1933). N. Luhmann, in his introduction to the German translation (1977), points out that the economic phenomenon of the division of labor provided Durkheim with a model for conceiving of social history as a progressive differentiation of social subsystems (20f.). For Luhmann's own application of this concept, see, e.g., his book *Die Funktion der Religion* (1977), 34f., 89f., 228f., 232f., 237f.

tasks and are combined in one form or another.

This circumstance is highly significant for the theological interpretation of institutionalization. The elements of particularism and mutuality that are combined in the development of an institutionalized reciprocal behavior recall the tension, described in the first part of this exposition of anthropology, between exocentricity and centrality in human behavior. We have now seen that the institutionalization of human behavior at the level of the reciprocity in the interaction of individuals links precisely these two factors and must integrate them with one another in every form of enduring communal life.[21] Social anthropology is thus referred back to the foundations of anthropology as such.

The description of the way in which particularism and mutuality are combined in the process of institutionalization—and, consequently, in the vital use of the setting created by the institution—must be such that it can suitably replace the traditional theological doctrine of the orders of creation and conservation. The function of this doctrine in modern theological ethics has been "to differentiate between the individual spheres of life" in which human beings find themselves and within which the divine will lay claim to them in various concrete ways.[22]

[21]Conversely, it becomes understandable that the institutional forms for the social interpretation of individual behavior must constantly take into account the appearance of *deviant behavior* (see Parsons, *The Social System* [n. 5, above], 249–97). The relation of such behavior to society is ambivalent. On the one hand, it is regarded as wicked, as a violation of the obligation to the community that is present in all social relations because of their reciprocal character. Deviant behavior is therefore subject to social sanctions. On the other hand, however, the individual's deviant behavior can be for the society an indispensable source of social innovation and change, and thus a condition of the continuing vital development of the society itself. From this second point of view, it is one of the strengths of a society that it can tolerate a high degree of deviant behavior. But pluralism becomes a weakness and contributes to the decay of a society when the outlines of normality are no longer recognizable and there is consequently no need for deviant behavior to come to grips with the norm. When a distinction is no longer made between normality and deviancy the concept of tolerance itself becomes invalid and is replaced by the public indifference that accompanies the state of anomie.

[22]F. Lau, "Schöpfungsordnung," *RGG*[3] V (1961), 1492. See the remarks of E. Brunner in his *The Divine Imperative,* trans. O. Wyon (New York, 1947). Brunner announced his intention "to show how the individual social groupings spring out of the nature of man, and [to] describe their peculiar characteristics" (291). In fact, however, he was satisfied to represent these creations as "produced by human, natural, and rational impulse" (337; see 333ff.), with natural impulse operating in marriage and family, the economy, the state, and the legal organization of society, and rational impulse operating in the cultural community, which is given a distinct place over against the church. This argument is vaguely reminiscent of Malinowski's derivation of institutions from human "basic needs."

While Brunner was at least concerned to provide an anthropological basis of some kind, others—such as P. Althaus, *Theologie der Ordnungen* (1934; 1935[2]), 9f.—simply accepted as given a plurality of "forms of human communal life" (9) and turned immediately to a

In conversations between German legal scholars and theologians after World War II the concept of order was replaced by that of institution. The latter seemed unencumbered by the two chief misgivings that the concept of order caused. On the one hand, it was not open to the suspicion that what was being asserted here was an order of human communal life still untouched by human sin. On the other, it did not connote, as did the idea of an order, a basic pattern that in fact exists and cannot be altered.[23]

Once again, however, in the work done by the Commission on Institutions of the Evangelical Church of Germany no systematic viewpoint is presented that renders intelligible the plurality of institutions. Only anthropology can supply such a viewpoint. Moreover, if a basis is to be provided for a theological doctrine of institutions, there is need for anthropological positions that have been submitted to theological reflection and thought through in the light of theology; a mere takeover of data established in a pretheological manner will not do. The distinction and coordination of the viewpoints of particularism and mutuality in the living of human life could serve this purpose, and in fact these have, at least since Schleiermacher's *Ethics,* played an appropriate part in establishing a theological doctrine of the forms of human community.[24] As I have pointed out, however, the resultant anthropological conditions for the social institutionalization of human behavior remain abstract in themselves. If they are to take historical form, they must be concretized in the spirit of the consciousness of meaning that is at the basis of each particular culture.

II. Property, Work, and Economy

Of all the social institutions, property is the one that most clearly shows the element of particularism in contrast to mutuality. The essence of

---

theological interpretation of these. In the ensuing period the givenness of the orders and their historical character (a point stressed by Althaus) were even more strongly emphasized. D. Bonhoeffer, in his *Ethics,* trans. N. H. Smith (New York, 1955; paperback ed., 1965), seeks to derive the orders directly from Scripture as "mandates" instead of arguing to them as already given in some other way (266ff.)—but why, then, does he choose work, marriage, authority, and the church?

[23]In the "Conversation on Institutions" in the Evangelical Church in Germany (from 1955 on) it was hoped that the use of "institution" instead of "order" would eliminate the element of the "static" that is associated with "order." According to H. Dombois, "Zur Begegnung zwischen Rechtswissenschaft und Theologie," *KuD* 31 (1957), 61–74 at 74 (see 69ff.), "the processual character of law" is associated with institutions. But even then the question of the "establishment and nature of institutions" remained ultimately "unanswered"; so Callies (n. 19, above), 61.

[24]See D. F. Schleiermacher, *Philosophische Ethik,* ed. A. Twesten (1841), 65 ff., 72–122. But Schleiermacher offers no further argument for the distinction between the "typical" and the "identical" (common), which he connects with the distinction between creative and organizational activity.

property is the exclusive right to dispose of a thing.[25] Were the element of exclusivity eliminated from the concept of property, this would become simply a right of access and participation;[26] the end result would be the elimination of property itself. It is true that there are forms of property involving rights of participation or sharing, but, first of all, these rights are more or less clearly defined in relation to one another and, second, even communal property is constituted property by the exclusion of those who have no share in it.

Property thus understood, and even individually owned property, seems to have existed since the beginnings of humankind, as can be inferred from burial gifts. Moreover, in the behavior of the higher animals who occupy a territory in an exclusive manner and defend it against inroads by others of the same species there is an analogue of human property; that is, there is a sphere of which the individual has disposal. Among animals who live in nomadic communities individual property may develop if the relation of ownership of *things* is separable from a connection with a particular place. This is the case at least among human beings. Human behavior with its openness to the world finds that objects can be used in many ways. They are therefore "kept" and "taken along" for future use (e.g., as tools).[27] In the identity of the objects that they treat in this way human beings see reflected their own identity.

Even in illiterate hunting and food-collecting cultures, which, like the Pygmies and the Bushmen down to our own day, did not have individual property in land, there was individual ownership of movable and immovable objects. Such property was indeed narrow in its scope, since money was unknown and it was not feasible to store up provisions in any large amount.[28] The range of property expanded only with the domestication of animals and reached its full extent only with the transition to a sedentary mode of life and to farming.

The bases for the claim to ownership are the appropriation of ownerless

[25]Thus J. Schapp, *Sein und Ort der Rechtsgebilde. Eine Untersuchung über Eigentum und Vertrag* (The Hague, 1968), 58, defines property as "the most comprehensive right of control over a thing." K. Larenz likewise interprets the concept of property in terms of the right of disposal; see his "Die rechtsphilosophische Problematik des Eigentums," in Th. Heckel, ed., *Eigentum und Eigentumsverteilung* (1962), 21–41 (at 25, 37f.).

[26]C. B. Macpherson, *Property: Mainstream and Critical Positions* (Toronto, 1978), 201, 205, makes this suggestion in order to avoid the contradiction between the liberal concept of property and the equal right of all to the development of their individual personalities (199). But he limits his suggestion to property in the form of land and capital and does not extend it to consumer goods, because these can be used only as "exclusive property" (206).

[27]Gehlen (n. 8, above), 51f.

[28]W. Nippold, *Die Anfänge des Eigentums bei den Naturvölkern und die Entstehung des Privateigentums* (The Hague, 1954), 28ff., 91f. On the assignment of property to individuals, see 75f., 90.

property and/or personal work.[29] Only the derivation of property from work corresponds to the specifically human way of dealing with the realities of the world. For work is necessary because of the deficient bodily adaptation of human beings to their natural surroundings. It is the means whereby they turn their natural surroundings into an artificial world that serves to satisfy their needs.[30]

Here again there are anticipations in prehuman behavior; especially striking in this regard are the nest-building of birds, the dam-building of beavers, and the colony-building of certain insects. These, however, are products peculiar to a given species, whereas human toil is not ordered to the production of a particular form of artificial environment. For this reason, human beings can increasingly extend their transformation of the living conditions provided by nature in the direction of a control of earthly nature and its resources. Theologians have therefore legitimately interpreted human work in the light of the mandate that the creator God of the Bible gave human beings to master the earth.[31] The transformation of the natural environment into a cultural world is a communal accomplishment of human beings; their work is, however, always individual and as such is the basis for the individual's claim to property.

The distinction between work and enjoyment[32] is constitutive for the concept of work. Consequently, when human beings nourish themselves on the fruits of nature that are at hand (even if they may first have to engage in a laborious search), they do not perform work. On the other hand, the gathering of these fruits for subsequent use, and especially in order to lay in a supply for the winter or other times of shortage, is to be considered work. Like the preparation of meals, which are only to be eaten

[29]Nippold, 82ff. While Nippold stresses individual work as the "ultimate and oldest source" of individual property (91), Gehlen emphasizes in addition the independent importance of "retention" *(Behalten)*. According to Hegel, *Jenaer Vorlesungen zur Realphilosophie* (1805–6), ed. J. Hoffmeister (PhB 67), work presupposes a taking possession of the object to be worked on (207f.), so that in his view this taking of possession is fundamental to the idea of property. See Hegel, *Philosophy of Right,* trans. T. M. Knox (Oxford, 1942), 54ff.

[30]Callies (n. 19, above), 23ff. (on B. Malinowski).

[31]Thus, e.g., M. D. Chenu, *The Theology of Work: An Exploration,* trans. L. Soiron (Dublin, 1963), 7, etc.; W. Zimmerli, "Mensch und Arbeit im Alten Testament," in J. Moltmann et al., *Recht auf Arbeit—Sinn der Arbeit* (1979), 40–58, esp. 43ff.

[32]In his *Phenomenology of Spirit,* Hegel represented the separation of work from enjoyment as being a result of the rise of relations of domination in which the slave must work for the enjoyment of the master (PhB 114, 146f.). In the *Jenaer Vorlesungen zur Realphilosophie,* on the contrary, property and work precede the "struggle for recognition" in the state of nature (PhB 67, 205ff.), a struggle that did not as yet end in the establishment of the opposition between master and slave but, more generally, in the "recognition" of the real state of society (212ff.). As a matter of fact, the difference between work and enjoyment is one of the bases for the development of relations of domination, but precisely for this reason it is presupposed by these relations.

after the preparation, the process of collection and storage postpones enjoyment and thus shows itself to be a behavior that has been cultivated. Work provides food not only for the moment but for an anticipated future and thus, in a preliminary way, for the whole of life. Through such postponement of enjoyment work creates property which to a large extent frees human beings from the immediate pressure of their primary needs,[33] since the products of their work are now at their disposition for future use. This opens the way for the "subsequent need of a more comprehensive mastery of things" (R.-P. Callies) and of the security this mastery bestows on one's life.

At this point we glimpse the ambiguity of property and its inherent tendency to expansion, which long ago drew the criticism of the prophets and especially of Jesus. The accumulation of property can present itself as the way to complete security in life and thus to the complete satisfaction of vital interests. But when it takes this form it begins to compete with the religious dimension of life.[34] In his criticism (e.g., Luke 12:15–21), Jesus shows up as illusory any exaggerated expectations that property will bring security; he also denounces the resultant social consequences of such expectations: neglect of our fellow human beings and their needs for the sake of our own private enrichment.

This criticism does not, however, mean that property as such is unjust.[35]

---

[33]Callies, 82; see Gehlen (n., 8, above), 52f. K. Stopp, "Einkommen und Eigentum," in *Christ und Eigentum* (1963), 12–120, esp. 24ff., disputes the origin of property in "individual performance," at least in the case of property acquired as the result of agreed-on recompense for work: "Social production excludes the element of individual performance as a constitutive feature of property" (27). This conclusion is extreme, for although the distribution of property is certainly *also* "the result of political power-group alliances and political decisions" (29), individual performance remains even then the constitutive factor; only the *value* set upon it changes under the influence of the political situation.

[34]T. Rendtorff, *Ethik* II (1981), 65. The tendency, connected with having, to an inversion of the proper relationship between being and having, has been described by G. Marcel in his *Being and Having,* trans. K. Farrer (London, 1949; Boston, 1951), as an inversion of the relation of disposal: "Our possessions eat us up" (165). "Having as such seems to have a tendency to destroy and lose itself in the very thing it began by possessing, but which now absorbs the master who thought he controlled it" (164). This tendency to inversion is due to the fact that the tendency of the ego to gain complete independence and self-disposal contradicts its exocentric structure (that is, the grounding of its being *extra se,* "outside itself"). As a result, while expecting to become independent by means of things, the ego only becomes dependent *on things.*

[35]Under the influence of Stoic ideas the theologians of the early church developed a very reserved attitude toward private property as being a consequence of original sin; see M. Hengel, *Property and Riches in the Early Church: Aspects of a Social History of Early Christianity,* trans. J. Bowden (Philadelphia, 1974), 1ff. This contrasted with the "free attitude to property" which Jesus himself maintained amid all his criticism of it (26ff.; see 23ff.). But see also ibid., 74ff., for Clement of Alexandria's remarks on possession as a form of freedom and a God-given tool.

On the contrary, it is part of our humanness to make provision for the
future and for our life as a whole (see Prov. 20:4), and one way in which
this relation to our life in its entirety manifests itself is the acquisition of
property. The point of Jesus' warning against yielding to worry about the
future, even if this is only the morrow (Matt. 6:25ff.), is that we must leave
room for trust in the divine source of life; human beings need this source
and must not cut themselves off from it through worry. This proper
attitude does not exclude responsibility for the future (and for the past in
view of the future) and a responsible management of what is presently
given to us with a view to the totality both of our individual lives and of
the community. Nor (despite Luke 10:41f.) does Jesus dispute the necessity of work; in fact, this necessity was even heavily stressed in early
Christianity.[36]

Since, however, the security associated with the acquisition of property
and with work is ambiguous, it should make us reserved toward the
interpretation of either work or property as a way to human liberation.
Work and property do indeed free human beings from the immediate
pressure of the quest, necessitated by human limitations, for food, shelter,
and clothing. But freedom in the full sense of human identity and self-
fulfillment is not thereby attained.[37] On the contrary, both work and
property become means of self-deception and self-alienation for human
beings when they believe they can gain this fuller freedom through
them.

Nonetheless work and property do contribute substantially to establishing the sphere in which true freedom can develop and be active once it
is given and received from another source. In this context it is important
to realize that neither work nor property can be understood solely in terms
of the isolated individual. Though it is not possible to describe work as

[36]See Hengel, 60ff. One need only recall what Paul says in 1 Thess. 4:11 (see 2 Thess.
3:10). On the entire subject, see also W. Bienert, *Die Arbeit nach der Lehre der Bibel. Eine
Grundlegung evangelischer Sozialethik* (1954).

[37]Such an exaggerated and even Promethean view of work is typical of both bourgeois
liberalism and Marxism; see M. Honecker, "Arbeit (VII)," *TRE* 3 (1978), 644f. This
judgment is valid despite the fact that Marx conceived of work alone as the human "act of
self-generation" and believed that he had found this idea in Hegel (see Marx, *Nationalökonomie und Philosophie* [1844], in *Die Frühschriften,* ed. S. Landshut [Kroner ed.], 281; see
247ff.), whereas he resisted private property as an alienated form of work. Chenu (n. 31,
above) accepts this view of work too uncritically when he praises it as a "liberating force"
(12), although elsewhere he does warn against a deification of work (16). Hegel, in his
Philosophy of Right (n. 29, above), had emphasized the ambivalence of the "liberation intrinsic
to work" (§ 194), because the multiplication of needs means that "dependence and want
increase *ad infinitum*" (§ 195). H. Arvon, *La philosophie du travail* (Paris, 1969), correctly
insists that the "material liberation" of human beings through work leaves unanswered the
question of the meaning of this victory over nature, unless it is supplemented by a "spiritual
liberation" (19).

antecedently and by its nature a social activity, the productivity aspect of even individual work gives the latter an impulse toward socialization.[38] For to the extent that private producers produce more of a thing than they individually need, while at the same time they desire the products of others, there is an exchange of products; this leads to the development of trade which mediates this exchange and in turn increases the need felt by individuals for the products of others. Adam Smith in his day described how the self-interest of productive individuals led, via the exchange of products, to the socialization of production through a division of labor, as individuals began to produce precisely for purposes of exchange.[39]

Adam Smith himself, and many others after him, saw the danger in the imbalance associated with the increasing division of labor. Marx believed he had found the source of this imbalance in the self-alienation of human activity that makes possible both exchange and dependent work. He regarded the division of labor and exchange as expressions of an alienation of laboring human beings from their human nature.[40] This alienation, according to Marx, reaches its extreme form in salaried work, where money is exchanged for the capacity for work.

Durkheim, on the other hand, regarded the division of labor as a condition for the progressive development of society into a state of "organic" solidarity, because such a division requires individuals to see their fellow workers as complementing their own activities.[41] The question therefore arises: Does the division of labor mean a progressive limitation and impoverishment of individuals, along with the creation of false needs, or, on the contrary, does it provide the opportunity for mutual enrichment and completion both in the work process itself and in the participation in its products?

The dehumanizing effect of the division of labor, especially in modern industrial work with its extensive specialization and monotony, has been repeatedly denounced both before and after Karl Marx and Friedrich

[38]This point is stressed by Rendtorff (n. 34, above), 30.

[39]A. Smith, *An Inquiry Into the Nature and Causes of the Wealth of Nations* (1776), Book I, ch. 2.

[40]Marx, (n. 37, above), 254ff., 289ff.; see *Die deutsche Ideologie* (1845–46), in Die *Frühschriften*, 357ff., 361ff. A. Wildermuth, *Marx und die Verwirklichung der Philosophie* II (1970), has shown how the market-oriented conception of economic processes as "processes for the exchange of materials" (591–692) led to the interpretation of capital as a "transcendental structure of the civilizing process and of communication."

[41]Durkheim, *The Division of Labor in Society,* (n. 20, above), 68ff., 111ff. The unbalancing effect often criticized in the division of labor is ascribed by Durkheim not to the division of labor as such but to its "anomic" variants in which the reciprocal complementarity of the functions distributed among workers is not found or does not determine consciousness (see 353ff.).

Engels.[42] Recent research, however, has shown the need for a more nuanced description and appraisal of the situation. In 1957, H. Popitz established that according to empirical observation only in "borderline cases" did the work situation in iron and steel foundries lead to problems of monotony (which in addition varied in the degree of oppressiveness they produced) and that in individual special cases the "compulsion to a minimal response" could even be felt as "comfortable."[43] In addition, Popitz observed that both in teamwork and in a "structured" collaboration at machines and on the assembly line there was a very intense social relationship among the workers, and that the hands felt "challenged" to "do what they could" by a work situation that did not reduce them to technological functions or mere parts of a whole.[44]

Such findings support Durkheim rather than Marx. The degradation of the human being to a mere "hand"[45] that exercises only a partial function is not a necessary consequence of private property, exchange, and the division of labor. Just as exchange can help make life rich and many-sided and is sought for precisely this reason, so too the division of labor provides the springboard for a "participation in a common work."[46] Indeed, it is

[42]In 1840, A. de Tocqueville wrote in Part II, Book II, ch. 20 of his *Democracy in America,* trans. H. Reeves, revised by F. Bowen and P. Bradley (New York, 1945), that "in proportion as the principle of the division of labor is more extensively applied, the workman becomes more weak, more narrow-minded, and more dependent" (II, 159). References on this point from the German development prior to Marx are collected in H. Popitz, *Der entfremdete Mensch. Zeitkritik und Geschichtsphilosophie des jungen Marx* (1953). The present-day situation elicits similar sentiments from F. Vilmar, *Industrielle Arbeitswelt. Grundlagen einer kritischen Betriebssoziologie* (1974), 63ff., and from A. Rich, *Christliche Existenz in der industriellen Welt* (1957), 60ff.

[43]H. Popitz et al., *Technik und Industriearbeit. Soziologische Untersuchungen in der Hüttenindustrie* (1957), 164 (156ff.), 201ff., 203; see 207.

[44]Ibid., 175f.

[45]Rendtorff (n. 34, above), 95, sees in this the "essence of exploitation." According to Arvon (n. 37, above), it is one of the consequences of a one-sided utilitarianism (100). Nonetheless it is not inevitable that this tendency should determine the spirit of a society, as has been claimed not only by Marx (from the standpoint of economic interest) but also (from other standpoints) by such critical analysts of culture as F. Jonas, *Sozialphilosophie der industriellen Arbeitswelt* (1960), esp. 189–218, and J. Ellul, *The Technological Society* (1964), trans. J. Wilkinson (New York, 1973), 133ff., and *The Technological System,* trans. J. Neugroschel (New York, 1980), 310ff., and also, following Ellul, by H. Schelsky, *Der Mensch in der wissenschaftlichen Zivilisation* (1961). In 1968, J. Habermas described such fatalistic theses as a "new ideology" which neglects the relevance of "morality" for the shaping of social life; see his *Technik und Wissenschaft als "Ideologie"* (1968), 48–103, esp. 90f. It was only because religion and, later on, traditional political structures lost their power that the interests of capital acquired for a time the "autonomy" described by Marx.

[46]Arvon, 104. It was this kind of consciousness that gave rise to the Protestant ethics of vocation, according to which individuals regarded their particular activity as a special call from God to the service of the common life. On the origin of this outlook in Luther, who gives a universal application to the idea of calling that had previously been limited to the

evidently this kind of community spirit which the socialist countries seek to awaken in their laboring populations, once the supposed obstacle thereto, namely, private ownership of the means of the production, has been overcome. But is it really property that is the barrier? Marxism claims it is, because of the opposition between communal production and private appropriation. It is doubtful, however, whether there is any real opposition here, since property itself has the character of a social institution.

Whereas the work of an individual is integrated into a social process of production only through a progressive division of labor, property is already a social entity because of its legal form. That is, possession becomes ownership only when legally recognized. Those who possess things have them actually under their control, but they may have gained this control illegally through theft, robbery, etc. Possessors become legal owners only when their possession is recognized by society.[47] This fact shows a priority of society over owners in the establishment of property, but it shows at the same time that the community organized under law affirms specific owners, whether these are families, associations, or individuals.

This affirmation is especially important in regard to individual property, since in recognizing the latter the society is affirming and respecting individual persons and their independent right to dispose of a perhaps quite limited realm of things. Of course, this affirmation takes the form not simply of recognizing ownership but also of guaranteeing other personal rights. In the history of modern law, however, the guarantee of property has been an essential facet of the guarantee of the individual freedom of persons. Admittedly, the guarantee is not an unlimited one but entails an obligation to use property in a proper manner,[48] even if this obligation is not always explicitly stressed in the law governing property. In addition, there is usually a "community proviso"[49] which can be the basis for a general "social obligation" attaching to property and makes it possible, at least in emergencies and in cases of an overriding community interest, to limit the right of persons to dispose of their property, or even to take the property from them (usually while compensating them for it).

The precedence of community over individual found expression in

religious state and on the contemporary problematic associated with the idea, see Rendtorff (n. 34, above), II, 46f.

[47]A. Antweiler, *Eigentum* (1967), 23f., 36f.; see also Schapp (n. 25, above), 106ff.

[48]Thus F. Brunstäd, "Rechtsidee und Staatsgedanke," in *Festschrift für J. Binder* (1930), 122f., cited in K. Larenz, "Die rechtsphilosophische Problematik des Eigentums," in Heckel (n. 25, above), 21–41 at 34f.

[49]E. Brunner gives this argument in his *Gerechtigkeit. Die Lehre von den Grundgesetzen der Gesellschaftsordnung* (Zurich, 1943), 176: "All property is acquired under conditions that the acquirers themselves have not created. They acquire property under the protection of the state and in a cultural world they did not produce. Therefore society too has a right to the property they have acquired, since society has been a silent partner in producing it."

ancient natural law in the view that in the state of nature humankind possessed all things in common. The Christian fathers and after them the Scholastics of the Middle Ages accepted these views to a great extent; not the least of the influences at work here was the biblical criticism of wealth. The argument of the fathers and the Scholastics was that when God created the world he intended worldly goods for the use of human beings as a group. Only in the Late Middle Ages did the viewpoint of the independence of the individual prevail. According to F. Suarez, even in paradise human beings had a specific right to the fruits of their work, that is, the fruits they themselves had collected.[50] John Locke then set down as a universal principle that the acquisition of property belongs to the very nature of the human being.

The decisive reason, it must be said, why ancient natural law adopted such a reserved attitude toward individual property was that the metaphysics of antiquity was as yet unfamiliar with the concept of person and assumed a priority of the universal over the particular.[51] Why did the Christian fathers and the Scholastics accept this view? The reason may be that "there was doubtless a certain conflict between the Christian commandment of love and the element of isolation and concentration on personal interest which accompanied private property."[52] On the other hand, it is consistent with Christian respect for the dignity of the individual person that in modern thought since Locke and in Germany especially since Kant individual property should be understood as "an external space for personal freedom and as a means and expression of a personal way of life."[53]

Locke saw individual property as having its basis in the individual nature of the human being, prior to any association with others in a state. German idealism, on the other hand, understood such property to be commanded by universal reason as embodied in the ethical state. This was especially true of Hegel, who regarded the ethical state as "the actuality of concrete freedom," in which "personal individuality and its particular interests . . . achieve their complete *development* and gain explicit recognition for *their right.*" But individuality and its interests also "pass over of their own

[50]F. Suarez, *De opere sex dierum,* Tract. I, Lib. 5, c. 7, n. 1, cited in F. Beutter, *Die Eigentumsbegründung in der Moraltheologie des 19. Jahrhunderts* (1971), 93. See also Beutter's summary of patristic views, 49–85.

[51]Beutter, 82f.

[52]Larenz (n. 48, above), 27.

[53]Ibid., 26. Larenz concludes from this that for Kant the condition of being without property is "a condition of nonfreedom and therefore one unworthy of a human being" (31). See also the fourth thesis in the 1962 *Memorandum on Property* of the Evangelical Church in Germany: "A human being must be able to say 'mine' if he or she is to be free" (*Die Denkschriften der Evangelischen Kirche in Deutschland,* 2: *Soziale Ordnung* [1978], 21.

accord into the interest of the universal" or, as the case may be, "even recognize it as their own *substantive mind*, . . . take it as their *end and aim* and are *active* in its pursuit" (*Philosophy of Right* § 260).

The "general principle that underlies Plato's ideal state" and forbids "the holding of private property" is therefore, according to Hegel, one that "violates the right of personality" (§ 46). For a person "must translate his freedom into an external sphere in order to exist as Idea" (§ 41). In fact, Hegel even says that it is a *"duty* to possess things as *property,* that is, to exist as a person."[54]

According to Hegel, this conception of property as an expression of personal freedom goes back ultimately to the Christian discovery of the personal freedom of the human being as such. "Only yesterday" indeed was the conclusion drawn from the principle, and Hegel sees in this delay an "example from history" which serves "to show the length of time that mind requires for progress in its self-consciousness" (§ 62). The conditional character of the social conditionedness of property generally and therefore of private property as well is here sublimated by means of the religious attitude that conditions the ethical unity of the life of society as a state. This attitude is ultimately responsible for the position allotted to the individual in the community and thus for the shape and justification of the right of property.[55] When viewed in this perspective, Marx's critique of private property is the sign of a failure to allow due importance to the individual in the life of society.

The fact that property is conditioned by the legally organized community finds expression in limitations put on the owner's right of disposal. Property is thus always accompanied by an obligation to use it in a proper

---

[54]G. W. F. Hegel, *Encyclopädie der philosophischen Wissenschaften.* (1817), § 486. This statement is to be understood as meaning that because ethical reason (in Kant's sense) establishes the freedom of the person, the rights of the individual are at the same time duties, and vice versa. See on this point the interpretation, much favored in Evangelical theological writing on the problem of property, of property as a divine "fief" bestowed for the service of one's fellows; see, for example, G. W. Locher, *Der Eigentumsbegriff als Problem evangelischer Theologie* (1954), 160 (see also 40f. on Calvin). Hengel (n. 35, above), 34ff., points out the pre-Christian origin of this idea in Euripides (*The Phoenician Women,* 553ff.). For criticism, see G. Breidenstein, *Das Eigentum und seine Verteilung. Eine sozial-wissenschaftliche und evangelisch-ethische Untersuchung zum Eigentum und zur socialen Gerechtigkeit* (1968), 160.

[55]As Beutter (n. 50, above), 86–140, has explained, in the natural law argument for property which it used in the nineteenth century, Catholic theology adopted the modern idea of individual freedom as the justification for private property. Nonetheless the idea of earthly goods as destined by the creator for all human beings remained operative as a corrective of an individualistic understanding of property; see the passage in DS 3726 from Pius XI's encyclical *Quadragesimo Anno.* The argument linking both viewpoints—the affirmation of the individual in the revelation of divine love which commands us to deal with our fellows in the same spirit of love—is here, however, only implicit at best, since the discussion stays on the level solely of the theology of creation.

manner. The arbitrary destruction of property, for example, is in most cases a misuse of the right. For the rest, the limits set on the owner's right of disposal differ according to the kind of property in question.[56] There are essential differences between property in consumer goods and property in buildings and land (whether these are used for a residence or for an agricultural or other business). These differences are based on "the nature of things" and justify limits set on the power of disposal in the case of the second kind of property. The same is true of property in economic goods and the means of production, where private property becomes the basis for relations of dependence and therefore also of special kinds of social responsibility.

At our present stage of social development doubts have occasionally been raised as to whether personal property and individual freedom have to go together. At times the assertion of this connection has even been held suspect as representing a "property ideology."[57] The point is made that the function of property as a source of security has largely been taken over by other institutional arrangements: guarantees of income and employment, rights to annuities and pensions, health insurance established by law; in other words, payments guaranteed by the state and rights of social participation.[58] Thus the free development of individual creativity is ensured by other means than personal property. Only in the case of consumer and residential property do the critics admit that the ancient functions of free development and provision for one's future continue to be ensured by property.[59]

In regard to provision for the future, it is clear that this concern has in large measure been shifted to the institutions of the welfare state. In addition, property is now far from being the only means of ensuring individuals a measure of independence from social and civil constraints. It continues, however, to be a more important factor in this area than many

[56]Larenz (n. 48, above), 37ff. Stopp (n. 33, above) formulated the following rule for this situation: "As property becomes more and more remote from the sphere of human intimacy, the social obligations connected with it increase" (193). The rule sounds plausible but overlooks the fact, first, that no general limits can be set on the sphere of intimacy (in the eyes of an entrepreneur who is also sole owner his business may be very much a part of the intimate sphere) and, second, that the sphere of intimacy is here represented as itself not socially conditioned. The pseudo-objectivity of the concept of "sphere of intimacy" hides the fact that the extent and nature of the realm of freedom are constituted only when *recognized* by society.

[57]Thus Stopp, 115ff., as well as Breidenstein (n. 54, above), 298ff.

[58]Breidenstein, 223ff. (critique of the fourth thesis in the *Memorandum on Property* of the Evangelical Church in Germany); similar idea already expressed in Callies (n. 19, above), 119ff., who follows A. Gehlen, *Eigentum und Eigentümer in unserer Gesellschaftsordnung* (1960), 169ff. See also E. Wolf in *ZEE* 6 (1962), 1–17, esp. 12ff.

[59]Breidenstein, 313; Callies, 124f.

of the critics are ready to admit who are too one-sidedly bent on expanding the scope of the institutions of the welfare state. Admittedly, in this context property functions primarily as means, that is, as something that is redeemable for money. But the role of property as means is only a partial aspect—and a rather marginal one at that—of the anthropological function of property as a factor in establishing a sphere of personal freedom. Individuals will not be prepared to surrender without further ado what belongs to them in this way. Modern discussion of the concept of property has paid too little attention to the extent of this internal tension between the basic anthropological significance of property and the function of property as means; yet it is a tension that affects even the problems of social policy.

We have seen that at the heart of the problem of property is society's recognition of individuals and their independent way of life. The close connection between property and work has the same basis. The establishment of property as a social institution guarantees individuals the freedom to develop their lives on a foundation of regulated and therefore comprehensible authorization; at the same time, it protects them against encroachments by others. The same two purposes apply analogously to institutionalized job security, which, however, is connected with a specific form of activity in the context of society as organized on the basis of the division of labor.

In addition, society's recognition of property has the characteristic that it looks not only to individuals but also to groups of individuals and, as the case may be, juridical persons. The oldest and still one of the most important examples of such a group is the family. The law governing inheritance shows that the social recognition of property does not envisage only the individual person in isolation but extends also to the communal relationships of which the individual is a part. As a result, the law of inheritance ensures both the permanence of property values beyond the lifetime of the individual and the institution of the family. On the other hand, the modern principle that inheritances are to be taxed counteracts the tendency, inherent in the law of inheritance, to cause an excessive and long-term inequality in the distribution of property.

III. Sexuality, Marriage, and Family

The integration of sexuality into the life of family and kinship group provides an especially instructive example of the anthropological function of institutionalization. Marriage and family show in an exemplary way that individual institutions are not simply geared each to a particular need but, rather, aid in the social integration of human behavior generally and thereby in the attainment of individual identity as well.

The specifically human traits in the natural conditioning of human sexuality exemplify in a striking way the blending of drives that is universally characteristic of the human system of drives. The importance of instinctive reactions that run their course in isolation becomes secondary as compared with the integration of phylogenetic adaptations into human behavior as a totality.[60] The tendency to this kind of integration is natural to humans, being determined by peculiarities of behavior that are peculiar to the species.

Thus human sexuality is set apart by the fact that it is not linked to periods that are seasonally limited and recur in a seasonal rhythm. This "permanent actuality" (H. Schelsky) of human sexuality is matched by the interweaving and interpenetration of all the other human drives and activities that have motifs of sexual origin. One consequence of this is a sexualization of the entire human instinctual life. On the other hand, it is also responsible for the fact that human sexuality can be influenced through linkage with other vital functions and that feelings of erotic pleasure can be separated from sexual activity[61] with the resultant potential eroticization of all areas of social and cultural life.

The elimination of seasonal restrictions on sexuality can be seen, in its beginnings, in the development of the primates.[62] Only in human beings, however, is it integrated into the structure of a cultural world which imposes a new form on human sexuality and "cultivates" it as it does all other human behavioral dispositions. This does not as yet signify in principle any "suppression" of human sexuality,[63] since social and cultural

[60]In older expositions of the subject this process was described as a "reduction of instinct" (A. Gehlen) whereby human drives lost the univocal character proper to a naturally preformed orientation to objects, while at the same time the clear boundaries between the individual drives were blurred. I. Eibl-Eibesfeldt, for his part, criticizes the view that human behavior shows an "almost unlimited plasticity" (E. Timaeus) in contrast to the instinct-bound behavior of animals and points instead to the phylogenetic adaptations which recent research has shown and by which human behavior (e.g., in the mother-child relationship) is in many respects "preprogrammed"; see G. Kurth and I. Eibl-Eibesfeldt, eds., *Hominisation und Verhalten* (1975), 395. On the other hand, Eibl-Eibesfeldt himself stresses the point that human behavior is "much less rigidly fixed" by this preprogramming than is the case in the higher animals (387). As a result, human behavior remains dependent on regulation by culture and the development of habits.

[61]This was pointed out in 1944 by A. Portmann, *Biologische Fragmente zu einer Lehre vom Menschen*, 61ff. (published as *Zoologie und das neue Bild des Menschen* [rde 20, 1956]), 63f.

[62]Chr. Vogel, "Praedispositionen bzw. Praeadaptationen der Primatenevolution im Hinblick auf die Hominisation," in Kurth and Eibl-Eibesfeldt (n. 60, above), 21f.

[63]Freud took too one-sided a view when he conceived of culture as built on renunciation of instinct and the suppression or repression "of powerful instincts"; see his *Civilization and Its Discontents*, trans. J. Strachey (New York, 1961). Freud's theory of culture supposes a concept of instinct that does not pay sufficient attention to the unique biological character

formation is always at every point essential to human nature and therefore to human sexuality as well. The principle that human beings are "by their nature cultural beings" (Adolf Portmann) also applies to this sphere of human behavior. Schelsky is therefore on the mark when he finds among the anthropological foundations of human sexuality a "dependence of the human sexual drive on social and cultural molding."[64] Of course, this molding, or formation, also reflects the many types of human culture.

The integration of sexual behavior into the cultural form taken by human communal life is connected with the institutions of marriage and family. Nonetheless, neither family nor marriage has for its primary purpose to regulate sexual relations. On the contrary, in most cultures the institution of marriage makes only limited claims on sexual behavior.[65] This is especially so in regard to the sexuality of the male, whereas stricter demands are made of the woman in this regard because her sexuality is immediately linked to birth and the child and therefore to the family as a set of long-term relationships. Only "from the familial community as a permanent moral relationship did influences emerge that defined the relation of man and woman in terms of the tendency to restrict sexual relations to marriage."[66]

It is also true, however, that by reason of the biological conditions underlying them, relations between the human sexes antecedently show a tendency to a "permanence of relationship" which is also "an inherited

---

of human instinctual life with its openness to cultural molding. The same is even more true of W. Reich, who sought to liberate instinct, conceived as a pure force of nature, by making Freud's description of the origin of culture through suppression of instinct apply only to patriarchal culture; see W. Reich, *The Sexual Revolution: Toward a Self-Regulating Character Structure*, trans. T. Pol (New York, 1974). The defect in his argument is not the principle that "the sex-economic regulation of biological energy requires the possibility of sexual gratification corresponding to each age group" (15–16) but, rather, the physicalist conception of instinct that is behind this principle.

[64]H. Schelsky, *Soziologie der Sexualität. Über die Beziehungen zwischen Geschlecht, Moral und Gesellschaft* (rde 2, 1955), 15.

[65]R. König, *Die Familie der Gegenwart. Ein interkultureller Vergleich* (1974), 55ff. König emphasizes the point that an excessive focusing of our understanding of family and marriage on sexuality must lead to misinterpretations: "What matters in the family is not simply physical generation or rearing but the 'second birth' of the human being as a sociocultural personality" (59). See H. Schelsky, "Die sozialen Formen der sexuellen Beziehungen," in *Die Sexualität des Menschen* (1954). Also C. Lévi-Strauss, "The Family," in H. L. Shapiro, ed., *Man, Culture and Society* (New York, 1955), 261–85, esp. 274 and 276. See also B. Malinowski, "Parenthood, the Basis of Social Structure," in R. L. Coser, ed., *The Family: Its Structure and Functions* (New York, 1964), 3–19, esp. 15ff.

[66]H. Begemann, *Strukturwandel der Familie. Eine sozialethisch-theologische Untersuchung über die Wandlung von der patriarchalischem zur partnerschaftlichen Familie* (1966²), 43.

tendency in many higher species of animals."[67] This permanency is not simply "natural" to human beings because of "the very long period during which children remain in a state of need."[68] It has an essentially broader basis in the peculiar character of human behavior. The tendency to a permanent relationship springs from the fact that because of its permanent actuality, the sexual life of human beings is not limited to the act of reproduction but also has "the function of binding the partners to one another."[69] This function must in turn be connected with the fact that human nature with its capacity for foresight and remembrance is disposed to long-term enterprises.[70]

The consciousness of time makes available to human beings—primarily in the form of feeling—a relation to their life as a totality; in their social life this relationship becomes thematic precisely in the relation of the sexes and gives the latter personal depth. It finds expression in the "tenderness" without which the encounter of the sexes remains humanly empty.[71] It is inseparable from the fact that sexual affection is directed to the entire person of the partner. This includes a directedness to the whole person as one whose life is characterized by extension in time. That is, given the temporality of human beings and the important part played in their lives by knowledge of past and future, the affirmation of the whole person of the partner necessarily implies at least the intention of a lasting relationship with that person.[72] Implications of this kind play a part in all human

[67]König, 9f., referring to H. M. Peters, "Gesellungsformen der Tiere," in W. Ziegenfuss, ed., *Handbuch der Soziologie* (1956), 613–40, esp. 633. See also R. Linton, "The Natural History of the Family," in R. N. Anshen, ed., *The Family: Its Function and Destiny* (New York, 1949), 18–38, esp. 19f.

[68]Thus Gehlen, *Urmensch und Spätkultur* (n. 8, above), 194.

[69]On the bonding function, see I. Eibl-Eibesfeldt, *Love and Hate: The Natural History of Behavior Patterns,* trans. G. Strachan (New York, 1974), 155ff.

[70]M. Midgley, *Beast and Man: The Roots of Human Nature* (Ithaca, N.Y., 1978), 301ff.

[71]The importance of tenderness for an "enduring sexual relationship" is emphasized even by an author like W. Reich (n. 63, above), 122ff. When persons engage only in transient relationships this is due (says Reich) to "the absence of tenderness toward the sexual partner" (123). "The constant absence of tenderness . . . diminishes the sensual experience" (ibid.). Reich also recognizes that the presence of such tenderness could lead to the "moralistic concept of permanent monogamy" (which he rejects as "compulsory morality"). He avoids this logical conclusion in a rather forced way by remarking that an "enduring" relationship "has no set time span" (125). But in fact an objectively determined period of time does not play a decisive role in monogamy; the decisive thing is the inherent tendency of the relationship to extend to the entire person and therefore to the entire life of the partner.

[72]H. Ringeling, *Theologie und Sexualität. Das private Verhalten als Thema der Sozialethik* (1968), 227ff., also calls attention to this point (esp. 229f.). He goes on, however, to express the view that an egalitarian society has relativized "the idea of personal totality and definitively reduced it to a form of private life" (234). Is it really possible to tackle the theme of personal totality from the viewpoint of a critique of ideologies and "reveal it to be a concern

relations in which persons bind themselves to one another. Precisely for this reason they are especially characteristic of the relation of the sexes.

The institution of marriage absorbs the tendency found in human sexual life to a lasting union with the partner and imposes on it the form of a fixed way of life which is entered into publicly and is sanctioned and protected by society. At the same time, however, in archaic societies marriage is itself firmly embedded in more comprehensive social contexts, namely, the family and the kinship group. Only in modern society has marriage become the basis of the family (in the form of the nuclear family). In older cultures "the family as the broader group took precedence over marriage or rather the association of two individual human beings."[73] This priority is made especially clear in the fact that it was the family, and originally the leaders of the clan, who chose the partners in a marriage.

The reason for this was the close connection between family and property; because of this connection the clan exercised a comprehensive care of its members in regard to food, shelter, work, and most of the other vital needs. The marriage of the young meant, therefore, the establishment of a connection between kinship groups. It was accompanied by acts of property transfer in the form of gifts given according to rules of reciprocity. But the most important transfer of property took place in the marriage ceremony itself,[74] and here again reciprocity in the sense of an equivalent exchange had to be observed, either in the form of the price paid for the bride or in the form of an exchange of women between the kinship groups.

People nowadays may regard as offensive the combination of marriage and family with property relationships that seems to have been especially characteristic of these institutions in the early stages of their development. Where this combination exists, relations between persons, which ought to be based on a free and reciprocal self-donation, are subordinated to forms of economic dependency. The emancipation of the choice of partner from such dependencies and considerations is a recent advance in the history of culture and even today cannot be regarded as complete as far as personal relations in marriage are concerned.

---

of the bourgeois personality" (240)? The bourgeois ideal of personality is, after all, only a specific expression of the relation (which is much more fundamental from an anthropological standpoint) of human beings to their wholeness. And in fact, the subjectivity that is in process of liberating itself and is seeking to evade the implications of personality is, rather, to be regarded as itself a phenomenon linked to the bourgeois cultural world. See also D. Rössler's discussion of the concept of "the whole man" in *HWP* 5 (1980), 1106–11.

[73]R. König, "Soziologie der Familie," in A. Gehlen and H. Schelsky, eds., *Soziologie* (1955[3]), 121–58 at 125.

[74]C. Lévi-Strauss, "Reciprocity, the Essence of Social Life" (1957), in Coser (n. 65, above), 36–48, esp. 45f.

On the other hand, we should not judge the close connection between marriage, family, and economic life solely from the viewpoint of the limitations it put on the personal freedom of the individual. First of all, originally and right down into the early modern age, economic life was organized in terms of the family and groups of families. Second, the fact that the place of women and children in family and clan was determined by property rights did not automatically mean that they were at the mercy of arbitrary decisions by those who ruled family and clan. For, third, the legal forms imposed on communal life in the kinship group, as well as the giving and receiving that went on between individuals and communities, were rooted in religious convictions and norms. These determined the self-understanding of individuals, while they also legitimized and regulated the way in which kinship groups combined with one another to form the context in which life was lived in a society. This meant, according to Claude Lévi-Strauss,[75] that these religious convictions and norms originally made possible the transition from nature to culture.

Arnold Gehlen, in his interpretation of the totemic organization of society (in which he disagrees with Lévi-Strauss), has brought out the importance of religion for this passage to human socialization, for the consequent regulation of relations between clans, and therefore also for the identity of the individual kinship group with the families belonging to it. The phenomenon of totemism is especially interesting in this regard, since it offers a unique opportunity for reconstructing the process whereby society as a whole developed out of kinship groups or, as the case may be, arose simultaneously with the kinship groups. Franz Boas (1916) and, following him, A. R. Radcliffe-Brown (1929) had recognized the connection between, on the one hand, totemic identifications of interrelated kinship groups with various species of animals or plants and, on the other, certain forms of social organization, namely, exogamy and the correlative prohibition of incest.[76]

Lévi-Strauss traced prohibitions of incest back to the requirement that the women of a family (or clan) be reserved for exchange for women of another kinship group. Malinowski had realized, and Marcel Mauss had expounded at length, the importance of reciprocal giving and receiving for social relations in primitive society. Lévi-Strauss was now extending this insight to the description of the familial structures of primitive societies.

The "totemic" association of various kinship groups with various spe-

---

[75]Lévi-Strauss defines the scope of the incest taboo along these lines in his *The Elementary Structures of Kinship*, trans. J. H. Bell and J. R. von Sturmer (Boston, 1969), chs. 2–3.

[76]C. Lévi-Strauss, *Totemism*, trans. R. Needham (Boston, 1963), 10ff. The page references that follow in the text are to this book.

ies of animals or plants was interpreted by Lévi-Strauss as a means of inking the kinship groups among themselves, since "opposition, instead of being an obstacle to integration, serve[s] rather to produce it" (89). At the same time, however, he regarded these totemic ideas themselves as simply metaphors, "tropes" (102), for expressing an intellectual content: the unity of what is distinct, which primitive human beings were as yet unable to grasp in an abstract way (100). In his view, then, the supposed religious meaning of these notions must fade into thin air, and in this disappearance he saw the "end" of totemism as a "religious anthropology": "The alleged totemism pertains to the understanding, and the demands to which it responds and the way in which it tries to meet them are primarily of an intellectual kind. In this sense, there is nothing archaic or remote about it. Its image is projected, not received; it does not derive its substance from without."[77]

Gehlen took an entirely different approach to the problem of totemism and its significance for the development of the institutions of marriage and the family.[78] He took as his starting point the question of how the rise of "unilineal" assignments of kinship—that is, the assessment of family membership on the basis of the paternal line alone or of the maternal line alone —is to be explained. This kind of unilineal assignment of kinship is indispensable for forming unified kinship groups and for deciding unambiguously on the membership of a person in only a single kinship group. Only in large-scale societies, in which cohesion depends no longer on clan identity but on other factors, and especially on political organization, can

[77]Ibid., 104. The fact that this judgment on totemism is inspired by a general attitude to the phenomenon of religion is made clear in Lévi-Strauss's introduction to M. Mauss, *Soziologie und Anthropologie* I (1974). There he discusses the function of *mana* in Mauss's interpretation of magic as a linking of diverse manifestations by means of *mana*, a linking that corresponds to the role of the copula in a judgment. But (says Lévi-Strauss) *mana* (which Mauss considers to be analogous to the Indian *brahman* and the "holy" of the phenomenology of religions) is not based, as Mauss maintains, "in a different order of reality than the relations which are formed with its help" (36). For if we regard it as based "on the level of feelings, volition and convictions" (ibid.) and see these as expressing an unconscious, the question must arise as to whether this substratum is acquired or innate. If it is acquired, then we face the problem of the inheritance of acquired characteristics. If it is innate, then (according to Lévi-Strauss) the following difficulty arises: "It is unthinkable, unless we invoke a theological hypothesis, that the content of experience should be prior to it" (25). In Lévi-Strauss's view, it is evidently enough simply to mention such a consequence in order to demonstrate the untenability of the assumption. In other words, ethnology, as understood by Lévi-Strauss, antecedently excludes the possibility of theological hypotheses, that is, any assumption that the religious manifestations found in human life have a specifically religious real content. Such an objective content cannot exist or, as the case may be, may not be permitted to exist.

[78]Gehlen, *Urmensch und Spätkultur* (n. 8, above), 199ff., and idem, "Die Sozialstrukturen primitiver Gesellschaften," in Gehlen and Schelsky (n. 73, above), 13–45, esp. 32ff.

a unilineal assignment of kinship be dropped and replaced by a bilineal.[79]

But how account for the origin of this unilineal assignment of kinship, without which the formation of identifiable kinship groups would not have been possible? Gehlen found the answer in totemism. According to Gehlen, the point of departure for totemism was the rituals in which the Stone Age hunters imitated animals; the existence of these rituals can be inferred from cave paintings. In Gehlen's hypothesis the passage from these rituals to totemism was due to groups defining themselves through identification with a particular species of animal.[80] Because of the analogy between the unilineal group, which lived dispersed, and the members of a particular species of animal, the totemist form of animal worship created the we-consciousness, or social identity, of the kinship group and at the same time made binding the rules governing incest and marriage. The unilineal kinship group was not a natural entity but an artificial, cultural creation; it could not, however, have been produced by purposeful reason for the sake of establishing a social unit, since such a function and the order thus established could be known only after the fact. It can therefore have originated, according to Gehlen, only as a product of the "ideative" religious consciousness.[81]

According to Gehlen, then, and in contrast to Lévi-Strauss, the religious experience of reality was constitutive for the institutional structures themselves. An important reason for the difference between these two interpretations is doubtless the fact that, unlike Lévi-Strauss, Gehlen is not satisfied with a "synchronic" description of the structures but also takes a "diachronic" approach and asks how they arose. Gehlen was probably wrong, however, in regarding the connection between totemism and exogamy as secondary.[82] It may well be that the need of the kinship group for identification arose simultaneously with the need for distinguishing it from similar associations and for regulating its relationships with these other groups. On the other hand, while the regulations concerning marriage and the prohibitions of incest certainly contributed in a substantial way to stabilize the clan organization and the authority of its leaders, they could hardly have accounted by themselves for the rise of the unilineal kinship system

---

[79]Gehlen, "Die Sozialstrukturen," 24. In present-day Western industrialized societies, kinship is reckoned bilineally, although family names are usually unilineal, being taken from the father's name; see König, *Die Familie der Gegenwart* (n. 65, above), 28.

[80]Gehlen, 34f., also links with this the belief that the dead members of the clan survive in the totem animals, and the consequent prohibition against killing these, as well as the idea of the "clan leader" as embodying the totem animal (or, as the case be, the ancestor).

[81]On this, see Begemann (n. 66, above), 43f. I will simply call attention in passing to the tension between this conception and the fundamental role assigned to the concept of action in Gehlen's anthropology.

[82]Ibid., 33f.

(which would then have been produced by rational purpose). The system must have sprung from the religious root described by Gehlen.

The religious basis for the institutions of family and clan has remained normative despite all the historical changes that not only the structures of family and marriage but also religion itself have undergone, and despite the more or less marked secularization of these institutions as a result of a greater differentiation within the social system.[83] The normative importance of religion can be seen in, for example, the fact that the patriarchal family became independent of the kinship group.[84]

The separation of the individual family from the clan could have been religiously motivated, with the result that henceforth God was to be the true father, the true leader of the clan.[85] At the same time, this God may have become, as he did in the Jewish family, the prototype for the father of the earthly, patriarchal family. On the other hand, the ancestors too could be venerated as prototypes of paternal authority and thus be relieved of their connections with the living heads of the clan. In the polytheistic religions the community of the gods themselves could be thought of as a community of families of a patriarchal type

[83]Gehlen, "Die Sozialstrukturen," 15, following R. H. Lowie (1921) and R. Piddington (1950), notes that even among "primitives" marriage proves to have become relatively secularized.

[84]König has argued that "separation from the kinship group must inevitably have brought an emphasis on the *patria potestas,* if the *pater familias* were to assert himself against the clan authorities"; see his "Abhängigkeit und Selbstständigkeit in der Familie," in L. von Wiese, ed., *Abhängigkeit und Selbstständigkeit im sozialen Leben* I (1951), 239, cited in H. Schelsky, *Wandlungen der deutschen Familie in der Gegenwart* (1960⁴), 323. Contrary to what Freud claimed in *Totem and Taboo* (1913), the patriarchal family was not the original form of the human family. Speaking of Freud's idea of the original tyrannical father who drove away his sons because they were his rivals for the favors of the women, Linton (n. 67, above) has remarked that such behavior is not observable in today's primates and that a human community adopting such practices could not have survived. With regard to the separation of the family from the kinship group despite the security which the latter offered to its members, Linton writes: "When the value of this security becomes less than the handicap imposed on the individual by the associated obligations, he is willing to sacrifice the former in order to avoid the latter. Colloquially speaking, when a man can do better without relatives than with them, he will tend to ignore the ties of kinship" (32).

[85]Thus a break with the patriarchal kinship group stands at the beginning of the traditions about Abraham in Genesis, and the break is legitimated by a divine election (Gen. 12:1). On this point, see R. Hamerton-Kelly, *God the Father: Theology and Patriarchality in the Teaching of Jesus* (Philadelphia, 1979), 30f. The description of God as father is relatively rare in the Old Testament (ibid., 20). Except in connection with the king's relation to God (2 Sam. 7:14; Ps. 89:26; see Ps. 2:7), it occurs only beginning with Hosea (11:1); see the commentary on Hosea by H. W. Wolff, *Hosea,* trans. G. Stansell (Philadelphia, 1974), 197f. It does, however, occur as an element in theophoric names such as Joab, Abiram, and, not least, Abraham, which came from an earlier age. On the authority of the father in the Jewish family, see Hamerton-Kelly, 43f., 55ff.

and thus be understood to form a unity.

In this phase of the reciprocal relations between family structure and religion there was the question largely of projections of social structures into the conception of divine reality, although these projections also represented to some extent a reaction against the patriarchal organization of the clan.[86] At the same time, however, we can see in this phase a need for religious legitimation, and this need in turn presupposes that the institutional order and its authority over individuals had a basis in religious convictions.

This state of affairs must be regarded as constitutive for the specifically institutional character of marriage and family as institutions that are not left to the discretion of their individual members. For if the family is not to be understood as simply a social group, even though of special kind,[87] and marriage is not to be understood as simply a contractual relationship,[88] and if on the contrary both of these, as institutions, confront their members with the binding claim of a reality that takes precedence over them, then this claim must ultimately have a religious basis.[89]

The significance of the public character of marriage and the wedding for their institutional character[90] is also connected with this religious dimension. For the commitment that the marriage partners make in relation to society as a whole (which is present by reason of the public character of marriage) is made not so much to society as an authoritative agency as to society in its role as witness. The commitment of the marriage partners becomes binding only in the context of the values on which the society is based and which in their turn point to the religious authority that stands behind them.

The same must be said of the structure of authority that is inherent in

---

[86]This may be the partial truth expressed in Freud's theory of religion. The cult of the ancestors, like the installation of the divinity as father, could be viewed as a compensation for the rejected authority of the clan.

[87]On this point, see Schelsky's analysis of König's views in Schelsky's *Wandlungen* (n. 84, above), 26ff. and 323.

[88]König, "Soziologie der Familie" (n. 73, above), 121–58, esp. 135, 139ff. On this question, see also Hegel's *Philosophy of Right*, § 75, where he opposes Kant's *Metaphysik der Sitten* I, §§ 24–27.

[89]See the remarks of König, "Soziologie der Familie," 141, on the Christian explanation of marriage as a community of married persons. But the fact that this meaning is antecedently present does not depend (as König claims, 126) on the priority of family over marriage.

[90]König, 144; idem, *Die Familie der Gegenwart* (n. 65, above), 52f. According to Schelsky, *Wandlungen* (n. 84, above), 30, the recognition of marriage by a public act is the act—in the sense which this term has in the juridical theory of institutions—whereby the individual marriage acquires the character of an institution. T. Rendtorff, *Ethik* II, 20 and 41f., emphasizes the ethical relevance of the public aspect of the wedding and of marriage as an institution. It is in this context that a theology of marriage must evaluate the significance of a church ceremony, as a public act, for the coming into existence of a marriage.

marriage and family. According to Schelsky, the "natural authority" possessed by certain members of the family over the familial community is due to the fact that by reason of their special function or contribution they represent the "communal we" of the family.[91] The claims of the communal we may find their expression more in the figure of the father or in that of the mother or in both together as exercising complementary functions and spheres of authority. In every case, however, the necessary presupposition is that the community is experienced by its members as meaningful and its claims on the individual as justified. Only if this supposition is verified can the family become, not only for the children but also for the married couple and the parents themselves, the place where human beings undergo a "second birth" as "sociocultural personalities."[92] When this presupposed priority of the community over the individual is no longer acknowledged, the individuals involved will experience the claims of marital and familial obligations as a suppression of their freedom, and not least of their sexual freedom,[93] and they will seek emancipation from these fetters.

But the priority of the community over the individual is not self-evidently valid. It requires a justification and legitimation which in the final analysis can be found only in religion. Crises affecting the structure of authority in marriage and family will therefore always be religious crises as well, whether these be limited to individuals or have broader implications, and whether the institutional crises have to do with changes in the form of the community or with its dissolution.

The process whereby the patriarchal family has disintegrated in the advanced industrial societies[94] provides an especially relevant example of what I have been saying. Whatever may be the truth of Freud's explanation of religion as originating in the Oedipus complex, this explanation is itself evidence of the close connection between the conception of the

---

[91]Schelsky, *Wandlungen,* 316ff.

[92]König, "Soziologie der Familie," 127 and 124, as well as 145ff.

[93]According to Ringeling (n. 72, above), the Kinsey reports and the facts detailed in them are to be seen as a protest against the absorption of human beings by the institution (150ff.). But, of course, it is possible to speak of such a protest only where the institutions of marriage and family are experienced no longer as forms of vital community but only as external constraints. On the other hand, Ringeling also opposes the illusion of "immediate romantic self-fulfillment" through sexual emancipation (158). Those subject to this illusion cannot but fail to achieve the identity they seek, because this is obtainable only in a lasting community of life, the institutional character of which relieves individuals of anxiety about whether the community will last. Ringeling justifiably remarks on the way in which people in the industrial age are seduced by an economically motivated "cult of eros" which presents immediate self-fulfillment as obtainable (161ff., 171ff.). See also his remarks in *Handbuch der christlichen Ethik* II (Freiburg, 1978), 167–71

[94]See Schelsky's remark on "tertiary patriarchalism" in *Wandlungen,* 325f.

family as patriarchally structured and a corresponding interpretation of it in religious tradition, and especially in the biblical tradition. For this reason, emancipation from the patriarchal family structure was inevitably associated in the minds of many people with a rejection of the religious convictions that had legitimated that structure. Thus Wilhelm Reich thought of his program of sexual emancipation as being "in flagrant contradiction" to "every patriarchal religion."[95] Conversely, efforts for the social emancipation of women have found a counterpart in a feminist theology which not only rejects the justification of patriarchal family structures in the Jewish and Christian traditions but also demands that the conception of God in these traditions be purified of all patriarchal traits.

It is in fact undeniable that the biblical tradition has legitimated a patriarchal order of the family and, in particular the subordination of wife to husband as his possession (Ex. 20:17). The Yahwist story of creation sees the relation of wife to husband as regulated by the divine words spoken at the end of the story of paradise: "He shall rule over you."[96] The New Testament writings continue to reflect the Jewish organization of the family and to call for the subordination of wife to husband (1 Cor. 14:34; see Col. 3:18; 1 Peter 3:1; Titus 2:5).

At the same time, however, the basis for a breakthrough and for the elimination of patriarchal structures is to be found in early Christianity and, above all, in the behavior of Jesus himself. But the Old Testament recognized the possibility of conflict between obedience to God and loyalty to the patriarchally organized family. In such cases, obedience to God had to take precedence. Thus Abraham was summoned by God to leave his father's house (Gen. 12:1). There is a saying of Jesus that points in the same direction: "If any one comes to me and does not hate his own father and mother and wife and children and brothers and sisters, yes, and even his own life, he cannot be my disciple" (Luke 14:26).

These and similar sayings of Jesus, however, are not directed against the patriarchal family structure in particular but first and foremost against the absolutizing of family loyalty as such. Obedience to God takes priority over family ties. But since this demand binds all human beings alike, it has consequences that in the name of God the Father shatter the patriarchal family order. This can be seen especially in Jesus' dealings with women.[97] Even though the early Christian tradition was rather strongly prejudiced on the side of patriarchal views, it did at decisive points speak out against

[95]Reich (n. 63, above), 19.

[96]See also the discussion in Begemann (n. 66, above), 75ff., and Hamerton-Kelly (n. 85, above), 55ff.

[97]See Hamerton-Kelly, 60f. as well as 63f., where, referring to sayings such as those in Mark 3:31–35 and Luke 9:60, he speaks of a "liberation" of children too from the absolute sway of familial duties.

the neglect of woman in comparison with men, as, for example, when it emphasized the equality of men and women in Christ (Gal. 3:28) and called married people to mutual love after the example of Christ (Eph. 5:25ff.).

These impulses were also at work in the subsequent history of Christianity. This is especially true of Jesus' condemnation of divorce, which Jewish law allowed husbands to declare unilaterally (Mark 10:2–12). By making divorce difficult, but also by requiring marital consent from both partners and abolishing the right that Roman law granted to the *pater familias* over the life and death of family members, the legislation of the early Byzantine emperors significantly improved the position of married women.[98] We may see this legislation as paving the way for a conception of marriage as more of a partnership, even if it left untouched the basic patriarchal structure of the family, a structure that was indeed also based on the economic and political conditions of the age. In any case, in the light of those beginnings it is possible to see the dissolution of the patriarchal family structure, which resulted from political and economic changes in modern society, as an opportunity to reshape marriage and family in the spirit of the Christian idea of mutual love.[99]

It is essential for any such reshaping that marriage no longer be viewed from the standpoint of the family but, rather, the family from the standpoint of marriage.[100] This means, first of all, that marriage, being a communion of love between the partners, is an end in itself and does not need to be justified by any further purposes, not even the generation of new life.[101] Only if the community of marriage is understood as an end in itself

---

[98]H. J. Berman, *The Interaction of Law and Religion* (New York, 1974), 52ff.

[99]In chs. 6 and 7 of the third part of his book, Begemann (n. 66, above) presents a sketch of such a view of marriage (134–60).

[100]This is in keeping with the sociological structure of the modern family as a nuclear family. "Today the married couple is the controlling center of the family; the children are then added" (König, "Soziologie der Familie," 135; see 138f. and idem, *Die Familie der Gegenwart*, 67f.). König's view of this situation was ambivalent. On the one hand, he saw the family as jeopardized by individualism ("Soziologie der Familie," 142ff.) and was therefore inclined to conceive of marriage simply as the "beginning of a family group" (144), the idea being that "at bottom, even today marriage must still have its basis in the family and not vice versa" (126). On the other hand, he recognized that a new formulation of the concept of family is possible if marriage is understood as "a community extending to the whole of life": "All that makes up marriage and the family will then be put in the service of this community that is based on the self-worth of the person as understood in Christianity" (141).

[101]Rendtorff, *Ethik* II, 16ff., lays particular emphasis on the point that marriage as a "model community of life" is an end in itself. In this he is opposing the view, dominant even in traditional Christian teaching on marriage, that marriage derives its orientation from ends distinct from the communion of life among the partners. See also Chr. Greif, *Die Ordnung der Ehe. Eine rechtsphilosophische Studie* (Berlin, 1977), 71.

can marriage serve as an exemplar of the human destination to that life in communion with others to which individual personhood owes its substance and cohesion. Marriage can represent the priority of the community over individuals because it embraces the entire life of the individuals in it. To that extent, individuals entering marriage surrender their isolated individuality.

On the other hand, the precedence, thus manifested, of the community over the individual is no longer naturally present in a marriage whose partners dismiss all external considerations. It is mediated, rather, by free reciprocity and remains operative only in the medium of this free reciprocity. The latter includes a readiness to accept the new life that emerges from marital intercourse, because otherwise the isolated individualities of the partners that had been surrendered in the decision to marry would once again become the ultimate goal of their communion. Without the readiness in principle to accept children, the essential combination—which is creative of marital communion—of an acceptance of one's own life as a gift with a readiness to give life in turn[102] would be dissolved.

The replacement of a patriarchal organization of marriage and family by a model in which marriage is a community of partners implies neither a rejection of the idea of monogamy nor a renunciation of the idea that the sexual roles of man and woman are culturally differentiated. For, on the one hand, the idea of marriage as a communion of life can be a suitable basis for the renewal of the institution of marriage only if the marital communion of life is understood as extending to the entire life of the couple.[103] On the other hand, apart from happy accidents, the mutual complementarity of man and woman that is thus realized will acquire significance for the functions of marriage and family in relation to society as a whole only if the understanding of sexual roles that has been formed by cultural tradition and education is compatible with this kind of mutual complementarity.

In the past, many distinctions between the sexes in mentality as well as in typical behaviors and activities were considered to be due to nature; today they are recognized as culturally conditioned. "Belief in the 'naturalness' of sexual differences and of the resultant divergences in social and cultural behavior is itself only a modern way of legitimizing the bases of the particular culture and the particular conception of society."[104] It does not, however, follow from this realization that such distinctions arose solely as a way of protecting the structures of patriarchal domination and

[102]The unity of these two aspects is the controlling idea in Rendtorff's description of "real ethical life": *Ethik* I (1980), 32–61. It is also the basis of his presentation of the unity of marriage and parenthood (II, 77).

[103]König, "Soziologie der Familie" (n. 73, above), 141.

[104]Schelsky, *Soziologie der Sexualität* (n. 64, above), 16.

that they are to be done away with in the name of a "return to (undistorted) nature." For human beings will inevitably develop one or another sort of lasting and reciprocal forms of behavior in their mutual dealings.

This means that the cultural shaping of behavior in the various areas of human activity takes its direction from the requirements of life in society. In the economic sphere such a direction is imposed by the principle of reciprocity or mutuality, which then goes on to influence many other spheres of behavior as well. In the area of relations between the sexes the requirement that the roles of man and woman be different yet complementary has a similar function.

> From each sex, society has asked that they so live that others may be born, that they cherish their masculinity and femininity, discipline it to the demands of parenthood, and leave new lives behind them when they die. This has meant that men had to be willing to choose, win, and keep women as lovers, protect and provide for them as husbands, and protect and provide for their children as fathers. It has meant that women have had to be willing to accept men as lovers, live with them as wives, and conceive, bear, feed, and cherish their children. Any society disappears which fails to make these demands on its members and to receive this much from them.[105]

The best insurance that these demands will be met is the stylization of the social roles of the sexes as opposed yet complementary. This state of affairs leads individuals to seek in a person of the opposite sex a comprehensive *complement* to their own being and existence; it also ensures that they will find this complement, despite all the limitations that the imperfection of human beings unavoidably imposes in each case. Because the roles of the sexes are stylized so as to be complementary, men and women, oriented as they are to other human beings and needing love and recognition from others, can concentrate on a relationship with a particular person of the other sex. As a result, they can, in an otherwise highly imperfect world, find in this relation to a person of the other sex an exemplary fulfillment of their destination to live in society. For this reason, early Christianity could look upon marriage as representing the entire human community as renewed by Jesus Christ.

As a regulated coordination of the roles of the sexes is fundamental to every society, so too the cultural world that takes its stamp from Christianity is based "on a formation of the sexes to play specific and opposed roles."[106] This formation is carried out in the light of a norm: the unqualified worth and validity of monogamous marriage in which each partner embraces the entire life of the other. This view of marriage was not

---

[105]M. Mead, *Male and Female: A Study of the Sexes in a Changing World* (New York, 1949), 380–81.
[106]Schelsky, 53.

a product of Christianity. It had become the norm in Hellenistic and, above all, Roman culture. In other cultures too, and to some extent despite official authorization of other types of marriage, monogamy was far more widespread in practice than was temporary marriage.[107]

Christianity did, however, give monogamy a new and humanly central meaning. Contrary to what Max Weber thought, it did not simply "make monogamy an absolute norm for ascetical reasons."[108] On the contrary, Jesus' condemnation of divorce (Mark 10:5f.) is connected with the idea that the union of man and woman as intended by God the creator is inviolable. Moreover, the early church understood marital communion as being a relationship of mutual love, analogous to that which exists between Christ and the church (Eph. 5:22ff.). This view of marriage was by no means obvious in Hellenistic culture.

Christianity thus gave monogamy a dimension of religious meaning because of which it "became the womb of our Western culture and of its spiritual and psychic attitudes."

> This tradition gave rise to an ideal of marriage which, while limiting sexual relations to the two partners in the marriage, attempts to lift each partner above the striving for personal and especially for sexual happiness. Its high point is the creation of a partnership between man and woman and of a shared destiny that will last beyond death. This partnership, this shared destiny, becomes the foundation of the marriage and of the fulfillment of the two personalities. This ideal integrates human sexuality with the sublimest heights of human existence and spirituality. Precisely for this reason, and despite all the statistical and psychological proofs that its realization is rare and improbable, it will always remain the ultimate claim made on the relationship of man and woman in our culture.[109]

The validity of monogamy as the social norm in a cultural world that bears the mark of Christianity is nonetheless jeopardized today and has even been extensively eroded. This should not be regarded as the result primarily of the contrast between the ideal of Christian marriage as a communion and the very imperfect way in which it is fulfilled because of the conflicts that mark human life in community. Such contrasts between

[107]This point is emphasized in C. Lévi-Strauss, "The Family," in Shapiro (n. 65, above), 261–85, esp. 266 and 267ff. See also C. Ratschow in *RGG*[3] II (1958), 315f.

[108]M. Weber, *Wirtschaft und Gesellschaft* (1922), 207.

[109]Schelsky, 34. According to Greif (n. 101, above), 49, monogamy in the form it takes in Christianity is "not a chance historical 'form' alongside others, but the embodiment of a primordial human content that is at the same time the natural order of things which lies behind the whole multiplicity of forms." In this context he calls attention in particular to the idea of equality in marriage and the requirement of mutual marital fidelity (50f.). Ringeling (n. 72, above), 245, offers a similar judgment: "Monogamy is still to be regarded as the highest cultural form of sexual behavior."

norm and everyday reality are not unusual, and the Christian consciousness of human sinfulness provides an adequate explanation of the situation. It can enable the partners to endure the reality of the situation by
promoting a readiness for mutual forgiveness, and, in the extreme case,
it can even lead them to accept the failure of a marriage.

There are in fact other reasons why the institution of monogamous
marriage is jeopardized and undermined. The chief reason is the disintegration, in the public social consciousness, of the religious foundations of
monogamy. In monogamy the communion entered into before God takes
precedence over the individual partners' expectations of happiness, while
the latter must depend for their fulfillment on the mutual love that is
grounded in the communion and arises out of it ever anew. In the modern
mind, however, communion before God has been replaced by the communion of love between the partners themselves as the basis for marriage.

But, even if (as Schelsky claims) the romantic idea of love emerged
from the Christian understanding of marital communion, it cannot ensure
the permanence of the communion. The feeling of affection may very
well, like every feeling, embrace the whole of life and in this case affirm
the partner in the entirety of his or her life, but of itself it remains a
momentary thing. Only if this feeling were to retain its intensity undimin-
ished could it ensure that the mutual relationship would last. In practice,
each partner is overtaxed by demands for love that cannot be met in
everyday family life. Schelsky has described how this experience results
in disillusion and a turning away from the partner. "The very fact that the
partners cling to their original expectations of a love appropriate to a
monogamous marriage leads to a need for erotic experiences outside
marriage, to an exchange of lovers, and to marital infidelity."[110]

I need only add that this diagnosis describes the disintegrative tendency
at work in modern society's "marriage for love" which is cut off from its
Christian roots and has been "secularized." Marriage, in the Christian
understanding of it, is precisely not built on the mutual affection of the
partners and their feeling of oneness, even though these may have motivated the decision to marry. The permanence of Christian marriage is
based on the fact that it was entered into before God. In a Christian
marriage, therefore, the love of the partners for each other must be
constantly renewed from the forgiving love of Christ for them. This will
make it possible for each partner to put up with the imperfection of the
other and the consciousness of his or her own imperfection and to advance
to a deeper consciousness of union by way of the experience of mutual
understanding and mutual forgiveness.

[110]Schelsky, 35.

IV. Political Order, Justice, and Religion

1. Anthropology and the State

Should a discussion of the state[111] be included in a book on anthropology? Has the organization of political power anything to do with human nature, or is it simply an emergency organization of power that should really be unnecessary and, if anything, distorts the achievement of the true human destiny since it suppresses the individual's striving for freedom?

According to Aristotle, human "nature" finds its completion only in the state, for human beings are by nature "political animals."[112] This does not mean that the political life can be traced back to a biological disposition in the sense of a natural drive.[113] Aristotle's point is, rather, that the essential nature of human beings, their destiny as humans, achieves its fulfillment only in an ethical way of life.[114] But, according to both Aristotle and Plato, a human moral life is in turn fulfilled only in the political community.

For Plato this claim is based on the fact that the individual is not self-sufficient but needs the cooperation of others.[115] The division of labor is therefore the basis for the political union of human beings in the state. However, again according to Plato, the actual rise of the state was occasioned by threats from without and, according to the myth told by Protagoras, was made possible by the gifts of shame and justice which Zeus bestowed "to be the organizing principles and bonds of the state and the mediators of affection *(philia)*."[116] In the community of the polis individu-

---

[111]With H. Quaritsch, *Staat und Souveränität* I (1970), 230, "state" is here usually understood in a broad sense as "an abstract designation for every kind of suprafamilial, independent ruling group," and not simply as referring to the specifically modern concept of the state. On the applicability of the concept of the state, see also G. Balandier, *Political Anthropology*, trans. M. M. Sheridan Smith (New York, 1970), 123ff.

[112]Aristotle, *Polit.* 1253a2 and 9. On this formula, see J. Ritter, *Metaphysik und Politik. Studien zu Aristoteles und Hegel* (1969), 75ff. and 126ff., and M. Riedel, *Metaphysik und Politik. Studien zu Aristoteles und zur politischen Sprache der neuzeitlichen Philosophie* (1975), 59f.

[113]This misunderstanding is to be found even in H. Heller's *Staatslehre* (1934); see his *Gesammelte Schriften*, vol. III: *Staatslehre als politische Wissenschaft*, ed. G. Niemeyer (Leiden, 1971), 170f., while Riedel, despite his insight into the teleological meaning of the Aristotelian concept of physis, also speaks of a "false naturalistic conclusion drawn by the Aristotelian political tradition" (62).

[114]Ritter has this pithy statement: Unlike other living things "human beings fulfill their nature not by force of this nature but 'ethically' " (127).

[115]Plato, *Respub.* 369b5ff. and e2ff.

[116]Plato, *Protag.* 322c2f. According to Aristotle too, *philia* is the most important bond between the citizens of the polis: *Polit.* 1259b24ff.; see *Eth. Nic.* 115a22ff., and see P.

als find the self-sufficiency they lacked.

Aristotle for his part expressly noted that neither the family and the individual "house" nor the village are "self-sufficient" communities, that is, are not ends in themselves. Self-sufficiency can be predicated only of the union of several villages into the city-state, or polis, which "came into existence for the sake of survival but continues to exist for the sake of the good life."[117] It is therefore in the polis that the human destination to community is definitively fulfilled, and for this reason Aristotle could define the human person as a "political" animal.

Aristotle—and Plato in substance—maintained this position in opposition to Sophists like Antiphon and Hippias, whose opinion was that the state and its laws are based solely on convention and not on a natural order of things.[118] This thesis of the Later Sophistic was adopted once again in the modern liberal philosophy of the state. According to this philosophy, the political organization of society is the result of a contract that prevents the destructive consequences of unrestrained individual egoism.[119] In this view, then, the political community is not the result of a need for community that is rooted in human nature. Reinhold Niebuhr could therefore accuse the liberal theory of society of failing to recognize "the primordial character of the human community."[120]

The positive points made by Niebuhr in his criticism have been included in the second part of this book, in my discussion of the way in which individuals and their identity are established through dealings with their

---

Koslowski, *Zum Verhältnis von Polis und Oikos bei Aristoteles* (Münchener Hochschulschriften; 1976), 37ff., on the difference here between Aristotle and Plato.

[117]Aristotle, *Polit.* 1252b29f. Riedel (n. 112, above), 58f., interprets the concept of autarky to mean that the political community is an end in itself. This notion may well be one root of the modern concept of sovereignty; see the discussion in Quaritsch (n. 111, above), 279ff., of Jean Bodin's insistence on an earthly life of virtue as an end in itself, in opposition to Thomas Aquinas. But Quaritsch does not examine in detail the relation between sovereignty and the Aristotelian concept of autarky.

[118]F. Heinimann, *Nomos und Physis. Herkunft und Bedeutung einer Antithese im griechischen Denken des 5. Jh.* (1945; repr., 1972), 139ff. R. Bubner, in *Philosophische Rundschau* 22 (1976), 1–34 at 6, doubts that Aristotle was still carrying on Plato's debate with the Sophists (as Ritter [n. 112, above] assumed, 121). Yet we must agree with Ritter if we are to accept, with E. Havelock, *The Liberal Temper in Greek Politics* (London, 1957, 1964²), 339–75, that Aristotle in his *Politics* borrowed extensively from the arguments of the Sophistic "liberals" and bent these to his own purposes (see especially 378f., 388ff., on the description of humans as political beings in contrast to the conception of the state as a free association of equal individuals).

[119]See above, chapter 4, sec. II, 2. In Hobbes, however, the influence of the Christian doctrine of sin still prevents a complete reversion to the arguments of the Sophists.

[120]R. Niebuhr, *The Children of Light and the Children of Darkness* (New York, 1944), 53 (cited earlier in chapter 4 at n. 40).

fellow human beings.[121] In that context the point to be made is not simply that the developing individuality is conditioned by the symbiotic web of life that is the family. The family is but the ontogenetically and probably also phylogenetically first manifestation of the larger social web of life that makes individual identity possible.[122] Even the identity of the adult individual is still grounded in a reality that transcends it and therefore binds it to others, although this reality proves to be not only social but at the same time, and in addition, religious. In the third part of this present book, we have seen this to mean that culture and therefore individual identity have a religious basis which is mediated through play and language.[123]

Human "nature" is not social and political in the sense that the individual possesses no independence in relation to society and its institutional forms, whether family or state. On the other hand, the independence of individuals in relation to family and state is not based on a neutrality toward all forms of human community. Rather, their independence is due to the fact that the institutional structure of the human community has itself a religious foundation to which individuals can appeal even against the concrete forms of their shared world. Only at this level is it possible to resolve the antagonism between the individual and the institutional order of society, that is, because the same truth in which the social order is founded simultaneously makes possible the independence of individuals in the face of the concrete forms this order takes. Conversely, however, precisely because individuals derive their independence in this manner they are also dependent on the life of the shared world in which they have their place.

In the history of European culture it was Christianity that first made possible the full development of these relations between individual, social order, and religion. It did so because in its message of redemption it

[121]See above, chapter 4, secs. III–IV, and all of chapter 5.

[122]According to Havelock (n. 118, above), 340f., 381f., Aristotle, like Plato and Homer before him, took the patriarchal family as the model for the state. In fact, Aristotle does see an analogy between monarchy and the relation of a father to his sons and between aristocracy and the relation of a husband to his wife (*Eth. Nic.* 1160b24ff.). He does not, however, derive from this analogy a justification of either the monarchic or the aristocratic form of government. In opposition to such a derivation John Locke made a distinction between the natural subjection of human beings to parental authority and a voluntary submission to political control (see above, chapter 4, at n. 39). As a matter of fact, the legal form of political organization differs radically from the natural development of the family group, although even the family must be regarded as a social or cultural institution and not simply a product of nature. Both forms of community, however, show the priority of the community over the individual. When adolescents reach maturity they simply pass to a personally responsible awareness of their membership in the larger political community. They do not make a radical decision as to whether or not they will be members of a political community at all.

[123]See chapter 7.

explicitly assigned the individual an eternal significance and importance. That message goes back to the parables in which Jesus depicts God addressing himself to every individual with an everlasting love and therefore seeking them out when they were lost. It found its anthropological expression in the development of the Christian hope of resurrection as a hope that the life of each individual, as a body-soul unity, would find its completion in communion with God and his immortal life.[124]

On the one hand, this teaching made the individual independent of the family and the state as forms of community based on nature. On the other hand, it incorporated the individual into the community of Christ's body and of the future kingdom of God, which is not simply a negation of natural forms of community but recognizes them as provisional forms taken by the human destination to community, although in recognizing them as only provisional it at the same time relativizes them.

In this perspective, the statement that human beings are political animals acquires a richer content than Aristotle intended. In his political philosophy Aristotle, unlike Plato, paid no special attention to the religious foundations of the state. This is probably due to his conception of the polis as an end in itself (as possessing autarky) and to the obscurities in this view,[125] and especially to the fact that he does not use the principle of the political nature of human beings to ground a theory of the just form of the state.

Plato had done precisely that and, especially in his *Laws,* had shown that the legitimacy of the political order and the obligation of individuals to accept it have their basis in religion.[126] On the other hand, Plato's conception of the state as an organization of classes remains indifferent to individuals and relations between individuals, whereas Aristotle, in his criticism of this blueprint which focuses wholly on the unity of the state,

---

[124]On this point, see the remarks in my *Die Bestimmung des Menschen. Menschsein, Erwählung und Geschichte* (1978), 10f., and further on in the present book, pp. 476f., as well as above, chapter 4, sec. II, 1.

[125]The "obscurity" in Aristotle's doctrine on the political nature of human beings (Riedel [n. 112, above], 60f., 259f.) is to be seen in the fact that this doctrine does not function as a basis for political theory (74); it has to do with the foundations of the political order and therefore explains the existence of the political order as such but not the difference between good and bad constitutions. This second function is provided to some extent by the distinction between despotic rule over a household and a government exercised over free citizens (*Polit.* 1277b7ff., etc.). However, this criterion is difficult to apply because of the disagreement over what constitutes the common good. In addition, it cannot base a decision for a particular form of constitution as unqualifiedly appropriate for a political community. As a result (according to Riedel), Aristotelian political theory provides only "a kind of natural history of the forms of government" (260).

[126]P. Koslowski, *Gesellschaft und Staat. Ein unvermeidlicher Dualismus* (1982), 30ff., 42ff. All that Aristotle can suggest at this point is the power of ethos (habit) (*Polit.* 1269a20–24). See Ritter (n. 112, above), 160ff.

emphasizes the fact that a state is made up of many individuals, and he is therefore led to his more empirical presentation of the forms of political organization.[127]

Both men, in any case, established too close a connection between the political destination of human beings and the city-state model. Their argument cannot be retained in this limited form, as if the city-state represented the fulfillment of humanity. In fact, the Stoics soon took the principle that human beings are political animals and applied it to the human race as such; the result was the idea of the world-state. At the same time, they asserted the right of all human beings to citizenship in this state, thus rejecting the assumption that nature has divided human beings into slave and free.[128] Only in this nonrestrictive form could Christianity accept the idea of human beings as having a political destiny; even then it profoundly altered the concept.

To begin with, Christianity could not accept without qualification the thesis that human nature finds its fulfillment in the state, even when "state" was interpreted as the "state which is the entire world." In the Christian view, human beings are created in the image of the transcendent God. This destiny directs them beyond this world and therefore beyond its political order as well. Individuals are thus assigned a much more radical independence of the state than the kind of independence in relation to the concrete forms of political rule for which the Stoic doctrine of the world-state had paved the way.

At the same time, however, Christians are obliged to see embodied in the laws of the state God's will that order be observed.[129] The seriousness of this will is manifested in the present world in the authority that the state has to punish evildoers. Early Christian theologians looked upon the political order as primarily God's way of preserving order in the face of the sins of human beings, so that the latter "might not swallow each other up as fish do, but rather, aided by the provisions of the laws, prevent the many injustices of the pagans." Through subjection to human authority and human law they should "at least in some degree attain to justice and curb one another from fear of the sword that is unsheathed before their eyes."[130]

Christian teaching on the political order has often looked no farther than its function of curbing evil *(coercere malum).* This is especially true of the teaching of the Reformers on the state and secular authority.[131] The

[127]Aristotle, *Polit.* 1261a15ff. See Ritter, 95ff.

[128]See M. Pohlenz, *Die Stoa. Geschichte einer geistigen Bewegung* I (1948), 135ff.

[129]1 Peter 2:13ff.; Rom. 13:1–8. See M. Hengel, *Christ and Power,* trans. E. Kalin (Philadelphia, 1977), 33ff.

[130]Irenaeus, *Adv. haer.* V, 24, 2.

[131]See M. Luther, *Vom weltlicher Obrigkeit* (1523), WA 11:248 and 251. See WA 42:79, 7–19.

reason for the narrow focus is that this aspect is in fact emphasized in what the Bible says on the subject. Nonetheless even in the function of political rule that is thus singled out there is an element that looks beyond it; I mean the idea that there is a correspondence between the justice of the state and the divine will to justice, the definitive accomplishment of which Christians await in the future of the reign of God.

This divine will cannot be adequately conceived as simply a reaction of God to sin. It looks, rather, to the order that God wants to see realized in the communal life of his creatures.[132] Moreover, this divine will does not remain simply external to the real life of creatures, as if the God who issues commands in the law were a stranger and not the creator of human beings. The truth is, rather, that the creator's will to order is imprinted in creation itself; not only in the laws of nature but also in the communal life of human beings does order emerge from the concrete life of creatures themselves, and this despite all the antagonism between individuals. Even in the institutional and political organization of their communal life human beings are "a law to themselves," as Paul says of the individual conscience (Rom. 2:14). The political order is thus based on human "nature" insofar as this is intrinsically disposed and oriented to a communal life.

The Christian idea of natural law is, in principle, a correct reflection of this situation. We need not see it as asserting the existence of a fundamental creatureliness that retains its original form and is supposedly untouched by sin. Human life is perverted by sin in its orientation to community no less than in its other aspects. But even amid all the sinful distortion precisely of political relations among human beings the divine will to order and justice asserts itself over and over, using as means to its ends even human jealousy and the desire to dominate. The political "nature" of human beings is therefore not a remnant left over from an originally perfect creation and still untouched by sin, but is part of the human *destiny* which, like creation as a whole, will be fulfilled only in the future and will only then be definitively known.

For this reason, Christian theology can also unhesitatingly appeal to the teleological meaning of the Aristotelian concept of nature. It must, however, see human beings as achieving their destiny of full "autarky," not

---

[132]The order willed by the creator need not be understood, as in the neo-Lutheran theology of the nineteenth and twentieth centuries, as an "order of creation" in the sense of an original order that is static, precedes subsequent history, and is untouched by the latter's aberrations. For a critique of this idea, see W. Künneth, *Politik zwischen Dämon und Gott. Eine christliche Ethik des Politischen* (1954), 120ff. The order willed by the creator is, rather, to be understood—as Künneth intends with his concept of the "order of conservation," 135ff.— as the divine will to justice that is at work in history itself, is the content of the proclamation of divine law on Sinai as well as of Jesus' interpretation of the law, and will be definitively fulfilled in the kingdom of God in the end time.

in the political order of the state but only in their relation to God and in the community of God's kingdom.[133] Even the aporias in the Aristotelian idea of autarky, or self-sufficiency, which was contradicted by the controversies over the constitution of the polis, point beyond the earthly polis. Christians must regard the latter as simply a provisional form of the human political destiny (Heb. 13:14), which will find its fulfillment only in the kingdom of God, after all domination of human beings over one another has been done away with.

It is also from the relation to the kingdom of God and its justice that the present political order, insofar as it has not been perverted into a tyranny, receives its limited legitimacy—limited, because it is not identical with the kingdom of God but is only the provisional representative of the divine will to justice. The mark of a tyrannical state is that it fails to recognize the limits of its authority and instead lays total claim to the lives of its citizens. It is the primary political function of the church, on the other hand, to keep the state conscious that it is not the kingdom of God. The church does this because, unlike the political order, it permits human beings to share even now, though only through faith and in symbolic form, in the future of God and his kingdom.

The role of the political order is to point ahead to the kingdom of God as a reality distinct from itself. In Augustine's teaching on earthly and heavenly peace this role is explained in such a way that the Aristotelian idea of human beings as destined to a political life is sublimated and absorbed into it. In his teaching on peace Augustine moves beyond the interpretation of the state as simply God's response to sin and intended for the curbing of evil.[134] For this reason, his conception of the political order can be understood as a more profound and critically nuanced version of the correspondence—already worked out in Origen and, after him, in the early Byzantine theology of empire—between Christ's messianic kingdom of peace and the peaceful order established by the Roman Empire.[135] This interpretation of Augustine's thought seems valid despite his

[133]Thus according to Thomas Aquinas the goal of the "good life"—i.e., of a communal life, in the political order and made possible by virtue (see Aristotle, *Polit.* 1252b29f., and n. 117, above)—is attained only in the human relationship with God. See Aquinas, *De regimine principum* I, 14 (*Opera*, ed. Leoniana, XVI, 236f.).

[134]From this standpoint Luther in his statements about the two modes of divine rule (n. 131, above) does not go as far as his model, Augustine. What he says about the task of preserving peace (see U. Duchrow, *Christenheit und Weltverantwortung. Traditionsgeschichte und systematische Struktur der Zweireichelehre* [1970], 486–94) is still clearly subordinated to the coercive function of the law in curbing evil. On the other hand, Luther could lay greater stress than Augustine had on the independence of the secular power (Duchrow, 511f.).

[135]On this, see Hengel (n. 129, above), 51ff. See also my own remarks in *Die Bestimmung des Menschen* (n. 124, above), 64ff., and, in greater detail, H. Fuchs, *Augustin und der antike Friedensgedanke* (1926). On what follows, see especially Fuchs, 44–52.

criticism of the gospel of civilization that was part of the Roman understanding of the state, and despite his references to the repression that was
the dark side of the *pax Romana*.

In Augustine's thinking, peace is a universal ontological category. All
things seek peace, since every being requires for its continuance a condition of ordered repose.[136] This is true even of the parts of the body in
their relations with one another and of the relation of body and soul.
Every being suffers when its natural order is disturbed (XIX, 13, 1), and
even that which is out of order must be at peace with something, since
otherwise it would not exist at all (XIX, 12, 3). So too human beings are
induced by their nature to seek social ties and peace with their fellows
(XIX, 12, 2). It can be seen, then, that for Augustine the political destination of the human being represents the application of the idea of peace
not simply to the individual but to the human community.[137] Even the
arrogant, who despise the divine order and the peace that is based on the
justice of *suum cuique* (XIX, 21, 1), likewise seek peace, even if according
to their own ideas of it (XIX, 21, 2). Wars are conducted in order that
some may impose their version of peace on others (XIX, 15, 4).

Genuine peace, however, is based on harmony *(concordia)*: harmony
among household members in home and family, harmony among citizens
of a state (XIX, 14 and 16).[138] The idea of harmony includes for Augustine, as it had for Plato and Aristotle, the element of superiority and
subordination. In his view, such an "ordered harmony in commanding
and obeying" *(ordinata imperandi oboediendique concordia)* belongs to the
very nature of things in family and state (XIX, 16), just as it is natural for
reason to command the desires, soul to command body, and God to
command human beings (XIX, 21, 2).

The governance exercised in these cases is not, according to Augustine,
the kind of lordship *(dominium)* in which a master issues orders to a slave;
that kind of domination of one human being over another came into
existence, according to Augustine, only as a result of sin (XIX, 15). On
the other hand, subordination for the common good in relationships of
command and obedience springs from the nature of things and therefore
of human beings as well. In Augustine's view, as in that of Aristotle before

---

[136]Augustine, *De civ. Dei* XIX, 13, 1 *(tranquillitas ordinis)*. The references that follow in
the text are to book, chapter, and section of this work.

[137]Augustine derived another argument for this position from the dependence of human
beings on God, whose law calls not only for love of God but also for love of neighbor.
This love of neighbor is meant to lead the neighbor to love of God. As a result, the
Christian will live with that neighbor in the "ordered harmony" that yields peace in the
home and in the political order (XIX, 14).

[138]See in this context the Platonic and Aristotelian idea of friendship (n. 116, above).

him,[139] this kind of *imperium* is to be carefully distinguished from the *dominium* of a master over a slave, since the former is inspired by a concern *(providentia)* for the good of the one obeying (XIX, 14).

Augustine does correct Aristotle, however, inasmuch as he asserts a natural subordination of human beings as such to God (XIX, 21, 1). When this proper order is not maintained, earthly peace is no longer related to future, heavenly peace (XIX, 17), and the order of justice is violated, because human beings refuse God his right over them (XIX, 21). But those who refuse God what is rightly his will also fail to curb their own desires as they should. This means that in a social fellowship in which God is refused his rights no true justice can prevail (XIX, 21, 2). The result is upheavals and wars in which, says Augustine, each party seeks to impose its own ideas of true peace.

At first glance, Augustine's acceptance, within his own teaching on peace, of Aristotle's thesis on the political destination of human beings seems surprisingly unreserved. It can be seen in the details of the argument as well as in the derivation of the political order from the family, the emphasis on harmony as a condition for the cohesion of that order, and the distinction between government for the good of the whole and despotic domination. All the more striking, therefore, is his criticism, aimed directly at Cicero but touching Aristotle as well, of the claim that justice can be found in a political order in which, as he sees it, true worship of God is lacking. In taking this position, Augustine prepared the way for the medieval union of church and state, even though he himself developed no theory of how the two are to work together in a society molded by Christianity.

In this context Augustine limited himself to the remark that the *civitas Dei,* the present form of which was for him the Christian church, makes use of earthly peace and promotes it (XIX, 17). He did not bring out the fact that the political order, as distinct from the church, has its own special relationship, even if a broken one, to the future kingdom of God. This is so because the latter itself has a political character inasmuch as, in contrast to any rule that human beings exercise over one another, it will accomplish the proper task of the political order: the sway of justice and peace.[140] For this reason, Augustine, unlike the Byzantine theology of

[139]Aristotle, *Polit.* III, 6 (1278b30—1279a21). In Aristotle's view, this distinction is the basis for the important difference between the polis as a community of free persons and all despotisms.

[140]The prophetic promises of a future of peace and justice (e.g., Isa. 2:2–4 = Micah 4:1–4; Isa. 9:6f. and 11:4f.) are brought together by Daniel in the visionary picture of a kingdom that comes from God and, like a stone falling from heaven, crushes the empires in which human beings exercise dominion (Dan. 2:31–45; see 9:2–27). On this point, see K. Koch, "Spätisraelitisches Geschichtsdenken am Beispiel des Buches Daniel," *HZ* 193 (1961),

empire, makes no attempt at a positive theological interpretation of the political order in relation to a society that has been molded by Christianity.[141] The consequence is that his acceptance of the Aristotelian thesis on the political destination of human beings is qualified far more than it need have been in the direction of a detachment from the concerns of this world.

Augustine also departed from the Aristotelian view in a second important respect when he traced the existence of despotic rule to the fall of Adam and understood the institution of slavery to be likewise a consequence of sin (XIX, 15). By so doing, he made his own the strand of patristic tradition that was critical of political domination, as well as the Stoic criticism of slavery, and added his considerable weight to the political theorists who were critical of political domination. Yet, given the universality of sin among human beings, we must ask whether it is possible to make such a categorical distinction between rule in the sense of the *imperium* that is concerned for the common good and *dominium* or despotic rule, as Augustine supposes in adopting the patriarchal outlook of the tradition, even though he had denied that any political order could claim to be just apart from authentic worship of God. This question remained in the background of attention because it was assumed that rulers possessed authority from God. For this reason, only in the modern age did it make its force felt to the full.

2. Power and Rule

Following the line established by Machiavelli and Hobbes, the political theorists of the modern age have treated the question of the political order as a question of rule and have reduced rule in turn to the phenomenon of power. No longer does the human need of community provide the key to an understanding of the processes of socialization. It has been replaced by the striving for power, on the one hand, and the readiness, on the other, of human beings to submit to claims to power for the sake of a life of peace and security. This reconstruction of the anthropological foundations of political rule (a reconstruction that Hobbes had projected on lines suggested by mechanical science) is based on a reduction of the order of common life to the striving for self-assertion and self-expansion.[142]

1–32. On the relation between Jesus' message of the kingdom of God and the originally political meaning of God's expected reign, see my remarks in *Die Bestimmung des Menschen* (n. 124, above), 23ff.

[141]Further details are in *Die Bestimmung des Menschen,* 67ff.

[142]In his article on the history of the concept of power, *HWP* 5 (1980), 588–604, K. Röttgers traces this view back to William of Occam, who, he says, applied the Roman legal principle for the acquisition of unowned property to political power as a *potestas acquirendi*

But does this represent a valid description of the phenomenon of power? Must it not, rather, be said that as modern physics has made force independent of the concept of body and thinks of it as a field, so power in the life of society is primarily a supraindividual reality, namely, the power of society over the individual?[143] If so, then it becomes necessary to distinguish between power as connected with the social "nature" of the human being and the appropriation of power by an individual ruler. Then too, the fact that an individual can have and exercise power must be understood in the light of that individual's special relation to the foundations and conditions of common life.

Even Max Weber's well-known and influential definition of power as "the chance of a man or of a number of men to realize their own will in a communal action even against the resistance of others who are participating in the action" neglected "the fundamentally social character of power," because it "conceived power solely as the exercise of an individual will."[144] Since Weber's time, scholars with various points of view have shown the dependence of power on aspects of social agreement. This need not mean that the possession of power implies recognition and consensus.[145] It does, however, presuppose at least an agreement between the ruler and those subject to his power on the possibilities at the ruler's disposal and the relevance of these to the subjects.[146]

---

dominium ("a power of acquiring dominion") and in so doing "already conceived the establishment of a family as an exercise of the male's power to appropriate females and, via them, offspring as well" (591). The Aristotelian derivation of the state from the family is thus transposed into a derivation of political rule from the idea of power. It is worth noting that the disintegration of the primacy (expressed in family life) of the community over the individual and its replacement by the particular interests that play the controlling role in property form a bridge to the modern basing of the state on the idea of power.

[143]According to P. Tillich, *Love, Power, and Justice: Ontological Analysis and Ethical Applications* (New York, 1954; Oxford Galaxy Books, 1964), 43, "everything real is an individual power of being within an embracing whole." The power of this whole manifests itself in each case through a center; this is true of social power as well (45; see 91ff.). In a quite different manner, M. Foucault, *Mikrophysik der Macht* (1976), 99, expressly speaks of the way in which power is at work in the whole of the "social field," but in fact he sees power as a set of elementary particles rather than a field.

[144]Thus T. Rendtorff, *Ethik* II, 24, citing M. Weber, *Wirtschaft und Gesellschaft* (1922), 28. [Weber's definition is here cited from H. H. Gerth and C. W. Mills, eds. and trs., *From Max Weber: Essays in Sociology* (New York, 1946), 180, where it is inserted into a different context (see 180, note).]

[145]H. Arendt, *On Violence* (New York, 1969, 1970), so one-sidedly emphasizes the viewpoint of power as exercised through consensus that power and force come to be mutually exclusive (esp. 44f.). This may be true of the supraindividual essence of power (e.g., the power of truth over the souls of human beings), but it is not true of those who exercise power over others, since the possession of power is inseparable from the ability to impose sanctions on those who resist it.

[146]On this point, see N. Luhmann, *Macht* (1975), 7ff.

The possession of power resembles the ownership of property in that both involve the aspect of means. Means can be used or not used. But, unlike property viewed as means, the possession of power is explicitly (and not merely implicitly) connected with the relevance of its use not only to the one who disposes of the power but also to others who are subject to it. Property (like personal prestige and the authority to make official decisions) can be used as a means to power; but it is then being used not as property but precisely as means, and specifically for the purpose of influencing others.

This can happen only if, and to the extent that, the life-style of others depends on or at least will be influenced by the use that the possessors make of their means to power. If all that is involved is the personal interests of the possessor, we will be inclined to speak of an illegitimate use of power. At this point a tension between power and property manifests itself; it is due to the fact that power is related directly to others and therefore to the problems of common life, while property is related only indirectly through its dependence on society which can refuse it out of envy but also through its potential social relevance when used as means.

According to K. O. Hondrich, the basis for the exercise of power is the ability of an agent to satisfy certain needs of others or to deny them this satisfaction.[147] In this description, power is linked to the positive goods that are the object of human needs. Disposal of these goods then provides the basis of the possession of power by the powerful, and this power itself consists in the ability to deny the satisfaction of needs that the acquisition of these goods brings.

But does power always have its basis in this kind of positive service rendered to others? Does not the simple ability to do harm already bring power? Nor may we simply view the decision not to do harm as equivalent to the positive satisfaction of a need. Yet it is true of both uses of power that "possibilities are given, the actualization of which is *avoided,*"[148] whether what is avoided is the denial of a positive benefit or the doing of threatened harm. The exercise of power, then, does not consist so much in the actual carrying out of decisions by the powerful which are unpleasant for those affected by them; the mere possibility of such decisions is usually enough to elicit obedience to their will. It is characteristic of power that "the mere possibility that the so-called means of power may be used is already effective, without any actual use being required"; in other words, all that is needed is that those affected know the disadvantages or

[147]K. O. Hondrich, *Theorie der Herrschaft* (1973), 56; see also Luhmann, 24.

[148]Thus Luhmann's formulation (23), which is couched in general terms and is more cautious regarding the connection of power with positive benefits to others.

advantages the use of power will bring.[149]

According to Niklaus Luhmann, however, the occasional use of the means of power, that is, of force, is needed in order to render the possession of power credible. Hondrich, on the other hand, believes that while the possession of power depends on the ability to deny satisfaction of needs, the actual denial will lead to a "breakdown of power in the form of a decline in authority." This brings him to the paradoxical conclusion that power exists only as long as it is not used.[150]

Hondrich bases his argument too exclusively on one specific case of power and its use: the use of it which in the history of culture seems to have led to the establishment of political rule. This narrow focus is especially clear in his linking of power and authority: the more the power of an agent is based on its being used to satisfy needs, the greater will be its *authority,* that is, the *recognition* of it in the sense of an *approval* of it and of the way in which it is used.[151]

In fact, however, not all power is linked to authority: not the power of an enemy or a criminal, nor that which has beneficial effects but whose use, as everyone realizes, is inspired by the special private interests of its possessor. Authority is acquired only when power is used for the good of a community and its members. But the power of a family head seems to be of this kind, as does that of the prehistoric chieftain over a number of families or village communities. Those early governments consolidated their position "by doing their economic and religious jobs well—by providing benefits—rather than by using physical force."[152] Under those special conditions the actual use of force could indeed lead to the "breakdown of power in the form of a decline in authority," but that would not be true of types of power that have a different basis.

Elman R. Service sees economic and religious functions as having led to the establishment, in the form of a chiefdom, of a suprafamilial authority. In the economic sphere the role of this authority was, above all, to "redistribute" goods in an economy based on storage and to regulate economic exchanges with other villages.[153] How did religious functions come into the picture? Was there an intrinsic connection between economic and religious tasks?

[149]Ibid., 27.

[150]Hondrich (n. 147, above), 79. The paradox disappears if we view power not (with Hondrich) as arising only from an actual and continual bestowal of benefits that confers authority but as already given with the possibility or, as the case may be, ability to benefit or harm others.

[151]Hondrich, 78f. and 36.

[152]E. R. Service, *Origins of the State and Civilization: The Process of Cultural Evolution* (New York, 1955), 8.

[153]Ibid., 75ff.

It was while looking for criteria to measure social power that Hondrich developed his thesis that power is based on the positive satisfaction of others' needs. In his view, the measure of power depends on the degree of need satisfaction (and, therefore, of potential refusal of such satisfaction). He recognizes, however, that "the central theoretical problem" can be expressed in the question, "Can needs be even conceived as socially independent of power relations?"[154] He sees the possibility of manipulating needs but fails to see that at the base of this very possibility itself there is the general dependence of needs on interpretation. He believes, therefore, that the opposed interests of those with lesser power are experienced in the form of "resistance" to the rule of the powerful. But in taking this approach, he still treats needs and opposed interests as if they were fixed quantities.

It is characteristic of the human situation in the world that needs change. Since human drives are not determined by instinctual mechanisms, they always need interpretation to give them direction. Only when a drive is directed by interpretation and experience to a determined content should it be called a need.[155] As human beings direct and redirect their drives through experience of their world and through dealing with their environment, they also develop and modify their needs, their inclinations toward well-worn ways of satisfying drives. In the process, the content of particular needs may change, as may the relative status of these needs in the context of the life that individuals project for themselves.

There is no doubt, of course, that in their *general form* the direction taken by certain drives—the need for food or the sexual drive—has a biological basis. But even these "primary" needs (Edward C. Tolman) undergo change as a result of selectivity being exercised in regard to the objects by which they are satisfied and in regard to the place they are to have in the overall picture of the individual's life. A basic need that is so fundamental biologically as the need for nourishment can in extreme situations be made secondary to (supposedly) more urgent goals; asceticism and hunger strikes are illustrations of this. Indoctrination or an autonomous decision can engender a readiness for sacrifice to the point of surrendering life itself. This mutability in the relative value assigned to needs shows that needs depend on the *context of meaning* that is provided by the life that individuals project for themselves and by the social world; it is in that context that individuals define themselves and their needs, as they base their judgments on what is "good" for them and for everyone.[156]

---

[154]Hondrich, 58. On starting with the question of a measure for social power, 52ff. The next citation in the text is from 61.

[155]See K. Lewin, "Untersuchungen zur Handlungs- und Affektpsychologie," *Psychologische Forschungen* 7 (1926), 294–385, esp. 378 (critique of the idea of "drive").

[156]See my *Theology and the Kingdom of God*, ed. R. J. Neuhaus (Philadelphia, 1969), 107.

The "context of meaning" is also the basis for the manipulation of needs. The manipulator influences the consciousness of meaning in a direction that is determined not by the quest of truth but by the (concealed) special interests of others. Advertising, for example, creates a need for the goods it extols by exaggerating their importance to the buyer. This example also helps us understand a broader phenomenon: the dependence of social power on control of the information and public opinion media.

Since the concept of need cannot be defined independently of the understanding and consciousness of meaning, the specific power of bestowing benefits that is the basis of political rule must also be traced back to the consciousness of meaning. This can be done in two ways: by showing that the satisfaction of need supposes an interpretation of need that comes from some other source, or by showing that power is measured by its ability both to interpret need and to satisfy it. In either case, however, since the interpretation of need depends on a comprehensive consciousness of meaning that has been articulated in the course of the race's development, the result is a connection between the economic accomplishments of political power and religion. In this light, the "thoroughly theocratic nature" (emphasized by Service) of the "classical forms" of early political rule becomes intelligible, as does the fact that these early governments managed "without regular recourse to violent coercion."[157]

An interpretation of need to which the other assents is already a fundamental way of satisfying need, namely, satisfying the need of meaning. Moreover, it is only with reference to the satisfaction of this particular need that Hondrich's thesis can be accepted without reservation: the withdrawal of satisfaction entails a loss of power through a decline of authority. For this reason, there was very likely not a single ruler in the archaic societies who deliberately refused to satisfy this need. This meant, of course, that the exercise of political power was dependent on the religious authorities. By the same token, however, the political ruler was preserved in principle, though not in every particular instance, from the suspicion of serving special interests. To the extent that government was nourished by the spirit of religion, it could rely on the consensus of the group and dispense with the constant use of repressive force. For this reason, "the state as a repressive institution based on secular force is not coterminous with civilization in the classical, primary developments."[158] This does not mean that in those developments the behavior of individuals

[157]Service, 307; see 78 and 296. K. Eder, in a volume edited by him, *Die Entstehung von Klassengesellschaften* (1973), observes that "sacral rule may be the oldest form of rule and may have been the point of departure for the development of the high cultures" (24). See M. Fortes, in Eder, 276, and Balandier (n. 111, above), 38 and 101f.

[158]Service, 307; see 303ff. R. M. Glassmann, "Rational and Irrational Legitimacy," in R. M. Glassman and A. J. Vidich, eds., *Conflict and Control: Challenge to Legitimacy of Modern*

was not subject to any compulsions. The point is, rather, that individuality in the modern sense, with its claims to autonomy over against society, was still unknown.

In the modern history of the concept of rule, political rule has been increasingly conceived on the model of the master-servant relationship. Hobbes still thought of "dominion" as having a twofold origin: on the one hand, the power exercised by parents and, on the other, military subjection which produces servitude.[159] Kant, however, was subsuming all traditional constitutions under despotism, that is, the rule of a master over servants, whereas Aristotle had distinguished political rule precisely from that of a master over slaves.[160] In Kant's view, it was only the modern principles of the division of powers and representation that made republicanism possible as an alternative to despotic rule.[161]

The historical presupposition for such a radical criticism of rule as such was established with the advent of the "absolutist monopolization of political power."[162] In this—a secularized version of the papal "fullness of power" *(plenitudo potestatis)*[163]—the ruler's specific claims to power replaced the divine origin of political power and of justice itself. By way of reaction such a monopolization provoked a return to the ideal of freedom from all rule. On the one hand, then, the reduction of political rule to the master-servant relationship was connected with the assumption that the state had its historical origin in military conquest.[164] On the other hand, especially under the influence of Marxism, the origin of the repressive state was traced back to the development of private property, with the state serving as the means by which a propertied class was able to continue its exploitation of human labor.[165] In both cases, the controlling idea was the reduction of political rule to the special interests of those in power, that is, to despotism. This means, however, that the entire modern discus-

---

Governments (London, 1979), 49–73, paints a much darker picture of the ethnological scene, as least in societies that have developed since the beginnings of agriculture.

[159]T. Hobbes, *Leviathan* II, 20. But Hobbes already thought that the consequences and rights of paternal and despotic rule, as well as of rule based on contract, are ultimately same.

[160]I. Kant, *Zum ewigen Frieden* (1795), II, 1 (AA VIII, 352f.); see Aristotle, *Polit.* 1277b7ff., 1252a7ff., 1253b18ff.

[161]See G. Bien, "Herrschaftsformen," *HWP* 3 (1974), 1096–99, esp. 1098.

[162]J. C. Papalekas, "Herrschaft," *HWP* 3 (1974), 1084.

[163]See Koslowski (n. 126, above), 131ff. See also Quaritsch (n. 111, above), 61ff., although he stresses the point that because of its biblical derivation, papal "omnipotence" does not claim sovereignty in Jean Bodin's sense of the term.

[164]This assumption is behind Hegel's influential definition of power as a master-servant relationship in his *Phenomenology of Spirit* (1807; ed. Hoffmeister), 114ff.

[165]See esp. F. Engels, *Origins of the Family, Private Property and the State* (1884; New York, 1942).

sion of these two types of explanation has been based on an already one-sided and reductive understanding of the nature of political rule.

The "conquest theory" of the origin of political rule is usually rejected today, because "the only instances we find of permanent subordination from war are when government already exists."[166] On the other hand, variants of the view that repressive rule came into existence for the purpose of preserving an economically based class system are still discussed even today. In its original form, however, Engels' theory breaks down at the very outset because "there is absolutely no evidence in the early archaic civilizations themselves of any important private dealings."[167] On the contrary, political rule first appeared because of the development of the functions of chieftains, which led to "political strata, not strata of ownership groups."[168]

The explanation of such a process requires a different basic conception of political rule than is supplied by the model of despotic power. Only secondarily could political rulers have been involved in producing an economic class system that in turn had to be maintained by repression.

Thus K. Eder is of the opinion that when kings came on the scene they had to depend on the services of an aristocratic class of warriors and a priestly class, both of which were recompensed with land rights. In this way, the "development and stabilization of rule" engendered "an expanding group of nonproductive members of society" and, in order to secure their claims, had to "have recourse to mechanisms that put structural *force* in the place of simple *legitimacy* and the limitations which legitimacy placed on the collection of taxes."[169] Service, on the other hand, thinks that repressive force was not used extensively until the political system "malfunctions and centrifugal tendencies prevail." Moreover, the result of the stabilization of rule was a return to a state of "peaceful theocracy."[170]

Eder himself recognizes the importance of religion and sacral kingship for the political integration of archaic societies. He believes, however, that the "structural basis" of a sacral kingship connected with ancestor worship, namely, kinship with all the tribes belonging to the ruler's territory, was eliminated by differentiation in the social order, especially in the cities. As a result (according to Eder), religious ideas that focused on

[166]Service, 270–71; see 271ff. See also R. Carneiro, "Eine Theorie zur Entstehung des Staates," in Eder (n. 157, above), 153–75, esp. 158ff., and M. Fried, *The Evolution of Political Society* (New York, 1967), 213–23.

[167]Service, 283.

[168]Ibid., 285.

[169]Eder, 25f.; see 20f., where the rise of the commercial classes is named as a third factor along with a warrior caste and a priesthood.

[170]Service, 303.

family relationship lost their power to confer legitimacy and, "belied by reality," remained operative only as a reminder of a golden age or a hope of an eschatological future; meanwhile, therefore, rulers had to "rely on structural force."[171]

But apart even from the fact that not all the archaic cultures developed cities,[172] Eder's assumptions regarding the history of religions appear quite unconvincing. The assertion that archaic religion is to be explained as primarily a "reflection of the structures of familial interaction"[173] neglects the cosmological aspect of the mythical consciousness as well as encounters with the *numina* (divine powers) that became significant for the life history of the individual or the group. As compared with these two factors in the development of religions, the structures of familial interaction are of secondary importance for sacral kingship, especially since the conception of the king as "son" of the divinity is to be understood less as a reflection of familial interaction than as a way of representing the divinity. Finally, the mythical primordial time, though different from the present time of society, is not to be understood as though that original period, now "belied by reality," were only a lost golden age, since what is primordial according to myth is constantly rendered present in cult.

True enough, along with other aspects of world order and of the threats to it, "latent conflicts" too "are represented in ritual." This, however, is not simply a transitional phenomenon in a process of dissolution; rather, it is part of the ongoing sanctification of the profane everyday world by cult.[174] Religious consciousness reaches the stage of depicting an alternative, opposed world only when cult no longer succeeds in rendering present the archetypal world of myth. But, except in cases of political and military catastrophe, such a stage is reached chiefly in the late phases of the development of the high cultures, as in Israel, Greece, or India. Moreover, it presupposes that the order of political rule has been subjected to secularizing processes of one origin or another. All this supports Service's thesis that only a political rule that is secular or has been stripped

---

[171]Eder, 296f. and, earlier, 293ff. Therefore the "basic problem," according to Eder, is "the incompatibility between asymmetrical social relations and the promise of meaning that will adequately motivate" (295). See also 271.

[172]Service, 225ff., refers to the example of ancient Egypt which, unlike Mesopotamia, was not an urban culture. Service also gives (280ff.) a radical criticism of "urbanism," claiming that the rise of cities is a consequence rather than the cause of the institutional state.

[173]Eder, 296.

[174]R. Döbert, "Zur Logik des Übergangs von archaischen zu hochkulturellen Religionssystemen," in Eder, 330–63 at 351. For the interpretation of the phenomenon that is given in the text, see Balandier (n. 111, above), ch. 5.

of its legitimacy by religious institutions will be experienced as repressive and must in turn act repressively if it is to hold its ground.

3. Legitimacy and Representation

Max Weber linked the nature of rule so closely with its claim to legitimacy that he distinguished the typical forms of rule according to the source of their legitimacy and thus came up with three basic types of rule: traditional, charismatic, and bureaucratic.[175] The objection has been raised against this approach that as a result of it Weber never really discusses the possibility of illegitimate rule and its distinction from legitimate rule.[176] This objection is closely associated with another: Weber neglects the ethical meaning of legitimacy as distinct from its sociological function for the authority of the ruler[177] or, as others put it, he makes no distinction between the sense of legitimacy which those subject to a ruler have and the question of the truth of the ruler's claim to legitimacy.[178] This is due in turn to the fact that Weber does not take the step from the sociological datum to the determination of a norm by which the validity of a meaningful claim to rule can be assessed.[179]

A rule or government and a state are in fact not legitimated simply by the fact that they must claim legitimacy if they are to achieve a stable existence.[180] There is such a thing as illegitimate rule. Consequently the concepts of government and state must first be defined independently of any claim to legitimacy.

In opposition to H. Kelsen, H. Heller has emphasized the point that a state must be understood not as a function of a system of laws but primarily

---

[175]M. Weber, *Wirtschaft und Gesellschaft* (1922; 1972⁵), 122–76; see 16ff. on the concept of legitimacy.

[176]Thus C. J. Friedrich, *Politik als Prozess der Gemeinschaftsbildung* (1963; German tr., 1970), 55. (English original: *Man and His Government: An Empirical Theory of Politics* [New York, 1967].)

[177]See Th. Würtenberger, Jr., *Die Legitimität staatlicher Herrschaft. Eine staatsrechtlich-politische Begriffsgeschichte* (1973), 301f.

[178]It is here that J. Habermas locates the ambiguity in Weber's concept of legitimacy; see Habermas, *Legitimation Crisis*, trans. T. McCarthy (Boston, 1975), 97ff.

[179]It is to this that J. Winckelmann, *Legitimität und Legalität in Max Webers Herrschaftssoziologie* (1952), 47, is referring when he objects to legitimation through legality on the grounds that in such an interpretation the ruling system really functions as the basis of its own legitimacy. Habermas, 100, in turn criticizes Winckelmann's interpretation of Weber (value-based principles of material legitimacy have priority over legality). If we want to avoid the difficulty mentioned, we must distinguish between legitimacy and mere legality, as C. Schmitt did, in his own fashion, many years ago in his *Legalität und Legitimität* (1932), when he sought to bestow legitimacy on the legally binding code of law by an appeal to the people, that is, by recourse to the principle of popular sovereignty.

[180]Weber himself saw this quite clearly: *Wirtschaft und Gesellschaft*, 123, n. 3.

as an association under rule.[181] Rule, moreover, is always characterized by a system of command and obedience,[182] and this in such a way that the competence to issue commands and the obligation to obey them are distributed in an unambiguous manner among the members of the association.[183] If the command is obeyed freely and with inward consent, we may speak of "leadership," but leadership is always a form of rule and must not be opposed to rule as if it fell into a different category.[184]

Any form of rule is the basis for the unity of a group under rule. This is especially true of political rule, because it lays claim to the entire life of the members of the association. This is true even when individuals are allowed areas of free disposition and decision, for these areas are given to them precisely by the state itself, that is, by its constitution.[185] By "state" in the narrower (modern) sense of the term is meant the fully developed form of political rule that claims and asserts a monopoly on the exercise of power within the area it rules. Herein can be seen the tendency, peculiar to political rule, to integrate the association in a total way.[186] Apart from this tendency, the claim of political systems to autarky, or sovereignty, becomes unintelligible, as does their claim to a territory over which they claim an authority from which there is no appeal.[187]

Rule can mean repression. It does so when it is exercised to the advantage of the ruler and not for the service of the common good. On this basis, Aristotle long ago distinguished between just and unjust re-

[181]H. Heller, *Staat*, in A. Vierkandt et al., *Handwörterbuch der Soziologie* (1931), 606–16. An order of civil justice exists "only because and insofar as there is a real unity of civil rule" (615).

[182]"System" here connotes that there is a reciprocal agreement, the "ordered harmony in commanding and obeying" *(ordinata imperandi oboediendique concordia)* of which Augustine speaks with reference to both the home and the state *(De civ. Dei* XIX, 16). See Aristotle, *Polit.* I, 5 (1254a21–33).

[183]Only because of this could Weber (n. 180, above), 128, describe power as the "chance" that "a specific command will be obeyed by persons singled out." The "capacity for gaining obedience without caring whether the one obeying gives an interior consent," which Heller, 614, gives as his definition of political rule, is likewise based on the "order" which rule presupposes. Hondrich (n. 147, above), 90, defines rule as an exercise of power that is limited by its being tied to a "formally regulated authority to make decisions." This definition is incomplete, however.

[184]Friedrich (n. 176, above), 39ff., 55, and F. A. Hermens, *Verfassungslehre* (1968), 38–46. For an opposing view, see O. Brunner, "Bemerkungen zu den Begriffen 'Herrschaft' und 'Legitimität,' " in his *Neue Wege der Verfassungs- und Sozialgeschichte* (1956; 1968²). 70.

[185]Weber, 29f.

[186]It was the basic thesis of R. Smend's *Verfassung und Verfassungsrecht* (1928), now in his *Staatsrechtliche Abhandlungen* (1955; 1968²), 119–276, that the state owes the unity of its "total life" to a continuous process of integration in which various factors play a part.

[187]This characteristic, which in Heller's view distinguishes the state from other associations under rule (616; see Weber, 29), is also treated by Smend as a special factor, among others, in the process whereby a state is made an integral whole.

gimes,[188] while later on a distinction was made between *imperium* and *dominium* on the same basis. Rule in the sense of *imperium*, that is, rule that serves not the personal advantage of the ruler but the well-being of the association and its members, is essential for legitimacy. As the word *imperium* indicates,[189] this is a rule that is guided by law and justice; these, however, serve—or ought to serve—the common good, since "just" *(dikaiōn)* is predicated precisely of what benefits the common good.[190] The aim of the state, therefore, is justice, since the entire association is benefited when each of its members is treated equally, that is, when each receives what is due to him or her.[191] As Aristotle puts it, a political rule that serves justice "ought not to be regarded as slavery, but rather as salvation."[192]

Modern political science likewise regards the commitment of the state to justice as the sole justification for political rule: "Only insofar as it strives for a just order are its vast claims justified."[193] Political rule seems indeed to have been connected with the development of law from the very beginning, if it is the case that such rule did not result first and foremost from military conquest but came into existence in natural human communities. It arose, specifically, when the transition from the life of hunters and food collectors to the domestication of animals and plants led to the formation of larger communities. Modern scholars like to describe this transition, which introduced the sedentary, nonnomadic way of life, as the neolithic "revolution" in human living.

In the development of communities that extended beyond a single kinship group, there was need not only of a suprafamilial authority who could arbitrate in disputes but also, and above all, of a central agency for storing provisions and distributing these in time of need. The function of redistribution seems to have played a fundamental role in the develop-

---

[188]Aristotle, *Polit.* 1279a17–21 (see, earlier, 1278b30ff.).

[189]See Würtenberger (n. 177, above), 32ff., on the meaning of *imperium legitimum* in Roman law.

[190]Aristotle, *Eth. Nic.* 1129b14f. and 1160a13f. See, at an earlier time, Heraclitus, Frag. 114, where the law of the city is offered as a model for the basing of strength on what is common to all (i.e., on what is rational).

[191]Aristotle, *Polit.* 1282b16–18.

[192]Aristotle, *Polit.* 1310a34–36, in *The Politics of Aristotle,* ed. and trans. E. Barker (New York, 1958 [1946]; Oxford Galaxy Books, 1962), 234. In this remark, which is very relevant to the modern discussion of political rule, Aristotle is reacting to what he calls a false definition of freedom, according to which they alone are free who can do whatever they wish (1310a27ff.).

[193]Heller, *Staatslehre* (n. 113, above), *Gesammelte Schriften* III, 327. Though the state, according to Heller, has its origin in the phenomenon of political rule and not in justice, it acquires legitimacy only as an "organization for the safeguarding of justice" (III, 333).

ment of the early chiefdoms.[194] With that function may have been linked the authority exercised by an arbiter who stood outside the hierarchy of the family.

There is disagreement about whether we should speak of a system of justice in connection with such manifestations. There are good reasons for saying that only the emerging state developed a judicial system that was independent of the clans and could conduct trials and enforce decisions regarding justice.[195] On the other hand, the origins of a system of justice are undoubtedly to be seen in the rules of reciprocity that decided how communal life was to be lived in the hunting and food-gathering period and that are reflected in the *ius talionis* (law of retaliation) which regulated offenses against the community.[196] As Aristotle insisted, formulated law has its roots in custom and habit.[197] It takes the institutional forms of communal life, the reciprocity of giving and receiving, and the therein implied mutual recognition of persons and their spheres of freedom, and gives these explicit force for a political community that now extends beyond the easily surveyed membership of the kinship group.

To that extent the translation of justice into positive law as the order governing common life is closely linked objectively with the peculiar character of political associations and especially with political rule, which has the task of maintaining the unity of the associations and the conditions required for it. In the process, of course, the content of inherited order and custom is also reformulated. With good reason, therefore, does Heller speak of a reciprocity in the relation between justice and the state. The state legislates, and the organized political power ensures its enforcement. On the other hand, in its origin justice precedes the state, and the legitimacy of the state itself is bound up with "the ethical principles of justice that transcend the state and its

---

[194]According to Fried (n. 166, above), 163 and, earlier, 116ff., the role of "village redistributor" may have fallen to those individuals who stood out in the "reciprocal economy" of hunters and food gatherers (with its "obligation to reciprocate," 35f.) because they gave more than they retained for themselves (115). See also Service (n. 152, above), 75ff., and his remark on 8: "Political power organized the economy, and not vice versa."

[195]Thus Fried, 14ff. It is not possible in the case either of the stone age hunting and food gathering societies (90ff.) or of the chiefdoms that preceded the state (144–53) to speak of justice as distinct from custom and tradition.

[196]See B. Malinowski, *Crime and Custom in Savage Society* (New York, 1926), 24ff., 39ff., 46ff. On the terminological problems connected with the concepts of custom *(Sitte)*, usage *(Brauch)*, and convention, see my remarks in *Handbuch der christlichen Ethik* 2 (1978), 329, n. 29.

[197]Aristotle, *Eth. Nic.* 1134b13–15; see *Polit.* 1269a20–25 and 1287b5, and J. Ritter, " 'Naturrecht' bei Aristoteles," in his *Metaphysik und Politik* (n. 112, above), 133–79, esp. 149ff., 160ff., 166. See also 113f.

laws and by that fact ground them."[198]

The reciprocity of state and justice shows itself somewhat problematical once we raise the question of the legitimacy of the state's power. If justice is the criterion of legitimacy and if, on the other hand, justice is formulated as laws by the state and can be altered in the process, is not the state legitimating itself, since it can alter "justice" at need? If so, is not the question of legitimacy reduced to the fact of possessing power to rule?

The crisis that the Greek city-state experienced in the fifth and fourth centuries B.C., the age of the Sophistic Enlightenment, has become a paradigm for discussing the problems raised by the reciprocity of state and justice. Until the time of the Sophists, custom and tradition had been thought of as grounded in the divine order of things, as Heraclitus had said (Frag. 114). Now, however, *nomos* (usage, custom) was opposed to *physis* and understood as that which could be altered by arbitrary human decision.[199] But what is the standard for deciding the order that corresponds to the nature of things?

The Socratic school sought to develop such a standard by inquiring into the nature of the human being. Plato concluded to a threefold division of the human soul and to the requirement that reason be in charge of the whole. In the light of this theory he divided the state into three classes, among which leadership was to belong to the philosophers. Aristotle abandoned this model. His answer to the question of the criterion for an order of communal life that would correspond to the nature of things was to the effect that political society actually brings human nature to its completion. It too, therefore, must be a criterion for what is just.

In fact, for Aristotle and the tradition dependent on him, the criterion for the legitimacy of political rule is that it is exercised for the common good and not for the personal advantage of the ruler. This does not yet tell us, however, in what the common good consists or what concrete organization of the community is to be derived from this criterion.[200] Moreover, the appeal to the common good seems to presuppose some idea of what the just order of things is.

At this point, the question of the legitimacy of a political rule becomes the question of representation, that is, of what (presupposed) true order of things is being represented by the political organization and whether it is being adequately represented. Here we see the connection between, on the one hand, the responsibility for a just order that went with and grew

[198]Heller, *Staatslehre,* 182–98 at 197, *Gesammelte Schriften* II (1971), 287–305.

[199]On the development of the concept of nomos, see Heinimann, *Nomos und Physis* (n. 118, above), 59–89 and 121ff. On its significance for political theory, see also A. Eberhardt, *Politische Metaphysik von Solon bis Augustin* I (1959), 17ff., esp. 24ff.

[200]See the observation of Riedel, referred to above in n. 125, on the "obscurity" in Aristotle's doctrine of the political nature of human beings.

out of the redistributive function of political rule and, on the other, the theocratic character of archaic political systems.

> All the early empires, Near Eastern as well as Far Eastern, understood themselves as representatives of a transcendent order, of the order of the cosmos. . . . Whether one turns to the earliest Chinese sources in the *Shu King* or to the inscriptions of Egypt, Babylonia, Assyria, or Persia, one uniformly finds the order of the empire interpreted as a representation of the cosmic order in the medium of human society. . . . Rulership becomes the task of securing the order of society in harmony with cosmic order; the territory of the empire is an analogical representation of the world with its four quarters; the great ceremonies of the empire represent the rhythm of the cosmos; festivals and sacrifices are a cosmic liturgy, a symbolic participation of the cosmion in the cosmos; and the ruler himself represents society, because on earth he represents the transcendent power which maintains cosmic order.[201]

Two elements are combined from the outset in the idea of representation: On the one hand, the king represents the cosmic order and the divine rulership that is manifested in it; on the other, he also represents the *corporate personality* of the people. The latter aspect has its basis in the former, since the unity of the people, represented by the king, depends on an identity that has been shaped by culture and history and that transcends pure contingency by reason of its religious roots. To the extent that the ruler represents in his own person these forces grounding the identity of the political community, he represents at the same time the very unity of the people. Only because of this does the representative function of political rule become, in the agents of this rule, an integrative factor.[202]

Modern discussion of the subject of political representation is often

[201]E. Voegelin, *The New Science of Politics: An Introduction* (Chicago, 1952), 54. See also Balandier (n. 111, above), 101ff., 108f. According to Voegelin, in both Greek thought and Christianity the political order is no longer understood as directly related to the cosmic order; it is seen instead as based on human nature and its relationship to the divine origin of both humankind and the world. But, with this modification, the idea of political representation of the cosmic order still applies to Christian emperorship and to the Christian kings as holding office by divine right (see my remarks in *Die Bestimmung des Menschen*, 65ff.). The idea that the heavenly lordship of Christ is represented in the political order by the earthly ruler need not detract from the uniqueness of divine revelation, as Koslowski (n. 126, above), 94, seems to think. On the other hand, in Christianity this kind of representation cannot be taken to mean that the ruler is a direct image of God. Such a claim would indeed be in opposition to God's revelation in Christ. The king can be understood as a representative only in the sense of being a deputy in the service of Christ's heavenly lordship.

[202]Thus according to Smend (n. 186, above), the "fullness of cultural values" in virtue of which the state rules (162) effects integration through representation (ibid.), and this representation is accomplished by the agencies of the state (198ff., 204), on the one hand, and by political symbols, such as flags, coats of arms, ceremonies, and festivals, on the other (163). But Smend also has the head of state functioning as a political symbol (ibid.). The head of state thus has a special place among the organs of the state.

limited to representation of the people by their elected representatives, as institutionalized in the parliamentary system.[203] The reason for this shift in focus is the modern doctrine of popular sovereignty. Th. Würtenberger aptly remarks, in connection with the start of this doctrine in Rousseau, that it signifies "the replacement of God by the people and its infallibility."[204] Once the people had been put in the place of God, it was possible for the modern consciousness to forget in great measure the religious roots of political representation and the political order.

As a matter of fact, this development got under way as soon as the modern idea of sovereignty was launched, for the claim to a *potestas legibus soluta* ("power not bound by laws") meant that "the sovereign took the place of God."[205] Jean Bodin even developed his teaching on sovereignty as a conscious alternative to a Christian and religious justification for and limitation on political rule.[206] By linking the idea of representation with the ancient notion of the person as a mask, Hobbes limited God's representatives to the figures of the revealers—Moses, Jesus, and the Holy Spirit—and thereby at the same time restricted the idea of political representation to the representation of the people by their deputies.[207] Even the

[203]Thus, e.g., in Hermens (n. 184, above), 204–24. See also the discussion of this theme in C. Schmitt, *Verfassungslehre* (1928), 205–16. Schmitt, however, like Rousseau (*The Social Contract* III, 15) and Sieyès (80), regarded the idea of representation as incompatible with the concept of democracy (218), because the people are mediatized when representatives are delegated to make decisions for them. Schmitt's controversy with W. R. Thomas on the relation between democracy and parliamentary representation was resolved by E. Fraenkel, *Die repräsentative und die plebiszitäre Komponente im demokratischen Verfassungsstaat* (1958) with the thesis that representation of the people by delegates is not directly related to the popular will but to the common good which takes precedence over individual interests (11ff.). In this solution two aspects of representation once again become visible. But the view proposed by G. Leibholz, *Strukturprobleme der modernen Demokratie* (1958), is more realistic: There is hardly any room left in modern democracy for an institutional expression of that difference between popular will and common good which lies behind the principle, still formally accepted, of the delegate's freedom of conscience (esp. 96ff., 112ff., 119).

[204]Würtenberger (n. 177, above), 107. See also Schmitt, *Verfassungslehre*, 77f., on the investiture of the people as the *pouvoir constituant* by Sieyès.

[205]Koslowski (n. 126, above), following Schmitt and (for the connection with the doctrine of divine omnipotence in the form of it that goes back to Occam) K. Th. Buddeberg. But Koslowski also correctly notes that a political theology based on the Christian doctrine of the Trinity must assert that the political authorities are bound by the law just as God binds himself by the revelation of his Son (105ff. in a discussion of H. Kelsen's essay, "Gott und Staat" [1922–23]).

[206]Quaritsch (n. 111, above) has pointed out that Bodin could appeal here to the secular character of Aristotle's *Politics* (280). On the historical roots of Bodin's endeavors during the confessional conflicts of the late sixteenth century, see 288.

[207]Hobbes, *Leviathan* I, 16. On the modalist doctrine of the Trinity that is latent here, see D. Braun, *Der sterbliche Gott oder Leviathan gegen Behemoth* (1963), 19ff. But when Braun in his concluding remarks describes Hobbes's sovereign state as also a *larva Dei* ("mask of God") (191f.), he takes a step that Hobbes exerted himself to avoid (as Braun himself

doctrines of Pufendorf and his followers on the contractual state were directed less against political absolutism than "against any theological grounding of rulership."[208]

The rise of absolutism, however, also brought with it the modern problem of legitimacy.[209] That is, emancipation from any and every religious foundation for the state created the problem of how to legitimize human rulership as such. True enough, even at this point thinkers still appealed to the concept of justice.[210] In the seventeenth and eighteenth centuries they could still maintain that justice provided a norm by which the power of the state was to be judged. But this norm itself collapsed, and the collapse did not wait upon the undermining of natural law doctrines by historical relativism. It was caused even earlier by the fact that the consciousness of right came to be based on the principle of popular sovereignty.

Three modern developments played a role here: the principle that a written constitution is to be the criterion of the state's action; the concomitant division of political powers; and especially the independence of the judiciary. On the one hand, all these gave consistent expression to the obligation of the state to pursue justice while at the same time providing hitherto unknown institutional guarantees that this obligation would be met. On the other hand, these foundations of justice were relativized because it was possible for the popular will to be constantly altering them in the form of changes in the constitution. Under the influence of Rousseau the popular will—but a will now detached from the fictions of the contractual theories and reduced to a consent to the form of government in power at the moment—came increasingly to be seen as the ultimate

---

recognizes, 112ff.). It is better not to assign any systematic implications for Hobbes's doctrine of the state to the remark in the 45th chapter of *Leviathan* (therefore not in the discussion of the Christian commonwealth but in the fourth part, on the kingdom of darkness) according to which an "earthly sovereign" can be described as an "image" of God in the broad sense of the term. More important is the consistent distinction made between the kingdom of Christ, which is reserved to the future when the dead arise (III, 41), and the political regimes of this world (III, 42).

[208]D. Klippel, *Politische Freiheit und Freiheitsrechte im deutschen Naturrecht des 18. Jahrhunderts* (1976), 46. The doctrine of the implicit or tacit contract shows (Klippel says) that even the idea of a contract could serve as the basis of a radical absolutism by releasing "the power of the ruler from unwelcome legal and moral ties" (46f.).

[209]See W. Hennis, "Legitimität. Zu einer Kategorie der bürgerlichen Gesellschaft," in *Politik und praktische Philosophie* (1977), 198–242 at 222ff.

[210]Already in Bodin, according to Quaritsch (n. 111, above), 387. For later conceptions of legitimacy and its relation to justice, see Würtenberger (n. 177, above), 122f., 155ff. As natural law norms were abandoned along with the idea of parliament as the representative of common interests against individual interests (see also Friedrich [n. 176, above], 173), the process led to "a reduction of legitimacy to simple legality" (252). It was against this reduction that Schmitt pitted the idea of legitimacy based on a plebiscite.

foundation of the state's legitimacy, but also as the authority that could by plebiscite legitimate the overthrow of the government.

While the idea of popular sovereignty was becoming the foundational political concept, society was becoming an independent entity over against the political order, to the point where the state was conceived as a function of society. This is another specifically modern development. It can of course be said that there had been a dualism in a broad sense between state and society ever since the first states arose out of the archaic chiefdoms,[211] inasmuch as there was the constant task of welding the particularist interests of the individual clans or "houses" into a unified political order. What is special, however, about society in the modern sense of the term is that the manifold particular interests have become functions of a system of universal interdependence due to the mechanisms of the market. This system of interdependence, as the form in which particular interests are combined in a single society, could then be in competition with the political order of the state. This system of universal interdependence was described in the new economics of nations that replaced the doctrine of an economy which operated at the domestic level. Hegel called it "bourgeois" society and distinguished it from, and opposed it to, the state.[212]

According to C. Schmitt, the point of departure for this development was the privatization of religion after the religious wars of the sixteenth and seventeenth centuries. This privatization, he says, brought "a relativization and even a devaluation of the state and of public life generally" and turned individual freedom into the highest value.[213] This conception of freedom had its historical origin in the value set upon the individual in Christianity, but it was turned into the basis for the decision whether or not to accept a divine revelation. The liberal doctrine of natural law developed it still further into a shield that would protect the private sphere

[211]This is the main thesis of Koslowski's book *Gesellschaft und Staat. Ein unvermeidlicher Dualismus* (n. 126, above). According to Koslowski, the connected disjunction between individual good and common good corresponds to the consequences of the fall in Augustine's interpretation: the shattering of the unity of love of God and love of self (1).

[212]M. Riedel has shown that prior to Hegel there was "as yet simply no" concept of society in this sense; see his *Studien zu Hegels Rechtsphilosophie* (1969), 156. Until then the concept of society *(societas)* included both *domestic* and *civil* society, the latter being identical with political society (128, on Thomasius, 1725). In Hegel, unlike Kant, the economic unit that was the "house" became the "family" which had been stripped of its economic role, while the economic functions earlier connected with the "house" now formed a social system of universal interdependence and constituted a third sphere between family and state (120f., 129).

[213]Schmitt, *Verfassungslehre*, 158f.: "Religion as what is highest and most absolute becomes the affair of the individual, and everything else, every type of social organization—church as well as state—is relativized and can claim value only as a help to that absolute value, which alone is normative."

against the absolute state and against the latter's "good policy" whereby it sought to promote the welfare of the citizens along the lines it thought right. The chief aim of the protective shield was to keep the state from intervening in the economy.[214]

In the vacuum thus created the self-regulating system of modern society came into existence as the result of market mechanisms that were at last freed of the limitations imposed by extrinsic considerations. The rules of reciprocity that were at the base of this system could take form in justice and ethics as a "complement to a market model of society," that is, as a corrective of purely utilitarian individual interests and of the antagonisms between individuals.[215] When thus conceived as a liberal state under the rule of law, the state became a function of society. But within such a framework—as Hegel and, following him, Marx saw more clearly than Kant—the antagonisms between opposed special interests cannot be resolved. On the other hand, a half century after the revolution that these antagonisms led Marx to look for, we can hardly expect any longer that such a resolution will come as a quasi-natural consequence of sweeping revolutionary change in bourgeois society.

The disillusionment that inevitably affects revolutionary enthusiasm in the long run will find in Hegel's idea of the ethical state a sounder solution of social antagonisms and therefore of the "problem of distribution."[216] Yet even in Hegel's model of the state the idea that the structure of political rule represents a metaphysically based order is, if anything, too weak rather than too strong. To an even greater degree, however, the moral authority given by "anticipation of a possible consensus"[217] is lacking in a state that is based on the principles of popular sovereignty and organized as the rule of the majority. The content of this kind of anticipation will have credibility only if it embodies the truth that precedes and

---

[214]Klippel (n. 208, above), 143f.

[215]Koslowski (n. 126, above), 204, on Kant's theory of right. According to Kant, the "hidden plan of nature" is promoted by the antagonism between individuals (*Idea for a Universal History from a Cosmopolitan Point of View*, trans. L. W. Beck, in I. Kant, *On History*, ed. L. W. Beck [Indianapolis, 1963], Thesis 4), and the system of justice has only to "stabilize the order that arises in this spontaneous way" (Koslowski, 206). See also Kant, *Zum ewigen Frieden*, AA VIII, 341f. On ethics as a "complement to the order of justice and the economic order," see Koslowski, 225; for Kant's critique of utilitarianism, 230ff.

[216]See Koslowski, 284–92. In a similar way, but using Marxist terminology, Habermas (n. 178, above), 132, formulates the problem of legitimating political rule as the task of "distributing the social surplus product unequally yet legitimately." Of course, if we prescind from the problems raised by the concept of "surplus product," the problem of distribution does not arise solely in "class societies."

[217]Koslowski, 290f., 299ff., following R. Spaemann, *Zur Kritik der politischen Utopie* (1977), 123. According to Spaemann, this idea, like the Aristotelian concept of justice, implies "the willingness and ability to give fairness priority over self-interest in exchange and distribution" (ibid.).

grounds the formation of consensus, and it must find corresponding representation in the institutional order of society. But a state that represents only the people, or society and its antagonisms, and no longer the divine truth revealed in the cosmic order or in history does not have available to it the possibility of legitimating its political order anywhere but in itself.

Even the welfare state does not provide a lasting substitute for such legitimation since no state can permanently satisfy all the needs of its citizens and guarantee their happiness. When the political order takes the form of the welfare state, it once again usurps the place of religion,[218] instead of carrying out the limited function that is assigned to it on the basis of a religiously grounded consciousness of meaning and that therefore gives it a truth distinct from that grasped by the religious consciousness. In addition, when it takes the form of the welfare state, the political order is in danger of losing its legitimacy every time the economic situation deteriorates.[219] As a result, the welfare state provides only a temporary solution to the legitimacy crisis of the secular state.

The legitimacy crisis of the secular state is not a question solely of public morality and of appropriate political reforms. It has deeper roots in the loss of the religious foundation for moral obligation and the authority of law. The crisis is repeated every time the discovery is made that the state is justifying its power by manipulating public awareness.[220] But while the

[218]Compare Augustine's criticism of the ancient (and Aristotelian) idea that the good life is realized in the state; he regards this as an expression of human arrogance (*De civ. Dei* XIX, 5 and 12; see Koslowski, 74ff.). Human beings achieve happiness only through communion with God in the life to come. Kant's "rejection of the welfare state" in favor of a state formally under the rule of law is strikingly analogous to Augustine's view (Koslowski, 218). "When the principle of promoting happiness instead of the principle of justice is made the basis of the legislator's action, conflicts and quarrels are the inevitable result, since no agreement will be reached on the material concept of happiness" (198). A. Altmann, *Prinzipien politischer Theorie bei Mendelssohn und Kant* (Trierer Universitätsreden 9; Trier, 1981), 20ff., discusses the opposition between Kant and Mendelssohn on this point. Klippel, 132, emphasizes the fact that Kant's thesis is directed against the absolutist state.

[219]Thus E. W. Böckenförde, *Staat, Gesellschaft, Freiheit. Studien zur Staatstheorie und zum Verfassungsrecht* (1976), 60f., as well as J. Rothschild's criticism of the reduction of legitimacy to efficiency as an "essentially shallow and even desperate perspective because such a pseudo-ideology will leave them [political regimes] naked and without principled authority if their efficiency declines," in B. Denitch, ed., *Legitimation of Regimes: International Framework for Analysis* (London, 1979), 37–54 at 39.

[220]At one time the point of legitimation was to impose control on political regimes. It came, however, to mean a manipulative creation—hardly to be called demagogic, because *unnoticed*—of consent to the existing forms of government. The change is described by P. L. Rosen, "Legitimacy, Domination, and Ego-Displacement," in Glassmann and Vidich (n. 158, above), 75–95, esp. 92f. "There is no doubt that legitimacy can be manufactured through the manipulation of beliefs and attitudes in much the same way consumers are led to mouthwash" (84). Political rulers cannot escape the pressure to engage in this kind of self-justification, because belief in the legitimacy of a regime "can minimize the cost of

collapse of legitimacy makes "governing" more difficult, it does not immediately and without some further impetus from outside lead to the breakup of the system of government. For, especially when the collapse is due to uncertainty about moral direction on the part of society as a whole as well as of the rulers, not only is there a decline of confidence in the legitimacy of the existing political order, but in addition the strength to choose an alternative wanes,[221] so that the only immediate result is a spreading but ineffective malaise.

V. Religion in the Cultural System

The function of religion in the political order of society is inevitably defined too narrowly when it is discussed only in the context of problems affecting the legitimacy of institutions that already exist and have their justification from some other source. If religion is to be claimed as a real source of legitimacy, it must have a more fundamental and radical function in the life of society.[222]

This function is to be seen, first, in the fact that religion has for its object the unity of the world as such in relation to its divine source and its possible fulfillment from that same source. Its function is to be seen also and above all in the fact that in this context of unity it thematizes the meaning of human life and the meaningful order found in the social life of human beings. As the young Schleiermacher explained, religion deals with the universe. The universe of the life-world (or the divine reality that gives this universe its unified meaning) manifests itself historically in ever

repression, surveillance, and police work" (J. Bensman, in Glassmann and Vidich, 146). See, earlier, C. J. Friedrich (n. 176, above), 105f.

[221]See R. E. Lane, "The Legitimacy Bias," in Denitch (n. 219, above), 55–79, esp. 56.

[222]Therefore P. Berger, in his *The Sacred Canopy: Elements of a Sociological Theory of Religion* (Garden City, N.Y., 1967), correctly begins with a chapter on the religious constitution of the social world ("Religion and World-Construction," 3–28) and only then moves on to the function of religion as a source of legitimacy ("Religion and World-Maintenance," 29–51). Similarly, in the book Berger wrote with T. Luckmann, *The Social Construction of Reality: A Treatise in the Sociology of Knowledge* (Garden City, N.Y., 1966), the integration of institutions via the "detour" of "shared universes of meaning" (61) is kept distinct from the problem of legitimation, this last being regarded as a second-order objectivation of meaning (85ff.). But, just as Berger and Luckmann derive institutionalization from the reciprocal interrelatedness of the *actions* of individuals (52ff.), so Berger in *The Sacred Canopy* speaks of human beings as exercising a "world-building activity" as they "impose a meaningful order on reality" (22)—as though the point of the religions were not that such meaning is precisely not *imposed* by human beings but is *perceived* by them as grounded in itself, and as though it were agreed that a modern theory of the constitution of meaning must reduce meaning to action. My remarks in chapter 7, sec. III, above, suggest that, on the contrary, language (and therefore meaning) precedes action and provides the medium in which the identity of the subject—which the concept of action must presuppose—is initially constituted.

varying particular shapes or occurrences that serve the religious consciousness as points on which to focus its unity,[223] and this with regard both to
the unity of the world and to the identity and integration of individual
lives.

Because religions are concerned with the unity of all reality, it is possible and necessary to seek and find in religion the ultimate frame of reference for the order of human life in society. For only the religions—and,
at need, the worldviews that have been substituted for the religions in the
modern age—apprehend the universe as a meaningful order in which,
through embeddedness in it, the order of life in society also becomes
meaningful. On the other hand, since political rule has for its task the
unification and ongoing integration of society, it must derive its legitimacy
from the religious foundations that make reality intelligible as an ordered
and meaningful whole.

It may therefore be claimed that there is no longer any legitimacy for
the secular state of the modern age, since it is no longer related to any
religious foundation.[224] Conversely, and for the same reason, the modern
state, having cut its ties with the religious basis of culture, has been
confronted in an incomparably radical way with the problem of legitimacy:
the legitimacy of its own organization of power and indeed the legitimacy
of political rule as such.[225]

As far as religion is concerned, the legitimation of an existing or projected political order is a quite secondary concern. Religion does not
become meaningful in human life simply because it proves itself relevant
for the continued existence of a particular social order and particular forms
of political rule. If that is the sole source of its vitality, then religion is
already hopelessly corrupt. Political rule, on the other hand, does need
legitimation as a defense against the continually renewed suspicion that it
represents the presumptuous misuse of power by individuals or groups in
government. Even the modern state has not been able to do without such
legitimation, even though in the course of time it has ceased to invoke
religion. Religion has been replaced by ideologies, chiefly the appeal to
the place a particular nation deserves to occupy in the community of
peoples, and secondarily the views on justice and popular sovereignty that
were discussed in the preceding section of this chapter.

Disillusionment with all these claimed foundations of legitimacy is now
widespread. As a result, recent years have seen a new awareness that the

[223]D. F. Schleiermacher, *On Religion: Addresses in Response to Its Cultured Critics,* trans. T.
N. Tice (Richmond, 1969), 67ff. (second address) and 272ff. (fifth address). The interpretation of Schleiermacher's term *Universum* as "universe of meaning" seems to do most justice
to the complex structure of this term in Schleiermacher's theory of religion.

[224]Thus U. Matz, *Politik und Gewalt* (1975), 116ff., 134.

[225]Hennis (n. 209, above), 224f.

secular state in all its forms suffers from a chronic defect of legitimacy. We are therefore justified in asking whether modern secular society can exist indefinitely without a religiously based legitimation. In the period when modern secularism had reached the high point of its success many people thought religion might simply wither away. What seems endangered today, at least if one takes the long view, is, rather, the continued existence of a social order that is cut off from its religious roots and defines itself in purely secular terms.

It is not self-evident, however, that religion should serve to legitimate an order of political rule. True enough, both religion and the order of political rule are concerned, each in its own way, with the total context in which individuals live their lives. Religion focuses on the origin and fulfillment of the unity of reality and on the salvation of human beings through participation in that unity. Political power, for its part, focuses on the political integration of society and on the well-being of individuals that such integration makes possible. But precisely because their concerns are so closely related, conflict between religion and the political powers can very easily arise.

Political power can be a manifestation of that rule of the Most High God over the world that gives the world order its unity. It will then be aureoled in messianic glory and enable human beings to share in that "unbroken world" *(die heile Welt)* which is the divine order for human life. Political power may also, however, claim to fulfill the human destiny; then it becomes God's competitor. In that case, the state presents itself, to Christian eyes, with the features of the Antichrist. The center to which the exocentricity of human life is directed (says the state) is the political order. Only through integration into the political order can individuals unify their lives and achieve personal identity. Individuals enjoy no independence of the political order and therefore no rights against the power of the ruler.

This kind of absolute political claim over human beings—no matter whether in the name of a kingdom or a nation or the sovereign people or a social order—is always tyrannical, even when it does not involve any recognizably arbitrary exercise of power by the ruler. Political gospels of salvation with their boundless claims are essentially lies, since they do not coincide with the divergent interests that constitute social reality and since their pretenses can be maintained only by repression. If in fact the self-destinations of individuals coincided in the form of a *volonté générale,* there would be no need for political rule, for a special coordination of the particular interests of individuals and groups. Political rule is indispensable precisely because the special interests of the members of a society are not automatically in harmony. For this reason, political rule always has an aspect of compulsion about it. This is true even of a democratic regime, especially since its decisions are carried out in the name of the majority of the moment and against the desires of the minority.

Moreover, even when a regime intends to represent not only a party or the majority of voters who stand behind the regime but the entire people, and when it endeavors to take the interests of the minority into account and treat them equitably, the rulers, being human, are limited in their insight, resolution, and energy. For this reason, if for no other, any political order established by human beings is limited in its ability to do justice to all, and it is not possible for the individual citizens to attain to the definitive fulfillment of their human destiny in any such order of things. Human beings are indeed destined for a social life, and only in society can they live in a way that accords with their destiny. Their destiny is therefore in fact political, but it cannot be fully and definitively realized in any order of political rule. The only organization of common life in which the destiny of individuals can be fully realized is the kingdom of God, which no political integration by human rule can possibly bring about.

At this point the inadequacy of any and every organization of political power becomes clear. Religion therefore becomes a court of appeal for the individual against the claim of any political order to be definitive. It becomes an authority capable of showing up the limitations of the political principles behind any such order as well as the failures and the usurpative and exaggerated claims of its rulers.

The relation between religion and political power is therefore an ambivalent one. The ambivalence is inherent in the role of political rulers as representatives of God's rule over the world. For, on the one hand, rulers may accept their role as representatives while recognizing the factual inadequacy of the order they are able to ensure; they therefore accept this order as being only a symbolic representation of the true order of things. But rulers can also use their function as representatives of God's rule in the earthly world to justify claims to exclusive authority and therefore to deny any human agency the right to criticize them. In so doing, rulers provoke conflict with religious institutions as well as others.

In the archaic cultures, rulers were conscious in the main of the positive aspect of their role as representatives, that is, the harmony between their rule and the authority of religion. This was probably due to the relative lack of tension between religion and the political order in the mythical religions, but also to the small value placed on the independence of the individual in relation to the people as a whole. Yet even in the archaic cultures, rulers doubtless had to suffer being judged by the lofty demands connected with their role as representatives of the divinity.

The familiar modern distinction between religion and the political order goes back, on the one hand, to the anthropological justification for political rule in Greek thought.[226] On the other, it can be traced back to the religion of Israel, to the exclusivity of the God of the Jews, and, from the standpoint of particular historical events, to the ministry of the prophets. The latter strongly emphasized the failures of the kings to carry out God's call for justice; they also directed the gaze of their people beyond the resultant historical catastrophes to an eschatological future in which the justice and peace willed by God would finally prevail.

In Christianity the anthropological justification of the political order and the Jewish dualism of Yahwistic faith and monarchy were welded together in the conviction that the human destiny of the individual can never be adequately fulfilled by the political order. The latter has but a provisional function: to ensure a peaceful communal life for human beings. Human salvation, however, can only be awaited in the coming world of God, and any participation in that future world is mediated in the present life not by the state but only by the sacramental and symbolic communion of the church. For this reason, even in the Byzantine empire the church and its bishops were, in principle, independent of the emperor and his rule.

But this linking of the transcendent biblical God with the transcendent human destiny that looks beyond the present world and its political life also made possible another and quite different development. At the beginning of the modern age in the West, and for an entirely new kind of reason —the hopelessness engendered by the religious civil wars—the connection I have just described made it possible to declare the individual's religious confession to be a wholly personal and private matter. Since that time, limits have been set on the claim of the church or, as the case may be, the competing claims of the confessional churches, to set a uniform stamp on the political order and the public culture along lines determined by the given church's dogmatic understanding of its faith. Moreover, it has been possible to justify these limits by an appeal to the spirit of Christianity itself.

On the other hand, the modern state still required a religious legitimation of its rule. In these new circumstances, however, doubts were soon raised about the state's having any confessional ties. Given the inclusiveness of the civic order and of the public culture that this order guarantees, it did not seem appropriate that the state should be founded on a particular confession.

Since there was no institutional form of the Christian religion that

---

[226]In the second and third volumes of his *Order and History* (Baton Rouge, 1957), E. Voegelin brings out the epochal significance of the anthropological justification that Greek thinkers gave for the civic order. This current of thought arose in the fifth century and reached its high point in the political theories of Plato and Aristotle. To this way of thinking Voegelin contrasts the "cosmological empires" of the ancient East (II, 168ff., 229ff.; III, *passim*).

transcended confessional particularism, the modern age looked to philosophy and science to create or bring to light a universally binding basis for a public culture and thus give legitimacy to political rule.[227] The expectations have been repeatedly disappointed. As scientific knowledge has expanded, its relevance to the culture at large has become increasingly limited.[228] Meanwhile various ideologies—absolutism, nationalism, liberalism, socialism, and fascism—have appealed to their supposedly scientific and therefore universally valid character and been able for a time to take over the political function of religion. Today such claims have lost their credibility, and it is clear that the ideologies are actually exercising a quasi-religious function without having the basis that authentic religion has in a self-revelation of God that precedes any human judgment, even though it is accessible only through human interpretation.

Disillusionment in this area is one factor, along with others discussed in the preceding section, in the decline of the modern state's legitimacy. We may expect the decline to continue as long as the needed reflection on the religious foundations of Western ideas that are normative for political life and the political order is avoided or deferred.[229] But this new reflection itself is not possible without a revision of those decisions in modern constitutional history that have put ruler or people in the place of God. As Augustine said with good reason, no political order can be called just in which God is denied what belongs to him, namely, his claim to the human beings he created.[230]

While any political order is ultimately dependent on religion for its legitimation, the religions are not dependent on the existence of any determinate political order. This is true at least of the missionary world religions whose message is directed to the human being as such. Not only are they independent of the continued existence of particular states and forms of government, but they may even survive the collapse of entire cultures. Culture has its roots in religion, but the world religions do not stand or fall with a particular culture. In this sense too religion transcends

[227]See the important remarks of F. H. Tenbruck, "Der Fortschritt der Wissenschaft als Trivialisierungsprozess," *Kölner Zeitschrift für Soziologie und Sozialpsychologie,* Sonderheft 18 (Wissenschaftssoziologie; 1975), 19–47, esp. 29ff.

[228]Ibid., 23ff., 35f.

[229]See my essay "Die theokratische Alternative," in R. Löw et al., *Fortschritt ohne Mass? Eine Ortsbestimmung der wissenschaftlich-technischen Zivilisation* (1981), 235–51.

[230]Augustine, *De civ. Dei* XIX, 21, 1: "What kind of human justice is it that takes human beings themselves away from the true God and subjects them to evil demons? Is that what it means to 'give each what is his own'? Is it not unjust to take an estate from the person who has bought it and give it to another who has no right to it? Well, then, are they to be considered just who remove themselves from the authority of God who made them and serve evil spirits?" On Cicero's thesis that there can be no state without justice, see his *Resp.* III, 8, 45.

the social order. It is far from being simply an expression of the universal character of society and of the latter's precedence over the particularity of individuals and groups.[231] It is capable of grounding the unity of a culture and a particular society precisely because it transcends them. Only within the horizon of this transcendence can a culture or an individual society be seen as a totality.

The transcendence of religion over society also grounds the independence of individuals in relation to the particular order in which they live. Even in the mythical religions human beings transcend the actual form of their social world and get behind it, as it were, when they celebrate in cult the primordial event of which the myth tells. All the more in the world religions are individuals raised above the confines of their social and cultural world. Thus Christians, through the communion with Christ that unites them to all other Christians, are freed from the bonds of this unredeemed world, although they are at the same time called to serve others within the orders proper to the present world. They are now no longer simply members of this world with its ways of life and its culture but are citizens of another world, the world of God, whom they serve by laboring to improve the present world and its culture.

The independence of individuals in relation to their society and its organization has been the product of the religions, for these have taught them to regard men and women no longer as mere members of their people and the sacrosanct order of their world but, rather, simply as

[231]As everyone knows, this was Durkheim's view in his *The Elementary Forms of the Religious Life: A Study in Religious Sociology,* trans. J. W. Swann (London, 1915; repr., Glencoe, Ill., 1947). "Nearly all the great social institutions have been born in religion" (418–19). Even the linguistic formulation of universal concepts was the work of religion (433). Yet Durkheim believed that "the idea of society is the soul of religion" (419). Following Feuerbach —but distancing himself from the historical materialism of Marx (423)—Durkheim wrote that "religious force is only the sentiment inspired by the group in its members, but projected outside of the consciousnesses that experience them, and objectified" (229). The close connection between society and religion is recognized in this statement, but the causal relation between them as seen in the religions is inverted: No longer does religion ground the unity of the social order; instead, the unity of society expresses itself in the objectivations of religion. But on what, then, is the unity of society itself based? As a cultural creation it cannot be understood simply in terms of Feuerbach's unity of the species, even if we prescind from the fact that the species is simply a universal concept and not an active subject (such as Durkheim repeatedly represents it as being, e.g., 418). Durkheim is unable to explain the integration of society, which religion for its part traces back to the divine order of things; he can only posit it as a primordial datum. Why, then, does he not respect the witness of the religious traditions, instead of reversing the causal relation between religion and society? The reason is evidently that what cannot be allowed must not be: Recourse to "some super-experimental reality which was postulated, but whose existence could be established by no observation" (447), must simply be excluded. But the positivistic conception of experience that is at work here is itself acknowledged today to be untenable, for it would not permit even the assumptions made by the natural sciences.

human beings. Thus Jesus of Nazareth addressed every human being as
one who is loved with an infinite love by the heavenly Father who seeks
out the lost.[232] Subsequently the resurrection of this man who had been
rejected by his people and condemned and crucified by the Roman Empire
freed his disciples from every unconditional tie to people and state.[233]
This did not mean a turning away from the tasks of the present world. It
meant, rather, a liberation for the service of the neighbor as a sign of the
coming reign of God and thus also for an active collaboration in the work
of advancing and preserving earthly justice and peace.

In all of this there emerges with crystal clarity a trait that in other areas
as well characterizes the relation of human beings to God, on the one
hand, and to the social order, on the other. I refer to the fact that while
the identity of individuals is indeed mediated through the social context
of their lives, nonetheless it has its root and ground only in their relation
to God. Human exocentricity compels men and women to find outside
themselves a center that will give unity and identity to their lives. As a
result, from the first moment of their existence they live ecstatically in a
symbiotic web of life within the security of which—and by reason of
whose fragility—they first awaken to themselves—that is, to the question
of themselves.

The norms that spring from social relations are never able fully to
guarantee the integrity and identity of the individual. Identity and integrity that are whole and entire is the salvation that religion alone bestows
and that human beings can acquire in it despite all the damage and failures
that earthly life inflicts on them. Only from religion can they gain the
strength to stand up to earthly life with its challenges. Despite its inevitable fragmentariness the earthly life of individuals can become the embodiment of a personal identity and integrity that transcend life's limitations
and weaknesses.

If individuals seek to achieve their identity directly through their social
life, they will consistently overtax the capacities of the institutions of
communal life. This is true of marriage, family life, and the state as well
as of work and property. Then the individual will either be consumed by
these institutions or estranged from the life they provide, or else the
institutions themselves will break down because too much is demanded of
them. The communal life of individuals can be successful only if they avoid
this overtaxing of institutions and of institutionally organized personal
relations, and if those who play social roles keep a certain distance from

---

[232]On this, see my *Die Bestimmung des Menschen* (n. 124, above), 7–22, esp. 10ff. on Luke
15:4–32.
[233]Hegel made this point in his *Vorlesungen über die Philosophie der Religion* (1821), in
Religionsphilosophie, ed. K. H. Iltung, I (1978), 641 = G. Lasson, III (PhB 63), 161f.

them in dealing both with others and with themselves. Only then can social institutions and the role behavior of individuals in them become a medium for *representing* or bodying forth persons and their more deeply grounded relationships with one another in the light of their religious vocation to union with God.

Any institution of the shared human world will reveal its true nature only to the extent that it is understood and lived as representational, that is, as representing or manifesting that destiny of human beings and their community which transcends the limitations of our earthly condition. In this way it becomes possible to bear the countless shortcomings of everyday life, but also to make them more tolerable.

What I have been saying holds even for the institutions of religion itself. They too are only a representation of the human being's relation to God, although in this symbolic form the very union itself takes place. In cult and other religious institutions there is represented, along with the action of the gods, the nature of human being and world as such, a nature that transcends the world of everyday life. There is need for this kind of representation, in which the arts are closely associated with religion, in order to keep both the profane institutions of communal life and human beings themselves from claiming, despite their limitations, an equality with God. The sanctification of life in all its aspects can come only from religion that elevates human beings above their limited goals.

Conversely, however, religious institutions and rituals can be made to serve finite human interests and misused as means to a magical disposal of things holy. This kind of distortion of the relation to God can find expression in religious conceptions of the form the divine reality takes as well as in the limitation of the religious relationship to a sacral realm and to special sacred times and in the subordination of cultic actions to the profane ends and needs of the participants.

In religions as they have existed and exist now, it is impossible not to see these two tendencies constantly at work and in conflict with each other. The world of the religions and their history does not display only idolatry, superstition, and enigmatic practices, though it is certainly full of such things. But it always contains as well examples of devout and reverential behavior and of a disposition to holiness of life. In this last respect at least, the men and women of a world that has succumbed to secularism and therefore grown meaningless have little reason to feel superior to the religions of the peoples and to the ways of communal life that these have shaped.

The secular world of modern life does indeed have its roots in the Christian distinction between the order of this passing world and the coming world of God that reaches into our present world in the worship of the church and in the faith of the individual. The fundamental secular idea of the autonomy of the individual is certainly anchored in the Christian idea of freedom, the radical importance of which for the Christian's life of faith as well as for the Christian's independence amid the affairs of earthly life was brought out anew by the Reformers.

At the same time, however, the secular world of the modern state and its culture is alienated from these roots. Only in individual cases, moreover, has the rebellion of human self-assertion against the authority of the Christian tradition given an emotional impetus to the process of alienation. On the whole, the alienation has been the inevitable, even if only hesitatingly accepted consequence of the division of the church in the West and of the indecisive outcome of the subsequent confessional wars. At that time it was necessary, for survival's sake, to place the state and public culture on a foundation that would be unaffected by confessional strife. But this led to a separation from the sources of religion, even though the intellectual elites of that transitional age thought they could easily restrict the surrender to only certain elements in those sources.

As public culture and social institutions have come to be increasingly emptied of meaning, the process of detachment from the sources of religion has imperiled the continued existence of secular society itself. This society must recollect itself and reflect on its religious sources if it is not to be destroyed by the collapse of all binding norms and the antagonisms produced by unfettered selfish interests. But that kind of reflection will come only from a realization that religion is not a collection of transmitted or newly proliferating superstitions, but a constant factor in human existence from the very beginning[234] and a specifically human trait.

---

[234]In his "Beiträge der Urgeschichte zur Kenntnis der Menschennatur," in H. G. Gadamer and P. Vogler, eds., *Kulturanthropologie,* Neue Anthropologie 4 (1973), 3–62, K. J. Narr regards the existence of burials from at least the middle of the Early Stone Age as a decisive criterion in answering the question of when the "transition from animal to human" came to an end. Since such burials, which may in fact be found even farther back in the Early Stone Age (31f.), imply ideas of "some kind of survival after death" (37; see 31), Narr concludes: "We must regard as *in principle fully human* any living entity to which such a world of ideas is to be attributed" (37).

See idem, "Vom Wesen des Frühmenschen. Halbtier oder Mensch?" *Saeculum* 25 (1974), 293–324, where he argues that the appearance of *Homo sapiens* is not to be thought of as coinciding with the beginnings of art ca. 30,000 B.C. (319f.) but is to be connected, rather, with the Early Stone Age by reason of the antiquity of burials. An even earlier date for the custom of burial than is presently attested is suggested by the fact that proven burials have survived only in caves (321), whereas early human beings lived not in caves but in open country and in man-made shelters (322).

A. F. C. Wallace, *Religion: An Anthropological View* (New York, 1966), likewise connects the beginnings of religion with the practice of burial (224ff.). According to Wallace, the self-consciousness therein expressed of human beings who knew they too must die distinguishes human ritual behavior from rituals attested among the higher animals (233; see 217–24).

Once the true place of religion is grasped, it will no longer be left to individual preference but will claim the universal and public attention and place that belong to the fundamental things of human existence. Only on this basis is it possible to give concrete shape to Paul Tillich's vision of a theonomous culture that embraces both heteronomy and autonomy and reconciles the two at a higher level.[235]

The coming of such a culture will be aided by the fact that in this ecumenical age of Christianity the churches in their consciousness of faith have to a large extent risen above the dogmatism that, together with clerical claims to ascendancy, was chiefly responsible for the division of past centuries. This development is not a matter simply of outward accommodation but has originated in a deeper and more nuanced understanding of Christian revelation and the Christian faith. As a result, the basic modern idea of tolerance is today deeply rooted in the Christian consciousness of faith itself and has even altered Christian attitudes to the non-Christian religions. A revitalization, therefore, of the Christian foundations of such social systems as have arisen because of the historical influence of Christianity, and a renewed grasp of their importance for the cultural and political identity of these systems, should not cause a relapse into the intolerance of the religious wars from which the modern state emerged.

In view, moreover, of the history of Christianity a renewed theonomous culture will not mean a fusion of church and state. On the contrary, it will be marked by that distinction between church and state which has characterized the entire history of Christianity, although it is a distinction that does not imply a separation or religious neutrality of the state but is, rather, an expression of a Christian understanding of the political order as a provisional order proper to the present world. It is precisely this provisional character which enables the institutional order of society to be understood as a representation or manifestation of the order of God himself and of his will to justice.

This institutional order might also once again regain its connection with the arts. In the culture business of a secularistic public life the arts have

---

On the other hand, there is no basis at all for P. Radin's claim, in his *Primitive Religion* (New York, 1937), that religion originated in a "religious formulator" comparable to a shaman (2d ed., 1957; 15–29). Despite the opposition between Radin's reduction of religion to discovery by an individual and Durkheim's and Lévy-Bruhl's conception of it as having a collective origin, the thought of all three is fundamentally the same. As Radin puts it, "man postulated the supernatural" (15; see 6). But this assertion is itself a mere assumption. Before human beings can "postulate" anything, they must themselves be first constituted subjects. But the constitution of the human being as a subject, as well as the constitution of the social group as a collective unit, seems from the beginning to have been the work of religion.

[235]P. Tillich, *Religionsphilosophie* (1925; repr. 1962), 61ff. See J. L. Adams, *Paul Tillich's Philosophy of Culture, Science, and Religion* (New York, 1970), esp. 77–85, and G. Wenz, *Subjekt und Sein. Die Entwicklung der Theologie Paul Tillichs* (1979), 13ff.

been deprived of their religious context. Their practice has been left to individual "artistic personalities" and to the agencies that market their products; all of these may arbitrarily declare a given representational activity to be art. A society, however, that understood itself to manifest the divine will to justice, that is, a Trinitarian self-commitment of divine omnipotence to justice,[236] would also be capable of developing a life-style that transcends while at the same time incorporates pragmatic needs.

Such a life-style would permeate all institutional forms and, far from stifling the creativity that manifests itself in individual variants, would truly inspire these. In a world marked by an indifferentist pluralism, on the other hand, fundamental cultural models and the impulse that leads to variants of them have become unintelligible, and their cultivation has suffered the fate of isolation, devitalization, and barbarization.

A word, finally, on the economy. The period when this was allowed to run rampant without hindrance is in any case long since past and has been followed by more or less successful efforts to channel economic activity within restrictions set by the state on competition in this area. In a theonomous culture even the economy with its competitiveness could once again be incorporated into a model of culture seen as representational play.[237]

---

[236]See the interesting observations of Koslowski (n. 126, above), 101–8, on the idea of the Trinitarian monarchy in Gregory of Nazianzus (*Or. theol.* III, 2 = PG 36:76) and its revival by L. G. A. de Bonald in 1796, as well as on the analogy, noted by H. Kelsen, between the doctrine of the Trinity and the idea of the state obliging itself to act justly (105ff.)—an analogy that Kelsen himself, however, felt obliged to reject (see, farther on, 116f.).

[237]According to F. A. von Hayek, the activity of the market is comparable to a game, and the economic activity of individuals to a "contest according to rules, which will be decided by superior ability, but also by luck": *Drei Vorlesungen über Demokratie, Gerechtigkeit und Sozialismus* (1977), 27. The end result of the game, however, does not automatically satisfy the requirement of a just distribution of goods (24). The economic contest therefore needs to be played within the framework of justly ordered human relations. On the problem of distribution as a limitation on the market, see Koslowski, 280ff.; on the questions it raises for the relation between the economy and religion, 301–6.

9

Human Beings
and History

Human life, whether it is the life span of the individual or the larger story of peoples and states, takes concrete form in history. When compared with this concreteness, the approaches taken in human biology, sociology, and psychology show themselves to be only abstract approximations to human reality. History is the *principium individuationis* ("principle of individuation") in the life both of individuals and of peoples and cultures. It is true, of course, that a historical account is still selective and therefore fails to convey the full richness of concrete life. Nonetheless, of all the disciplines that have the human being for their subject, the science of history and historiography come closest to grasping human reality as it is experienced.

Can history be considered part of the shared world in which individuals live their lives? Does it not have to do, rather, with the coming into being and passing away of this shared world, and do these processes not take place despite all the efforts that human beings make to preserve the order of their world against its slow erosion by time and against the sudden vicissitudes of fate?

On the other hand, does history not take two forms: the history of individuals and the history of peoples and states? But the history of individuals is interwoven with that of the world in which they live, and conversely the history of institutions and communities shows that these do not exist independently of their members but are determined by the experiences and activities of individuals. Institutions, communities, and individuals alike have real existence only in the history of their coming into existence and their passing away. What takes place in history is not simply a process of individuation but also an integration of individuals into the shared world of groups. And this integration takes place not least as a result of conflicts among individuals that call for solutions reached conjointly. It is through common interests, exchanges, and conflicts that even peoples and states are drawn into the process of a single all-embracing history.

Because of its ecumenical character, this history, being the history of a human community that has not yet taken shape in an order of life, has to be understood as the history of the human race. Precisely because it forms an all-embracing web into which everything is dynamically woven, the process of history transcends the shared world of each particular community and culture. In this it resembles, on the one hand, the world religions with their universalist thrust and, on the other, the impulse to domination that characterizes empires with their insatiable thirst for more. The universality of history marks human life itself and is inseparable from the coming into existence and passing away of this life. As a result, history belongs to the shared world of human beings, despite the fact that historical processes repeatedly dissolve, transform, and destroy the order of the shared human world.

The course of history is thus comparable to the exocentricity of human beings, since this too constantly moves beyond all that is at hand and given. The exocentric movement of human life, however, reaches out for a comprehensive fulfillment, whereas the response given by history—at least by history thus far, which alone can be the object of historiography —remains ambivalent with its successes and failures, its rises and falls, its preservation of the past and its judgments upon it. The fulfillment that is the goal of human beings in history transcends the limits of every historical present and rejects this present, for while the present too may seem to show a likeness to an everlasting order of things, it deserves, from another viewpoint, to pass away.

If history is thus the element, as it were, in which human beings live their concrete lives, it would seem natural to thematize history as the sphere in which the order of the shared cultural world and all the anthropological approaches hitherto discussed are seen in a new light. History and the philosophy of history would then serve to make possible a concluding and summarizing presentation of human reality: history as a description of the shaping of the human being that has already been accomplished, and the philosophy of history as providing a perspective on the still open future of humanity.

But the unfinished character of the historical process challenges the claim of either the philosopher of history or the historian to grasp the whole of human reality. In addition, a historical exposition too has its anthropological presuppositions, and although the relation of these to concrete history is by no means unproblematic, they nonetheless do embrace human nature in its totality, even if in the abstract form of universality; a concrete exposition of history, on the other hand, is incapable of grasping that totality. A distinction must therefore be made between anthropology and the historical description of human beings and the world they live in. Consequently, the following remarks will be limited to a reflection on the relation between anthropology and history, and no attempt will be made to present human reality in its concrete historical development.

I. Historicity and Human Nature

1. The Modern State of the Problem

As the concept of anthropology developed in the modern age, this discipline was repeatedly contrasted with the understanding of human beings that is gained from their history. Anthropology, it was said, deals with the universal and always valid structures of humanness, with human "nature," whereas the philosophy of history focuses not on the always identical nature of human beings but precisely on the process whereby they attain to their "destiny."[1] Ever since the development of a "natural system" of human sciences[2] in the seventeenth century, the focus on the universal "nature" of the human being has been accompanied by an indifference to the Christian understanding (itself an object of confessional dispute) of human beings and their destiny. On the other hand, when Herder and Hegel set the philosophy of history on a new basis, they pointed out that the understanding of the human person as subject originated in Christianity.

The focus on the philosophy of history was ambivalent, however, inasmuch as this philosophy made providence responsible for the unity of history, while at the same time it presupposed human beings to be the active subjects of history. Even Hegel's philosophy of history shows this ambiguity, since it defines history as the active self-fulfillment of the spirit. Spirit, in this context, is hardly the absolute spirit; it is, rather, the spirit as it lives in a people and impels them to liberate themselves,[3] although,

---

[1]This contrast is developed especially in O. Marquard, "Anthropologie," *HWP* 1 (1971), 362–74, esp. 368ff., and in his "Zur Geschichte des Begriffs Anthropologie seit dem 18. Jahrhundert" (1965), reprinted in his *Schwierigkeiten mit der Geschichtsphilosophie* (1973), 122–44. Of interest is the ambivalent attitude that Marquard sees Kant adopting in this matter; despite his conversion to anthropology, he gives priority (according to Marquard) to the philosophy of history and its question about human destiny as ultimate goal of freedom —in "its provisional and abstract form, which is ethics, but also in its boldly concrete form, which is the philosophy of a 'universal history from a cosmopolitan point of view' " (128).

[2]W. Dilthey, "Das natürliche System der Geisteswissenschaften," in *Gesammelte Schriften* II (1914), 90–245. See ibid., 246ff., and the evidence, 439–52, for the acceptance of Stoic ideas in this process.

[3]G. W. F. Hegel, *Encyclopädie der philosophischen Wissenschaften* (3d ed., 1830), § 549. Hegel there describes the "movement" of world history as "the path of liberation for the spiritual substance, the deed by which the absolute final aim of the world is realized in it, and the merely implicit mind achieves consciousness and self-consciousness. It is thus the revelation and actuality of its essential and completed essence, whereby it becomes to the outward eye a universal spirit—a world-mind." Although the "deed" of history is linked

according to Hegel, their freedom can be won only through consciousness of unity with the absolute spirit.[4]

It is this lack of clarity in the foundations of the idealist philosophy of history, rather than any disillusionment about the actual course of history,[5] that explains why in the period after Hegel the philosophy of history again took a general anthropology as its basis. This was the case with Feuerbach and even Marx,[6] with Nietzsche and even the early Dilthey. In his critique of historical reason Dilthey originally aimed at reducing the manifold of history to its anthropological presuppositions and conditions. In the words of O. Marquard, this program led to a "destruction of the philosophy of history," since, according to Dilthey (before his shift to hermeneutics), history teaches us that "human nature" is "always the same."[7] The young Dilthey intended therefore to apply a general psychology and in this way explain the structures of human experience and action that underlie historical phenomena.

Though their ultimate intentions differed from those of Dilthey, Heidegger in his analysis of Dasein (in *Being and Time*) and, following him, Bultmann and his school in their theology of existence all reduced concrete history to the "possibilities" of the Dasein and its self-understanding that find expression in this history; it is these possibilities in turn which are the basis of the historicity of the Dasein.

Reserve toward the philosophy of history and its answering of the question of human nature by an appeal to history emerges even more decisively (because it is now part of the program and not simply a result) in "philosophical anthropology" from Scheler and Plessner to Gehlen. The same is true of structuralism. On the other hand, such a problem did not even exist for the physicalist anthropology of behaviorism. Whenever

---

here to "the absolute final aim of the world," the preceding and following sections of the *Encyclopädie* deal with the spirit or self-consciousness of a "particular nation" as "vehicle" for the "liberation of mind, in which it proceeds to come to itself and to realize its truth" (§ 550). [The passage is here cited from *Hegel: Selections*, ed. J. Loewenberg (New York, 1920), 262 and 267.]

[4]Thus Hegel in the additions to § 552 in the third edition of the *Encyclopädie;* see also *Vorlesungen über die Geschichte der Philosophie* I (ed. Hoffmeister; PhB 166), 245f., and *Philosophie der Geschichte* (ed. Brunståd, 1961), 459 and 101.

[5]This last is given by Marquard, 1973 (see n. 1, above), as the reason for the rejection of the philosophy of history, both in the period around 1800 and in our own day (128f., 135).

[6]Though Marquard, 1971 (see n. 1, above), 370, puts Marx on the side of the philosophy of history as against anthropology, there are good reasons for describing the materialistic conception of history as a naturalistic reduction of history, as M. Theunissen does in his debate with the critical theory of the Frankfurt School; see his *Gesellschaft und Geschichte. Zur Kritik der kritischen Theorie* (1969), 13f., 23f.

[7]Dilthey, *Gesammelte Schriften* VIII, 79. Marquard (1973, 132) takes this statement as evidence for his thesis that Dilthey "destroyed" the philosophy of history.

a universal, essential human nature, remaining the same at all periods, is taken as the starting point for systematic thought, history can play only a secondary role in knowledge of the human. It provides simply a collection of variants on this universal and essential nature and thus supplies material for cultural anthropology, which now exercises the function formerly assigned to the philosophy of history. Marquard can therefore say: "A turning to the philosophy of history must mean a turning away from anthropology, and a turning to anthropology must mean a turning away from the philosophy of history"; "A rejection of anthropology is even today part of any theory of human destiny based on the philosophy of history."[8]

Marquard is able to interpret even the development of the historical sense in the nineteenth century as an expression of a turn from the philosophy of history to anthropology.[9] And in fact the young Dilthey was not alone in considering a universal and immutable human nature as a necessary presupposition for understanding and assessing the multiplicity of its historical manifestations. Even present-day practitioners of historical science demand an anthropological basis for historical knowledge, which has for its purpose to bring to light a "fundamental human substance" that escapes all historical change.[10]

At the same time, however, even though Jacob Burckhardt spoke of "man, suffering, striving, doing, as he is and was and ever shall be" as being "the one point accessible to us, the one eternal center of all things," he nonetheless emphasized the mutability of the human world as compared with the world of nature: "The essence of history is change."[11] And while the question of the anthropological bases for the knowledge and presentation of history is indispensable, we must also realize that "even anthropological structures are historically mutable."[12] This holds for both the psychological structures of individual behavior and the social struc-

---

[8]Marquard, 1973, 134.

[9]Ibid., 115; see 81: Historical meaning as "toning down the philosophy of history to history."

[10]Thus K.-G. Faber, *Theorie der Geschichtswissenschaft* (1971), 209; see 210ff. Critical response in *Philosophische Rundschau* 21 (1975), 33f. G. J. Renier, *History: Its Purpose and Method* (London, 1950; Macon, Ga., 1983), 189ff., devoted a section to the question, "Does human nature change?" and concluded with H. Pirenne, against R. G. Collingwood, that at least in practice historians take it for granted "that human nature in the past was what it is now" (192).

[11]J. Burckhardt, *Reflections on History*. trans. M. D. Hottinger (London and New York, 1943; new ed., Indianapolis, 1979), 34 and 57. See the observations, based on Burckhardt, of Th. Schieder, *Geschichte als Wissenschaft* (1965), 96ff. and 99f., where, however—and probably not by accident—only the first of these two statements of Burckhardt is cited.

[12]Th. Nipperdey, "Die anthropologische Dimension der Geschichtswissenschaft," in G. Schulz, ed., *Geschichte heute—Positionen. Tendenzen. Probleme* (1973), 225–55 at 227.

tures of human communal life. The two kinds of structure are only "relatively constant,"[13] although the constancy is significant enough in comparison with the much greater mutability of historical situations and conditions.

The reason for the mutability is doubtless to be found in the exocentricity that enables human beings to distance themselves from the immediately given.[14] The result is the specifically human relationship between individuals and community, in which individuals exert an influence on the organization of social life, as Burckhardt pointed out in his day.[15] It is also true, of course, that changes originating in individuals become significant and effective only in the medium of the shared world and its institutions.[16] This fact too becomes intelligible in the light of exocentricity as the fundamental form of human behavior. Human beings find their center outside themselves in the shared world and its order, although only to the extent that these become for them the place where the divine reality is present.

The religious meaning of the social order and its presupposed correspondence to the cosmic order explain why throughout lengthy periods of human history any changes in the social order were contained within narrow bounds and, above all, why changes in this order could not be regarded as valuable in themselves. "For the greatest part of their history human beings dedicated themselves to permanence; only five thousand

[13]Ibid., 232. For the psychological side, see the important book, mentioned by Nipperdey, of J. H. Van den Berg, *Metabletica. Über die Wandlung des Menschen. Grundlinien einer historischen Psychologie* (1960).

[14]K.-G. Faber, "Objektivität in der Geschichtswissenschaft?" in J. Rüsen, ed., *Historische Objektivität* (1975), 9–32 at 28, is therefore wrong to oppose human exocentricity as an anthropological constant to historicity (see also Rüsen's criticism, ibid., 91). In fact, historicity has its anthropological roots in "the capacity of human beings to distance themselves from their situation" (Faber, 28).

[15]Burckhardt (n. 11, above), 57. E. H. Carr, on the other hand, in his *What Is History?* (New York, 1962), has not paid any special attention to this fact in his observations on the historical relation between society and individual (36ff.). Similarly, R. Wittram, *Anspruch und Fragwürdigkeit in der Geschichte* (1969), 66f., follows Carr and does not go into this point but limits himself to emphasizing the irreducibility of the individual in relation to the social.

[16]This point is rightly emphasized by A. Heuss, "Zum Problem einer geschichtlichen Anthropologie," in H. G. Gadamer and P. Vogler, eds., *Kulturanthropologie. Neue Anthropologie 4* (1973), 150–94 at 178ff., esp. 182f., 185f. Heuss is here thinking primarily of the political order as the medium for changes that emanate from individuals. But, as his rather unpersuasive critique of A. Gehlen shows (156), he underestimates the importance of religion for the justification of institutions in archaic societies. For in those societies "ritual" is by no means simply "one institution among many," as it is in modern secular society. In consequence, Heuss does not do justice to the role of religion in the stability of those societies, or to the significance of changes in religious consciousness for the increasing mutability of social institutions.

years ago did they abandon the rule according to which they had lived for hundreds of thousands of years."[17]

Yet the rise of the high cultures did not bring any radically new attitude to historical change, even though the transition to high culture and its imperialist expansion, as well as the previous neolithic "revolution" with its shift to the domestication of animals and plants and to a sedentary way of life, look to us like revolutionary changes. In the consciousness of their members the "cosmological empires" of the early high cultures were still strongly committed to a cosmological justification for the social order, which was traced back to a primordial mythical time. Only when the experience of actual change penetrated the religious consciousness and when the divinity itself came to be thought of as the origin of changes in the social order and therefore as less closely associated with the form this order took at any given time, was the way prepared for the approval of change as such and for a consciousness of historicity.

Heidegger conceived of the historicality or historicity of human beings as a constant of their existential structure and one that precedes any and all historical experience.[18] As a result, in his *Being and Time* he did not completely follow Dilthey in the latter's radical turn from an anthropological and psychological explanation of historical experience to hermeneutics.[19] He took this step only later on in his concept of a "history of being." The conception of historicity as an existential structure which alone makes history possible still followed Dilthey in the latter's early efforts to provide a psychological basis for historical experience; Dilthey conceived of this basis as being transcendental, like Heidegger's *Existenzialien* ("*existentialia*" in the Macquarrie-Robinson translation).

As a matter of fact, however, historicity itself is not independent of the experience of history. It develops only in the process of such experience and, like all other anthropological structures, is changeable. Thus, with the development of a historical consciousness, and as a repercussion of its penetration into the religious consciousness, human exocentricity has altered its meaning and become historicity. Historicity itself, in turn, has

[17]Heuss, 187.

[18]According to M. Heidegger, *Being and Time*. trans. J. Macquarrie and E. Robinson (New York, 1962), the Dasein can have a history, "because the Being of this entity is constituted by historicality" (434; German 382). For a critique of this thesis and on its adoption by R. Bultmann and F. Gogarten, see my remarks in "Redemptive Event and History" (1959), now in *Basic Questions in Theology* I, trans. G. H. Kehm (Philadelphia, 1970), 15ff., where I argue for an inversion of Heidegger's thesis and a dependence of human historicity on the experience of history.

[19]See B. Groethuysen's introduction to vol. VII of Dilthey's *Gesammelte Schriften*. pp. VIff. See also my remarks in *Theology and the Philosophy of Science*. trans. F. McDonagh (Philadelphia, 1976), 160ff.

changed its meaning on the journey leading from the Jewish and Christian conception of the human person, which has for its context a divinely effected human history, to the conception of the person as an autonomous subject of historical action.

2. The Development of Historicity

There is a great deal to be said for the assumption that the beginnings of historical consciousness were connected with the rise of a civic order more comprehensive than that of the chiefdoms.[20] It may be that in the period prior to the formation of states, human institutions, customs, and usages were already being traced back to a mythical primordial time. It seems nonetheless that the formation of a political order that unified the entire life of a society was what created a felt need for an identity persisting through the ages ever since the mythical beginnings.

In normal circumstances the periodically recurring ritual revitalization of the system of rule[21] may have been enough to counteract the wear and tear and pollution caused by the activities of everyday political life. In times of danger, however, or after a temporary hiatus in the political order it was evidently necessary that this order receive a particular assurance of its identity with its mythical origins despite all the vicissitudes of time. Thus the Sumerian King List,[22] which dates from about the end of the third millennium B.C., gives the history of the Sumerian city-states its place in the picture of a single royal rule that in the course of time has passed in succession to various cities. "One cosmos, it appears, can have only one imperial order, and the sin of coexistence must be atoned by posthumous integration into the one history whose goal has been demonstrated

---

[20]Thus G. Balandier, *Political Anthropology*. trans. M. M. Sheridan Smith (New York, 1970), 189. The assumption is consistent with E. Voegelin's basic idea that "the order of history emerges from the history of order": *Order and History* I (Baton Rouge, 1956), IX. According to Voegelin, the cosmological myth itself is linked to the advance in the organization of human communal life beyond the stage of clan organization (ibid., 14).

[21]We may recall the ancient Egyptian feast of Seth, the purpose of which was to revitalize the monarchy after a period equal to a human life span (see E. Otto, "Religionsgeschichte des Alten Orients," in *Handbuch der Orientalistik* I, 8, 1 [1964], 27), or the importance of the Pharaoh's enthronement as a "repetition and renewal of the creation of the world" (E. Otto, *Ägypten. Der Weg des Pharaonenreiches* [1953], 68), or the renewal of the monarchy at the Babylonian New Year Festival. According to E. Hornung, *Geschichte als Fest* (1966), 19, in the view of the ancient Egyptians history itself was a cultic event which the king celebrated by repeating such mythical actions as the crushing of enemies or the unification of the two kingdoms (see 26f., 29).

[22]*ANET* 265f. On the function of the Egyptian annals, which were much more heavily weighted toward the repetition of the typical tasks of the kings, see Hornung, 19ff.

through the success of the conqueror."[23] The Sumerian myth also speaks a number of times of Enlil, the storm-god, transferring royal rule from one city to another.[24]

These documents show that experience of historical change had already influenced the consciousness that people had of the divine activity. The main concern, however, was to resist the destructive powers of chaos and restore the original order of things or, in other words, to undo the fact of historical change. Thus the prophecy by Nefer-rohu (under King Sne-fru of the Fifth Dynasty) of the fall of the Old Kingdom was transmitted in the days of the early Middle Kingdom in order to foster a consciousness that the kingdom had remained identical through the interim period.[25] The account of the deeds of Queen Hatshepsut, which tells of her restoration of the order originally established by Re, the sun-god, had a similar function.[26] Other accounts of the deeds of ancient Eastern kings are likewise to be understood primarily as referring to the restoration and consolidation by these rulers of the divine order which they represented.

The fact is, nonetheless, that "the vicissitudes of social order in history, with their undercurrent of anxiety, will ultimately destroy the faith in cosmic order."[27] A transition can be seen in Hittite historiography where history becomes of interest for its own sake. This phenomenon was closely linked with the kings and their belief in their divine election.[28] Similar notions were also to be found elsewhere in the ancient East, wherever individuals achieved royal rank by other than the normal ways of transmission. Thus a stela tells how Thutmose IV (1409–1400), a prince of the second rank, learned in a dream at the foot of the great sphinx at Gizeh that he was chosen to be king.[29] Yet even these extraordinary ways to kingship always led ultimately to a renewal of the existing order of government, and the accounts of the divine initiative at work in these ways served to legitimate the irregularities that occurred at the succession. In the Hittite royal annals and comparable historical texts not only does the idea of election emerge more forcibly but, along with the continuing idea that the king is divinely guided, there is an interest in historical detail for its own sake.

[23]Voegelin, *Order and History* IV (Baton Rouge, 1974), 63, following Th. Jacobsen.
[24]See Th. Jacobsen, "Mesopotamia," in H. Frankfort et al., *The Intellectual Adventure of Ancient Man* (Chicago, 1946; rev. ed., 1977), 125ff., as well as H. Schmökel, *Das Land Sumer* (1956), 76ff.
[25]*ANET* 444–46.
[26]*ANET* 231a, and see Voegelin (n. 23, above), 69f.
[27]Voegelin, IV, 71.
[28]See H. Cancik, *Mythische und historische Wahrheit* (1970), 47, 65f.
[29]*ANET* 449. See also the nomination of Thutmose III by Re, ibid., 446f.

In Israel, belief in election was extended to include the people[30] and not simply the king or dynasty.[31] The peculiar position that this people occupied in the world of the nations was itself explained by their divine election.[32] The God of Israel was thus understood as the source of the people's history and at the same time as the mighty one who through his fidelity to his promises and his election ensures this history its unity and fulfillment. Consequently the understanding of God was no longer tied either to a cosmic order established in primordial time or to society, and the God of Israel became what was dimly anticipated in the storm-gods of Sumer and Hatti: the master of historical change and its dynamism, which was controlled by his plan.[33]

History itself, as the embodiment of the divine action,[34] was understood in Israel to be a goal-oriented process in the course of which human aims are constantly frustrated, whereas God through this very frustration pursues the goal he intends in his dealings with human beings. In this outlook we see the basis for the difference between the ancient Israelite understanding of history and that of Greek and Roman antiquity. The latter, too, broke the ties to an order established in the primordial time of myth and, even more radically than in Israel, organized its own political life with an eye on other peoples and their representatives.[35] On the other hand, in Greece and Rome the unity of the historical process could not be based on the unity of a God who elected human beings and guaranteed the

[30]Deut. 7:6; Isa. 41:8ff.; 1 Kings 3:8. On the various terminologies used to express the concept of election and on their development, see K. Koch, "Zur Geschichte der Erwählungsvorstellung in Israel," *Zeitschrift für die alttestamentliche Wissenschaft* 67 (1955), 205–256. For a comparison with Hittite thinking on history it is important to observe that in the latter "it was never 'the people' but always the king and the dynasty that were the vehicle (subject) of history" (Cancik, 70).

[31]1 Sam. 10:24; 16:1–13; 1 Kings 8:16 (see 2 Sam. 7:8–16).

[32]In this regard, the Sinai covenant plays a critical role in Israel's later understanding of itself: Ex. 19:5f.; Deut. 7:6ff.; 26:16ff. In comparison with the rest of the ancient Near East and especially the Sumerian King List, it is characteristic of Israelite thought that the Yahwist never traces the political order of the Israelite monarchy back directly to a model originating in the divine world, but presents it, rather, as the result of a history of election that begins with Abraham and in him marks a new beginning within the broad world of the peoples represented in the Table of Nations in Genesis 10. See G. von Rad, *Genesis. A Commentary*, trans. J. H. Marks (Philadelphia, 1972²), 139f.

[33]See, e.g., the remarks of K. Koch on Isaiah's theology of history in *Die Propheten* I (1978), 157ff., and especially 167f. on Isaiah's conception of the "plan" of Yahweh. See also 84ff. on Amos, and vol. II (1980), 77ff. on Jeremiah and 151ff. on Second Isaiah.

[34]On the Israelite conception of history as the embodiment of God's action or "work" *(ma'aśe)*, see Koch, *Die Propheten* I, 167f., and my remarks in *Grundfragen systematischer Theologie* II (1980), 194.

[35]Voegelin, *Order and History* IV, 104f. See 106: "Only the Hellenes have made neither an imperial society, nor the open society of all Hellenes, but ecumenic mankind the subject of history."

fulfillment of his own promises. Instead, the historical thinking of the Greek Herodotus was guided by the idea, found everywhere in the ancient world, of an inescapable connection between act and consequence. Anaximander had elevated this idea to the rank of the divine *archē* by linking it closely with his own idea of the infinite, from which things emerge and into which they pass away "according to necessity; for they give justice and make reparation to one another for their injustice, according to the arrangement of Time."[36]

The inevitable connection between act and consequence was not unknown to biblical thought about history,[37] but here it was subordinated to the action of the God who elects and is faithful to his choices. Greek historical thought, on the contrary, was confronted with pitiless Nemesis and could only cling to the idea that human beings are worth remembering as they reveal their wretchedness and their greatness in their rise and fall. Herein, in fact, is to be seen the universality peculiar to this historical thinking.[38] But in this approach human beings themselves were not thought of as history. This step was taken in the perspective opened up by the Jewish history of God as this was broadened to include others besides the Jews and thus became a history of humankind and of the human being as such.

3. The Christian Idea of Human Historicity

Christian missionaries took to heart the eschatological significance of Jesus Christ not only for the Jewish people, whose Messiah they proclaimed him to be, but also for every human being. This conviction led in early Christianity to the thesis that only in the story of Jesus do human beings find their true destiny and only in communion with him do they achieve it. Here a claim was being made that was felt to be paradoxical long before the modern age: the claim that a particular historical event had universal human validity. This claim and the Christological concern behind it led to the historicization of human self-understanding.

[36]Anaximander, frag. 1, trans. in K. Freeman, *Ancilla to the Pre-Socratic Philosophers* (Cambridge, Mass., 1961), 19. On the relation of Herodotus' history to this thought of Anaximander, see Voegelin II, 336–44, and IV, 105f.

[37]See K. Koch, "Is There a Doctrine of Retribution in the Old Testament?" trans. in J. L. Crenshaw, ed., *Theodicy in the Old Testament* (Philadelphia, 1983), 57–88, and G. von Rad, *Wisdom in Israel* (Nashville, 1972), 124–39.

[38]This is a universality of a different kind from that which found expression in the enterprise of founding universal empires, from the Persian Empire to the rise of Rome. Voegelin describes this period, whose historian was Polybius, as the "ecumenic age" (*Order and History* IV, 114–211) and thus sheds light on the vanity of the concupiscential urge to imperial expansion (208), while also emphasizing its connection with the rise of the universalist civilizations and religions (209f.).

Paul's interpretation of Jesus Christ as a new, second Adam played a fundamental role here: "The first man was from the earth, a man of dust; the second man is from heaven. . . . Just as we have borne the image of the man of dust, we shall also bear the image of the man of heaven" (1 Cor. 15:47, 49). If we are to appreciate the scope of these statements, we must keep in mind the mythical background of the biblical conception of the creation of Adam—and therefore of the human being as such—at the beginning of world history.

Mythical thought interpreted both the order of the human world and the setting in which human beings live their lives in the light of events that took place at the very beginning of time, when the gods gave the world its form and organization.[39] The mythical consciousness regarded those primordial events, which cult renders present so that those now alive may participate in that order of things, as possessing a higher reality. This kind of mythical basis was provided not least for human beings themselves and their place in the cosmos.

This is still the case in the biblical account of primeval history, even though the polytheistic traits in related ancient Near Eastern traditions were removed before use was made of these traditions. Thus Adam is both the first human being and the human being as such. His history is repeated in all human individuals and provides the key for explaining such peculiarities of human existence as need explaining: the power that human beings have over creatures (via knowledge of their names); the difference and solidarity of the sexes; the tribulations of work; the pains accompanying the birth of new life; the inevitability of death. The biblical stories of creation are indeed no longer myths in the proper sense, but rather etiological sagas. Nonetheless the form in which they are presented is clearly that of myth, since the basic characteristics of human life are shown to be based on happenings of the primordial time.

In Christian dogmatic teaching on the original state of the first human pair this outlook, rooted in mythical thinking, has continued to be influential right into the modern period.[40] A late, even if fully secularized, echo of that teaching on the original state may still be heard in Marxist notions of the original human society, which anteceded the fall into the division of labor, and in Nietzsche's idea that human beings originally enjoyed an animal-like health before being rendered psychically ill through the development of morality and conscience. All the more astonishing, then, is

[39]See the remarks of B. Malinowski, H. Preuss, M. Eliade, and others that are cited in my essay "Christentum und Mythos," in my *Grundfragen systematischer Theologie* II, 13–65.

[40]In my essay "Gottebenbildlichkeit als Bestimmung des Menschen in der neueren Theologiegeschichte," *Sitzungsberichte der Bayer. Akad. der Wissenschaften* (Phil.-Hist. Klasse), 1979, Heft 8, I have studied in greater detail the replacement of this view, since the late eighteenth century, by the interpretation of the divine image as the human destiny.

Paul's reorientation of the concept of the human person as he turns away from the past and looks to the future of a new human being.

The apostle's eschatological redirection of anthropology was in tension not only with the orientation of myth to primordial time but also with the philosophical thought of Greek antiquity. The philosophers identified as truly real not that which came at the very beginning but, rather, that which is everlasting and underlies the fleeting succession of phenomena. This characteristic of philosophical thought found its purest expression in Parmenides and in Plato's doctrine of the ideas. But it showed itself on a far broader scene, namely, wherever an effort was made to reduce phenomena to unchanging structures or laws, as has been done down even to the present time in the sciences. Now, whenever that which abides in and behind appearances was regarded as the true essence of these, the essential nature of the human person was also thought of as the same at all times and in all individuals.

As a result, philosophical thinking, focused as it was on what is universal and unchanging, may have differed in many other respects from mythical thinking, but it shared with the latter a reserve toward history. The mythical focus on primordial time gave human beings security against the uncertain historical future.[41] Historical changes were suppressed from consciousness because that which abided through change was projected back into primordial time and connected with the foundational events.[42] Human beings focused their gaze not on the future but on primordial time and turned their backs on the future.[43] But to the extent that it was shaped by the Parmenidean outlook the philosophical consciousness likewise distanced itself from the fact of historical change. It regarded historical changes as unimportant as long as it identified the essential with the abiding. Therefore, according to Aristotle, there can be no science of history.[44]

[41]In his book *The Myth of the Eternal Return,* trans. W. R. Trask (New York, 1954; Harper Torchbooks, 1959, with the title *Cosmos and History: The Myth of the Eternal Return*), M. Eliade speaks not only of an abolition of profane time by its projection into mythical time (35f., 85f.) but even of "archaic man's refusal to accept himself as a historical being" (85). In view of the development of historical consciousness in the early high cultures, this thesis is surely overstated. See my remarks in *Grundfragen systematischer Theologie* II, 191.

[42]For examples from the legal history and other traditions of ancient Israel, see my essay "Christentum und Mythos" (n. 39, above), 32f.

[43]See my *Grundfragen systematischer Theologie* II, 152f.

[44]In his *Poetics,* ch. 9 (1451b3ff.), Aristotle says that poetry is closer than history to philosophy because poetry is concerned more with the universal than with the particular. Augustine was the first to regard *historia* as *scientia* (*De Trin.* XIII, 1). On this, see L. Boehm, "Der wissenschaftstheoretische Ort der *historia* im früheren Mittelalter. Die Geschichte auf dem Weg zur Geschichtswissenschaft," in *Speculum Historiale (Festschrift für J. Spörl)* (1965), 663–93, esp. 686f.

On this point the Christian faith brought a very radical and momentous departure from both the mythical consciousness and ancient philosophy in the understanding of the human person. For Paul, apostle to the nations, the appearance of Christ meant that what had previously been regarded as humanity was now replaced by a radically new kind of humanity. The first Adam was confronted in Jesus—and definitively so in the resurrection of Jesus[45]—by a new and final form of human being whose "image" we all bear, that is, to whom we are all to be conformed (Rom. 8:29).

This new Adam is no longer simply a living being and, as such, subject to death; rather, his life is permeated by the source of all life and is therefore immortal. He is therefore a life-giving spirit (1 Cor. 15:45ff.). In this context, what is first and original is no longer to be regarded as the highest.[46] In Paul's view, the first human being was created earthly and mortal, the second and final human being, on the other hand, heavenly and immortal—as he has emerged in the resurrection of Jesus. According to Paul, therefore, only Jesus Christ, the eschatological human being, is that image of God (2 Cor. 4:4) of which the first of the two biblical creation stories speaks (Gen. 1:27).

At the same time, however, we still find Paul following the traditional view, namely, that in accordance with Gen. 1:27 the image of God is at every point already a feature of the human being, and especially of the

[45] 1 Cor. 15:42ff. Only later, in the letter to the Romans, does Paul also apply his interpretation of Jesus Christ as the new and eschatological Adam to the earthly life of Jesus and relate it to the obedience of Jesus to his Father. See U. Wilckens, *Der Brief an die Römer* (Evang.-kath. Kommentar zum Neuen Testament VI/1; 1978), 307ff., esp. 312ff.

[46] In the background here is the problem of how to interpret the double account of the creation of human beings in Genesis. The first or Priestly account speaks of the creation of human beings in the image of God (Gen. 1:27); the older or Yahwist account speaks of the making of the human form from the dust of the ground (Gen. 2:7). Jewish interpreters distinguished two separate acts of creation. Thus Philo distinguished between the heavenly human being of Genesis 1 and the earthly human being of Genesis 2. See E. Brandenburger, *Adam und Christus. Exegetisch-religionsgeschichtliche Untersuchung zu Röm. 5, 12–21 (1 Kor. 15)* (1962), 77–131.

U. Wilckens regards it as probable that at Corinth (and perhaps elsewhere in primitive Hellenistic Christianity) the exalted Christ was identified with the heavenly primal man of Genesis 1. Paul, on the other hand (says Wilckens), explained that this earthly human being of Genesis 2 is the "first" human being (1 Cor. 15:45, 47) and thus separated the eschatological character of the risen Christ as the last human being from any basis in protology; see U. Wilckens, "Christus, der 'letzte Adam,' und der Menschensohn," in R. Pesch and R. Schnackenburg, eds., *Jesus und der Menschensohn. Festschrift für A. Vögtle* (1975), 387–403. But does not the Pauline description of Christ as the image of God (2 Cor. 4:4) imply an identification with the primal human being of Gen. 1:26f.? That is why his appearance *in time* could be thought of as that of the "last man." In this way, too, it becomes easier to understand what is said about the mission of the Son in the later Pauline letters (Gal. 4:4; Rom. 8:3), as well as the acceptance of statements about preexistence in such early Christian hymns as Phil. 2:6ff.

male (1 Cor. 11:7). The early Christian theologians reduced the tension between these two approaches by conceiving Christ as the prototype in view of which the first human being was created "in the image," that is, as a copy of this prototype. In order to explain the connection between that first human being and the new human being who has been manifested in Christ, these theologians maintained that only the visible appearance of this prototype itself in the incarnation could bring the image of God in us to its completion.[47]

In this kind of platonizing exegesis the historical once-for-all of the saving event, in which the eschatological destiny of the human person becomes present and operative, caused the concept of human nature to be, as it were, liquefied and remolded into that of a salvation history *(oeconomia)* which leads "to Jesus Christ, the new man." This conception, formulated by Ignatius of Antioch *(Ad Eph.* 20, 1), occupied in early Christian thinking the identical place that the concept of the human essence, or human "nature," had occupied in philosophy. Salvation history was not tacked on to the concept of the human being but, rather, replaced it. At the same time (as early as Irenaeus), the concept of the divine image, in which the first human being was created but which is brought to completion only by Jesus Christ, served as the clamp that held the beginning and the end of this process together in the unity of a single history of the human race. In this way the theologians avoided the danger to which the Christian gnostics succumbed: the error of a dualistic separation between the first Adam and the second, the earthly man and the heavenly,[48] and, ultimately, the God who creates and the God who redeems.

The Christian view of the human race as a history that runs from the first Adam to the new and final Adam replaced the philosophical concept of an essential human nature that is independent of time with a concept of the human being as historical or, rather, as caught up in the movement of that concrete history. The situation with which we are dealing here is better described in that way than by speaking of a "supernatural" destiny and completion to which human beings are ordered.[49]

The latter way of speaking does admittedly bring out in its own way the historical character of the human being as in movement from the first Adam to the second. But it is also burdened with difficulties, since an "essential nature" understood according to the philosophical concept of *physis* is incapable of any supernatural completion. Conversely, a "nature" that is ordered to a supernatural fulfillment no longer corresponds to the

---

[47]Irenaeus, *Adv. haer.* V, 16, 1f.

[48]H. Langerbeck, *Aufsätze zur Gnosis,* ed. H. Dörries (1967), 56.

[49]As in Thomas Aquinas, *Summa theologiae* I-II, q. 109, a. 5 *(finis excedens proportionem humanae naturae,* "an end beyond the powers of human nature to attain").

concept of nature in classical Greek philosophy. In fact, it resembles, rather, the assumption that human existence is subject to natural conditions which provide the starting position for a concrete history that will decide, one way or another, what the nature of the human being is. Given that there is a possible, still unrealized fulfillment (the possibility of which, however, is knowable only in retrospect once the possibility is realized), such a starting position is characterized by a certain openness that looks beyond what is already at hand. When viewed from the vantage point of the future fulfillment, this openness proves to be an openness precisely to that kind of fulfillment. But when looked at from the vantage point of the starting position itself, the content of that future destiny is not yet determined and guaranteed.

The historical uniqueness of the saving event thus calls for a conception of human history as starting with a state of pure openness which, however, in the light of its future fulfillment can be understood precisely as a destination to that fulfillment. In the history of Christian anthropology, however, the picture was distorted by the doctrine of the original state and its idea of Adam as having been originally perfect. Here the introduction of a mythological orientation to a primordial time blurred the conception of humans as historical beings. The situation was not much improved when the beginning and the end of history were linked in the Neoplatonic schema of *exitus* and *reditus* ("departure" and "return").[50] Such a correspondence between time of origin and end time is itself mythological rather than historical in character.

The historical dimension in the Christian conception of the human person did not emerge fully until the doctrine of the original state was dismantled. This dismantling itself became possible only in the context of modern views on the beginnings of humankind and as a result of the critical historical interpretation of the biblical primeval history. This new way of looking at the human person was presupposed in Herder's conception of the divine image as not ready-made in the beginning but needing to be completed. Since J. G. Eichhorn's historical study of the biblical primeval history[51] it has become increasingly prevalent in modern theology.[52]

---

[50]M. Seckler, *Das Heil in der Geschichte. Geschichtstheologisches Denken bei Thomas von Aquin* (1964), shows the importance of this idea in the anthropology of Thomas Aquinas.

[51]J. G. Eichhorn's study, which appeared first in 1779, was reedited by J. Ph. Gabler in two volumes with notes, from 1790 to 1793.

[52]In his *Dogmatik*, which first appeared in 1814, K. G. Bretschneider explicitly rejected the doctrine of the original state and spoke of human beings as created in the image of God in the sense that this image as realized in Jesus Christ is the "destiny" of human beings: *Handbuch der Dogmatik des ev.-luth. Kirche* (Leipzig, 1828³) I, 748; see 752 and 754, as well as II, 77.

Herder understood the natural conditions of human existence in the way I described just above; moreover, he understood the resultant "natural" starting point of human history to be one of openness to a destiny not yet achieved. To that extent, he rendered possible and prepared the way for a reformulation, in the context of modern thought, of those tentative early Christian interpretations of the human being as a history. On the other hand, Herder left Christology out of the picture. He has nothing corresponding to the idea, found in Paul and, following him, in the early Christian recapitulation theory of Irenaeus, that human nature attains to its fulfillment only in Jesus Christ and in the communion with God which he brings about.[53]

As a result, the relation between anthropology and the philosophy of history remains ambivalent in Herder. Anthropology is indeed conceived as being the basis for the philosophy of history, especially in the *Outlines of a Philosophy of the History of Man,* from Herder's late period. But in the process the philosophy of history is based entirely on general anthropology, with history being the development of those dispositions which make up human nature. In addition, human beings find their fulfillment not in history but only beyond it in a state of immortality.

In a more decisive way than Herder, Hegel attempted, by accepting the idea of the incarnation, to integrate general anthropology into the historical process. Nonetheless even Hegel's philosophy of history remained ambiguous on this point, for, on the one hand, the concept of the human being is realized only through its history but, on the other, this history is itself only the unfolding of what is already contained in the concept of the human being as such. The logical apriorism of the concept renders dubious not only Hegel's interpretation of Christianity but also his intended sublimation of anthropology into a philosophy of history. The

[53]Schleiermacher, on the other hand, did express this idea when he described the institution by Jesus Christ of a new "corporate life," a new society no longer corrupted by sin, as "the completion, only now accomplished, of the creation of human nature": *The Christian Faith.* ed. and trans. H. R. Mackintosh and J. S. Stewart (Edinburgh, 1928; Philadelphia, 1976), § 89, title. But Schleiermacher voiced this idea only in a book on faith and as the expression of the subjective Christian belief in redemption. That the idea implies, however, a philosophy of history becomes clear if we attend to the link with Kant's ideas on the founding of an ethical commonwealth as a people of God under ethical laws (see I. Kant, *Religion Within the Limits of Reason Alone.* trans. T. M. Greene and H. H. Hudson [Chicago, 1934], 88ff.) and, in addition, to the material analogy with Marxist belief in the possibility of the establishment, through a revolution, of a new society that has been purified of sinful class rule. All these conceptions show a remarkable structural similarity, despite the no less notable difference that in Kant and Schleiermacher (who place their emphases differently) this new humanity is to emerge from a morality mediated by religion, whereas in Marxism it is to emerge from the dialectic of the history of the human species itself, with the assistance of the dictatorship of the proletariat.

two results may in fact be closely connected.

In the post-Hegelian history of the problem the same ambiguity manifests itself in Dilthey in the tension between the once-onlyness and particularity of history and Dilthey's effort to base the knowledge of history on a general psychology. The problem appears in its most radical conceptual form in the question of the subject of history, a question that is in turn closely connected with the question of the relation between history and human action. Are human beings merely the objects with which history deals, or are they also the subjects who by their action attain to fulfillment via the historical process? This is the ambiguity that clings to the modern concept of historicity when it connects historicity with the "possibilities" of the Dasein.[54]

The modern historical consciousness has declared its independence from its Christian origins. As a result, the historicity of the human being has had to be explained in terms of an anthropological basis that antecedes history. But this still leaves unanswered the question of how the identity of the subject itself is related to the subject's history. History is indeed made up largely of human actions, but by what means are the acting subjects themselves constituted? Are they constituted as subjects prior to history, or does the development of subjectivity itself take the form of a history? The response to this question is decisive for determining the relation between anthropology and history.

II. History as a Process of Subject Formation

When Herodotus inaugurated the historiography of classical antiquity he took for his object the deeds and works of human beings, with the intention of preserving these from oblivion.[55] Augustine, on the other hand, while admitting that historical narrative does also deal with the creations *(instituta)* of human beings, emphasized the point that history itself *(ipsa historia)* is not to be accounted a human creation, since God is author and governor of the order of time.[56] The temporal order, which

---

[54]Heidegger, *Being and Time.* 434ff. (German 382ff.), does not immediately connect the viewpoint of potentiality with the concept of action (see, however, 373f.; German 326), but he does connect it with "resoluteness" (434ff.; German 383ff.) and speaks of the "factical existentiell *choice* of Dasein's historicality" (447; German 395), so that the practical bearing of his analysis of the concept is unmistakable. In all of this he expressly presupposes that the human Dasein is the primary "subject" of history (433; German 382).

[55]Thus Herodotus in the Introduction to his *History.* On this, see Chr. Meier, "Die Entstehung der Historie," in R. Koselleck and W. D. Stempel, eds., *Geschichte—Ereignis und Erzählung.* Poetik und Hermeneutik 5 (Munich, 1973), 251–305, esp. 258ff.

[56]Augustine, *De doctrina christiana* II, 28, 44: "Although historical accounts tell of institutions established by human beings in the past, history itself is not to be regarded as a human institution. For since events cannot be undone, they belong to the order of time whose

is established by divine providence and which according to Augustine is "the essential point" of the Christian religion,[57] thus became the real object of historical knowledge, and as a result the latter in turn became "a means of reaching objective truth."[58]

Only in the humanist period did a new understanding of history begin that would ultimately shatter the Augustinian framework. As early as Petrarch the human person was viewed as "the subject of history," so that historical reality "was conceived according to categories proper to human action."[59] On the other hand, for Vico this new viewpoint did not exclude the Augustinian idea of providence. He did indeed base the knowability of the historical world on the principle that "man makes history,"[60] but he nonetheless retained the idea of divine providence as the basis for the unity of the course of history, since "an orderly historical development is the result of human actions but not of human intentions."[61] Only from Voltaire and Condorcet on has divine providence been replaced by the human foresight that guides the progress of civilization.[62]

In the historical thinking of our day providence has disappeared, but there is also doubt about progress. What is left is "the concept of action as basic to a historical anthropology."[63] True enough, human actions certainly belong to the stuff of history. But are they whole stuff? Back in 1958, Bultmann made the point, against R. G. Collingwood, that along

---

creator and administrator is God." See Boehm (n. 44, above), 669–93, esp. 684f. Also E. Kessler, "Das rhetorische Modell der Historiographie," in R. Koselleck, H. Lutz, and J. Rüsen, eds., *Formen der Geschichtsschreibung* (1982), 37ff. and 59: "History became a divine institution, in the realization of which human beings play an instrumental role but the subject of which is divine *providentia.*"

[57]Augustine, *De vera religione* I, 7, 13: "In this religion the essential point to be admitted is history and the prophecy of the way in which divine providence accomplishes the salvation of the human race within time by restoring and renewing it for eternal life." See I, 26 and 27, as well as *De civ. Dei* X, 32, 3, and XVIII, 40, and see my remarks in "Erfordert die Einheit der Geschichte ein Subjekt?" in Koselleck and Stempel (n. 55, above), 478–90 at 487.

[58]Kessler (n. 56, above), 59.

[59]Ibid., 67, and see 73f.

[60]G. Vico, *La sciencia nuova seconda.* ed. E. Auerbach (Munich, 1924), 125.

[61]F. Fellmann, *Das Vico-Axiom: Der Mensch macht die Geschichte* (Munich, 1976), 125, n. 21. In other remarks (19ff.), however, Fellmann comes close to the antitheological interpretation which K. Löwith rejects in his *Meaning in History: The Theological Implications of the Philosophy of History* (Chicago, 1949), "as though Vico had intended to say that the civilized world of man is nothing else than the product of his spontaneous creativity" (121). Löwith here appeals to B. Croce, *The Philosophy of G. Vico.* trans. R. G. Collingwood (New York, 1913).

[62]Löwith, 104; see 91ff.

[63]Heuss (n. 16, above), 196, and see earlier, 173ff. See also L. Landgrebe, "Das philosophische Problem des Endes der Geschichte," in his *Phänomenologie und Geschichte* (1968), 182ff., esp. 200.

with actions the "events that encounter one" are also part of history.[64] Since then W. Kamlah has called attention to the reciprocal ties between actions and things experienced; in the interplay of partners, for example, "the actions of one are things experienced by the other."[65] But Kamlah also gives examples showing that the class of things experienced includes more than just the actions of others: since the concept of "events that encounter one" relates to humans as needy (and vulnerable) beings, it also includes technological disruptions and natural occurrences such as birth and death. It is not the category of human actions but only the more inclusive category of things experienced (which includes actions) that is coextensive with the category of historical events, for we "do not speak of 'events' when something happens that is not a 'thing experienced' by someone."[66]

History is not made up, therefore, solely of human actions. For this reason, it is antecedently unlikely that actions could explain the connection and continuity in the course of historical events. As a matter of fact, we grasp the continuity in a series of events, not by thinking of it as a series of actions linking means to ends, but by remembering[67] our own and others' actions and the "events that encounter us." Actions and the human plans and intentions behind them cannot render the course of history intelligible, because human beings thwart one another's plans and intentions. For this reason and also because actions have unintended side effects, the course of events usually produces something other than what the active participants intended.[68] For this reason, traditional reflection on history, which on this point was still shared by Vico, ascribed the actual course of events to a superhuman agency, namely, the divine providence that directs history.[69]

Only if the antagonistic goals and actions of individuals were ultimately

---

[64]R. Bultmann, *History and Eschatology: The Presence of Eternity* (New York, 1957; Harper Torchbooks, 1962), 136f.; see 130f.

[65]W. Kamlah, *Philosophische Anthropologie. Sprachliche Grundlegung und Ethik* (1973), 37. H. Lübbe makes use of this example in his reflections on the role of the concept of action in a theory of history: *Geschichtsbegriff und Geschichtsinteresse. Analytik und Pragmatik der Historie* (1977), 59.

[66]Kamlah, 35.

[67]Thus H. M. Baumgartner, *Kontinuität und Geschichte. Zur Kritik und Methodik der historischen Vernunft* (1972), in his discussion of Landgrebe (202–16, esp. 211).

[68]Lübbe (n. 65, above) uses this fact in order to delimit what is specifically historical: "Histories are processes that do not adapt themselves to the rationales of the acting participants. They do not follow a rational plan of action" (55; see 38f., 82, 275).

[69]The early Israelite sapiential writers understood this: "The horse is made ready for the day of battle, but the victory belongs to the Lord" (Prov. 21:31); "Many are the plans in the mind of a man, but it is the purpose of the Lord that will be established" (19:21; see 16:9; 14:12; etc.)

to serve a common interest (as liberal economics assumed) or could be assimilated in a collective planning process (as socialism seeks to do), and if all the side effects of human action could be grasped in advance, could the course of history be controlled by human beings and guided in the direction of continuous progress in civilization. But hopes of this kind that were cultivated by an "enlightened" faith in progress seem unrealistic today. The conflict between individual and collective interests can be overcome in this or that instance but not in principle. Furthermore, every new advance is accompanied by unanticipated side effects. For this reason no rational planning of the course of history is possible. Therefore, too, the continuity that results from the sequence of events can be conceived as a manifestation of a divine activity but not as the result of human action. The divine subject which in the Christian theology of history guarantees the unity of history cannot be replaced by a human subject—not by hypostatized collective subjects[70] nor by the "collective singular" of history itself.[71]

The idea of a divine providence that not only conserves the world but also guides the course of history is admittedly so problematic to the modern mind that any return to it, at least in its traditional form, can hardly be expected. The problem of theodicy, which so occupied eighteenth-century thinkers,[72] is the least of these difficulties. The only reason why that problem attracted such disproportionate attention was that its Christian solution through faith in the reconciliation of the world with its creator through Jesus Christ had already been lost sight of for other reasons. A more serious factor today is the replacement of a divine conservation of the world by the self-conservation of material structures and of human beings.[73] It is likely too that the idea of self-conservation has also

---

[70]For a critique of the assumption that associations, institutions, nations, and even the human race are collective subjects capable of acting, see my remarks on the question, "Erfordert die Einheit der Geschichte ein Subjekt?" (n. 57, above), 478–90, esp. 479f. on the criticism of such notions by K. Marx and N. Hartmann. Lübbe, following F. Kambartel (ibid., 477f.) and even going beyond him, claims that the assumption of "institutional subjects of actions" causes "no difficulties"; see his *Geschichtsbegriff* (n. 65, above), 72. But actions can be attributed to states and other institutions as legal subjects only in an applied sense, namely, insofar as they have representatives who act in the name of the institution or collectivity.

[71]R. Koselleck coined this term in order to describe the modern hypostatization of "history" (singular) as an active subject; see his *"Historia Magistra Vitae. Über die Auflösung des Topos im Horizont neuzeitlich bewegter Geschichte"* (1967), reprinted in his *Vergangene Zukunft. Zur Semantik geschichtlicher Zeiten* (1979), 38–66, esp. 50ff., 53f.

[72]For O. Marquard it was this question that gave rise to the idealist philosophy of history; see his *Schwierigkeiten mit der Geschichtsphilosophie* (n. 1, above), 52ff., 66ff.

[73]See the essay of H. Blumenberg, "Selbsterhaltung und Beharrung," and of D. Henrich, "Die Grundstruktur der modernen Philosophie," in H. Ebeling, ed., *Subjektivität und Selbsterhaltung. Beiträge zur Diagnose der Moderne* (Frankfurt, 1976), 77ff., and 144ff.

become influential in modern thinking about history.[74]

But the really decisive cause at work in the rejection of a divine guidance of history is the motif of human freedom that is behind the substitution of self-conservation for conservation by an outside power. Freedom seems to be incompatible with the idea of a divine providence that completely determines the course of history in advance.[75] Moreover, an infallible foreknowledge would destroy not only human freedom but the entire contingency of historical events and thus the real nature of time and history, which is to be seen in the asymmetry between unchangeable past and open future.[76] For this reason, historical knowledge can only take the form of retrospective narration that begins with the state of affairs at a given moment and then reports the course of events that led to this outcome.

A historian narrates a sequence of events—for example, the prehistory of the Thirty Years War—as one who already knows the outcome and therefore adopts a perspective that is different in principle from that of any contemporary observer, no matter how well informed.[77] For historians know the outcome which at that time was still hidden in the womb of the future. But for the same reason, and because they are concerned only with the process that led to the outcome still hidden from contemporaries, they do not need to know and tell everything that happened at that period but only that which played a significant part in the end result of the historical process. Historical narrative is therefore always selective.[78] On the other hand, the events reported may also become factors in other stories,[79] especially since the location of historians themselves within history changes and history must therefore be repeatedly rewrit-

---

[74]Thus Henrich, 303ff.: "Selbsterhaltung und Geschichtlichkeit" (esp. 309ff.). See also G. Buck, "Selbsterhaltung und Historizität," in Koselleck and Stempel (n. 55, above), 29–94.

[75]The Christian Scholastics of the Middle Ages tried to solve this problem by explaining the eternity of God as a contemporaneity with all points in time. See the remarks in my *Die Prädestinationslehre des Duns Scotus* (1954), 24ff., 60ff., 67f., and K. Bannach, *Die Lehre von der doppelten Macht Gottes bei Wilhelm von Ockham* (1975), 200ff., 221ff. But is it still possible to speak of a foreknowledge in the sense of a knowledge that precedes in time that which is known?

[76]A. C. Danto, *Analytical Philosophy of History* (Cambridge, 1965), 199f.

[77]Danto, 170f. The example of the Thirty Years War as having its beginnings in the actions of Frederick, the Palatine Elector, is given ibid., 182f. In connection with Aristotle's well-known discussion of contingent futures in *Peri Hermeneias* 9 (18a28—19a32), Danto writes: "God, even if omniscient, cannot *know* what the significance of events is before they in fact *have* this significance" (197; see 189ff.).

[78]Danto, 141f.; see also W. H. Dray, *Philosophy of History* (Englewood Cliffs, N.J., 1964), 28ff.

[79]Danto, 136.

ten.[80] This brings us to the problem of whether narrated history has its unity and continuity in itself or only in the historian's narration of it.

According to Arthur C. Danto, a historical narrative must have a correspondingly continuous object in the sequence of events: "A narrative requires a continuant subject."[81] This is connected with the fact that the very concept of a historical report already asserts a historical reality corresponding to the narrative.[82] And the assertion applies not only to the details but also to the continuity of the historical description. To challenge the assumption that a narrative has a correspondingly unified object is to deny the very historicity of the narrative.[83]

But what is the nature of this unity in the object? W. D. Stempel introduced the term "referential subject,"[84] and in the 1970 discussions of the Poetik und Hermeneutik group, Dieter Henrich distinguished between referential subject and acting subject.[85] But is the assumption of a unified object in the sense of a referential subject enough to ensure the unity of that object's history? When we speak of the unity of a history do we not mean a unity that arises only from the sequence of events and is

[80]R. G. Collingwood laid special emphasis on this point in his interpretation of historical accounts as reconstructions; see his *The Idea of History* (Oxford, 1946), 266ff., 275ff.; see 234ff.

[81]Danto, 250. A necessary condition for the unity of a narrative is that *"N* [narrative] is about the same subject" (251).

[82]Danto, 91. Without this objective reference, it would be meaningless to speak of historical documents (95; see 89). Danto seems, however, not to see that history as a science is not coextensive with historical narrative. He does emphasize, against W. H. Walsh, *Philosophy of History* (New York, 1951; London, 1958[2]; Harper Torchbooks, 1960), 18f., and rightly so, that even the ascertainment of facts supposes connections that only a continuous narrative can render explicit (140ff.). Nonetheless a distinction still needs to be made between, on the one hand, the ascertainment and reconstruction of facts and, on the other, a simple narrative.

[83]Baumgartner (n. 67, above), 291, characterizes Danto's assumption "of a narrative reality preceding any narrative organization" as inconsistent and contradictory. He opposes to that view the claim that "historical continuity is constructively produced in the same sense as history itself" (292; see 293f., 296f.). But here, as in Danto, no distinction is made between construction and narration, and if the construction is purely subjective, there is no way of determining how the claim of a narrative to be truthful (318) is compatible with the element of construction. It is hardly enough to maintain that the object has an "identity" through time that is different from historical continuity (298; see 336). See also Rüsen's comments on Baumgartner's observations regarding "Narrative Struktur und Objektivität," in Rüsen (n. 14, above), 94f., esp. 96.

[84]W. D. Stempel, "Erzählung, Beschreibung und historischer Diskurs," in Koselleck and Stempel (n. 55, above), 325–46, esp. 329: "The referential identity of the subject in whom and through whom the change is effected."

[85]Mentioned in Koselleck and Stempel, 481. Lübbe (n. 65, above) then accepted and developed this distinction (16, 75f., 84, 154).

precisely not something already underlying this sequence? Or is the referential subject of a historical narrative identical with this unity which arises only in the course of the narrated sequence?

Here once again a more precise distinction must be made. The subject of whom a story is told may be one of which many different stories are told, among them the one under discussion. If this is so, then the subject to whom all the stories refer stands behind these, as it were. His unity (or hers, as the case may be) is to be distinguished from the unity of each particular story, and while it unites the various stories among themselves, it does not automatically explain the particular unity of each story. The narrative unity of an anecdote about Frederick II of Prussia is not due simply to his person.

The situation is different when we are dealing with the history of this subject himself. In the case of this kind of narrative it is in the course of the history told by the narrator that the subject has become what he is as seen by the narrator. Here the narrative unity of the history is supplied by its referential subject, insofar as it is that subject's history that is being told, namely, the history that has established that subject's individual identity.[86]

At this point, however, it seems a dubious procedure to assume for the same subject a second, "numerical" identity that is independent of his history and to make this second identity the referential subject of the history.[87] Such an assumption seems justified only in the first type of story, that is, stories told about a subject who is already there independently of the stories. In any case, even in the story that tells the history of the represented subject himself, the referential subject cannot ground the unity of this history, since on the contrary it is this very history which is constitutive of the subject's own identity. This history does, however, derive its thematic unity from the process whereby the subject of which it tells was formed.

In this sense, histories describe the process whereby the identity of their object was established. This is true not only of histories of an institution

[86]Lübbe, 146ff.; see 185, 203.

[87]Ibid., 145f. This idea is also in the background when Lübbe describes histories as "processes whereby systems are individualized" (146; see 90ff., 98). He seems to presuppose that the system which functions as the referent of a history is already at hand even apart from the history. Does this mean, therefore, that the process whereby it is individualized remains external to it? Or, on the contrary, does not the system exist at all only as something individual and concrete? But if so, then it would have to be thought of as at every point already constituted by its history. The distinction between a numerical and a historical identity of an object can mean at most a rough, abstract, and approximate grasp of it as distinct from a grasp of it in its individual concretion.

(e.g., the history of a university) or of an individual (in the form of his or her biography) or of a nation (its rise and decline) but also of stories of the first type mentioned above, that is, stories that are told about someone but without narrating the person's history. Consequently, only two referential subjects are to be distinguished: the person of whom an anecdote (for example) is told, and the theme of the narrative itself. Only of the second is it true that it is at the same time the result of the history, or that the history is to be understood as the process whereby this referential subject was formed.

Thus Frederick's sense of justice was the result of the experience at the mill at Sans Souci. It follows from this story that for all his royal power Frederick was a man who thought in terms of law. On the other hand, this trait does not depend on this one story alone. For this reason, the story serves simply to illustrate an objective quality that was there independently of the story, although the quality would not have been quite the same if Frederick had acted differently in the episode reported.

The history of the Thirty Years War or of the First Crusade is to be understood as a formative process in a different way: the history describes only the origin and special characteristics of these events. At the same time, however, attention must be paid to a wider interest that the expositor has which is not identical with the object of the history. In contrast, a presentation of the history of an institution or a nation or a person still living usually has for its purpose to describe the process by which the identity of these still existing "subjects" was formed. In this case, historiography has in a special sense the function of "presenting an identity."[88] Etiological myths used to fulfill a similar function. So too, in a different way, did the early lists of kings and, in still another way, accounts of the rise of the monarchy or ascent of a dynasty among the Hittites and in the Old Testament or, finally, the growth of the Roman Empire in Polybius.

In those cases in which a historical account functions as a presentation of an identity, the history of its object is usually not yet complete. This means in turn that the process whereby the identity of the persons, institutions, or nations in question is formed is itself also not yet complete. Here if anywhere, Dilthey's statement is valid: Only in the hour of death is it

---

[88]See Lübbe, 168ff., 185, and J. Rüsen, "Probleme und Funktion der Historie," in W. Oelmüller, ed., *Wozu noch Geschichte?* (1977), 19–34 at 133: "Historical science is an institutionalized feat of memory that is necessary for the society that accomplishes it, if that society is to identify itself and be able to enter the future." This may be taken as a more precise description of what Baumgartner (n. 67, above) says, 200f., from the standpoint of the practical use of history: this practicality does not mean an immediate relation to action and goals of action, but first and foremost an identity which when grasped will become the basis for reflection that leads to action.

possible to survey the whole which determines the meaning of the parts of a life.[89] If, then, a "presentation of identity" is possible that looks back to a history of origins but at the same time takes place in the midst of the ongoing stream of events, it is possible only through anticipation.[90]

This last assertion also holds, though in a different way, for the presentation of historical processes already completed, because the history of their interpretation is still going on. However, a historical "presentation of identity" through anticipation of the whole history of one's own life or one's own society and its institutions has this special peculiarity, that it includes an element of self-reflection in relation to the object being presented; this element of self-reflection is characteristic of the idea of history as a process of formation, as understood by Jürgen Habermas.[91]

Self-reflection does not, however, imply self-constitution. Habermas spoke in 1968 (and claimed later to be following Marx[92]) of a "self-constitution of the human species" through work and interaction and by way of a "self-formative process, in which the species subject first constitutes itself."[93] Habermas was here envisaging the human race as in fact the active subject of its own history,[94] although in such a way that only

---

[89]Dilthey, *Gesammelte Schriften* VII, 233; see 237. See the remarks on this statement in my essay "On Historical and Theological Hermeneutic," in *Basic Questions in Theology* I (n. 18, above), 163f.

[90]See my remarks, ibid., 169ff. This kind of anticipation is not simply the expression of "an evaluation, an interest, that takes shape in concrete communication," as Baumgartner (n. 67, above), 281, puts it, nor is it simply the expression of a subjective hope, as P. Ricoeur maintains in his "Événement et sens," in E. Castelli, ed., *Révélation et histoire* (Paris, 1971), 15–34 at 32. Rather, it implies the objective meaning structures of lived experience. This kind of anticipation is explicitly thematized in philosophical reflection on history, although there cannot at yet be a concrete knowledge of future events (Danto, 174ff., 189ff.; also Baumgartner, 277ff.).

As the viewpoint that guides the presentation, this kind of anticipation also implicitly underlies the historian's reconstruction of past events. See the remarks of Rüsen in *Historische Objektivität* (n. 14, above), 94f., on the inevitability of a reference to the "totality" of history. This, however, ought not to be immediately connected with the "determinations of the meaning of social action," for it has its basis first of all in the experience of meaning that precedes all reflection on action and is bound up with the question of the identity of the historian's own social world in the larger framework of the world as a whole.

[91]J. Habermas, *Zur Logik der Sozialwissenschaften* (1967), 189. See his criticism, under this rubric, of H. G. Gadamer (174ff.), as well as the corresponding criticism of Dilthey in his *Knowledge and Human Interests,* trans. J. J. Shapiro (Boston, 1971), 177ff., and the acceptance of psychoanalysis, again under this rubric, 214ff.

[92]J. Habermas, "Theorie der Gesellschaft oder Socialtechnologie?" in the book of the same title written with N. Luhmann (1971), 179f. We may recall in this context various statements of Marx on "self-generation" in *Die Frühschriften,* ed. S. Landshut, 247f., 269, 281. See Habermas, *Knowledge and Human Interests,* 285.

[93]Habermas, *Knowledge and Human Interests,* 197; see 194ff.

[94]See J. Habermas, *Theorie und Praxis* (1963), 206ff.

in this historical process was it constituted a subject. In taking this approach, Habermas was opening himself to the question of "how the self-identity which is a necessary presupposition for the idea of a self-formative process on the part of the human species" could be conceived without recourse to Hegel's concept of reason or, as the case may be, the spirit. Furthermore, "How is the formative process, which presupposes the unity of the species subject, to be expressed *without* equivocation by the concept of formation when the subject's totality and unity, themselves historical occurrences, make their appearance only within this process?"[95]

The fact is that by the time this criticism was published Habermas had changed his mind about the asserted self-constitution.[96] The correction did not invalidate his conception of history as a process of formation but, rather, gave it greater coherence, since we know from elsewhere that processes of identity formation take the form of histories which are in principle incapable of being reduced to rational plans of action and which have no active subject because it is they that first constitute the identity of such a subject (H. Lübbe). Lübbe describes histories as processes that derive their unity not from rational plans of action but rather from a referential subject whose identity can be represented only as being the result of a history and can therefore motivate the telling of this history.[97] Such a description makes history a process of identity formation, since the identity of the referential subject is not to be thought of as prior to the historical process but is to be understood as the theme of the process itself. Of course, the question once again arises of the basis for the unity of such a history itself, inasmuch as the identity of the subject is the result of it, not its presupposition.

Dilthey has taught us to see the unity of historical processes as provided by continuities of meaning in which the detail and the whole reciprocally condition one another.[98] The significance of the particular event is grasped only when in lived experience the particular impression is related to the whole of life. This "whole" is first of all the whole of the person's own life. Dilthey had initially supposed, with Kant, that the unity of self-consciousness is also a condition for historical experience. His later

[95]Baumgartner (n. 67, above), 229. See the criticism based on these questions, 238f., 242ff.

[96]See the 1971 statement referred to above at n. 92. See, in addition, Habermas' observations "Über das Subjekt der Geschichte," in Koselleck and Stempel (n. 55, above), 470–76, esp. 473 and the statement on 476: "The self-creating subject of history was and is a fiction," along with the addendum that we must nevertheless keep to the "intention" of linking "the development of sociocultural systems with reflection on the self as a guidance system."

[97]See especially Lübbe's formulation, 203.

[98]Detailed evidence for the following remarks is given in my book *Theology and the Philosophy of Science* (n. 19, above), 72–80, 160–63.

shift to hermeneutics[99] really consisted in integrating this very presupposition itself into the historical process. History as such is now expressly declared to be an instrument of self-knowledge. But in each moment of the process the whole of life is still open-ended. That whole becomes visible for the individual life only at the moment of death and for the human race only at the end of its history (VII, 233, 237).

We blunt the edge of these statements if we suppose that in Dilthey's view the "parts" of life even now have their meaning "only as moments in the life of one and the same subject."[100] It is true indeed that statements are still to be found in Dilthey that point in that direction.[101] They fit in with the notion that understanding of others comes about only through "empathy" (VII, 214). But there are also statements that suggest an immediate connection between the individual life and life in its totality. "What we grasp through experience and understanding is life as the interweaving of all mankind" (VII, 131), and each individual experiences, thinks, acts, and understands only in a "sphere of communality" (146f.). Such reflections, like the insight into the historicity of the individual life, do not simply lead beyond the unity of consciousness in each present moment; they also anchor the individual's life and experience in a comprehensive web of life in which the person's "individuality is inseparable from the human community" (159; see 213).

Dilthey did not explicitly develop the consequences of all this for the experience of meaning and significance. It is clear, however, that the supraindividual interrelations of meaning between parts and whole must be anchored in this all-inclusive web of life, even though they are grasped from within the perspective proper to any given moment of life. In that anchoring, the preapprehension of the whole of the personal individual life and the preapprehension of universal life as a meaningful whole are distinguishable only by a further operation.

Looking back to my earlier discussion of the formation of individual identity in the framework of a primarily symbiotic web of life,[102] I can now say that the unity of an individual life can be grasped by the individual only

----

[99]See on this point the introduction by B. Groethuysen to vol. VII of Dilthey's *Gesammelte Schriften* (1926), as well as ibid., 70–75. The page references that follow in the text are to this volume. The translation of the short sentence from VII, 131, is taken from *W. Dilthey: Selected Writings,* ed. and trans. H. P. Rickman (Cambridge, 1976), 177f.

[100]Thus Baumgartner, 98. In his interpretation and criticism, Baumgartner does not go into Dilthey's shift from a psychological foundation for the human sciences to hermeneutics.

[101]Especially in VII, 230, note. The remarks made there show in any case that the question had become a problem for Dilthey. On the contrary, VII, 195, says only that we *grasp* the continuity of experience "in virtue of the unity of consciousness," while VII, 203, on the question of the "subject" of the categories, says only that the question deals "first and foremost" with the (individual's) life.

[102]See above, chapter 5, pp. 220ff., especially pp. 225ff.

on the basis of an experience of all-inclusive continuities of meaning and that it is constituted as a unity of consciousness. The unity of consciousness itself emerges only from a process in which the relations of experienced elements of meaning to the totality are increasingly differentiated. If Dilthey had analyzed more closely the way in which the unity of an individual life is constituted on the basis of the more comprehensive "sphere of communality," he would not have laid himself open to the objection that his application of "the structures of individual life history to nonindividual and independent complexes of reality that are centered on meaning"[103] amounts to a secondary hypostatization of structural contexts.

To the extent that the individual's whole identity and unity of consciousness are constituted only in a process in which the individual experiences meanings and contexts or continuities of meaning, it is possible to speak of experience as having priority over action. Unlike experience, action presupposes the identity of the acting subject. Not only must agents grasp in advance the connection between means and ends, as well as the possible side effects of their action; in addition, they themselves establish the connection between means and ends by actually using the means in order to achieve their purposes. The unity of the connection is based on the identity of the acting subject through time. But the identity of the subject itself is constituted by a process of identity formation that takes the form of a history in which the particularity of the individual's existence is grasped in the context of more inclusive continuities of meaning and in the medium of linguistic articulation and communication.

The existence of these contexts or continuities of meaning cannot be due to a positing of meaning by subjects, since the latter for their part are not constituted except by a process of experience of meaning. On the other hand, subjects do not have their existence independently of all human assistance. They gain their subjectivity through the continuity of social life and in the framework of a shared cultural life-world in which the experience of meaning and the interpretation of meaning interpenetrate in processes of transmission and reception. Only in a passage through these and by participation in them do histories themselves have their thematic unity.[104]

Despite the priority of experience over action, human action does play a part in these historical processes of formation. How is this to be under-

[103]Baumgartner, 106. See also the criticism of H. G. Gadamer in his *Truth and Method*, tr. G. Barden and J. Cumming (New York, 1975), 192ff., which is, however, more restrained.

[104]That is, "by the identity of the horizon of expectations" (Habermas, *Knowledge and Human Interests*, 262). The decisive point here, however, is that such horizons of expectations cannot be arbitrarily chosen, but are mediated through the meaning structures of historical experience, insofar as this is itself open to future completion.

stood, if history must be regarded as not having an active subject and as being, instead, constitutive of active subjects? Is there an identity that is not simply a result but is already present in the course of history, so that an activity based on this identity can intervene in the process of the subject's own formation?

We must recall here that the function of histories as presentations of identity is based on an anticipation of the totality of an as yet uncompleted history. It is this kind of anticipation that makes possible a consciousness of personal identity amid the flow of events and thus makes it possible for a self-comporting to react upon the individual's own formative history and thereby the cultural tradition as well. The anticipation of the unbroken meaning of one's own being throughout the historical process of a life interwoven with world and society is the basis for that familiarity with the self which makes possible a concern for the permanence of one's being and a striving for self-preservation[105] and identity throughout the course of one's life history. The reflexive action of life upon itself is thus mediated through anticipation.

The one who does the anticipating here is not the historian but the human being who lives and acts in history and "with a view to praxis" anticipates "final states in the light of which the manifold of events is freely structured into action-oriented histories."[106] The work of historians has reference to praxis, but what they directly intend is not guidance for action but a presentation of identity, although such a presentation does have implications for the direction of action. To the extent that historians in their descriptions anticipate final outcomes, they do so because the history they are presenting of a nation, an institution, or even a culture is still unfinished.

Human beings living in history likewise anticipate final outcomes but primarily from the viewpoint of the identity both of their own lives and of the social and cultural world to which they belong. Only secondarily do they engage in such anticipation for the sake of deciding goals for their action, the content of which is determined rather by their consciousness of their own identity. As they decide on the goals of their action, they may realize that by setting goals and acting they can contribute to the historical formation of their society, their own individual lives, and of the race as a whole. They will also realize, however, that they cannot by their action

---

[105]In his discussion of the connection between self-consciousness and self-preservation, Henrich (n. 73, above) stresses the point that a being which has to preserve itself needs self-consciousness precisely because it does not have its ground wholly in itself: "That which must preserve itself must know that it does not always and, above all, does not unqualifiedly have its ground in itself" (11; see also 137f.).

[106]Habermas, *Zur Logik der Sozialwissenschaften* (n. 91, above), 166.

really produce the identity of their own lives or of the life of society or the race.

This is to say that human beings will not produce the new human being in whom the human destiny will be fulfilled. They are prevented from doing so by many factors: the discord between individual and collective goals, the contingent "events that encounter us" and contingent side effects of human action that cannot be foreseen or controlled, the limited resources and possibilities of action available to human beings. If the history of the human race is to be a formative process leading to a fulfilled humanity, it can be such only under the guidance of divine providence.

This guidance need not, of course, be understood as a determination of events prior to the actual course of history. Neither, when properly understood, does it preclude the participation of human beings and their actions in the formative process that is history. Rather, an understanding of God as the goal of history and, in this limited form, an understanding of God's aims in dealing with humankind can inspire their anticipation of the final form of human identity and thus the orientational framework in which they decide on the goals of their own action. God strives for and reaches his ends not apart from human beings but with the cooperation of his creatures and through the conflicts between human purposes and interests.

III. History and Spirit

1. The Incompleteness of History and the Presence of Truth

The formative process that is history remains incomplete in every historical present. Future events may destroy what has been gained, but they may also lead us beyond periods of decadence. They may disclose unsuspected ranges of problems but also give plausibility to new conceptions of order. At the same time, however, there is present in every historical moment the whole of the life that in its historical course is still unfinished. Only on this condition is identity possible amid the stream of history, only on this condition can the narration and portrayal of history be a presentation of identity.

The identity of individuals and peoples that has already emerged in the course of history and been brought into focus at significant moments is, of course, always a provisional identity. Events still hidden in the womb of the future will appear and contribute to defining the being of individuals and cultures and will show the identity of these in a new light. Nonetheless events of epochal significance in the life of individuals and in the memory of nations and cultures claim a permanent place despite the vicissitudes the future will bring and even in the face of possible decline and fall. Over against these epochal events that serve as points of reference and orientation for identity consciousness stand others that remain like fiery wounds in the consciousness of individuals and peoples. Both kinds of events influence human behavior and must keep their place in any future interpretation of individual or national identity.

What is final and definitive is thus present in the relativity and flow of history, not indeed in the mode of finality but in the form of anticipation (see above, n. 90). On the other hand, the presence of the definitive and truly real is experienced not as something anticipated but as the eternal and abiding in its contrast to the realm of the temporarily mutable and transient. Only through reflection on the historical character of this experience of the eternal and abiding does the experience reveal itself to be an anticipation.

To speak of the experience as one of anticipation is not to detract in any way from the presence of the eternal. Quite the contrary: the understanding that the experience is one of anticipation alone makes it possible to preserve the conviction that it is a true experience despite changing interpretations of it as our historical experience expands. The viewpoint of anticipation enables us to understand that later interpretations are simply looking at the same totality of meaning and significance in different ways. Therefore the anticipatory consciousness of the truly real in historical form represents a higher stage of the general consciousness that the true and abiding are present in human life.

At issue in this experience is not only the unity of individual life and its meaning but also and at the same time the identity of the being and things of our world and, in addition, the world itself and the foundations of its unity. Because human beings are exocentric beings who experience themselves only via their world, they can become aware of the unity of their own Dasein only along with the unity of the world.[107] The awareness extends both to the social world and the world of nature. Just as the meaningful unity of the social world is the basis for the formation of individual identity, so in the early cultures the unity of the social world was in turn traced back to the unity of the cosmos. In the modern age the attempt has been made to explain the order both of the natural world and of social life as based on reason or, as the case might be, to reorganize it according to the standards of reason.

In its own way this outlook acknowledges that natural order and social order belong together as a basis for the identity of human beings (as rational beings). How could men and women identify themselves as rational beings if the natural order and the course of human history were not

---

[107]See above, chapter 2, pp. 67ff., and chapter 4, pp. 157ff.

ultimately in harmony with the requirements of reason? According to Kant's teaching on the supreme good, the assumption that such a harmony exists is indispensable for the unity of the human person as a natural being and as a rational being. But the harmony between reason and social reality (and therefore also between society and nature) cannot be asserted as a brute fact but can be thought of only as resulting from a history. Without the dimension of history the consciousness of the fulfillment not yet achieved in the present would be suppressed, as would our suffering from the contradictions, absurdities, and injustices of the present world. The unity of the natural and social worlds as the basis for the formation of individual identity can therefore be represented, if at all, only as a result of a still open history.

The unity of this history as deriving from its possible fulfillment— whether this fulfillment is expected from human action or solely from the operation of divine providence—is therefore presupposed, explicitly or implicitly, as the frame of reference for individual identity formation. When neither the social world nor the natural world nor even history can be experienced as having a meaningful unity, individual identity formation becomes an extremely difficult task, especially when religion too no longer supplies a basis for identity formation. As a matter of fact, even in these cases, and despite all the theoretical disagreements, individual experience still has available to it at least fragmentary indications of unity in nature, society, and history and of the religious basis of that unity, and these indications make it possible to achieve an individual identity.

The primary access to this whole that is given to us only in fragments[108] is through feeling. As we saw earlier, feeling is the place where human beings have a prereflective familiarity with the whole not only of their individual lives but also of their symbiotic sphere of existence.[109] In all the variants of the life of feelings, moods, and affects and even in private feelings of loneliness, anxiety, hatred, meaninglessness, and lostness the reference to the whole of life shows itself to be constitutive. But this reference to the whole that is based on feeling is of itself indeterminate. It is further articulated only in the light of the particular impressions of each moment and in relation to a gradually forming continuum of active and passive experience. In this way the person acquires that grasp of the whole in the detail and the detail in the whole which the early Schleier-

---

[108]In his study of the theology of history, H. Urs von Balthasar unfortunately does not provide the conceptual analysis that the title of his book, *Das Ganze im Fragment* ("The whole in the fragment") (1963), would lead us to expect, even though the tenor of his remarks (esp. 264–354) doubtless does correspond to the basic tone struck in the title. Balthasar's *Das Ganze im Fragment* has been translated into English as *A Theological Anthropology* (New York, 1967).

[109]See above, chapter 6, pp. 248ff.

macher made the central idea of his theory of religion and which later on
became the basis for Dilthey's descriptive psychology of lived experience
(Erleben). [110]

Because subject and object are not yet distinguished within the focus on
the whole that is proper to feeling (as distinct from sensation), feeling
provides the horizon not only for relating experiences to the whole of the
individual's existence but also for grasping impressions as parts of an
objective whole which in its turn has its place in the context of the world
in its entirety. At this root level, feeling and reason are bound together.
Out of it arises the differentiation, occasioned by sense impressions, between feelings, which refer to the self, and reason, which relates to the
totality that is the objective world. [111]

In lived experience these two sides are not yet separated. The meaning
of things and events, as grasped in lived experience, articulates both the
web of meaning in the individual's own life and the objective continuities
of the life-world, which in their turn are webs of meaning and significance.
The concrete grasp of meaning in the lived experience of the meaning of
things and events as parts of the wholes which they represent is not to be
regarded as a positing of meaning by a subject, because, apart from any
other consideration, its origins precede any separation between subjective
and objective. Only with the coming of language does the differentiation
become definitive, but with an initial focus on a quasi-mythical subjectivity
in things, which spontaneously manifest their being through the words
that name them. [112]

This predominance of the objective world shows human exocentricity
at work in lived experience. The feeling-related presence of the whole in
the open-ended process of the individual's life manifests itself in connec-

[110]In his early phase, however, Schleiermacher did not as yet recognize feeling to be the
place of the "presence of whole undivided Being" (*The Christian Faith,* § 3, where he is
citing Steffens). This explains the preponderance of *"Anschauung"* ("perspectivity," in Tice's
translation) in the *Addresses on Religion* (1799), whereas later on the tendency to give a
transcendental interpretation of feeling and to underestimate its indeterminacy apart from
contents deriving from *Anschauung* and imagination gave occasion for Hegel's criticism on
this point. But Hegel's criticism did not touch the key element in Schleiermacher's concept
of feeling, namely, the relation to a totality that is an element in feeling prior to any
conceptual determination. On this precise point, Dilthey's concept of lived experience
(Erlebnis) was true to Schleiermacher's intentions in a way that is not open to Hegel's
criticism, because experience is always connected with a particular impression. On the other
hand, Dilthey substituted for the concept of feeling the concept of life, which, in view of
its relation to the idealist philosophy of the subject (the transcendental ego), was even vaguer
and used the opportunities provided by the concept of feeling for coming to grips with this
basic idea of idealist philosophy.

[111]See my earlier remarks in chapter 7, at n. 183.

[112]See chapter 7, at n. 185 and, with reference to the child's acquisition of language, at
nn. 99f.

tion with the identity of things and in the medium of language. Because of the social nature of language this identity of things and of the order that manifests itself in them is an identity that has intersubjective validity and is not limited to the individual's lived experience.

The identity of things and of their order is called in question by the experience of mutability and of actual change and transience in the world of objects. Under the pressure of this experience the hunger for reality and for the presence of what is permanent and definitive forces a path through the transient appearances of things to their true and abiding essence which may be identified with, for example, their beauty. Or else the realization that human life fades like the grass combines with the experience, and confession, that God alone—his truth, his fidelity, his world—abides forever.[113] Nonetheless the identity of things in their transitory existence and of the order that manifests itself in them is the place where true being makes its appearance and God manifests his fidelity (see Ps. 119:160; compare Ps. 111:7f.).

The representation of this identity in the words of language provides the first articulation in human experience of the presence (which discloses itself in only an indeterminate way in feeling) of the whole and definitive, the permanently true and abiding. The unity of consciousness arises only in response to the linguistically apprehended identity of things and their order, in which the individual's own body has its place and in which therefore the little word "I" has its point of reference; the converse of this statement is false. The truth in this matter is more accurately conveyed by the mythical image in Plato's *Phaedrus,* according to which not only the human soul but the gods themselves nurture their immortality through association with the eternal ideas,[114] than it is in Kant's thesis that the identity of a static and abiding ego is presupposed by the content of experience.[115]

To this presence of the true and definitive amid the processes of history that always break off uncompleted and amid earthly failure and earthly transiency I give the name "spirit." In so doing, I am introducing at the end of this study of anthropology a concept which I earlier set aside that

[113]Ps. 103:15ff.; Isa. 40:6ff. On the concept of truth in Old Testament thought, see my remarks in the essay "What Is Truth?" in *Basic Questions in Theology* II, 1ff., and further in *Grundfragen systematischer Theologie* II, 229ff.

[114]Plato, *Phaedrus* 247d1ff., 249c5ff. See *Phaedo* 79b16f. and d1f. I read these sentences of Plato as explaining primarily the identity of the soul (on the supposition that human memory and its control depend on the availability of the words of the language) and not necessarily as also an argument for its immortality. In any case, the identity of the consciousness that bridges time can be conceived as a kind of participation in eternity, even when this identity takes the form of a perverted will to be like God.

[115]See earlier, chapter 5, sec. II, especially at nn. 85ff.

I might not bring uncriticized traditional notions into the investigation and interpretation of anthropological phenomena. It was for this last reason that I followed Helmuth Plessner and Arnold Gehlen in their effort to avoid the metaphysically burdened concept of spirit and to explain in some other manner those phenomena (especially the inhibition of instinct) which Max Scheler had assigned to spirit as an anthropological principle.[116]

Since that earlier decision, however, the discussion has repeatedly yielded conclusions pointing to the constitutive importance of a presence of meaning that does not arise from human action or a human positing of meaning but, on the contrary, underlies the constitution of human subjectivity as well as any and every human interpretation of meaning. We came to this kind of conclusion in discussing the problems of identity and especially the constitution of individual identity, and again in connection with the concept of feeling and with the questions raised by the origin and use of language, and in our discussion of the foundations of culture and institutions. Now, in order to provide a summary description of what is at issue here, I shall in conclusion return to the concept of spirit and discuss its importance for anthropology.

The traditional concept of spirit has to be revised. There is no reason why at the end of a study of the human person as a complex but nonetheless unitary phenomenon we should return to the anthropological dualism of Cartesian philosophy with its conception of the human being as composed of two substances, a *res extensa* and a *res cogitans*. The concept "spirit" as I intend it here is not to be understood in terms of consciousness. It is to be understood, rather, as that which alone makes possible both consciousness and subjectivity (in the sense of the unity of conscious life) and that, at the same time, makes possible the unity of social and cultural life as well as the continuity of history amid the open-endedness and incompleteness of its processes.

Common to all these phenomena is the operative presence of a sphere of meaning that precedes individuals and both constitutes and transcends their concrete existence. This sphere of meaning discloses itself to lived human experience, at least in a partial way; human beings even contribute to forming it, but they do not first bring it into existence as such. Hegel discusses it under the rubric of "the objective spirit," Dilthey under the rubric of "life." Both descriptions, however, are somewhat misleading and have led to distorted versions of what is being conveyed.

The concept of the objective spirit suggests the idea of an objectivation that has for its basis the activity of the subjective spirit, even though the

116See above, chapter 1, pp. 36ff.

objective spirit, as the power of the universal, is independent of individuals. On such a view, it is impossible to think of subjective consciousness as being constituted by the objective spirit. As a result, the idea of an objective spirit has led repeatedly to theories of alienation and to the demand that the supposedly objective spirit be seen instead as the reified product of the activity of individuals. Such a reinterpretation does not, however, explain either the constitution of individual identity or even a single one of the other phenomena that I mentioned a moment ago as occasions for reintroducing the concept of spirit.

Dilthey's idea of "life," on the other hand, remains tied to unclarified biological notions of a life-force that manifests itself, through the activity of individuals, as a power that is proper to the species and that is to explain how individuals are able to understand one another through empathy. In his analyses of the structural connections within lived experience Dilthey in fact transcends the ideas that serve as his point of departure. Nonetheless these ideas repeatedly make their presence felt as disturbing and unnecessary constraints on his argument—for example, in limiting the demonstration of structural connections to an already given unity of life.

Dilthey's reduction of the Hegelian concept of spirit to the concept of life represented an effort to overcome the limitations of the idealist philosophy of consciousness. That effort has certainly not lost its relevance. To achieve the purpose, however, it would have been enough to relate spirit as such primarily to the phenomenon of life and only then, within the framework thus created, to relate it to consciousness. There was no need first to make "spirit" disappear in the concept of "life" in order then to make it reappear by means of a "descriptive" psychology developed for that very purpose. Such a procedure could recommend itself only to one whose fascination with the rise of the natural sciences caused him to react against the idealist tradition and whose state of mind was such that he found the whole concept of spirit an embarrassment.

A book on anthropology is unfortunately not the place in which to give a systematic justification for introducing the concept of spirit. That would require that we discuss at a very general level our understanding of reality as such. This is especially the case since in the present context we cannot be satisfied with a narrow approach to spirit from the standpoint of the philosophy of consciousness. An adequate treatment of the problems needing to be discussed would be possible only in the framework of a general ontology. I must therefore be satisfied here with the indications already given of the problems that arise in justifying the concept of spirit. On the other hand, the phenomenon that the concept of spirit sums up can be allowed to speak for itself. It calls for a renewed reflection on the concept of spirit, while itself not depending on any particular version of it. For the moment, let me here again show the links that exist with the language of biblical tradition and Christian teaching.

2. Spirit, Person, and Community

When the Scriptures speak of "spirit" they are not thinking first and foremost of consciousness. Rather, they view the spirit primarily as the origin of life. Only inasmuch as consciousness and in particular a charismatically intensified and ecstatic consciousness is seen as an especially heightened form of life is it also regarded as emphatically the work of the spirit.

In addition, the spirit was regarded in ancient Israel as first and last the creative spirit of God (Gen. 1:2). When Isaiah contrasts "spirit" as life-giving power with the transient flesh (Isa. 31:3), he is evidently speaking of the divine reality. The spirit of God gives life to creatures, both plants and animals (Ps. 104:30), and their life lasts as long as God permits his spirit to work in them.[117] Human beings too have life because God breathes his own breath into their nostrils (Gen. 2:7). But because of their arrogance he willed that his spirit should not abide in them forever (Gen. 6:3), and therefore their lives, like those of other creatures, last for only a limited period. In death they give "their" spirit back to God, who gave it to them, while their bodies return to the earth, from which they were taken (Eccles. 12:7).

The spirit is, then, the source of life, but its being and action are not exhausted by phenomenal life, at least not by the form of it which is limited by death and involves the self-assertion of individuals against one another and against the divine source of their life. Only the future life of the resurrected state will be so united to the divine spirit as source of all life that it will be immortal. This Pauline interpretation of the hope of resurrection (1 Cor. 15:44ff.) goes beyond what the Old Testament says about the relation between spirit and life. Nonetheless it follows the same logic as they, since it applies their conception of spirit and life to the hope of resurrection that had made its appearance since the postexilic period.

In a Christian anthropology the statement that "man has spirit" must be understood as meaning that the spirit is "something that comes to man, something not essentially his own but to be received and actually received by him."[118] Human beings are body and soul, but they are not spirit in the same way. The spirit is the source of their life and is at work in them. "But while He is in man, He is not identical with him." For to say that

---

[117]It can also be called the spirit of creatures—but when God takes it away, "they . . . return to their dust" (Ps. 104:29).

[118]K. Barth, *Church Dogmatics* III/2, trans. H. Knight et al. (1960), 354.

the human being is such only through the spirit is the same as to say "that he is man, and therefore soul of his body, not without God but by God, i.e., by the ever new act of God."[119]

It is true that the word *pneuma* occurs now and then in the New Testament and in the literature of Hellenistic Judaism as meaning the human soul in its cognitive and emotive functions.[120] But wherever the New Testament writers speak independently and in an explicitly theological way, they always conceive of the spirit as the divine counterpart to the human soul.[121] In keeping with this, the Christian fathers too look upon human beings as not having by nature any share in the divine spirit, not even in virtue of their being rational creatures. Only rebirth through faith and baptism gives them a participation in the spirit and therewith the pledge of a new and immortal life that will be revealed in Christians at the resurrection of the dead, as it has already been revealed in Jesus Christ (2 Cor. 1:22; Rom. 8:23).[122]

The action of the Holy Spirit in human beings is concretized for us if we look at the biblical idea of the soul.[123] According to the Yahwist story of creation, the divine cause of life that is breathed into human beings makes of them a "living soul" (literal translation of Gen. 2:7). The expression means simply that the person is a living being. The soul *(nepeš)* is not another component part of a human being over and above the body, as in Cartesian or Platonic dualism; it is simply the bodily being as living. That is precisely what the medieval Latin Church intended to say when, using the conceptual language of Aristotle, it asserted the soul to be the essential form of the human body.[124]

But insofar as the soul is the life of its body it is an effect of the life-giving spirit. The divine creative spirit causes human beings to have life within them, and to that extent the spirit is internally present to them, although it does not on that account become a "part" of them. Conversely, the movement of life or the "soul" that is in every living thing consists in a

[119]Ibid., 364 and 356.

[120]See E. Schweizer, "Pneuma," *TDNT* 6:387, 396 (especially on Mark 2:8 and 8:12), 401 (on Matt. 5:3), 434ff. (on Paul); also 446 (on Heb. 4:12) and 449 (on Rev. 11:11 and 13:15).

[121]Ibid., 434f., on Paul.

[122]For what the early fathers say about the spirit, see W. D. Hauschild, *Gottes Geist und der Mensch. Studien zur frühchristlichen Pneumatologie* (1972), esp. 30ff., 36ff. (Clement of Alexandria), 201ff. (Tatian), and 204ff. (Irenaeus of Lyons).

[123]See H. W. Wolff, *Anthropology of the Old Testament*, trans. M. Kohl (Philadelphia, 1974), 10–25.

[124]DS 902 (Council of Vienne, 1311–1312). On this, see the remarks of J. B. Metz, "Seele III. Systematisch," *Lexikon für Theologie und Kirche* 9 (1964), 570f. (also, idem, "Leib," in ibid., 6 [1961], 903), as well as G. Ebeling, *Lutherstudien*, vol. II: *Disputatio de homine*, Part 1 (1977), 150ff., 187ff., and, on the Council of Vienne, 195ff.

movement beyond the limited corporeal life of the individual into the environment in which that life is lived. In this process the life of the soul is characterized by "neediness" (H. W. Wolff). Moreover, in this neediness, and not simply in the satisfaction of need, the life-giving action of the spirit manifests itself, since the living being is thereby enabled to act on its own and seek its food and other satisfactions from its environment or, as the case may be, "from God" (Ps. 104:21).

All life, then, is ecstatic and to that extent spiritual. But the ecstatic character found in all life reaches a new level of intensity, a new high point, in human beings. To the extent that human beings exist exocentrically in a presence to what is other than themselves, precisely as other, and experience themselves from that vantage point,[125] the life-giving power of the spirit, which raises them above their own finiteness, manifests itself in an intensified form.[126] This specific kind of action by the spirit finds expression especially in human consciousness, which is tied in with the behavioral structure just indicated. For by reason of their consciousness human beings exist outside themselves to a greater degree than do other living things. Human consciousness is therefore in an especially close relation to the action of the spirit only because, and to the extent that, human beings realize their exocentric mode of being primarily in their conscious life.

It is, however, in its temporal structure that the peculiar nature of the ecstatic self-transcendence found in all living things emerges most clearly, as does the importance and scope of its modification in human life. All living things are directed by their drives to a future that will bring a change in their condition: to a state of repletion as opposed to hunger and want, but also to dangers that must be avoided. Human beings alone, however, seem able to distinguish the future as future from the present.[127] Since they are present to what is other than themselves and present to it precisely as an other which they not only distinguish from themselves but also grasp in its distinctness from what is other than it and therefore in its uniqueness within the horizon of an all-embracing whole, they are also capable of distinguishing the present from the future which they strive for or fear and, conversely, of distinguishing the future from the present.

I need not emphasize once again the importance of the development of language for holding on to these distinctions and keeping them present.

---

[125]See above, chapter 2, pp. 51ff.

[126]On this, see also J. Zizioulas, "Human Capacity and Human Incapacity," *Scottish Journal of Theology* 28 (1975), 401–47, esp. 407f., and Chr. Yannaras, *Person und Eros. Eine Gegenüberstellung der Ontologie der griechischen Kirchenväter und der Existenzphilosophie des Westens* (1976; German tr., 1982), 48ff.

[127]See above, chapter 2, nn. 54f.

It is language that enables us to keep what is past and absent present in consciousness.[128]

Human beings are thus set apart by the development of a consciousness that bridges time, cancels (within the limits imposed on it) the distinction of things and times, and sublimates this in the unity and continuity of its own present, thus giving a presentiment of eternity. The continuity of this time-bridging consciousness derives from anticipation of the future. The constant anticipation of the future not only prevents the unity of consciousness from being continually disrupted by every new alteration but also allows it to see in things present and past what these perceived things are not yet in themselves but will or at least can become. Anticipation of the future by perceptual consciousness thus makes it possible to deal actively with things in the context of human goals.

More generally, it alone grasps the abiding identity of things, an identity that transcends the experience of them as changing and combines their past with their still open future in a single conception of their being. The identity of the knower's own self is also grasped and determined in a similar manner.

As I said above, the time-spanning present that is peculiar to human consciousness has an ecstatic character. It is an expression of the specifically human being-present to the other as other, an expression of the exocentricity of the human mode of life and thus an expression of the presence of the spirit, who is at work in the interrelationships of things. The ecstatic relation to the world has itself a temporal structure which depends on anticipation of the future.[129] It is from the future that the abiding essence of things discloses itself, because the future alone decides what is truly lasting.

All this was first consciously grasped in ancient Israel with its understanding of truth as historical.[130] The mythical mind, for its part, conceived of the true being of things as that which had perdured since primordial times, while classical Greek philosophy thought of it as a timeless and always identical essential form. Plato, however, did think of

---

[128]Ibid.

[129]See M. Heidegger, *Being and Time,* 372ff., 377f. (German 325ff., 329). But, contrary to what Heidegger says 369ff. (German 323ff.), this anticipation is not to be understood originally in the light of care *(Sorge)*. Rather, because of care the ecstatic meaning of being present to the other as other and the priority of the future for the temporal structure of this ecstatic mode of life are already turned back upon the present existence with which care is concerned. The very reference of care to the future points to a more original form of the ecstatic exercise of existence and of the priority of the future which that exercise entails.

[130]See my remarks on the Old Testament understanding of truth in my essay "What Is Truth?" (n. 113, above), and H. von Soden's summarizing formula cited there: "Truth is that which will show itself in the future" (3).

the idea of the good as being at the same time its future, for which eros strives in its yearning desire for completeness. This represented an approach to the understanding of time as historical, but in Plato himself its development was hindered by the Eleatic character of his doctrine of the ideas.

It did, however, serve as one of the points of contact for the Christian acceptance of Platonism. Thus Maximus the Confessor, following the Platonic tradition and the writings of Dionysius the Areopagite, was able to interpret the cosmic eros that is at work in the ecstatic self-transcendence characteristic of all life and especially human life, as an expression of the redemptive love of the biblical God, who has put eros in the hearts of his creatures so that "through their own nature he might draw to himself those set in motion by his call."[131] The movement of eros reaches beyond the transient to the permanent or, in biblical terms, to a future life that will no longer be separated from its source in the spirit but will be permeated by the spirit and therefore be immortal.

The striving proper to eros is, however, ambivalent. Anders Nygren has brought out its problematic side by contrasting eros as an egoistic striving for the completion and enrichment of the person's own ego with agape as love that gives.[132] That description is one-sided, inasmuch as eros too involves an ecstatic transcending of its own imperfect existence. From this point of view, the Christian acceptance of the Platonic eros in Maximus and others was legitimate. On the other hand, eros does need to be liberated from its entanglement with the egoistic striving by reason of which it becomes for human beings an "instrument of death."[133] This liberation is achieved only through the new birth in which human beings die to sin and its egoism, as is shown by the symbolic action of baptism.

The intention of eros in its ecstatic self-transcendence is to achieve liberation from its own inadequacy and wretchedness by means of the beauty and goodness to which its striving is directed. This orientation to the future of the good finds its purest and most comprehensive expression in trust and hope. These are attitudes which from the very beginnings of human life accompany the process whereby the person is formed; they give this process space to breathe in, so to speak.

Trust, no less than hope, is characterized by a reference to the future, because those who trust believe that the future of their own being is made secure by the one in whose hands they place themselves. Only the future,

[131]PG 91:1260, cited in Yannaras (n. 126, above), 47; see 122f. The erotic character of the human ecstatic mode of life is also emphasized by J. Zizioulas, *L'être ecclésial* (1981), 44f., 54.

[132]A. Nygren, *Agape and Eros*, trans. P. S. Watson (London, 1932, 1938, 1939; in one volume, Philadelphia, 1953).

[133]Thus Zizioulas, *L'être ecclésial*, 44f.

moreover, will show whether the foundation on which they build is able to bear the weight they place on it. Trust and hope too—and indeed trust and hope especially—can go astray. But in one way or another the foundational importance of trust for the process of personal formation shows that what the Letter to the Hebrews says about faith (Heb. 11:1) holds also for the person: the person lives by the future in which its trust is placed.[134] That is how the person lives in the present, for such is the ecstatic mode of existence proper to the person.

This last statement does not contradict my earlier statement that history is the *principium individuationis*. History as a formative process is the way to the future to which the individual is destined. As long as the journey is incomplete, it can only be described in terms anticipatory of its end and goal. It is in the light of that end and goal that human beings grasp the meaning of their lives and the task life sets them. Way and goal must, of course, be so related to each other that the way thus far traveled can be interpreted as a way to that goal, just as the actual life history of a person must be capable of being integrated into the identity he or she projects. For the human person as historical being is not only the goal but also the movement of the history that leads to the goal.

This movement, however, derives its unity from the future by which it will be completed. Therefore only through anticipation of this future can human beings presently exist as themselves.[135] If they do so exist, they will also understand their present concrete existence as being not simply a product of their own capricious choices but as a call and election with a view to that future.[136] Here, moreover, the identity of their present existence presupposes not only their personal future but also, in a way, the future of their people and their world and even the future of all humankind, since individuals are inseparable from their world. The content of this presupposition is admittedly very vague. It acquires determinateness only in the present existence of persons. In this existence their future destiny makes its appearance and, with it, that of all humankind, and this not only in a *single* person but in a plurality of persons and in a many-voiced manner.

[134]Heb. 11:1 uses here the term *hypostasis*, which ever since the fourth-century theological debates on the Trinity has been a Christian technical term for "person." When read in that light, the statement that faith is *"substantia rerum sperandarum"* ("the substance of things hoped for") suggests a correction of the traditional concept of substance along the lines of a "paradoxical hypostasis whose roots are located in the future and its branches in the present" (Zizioulas, *L'être ecclésial*, 51). See W. Joest, *Ontologie der Person bei Luther* (1967), 238–47, on the beginnings, in Luther's exegesis, of a biblically founded conception of the person as *hypostasis* in connection with Heb. 11:1.

[135]See the earlier discussion of Heidegger and Sartre in chapter 5, at nn. 122ff.

[136]See the discussion of the concept of election in my *Die Bestimmung des Menschen. Menschsein, Erwählung und Geschichte* (1978), esp. chs. 3 to 5.

If the person is thus the presence of the self in the instant of the ego,[137] personality is to be understood as a special instance of the working of the spirit, a special instance of the anticipatory presence of the final truth of things. Conversely, the essence of the identity of things and of what is perceived in them is more profoundly disclosed to personal presence with its ecstatic character. In the identity of their being, which the word names in the light of a preapprehension of final truth, things too are more than is at hand in them. Perception already sees, hears, and tastes more of the object than the senses show us in it. Insofar as we perceive existent things as objects centered in themselves and do not antecedently limit perception to a particular aspect of them, we grasp them in their truth which transcends the superficially discoverable.

But while lifeless things are grounded only in themselves and in a truth that transcends what is now manifested in them, living beings relate actively to their perdurance, identity, and truth, which transcend what is now manifested in them. To that extent, the spirit is more intensely present in the ecstatic movement of love and is, in addition, present in a special way in human consciousness as the medium of the presence of the person's own identity, as distinct from, though united with, the truth of things. Thus, in the medium of the human soul and in the place that is the ensouled body, the presence of the spirit constitutes the identity of the person as a presence of the self in the instant of the ego.

It is this identity of the person in a time-bridging present that alone makes possible the independence which characterizes human beings as subjects of responsible action. Throughout this presentation of anthropology I have repeatedly given the concept of action a secondary place. This procedure has not, however, meant that I disparage the concept. As a matter of fact, it is precisely as active beings that human beings manifest their personal independence in its full form. But this independence is based on conditions that cannot be described as products of human action; rather, they constitute the very subject who acts. These constitutive conditions of subjectivity may now be summed up in the following formula: the human being as person is a creation of the spirit.

It is only all too easy to describe as "self-constitution" the human personal independence that is connected with the capacity for action and with the unquestionable importance of action for the self-preservation and self-expansion of human life. This is by no means a purely theoretical illusion. On the contrary, as I showed earlier,[138] we are dealing here with that seductive self-misunderstanding of human independence which is the

[137]See above, chapter 5, at n. 128.
[138]See above, chapter 3, sec. II, and especially the discussion of Kierkegaard's description of this situation (at nn. 39ff.).

condition for the real brokenness and distortion of human subjectivity and life-style. Here I must return to this theme, but from the viewpoint of the concept of spirit.

The distortion to which I am referring means that human beings wrench their life away from its source in the divine spirit and try to ground it in itself. The result is that their life is now forfeited to death. Why do sinners not die on the spot? The answer, when viewed in terms of the derivation of all life from the action of the spirit, can only be that when sinners wrench themselves away from their source, which is the spirit, they carry away with them the spirit who works within them. This in turn is possible only on condition that God still grants sinners a life of their own, even if a limited one.

This complex state of affairs seems to be behind certain marginal statements of Scripture about a spirit in human beings that is distinct from the divine spirit. Even the life of sinners continues to be in its own way determined by spirit, although in a perverse form.[139] The divine spirit effects the life of the creature insofar as the latter goes out of itself ecstatically and shares in the operation of the spirit in such a way that this spirit, despite its transcendence, is present at the very heart of the creature's life. In sinners, the ecstasy proper to the life given them is perverted into the self-expansion of finite and isolatedly individual beings who set themselves against their divine source as well as other creatures. As a result, they destroy other lives and themselves perish because others resist them.

By contrast, one element in the authentic operation of the spirit is the formation of a community. This can be seen in the fact that the ecstatic movement of life reaches beyond the particular being. The movement is accompanied by a tendency to share in that to which it is directed.[140] This ecstatic movement of life in union with others is always concerned at the same time with the unity of that life itself, and this not only in the sense of preserving the unity of the particular life and its peaceful relations with its environment but also in the sense of preserving the species.

At the human level this tendency to a unity that transcends individuals and at the same time enfolds them manifests itself in the twofold form of reason and love. Through reason, first of all, human beings order themselves to the unity of the world in the totality of its manifestations, in order to find therein the basis for the identity of their own concrete existences. For them as exocentric beings the center that can give unity to their lives is not in themselves but must be based outside themselves.[141] Conse-

---

[139]See, e.g., 1 Sam. 16:14ff.; 1 Kings 22:21ff.; Isa. 29:10.

[140]Augustine saw in this basic striving the expression of a love. For this reason, much of the time he uses *voluntas* ("will") and *amor* ("love") almost as synonyms.

[141]See above, chapter 2, at nn. 62 and 68, and chapter 4, sec. I.

quently, they learn to understand themselves in the light of the order of their world or, as the case may be, in the light of the divine center in which they have their ground,[142] or even in the light of a new order that will transform the existent world and thus of the continuity of history and its supposed goal.

Reason is, however, also concerned with unity to the extent that it aims at an intersubjectively valid and shared knowledge. At this point, what is specific to love already makes its appearance in the operation of reason. That is, reason here does not simply presuppose the unity of the world and a center that grounds this unity but, by overcoming the oppositions between individuals, also produces unity where disunity previously reigned.

It is therefore part of the nature and operation of spirit to bring about a community that will transcend and overcome the isolation of individuals; conversely, a certain spirit manifests itself in every formation of a community. People are correct therefore when they talk of the spirit of a family or a school or a team, but also of the spirit of a period, an age, or a culture. In each case this "spirit" is an always unique manifestation of the spirit of God that is at work in all living things but that can also, as in human individuals, be cut off from its relation to God and become demonic. In fact, it is especially easy for the spirit—whether a corporate spirit or the spirit of the age—that prevails in social life to take on demonic traits so that human beings become blind to the demands of reason and deaf to the voice of love.

Perhaps this is because the experience of harmony with others seems to satisfy the exocentric human destiny and is taken as in itself an adequate sign of truth—of a truth, the possession of which seemingly authorizes us to ignore other voices or even to silence them as monstrous manifestations of evil. This kind of demonic perversion is based on the factual particularism of community interests that of course present themselves as universally binding. The perversion is so difficult to see through in individual instances because evil does in fact exist which refuses to submit to any order that transcends one's own particularism and which destroys every form of community. But the one-sidedness of the supposedly universal interest all too easily causes everything neglected by it to be branded as evil; by that very fact the prevailing communal spirit proves that it itself is evil.

Despite this danger of demonic perversion, harmony and community do remain marks of the true spirit. At the same time, however, the harmony and the community must be concrete forms of that comprehensive unity and community which are consonant with faith in the one God and which have for their criterion the universality of reason and the limitless-

---

[142]See above, chapter 7, at nn. 90ff. and 99, as well as chapter 8, at n. 201.

ness of love. In this light, Maximus the Confessor understood human beings as the beings who are called to unify creation and overcome the five primordial oppositions: the separations between man and woman, paradise and the actual state of the world, heaven and earth, idea and reality, and, finally, creator and creature.[143] By unification Maximus here means not a universal uniformity but a recognition of diversity both in its determinateness and in its limitation.

Perhaps it is along this line that we should conceive the destiny of human beings to be images of God and as such to exercise rule over creation. After all, the positive aim of rule that is not mere coercion is to bring unity and peace. The destiny of human beings to be images of God would then be fulfilled in the reconciliation of the world through the coming of the Messiah. In the New Testament, Christ is described, is he not, as the realized image of God (2 Cor. 4:4)? He is such not for himself alone but as head of his body, the church (Col. 1:15, 18), in which the community of a human race that is renewed and united under the reign of God already makes its appearance in signs. To that extent the image of God in human beings, when viewed from the standpoint of its realization in Jesus Christ, has in fact a "societal structure."[144]

In this perspective it is also possible to regard the creation of human beings in different sexes which are intended for sexual community as a sign pointing to their ultimate destiny, and marriage as a part and a sign of the mystery of salvation, of that plan, to be revealed at the end of time, by which God enters into a history of salvation with humanity.[145] It is true that if we stick to the literal sense of the Old Testament statement about the image of God in human beings, it is not possible to accept Barth's interpretation of it as referring to the relation of the sexes (see above, chapter 2, n. 77). But if we take into account the salvation-historical realization of the human image of God in Jesus Christ, this interpretation proves to be justified in a deeper sense.[146]

The correspondence between the image of God in human beings and the Trinitarian life of God is in fact fulfilled in the human community and specifically in the community of God's kingdom, whose King-Messiah is

---

[143]L. Thunberg, *Microcosm and Mediator: The Theological Anthropology of Maximus the Confessor* (Lund, 1965), 140ff., esp. 145ff. See also Yannaras (n. 126, above), 96ff.

[144]Thus E. Jüngel, "Der Gott entsprechende Mensch. Bemerkungen zur Gottebenbildlichkeit des Menschen als Grundfigur theologischer Anthropologie," in H. G. Gadamer and P. Vogler, eds., in vol. 6 (1975) of Neue Anthropologie, 342–72 at 354. In a still unpublished lecture, J. Moltmann explains the destiny of human beings to a community based on the image of God as originating in the Trinitarian community in God.

[145]Eph. 5:32. On the concept of mystery as the saving plan of God that is to be revealed at the end of history, see G. Bornkamm, "Mystērion," *TDNT* 4:802–28, esp. 822ff.

[146]But Eph. 5:32 refers explicitly to Gen. 2:24, not to Gen. 1:26.

Christ the Servant (Luke 22:28) and in which all dominion of human beings over one another will be eliminated. The corporeal reality of the risen Christ is therefore no longer limited to the isolated existence of the individual named Jesus of Nazareth. Jesus offered his individual life in sacrifice on the cross, and it is in keeping with that intention that the glorified life of the risen Jesus should extend, as to his own "body," to the community of his disciples in whom the unity of a renewed humanity in the coming kingdom of God already manifests itself.[147]

The presence of the eschatological future in the life of the church is in a special way the work of the spirit.[148] The life of the faithful and the life of the eucharistic community that is the church are characterized by an anticipatory participation in the final destiny of human beings through a sharing in the spirit. The spirit is the firstfruit and pledge of the new and immortal life that has already manifested itself in the risen Christ (Rom. 8:23; 2 Cor. 1:22; see 1 Cor. 15:20). This new life is no longer separated from its source in the divine spirit; rather, it is permeated by this spirit (1 Cor. 15:44f.) and is precisely for that reason immortal. The presence of the truth (on which all spiritual experience draws) of our own lives and of the world, the presence of eternity in the consciousness of our own identity and of the being of things within the totality of all that is—that presence will be made perfect in the final and definitive unity of spirit and body.

---

[147]See the more detailed exposition in my *Grundfragen systematischer Theologie* II, 174ff., esp. 184ff.

[148]J. Moltmann, *The Church in the Power of the Spirit: A Contribution to Messianic Ecclesiology,* trans. M. Kohl (New York, 1977), 197ff.

Index
of Scriptural References

Index
of Names

Index
of Subjects